The Easter Egg Fleet

American ship camouflage in WWI

Aryeh Wetherhorn

ISBN 978-965-92747-0-3
first edition - Oct 2020
published by Aryeh Wetherhorn

Foreword

I originally envisaged this book as a reference for American camouflage patterns carried by ships in the First World War. I quickly came to the realization that such a reference needed several additional chapters in order to set the context. I have endeavored to make the background chapters concise. Much of the data in those chapters has been covered, often in greater detail, by other publications. Any reader who feels he already knows enough about the subject of any of the background chapters could easily skip them, even though they are brief. Some contain specific facts that are sometimes omitted or distorted in other places covering this subject. In keeping with my original objective I have purposely tried to be very brief in the textual portions of this book. For anyone wanting more details I have included a small bibliography that includes many of the original sources I consulted as well as some secondary accounts.

Research for this book started nearly 20 years ago. But then it was just for my model collection. I wanted to paint models from my own collection in accurate WW I camouflage. My collection of ship models numbered over 6000 at one time. The total has gone down more recently, but it does include about 150 ships in WWI camouflage, as well as several hundred others in accurate Second World War colors. I have used pictures of some of my 1:1250 scale models to illustrate the patterns in the reference section. They are all hand painted. Other modelers have done similar or even better work. The slight inaccuracies on my models are indicative of a less steady hand wielding a 5-0 brush. A few of the models are ones I made myself from scrap wood, cardboard, wire and pins because a commercial model was not available at the time.

I need to emphasize here that this book is not intended to be primarily about art, but about warfare. Though how art and artists affected the war at sea is important. My approach starts from my years of experience as a sea-going naval officer. There is, therefore, a certain similarity to LCDR Norman Wilkinson RNVR who conceived of his version of "dazzle camouflage" while on active duty during the Great War. I have included much material about the American artists who were involved. For anyone interested primarily in Art and the artists a recent book titled *Dazzle*, by James Taylor, provides good coverage. There are also several books by Roy Behrens who taught art at an American University before his retirement.

I have been aided in preparing this book by a number of people who provided me with material or photographs that are found on the following pages. While many of the pictures are over 100 years old and the original copies reside in the public domain, I am still indebted to the individuals who provided them.

First among those who helped are my 2 researchers in Washington DC who found pictures and documents in the repositories of the US National Archives, Susan Strange, and Alison Lang. The special collections staff at the Fleet Library of the Rhode Island School of Design gave me access to their collection. Thank you to Claudia Covert and Ariel Bordeaux. Another of the major sources for data and leads to material is former Professor Roy Behrens, whom I mentioned above. His on-line blog and books often directed me to areas I had not yet explored. Others who helped include my artist, Talya Shachar-Albocher, Ted Woofendon of the Subchaser Archives, the crew that maintains the Navsource. Com site, The Naval History and Heritage Command, Ric Heineman of pigboats.org, The Great Lakes Maritime Historical Archives, and Mathew Reitzel of The state historical museum of North Dakota. I hope I haven't omitted anyone. I also spent many hours looking at the on-line collections of the Imperial War Museum.

Most of the photographs I have used come from the US National Archives. Others come from the Naval History and Heritage Center. Those items, being in the public domain, are credited only by the letters NARA , NHHC, or a photograph identification number such as NH107163 or 19-N-455.

Of course, none of them are responsible for any errors or omissions in the book. That responsibility remains entirely mine.

Contents

CHAPTER 1

The Lusitania is torpedoed

This was the top headline of the Boston Evening Globe on 7 May 1915.

Sunday Globe Adv'ts—Order Them Today. Autos For Sale? Summer Boarders Wanted? Cottages To Let? Advertise in the Globe.

Boston Evening Globe

Evening Edition 1c

VOL LXXXVII—NO 127 — BOSTON, FRIDAY EVENING, MAY 7, 1915—SIXTEEN PAGES — PRICE ONE CENT

EVENING EDITION—7:30 O'CLOCK—LATEST

LUSITANIA SUNK

Not Known How Many Passengers Saved

TORPEDOED BY GERMANS, REMAINED AFLOAT 12 HOURS

TORPEDOED OFF THE IRISH COAST

Left New York Last Saturday With 1253 Passengers.

WASHINGTON, May 7—Ambassador Page at London has cabled:

"Lusitania torpedoed and sunk within 30 minutes. No news of passengers yet."

LONDON, May 7—The Cunard Line steamer Lusitania, from New York May 1 for Liverpool with 1253 passengers on board, was torpedoed at about 2 o'clock this afternoon at a point about 10 miles off Old Head, Kinsale, Ireland, and later went down.

"It is believed that her passengers are safe. No details of how they may have been rescued, however, are at hand. One message received here says:

"It is not known how many of the Lusitania's passengers were saved."

QUEENSTOWN, 4:59 P M—Wire begins "About 20 boats of all sorts belonging to our line are in vicinity where Lusitania sunk. About 15 other boats are making for ship to render assist-

CUNARD STEAMSHIP LUSITANIA, TORPEDOED OFF THE HEAD OF KINSALE, IRE.

As the story raced across the United States other newspapers from Washington, DC to San Francisco began rearranging their front pages to feature the story. In some cases, the main headline was set in the largest type font they had. The Daily Oklahoman fairly screamed to its readers "More Than 1400 Lives Believed Lost". The number of dead was actually about 1198 and included 198 American citizens. It wasn't just the death toll that created such a stir. The Lusitania was a very large and well known passenger ship. The attack had taken place with no warning. The ship sank in about 20 minutes, leaving hundreds of passengers and crew members struggling in the water. Hundreds of others never managed to leave the ship. Most people believed that unannounced attacks on unarmed merchant ships or non-belligerent passengers were contrary to the way war should be conducted. The foundation for this belief will be examined in greater depth in the next chapter.

The death of nearly 200 Americans made the incident one of high interest for the US Government. President Wilson was not really in favor of entering the European conflict. His Secretary of State,

William Jennings Bryan, had pacifist leanings, and expressed his opinion to President Wilson that Americans taking passage on a belligerent (British) vessel passing through a declared 'War Zone' might be considered to have done so at their own risk. This position was also that of the German Government. In fact, The German representatives in America had paid for advertised warnings specifically saying this in several American newspapers.

NOTICE!

TRAVELLERS intending to embark on the Atlantic voyage are reminded that a state of war exists between Germany and her allies and Great Britain and her allies; that the zone of war includes the waters adjacent to the British Isles: that, in accordance with formal notice given by the Imperial German Government, vessels flying the flag of Great Britain, or of any of her allies, are liable to destruction in those waters and that travellers sailing in the war zone on ships of Great Britain or her allies do so at their own risk.

IMPERIAL GERMAN EMBASSY
WASHINGTON, D. C., APRIL 22, 1915.

A quite different view was taken by Robert Lansing who was then The Counselor for the State Department. He pointed out that on February 10th the US had advised Germany that the 'War Zone' did not restrict the rights of neutrals to trade freely and that the United States would hold Germany accountable for any loss of American lives or property in the zone.

Bryan sent the first American diplomatic protest to the German government on May 13th, 1915. It appealed for cooperation in solving the problem by strict adherence to neutral rights. Bryan seemed to me to be looking for a way to avoid a direct confrontation. The German response focused on claims that the Lusitania was armed (False), carrying troops (False), and carrying contraband (partly, but only marginally, true). It also reiterated the claim that they had warned potential passengers. The questions of adherence to accepted norms of warfare at sea and humanitarian protection for non-belligerents were not addressed. The next American notes pointed out the lack of attention to principles and rebutted the other German claims mentioned above, specifically noting that no prior printed warning could excuse the disregard for life exhibited by a sudden torpedoing of a passenger vessel without making any provision for the safety of those on board. President Wilson, himself, had a hand in drafting them. The final American note, sent on Jun 21st, contained a threat that any future such actions would be regarded as "deliberately unfriendly". That threat was enough for the Germans to reconsider their position and they issued instructions to their U-boat commanders to refrain from attacking any passenger ships and allow safe passage for other vessels displaying clear markings indicating their neutral status. This marked the end of the first German unrestricted submarine offensive.

The diplomatic tension between the US and Germany did result in some important changes. William J. Bryan resigned from the post of Secretary of State on Jun 9th. He felt Wilson was trying to involve the US in one of those foreign entanglements that George Washington had warned against. It is clear that the US was not really prepared for entering the war in Europe at that time.

But it did not mean that Wilson was afraid to use military force to support his policies. He sent a major expedition to Veracruz, Mexico, in April, 1914. The US Army later deployed large bodies of troops to "police" the border with Mexico and chase "bandits" in the years following the Veracruz intervention. The U.S. Marines were used again in Haiti on Jul 28th, 1915. On May 13th of the following year American forces occupied the Dominican Republic. But all those actions were in the Western

Hemisphere and could be interpreted as enforcement of the Monroe Doctrine. There doesn't seem to be any evidence that President Wilson intended to bring the US into the War in Europe in 1915.

Diplomacy aside, there was plenty of popular sentiment in America for immediately declaring war on Germany. Today, a century later, many people still think the sinking of the Lusitania was what brought the United States into the war. Of course, the entire Lusitania episode was just one part of the story. In the following chapters I intend to examine some of the background and connect this incident to an important, but not well known, chapter in the history of American art.

CHAPTER 2

Submarines

One of the often cited principles of war is surprise. It is easy to achieve if your enemy cannot see you. The most important advantage a submarine has is that it is invisible when it is beneath the surface. This allowed submersibles to creep up on unsuspecting enemies during the American Civil War, and thrust a spar with an explosive charge against the side of their target. The range of the weapon the submarine carried was limited to the length of the spar, and the speed it could make while submerged was dependent upon the brute strength of the crew. These limitations made it of very marginal utility as a weapon of war.

Internal combustion engines and electric motors powered by storage batteries made it possible to think of the submarine in a more positive light. The invention of a self-propelled torpedo was a partial solution to the limited range of the submarines offensive capability. Combining these elements gave an impetus to the design of submersible craft for use in war. Early submarines were just beginning to be used at the start of the 20th century. They were still small, and had only a limited range. Most were considered as defensive weapons for coastal protection. Contemporary thinking about submarines put them in that category. No one thought of them as commerce destroyers. Some larger submarines were considered useful for long range scouting or possibly reducing the strength of an enemy battle fleet by stealthy attacks. Most countries that built submarines contemplated using them in the same way they had been employed half a century earlier. The submarine had the potential to protect the coast and destroy enemy warships that might try to enforce a blockade.

The best known early self-propelled torpedoes were developed by an Englishman, Robert Whitehead. He was already employed in Fiume, a major Austro-Hungarian base, when he was asked to devise a mobile mine around 1860. The first version Whitehead torpedoes were slow (about 7 knots), had limited range (close to 700 meters), but had a unique, and effective, means of staying at a set depth. Torpedoes made in Austria-Hungary, and similar weapons made in other places, were constantly being improved. By 1895 gyroscopes were introduced to provide even more reliable depth keeping and reduce aiming errors to less than 1 degree. Among other changes made up to the start of the Great War were increased range, and variable speed settings. The standard German torpedo used in U-boats during the Great War could run at 27 knots for 3000 meters or at 31 knots for half that distance. That was quite an improvement over the first versions.

In order to avoid becoming a hazard when their fuel was expended torpedoes had little hole in the bottom that let in sea water when the torpedo was not moving. This made the torpedo sink if it failed to hit a target. International law, as discussed in the next chapter, required that floating mines should self-destruct or sink in order not to become a navigational hazard to non-combatants.

Torpedoes were much slower than projectiles fired from cannons. For that reason they had to be launched in a direction and speed (fixed) to intercept their target at some future expected position. It also had to strike the target nearly perpendicular to the target course in order to ignite a contact fuse that was only armed after the torpedo had run a short distance from the launching vessel. This also meant that a submarine needed to reach an optimal firing position before launching a torpedo. Both the selection of a launch position relative to the target, and how to reach that position from the current location, were relatively simple mathematical problems. But only if the course and speed of the target were known.

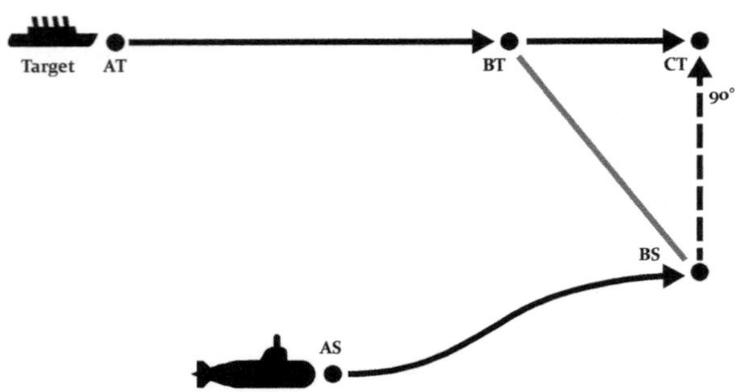

Submarine torpedo attack problem.
Submarine detects target at position A
At= target position, As =submarine position.
Submarine must move to position B , the firing position. Bt = target position, Bs = submarine position
Torpedo travels along line Bs-Ct in order to hit the target at a 90 degree angle.
At-Bt-Ct is the target track
As-Bs is the submarine track

These characteristics, or limitations, meant that there was an entire body of theoretical tactics that grew up around how they were to be used. Despite the fact that this chapter is focused primarily on submarines, the vast majority of tactical literature at that time was aimed at using torpedoes launched from surface ships. The torpedo had become a serious weapon long before the submarine became an effective launching platform. It was the main armament of a large number of small fast surface ships (torpedo boats). Such craft were more feared than submarines in tactical discussions at the time. They also had an impressive record. Torpedo boats had also been used as early as the American Civil War. The Russians employed them against the Turks less than 2 decades later. They had disabled major warships in the Russo-Japanese War in 1904. Many tactical discussions involved using numbers of torpedo boats for attacks against an enemy fleet that was in port or blockading the coast. The most common scenario involved night attacks. Coastal torpedo boat squadrons were therefore often painted black because it was thought, incorrectly, that black would be harder to see in the darkness. Night was the way a surface torpedo boat could acquire a measure of invisibility that would allow it to get close enough to launch a torpedo with some hope of striking the target. Hiding beneath the waves was an even better way to do this.

Robert Whitehead's invention had a profound effect on warship design. Major warships were protected by armor, and carried ever larger guns to enable them to defeat other armored ships in battle. But larger guns had slow rates of fire. While the crew prepared a main gun for another round a swift torpedo boat might slip in and deliver a fatal blow. Torpedo boats were small, and vulnerable to damage by smaller caliber weapons. It soon came to pass that large battleships bristled with secondary batteries of smaller guns that had higher rates of fire for protection against torpedo boats. Large searchlights were mounted on the masts and on special platforms to illuminate enemy vessels that tried to attack under the cover of night. An escort for the fleet to protect them was designed. It was originally called a torpedo boat destroyer. The long name quickly became shortened in practice to simply destroyer.

Professionally, naval officers devoted much time to discussing tactics. The prize essay of the Royal United Services Institute (RUSI) in 1894 was centered on how to best develop the power of existing weapons (gun, ram and torpedo) in multi ship actions. Different ideas were presented. The following year came the first test. Japan went to war with China in 1895 and defeated the Chinese fleet in actions where the faster Japanese column ran rings around the Chinese. Then came the Spanish American War, where a better armed and trained US fleet defeated Spanish squadrons in both Cuba and the Philippines. Five years later Japan was at war again, this time against Russia. This last war saw both the application of effective tactics and the utilization of new weapons in an integrated campaign. Following the Russian defeat, *Brassey's Naval Annual* of 1905 contained "A Plea for the Study of Tactics" along with an analysis of the fighting. There were similar essays published in Germany's *Marine Rundschau* and the American *U. S. Naval Institute Proceedings*. Much attention was devoted to destroyer and torpedo boats. Little was said of submarines. The prevailing attitude could probably be summarized in the following quote from a 1900 RUSI prize essay by a Royal Marines Major saying that submarines "are a confession of weakness and by no means to be recommended to our own Navy, whatever foreigners may think about them." This attitude could easily be supported at that time because of the extremely limited capabilities of submarines. But only 12 years later future Fleet Admiral C. W. Nimitz noted that "...leaving out the factor of mobility, which for submarine craft of the future will advance more rapidly than for surface craft, we find that submarine craft rank equally well, if not better, than surface craft".

Another advance that improved submarines was the invention of improved electrical storage batteries. The newer batteries allowed the submarine to operate submerged for a longer time. But that was the case only if the submarine traveled at a slow speed. The improved batteries did not make the submarine a true underwater vessel. When operating submerged the power available might last for several hours at low speed. When the submarine went faster she used up the stored power at a much faster rate. On the surface, many submarines could go a little faster than the average merchant ship. But under water the submarine was severely limited. Most German U-boats could not exceed 9 knots, and that speed soon used up all her reserve power. The expense and limited number of torpedoes carried by a submarine made it important to hit the target with nearly every launch. Even though the torpedo had a greater range, World War One German submarine doctrine recommended firing only at about 300 meters from the target. Longer ranges introduced the possibility of larger errors in the estimation of a target's course or speed. In addition it gave the target more time to maneuver if the torpedo wake was sighted.

German U-34 *nh43795*

Despite the technical advances in engineering, a submarine powered by diesel engines and with enlarged electrical storage batteries remained, primarily, a surface vessel with the ability to hide under water for a limited period of time. It could not operate tactically as a part of a fleet organization because it could not communicate while submerged. What could be done with submarines was to position them off enemy ports where they could attack warships entering or leaving the harbor, or to lay a trap in an area at sea into which an enemy fleet might be lured. There was still no discussion of using submarines as commerce raiders. The small size and cramped quarters of submarines made them unsuitable for traditional prize warfare. There was insufficient space to keep extra men for use as prize crews or for carrying survivors if the intended prize had to be sunk. This aspect will be discussed in the next chapter.

The cramped space inside the submarine had additional side effects. The amount of fresh water carried was insufficient to allow regular bathing or any laundry service. U-boat crews usually went for the duration of a cruise without bathing and often without being able to change to clean uniforms. There was always plenty of grease, oil, and dirt to soil any clothing in use. This also meant that the crew took on the appearance of a bunch of filthy pirates by the end of a long cruise. That description was quite apt when considering their use in unrestricted submarine warfare.

CHAPTER 3

A Brief Introduction to International Law

The following two books, published by the US Government, are the main sources for the content of this chapter. I found them to be excellent sources for the view of international law at the time of the First World War.

Harold Martin and Joseph Baker *Laws of Maritime Warfare* USGPO May 1918

Carleton Savage *Policy of the United States toward Maritime Commerce in War* Vol II 1914-18 USGPO 1936

In addition I have relied upon a text I found useful when I was assigned collateral duty as legal officer during service in the US Navy.

CDR Burdick H Brittin and L B Watson *International Law for Seagoing Officers* USNI Annapolis 1956.

Modern International Law started with Hague conventions, just a few years before the outbreak of WWI. The first conference convened at The Hague at the initiative of Czar Nicholas II of Russia. The meeting actually started on 18 May, 1899, which was also the Czar's birthday. It was intended as a conference to support disarmament. England, Germany, France, Italy, The United States, Spain, Sweden & Norway, The Netherlands, Belgium, Bulgaria, Japan, Persia, Siam, Mexico, Turkey, Austria-Hungary, Portugal, Denmark, Switzerland, Luxembourg, China, Rumania, Serbia, Greece, Russia, and even little Montenegro participated. The agreements signed fell far short of what many of the participants wanted.

A second conference was convened in 1907 with the participation of most of the Western Hemisphere nations that had not been present at the first conference. This time the results were much more detailed and far reaching. The 1907 convention defined rules for both belligerents and neutrals. With regard to war at sea, there was a strong emphasis on preservation of life. The former practice of privateering was outlawed. In its place came definitions that the participants trusted would cover the behavior of nations during war at sea. Other provisions governed war on land. The conversion of civilian vessels to warships was covered, as was the right of merchant ships belonging to a belligerent to immunity from capture if they were ignorant of the commencement of hostilities. At the time of the meeting most ships did not have radios, and much could take place while they traveled from one port to another.

Under the new rules blockades could be declared to prevent cargos with military use from reaching an enemy port. It was not a new concept, but it needed specific definition. Mines could be laid to limit access to a port. Coastal minefields had to be proclaimed and neutral shipping notified of their placement. Mines could also be laid in international waters as a tactic, but had to be neutralized after a brief period, in order to protect neutrals. Merchant vessels that were liable to capture could take refuge in neutral ports for the duration of the war. Ships or cargos belonging to an enemy could be seized. In order to do this, a warship had to stop and examine the suspected vessel. Flight after being called upon to stop was evidence of hostile intent. Seized ships had to be brought into a port where a Prize Court would determine disposition of the vessel or cargo. Neutral ships carrying contraband cargo were to be allowed to proceed after the cargo was either taken or destroyed. Even more important, no merchant vessel was to be destroyed at sea without making provision for the safety of her crew and passengers.

There were still differences of interpretation, especially with regard to contraband. A last try to establish agreement on these rules resulted in the London Declaration of 1909. It was not a ratified part of the conventions, but was expected by most countries to be a more detailed guideline for conducting legal blockades.

In summary, here are the parts of interest:

- There was an emphasis on preservation of life.
- Rights of belligerents, and of neutrals, were summarized.
- Rules for blockades were established, even though there was no agreement on contraband.
- Most important of all, there were no provisions for enforcement.

As noted in the chapter about submarines, subs are small, no room for lots of prisoners or for providing prize crews to take captured ships home. No one thought it was necessary to make any special provision for them.

Blockade allows seizure of goods destined for enemy belligerents. But what goods are being discussed? Those liable to be taken are defined as contraband. Originally, contraband was limited to items that were either directly used for combat or combat support (and specifically excluding food!) but later the idea was expanded by the British Admiralty to include almost anything. The USA maintained a right to trade with anyone, and especially other neutrals like Holland. When the British expanded their definition of conditional contraband during the war the Americans objected. There was even a possibility of US entry on the German side in defense of neutral rights to free trade.

With no international courts, the only reason to obey the rules was self-interest. If you violated the rules, your opponent would not feel bound to obey them either. This was articulated by the former First Sea Lord of the Admiralty in the following often quoted line:

> "The essence of war is violence, Moderation in warfare is imbecility."

When the war actually was declared, the British were quick to declare a blockade of Germany. Royal Navy ships were dispatched to hunt down German warships that were located outside Europe. The English Channel was blocked by an active naval patrol and mine fields. A patrol line of converted merchant cruisers covered the area between Norway and Scotland to intercept and examine all ships passing through that area. Germany also had a very large merchant marine. Those ships were liable to capture under the rules. To protect them, many were ordered to take refuge in the nearest neutral ports. Once there, they could remain safely for the duration of hostilities. Warships could also do this, but had to be disarmed and maintained by only a caretaker crew for the period of their internment. Many German ships were trapped in American ports. Some of their crew members were allowed to travel back to Germany. The British blockade soon resulted in the disappearance of German ships, and even cargos destined for Germany, from the seas around Europe.

The British blockade strangled Germany. During the decade before the war Germany had become an industrialized country, and did not even grow enough foodstuffs at home to feed her own population. But food, if you recall, was supposed to be exempt from seizure. The British decided otherwise and began adding food items to their lists of contraband. No raw materials for weapons or munitions could reach Germany. Even fuel found its way on to the contraband lists. The German government was well aware that they could not hold out for a period of several years. They planned on making the war short. Part of that plan included invading Belgium in order to outflank the French armies. The invaders seemed to have been unnecessarily cruel in their relations to Belgian civilians. There were even suggestions that the Germans may have fostered the image of the "Horrible Huns" in an attempt to shorten the war. Along the entire front it soon became clear that attacking entrenched positions was a very costly endeavor. The attempt to get past the French Northern flank was blocked by the arrival of the British Army. Both sides engaged in a sort of race to the sea as they extended their trenches. Attempts to break the stalemate by ground attacks by either side just resulted in extremely large lists of casualties in return for minimal geographical gains. It was going to be a long war.

Slow strangulation by blockade now became a real issue. Germany recognized that England, an island nation, was even more vulnerable to blockade. But the only means she had to conduct such a blockade was a handful of submarines. Germany declared a blockade of her own. Initially, German submarines followed the rules and made provisions for the crews of intercepted ships to reach safety before sinking the ships. One of the most important steps the British took in response was to provide a defensive gun and gun crew for their merchant vessels. According to the rules, a submarine had to come to the surface and call upon the merchant ship to halt. That meant giving up her main advantage, invisibility. Even worse was the position in which the submarine then found itself; facing an opponent with a large gun, often of greater size than that carried by the submarine, and being much more vulnerable. Even a hit by a single shell might permanently deprive the submarine of its ability to submerge. The Germans decision to attack without warning with a torpedo, might have been dictated more by a sense of self-preservation than by a conscious wish to violate the rules of war. The actual decision came about in a slightly different manner. The German Naval Commander, Admiral Hugo von Pohl, was looking for a way to counter the British blockade. He thought that a declared policy of sinking without warning of any ships in a declared "War Zone" might work. His reasoning was that the sinking of a few neutral merchant ships would be enough to frighten the rest away from trading with his English enemies. But there were some problems with his approach. He did not have enough U-boats capable of conducting an effective campaign of this sort, without even considering that it was a violation of international law. Another contributing factor to the failure of the first German attempt at unrestricted submarine warfare was the size of the British merchant navy relative to the numbers of submarines that could be deployed. When Germany officially announced that she would conduct an unrestrained campaign against merchant ships trading with England starting on 22 February, 1915 the Germans were simply unable to keep more than 4-5 submarines operating at sea. At that time there were some 5000 individual ship arrivals and departures at British ports every month. The U-boats only managed to attack fewer than 2 dozen of them.

On top of all this came the diplomatic outcry. Neutral nations complained that the Germans were violating the very agreements that they had accepted just a few years earlier. Foremost among the flurry of diplomatic notes was the American statement that they would hold Germany accountable for any loss of American ships or cargoes. The threat of having the United States enter the war against them was more than the German chancellor, Von Bethmann-Hollweg, was willing to risk. The German navy was instructed to spare neutral shipping. Despite this, some neutral ships were sunk; sometimes, perhaps, due to an error in identification. Civilian lives were lost because the provisions of the Hague convention were not being followed. This was the state of affairs when the Lusitania was attacked.

Following the German decision to give up their first attempt at unrestricted submarine warfare they concentrated on another idea. Submarines were capable of carrying mines instead of torpedoes. The Germans designed a series of submarine minelayers and employed them to sneak into the approaches of British harbors and deposit a small, but lethal, explosive package right in the path of entering vessels. The mine laying offensive caused some damage and sank a few ships. The British were prepared. Even though the British fishing fleet was supposed to be able to continue their work under the terms of the Hague conventions, the reality was that they could not do so. The Admiralty had an alternative for them. Hundreds of trawlers and drifters were enrolled in the Auxiliary Patrol. The vessels were equipped with wireless sets and armed with one or more small guns. The crews were augmented by radio operators and gunners. The vessels were then assigned to local commands along the British coast where they worked either as minesweepers or as part of the anti-submarine patrols. Some German minefields were discovered and swept up before they could claim a victim. Others resulted in only a brief closure of the port while the auxiliary patrol cleared the area. One of the most important jobs given to the auxiliary patrol was to watch for submarines. The entire English Channel off Dover was closed off, partly by mine fields, and partly by deep nets. The nets had indicator floats attached that would move if a submarine tried to penetrate the net. Trawlers and drifters maintained a constant surveillance of those indicators, and of the minefields. The mines were laid at depths that allowed the shallow draft fishing craft to sail over them, but would explode if a submerged U-boat ran into them.

The war went on for another 2 years and still neither side was able to force a decision on land. While this was happening, Germany was feeling the effect of the British blockade. To keep fish from neutral Norway from reaching Germany the British purchased more than three quarters of the annual Norwegian catch for themselves. Exporting any remaining fish to Germany would mean Norwegians would go hungry. German soldiers at the front continued to be fed, but their families at home had their rations progressively reduced. German troops were receiving about 3200 calories per day, and it soon dropped to 2900. To put this in perspective, British soldiers received about 4000 calories per day. German rationing programs provided the average citizen at home with one loaf of dark bread, one slice of sausage - which contained little or no fat - and three pounds of potatoes per week. Rations inside Germany were reduced to about one thousand calories a day. By 1918, the mortality rate among civilians was 38 percent higher than in 1913. By December 1918, the National Health Office in Berlin calculated that 763,000 persons had died as a result of the blockade. Meanwhile, Germany had constructed many more U-boats. The German army was still unable to break the stalemate on the Western Front. Admiral Von Pohl had died in 1916 and his successor, Admiral Rheinhold Scheer, led the German High Seas Fleet into a major fleet action in the North Sea. He managed to get most of his ships safely home, but was now certain that he could not break the British blockade by a naval battle. The only way to victory seemed to be a return to unrestricted submarine warfare. The German Navy claimed they could return to unrestricted submarine warfare and starve Britain before the US could intervene effectively. They were almost correct.

It is also clear that Germany returned to unrestricted submarine warfare with the certain understanding that it was a violation of the Geneva conventions regarding war. Here is a small part of the German Chancellor's speech announcing their decision.

> "The question of the U-boat war, as the gentlemen of the Reichstag will remember, has occupied us three times in this committee, namely, in March, May and September last year. On each occasion, in an exhaustive statement, I expounded points for and against in this question. I emphasized on each occasion that I was speaking *pro tempore*, and not as a supporter in principle or an opponent in principle of the unrestricted employment of the U-boats, but in consideration of the military, political and economic situation as a whole. I always proceeded from the standpoint as to whether an unrestricted U-boat war would bring us nearer to a victorious peace or not. Every means, I said in March, which is calculated to shorten the war is the humanest policy to follow. When the most ruthless methods are considered as the best calculated to lead us to a victory and to a swift victory, I said at that time, then they must be employed...
>
> The Admiralty Staff and the High Seas Fleet entertain the firm conviction - a conviction which has its practical support in the experience gained in the U-boat cruiser warfare - that Great Britain will be brought to peace by arms."

It is striking to note that he justified the return to unrestricted submarine warfare as being "humane".

The merchant marine crews that were on board ships torpedoed without warning frequently did not survive. Lifeboats could not always be lowered successfully before the ship went down. Hypothermia is the medical term used to describe the condition of a human body that is constantly exposed to cold. The usual standard is 4 degrees or less than the usual 98.6 degrees Fahrenheit normal body temperature. The body reacts by trying to keep the vital organs warm for as long as possible. A person in the ocean would experience numbness in his outer limbs, followed by slowly becoming comatose and then dying. The mean temperature of the Atlantic is less than 70 degrees for most of the year. Survivors of a torpedoing would not last long. Even being in a lifeboat when at a great distance from land was little help. The supply of fresh water carried in the boats was not large. Drinking sea water was a sure way to delirium and death. All of this simply emphasizes the reasons that the original formulations of international law for war at sea were constructed to save lives, while unrestricted submarine warfare increased the likelihood of sailors dying.

Neutral merchant ships often attempted to avoid submarine attack by painting the national flag of the country, or name of the ship or the shipping line on the side of the vessel in large letters. German u-boat commanders tended to ignore these markings because they assumed the British ships would use such schemes as a way to elude attack. In any case, under unrestricted submarine warfare even neutral shipping was frequently subject to being sunk without warning.

CHAPTER 4

Anti-submarine Warfare

Although most of the discussions of tactics regarding torpedo craft were focused on surface ships, it did not mean that submarines were ignored. Defense against submarines was actually a very difficult problem. The only way to attack a submarine was if you knew where it was. There were some passive weapons that could be used. Mines and nets could be placed to either destroy or detect a submarine that dared to venture into the areas where such devices were employed. But an active direct attack was dependent upon the submarine doing something that gave away its position. A submarine on the surface was an obvious target. So was a periscope. One early idea for defeating submarines was to employ small boats equipped with canvas bags and heavy hammers. On sighting a periscope, the boat crew would throw the bag over the end of the periscope to temporarily blind it, and then smash the glass under the bag to make it permanently sightless. I don't know of any case where this tactic was employed successfully, but many small craft off the English coast were actually given the equipment.

It was later noted that a submarine could also expose her position by firing a torpedo. The torpedo left a wake of either steam or compressed air that allowed one to follow it back to the point from which it was launched, and the bubble of compressed air that sent the torpedo on its way left a disturbance in the water. The problem became a bit more complicated after that. An attacker could attempt to ram the submarine since most of them submerged to a depth of only a few meters below the surface. If you passed over the spot where the submarine was thought to be you might see a shadow under water and could attack it. Some vessels were given an anti-submarine lance. It resembled a whaling harpoon, but with a tip containing a 7 pound explosive charge. It was thrown by hand, usually by one of the stronger crew members. In the absence of better weapons these were produced in quantity. About 20,000 were made. Unlike the hammer technique, there is one case of this weapon being given credit for sinking a U-boat. UB-18 was damaged by a lance bomb and ultimately destroyed.

The British Admiralty did devote some time to research in handling the submarine menace. Someone decided that a torpedo was nothing more than a self-propelled mine. The next step, to use modern parlance, was to decide that a submarine was just the first stage of a multi stage delivery system for that mine. Stationary mines were handled by sweeping the area ahead of the fleet. Usually this was done with a wire towed between two small ships. The wire encountered the mooring line of the mine and either pulled it into contact, where it exploded, or broke the mooring line and allowed the mine to float to the surface where it could be destroyed by gunfire. The Royal Navy tried using this sweep technique to find submarines. They even conducted live tests using an older submarine and a sweep towed by destroyers. The experiments were successful. The next step was to attach explosives to the sweep wire that could be detonated on command when the sweep found a submarine. Further refinements included using multiple contact fused explosive charges and adding devices called paravanes, kites, and otters to control the positioning and depth of the sweep and allow it to be employed by a single ship. The Admiralty was convinced that this was a sufficient answer to the submarine menace to the fleet. Several destroyers were equipped with it from early in 1912. Like the hand lance, there is actually a confirmed kill of a U-boat credited to this method.

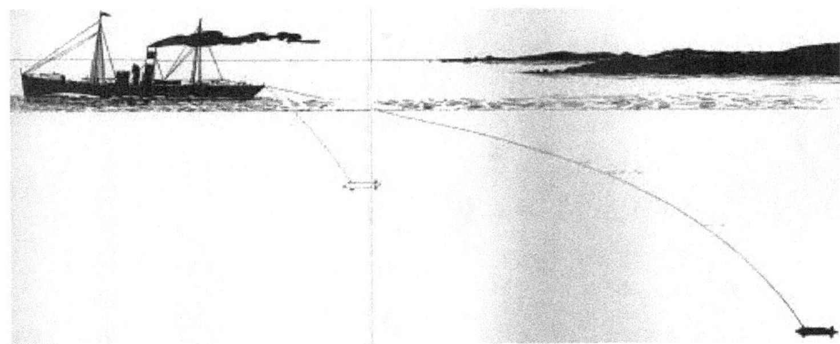

Towed sweep paravane deployed.
From 1917 admiralty manual on explosive sweep

The first depth charges were similar to the hand lance. They consisted of an explosive charge connected to a float by a lanyard of 25 to 100 feet in length. The length of the lanyard was set using a hand crank before throwing it over the side. The entire apparatus was thrown over the side at the place where the submarine was expected to be. The float stayed on the surface while the charge sank. When it reached a depth equal to the length of the lanyard the slight tug from the float activated the charge. The first American depth charge was the mark I produced by Sperry. It was almost identical the British Mark I. It was lethal only if it exploded within 10 feet of the submarine. The British soon adapted a small (65 pound) aerial bomb for the same purpose and produced it with both a float and, after 1916, a hydrostatic fuse. British craft assigned to the Harwich Force adapted the explosive charges from the anti-submarine sweep for use as depth charges. They were dropped in pairs, detonated electrically, and were expected to be more effective because their weight was nearly 5 times that of the Mark I or type A charges. The extra explosives made them lethal at a range almost 30 feet. Improved charges with a weight of 300 pounds and a greater lethal radius did not become available until much later.

Direct gunfire was one of the more effective early measures for sinking submarines. Merchant vessels were armed with guns, many taken from older warships that had been dropped from the roles of effective ships. Submarines spent most of their time on the surface, and had to expose a periscope when attacking. Gunfire offered a chance to fight back against a nearly invisible enemy. The wake of the torpedo also gave an indication of the U-boat's location. There are also documented cases where gunfire was directed at the torpedo itself, and caused it to miss the targeted ship.

The Royal Navy laid minefields and net barriers in restricted waters with the idea that a submarine that encountered a net would pull the net. Indicator buoys or floats on the upper part of the net would move, and small craft of the auxiliary patrol would detect the movement, report it, and be available to attack the U-boat if it chose to surface. Some nets had mines attached that could be activated by contact with the U-boat when it tried to pass through the net. Despite the hundreds of vessels and miles of nets, detection of a penetration at night during the early part of the war was almost impossible.

The above discussion probably makes it clear that no one, especially the Royal Navy, had an effective way of detecting and destroying U-boats. When the Germans declared a resumption of unrestricted submarine warfare it brought the United States into the war. One of the first things the US Navy did was to dispatch a division of American destroyers to assist the Royal Navy against the submarine menace. The US Navy is justifiably proud of the fact that when these ships arrived the British admiral asked when they would be ready to be employed the American commander replied "We are ready now, sir!" That response wasn't entirely correct. The American destroyers had no dedicated anti-submarine weapons at all. One of the first changes made to them was to weld two metal frames for holding and releasing depth charges on the fantail of the US Navy vessels. At the time, depth charge production was not creating the weapons at a rapid enough rate. The US craft went to sea to conduct their first patrols with empty racks. When more charges arrived, the initial allowance to each American destroyer was only 2 charges. By June 1917 the allowance of depth charges per ship went up to 4. Two months later it had doubled again to 8. In 1918 some ships carried 20 or more depth charges. It had become one of the best anti-submarine weapons available. Many ships were fitted with Y-gun projectors that allowed depth charges to be thrown to the side of the ship in addition to those rolled of the racks astern.

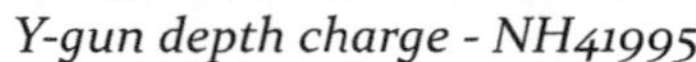

Y-gun depth charge - NH41995

Depth charge roller tracks on American Destroyers - NHHC photo NH 123835

The resumption of unrestricted submarine warfare found the Royal Navy using 2 ideas to control the U-boat threat. One of them was to restrict passage of the submarines and keep them away from potential targets. As mentioned above, the Dover straits had been covered with mines and nets and a large number of auxiliary patrol craft were utilized to support the barrier. The ideas seemed sound, but the German submarines actually had little difficulty in penetrating the supposedly closed barrage. It took a new commander, ADM Sir Roger Keyes, to take the steps needed to make the barrier effective. He was only appointed to the job in October 1917. The energetic Keyes quickly established systems to provide lighting for the barrier during the night. This forced any submarines to make the transit submerged for almost the entire time. He even tried bombarding the U-boat bases at Ostend and Zeebruge. He would later try to close the entrance to those ports with block ships. His actions turned the Channel passage, once merely an irritating obstacle for the German submarines, into a truly hazardous voyage. All larger U-boats made the trip to their operating areas by going around the Northern end of the British Isles because the Channel passage and its' extended minefields was simply too hazardous.

The second means for handling the U-boats was to try to find and destroy them at sea by extensive offensive patrols. The ocean is truly vast, and even concentrating the patrols near the areas where normal shipping lanes converged was still very much like looking for a needle in a haystack. U-boats spent most of their time on the surface. The offensive patrols tried to find them, but with little success. While on patrol a typical American destroyer would have from 6 to 8 sailors assigned as lookouts to scan the ocean and, hopefully, spot a submarine. At least one man was located in a tiny box high on the mast called a crow's nest. It was a boring assignment, and, in bad weather, downright uncomfortable. There was still a major problem with locating the submarine under water. Hydrophones and even directional hydrophones existed. Listening tubes gave directions, but not range. The Fessenden oscillator was installed on American submarines. It failed as a detector but worked as an underwater telephone. The idea of using trained California sea lions to locate submarines was even discussed.

Considerable effort was made to try to get the U-boats to expose themselves by coming to the surface. Merchant vessels carried a gun for self-defense. Some vessels were equipped as decoy traps for submarines. They carried several additional cannon hidden behind droppable bulwarks and inside false deck structures. Their holds were filled with empty barrels or other materials to help keep them afloat. When hit by a torpedo, part of the crew made a show of abandoning ship and lowered lifeboats. The ship remained afloat so the submarine would be tempted to surface and finish off her prey with gunfire or explosive charges rather than waste another torpedo. Despite some success, especially early in the war, the Germans soon became aware of the ruse and became much more cautious. The US Navy actually manned one such ship which was given to them by the British. She was damaged by a torpedo, but the U-boat declined to surface. The ship was towed back to port and repaired, but resumed service as a British ship. It should be noted that despite the increased range of the torpedo mentioned in the previous chapter, the German submarine operating instructions forbade firing at more than 3000 meters and considered the optimal range for launch to be between 250 and 300 meters.

The submarine problem that was confronting the British had been under investigation for quite a while on the Western side of the Atlantic. President Wilson had two very competent individuals dealing with the Navy Department. He had appointed Josephus Daniels as his Secretary of the Navy. Daniels was well aware that the Navy was America's first line of defense and wasted no time in ensuring that line would be well prepared. Major naval appropriations bills were sent to congress via his office. The Assistant Secretary of the Navy was Franklin D Roosevelt. He, too, was concerned about being prepared. Both men worked on programs of their own choosing that, fortuitously, complemented each other. Daniels, a former newspaper editor, was acquainted with a man with one of the sharpest minds in the US, the inventor Thomas A Edison. Edison was asked to assemble a group of the best people he could find as an unofficial source for recommending things the Navy could do to be prepared to enter the war if it became necessary. The group was called the Navy Consulting Board. It originally had 12 members with Edison as the figurehead chairman. The board first met and formed sub-committees to look at all aspects of anti-submarine warfare. They screened other people's ideas as well

Naval Consulting board - Library of Congress photo LC-DIG-npcc-27736

J. Daniels - NH2336

as making their own recommendations. Good ideas were forwarded to Daniels, and many of them were put to use.

Franklin Roosevelt came up with ideas of his own. When the American Motor Boat Club assembled in New York in September 1916 for a group cruise Roosevelt sent a team of naval officers to inspect and register the craft for potential future employment as a naval auxiliary for local patrols. They were placed on a numbered list with the prefix SP, for Section Patrol. The owners took many of their boats to the Brooklyn Navy Yard or to Charlestown Naval Yard in Boston for the inspection. This system was soon expanded to include all types of craft from fishing boats to ocean going steamers and the prefix SP gave way to ID for identification. By Jun 1917 there were 799 vessels listed in the register. It would grow to over 4000 before the war ended.

Assistant Secretary of the Navy Franklin D Roosevelt - NH19

Even before the second German declaration of unrestricted submarine warfare the depredations of the U-boats were reducing the numbers of merchant ships plying the oceans. By 1917 the net loss amounted to about 7.5 million tons of carrying capacity. American shipyards soon found they had many orders for new ships to replace those lost. Congress passed the Shipping Act (39 Stat. 729), on September 7, 1916. The U.S. Shipping Board was organized on January 30, 1917, pursuant to that act. The Emergency Fleet Corporation (EFC) was then established by the U.S. Shipping Board, on April 16, 1917, to acquire, maintain, and operate a fleet of merchant ships to meet the needs of national defense and foreign and domestic commerce. De facto, USSB owned the ships. The EFC contracted for new designs and construction. EFC covered the building of new shipyards, and the training of crews to operate the newly constructed ships.

Prior to the US declaration of war the president, himself, had issued a few executive orders to increase the size of the armed forces and control radio station operations. He also assigned a couple of experts on Maritime Insurance and War Risks to the US Treasury Department. US official activities after entering the war will be covered in a later chapter. Some of these actions helped make the Navy ready to respond faster once war was declared. This will be mentioned again in a later chapter.

Camouflage painting for ships, as will soon be shown, was a concern for the U S Navy well before the Royal Navy "invented" the concept of "dazzle". As an anti-submarine measure it offered a solution to a specific problem that would remain valid for only a limited time. It was a passive measure intended for defense. It degraded the accuracy of the submarine torpedo in use during that era. It was also relatively inexpensive and easy to apply. The advent of electronic sensors for detection and tracking rendered it obsolete.

Whatever weapons were used, a successful attack on a U-boat usually meant the death of the entire crew. Any penetration of the submarine's pressure hull meant a massive rush of seawater entering the craft. Crew members not killed outright could expect to drown fairly quickly. Those who were able to escape to a nearby intact compartment could look forward to slow asphyxiation as the oxygen in the air was consumed. The ability to escape from a sunken submarine was a development that would only come several decades later. Even a relatively small sea water leak might put the crew in mortal danger. Sea water that came in contact with the acid in the electrical storage batteries might result in the generation of chlorine gas. Inhaling chlorine in a confined space was a most uncomfortable way to die.

CHAPTER 5

Concealment and Confusion

The human eye is an amazing organ. It is almost full size at birth. The light impulses it collects are transferred to the brain, giving us the sense of sight. The inside of the eye, or retina, contains a number of sensory cells with different functions. They are referred to as rods and cones. There are about 120 million rods in an adult retina. They are more sensitive to light than the cones. But they are not sensitive to color. The 6 to 7 million cones provide the eye's color sensitivity and they are much more concentrated in the central yellow spot known as the macula. Rods give us black and white vision, without color. Their distribution over most of the retina makes them useful for detecting motion. There are three different types of cones, each type being responsive to a different wavelength spectrum of light. The "red" cones (64% of the total) have a peak response at about 575 nanometers, "green" cones (32%) peak at 535 nm, and "blue" cones (2%) at 445 nm. They all contain a protein called opsin which comes in three different forms. The molecule has the same composition, but the structure at one part connects at a different angle. Light energy breaks the molecule apart and causes an electro-chemical signal to be sent to the brain. Once the signal has been sent, the molecule recombines and can respond again to the next light stimulus. The brain interprets the signals as colors. Color blindness is caused by a deficiency of one or more types of opsin in the eye.

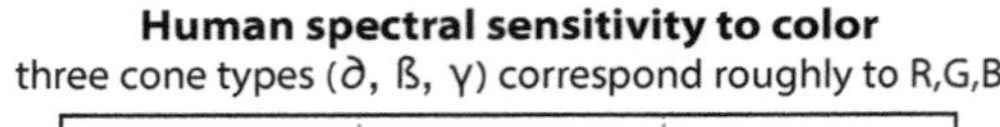

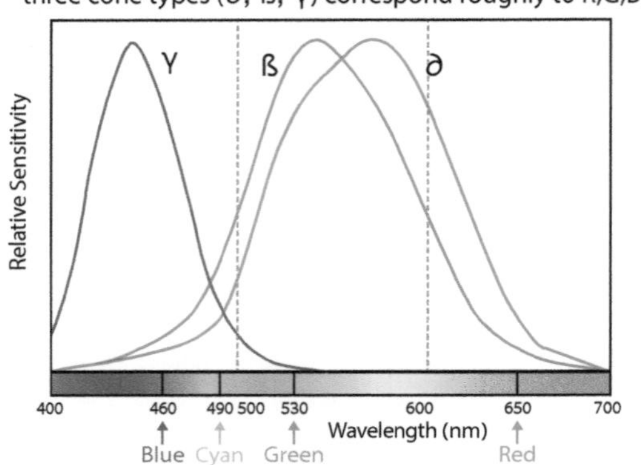

Television and computer screens do almost the same process. The screen is coated with phosphors or light emitting diodes (LEDs) that emit light energy at a particular wavelength when illuminated or selected by a beam of electronic energy.

The eye was the principal means of detecting another vessel at sea during the Great War. There was no radar, no sonar, and no electronic aids to navigation. But there is another aspect of vision that needs to be discussed. How do we detect movement? Humans have 2 eyes and compare the images in the brain in order to determine how far they are from an object. Changes in that perception of distance, or in the relation of one object to another, allow the viewer to detect motion. But not all creatures have binocular vision. Birds have 2 eyes, but they are positioned on opposite sides of their head. The perception of distance, and movement, comes from how much of their field of vision is taken up by the object being viewed. Artists have long struggled with the problem of transferring a 3 dimensional object to the 2 dimensions of their canvas. One of the earlier written discussions of perspective dates from the early 18th century. To deceive a human observer into thinking an object is moving at a different speed or in a different direction than it actually is, requires affecting perception. Art students all learn about this. The terms false perspective or forced perspective are familiar to artists. Other terms used for ways of inducing confusion in an observer include anamorphosis, quadrature, and trompe l'oeil. The latter is particularly appropriate. It is simply "fooling the eye" in French. Knowing something about this was a reason artists were selected for camouflage work.

Darwinian evolution is a widely known idea. The impact of camouflage in nature, and the individual who first wrote about it, are not nearly so well recognized. American artist and naturalist Abbott Henderson Thayer published his landmark book "Concealing Coloration in the Animal Kingdom" in 1909. It was the culmination of years of study of the subject. He had already presented part of it in an article for The Awk, The American Journal of Ornithology in 1896. That article was titled "*The Law Which Underlies Protective Colouration*". The larger book, which was officially co-authored by his son Gerald, developed the ideas further. The three principal ideas presented were countershading, blending with the background, and disruptive patterns. The concepts were not entirely new. Half a century earlier the British had adopted a tan color for the uniforms of soldiers serving in India. The color was called khaki. It was derived from an Urdu word for dust. One important contribution of Thayer's book lay in illustrating the idea that evolution favored the survival of species that developed coloration to make them less visible to possible predators. An interesting aside to this was that one of the greatest detractors of the book was Theodore Roosevelt. Roosevelt knew that zebras and giraffes were clearly visible on the African veldt from several miles away. He reportedly wrote "If you...sincerely desire to get at the truth you would realize that your position is literally nonsensical." It has nearly taken another century for science to examine the idea that the stripes on a zebra may be there to confuse predators about the animal's speed and direction of flight, and not for concealment.

Thayer proposed ideas for reducing the visibility of American warships during the brief war with Spain. The proposals weren't adopted, but they did later take the form of a patent issued to Thayer and George De Forest Brush for a "Process of Treating the Outsides of Ships, etc., for Making Them Less Visible" (*U.S. Patent No. 715,013*). When the Great War started, Thayer tried to get his ideas for ship concealment adopted. He even wrote a mini-essay in the New York Tribune titled "Teaching Britannia Her Job" (Sunday, August 18, 1916, page 4ff) which was reprinted in Professor Roy Behrens' book *Shipshape*. The Admiralty wasn't influenced by Thayer, but one of his fellow naturalists had better luck, at least for a short period.

Glasgow zoology professor John Graham Kerr offered his services on the subject of ship camouflage early in the war. He also was personally acquainted with the First Lord of the Admiralty, Winston Churchill. A letter to Churchill describing what Kerr termed "parti-coloring" was soon forwarded to commanders afloat. The result was adoption of the idea in several cases. The article by Hugh Murphy and Martin Bellamy in the Northern Mariner, vol 19 ("The Dazzling Zoologist, John Graham Kerr and the Early Development of Ship Camouflage") includes an excerpt from an officer's diary describing what happened.

"Ships have been painting their masts, and in some cases, their funnels, white in order to make ranging on them more difficult for the enemy. Some ships have painted their turrets black and white like the Spit fort but this does not seem to serve any useful purpose. We have wrapped strips of canvas loosely round the topgallant and topmasts so as to break the edge and have painted the masts white in between the strips of canvas. The funnels and lower masts have been painted with large irregular blobs of white"

Here is a photo of the Spit fort, and a couple of other ships painted in parti-coloring early in the war. The ships involved in the Dardanelles campaign included several that were painted this way. But the Dardanelles attacks failed. Churchill had to resign, and the camouflage ideas proposed for His Majesty's

Horse Sand Fort – Spithead
portsmouth.co.uk photo 3573249849

HMS Dartmouth at the Dardanelles
Australian War Museum photo p05194.012

HMS Agamemnon at the Dardanelles partly painted in Kerr splotches courtesy of Dr. Piotr Nykiel

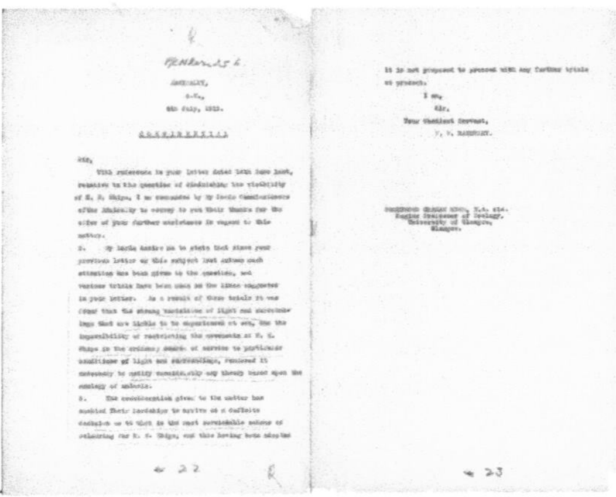

[illegible]

It is not proposed to proceed with any further trials at present.

I am,
Sir,
Your obedient Servant,
[illegible]

Rejection letter to Professor Kerr

Ships were quickly replaced with a coat of uniform, overall, grey. Kerr received a polite rejection letter from the Admiralty. This was where matters stood in Europe until the Germans returned to try unrestricted submarine warfare once more.

The study of color had been around for a long time. Isaac Newton aimed a beam of light through a prism and observed that it broke into distinct bands of color. He postulated that there were 7 basic colors; red, orange, yellow, green, blue, indigo, and violet. His theory held sway for a couple of centuries until the idea of 3 primary colors was proposed. A Scottish genius named James Clerk Maxwell looked at color theory and demonstrated conclusively that mixing different primary colors in varying amounts resulted in other colors. Maxwell, who also made important contributions to the study of electricity and magnetism, took colored discs with different sized sections of varied colors and spun them rapidly. The result was that the observer saw a new color. The spinning discs were called Maxwell Discs. They played an important role in the way one of the first American artists to investigate ship camouflage approached the problem. That artist, William Andrew Mackay, managed to get the US Navy to work with him in a series of experiments on ship camouflage. The original ideas came about via cooperation between Mackay and CDR Joseph Fisher. Fisher had just been given command of a division of the newest submarines. The year was 1913, before the onset of hostilities in Europe. While the submarine camouflage trials were being discussed, the US Navy painted a destroyer, USS Trippe, with a coat of outlandish colors and design. It was done in 1915 so the Trippe could be exhibited to a convention of state governors in Boston. The design might have been from Mackay, or even from Abbot Thayer. The pictures below come from contemporary news reports.

USS Trippe Port view - 5 Sep 1915 *navsource 0503308*

USS Trippe Starboard view *Baltimore Sun, 12 Sep 1915*

The submarine experiments were actually conducted in April, 1916 by CDR Fisher's successor. Mackay had the 4 K class submarines of the Atlantic Fleet painted with stripes in red, white, green and violet. Another round of tests was conducted with the submarines painted in different sized black and white checkerboard patterns and thin black and white angled stripes. Photographs suggest that each submarine may have carried more than one pattern. This is mentioned here to show the US was working on ship camouflage long before the country went to war. In fact, after the Admiralty dropped Professor Kerr's parti-coloring, the U.S. was the only country that was seriously looking at ship camouflage.

Four K class submarines alongside their mother ship, former monitor USS Tallahassee, during the experiments *Photo: Ric Heinemen at pigboats.com*

Most experiments involved reducing the visibility of a ship. No system of painting a ship can make it invisible. Even reduced visibility has limitations. Changes in the time of day, position of the sun, and weather all contribute to making a color scheme that might be effective in one set of circumstances, completely useless in another. Despite this, suggestions submitted to the Naval Advisory Board for using some kind of protective coloration were examined, and 5 of the proposals were considered by the board to have some merit. Examples of the 5 are shown in the chapter on the US goes to war. Only the Warner design was aimed at deception. The Advisory Board conducted extensive experiments on visibility. They used USS GEM, a converted yacht, as a test bed. They concluded that a blue grey that they called omega grey was the best color to avoid detection. They did not examine deception in the same way.

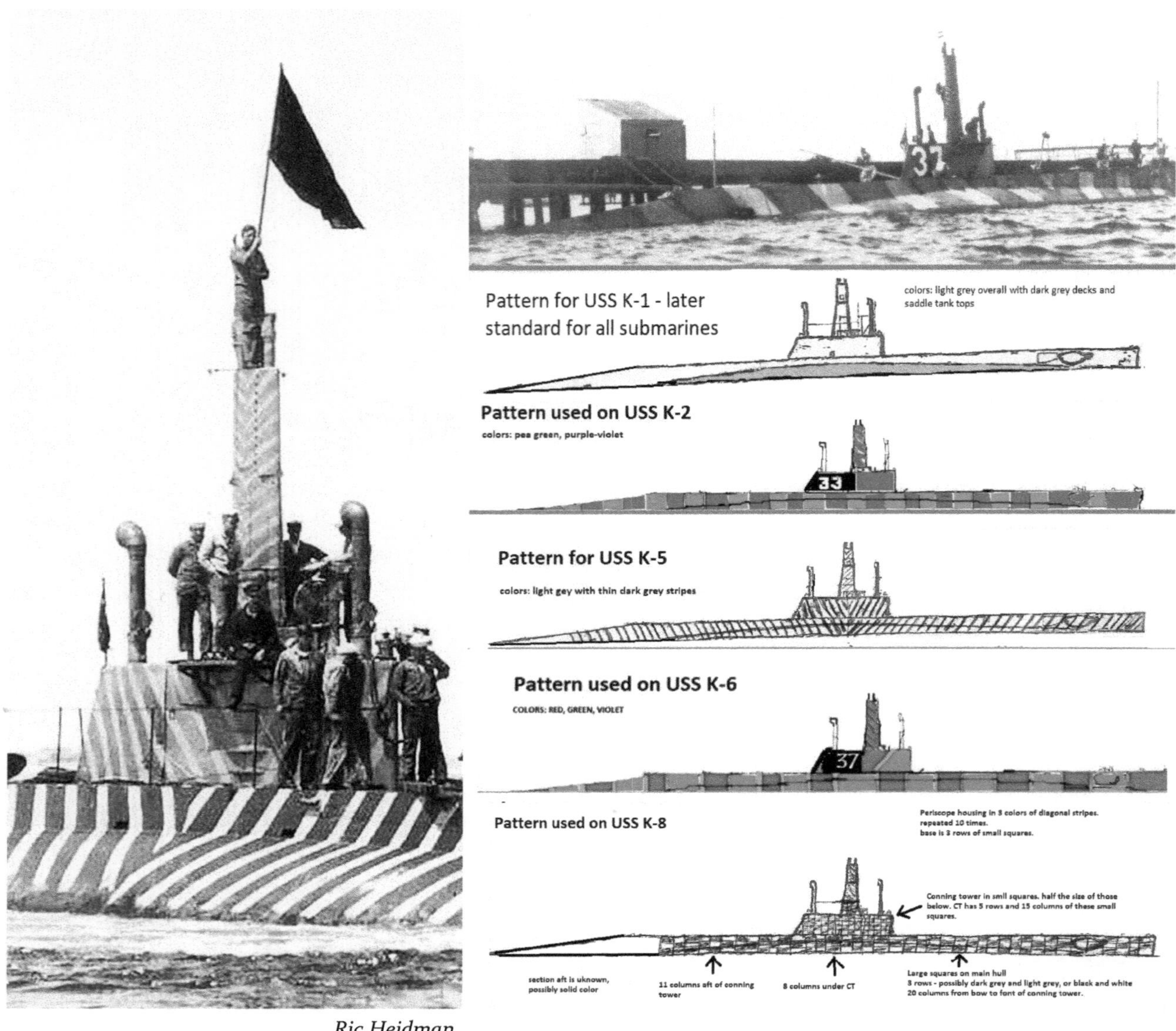

Ric Heidman

The result of the 5 designs mentioned above receiving board approval meant that ships painted using these designs would be eligible for reduced War Risk Insurance rates. This was a very big consideration. Painting an entire ship might cost a few hundred dollars. Operating costs were also in the neighborhood of $100 per day for cargo ships. Such vessels burned up about 30 tons of fuel every day. Building a ship then cost hundreds of thousands of dollars. Some small cargo ships of around 3000 tons were built in 1918 for a cost of around $300,000. We often forget the effect inflation has on prices, especially for items over a century old. The first Boeing 747 airliner cost $24M when it was built. Today it would be almost $300M for a single aircraft. But Cruise liners today cost more than 5 times as much! When disarmament and arms limitations were discussed after the Great War, the first item that was controlled was the construction of new major warships. It was obvious then, as it still is now, that large warships represent a bigger capital investment in a single item than any other piece of military hardware.

Figure 30
Photograph of the U. S. S. *Gem* Painted According to the Association's System

USS Gem *NH79363*

The Bureau of War Risk Insurance (BWRI) was established in the Treasury Department by the *War Risk Insurance* Act (38 Stat. 711), September 2, 1914, to administer an *insurance* program for U.S. merchant vessels and their cargoes. On 2 Oct 1917 the BWRI warned ship owners that an additional ½% premium would be required for ships not painted with one of the 5 approved schemes. Ship owners could to use any other camouflage design but then they had to get specific approval from the Chairman of the Naval Board. The British had a similar scheme in place from early in the war, but without the penalty incentive. Basic insurance premiums were based on the potential cost of replacing either the ship, its cargo, or both.

There are some interesting details about the operations of the BWRI. There were several sections. The most important here is the part that handled policies on hulls, cargoes, freight and personal effects. The BWRI issued some 27,215 policies during the war. The value of the insurance was over $2 billion. Ship owners paid insurance premiums of $46,746,709.33 for their coverage according to the Bureau's own 1920 report. Claims for insurance were filed for 55 ships that were lost, 11 that were damaged, and a further 5 that were detained or whose voyages were otherwise interfered with. Payments for those cases amounted to less than 29 Million dollars. In other words, the Bureau actually made a substantial profit for guaranteeing that American ships would continue to carry cargoes during the war.

On the Eastern side of the Atlantic there had been no progress in the field of ship camouflage for a few years after the Admiralty discarded the ideas proposed by Professor Kerr. Then LCDR Norman Wilkinson, an artist serving as commander of a small patrol boat, came up with what he later claimed was a completely new idea. Ships could never be truly invisible under the changing conditions of the maritime environment. But applying a high contrast coat of several colors of paint could break up the lines of the ship and deceive an observer into thinking she was going in a different direction or at a different speed than was actually the case. If an enemy submarine saw the ship he might not be able to reach a favorable position to launch a torpedo if he assumed an erroneous course or speed for his target.

Even an error of as little as 2 knots or 15 degrees off course would be nearly enough to ensure the safety of the ship. He sent his idea to the Admiralty and termed it a proposal for protecting merchant ships from submarine attack. Since he had not called for using protective coloration on warships, his paper received a favorable review. A Royal Fleet Auxiliary ship, RFA Industry, was selected as a trials ship. She was painted in a pattern and sent to sea to be observed. The results were very encouraging. The Admiralty ordered plans for painting 50 ships to be prepared immediately. The number was later extended to cover all ships that might be exposed to U-boat attack.

Wilkinson was put in charge of organizing a team for implementing his idea. He was given a large space in the Royal Academy for the Arts at Burlington House in London. His initial staff included 4 other artists who were given commissions as LT, RNVR, and 5 more to supervise painting the designs at major British ports. Within a short time he had a total team of 25 men, supported by at least 24 women (mostly art students) at work preparing camouflage designs for ships. More about how this was done will be found in the chapter on Process. What is important to note here is that the British designs placed heavy emphasis on confusion, and little on concealment. Even dazzle designs tended to fade into a single color at longer ranges. When Wilkinson brought samples of his dazzle designs to the US they were tested in the American installation. The results were of great interest to both sides. Wilkinson's design scored 14.0 in the test. It was the highest score of any design. Mackay used a design that scored less than 5. No American design came in above 10. That meant that the probability of initial detection of an Admiralty design was significantly higher than those developed in the USA. Wilkinson felt that the disruptive effects of his design would give a greater chance of the attacking submarine missing his target. In the end, it seems that both sides came away with the idea

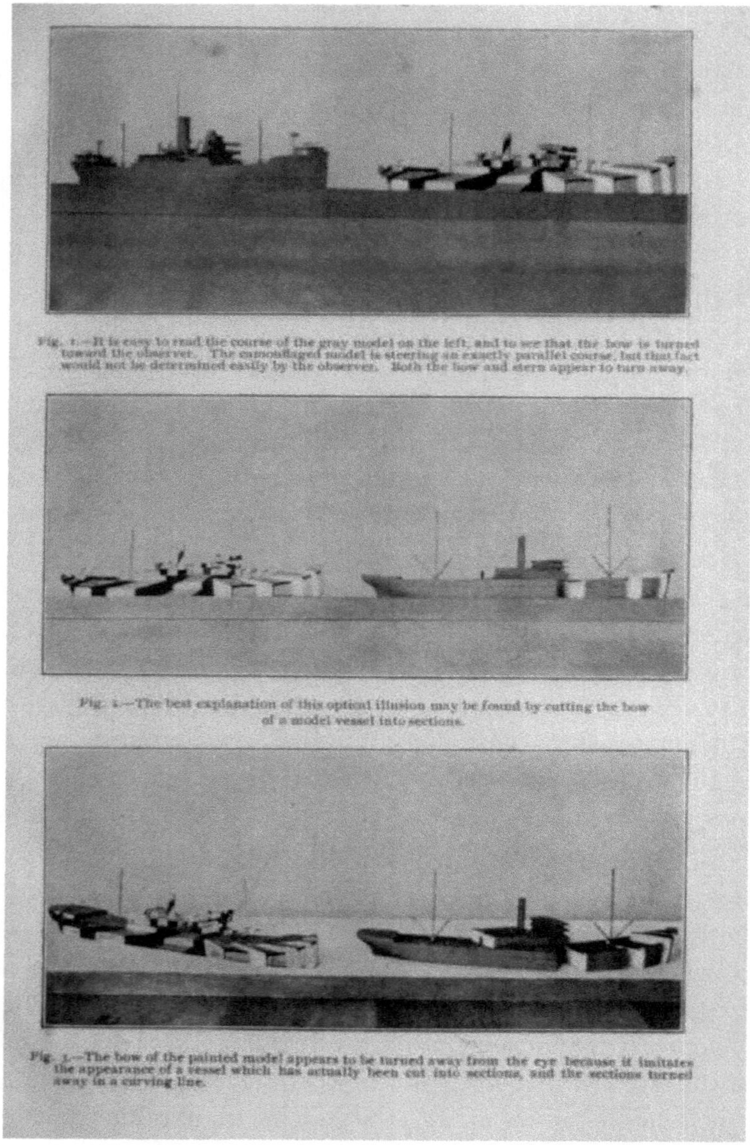

Fig. 1.—It is easy to read the course of the gray model on the left, and to see that the bow is turned toward the observer. The camouflaged model is steering an exactly parallel course, but that fact would not be determined easily by the observer. Both the bow and stern appear to turn away.

Fig. 2.—The best explanation of this optical illusion may be found by cutting the bow of a model vessel into sections.

Fig. 3.—The bow of the painted model appears to be turned away from the eye because it imitates the appearance of a vessel which has actually been cut into sections, and the sections turned away in a curving line.

from Warner: 'The Science of Marine Camouflage Design'

of making changes. The Americans completely abandoned pure concealment designs. The British, over time, revised their patterns in order to use more blue and reduce the total number of colors in their designs. Neither side seemed totally prepared to give much credit to their opposite numbers for making a contribution to these decisions.

Warner, in Washington, emphasized a scientific approach utilizing geometric models. The result was that he developed a regular system for approaching the design of deceptive camouflage. Naval architects also got involved. Newly constructed ships were designed to obscure common visual clues to the direction a ship was moving. The escort designs from near the end of the war for both the "Kil" class gunboats and the "24" class escort sloops were set up to look symmetric. The bow and stern were alike. To make it even more complicated, the single mast was positioned ahead of the funnel in some ships, and aft of the funnel in others. Mast positions were also an important consideration in the design of new standard cargo ships. The traditional masts forward and aft were designed with hinges at the base to allow them to be folded down when the ships left port. This took away the ability of the submarine skipper to use the separation distance between the masts to help gauge direction of travel.

Warner presented some of the ideas he had developed in post-war articles. One of them was the approach of using a cut up model. The model was sliced into several sections and the newly created surfaces given a contrasting color. The result is shown on the previous page, taken from Warner's own article "The Science of Marine Camouflage Design" in the July 1919 issue of the *Transactions of the Illuminating Engineering Society*.

Another approach was to take the outline of the ship and add overlays of geometric shapes that extended beyond the outline. Coloring the sections of the ship that were separated by the overlays in different, and contrasting, colors made the original shape harder to discern.

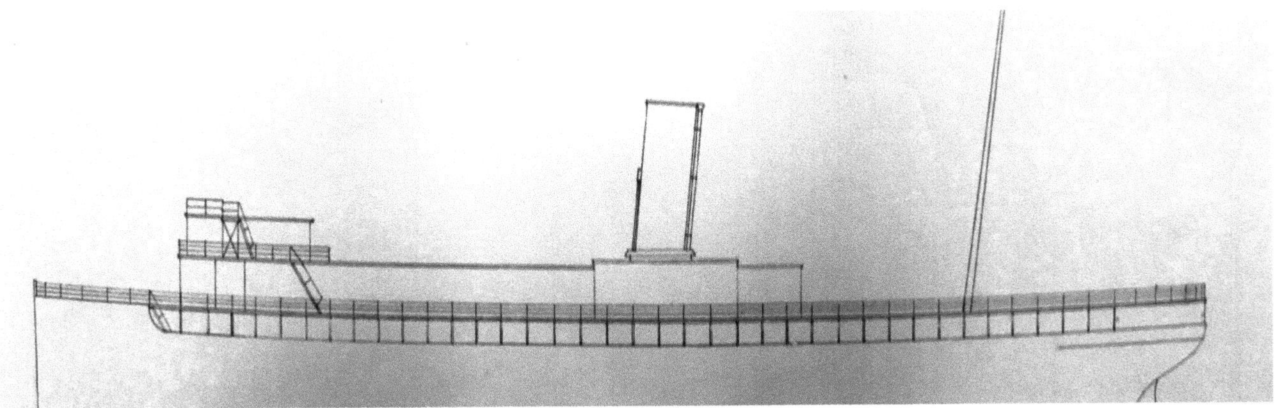

This is the original ship silhouette.

Here it is after overlaying triangles to separate sections.

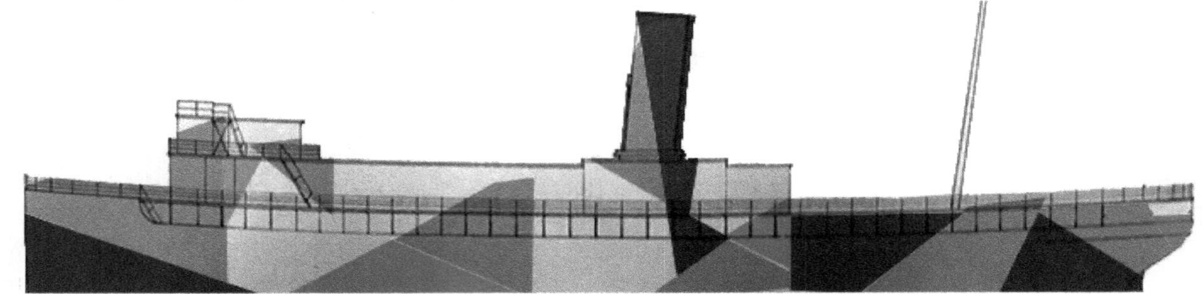

And, finally, here it is after adding colors to make a pattern to obscure significant features.

This illustration uses only straight lines. The artists would usually include curves.

CHAPTER 6

The US goes to war

The German decision to resume unrestricted submarine warfare was not an easy one. The war had dragged on for longer than anyone had envisaged. The British blockade was working, and Germany was no longer able to ignore it. The German high command had envisioned a swift war, similar to the one in 1871, when German armies drove through France and reached the edge of Paris. The German army had been expected to repeat that performance. But new technology, especially machine guns, held back the German advance. Those new weapons also resulted in thousands of battlefield casualties. By the end of 1916 the German army, once thought to be the best on the continent, could not make a decisive breakthrough on the Western Front. The German high command met at Pless on 9 January, 1917 with the Kaiser, the government representatives, headed by Chancellor Bethmann-Hollweg, and the heads of the Army and Navy. The Army chief, Gen. Von Falkenheyn, who had earlier favored unrestricted submarine warfare, and almost convinced Kaiser Wilhelm the previous year to take the step, had been replaced in Aug 1916 by Generals Hindenburg and Ludendorff. They, too, admitted they could not force a victory, and would soon need to find a way to end the war without facing total defeat. Could the Navy help? The new chief of the Navy, Admiral Von Holtzendorff, who had been appointed after Admiral Von Pohl's death, had spent some time looking at the problem. There could be no decisive naval battle because the High Seas Fleet was still too weak to engage the Royal Navy with any hope of victory. But the undersea arm offered an alternative. The fleet now had more U-boats than in 1914, and many of them were larger. These new submarines could travel further, and carry more torpedoes. They still could not follow the accepted rules of prize warfare at sea, but if they were to attack British commerce, the island nation of Great Britain would be brought to her knees for lack of food within a few months. Worries about American involvement were raised. Admiral von Holzendorff responded by promising that England would starve before the Americans could land any soldiers in Europe. He was almost correct. The German government announced on Jan 31st that unrestricted warfare, including unannounced attacks on neutral shipping, would commence again on February 1st.

In America, the first response was purely diplomatic. Diplomatic relations between Germany and the U.S. were broken off on Feb 3rd. But the situation became more serious when American ships were sunk. The President asked congress for authority to arm U.S. ships, but anti-war senators thwarted the passage of the bill with a filibuster. President Wilson then issued a series of Executive orders to prepare for war. He seems to have still harbored a vain hope that American ships would not be targeted. If so, that hope was soon dashed when American flag ships began to be torpedoed without warning, along with those of every other country. President Wilson eventually asked Congress to declare war on 2 April, 1917. By then U-boats were sinking ships at a rate of more than one a day, and England found her food reserves were down to about 2 months total.

Congress provided some legislation but the very first activities were carried out under President Wilson's executive orders. These included taking control of radio communications (order 2585, dated 6 Apr 1917) and transferring the Coast Guard to the control of the Navy Department (order 2587, dated 6 Apr 1917). He declared the approaches to the Panama Canal to be American Defensive Sea Areas (order

2592). On 12 May he officially began a series of executive orders which authorized taking possession of German ships in American ports and placing them under the control of either the US Shipping Board or the Navy Department. The small maintenance crews of those ships had already started to sabotage the ship's engines and other machinery, but the Navy shipyards soon discovered that they were able to repair the damage.

American ships were already being painted in various types of camouflage. Most of the cases used one of the recommended designs. But at least three ships, DEKALB. ANTIGONE, and VON STEUBEN, had the silhouette of a destroyer painted on their sides to frighten away prowling U-boats. The War Risk Insurance Bureau of the Treasury Department was convinced that ship camouflage was a viable and valuable aid in the struggle against the U-boats. They issued guidelines for applying camouflage based on 5 designs that had been accepted by the Naval Advisory Board. The designs were identified by the last name of the person who originated them; William Andrew Mackay, Gerome Brush, Maximilian Toch, Everett L. Warner, and Lewis Herzog. Samples of these designs from the Naval History and Heritage Command collection taken from the report of the Naval Advisory Board are shown below.

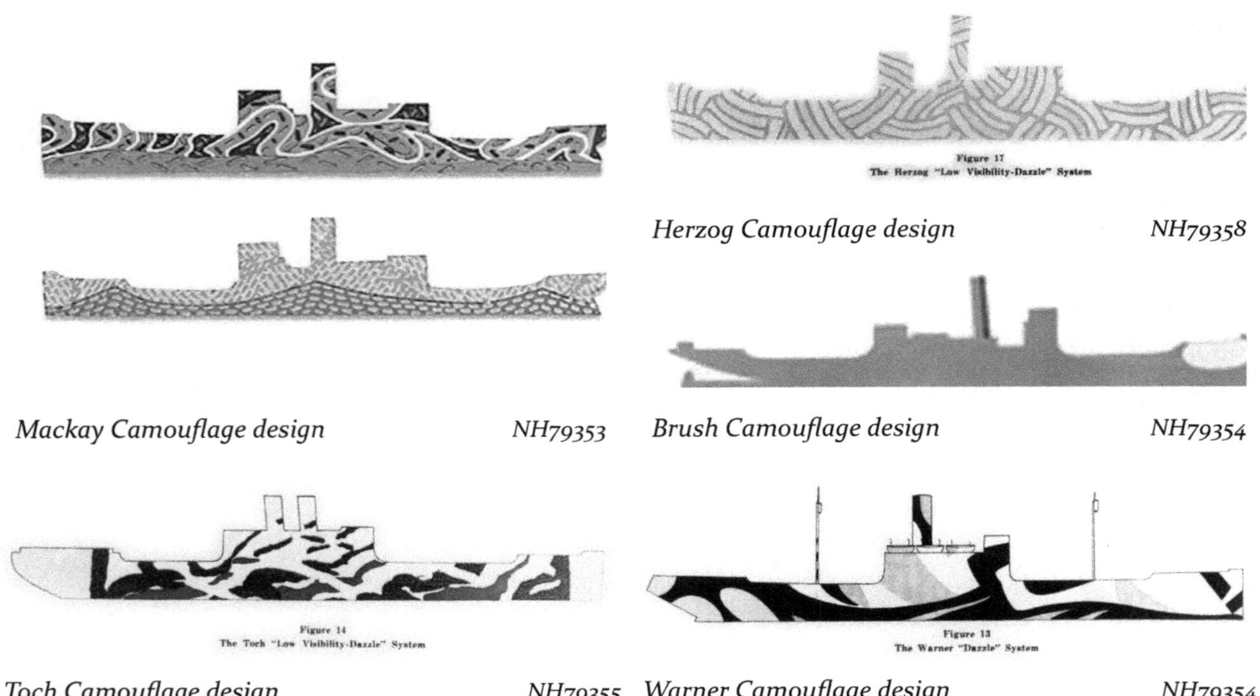

Herzog Camouflage design *NH79358*

Mackay Camouflage design *NH79353*

Brush Camouflage design *NH79354*

Toch Camouflage design *NH79355*

Warner Camouflage design *NH79354*

This measure received additional emphasis when British LCDR Norman Wilkinson, who was also a painter of some talent, convinced the Admiralty to use disruptive camouflage. Wilkinson made his pitch to the Admiralty a success by emphasizing it as a protective measure for merchant vessels. The Admiralty by this time was desperate to find a solution to the depredations of the U-boats. The best actual solution turned out to be the use of convoys. Meanwhile, the US Navy took several initial actions to defend America and to help the Royal Navy.

One way to keep ships flowing to England was to build new ones. If new vessels could be built faster than the submarines could sink them, England could survive. The USSB requisitioned all ships currently under construction in American shipyards, irrespective of who had ordered them. Some were ultimately delivered to their intended owners, but only a few. USSB made contracts for construction of new ships. Standardized designs were selected to streamline the first steps of construction. Some contracts were let with the existing yards for construction of masses of new ships. Others went to new shipyards that were to be built immediately. Many of the new ships ordered were to be built from wood in order to hold down the demand for steel. Special courses were formed to provide manpower for the shipyards and the ships. But these measures, even though implemented quickly, could only provide a long term solution.

In the near term, the U.S. Navy dispatched a squadron of destroyers to join the Royal Navy patrols in anti-submarine operations. These destroyers were assigned a Royal Navy liaison officer and given some minor modifications to prepare them for fighting submarines. This included fitting tracks for carrying the new heavy depth charges that the British had developed. The charges themselves were not supplied at the same time. It took several months for production to catch up with the demand. At first, each ship was given an allowance of only 2 of the new weapons. As stocks increased the number of charges carried grew.

At home, the Navy started to acquire many of the ships and craft that had already been registered. Some of the larger yachts were purchased, others chartered. There were even cases where yacht owners offered to donate their personal pleasure craft outright. These usually ended up being chartered for a symbolic payment. The first of the large yachts were sent to Navy shipyards where their opulent furnishings were stripped and sent to storage. The yachts were equipped with guns, radios, and berthing for their new and enlarged navy crews. The first group of these "draftee" ships sailed for the war zone within 2 months of the U.S. declaration of war. It took a longer time to train new soldiers, but the U.S. Navy was ready to join the war effort almost immediately.

Newly requisitioned former German ships were integrated into the war effort. Some were equipped as navy auxiliaries. Others were outfitted as troopships to ferry the American armies to France. Many of those remaining were incorporated into the Naval Overseas Transport Service (NOTS) to provide supplies for allied forces in France and England.

The total number of German and Austrian ships seized was 91. That total included some 19 passenger ships that would, in the near future, carry a large portion of the U S Army Expeditionary Force sent to turn the tide of the war on land.

None of these actions were having any real impact on the immediate problem of the massive loss of ships. Along with the introduction of convoys, the Admiralty accepted a suggestion by an officer serving on a vessel involved in the anti-submarine war. The officer was LCDR Norman Wilkinson, who was mentioned above. His idea was to camouflage ships. Wilkinson's camouflage was not going to make the ships harder to see. His idea was to paint the ships with high contrast colors in patches that would break up the features that a U-boat commander would look at in order to make a successful torpedo attack. The Dazzle Camouflage he proposed would make it harder to determine the course and speed of the ship. An error in either of those details could easily cause the submerged submarine to fail to get to a favorable position to fire a torpedo. A Royal Fleet Auxiliary ship named Industry was given a dazzle treatment in October, 1917. The trial was a success. Wilkinson was removed from command of the 83 foot minesweeper he had been given, and placed in charge of organizing the Dazzle Section at the Admiralty. He was given a set of 4 offices at Burlington House, the site of the Royal Academy for the Arts. His initial staff was composed of himself, LT Cecil George Charles King and 18 others, mostly with art backgrounds. The section included a model making section and a special viewing theater for assessing the effect of the painted design. Additional officers were detailed to supervise the application of the paint designs at the major ports of England. Foremost among them was Edward Wadsworth who was responsible for Bristol and Liverpool.

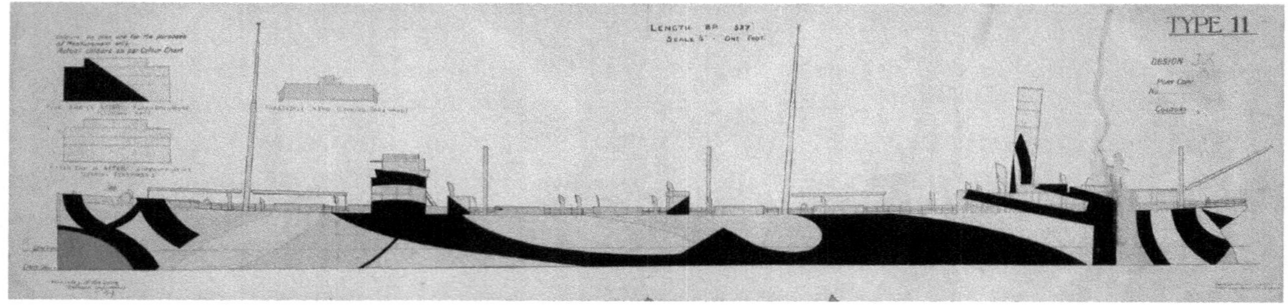

British Admiralty design for a tanker, Type 11 design JX port side *NARA RG19*

The Royal Navy also prepared dazzle camouflage designs for American ships that were already in Europe. Here is how the commander of the first American destroyers recorded the application of British camouflage to his ship in August, 1917.

> "We have been painting the Wadsworth with the new "camouflage" or dazzle effect. The colors used are white, black, blue (2 shades), gray (3 shades), green, and pink. The idea is not to obtain invisibility, but to obtain deception."
>
> From "The Queenstown Patrol 1917", the diary of CDR Joseph K Taussig, Naval War College Press, Newport, R.I.,1996.

All US destroyers in Europe were painted with the British designs. The American designs were applied to new destroyers as they were being built, and to a few ships that had either returned from the War zone, like USS Patterson, or that never went there, like USS Henley and USS Lawrence. The RN designs also included some of the converted yachts and former Coast guard cutters that were then based in Gibraltar or in France, where they patrolled the areas around Brest and the English Channel. USS Piqua was listed as admiralty order US 44, USS Marietta as order US 8, and USS Cythera as order US 21.

The Admiralty also integrated the American converted yachts into their own communications system and assigned them radio call signs from the British sequence. Under international agreements American stations were given call signs which began with the letter "N" or "L". The letters "K" and "W" were also assigned to the U.S., but were used for shore stations. British call letters for ships normally started with the letter "G". During the Great War, Piqua was known phonetically as "George Sail King Mike". The phonetic alphabet in use then was not the same as the one commonly used now. The pictures on the next page show examples.

USS Cythera in RN Camouflage *navsource 1217508* *USS Piqua in RN camouflage* *NH42427*

The US Forces based in France used the French communications network to send messages to American ships at sea. Assignments to escort ships or coastal convoys were often sent by radio, but it was a slow method. A change of orders to keep a yacht as an escort for a coastal convoy beyond the originally scheduled point might take 5 hours to send and receive confirmation. The range of radio transmissions at the time was also limited by both power and atmospheric conditions.

Norman Wilkinson, personally, sailed to the US in early 1918 with a large number (90) of camouflage patterns prepared by himself and his artists. These plans remained in Washington and are in the US National Archives. Wilkinson was escorted around American facilities by LT Everett Warner. Warner was then in the process of organizing his own design team in Washington. The two men appear to have had some differences of opinion as to how the problem of ship camouflage was to be approached. Warner later wrote that Wilkinson had no idea of how to formulate rules underlying the disruptive process while Wilkinson returned to England convinced that the Americans did not understand his theory of disruptive designs.

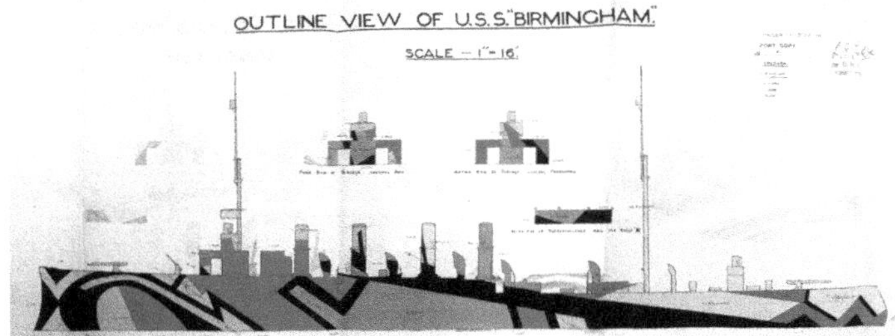

Birmingham design plan *NARA RG32*

The American National Archives includes an Admiralty design that was applied to the USS Birmingham, a cruiser employed as a convoy escort operating from Gibraltar. It was produced as Admiralty order USS 36 and was actually used on the ship. The American copy is labeled as copy no. 2 and dated Apr 1918 which indicates that it was produced after Wilkinson's visit to the U.S.

USS Birmingham *NH 56393*

Marietta *Navsource 120901515*

CHAPTER 7

Convoys

Maritime commerce has always been a target in times of conflict. One of the ways to protect it has been to provide an armed escort. For ships, this often meant collecting several merchant vessels and sending a warship to accompany them to their destination. But the idea of convoying British ships during the First World War had not been seriously considered. British merchants were still sailing independently. It seems the Admiralty had looked at the idea of convoy and turned it down. There were plenty of excuses. Operating in convoys required station keeping. The leaders of the fighting navy did not believe that merchant navy officers were up to doing that. Keeping several ships in close proximity, a necessity for visual signaling was also expected to substantially increase the risk of collision. Then there was the delay caused by waiting for a convoy to assemble and sailing at the speed of the slowest vessel. Additionally, the arrival of a convoy of several ships was expected to cause unacceptable congestion in the arrival port. The ships escorting a convoy were defenders, pure and simple. This did not sit well with Royal Navy Officers imbued with the spirit of offensive action. They preferred to go hunting for enemy craft in order to attack them. These were all beliefs shared by some of the senior admirals in the Royal Navy. Much of it was not based upon any serious investigation because the Admiralty did not have a staff to do that when the war started. Whenever the subject was raised it was dismissed as impractical because that was what had been decided on previous occasions when it came up for discussion. Even dissemination of probable submarine locations based on intercepted radio transmissions was initially limited to just a few admirals at Whitehall. Convoy was used for escorting troopships, ships sailing to neutral Scandinavian ports, and the cross-channel French coal trade and BEF supplies. The channel convoys were primarily a case of having sufficient auxiliary patrol vessels available for use as escorts. This was the situation in the Admiralty when Sir John Jellicoe took office as First Sea Lord in 1917.

The risk of collision was real. Destroyers Jarvis and Benham collided in July 1918. A heavy fog rather than their camouflage may have been the main reason for their crash. Stockton crumpled her bow in a nighttime collision with SS Slieve Bloom. Here, too, the major factor may have been darkness, not camouflage.

When the new phase of German unrestricted submarine warfare began to sink ships at a truly alarming rate, the statistics could be delivered to Admiral Jellicoe by the recently formed staff. The data was not accompanied by a recommendation for actions. The idea of convoy was brought up. But it was not immediately adopted. It was said that the intervention of American Admiral William S. Sims might have been the event that caused the change in Admiralty policy. Sims had been sent to England in March, before the US declaration of war the following month. He sailed on the U.S. passenger ship, New York , under the assumed name of S. J .Davidson. Less than a week after his arrival in Liverpool,

Sims sent his first cable message to the Secretary of the Navy, which stated: "The submarine issue is very much more serious than people realize in America." He is reported to have told Admiral Jellicoe that adopting convoys as a defensive measure was a good idea. However he may have approached it, the idea of convoys was soon adopted by the Admiralty.

The organizational effort to establish and control convoys was considerable. A port for assembling the ships involved had to be established and the ships gathered there to await a cruiser escort. The speed of the ships was considered. Fast ships sailed independently, depending on their speed to keep them safe. Slower ships were assigned to convoys. The convoy, of course, was restricted to best speed of the slowest ship. The merchant ships had to be assigned to positions in the convoy and given instructions regarding communications and emergency maneuvers. Signals for maneuvering, both visual and whistle, were printed in separate instruction books for this, and additional men were provided for visual signals, radio, and gun crews. Preparing the routes, printing the orders, and even training the additional crew required, all took time. Before long, special equipment was also supplied. Ships were equipped with special floats to tow in fog to allow the next astern to avoid creeping up and hitting them. As the war progressed, the merchant navy officers were even given tables of engine rpm change in order to increase or decrease speed, and times needed to move ahead or astern by a cable length. A cable, by the way, is a nautical measurement equal to 200 yards.

On the Navy side, Convoy routes and frequency of sailing had to be worked out. Shipping companies provided lists of ships to join convoys, and when they would be available. The cruiser escorts were initially taken from the local cruiser squadrons. The local squadrons had been on patrol to look for potential hostile surface raiders. Now they sailed just ahead of the convoy hoping to spot enemy submarines in time to divert their charges to a course where the U-boat would be unable to harm them. The cruisers also provided an answer to enemy surface raiders.

The first ocean convoy was organized from Gibraltar to Great Britain in May, 1917. That was the same month that the first trial ship using dazzle camouflage put to sea. All the convoy ships arrived safely. A second experimental convoy sailed from Hampton Roads the following month. HMS Roxburgh was the principal escort. Her captain reported that the 10 merchant vessels had managed to handle all the expected difficulties in keeping station, zig-zagging, and communicating, without any major problems. More convoys were arranged. A 4 or 8 day interval between sailings became standard. The convoys were given identification letters; HG, HH, HS, HD, and HN. The "H" stood for homeward bound/ the second letter indicated the port of origin; G – Gibraltar, H – Hampton Roads, N – New York, and S – Sydney, Nova Scotia. Each was escorted for the entire voyage by a large cruiser or armed merchant cruiser. Schedules were arranged to have each convoy met by a group of escorts, destroyers and sloops, at a rendezvous point near England.

Many senior officers from the retired list were recalled to act as convoy commodores. They conducted the pre-sailing conference at which the ship captains were briefed about sailing in a convoy. Ships were given assignments to specific stations by row and column within the convoy at this conference. Convoys had a specific route to follow that took them through a series of geographical check points. Between those check points the convoy commodore had a lot of room to maneuver. Ships that became separated could try to rejoin their convoy by heading for one of those points. The specific assignments and routes, and instructions for both visual and radio communications, were given to each ship at the conference or in a separate sealed envelope just before sailing. Additional information was contained in a separate sealed envelope that was to be opened only after the convoy sailed. Emergency procedures and signals were emphasized. It was standard procedure for any ship sighting a submarine, or what they thought was a submarine, to broadcast a radio warning giving the position prefaced by the code word "ALL O". Plots of these locations were kept at the admiralty and could be used to redirect convoys around areas of suspected submarine activity. The US Navy even made a briefing guide for the conduct of the convoy pre-sailing conference and the points to be covered.

A sample order based on actual orders for convoy H. G. 50 from Gibraltar follows. Note the scope and details in the instructions, for example, Masthead height was included to help the ships maintain station by using a sextant or stadimeter to get a visual estimate of the distance between lines and columns.

Convoy Order H. G. 50. H. M. Dockyard, Gibraltar,

Sailing Orders. *30 January, 1918.*

FORCES.

(*a*) *Convoy H. G. 50.*

Commodore, Acting Commander F. G. Thompson, R. N. R.;

Vice Commodore, Master of S. S. *Merchant Prince;*

17 merchant ships (see Appendix A and B).

(*b*) *Gibraltar Danger Zone Escort.*

Commander Cochrane, Ft. N,, S. O. until ocean escort joins.

H. M. S. *Dianthus,* senior officer's ship.

H. M. S. *Laggan.*

H. M. S. *Hibiscus.*

U. S. S. *Dale.*

(*c*) *Ocean escort.*

Captain C. L. Hussey, U. S. N., senior officer.

U. S. S. *Birmingham.*

1. Information of enemy forces and of our own convoys will be furnished commodore and commander of escorts, who will visit "Operations" just before sailing. An escort of destroyers and trawlers is to meet *Convoy* H. G. 50 at 9.30 a. m., 7 February in latitude ______ N.; longitude ______ W.

The destroyers of this escort will bring instructions as to route for *Convoy* H. G. 50 to follow in British waters and as to point when *Ocean Escort* will part company with convoy.

2. ______ The *Convoy* is to proceed in one body guarded by designated escorts from Gibraltar to the United Kingdom, passing through the following positions:

(I) ______ miles ______ Magnetic from ______

(II) ______ Latitude ______ N.; ______ Longitude ______ W.

(III) ______ Latitude ______ N.; ______ Longitude ______ W.

(IV) ______ Latitude ______ N.; ______ Longitude ______ W.

(V) ______ Latitude ______ N.; ______ Longitude ______ W.

(VI) ______ Thence toward __________________

3. ______ (*a*) *Convoy H. G. 50.* Leave Gibraltar noon, 1 February. 1918. Form up before leaving position 7 miles north (mag.) of ______ and proceed along designated route so as to arrive at latitude ______ N., longitude ______ W., at 9.30 a. m. 7 February. If time must be wasted, waste it on that part of the route south of latitude ______ N., and west of longitude ______ W. Speed, 7 knots. Detach S. S. *Basse Terre* in latitude ______ N. for ______.

(*b*) *Gibraltar Danger Zone Escort* guard convoy from Gibraltar to latitude ______ N., longitude ______ W., then proceed to meet O. M. 42 (see Art. 60, C. B,, 648).

(*c*) *Ocean Escort* leave Gibraltar in time to join convoy during daylight, and before convoy passes latitude ______ N., longitude ______ W., guard convoy from time of joining until relieved by destroyers.

4. Be governed by C. B. 648 (particular attention invited to Articles 38 and 51) ; C. B. 648A; and C. B. 585 with recent modifications to conform to C. B. 648.

5. The following papers are appended to this order:

(*a*) Plan of Convoy Formation.

(*b*) List and Data of Vessels in Convoy.

(*c*) Instructions to Masters.

(*d*) Information Relative to Enemy Submarines and Mines and our Convoys.

(*e*) Signals additional to those in C. B. 585 for use with this convoy only.

6. Report to Admiralty by W. T. via Brest (enter call letter here). Destroyers will answer (enter call letters here) call if they do not hear Brest answer. Use Convoy Cipher No. 2. Use G. M. T. For this convoy use call letters as follows: ______

____

(Signature.)

Copies to—

Commodore.

Vice Commodore, S. S. *Merchant Prince.*

Commanding Officer, U. S. S. *Birmingham.*

Commanding Officer, H. M. S. *Dianthus.*

Appendix A.

[Note.—Burn this sheet as soon as convoy finally disperses.)

Plan of convoy formation.

Convoy ______		W. T. Call ______
"Ocean Escort"	H. M. S. ______	Ships in column to be ______ yards apart.
	Call Flag ______	Columns to be ______ yards apart.
	W/T Call ______	Cruising speed to be ______ knots.
	M. H.[1] from water line ______ feet.	Convoy guide to be S. S. ______
Commodore in S. S. ______		Vice Commodore in S. S ______

Port Columns.					Starboard Columns.		
Spare Column S. A.	**Spare Column T. A.**	**Column U. A.**	**Column V. A.**	**Column W. A.**	**Column X. A.**	**Column Y. A.**	**Column Z. A.**
S. S. ______	S. S. ______	S. S. ______	S. S. ______	S. S. ______	S. S. ______	S. S. ______	S. S. ______
Flag ... S. A.	Flag .. T. A.	Flag .. U. A.	Flag .. V. A.	Flag .. W. A.	Flag .. X. A.	Flag .. Y. A.	Flag .Z. A.
W/T ______	W/T ______	W/T ______	W/T ______	W/T ______	W/T ______	W/T ______	W/T ______
M. H ... feet	M. H ... feet	M. H ... feet	M. H ... feet	M. H ... feet	M. H ... feet	M. H ... feet	M. H ... feet
S. S. ______	S. S. ______	S. S. ______	S. S. ______	S. S. ______	S. S. ______	S. S. ______	S. S. ______
Flag .. S. B.	Flag .. T. B.	Flag .. U. B.	Flag .. V. B.	Flag .. W. B.	Flag .. X. B.	Flag .. Y. B.	Flag ... Z. B.
W/T ______	W/T ______	W/T ______	W/T ______	W/T ______	W/T ______	W/T ______	W/T ______
M. H ... feet	M. H ... feet	M. H ... feet	M. H ... feet	M. H ... feet	M. H ... feet	M. H ... feet	M. H ... feet
S. S. ______	S. S. ______	S. S. ______	S. S. ______	S. S. ______	S. S. ______	S. S. ______	S. S. ______
Flag .. S. C.	Flag .. T. C.	Flag .. U. C.	Flag .. V. C.	Flag .. W. C.	Flag .. X. C.	Flag .. Y. C.	Flag .. Z.C.
W/T ______	W/T ______	W/T ______	W/T ______	W/T ______	W/T ______	W/T ______	W/T ______
M. H ... feet	M. H ... feet	M. H ... feet	M. H ... feet	M. H ... feet	M. H ... feet	M. H ... feet	M. H ... feet

[1] M. H. is height of mainmast head above water line.

List of ships in convoy No. ______ .

Name of ship.	Flag.	Gross tonnage.	Speed.	Des-tina-tion.	Cargo.	Nature of gun.	Whether fitted with W/T.	Number of W/T operators.	Number of signalers.	Position in convoy.	Remarks.

Instructions to masters ______form.

H. M. Dockyard ______

______, 1918.

Convoy Order ______

Instructions to Masters.

1. The ______, commanded by ______ ______, is Ocean Escort. ______, in ______ commands First Danger Zone Escort ______, is Senior Officer.

Add in this paragraph any additional information that may be deemed appropriate, but no orders should be in this paragraph.

2. The Convoy __________ is to proceed in one body guarded by Escorts from __________, to __________, through positions already communicated to the Commodore and Vice Commodore.

3. Have steam by __________ a. m. __________, p.m. __________, 1918.

Be at short stay by __________ a. m. __________, p.m. __________, 1918.

Weigh anchor at __________ a. m. __________, p.m. __________, 1918.

Then take assigned position in convoy astern of your column leader.

Column leaders by distinguishing flags of their columns below code pennant and form as follows:

Formation will proceed when and as directed by __________

4. Enter in this paragraph and references to printed instructions.

5. In the event of fog when forming the convoy you will ____________________

Fill in special instructions on dotted lines, but do not repeat instructions already contained in printed book of instructions.

In the event of fog at other times __________

6. __________ Enter in this paragraph all necessary instructions relating to reports to Admiralty, communication with escorts, cipher to he used, time to be used, and special call letters if they have not been given otherwise.

7. _________The following papers are appended:

(*a*) Plan of Convoy Formation.

(*b*)

(*c*)

____

(Signature.)

Copies to—

Masters.
Commodore.
Vice Commodore.
Commander First Zone Escort.
Commander Ocean Escort.
O. P., B. C. O., R. O.
Naval Secretary.

By August the results were impressive enough to add more routes; HL from Sierra Leone and HD from Dakar. Convoys for outbound vessels were also arranged; OM from Milford, OD from Devonport, OF from Falmouth, and OB from Buncara. The OB convoys were soon supplanted by OQ from Queenstown. When convoys were needed again in the Second World War, a similar naming convention was used.The officers in charge of the convoys, the convoy commodores, usually sailed only on one route. They were accompanied by a special staff of 3 signalmen and a wireless operator to supplement the regular merchant crew. This was in addition to any naval Armed Guard personnel assigned to man guns that had been fitted.

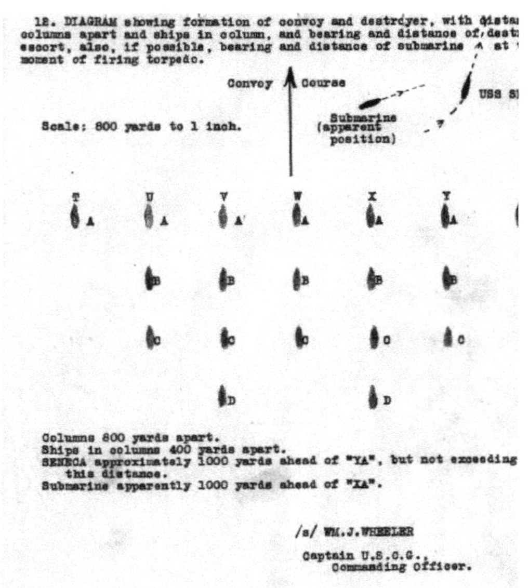

Here is a diagram of how a typical convoy formation would look. Note that both columns and rows are given letter designations. In the Second World War numbers were used for rows to avoid possible confusion. The ocean escort would usually be stationed ahead of the convoy until there was a rendezvous with the destroyers that escorted the convoy on the last day or so through the most dangerous areas.

Ultimately, it was the convoy system that resulted in the defeat of the U-boats. The probability of a submarine sighting a convoy of 10 ships was only slightly larger than that of locating a single ship. It was very much lower than the probability of finding even one of ten ships proceeding independently. In short, the submarines ran out of targets. Pressing home an attack with escorts present was dangerous to the submarine. Even if they did manage to launch a torpedo, there was almost no opportunity to conduct another attack on one of the other vessels in the convoy. The presence of escorting warships meant the U-boat was likely to be attacked. Launching a torpedo was certain to betray the existence of the submarine. Making extended or multiple periscope observations might do the same. The submarine had no chance to run away. Speed when submerged was very limited, and moving at higher speed used up battery power very quickly. If the U-boat dived deeper after firing a torpedo, it was not likely to see the convoy again when it returned to the surface. The failure of the German Unrestricted Submarine Warfare campaign was primarily due to the 1500 convoys that kept both England and the American Expeditionary Force supplied. There were nearly 84,000 ships that sailed in convoys. Only 257 of them were sunk by submarines. That's a loss rate of less than 1%. Ships sailing independently, not in convoy, often had a loss rate of nearly 25%.

There is one more thing to say about convoys. As more and more ships were being painted in dazzle camouflage each sailing of a convoy began to take on the appearance of a floating art exhibition. The ships were in place of the artists canvases and were much bigger. The side of a painted ship was often 300 to 400 feet long. Unfortunately for the artists, the designs were not for sale. The ships were all repainted when the war ended. None of the various ships painted to commemorate the 100th anniversary of the war were painted in designs that bore any real similarity to the designs actually used during the conflict. That was one contributing motivation for the writing of this book.

CHAPTER 8

Process

The design process started with the selection of a ship, or class of ships, that needed to be camouflaged. In the case of warships, the Bureau of Construction and Repair took existing blueprints and made a simplified version of the side view of the ship. This would become a standard Form number 2 for use in preparing the design. For merchant ships, the basic Form number 2 was adapted from the blueprints of an actual ship provided by the shipyard that had built her. Merchant type designs were prepared for one ship that matched the description of the type. Unlike warship designs, not all ships within the type were sister ships. The following illustration shows a blank form 1 pattern for USS Petrel with 3 pre-printed additions taped in place. This version was then sent to be lithographed and copies used for adding the designs.

Blank form 1 NARA RG36

The lower right hand section was for approval signatures.

The upper left hand side section was for a generic identifier.

The upper right hand section was for a specific identification. The actual number and design letter would be added later. Standard colors to be used would be stamped in the section provided for them, as shown in the next illustration.

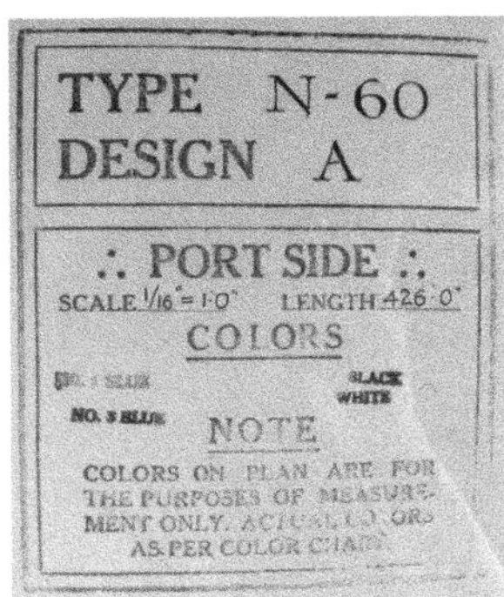

Form 1 identification and color guide box

One sheet was prepared for the starboard side view, and a mirror image was made for the port side. The starboard side was modified to include views from ahead and astern and fore or aft views of parts of the superstructure, like the bridge, that would receive camouflage. A standard identification table was prepared and added to the upper right hand corner of both sheets. The table included place for an identification number for the ship type and for the design letter. A section of the table was included for noting the actual colors to be used. Rubber stamps were made for each of the standard colors. Those needed for any particular design could then be stamped in the place reserved for them when the design was complete. It is interesting to note that the first Navy designs, N1 designs A, B, C, and D, were prepared before form 2 became standardized. The surviving file copies do not refer to standard colors. Indeed, they list colors and the sheet design identification in hand drafted lines, sometimes in different locations. This is as an indication that the design section already commenced working before deciding on how to keep track of what they were doing. Those 4 designs appear to have been sent to New Jersey very quickly. That was where the 4 former Morgan Line Passenger ships were being converted to minelayers. The ships sailed to Europe even before there was a supply of mines for them to plant. But they were camouflaged in those first designs prepared by the team. A later set of designs was prepared for the same vessels, but was never used.

NO 2

LITHOGRAPHS

TYPE	DESIGN	WHEN SENT	NO ORDERED		WHEN RETURNED	NO. RETURNED	
			PORT	STAR		PORT	STAR
9	J	7/10	300	300	7/17	272	262
1	E	"	"	"	"	271	272
2	J	"	"	"	"	284	284
10	D	"	"	"	"	267	267
9	I	"	"	"	"	279	277
3	J	"	"	"	"	280	277
6	J	"	"	"	"	268	268
7	H	"	"	"	"	264	264

Susan Strange *NARA RG19*

Lithograph copies were ordered in sufficient quantity to provide one for every location where they might be needed, here is an original receipt showing the orders and quantities received.

The model making room received both side and top views in order to make wooden models of the ships. Many models were made to a scale of about 1:500. Most naval vessels had only one design of camouflage prepared, but merchant ship patterns were often produced in many designs for each type. The model makers produced as many duplicates as were needed.

165-ww-70c-010

Note the chart of silhouettes on the wall in the photo.

The US prepared camouflage for 28 different standardized "types" of merchant vessels based on the physical characteristics of the ships. These included the number and placement of funnels, masts, and the size and location of any raised structures above the main deck. The British had 37 "types".

The models were the chief tools for the artists. They also received a blank copy of Form number 2 for each design. The designs were painted on the models by the artists.

Approved designs were tested to see how effective they were. There was a small local testing laboratory in Washington. William Mackay had his own testing lab in NY. Mackay often used plaster cast models for his testing. More serious testing was conducted at the Eastman facility in Rochester NY. That was where Loyd Jones and his team developed instruments for measurement as well as conducting tests of designs sent to them. The facility in Rochester used Lake Erie as a background for many tests and tried to examine the effectiveness of the designs under as wide a range of conditions of time and weather as possible.

U.S. Navy Department, National Archives and Record Service *165-ww-70c-007*

Designs that received approval were copied onto a fresh version of a Form number two with the colors to be used stamped in the corner. A team at the camouflage center did this. It included a number of women. A few may have been civilian employees, but others were enlisted in the navy as "yeomanettes". Women did not have the right to vote yet. That came in 1920. But the Secretary of the Navy, who supported women's suffrage, found a loophole in the law that allowed him to order their acceptance in shore based support jobs. Women who enlisted were given the rating of female yeoman (yeoman (F)) hence the appellation. In the picture below of the design room, almost half the personnel are female. Another interesting point is that the yeomanettes were given the same pay as their male counterparts, initially $28.75 per month. A century later we find that equal pay for equal work is still an issue in civilian life. Women appear in two of the following pictures.

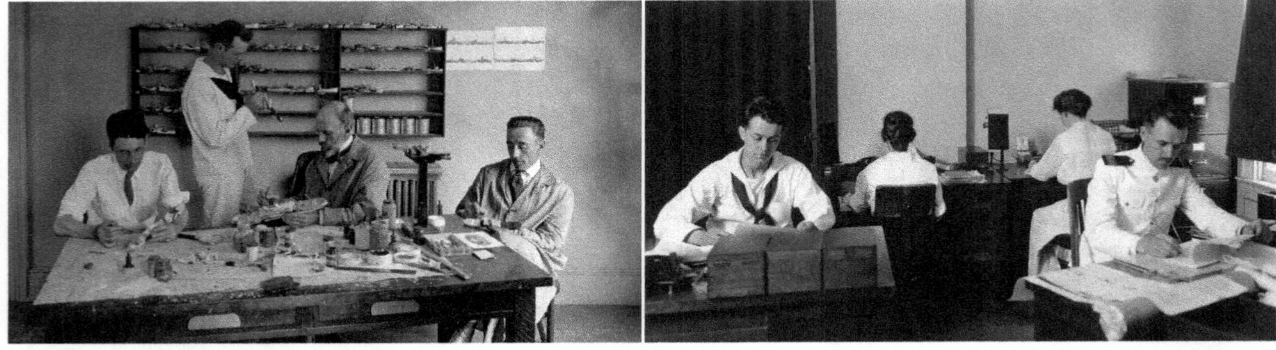

unknown, Stevenson, Waugh, Manley 165-ww-70c-001 *admin office, Lt. Van Buskirk on right* 165-ww-70c-004

Women on camo team camopedia.com *Model storage room* 165-ww-70c-008.

The newly colored patterns were signed by Acting Captain John D Beuret. He was a Naval Academy graduate who chose to serve in the construction corps rather than as a line officer at sea. A few years after the war President Warren Harding would appoint him Chief Constructor of the Navy and head of the Bureau of Construction and Repair. He was awarded the Navy Cross for his service during World War I. A total of 1298 such medals were awarded I World War I. But only two Construction Corps officers received them. The signed pattern became the master version from which multiple lithographed copies were made. The lithographed copies were distributed to the district camouflage supervisors in every location where camouflage could be applied.

The local artists supervised the adaptation of the design on the lithograph to full size versions on the ships. The limits of each colored section were drawn on the sides and structures of the ships with chalk. Sometimes an observer would look on from a distance and direct the application of the lines or paint by means of a megaphone, gestures, or even a signal mirror. Often, the color to be used was indicated somewhere within the delimited markings. At that point the shipyard painters came in and painted each section in the proper colors. The painting teams could be as many as 60 men, depending upon the size of the ship being camouflaged. They received 60 cents per hour for their work in March, 1918.

The lithographs had an additional note on the bottom part of the standard label underneath the section where the actual colors were stamped. It read: "Colors on plan are for the purposes of measurement only. Actual colors as per color chart." This warning was taken verbatim from the British plans supplied by LCDR Wilkinson. On the British plans it usually appeared on the top left side as a separate item. It was an important reminder. The artist often felt that any deviation from the specified colors might detract from the effect the pattern was supposed to cause. Other artists working in different projects had no qualms about taking "artistic license" and painting ships in red even though red was never one of the colors used for actual ship camouflage. Here is an example in a poster by Leon Alaric Shafer promoting war loans.

Poster from Naval Heritage and History Command *NHHC 99-064-p*

At the time of this writing one of the original British plans for SS Warlingham has been copied to several sites on the internet. The hull of the ship in those copies is bright red. The example probably comes from Imperial War museum catalog item DAZ 663. Here is the original plan for UK Type 4 design A. That plan calls for colors of Black, White, Yellow, Blue-Grey, and Green. The original color list indicates that the sections in red in the internet examples (and in reddish brown on the illustration below) should be yellow, those in yellow should be green, and the mauve/pink parts should be blue-grey. The internet example does not have the standard warning on the top left. My illustration is a public domain item from the US National Archives. This case shows how accepting uncorroborated internet materials might distort historical accuracy.

It is also important to mention some other small problems in researching World War I ship camouflage. First, as already noted, it should be obvious that the appearance of an item on the internet is not a guarantee of the accuracy of the information presented. Second, photographs do not lie. But contemporary photos from that era do suffer from a sort of color blindness in the blue range of the spectrum that can result in difficulties in discerning areas that were painted in blue or blue combinations. Finally, not all paint colors specified were always available at the time a ship was due to be camouflaged. This might have caused the camoufleur to make changes that had not been previously

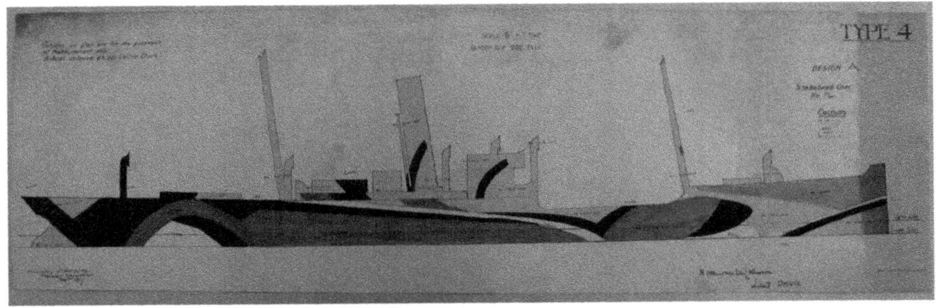

Public Domain image from US National Archives RG19

authorized. Also, adapting a pattern to a similar ship could result in deviations from the original. A careless camoufleur supervisor or painter could make mistakes. This is very evident when one reads the contemporary accounts of the Aides for Information in the US Navy Naval Districts when they reported on camouflaged ships entering the harbors where they were assigned.

The actual painting of the ship started with a camoufleur supervisor comparing the lithograph design to the actual ship and making measurements to allow him to copy the design to the ship. He did this by climbing scaffolding and walking around the decks in order to mark the lines between different colors with yellow chalk. In one of the early applications, an EFC camoufleur in Philadelphia found he could attach a bit of yellow chalk to the end of a bamboo pole in order to mark areas not easily reachable from the decks or scaffolding.

Tanker Sarah Thompson in port, 1918 — *NH 99781*

Workers Painting Ship 1918
courtesy of Prof Roy Behrens

The shipyard painters were called in once the pattern had been marked. The time available to finish the job was usually quite limited. Some ships were painted during a wait for forming the next convoy. Convoys sailed on a 4 or 8 day cycle. Paint crews could number 60 or more persons for very large ships. Each one worked on a particular area with the color specified. Smaller crews often worked many extra hours in order to finish before the ship was to sail. The crews skipped regular meals. Instead they brought sandwiches and ate them on the job.

Newly constructed ships might even be launched with their camouflage patterns already at least partially applied

The process followed by the British was almost the same. First they made one or more models representing a specific ship or class of ships. Each model was painted in a camouflage pattern.

The artists used wash colors to allow for rapid alteration after the next step if it was necessary.

The painted model was studied in a prepared theatre through a submarine periscope using differing backgrounds in order to assess its effectiveness. The British did not have a separate testing section like the one at Rochester, NY. Their instrumentation was not nearly as extensive as that used by the American testing section, but it appears to have been comparable to the smaller American testing theaters in Washington DC and in New York. The final painted version of the model was delivered to the plan makers who copied it on to a 1/16th inch profile plan of the ship on white paper showing both port and starboard sides. Many of the individuals working on this phase were female art students at Burlington House. The original British Camouflage team consisted of 3 modelers (1 female), 5 RNVR Lieutenants, and 15 women (later increased to 25) who did the painting and coloring of the designs. They were supported by another 10 RNVR officers who were assigned to oversee the application of camouflage at various ports. It appears that many of the original British patterns were colored in hues that did not actually match the colors specified. This was probably the origin of the standard caveat regarding color usage mentioned in an earlier paragraph. Finally, the plan was then sent to the port officer to oversee the application on the actual ship. Overall, the process followed on both sides of the Atlantic was nearly identical.

Launch of SS Everglades Courtesy, Tampa Hillsborough County Public Library System.

The insignia of rank on the sleeve of the officer and the zebra stripe style of camouflage on the model mark the picture below as being part of a British process.

Scheduling when a ship could have her camouflage painted was separate problem. It required cooperation between the camouflage painters, the supervising camoufleurs, the convoy schedulers, and the captain of the port where the convoys assembled. Army Lieutenant Frederick Alexander Pawla was in charge of embarkation in New York and was often credited as having made ships available for camouflage painting in some records now located in the US National Archives.

Admiralty testing lab *from Wolfson library*

CHAPTER 9

Artists

Thus far, all the technical considerations about weapons and countermeasures have focused on the ability to locate and identify a target. Submarines were invisible because they hid underwater. Could surface craft also be hidden? Abbot Thayer had approached the idea assuming that there was a positive answer to that question. But the environment that a ship existed in was not constant. It wasn't just that the light changed depending upon the time of day. Weather also played a major role. Clouds, wind, rainstorms and the height of the waves all affected visibility at sea. Steam powered ships usually burned coal. The type of coal used for fuel had an impact on the smoke emitted from the funnel. Hard anthracite coal made less smoke than softer varieties. The smoke, of course, could tower high above the horizon. It was often the first indication of the approach of another vessel. The relative position of the sun at different times of the day also had a major impact. When the sun was rising or setting behind a ship being observed, the color of the craft was immaterial. The question of using color to conceal the presence of a ship then became one of what color, or combination of colors, offered the best concealment over the largest range of probable conditions.

The U S Navy was the first to investigate the subject on a serious basis. Perhaps it isn't surprising that one of the prime movers of these investigations was an artist, William Andrew Mackay. Mackay had been interested in camouflage as concealment for some time. One example of this interest was the visibility experiments he conducted with the submarine flotilla originally commanded by CDR Fisher. Mackay used colored rotating disks, known as Maxwell disks, to illustrate his ideas in presentations before various bodies. One of those bodies was the Naval Advisory Board. One result of this was that his basic design was one of those approved for use on American ships. Mackay also initiated his own course for teaching camouflage of ships to other artists at the beginning of U.S. involvement in the war. At that time he was over 40 years old and possibly felt that his age and experience should have given him the status of a leader and pioneer in the field. He was chosen for the post of chief camoufleur for the Emergency Fleet Corporation (EFC) in New York. Mackay used his position to build his own testing theater and made his own plaster models for tests. This was completely independent of the official directives for all ship camouflage that came from the Navy Department based in Washington, DC. Among the younger artists who attended Mackey's original camouflage course were Kenneth Stevens MacIntire, Raymond John Richardson, and Charles Bittinger. Bittinger would later join the testing lab crew under Loyd Jones. Both of the others served as officers in the Navy Camouflage Section in Washington.

Before proceeding it's worth noting that Mackay went on to paint major murals on several American buildings. Probably the most famous of these is in the entrance to the American Museum of Natural history on the East side of New York City's Central Park. Other Mackay murals were done for the Library of Congress, the 1939 NY World's Fair, and the Minnesota House of Representatives. Mackay also took out a patent on his camouflage design. It combined small rectangles, or other shapes, in red, green and purple displayed on a blue or grey background. The use of small blobs of color makes his design reminiscent of the impressionist pointillism approach of Georges Seurat from an era nearly 30 years earlier.

The United States had decided that camouflage was to be used on ships soon after declaring war. Organizing and creating camouflage designs, however, was a bit more complicated. There was an early decision that the Navy would be responsible for camouflage designs, not only for warships, but for merchant vessels as well. It seems probable that Rear Admiral (RADM) William S. Sims, who had been sent to Europe to coordinate with the Royal Navy, had some influence in this. The Navy Bureau of Construction and Repair established a subsection for handling camouflage design. Harold Van Buskirk, a well-known architect, was given a commission as a Naval Reserve Force Lieutenant (LT) as of 21 Feb, 1918, and placed in charge of the administration of the new office. Two other men were given similar status and assigned as his subordinates. LT Loyd Ancil Jones had been a senior scientist at the Eastman Laboratories in Rochester, New York. He was placed in command of the testing group which, coincidentally, was located at the Eastman Labs in Rochester. The design development section was given to 5 foot 10 inch LT Everett Longley Warner. Warner had submitted the only design using confusion that was recommended by the Naval Advisory Board. The design section found a home in Washington, D.C., at the corner of 17th and Pennsylvania Avenue over a haberdasher's shop. Warner developed his own ideas about how disruptive camouflage should work. One of his better examples was to take a model of a ship and cut it into several parts. The parts were then placed on an arc so that each part was at a different angle to the observer's line of sight. Projecting this result back on to a flat plane resulted in the pattern that was used for Type 9 design K. This particular design was copied, intact, by the Japanese during the Second World War and applied to the converted armed merchant cruiser Hokoku Maru.

While the design section was just beginning to get organized Lieutenant Commander (LCDR) Norman Wilkinson RNVR, the originator of dazzle camouflage for the Admiralty, came to the United States. He was accompanied by his wife, and brought a large collection of about 90 Admiralty dazzle camouflage designs for merchant ships. As previously noted, Warner was his escort. While involved in that task Warner also looked to recruit some people to work in his new realm. Warner wrote to Frederick Judd Waugh and asked him to join the team as a civilian employee. Waugh was already 56 years old at the time, and had a well established reputation as a painter. When blue-eyed Raymond John Richardson, a tall slender architectural draftsman, joined the Navy he was sent on special duty to attend William Mackay's course on ship camouflage. He would later become head of the actual design subsection under Warner. The 23 year old Richardson had enlisted in Nov 1917 as a seaman 2nd class and was given service number 1068789. He spent a short time after the course attached to a receiving ship at Philadelphia before being sent to the Navy Yard at Washington D.C. He was given the provisional rank of Carpenter on 24 may 1918 and assigned to Bureau of Construction and Repair. His promotion to Ensign (ENS) dated from 22 Oct., 1918. That's probably after the time he was placed in charge of the design section's drafting room.

Both Warner and Waugh became notable artists in America. Both were able to make art their post war profession. Both also were among a number of well-known painters whose works are in the hands of major American art museums. Their paintings aren't always part of permanent exhibits, but they both have more than one item in the holdings of the Smithsonian Institute in Washington, D.C., and/or the Metropolitan in New York City. Camouflage for ships was an arena where people with art training had an opportunity to make an important contribution to the war effort. It isn't surprising to find several of the camouflage artists later appearing in *Who Was Who in American Art*. Warner was called back to active duty in the US Navy to serve, again, as head of the camouflage design department in the Second World War. The senior officer in charge of the department in World War II was CDR Charles Bittinger. The same Bittinger had been a subordinate of Loyd Jones in the Rochester testing facility. Bittinger had stayed in the Naval Reserve. He was promoted to CAPT and awarded the Legion of Merit for his work in the second conflict.

Kenneth Stevens MacIntire, another Mackay course graduate, was also made an ENS in the U.S. Naval Reserve Force (USNRF). His position was head of the model making room under Warner. The 27 year old Macintire had about 6 people, including both men and women, working for him. They made scaled wooden models of the ships from official blueprints. After the war he owned an art gallery in California and painted. He died on 19 Apr 1979, and never sold any of his own work during his lifetime.

Wooden ship model room 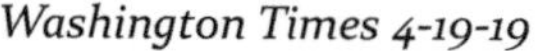 *Washington Times 4-19-19*

Model making team *NARA 165-ww-70c-005*

The other artists in the Washington team included; Frederick Charles Clayter, Douglas Dobel Ellington, Manley Kercheval Nash, and Gordon Stevenson.

Frederick Charles Clayter was assigned to the Navy Department in Washington, DC as a painter, 2nd class, when he was just shy of his 28th birthday. He worked with the model making team, and was promoted to painter, 1st class in July of 1918. The slim, grey-eyed Clayter became a professor of sculpture at Carnegie Institute in Pittsburgh where he was a master goldsmith and worked in both metalwork and industrial design.

Douglas Dobel Ellington was a 32 year old professor of architecture at Carnegie when he joined the Navy in Jun., 1918. He was assigned to Washington the following month as a chief carpenter's mate with the model making team. After the war he relocated to Asheville, North Carolina and was a highly respected architect. He designed many of the Art Deco style buildings in Asheville in the 1920's.

Manley Kercheval Nash was born in Kentucky in Jan 1881. He had been working as an artist since he was 19. When war was declared he took his wife and infant daughter from Texas, where they had been living, to Washington, D.C. When he registered for the selective service he was already working as a camouflage artist for the navy. He was 6 feet tall, weighed 170 pounds and had dark brown eyes and brown hair. His family home was at 1449 Park Road NW.

Gordon Stevenson was born in 1892 and worked as an artist and printmaker before he joined the navy in Newport, RI, on 28 June, 1917. He served on the destroyer USS Whipple until Dec 1917 as a Seaman 2nd class. Then someone found out about his background and he was promoted to painter 1st class. He was then assigned to the navy yard in Washington, and joined the camouflage section as a chief carpenters mate on 19 mar 1918. The tall, blue eyed Stevenson was released from active duty with the Armistice of 11 Nov., 1918. He may have stayed in the Naval Reserve Force because I found a mention of him being a USNRF officer in the 3rd Naval District on 25 Nov. 1918. He appears in several photographs of the design section where he can be easily identified by the glasses he wore.

Warner, Waugh, Nash & others *NARA 165-WW-70C-005*

The design team began work even before the formal process was in place. The first designs for U. S. Navy ships were prepared for a set of converted merchant vessels that were to become minelayers. The file copies that appear in the reference section below show that Type N1 designs A, B, C, and D, do not have the same format as later designs, and the colors indicated are not given in accordance with the later set of standardized colors and shades. The N2 designs, A and B, have the first examples of a standard legend box. But even they still have traces of the original versions before the standardized box was added. The colors even appear twice. All the originals of this set from the US National Archives are in very poor condition. They appear to have possibly been rescued from a fire.

USS DeGrasse, 1918 *NH94479a*

Swedish born Henry Reuterdahl was already well known as an artist with a deep involvement in naval affairs when the U.S. went to war. He received an appointment as a LT in the U S Naval Reserve Force in 1917. But he was not assigned to work on camouflage. He was promoted to LCDR in 1918 and was head of the Poster department. Much of the work done under his direction was aimed at recruitment. But that didn't keep him from dabbling in camouflage. A rather confused design was applied to the 81 foot long section patrol vessel, USS De Grasse, which was attributed to Reuterdahl. It seems he made no other contributions to actual ship camouflage. When he died in 1925 he was buried in Arlington National Cemetery because of his long association with the U.S. Navy.

The United States Shipping Board (USSB) had been created before the US declaration of War. It was empowered to direct the employment of American merchant ships. Additional legislation created the Emergency Fleet Corporation (EFC) to deal with acquisition of shipping. Since American ships were required to be camouflaged, the EFC formed a subordinate branch to supervise the actual painting of camouflage patterns of ships not under the control of the Navy. The creation and approval of patterns was expected to be left to the Navy. This wasn't always the case in practice.

Mr. Henry C. Grover went to Washington as the administrative head of the EFC camouflage department. He selected the people, mostly artists, who would deal with the day to day painting of shipping not assigned to the Navy. One of his early choices was to make William Mackay head of the EFC office in New York at 345 E. 33rd St. In keeping with the alignment of USSB districts with those of the Navy, The NY office became the 2nd District. At first, Mackay put his team to work painting ships with his own camouflage designs. Later, he was probably the driving force behind the creation of the American Society of Marine Camoufleurs. The organization was established in New York City and met monthly. There were 2 requirements. Members had to pay $1 per year dues, and they had to be appointed by the USSB. This looks to be a backhanded slap at the Navy organization.

The early months of American mobilization for war were marked with many inconsistencies. The Navy began adapting previously registered private vessels for section patrol. German ships that had taken refuge in what had been previously neutral American ports were taken over. The control of those ships formally belonged to the USSB. Shipyards, both private and Navy, found themselves heavily involved in converting some of the newly acquired ships for war service. The Navy Camouflage department was only created in March, 1918. Meanwhile, new ships were painted in whatever manner the local authorities felt was appropriate. Some Menhaden type fishing boats received their conversion to Navy colors in Charleston, SC. They were Amagansett (sp 693), Wilbert A. Edwards (sp 315) and Warren J. Courtney (sp 375), all shown below. They were painted in what looks to be a Toch pattern. Toch being one of the 5 patterns originally authorized, and named for its creator, Maximillian Toch. Toch designs were also made for USS Kajeruna (sp 389), USS Aeolus (id 3005) and USS Huron (id 1408). Aeolus and Huron were later repainted in standard Navy designs.

Two larger ships were painted with the black silhouette of a destroyer appearing prominently on the side of their hull. The Von Steuben (id 3017) and Antigone (id 3007) would keep this style of camouflage until they could be scheduled for repainting with a standard pattern issued by the Navy. The painted destroyer was expected to work like a scarecrow and frighten away hostile U-boats. It's doubtful that it was really effective.

Warren Courtney nh75516

Wilbert Edwards nh75514

Kajeruna NH 101951

Amagansett nh100664

Van Stuyben NH 101626 *Antigone* NH 57625

The small German maintenance crews on many of the interned vessels had attempted to sabotage their ships' machinery. They succeeded in doing a considerable amount of damage. American engineers and manufacturers were able to produce parts for repairing them in a much shorter time than the Germans believed would have been possible.

The EFC began hiring to set up their camoufleur teams wherever there were American shipyards. William Mackay added 36 year old Arthur Beecher Carles, an impressionist painter, to his team. Being 5'8" tall, Carles might not have stood out in a group photograph. But he did. He was the only one in the USBS NY office with a full beard. His younger sister, Sara Elizabeth Carles, was also an artist. She enlisted in the navy. She was given service number 184-81-52 and assigned as a landsman/yeoman(F). She served in Philadelphia at 4th naval district headquarters. She actually drew pictures of ships in camouflage that were submitted by the office of the district aide for information to Naval Intelligence headquarters in Washington. Other aides for information and their work are mentioned below.

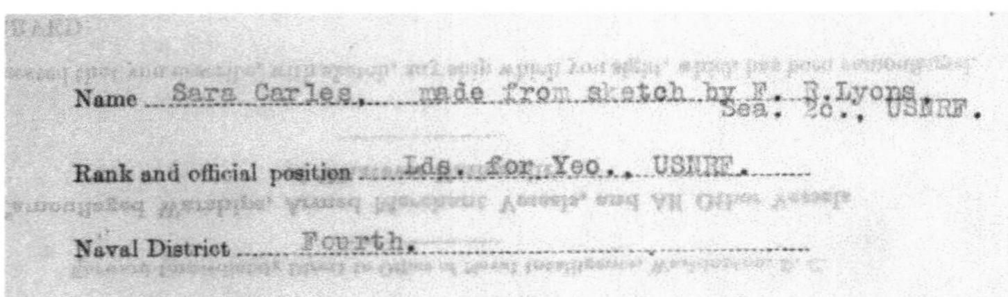
Name Sara Carles, made from sketch by F. B. Lyons, Sea. 2c., USNRF.

Rank and official position Lds. for Yeo., USNRF.

Naval District Fourth.

Sara Carles *NARA RG 38E*

Another member of the staff in New York was Frank Vinton Smith who would later be well known as a painter of marine subjects, especially of tall ships under sail. Smith was briefly sent to Philadelphia as assistant camoufleur in charge. The USSB 4th district office was located in the Medical Arts Building. Baltimore would later be separated and become the USSB's 3rd district. The arrival of Smith's official boss, Austin, was delayed. Meanwhile, Smith supervised the application of the Type 5 design A pattern on the SS Radnor (id 3023). He made a slight adaptation to the design, which, when it became known, resulted in some correspondence emphasizing that the officially supplied Navy patterns were to be strictly adhered to. Soon after, Smith returned to New York, and was later sent to Boston. The official plans were followed for most of the ships. There were, however, several instances of local camoufleurs either making changes or even creating their own designs. Another example of variations in application can be seen here.

Mackay had set up his own facilities for testing camouflage designs. With all the window dressing to indicate that the N.Y. EFC office might have designed their own ship camouflage, it would be easy to

Congaree – upper left, Lake Borgne – lower left, and Andra – right (from warshipporn.org). All in Type 2 design A.

conclude that they did so. But the Bridgeport Times reported on 22 July 1917 that there was an official agreement that assigned the Navy the job of preparing all camouflage designs, including those for merchant ships.

EFC district camoufleurs were assigned wherever ships were being built or converted. On the Gulf coast, EFC district 11 was centered in Houston. It included Beaumont, Orange and Morgan City, in Louisiana and Houston and Port Arthur in Texas. The EFC chief camoufleur there was Follette Israel Isaacson. He had been working as an EFC camoufleur in the Carter building in Houston when he registered for the draft. According to his WWI draft registration, Houston was, at that time, in District 6. The card also shows he was 33 years old, of medium height and build, and had brown eyes and black hair. Isaacson was a native of Massachusetts and a 1908 graduate of Dartmouth College. Prior to the war he had been working in New Orleans, and after the war he returned to New England. It's interesting to note that he seems to have had no background in art or architecture.

The USSB/EFC Camouflage department for the Great Lakes was located at 328 Superior Ave NW in Cleveland, Ohio. One of the more important camoufleurs working there was 33 year old David Orville Reasoner. In common with many others, he would make a mark in the American world of art after the war. Meanwhile, he had a room at the Holland Hotel in Cleveland, and visited shipyards on the Great Lakes where many of the EFC designed "Laker" cargo vessels were being built and painted in Type 2 camouflage designs.

On the West Coast the EFC main office was in San Francisco. Forty year old William Penhallow Henderson was the camoufleur in charge. His assistant, Bror Julius Olsson Nordfelt, was a year younger. Henderson had moved to Santa Fe, New Mexico in 1916. He returned there after the war, bringing his friend and colleague, Nordfelt, with him. They attracted a few other artists and made their group well known in the American art world.

Forty four year old Frank Bird Masters was the senior USSB camoufleur in Jacksonville, FL. His camoufleur work had also taken him to Tampa FL, Charleston, SC, Savannah, GA and Washington D.C. Masters had been a book illustrator before the war, and returned to that profession afterwards. Maurice Lisso Freedman was another former Mackay student. He enlisted in the Navy on 16 May 1917. That was barely a month after the US declared war on Germany. He was initially assigned to the 3rd naval district as a seaman 2nd class with service number 1515699. The N.Y. abstract of his military service indicates he was still in the Navy until 15 May 1918. At that time he was still required to register with the local draft board in Manhattan. When he did so, he reported he was employed as a camoufleur by the USSB at 816 Heard building, which was

EFC District 4 Camofleur team — *from Philadelphia in the Great War*

located in Jacksonville, FL. He supervised the camouflage of SS Everglades in Tampa; FL. Everglades might have been the first ship to be launched with her camouflage already in place. After the end of the war, Freedman donated some 455 lithograph plans of camouflage to the Rhode Island School of Design. The only other complete collection of these designs is in the National Archives in College Park, Maryland.

Philadelphia was the center from which EFC camoufleurs went out to shipyards all over the Delaware basin. Carles, Smith, and Austin were mentioned above because they spent time in both N.Y. and Philadelphia. Another artist whose later portrait work would earn him a place in the American art world was Franklin Chennault Watkins. He was only 22 years old when he joined the team in Philadelphia, but he was 6'2" tall and stands out in the center of the picture on p. 59. Carles is on the right with a cigarette and Smith is seated on the right with his pipe.

The EFC cleared an area at Hog Island, near Philadelphia, and built a shipyard for construction of a large number of new ships. It was one of the largest yards ever constructed up to that time and had 50 ways set up for the mass production of standardized ships. The war ended before it was able to make a real contribution. That didn't stop the EFC from assigning artist George Warren Lawlor to take care of camouflage for the new ships. Lawlor was just a bit less than 5' 11" tall and, at age 39, when he was put in charge of the Hog Island painting, already had prematurely greying hair. He worked from the office at 1601 Walnut in Philadelphia. Like many of his compatriots, he would later be mentioned in *Who Was Who in American Art*. The Hog Island shipyards built 2 types of ships, one for cargo, and one for passengers. Camouflage Type 27 design A was specifically created for the new cargo ships being built at Hog Island. Camouflage Type 28 design A was specifically created for the new passenger ships being built at Hog Island.

The Office of Naval Intelligence (ONI) assigned individuals to all 15 of the various naval districts as "aides for information" to the district commandant. Others were based in major American port cities. Their job was to visit, photograph, and sketch every ship in camouflage that visited ports in their district. Another aspect of their work was port security. The 7th Naval district office in Key West had 19 investigators working to look for potential spies and saboteurs. The New York City office had over 100 people assigned as inspectors. Assignment as an Aide for Information was obviously not restricted to artists. In fact, art work was only a part of the work they did. Few of them had backgrounds in art. The 4th Naval District at Philadelphia under Commandant CAPT George F Cooper, USN was the only one I have been able to identify as using women for preparing the art work in their ONI reports. ENS Earl Jukes USN (ret.) was the aide for information and he had at least 6 yeoman (F) girls that did the art work for the ONI reports. Sara Elizabeth Carles has already been mentioned. The others were: Ruth PrenticeThompson, Lilian A. Jones, Jean Knox, Sara Scott, and Florence Dorothea Fischer. This is an example of one of the sketches prepared by Florence Fischer.

Florence Fischer sketch *NARA RG 38E*

Among the other artists who were looking at visiting camouflaged ships were Frederick Remington, McClellan Barcley, Griffith Bailey Coale, and Thomas Hart Benton, all of whom became well-known names in the post-war art world. The ONI aides for information were issued a set of instructions using a standard blank form for reports. The reports had places for photographs, data, and drawings of camouflage.

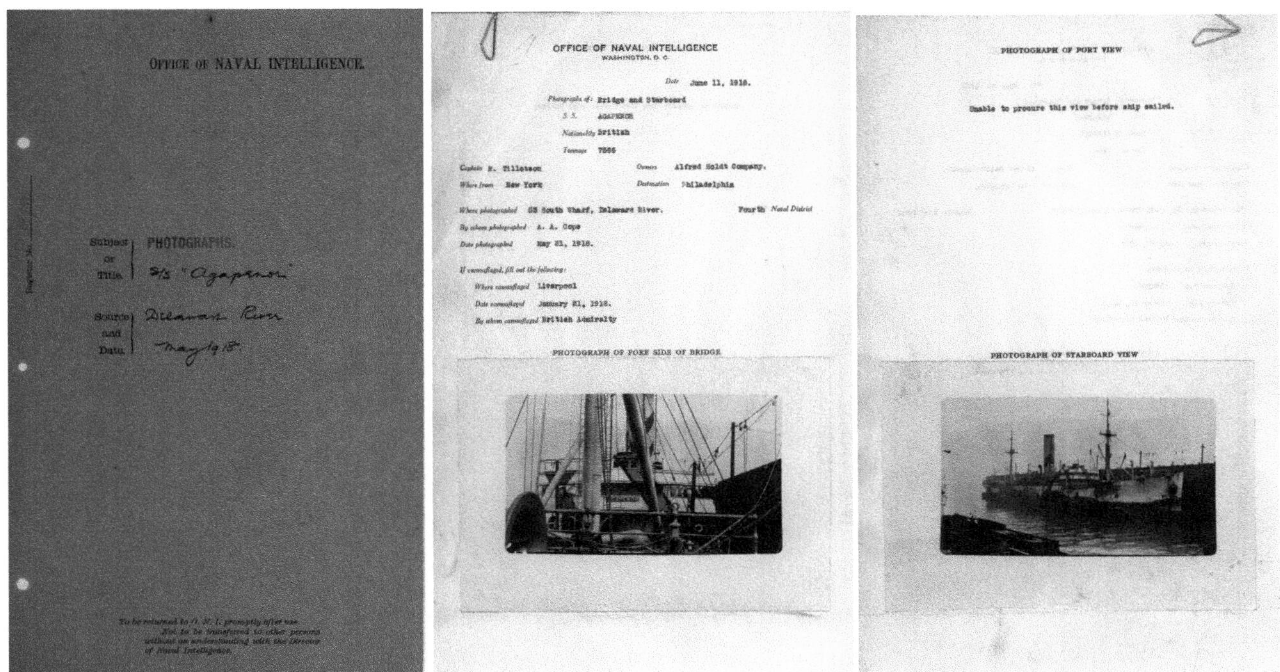

OFFICE OF NAVAL INTELLIGENCE.

Subject or Title: PHOTOGRAPHS. S/S "Agapenor"

Source and Data: Delaware River May 1918.

OFFICE OF NAVAL INTELLIGENCE
WASHINGTON, D. C.

Date June 11, 1918.

Photographs of: Bridge and Starboard

S. S. [illegible]

Nationality British

Tonnage 7586

Captain R. Tilleteon — Owners Alfred Holdt Company.

Where from New York — Destination Philadelphia

Where photographed 58 South Wharf, Delaware River. — Fourth Naval District

By whom photographed A. A. Cope

Date photographed May 21, 1918.

If camouflaged, fill out the following:

Where camouflaged Liverpool

Date camouflaged January 21, 1918.

By whom camouflaged British Admiralty

PHOTOGRAPH OF FORE SIDE OF BRIDGE

PHOTOGRAPH OF PORT VIEW

Unable to procure this view before ship sailed.

PHOTOGRAPH OF STARBOARD VIEW

NARA RG 38E

Despite the claims made in some biographies of the above named artists, none of them appear to have anything to do with actually designing ship camouflage patterns or with the application of those patterns. This was so even though many of them were later given a job description as camoufleurs. J. Boyd Dearborn, who was an aide for information in Charleston, SC, was enlisted as a seaman 2nd class and lived in the local YMCA during his service there. But others given similar jobs in other places were given, at least temporarily, more advanced ranks. F. W. Fischer, not related to Florence, was made a musician 1st class. In the 8th naval district, both A. P. Miller and M. Pons served as quartermaster 1st class. W. S. Clements in the 5th naval district was a chief master at arms. There were over 100 people who were assigned as aides for information. The leading artists in Washington all went on to make some kind of mark in the American Art world. Not so the aides for information. The four mentioned in the previous paragraph are exceptions. Two of them, Barclay and Coale, returned to work in the Second World War as official Navy Combat artists. McClelland Barclay also designed some unusual camouflage plans for aircraft. He was killed during the Second World War.

One last item that needs to be added here is the contribution of outsiders. There were a few people who came up with camouflage designs for ships that were outside the framework of the Navy/USSB groups. Philip Little managed to get the people in Boston to paint a couple of local patrol craft in designs he had created. The ideas were forwarded to Washington, but there was no follow up. The two ships referred to were USS Aztec (sp 590) and USS Yacona (sp 617).

Frank Morris Watson was a master painter at the Norfolk Navy Yard. He was 6 feet tall and had blue eyes and brown hair. He lived with his wife, Gertrude, at 1038 Ann Street in Portsmouth, Virginia. Watson was 37 years old when he came up with several experimental geometric camouflage designs. His ideas were tried out on USS Anniston (C-9), and USS Nebraska (BB-14). Anniston had different designs on each side. Nebraska used the same pattern on each side. Stephen J. Hoxie, who ran a paint store in Massachusetts, is credited with creating the design N11 A for USS Henderson (AP-1). He reportedly did the work according to instructions from Everett Warner. The design for the tugboat USS Narkeeta was possibly created by Gerome Brush.

Aztec NH59573

Yacona NH 102576

Anniston NH 100399

Nebraska NH 101208

Narkeeta NH 45637

At some point the question of whether camouflage was effective will always be asked. Only one case was recorded where later coverage specifically gave credit to dazzle camouflage. Here is a quote from the Naval History and Heritage Center chronology for the "United States Navy in World War I: 1914-1922" by Frank A. Blazich for 28 April, 1918.

"The destroyer Porter (DD-59) is on convoy duty when she spots a periscope 1,000 yards away on her starboard bow. She manages to close in to within 40 yards of the surfaced sub before it submerged. The German captain overestimated the destroyer's distance because of encroaching darkness and her dazzle camouflage. Porter drops 22 depth charges, badly damaging the German submarine U-108, and putting her out of service for two months."

There are many quotes from allied commanders and crewmen that can be found which mention how difficult it was for them to determine the course and speed of a ship painted in dazzle. The most telling support, however, comes from the German side. Several months after the introduction of convoys and dazzle paint the training course for new German submarine commanders and their crews had a new item added to the curriculum. Several German ships were formed into a convoy so the new skippers could practice attacking them. These training targets included vessels painted by the Germans to simulate dazzle camouflage. Imitation is the sincerest form of flattery. That imitation did not stop there. Check out the American Type 9 design K pattern copied by Japan in the Second World War on Hokoku Maru.

Hokuku Maru *Public domain from Japanese magazine The Maru Special No.53*

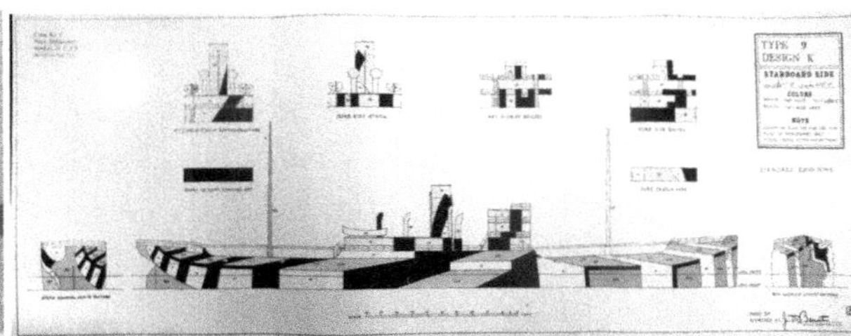

Type 9 Design K *Public domain from US National Archives, College Park, MD*

The question of how effective ship camouflage actually was has had arguments made both for and against. The British study, which is most often quoted, failed to find any convincing arguments for camouflage. An American study from 1919 supported its' use, but was based on models of ships. The French made their own study just after the war and concluded that there was insufficient data for a definitive conclusion, but, on the whole, they favored disruptive camouflage. One key fact in making a decision today is that ship camouflage was used during the Second World War by nearly all the major participants. It is still being used in the 21st century by several countries including The United States, Sweden, Norway, Finland, China, and Russia. Some WWII camouflage has been widely covered. Some has not. In the latter category, the Japanese painting of merchant ships and the flight decks of their carriers came later in the war. The Italian Navy made separate individual patterns for nearly all their warships, and many merchant vessels, too. German Kriegsmarine camouflage has been well documented, but mostly in German. The Royal Navy camouflage efforts have been widely covered, with the exception of the separate contribution from the Canadians. Canadian art professor, Rowley Murphy created several designs for RCN ships. One of them is similar to the confused patterns used in 1917 to such a degree that including pictures of a Second World War design seemed an appropriate way to conclude the coverage of World War One ship camouflage.

HMCS Hamilton *Navsource 0517005*

Photo # NH 70862 HMS Hamilton, photographed during World War II. She was originally USS Kalk (DD-170)

HMCS Hamilton p nh70862 *Navsource 0517003*

Chapter 10

Reference

This section contains patterns and ship photographs to illustrate the usage of ship camouflage. Each pattern page includes diagrams of the pattern for both sides of the ship. There are pictures showing at least one ship that actually carried the pattern, and frequently a list of additional ships that photographic evidence shows to have also been painted in the same pattern. There is also a listing of the official colors specified for the pattern. The Navy Bureau design section created more than 200 patterns for merchant ships and over 100 more for warships. The patterns for warships, and a few others, are the work of my graphic artist Talya Shachar-Albocher. Most patterns reproduced for the "T" series merchant ship designs are from public domain material in the US National Archive, College Park, MD. That collection, and the materials at the Rhode Island School of Design, are the only nearly complete collections of U S merchant ship camouflage designs that I know of that are still extant. Neither is 100% complete.

The criteria for inclusion of a pattern in this book are the availability of a copy of the actual pattern, or sufficient evidence to make a reconstruction of the pattern, and the existence of a contemporary photograph of a ship in that camouflage. I have also included cases where I have only a textual reference to the ship being camouflaged. They are marked with "(t)" after the name of the ship. There were many patterns that either were not used, or for which there isn't a picture or textual reference. Most patterns that lack confirmation of usage (or non-usage) have been omitted. There is an alphabetical index of ships known to have been camouflaged at the end of this section. It includes over 600 ship names. It does not include ships known to have been camouflaged but for whom there is no known pattern.

It is possible to confuse American merchant ship "Type" designs with "Type" designs provided by the Admiralty. Both countries chose examples of what they hoped could be used as a standard for certain kinds of ships. But a Type 1 in Washington was not the same as a Type 1 in London. The US dealt with 28 standard merchant ship types. The British had 37. The Americans used "N" series designs for Navy warships and some auxiliaries. The British identified their camouflage patterns by three separate series of order numbers. Orders with no prefix were used for merchant vessels. "HMS" orders were for Royal Navy vessel, especially those involved in convoy escort duties. "USN" orders were for American naval vessels. The British system is further complicated by the fact that almost all the original material is deposited at the Imperial War Museum. It is identified there by catalog numbers. The "DAZ" prefix is used for dazzle camouflage items. The "MOD" prefix is used to identify models, including the surviving original models used for pattern testing during World War One. Ship photographs are scattered in several places with many using the "Q" or "SP" prefixes. The Admiralty commissioned paintings of many camouflaged ships, but rarely by name or design. These works are identified by numbers in the "ART" series. It is possible that there are different curators responsible for each category. There doesn't appear to be any cross-reference or index to make connections between the various types of identification. As of the time of my writing this there are still a few items in the IWM collections that appear to be incorrectly identified, and many of the MOD models have pieces missing.

This book deals with American ship camouflage. Other countries had their own camouflage bureaus. The British had an extensive organization for making, and applying, their own patterns. The French also had a camouflage design bureau for their own ships. The British also provided and painted patterns for many ships of other countries including U S Navy ships that came to them in an overall standard grey. Some of these are mentioned here, but usually without the original patterns. Patterns that were derived from Admiralty designs are named with the suffix "ADM". There are also 2 designs for which I have found no official designation. I used the prefix "NX" for them. I have not included all Admiralty designs for which I found photographs.

It was not possible to locate original design sheets for several ships. British Admiralty plans used for American destroyers are not listed in the IWM catalog. Many photographs exist. But it was not possible to determine which colors were used. US Records only have examples for USS Birmingham, and for a destroyer design that is listed here as N8 A because it was found in the same folder as other N8 designs for USS Paul Jones. Similar designs are listed as N10-ADM, N12-ADM, and N24-ADM. No patterns for N4 A (id 1256 USS Aroostook), or N5 A (BB 17 USS Rhode Island) or the starboard side of N38 A (id 1408 USS Huron), have been located. The designs for N4 A, N4 B, and N5 A were recreated from the actual ship photographs and may not be entirely accurate. Note that those patterns do not have the title box in the upper right hand corner. I would be delighted to have any reader fill in these lacunae.

BRUSH

Colors used	Ships painted with this pattern
BLACK	ID 1644 LOUISVILLE
WHITE	ID 2216 JUPITER (T)
DARK GREY	SP 322 MESSICK (T)
LIGHT GREY	SP 391 THETIS (T)
	ID 4508 MT. VERNON Design prepared, maybe never used

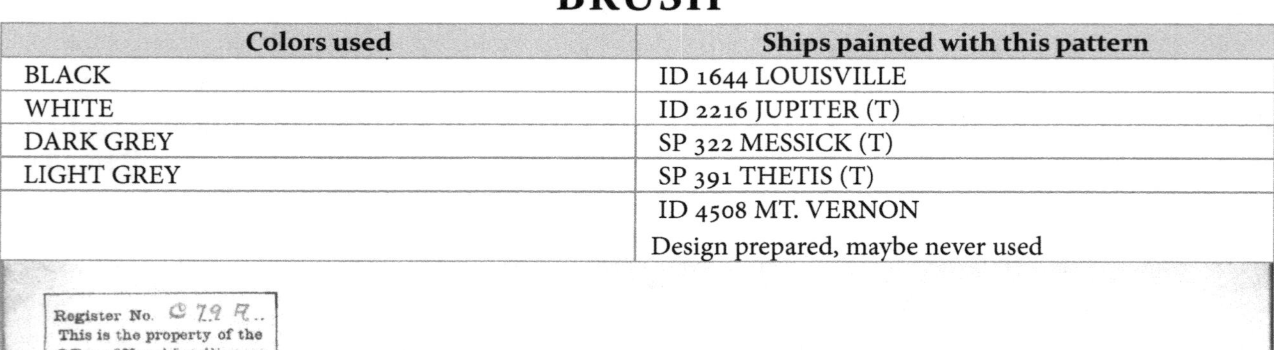

id 1644 Louisville *NARA RG38*

id 4508 Mount Vernon *NARA RG38*

MACKAY

Colors used	Ships painted with this pattern
RED	SP 314 M M DAVIS
GREEN	SP 493 WINFIELD S CAHILL
BLUE	SP 52 GREY FOX
MAUVE	SP 431 VENETIA

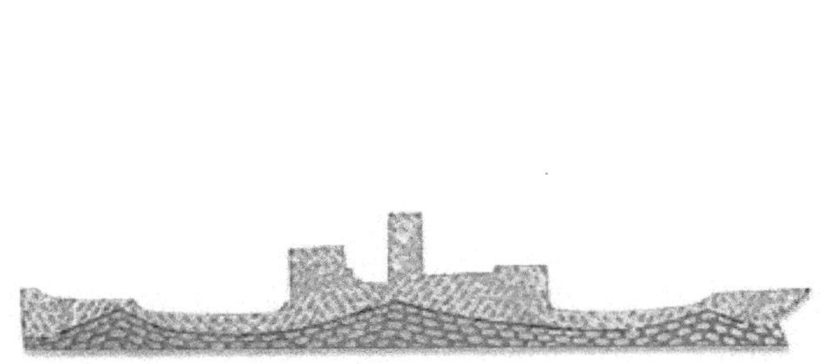

Mackay Pattern

Winfield S Cahill NH75515

Venetia NH47198

Grey Fox NH89748

MACKAY

Colors used	Ships painted with this pattern
RED	ID 4545 FINLAND
GREEN	ID 1614 TROY
BLUE	ID 1645 PLATTSBURG
MAUVE	ID 1643 ST PAUL

Finland NH53905

Troy model

Plattsburg NH42619

St. Paul NH53635

MACKAY

Colors used	Ships painted with this pattern
RED	BB 14 NEW JERSEY
GREEN	BM 8 TONOPAH
BLUE	DD 69 CALDWELL
MAUVE	ID 1565 J L LUCKENBACH

New Jersey NH100409

J L Luckenbach NH2774

Caldwell NH69832

Tonopah Navsource BOSTTS-1444

N1 A

Colors used	Ships painted with this pattern
BLACK	ID 1694 CANANDAIGUA
WHITE	
GRAY	

N1 A

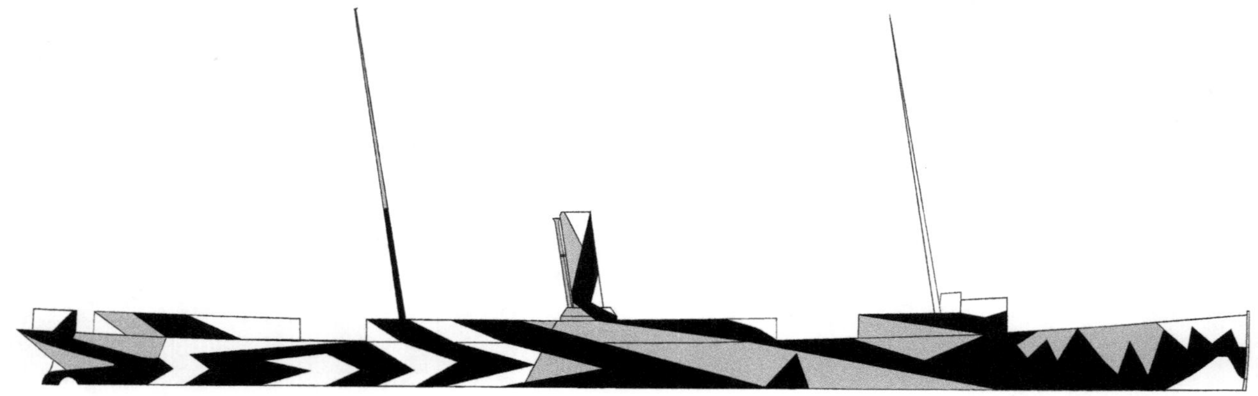

Starboard Side Pattern

N1 A

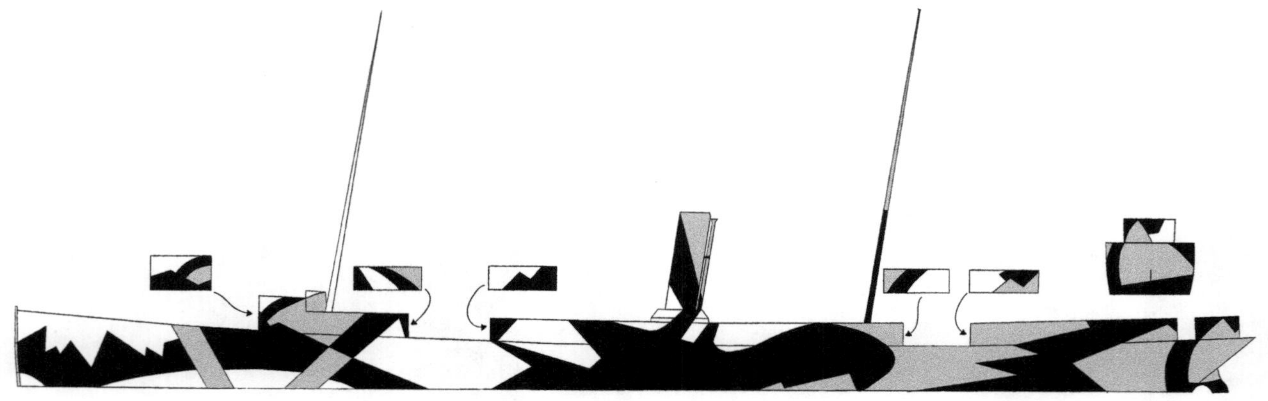

Port Side Pattern

N1 B

Colors used	Ships painted with this pattern
BLACK	ID 1696 CANONICUS
WHITE	
GRAY	

N1 B

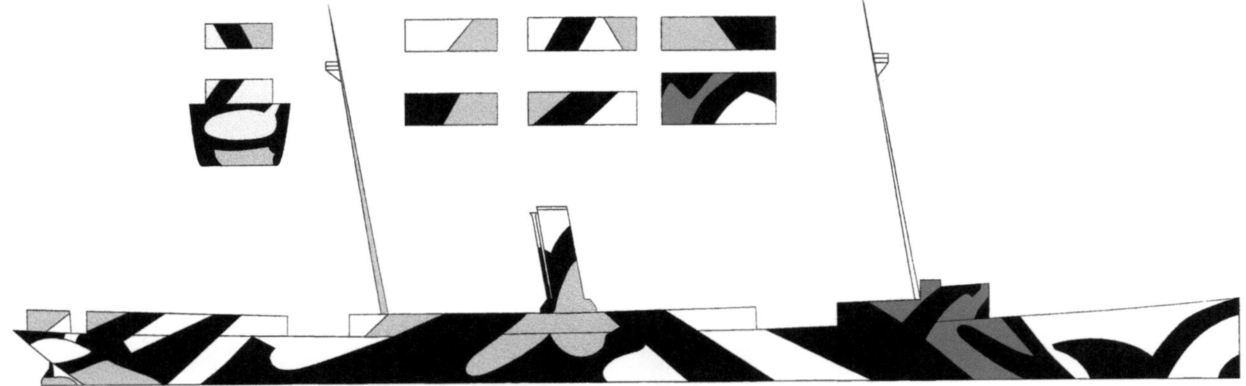

STARBOARD SIDE PATTERN

N1 B

PORT SIDE PATTERN

N1 C

Colors used	Ships painted with this pattern
BLACK	ID 1695 ROANOKE
WHITE	
BLUE	
GRAY	

N1 C

STARBOARD SIDE PATTERN

N1 C

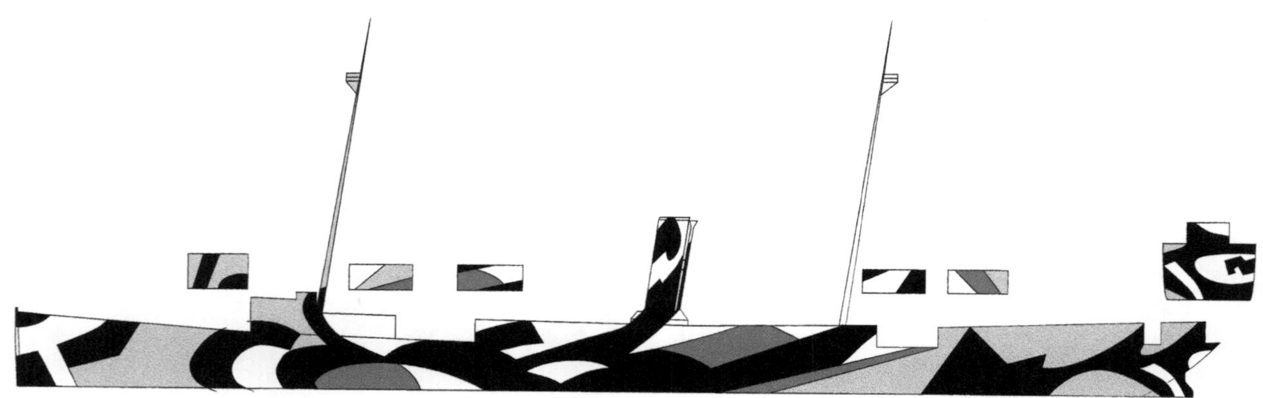

PORT SIDE PATTERN

N1 D

Colors used	Ships painted with this pattern
BLACK	ID 1697 HOUSATONIC
WHITE	
GRAY	
BLUE	

N1 D

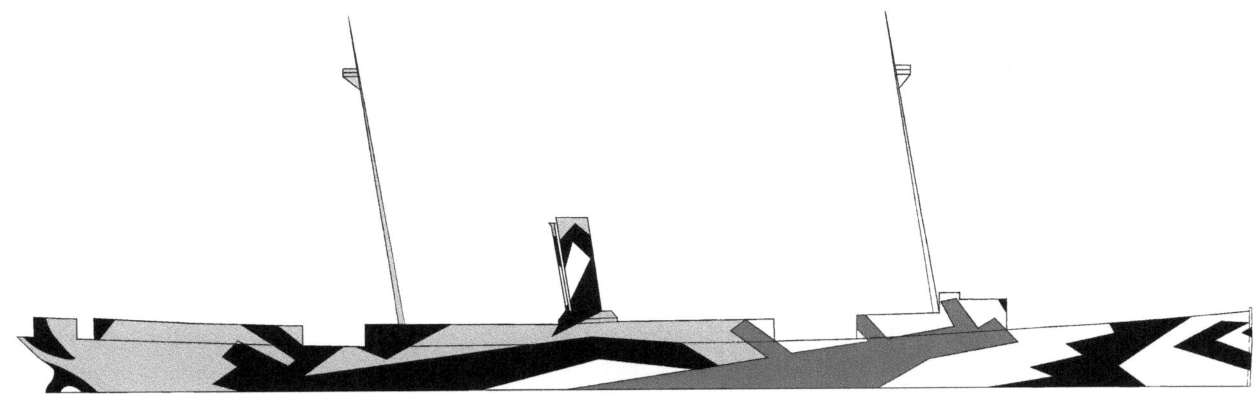

Starboard Side Pattern

N1 D

Port Side Pattern

N2 A

Colors used	Ships painted with this pattern
BLACK	ID 1687 QUINNEBAUG
WHITE	
#3 BLUE	
#1 BLUE-GRAY	

TYPE N·2
DESIGN A

PORT SIDE
SCALE 1/16" = 1'-0" LENGTH 351'-0"
COLORS
WHITE BLACK
NO. 3 BLUE NO. 1 BLUE GREY
NOTE
COLORS ON PLAN ARE FOR THE PURPOSES OF MEASUREMENT ONLY ACTUAL COLORS AS PER COLOR CHART.

TYPE N·2·
DESIGN A

STARBOARD SIDE
SCALE 1/16" = 1'-0" LENGTH 351'-0"
COLORS
NO. 1 BLUE GREY
NO. 3 BLUE
NOTE
COLORS ON PLAN ARE FOR THE PURPOSES OF MEASUREMENT ONLY ACTUAL COLORS AS PER COLOR CHART.

N2 A

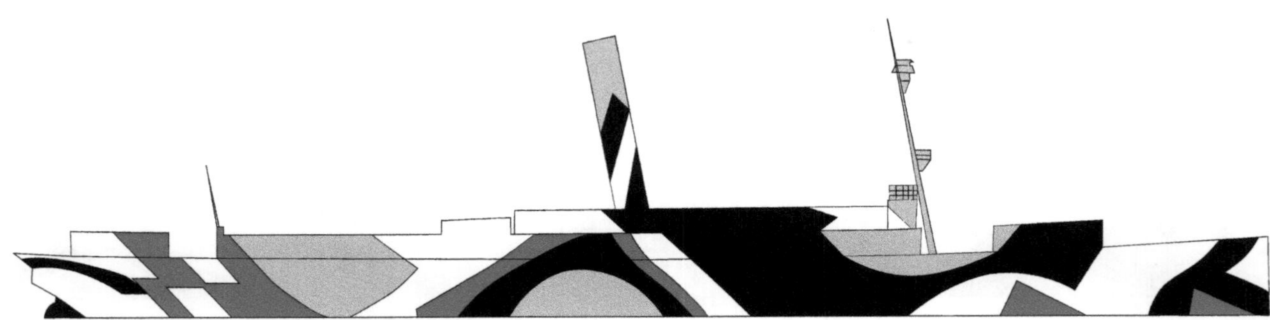

STARBOARD SIDE PATTERN

N2 A

PORT SIDE PATTERN

N2 B

Colors used	Ships painted with this pattern
BLACK	ID 1704 SARANAC
WHITE	
BLUE	
GRAY	

N2 B

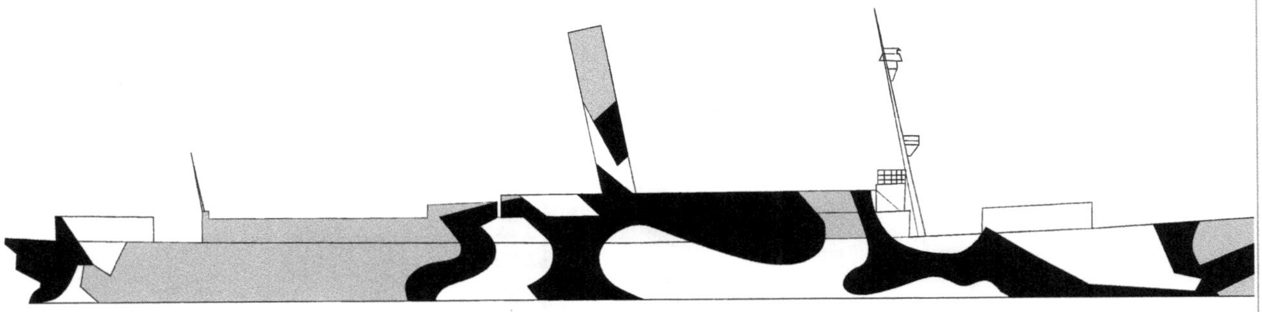

STARBOARD SIDE PATTERN

N2 B

PORT SIDE PATTERN

N3 A

Colors used	Ships painted with this pattern
BLACK	ID 2999 SIBONEY
WHITE	
#3 BLUE	
#2 BLUE-GRAY	

N3 A

STARBOARD SIDE PATTERN

N3 A

PORT SIDE PATTERN

N3 B

Colors used	Ships painted with this pattern
BLACK	ID 1536 ORIZABA
WHITE	
#3 BLUE	
#2 BLUE-GRAY	

TYPE N 3
DESIGN B
∴ PORT SIDE ∴
SCALE LENGTH
COLORS
NO. 3 BLUE WHITE
NO. 1 BLUE GREY BLACK
NOTE
COLORS ON PLAN ARE FOR THE PURPOSES OF MEASUREMENT ONLY. ACTUAL COLORS AS PER COLOR CHART.

TYPE N 3
DESIGN B
STARBOARD SIDE
SCALE LENGTH
COLORS
NO. 3 BLUE WHITE
NO. 1 BLUE GREY BLACK
NOTE
COLORS ON PLAN ARE FOR THE PURPOSES OF MEASUREMENT ONLY. ACTUAL COLORS AS PER COLOR CHART.

N3 B

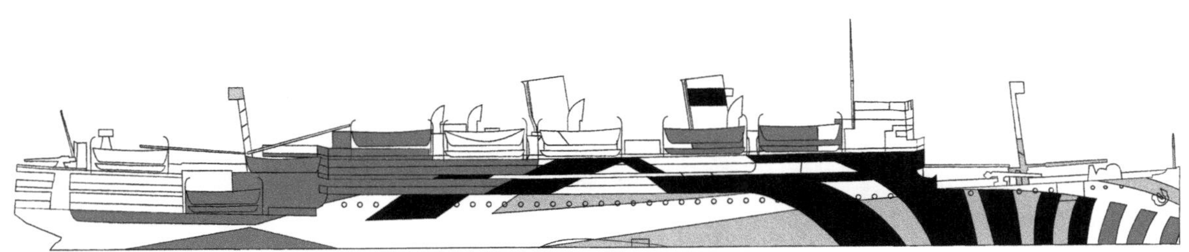

Starboard Side Pattern

N3 B

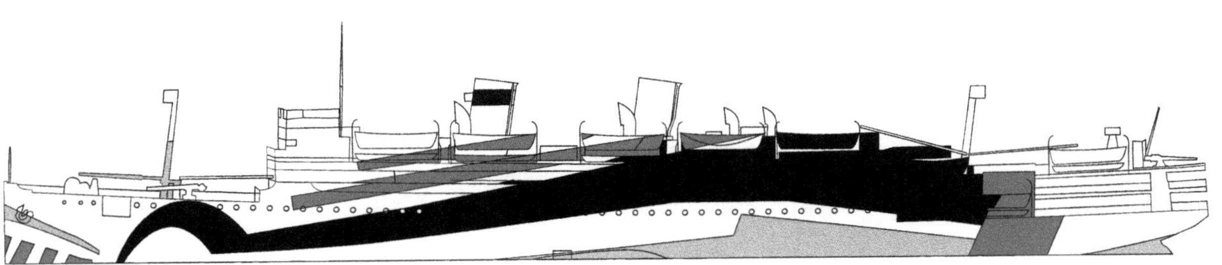

Port Side Pattern

N4 A

Colors used	Ships painted with this pattern
BLACK	ID 1255 SHAWMUT
WHITE	
#3 BLUE	
#1 BLUE-GRAY	

N4 A

Starboard Side Pattern

N4 A

Port Side Pattern

N4 B

Colors used	Ships painted with this pattern
BLACK	ID 1256 AROOSTOOK
WHITE	
#3 BLUE	
#1 BLUE-GRAY	

N4 B

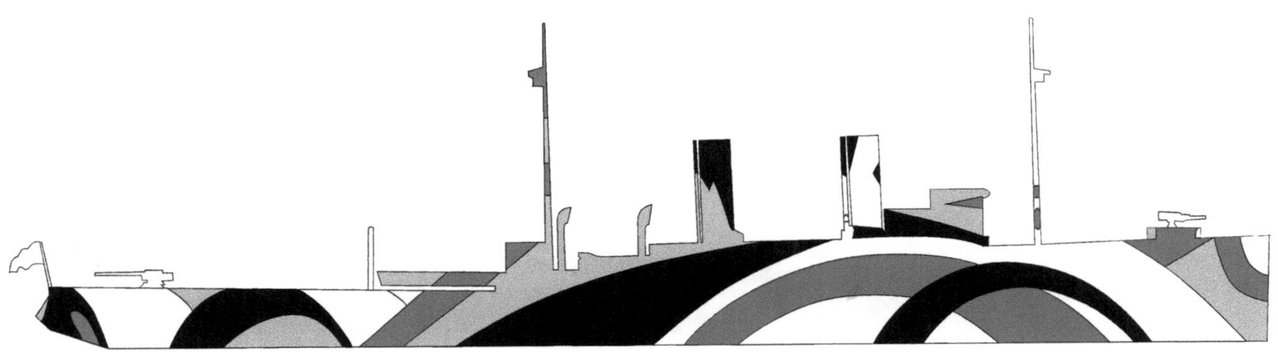

STARBOARD SIDE PATTERN

N4 B

PORT SIDE PATTERN

N5 A

Colors used	Ships painted with this pattern
BLACK	NEW JERSEY BB 17
WHITE	
#3 BLUE	
#2 BLUE-GRAY	
No original patterns. Colors assumed.	

N5 A

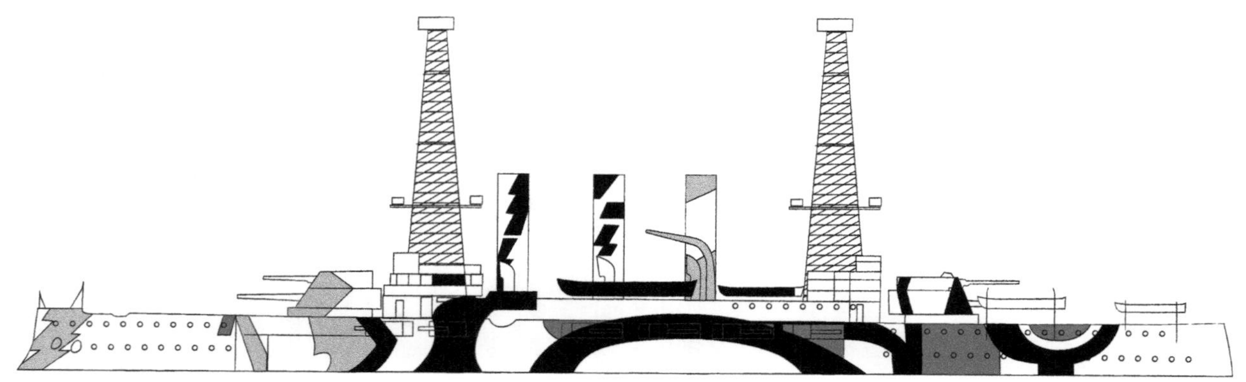

PORT SIDE PATTERN

No patterns or photos of starboard side

N6 A

Colors used	Ships painted with this pattern
BLACK	AD 5 PRAIRIE
WHITE	
#3 BLUE	
#1 BLUE-GRAY	

TYPE N 6 DESIGN A

PORT SIDE

SCALE ____ LENGTH ____

COLORS

NOTE

COLORS ON PLAN ARE FOR THE PURPOSES OF MEASUREMENT ONLY. ACTUAL COLORS AS PER COLOR CHART.

TYPE N 6 DESIGN A

STARBOARD SIDE

SCALE ____ LENGTH ____

COLORS

NO. 1 BLUE GREY

WHITE

NO. 3 BLUE

BLACK

NOTE

COLORS ON PLAN ARE FOR THE PURPOSES OF MEASUREMENT ONLY. ACTUAL COLORS AS PER COLOR CHART.

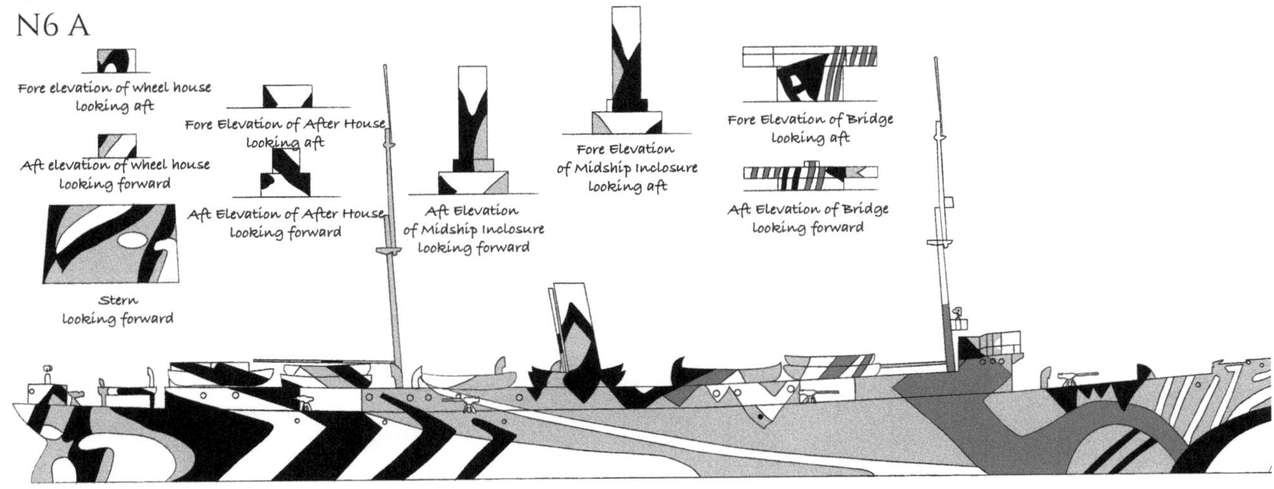

Starboard Side Pattern

Port Side Pattern

N6 B

Colors used	Ships painted with this pattern
BLACK	AD 8 BUFFALO
WHITE	
#3 BLUE	
#1 BLUE-GRAY	

TYPE 6 N
DESIGN - B -

· PORT · SIDE ·
SCALE 1/16 = 1·0 LENGTH 391'·0"
COLORS
BLACK NO. 3 BLUE
WHITE NO. 1 BLUE GREY
NOTE
COLORS ON PLAN ARE FOR THE PURPOSES OF MEASUREMENT ONLY ··· ACTUAL COLORS AS PER COLOR CHART ·

TYPE 6 N
DESIGN - B -

· STARBOARD · SIDE ·
SCALE 1/16 = 1·0 LENGTH 391'·0"
COLORS
BLACK NO. 3 BLUE
WHITE NO. 1 BLUE GREY
NOTE
COLORS ON PLAN ARE FOR THE PURPOSES OF MEASUREMENT ONLY ··· ACTUAL COLORS AS PER COLOR CHART ·

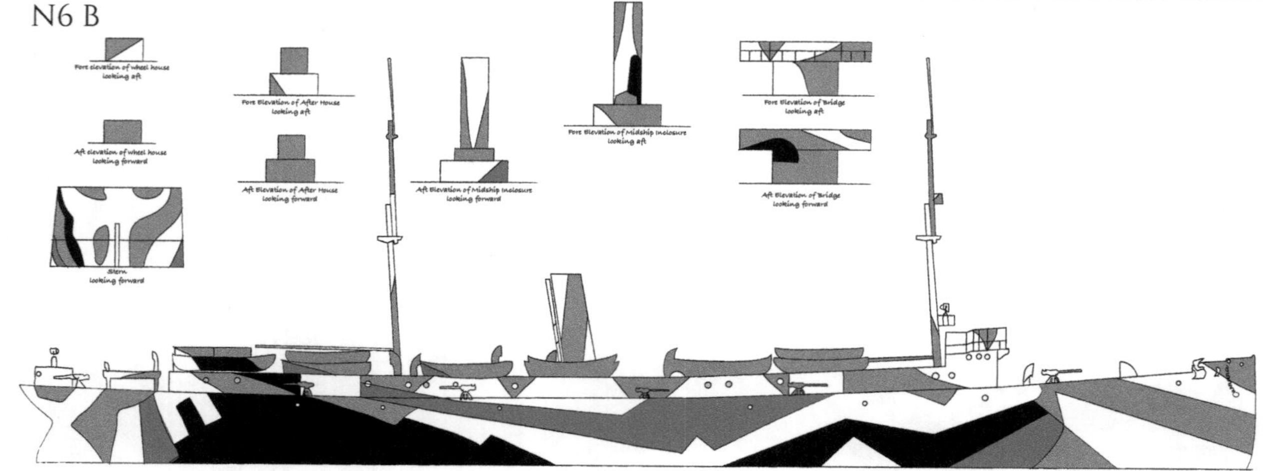

Starboard Side Pattern

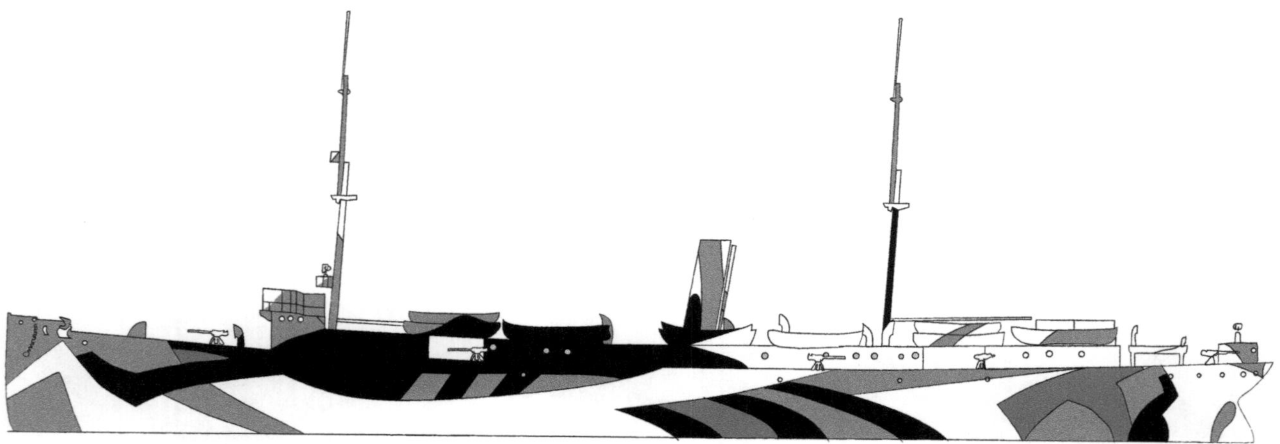

Port Side Pattern

N7 B

Colors used	Ships painted with this pattern
BLACK	AF 4 GLACIER
WHITE	
#3 BLUE	
#1 BLUE-GRAY	

TYPE N 7
DESIGN B

PORT SIDE
SCALE ____ LENGTH 371'-0"
COLORS
WHITE NO. 1 BLUE GREY
BLACK NO. 3 BLUE
NOTE
COLORS ON PLAN ARE FOR THE PURPOSES OF MEASUREMENT ONLY ... ACTUAL COLORS AS PER COLOR CHART

TYPE N 7
DESIGN B

STARBOARD SIDE
SCALE ____ LENGTH 371'-0"
COLORS
BLACK NO. 3 BLUE
WHITE NO. 1 BLUE GREY
NOTE
COLORS ON PLAN ARE FOR THE PURPOSES OF MEASUREMENT ONLY ... ACTUAL COLORS AS PER COLOR CHART

STARBOARD SIDE PATTERN

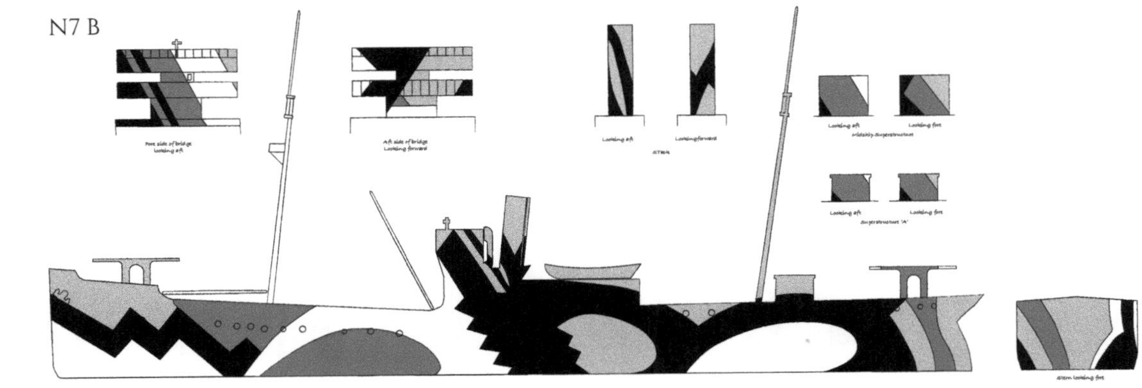

PORT SIDE PATTERN

N8 A

Colors used	Ships painted with this pattern
BLACK	PAUL JONES DD10
WHITE	
#3 BLUE	
#1 BLUE-GRAY	

N8 A

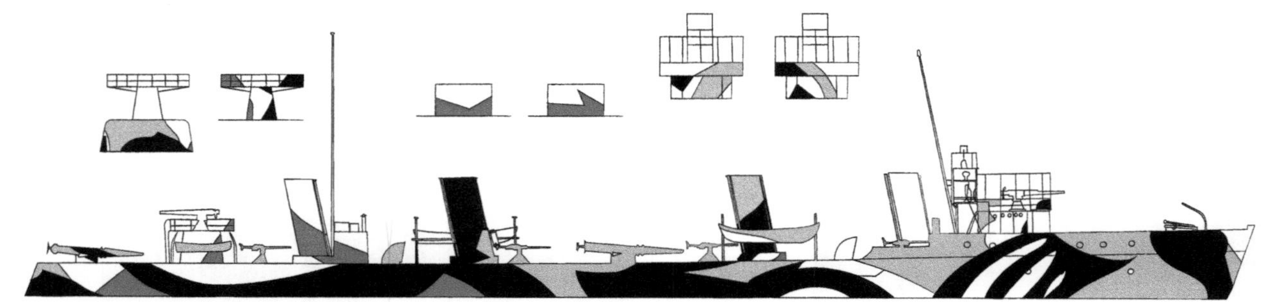

STARBOARD SIDE PATTERN

N8 A

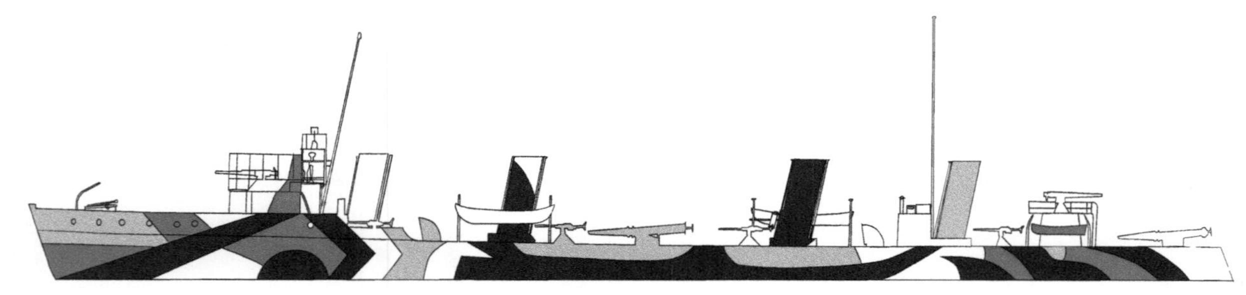

PORT SIDE PATTERN

N8-ADM

Colors used	Ships painted with this pattern
BLACK	DD10 PAUL JONES
WHITE	
#3 BLUE	Pattern adapted from photographs and comparison with a British pattern found on file
#1 BLUE-GRAY	
	This pattern was used as the base for other ADM destroyer patterns

N8 A

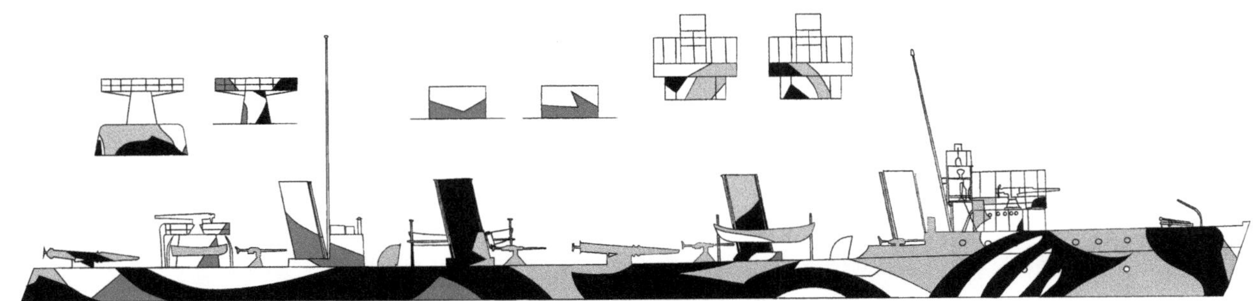

STARBOARD SIDE PATTERN

N8 A

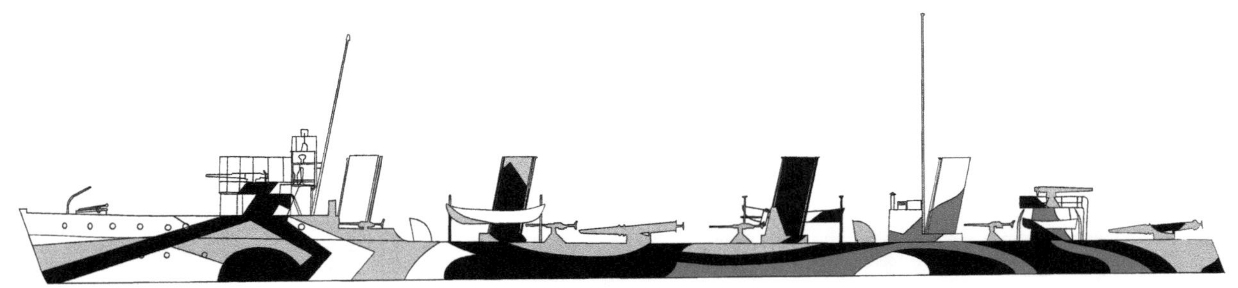

PORT SIDE PATTERN

N8 B

Colors used	Ships painted with this pattern
BLACK	DD 12 PREBLE
WHITE	
#3 BLUE	
#1 BLUE-GRAY	

TYPE N·8
DESIGN B

∴ PORT SIDE ∴
SCALE 3/32=1'0 LENGTH 245'0
COLORS
BLACK NO 1 BLUE GREY
WHITE NO 3 BLUE
NOTE
COLORS ON PLAN ARE FOR THE PURPOSES OF MEASUREMENT ONLY. ACTUAL COLORS AS PER COLOR CHART.

TYPE N·8
DESIGN B

STARBOARD SIDE
SCALE 3/32=1'0 LENGTH 245'0
COLORS
BLACK NO 1 BLUE GREY
WHITE NO 3 BLUE
NOTE
COLORS ON PLAN ARE FOR THE PURPOSES OF MEASUREMENT ONLY. ACTUAL COLORS AS PER COLOR CHART.

N8 A

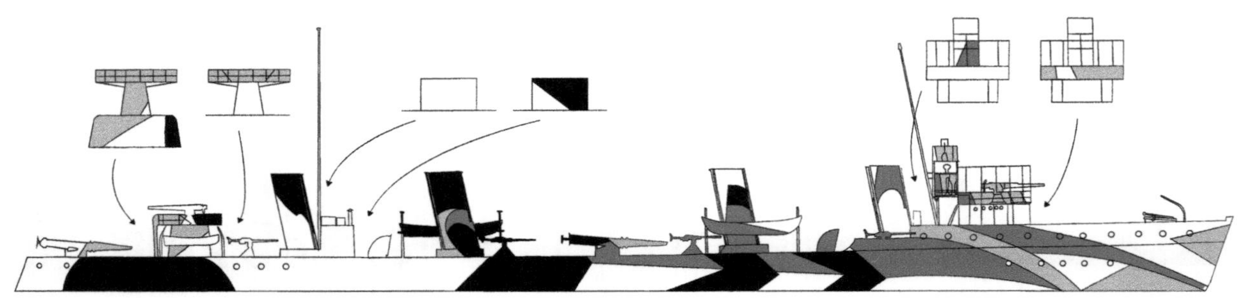

STARBOARD SIDE PATTERN

N8 A

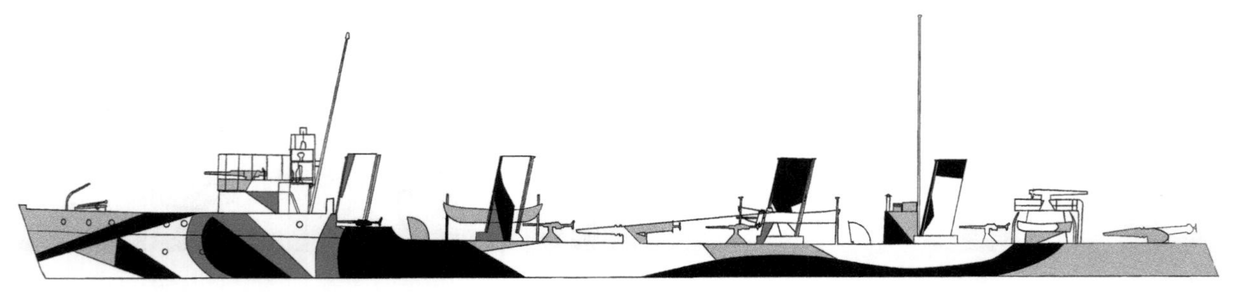

PORT SIDE PATTERN

N9 A

Colors used	Ships painted with this pattern
BLACK	ID 3015 SAVANNAH
WHITE	
#3 BLUE	
#1 BLUE-GRAY	

TYPE N9
DESIGN A

·PORT·SIDE·
SCALE LENGTH
COLORS
NOTE
COLORS·ON·PLAN ARE FOR THE·PURPOSES·OF MEASUREMENT·ONLY···ACTUAL COLORS AS·PER·COLOR·CHART·

TYPE N9
DESIGN A

·STARBOARD·SIDE·
SCALE LENGTH
COLORS
BLACK
WHITE
NO. 1 BLUE GREY
NO. 3 BLUE
NOTE
COLORS ON PLAN ARE FOR THE·PURPOSES OF MEASUREMENT·ONLY ··ACTUAL COLORS AS PER·COLOR CHART·

N9 A

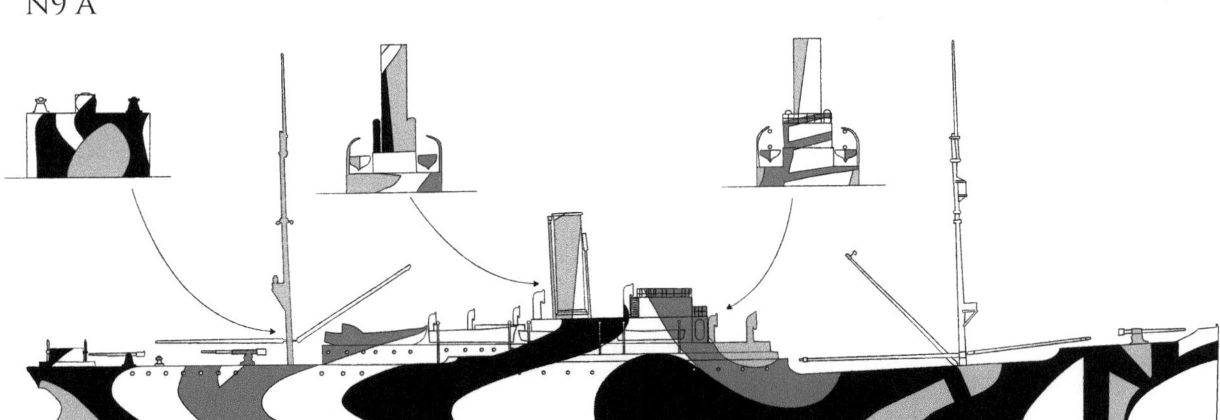

Starboard Side Pattern

N9 A

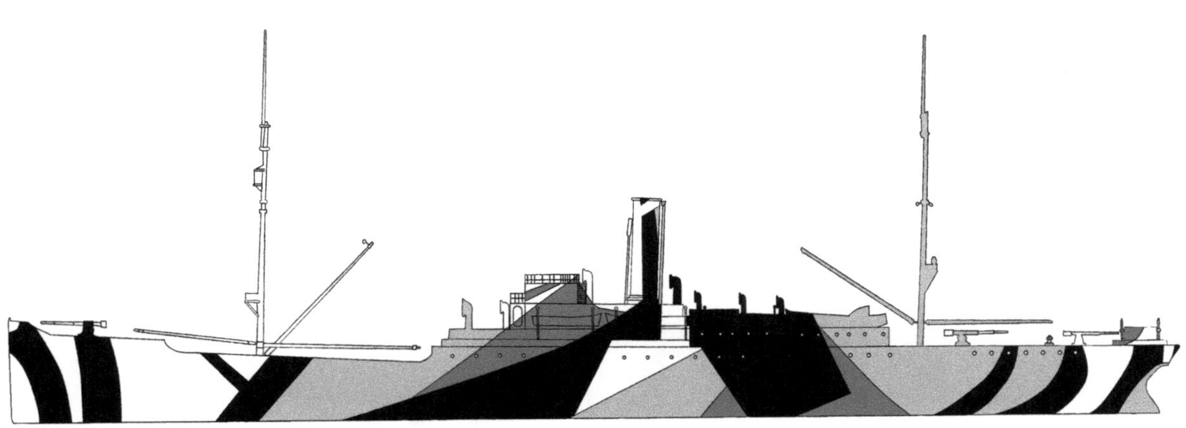

Port Side Pattern

N10 A

Colors used	Ships painted with this pattern
BLACK	DD 39 HENLEY
WHITE	
#3 BLUE	
#1 BLUE-GRAY	

TYPE · 10·N·
DESIGN·A·

·PORT·SIDE·
SCALE 3/32·10' LENGTH 310 FT
COLORS
W · White B · Black
1BG · № 1 Blue Gray
3B · № 3 Blue
NOTE
COLORS ON PLAN ARE FOR THE PURPOSES OF MEASUREMENT ONLY ··· ACTUAL COLORS AS PER COLOR CHART

TYPE 10-N
DESIGN A

·STARBOARD·SIDE·
SCALE 3/32·10' LENGTH 310 FT
COLORS
W · WHITE B · BLACK
1 BG · № 1 BLUE GRAY
3 B · № 3 BLUE
NOTE
COLORS ON PLAN ARE FOR THE PURPOSES OF MEASUREMENT ONLY ·· ACTUAL COLORS AS PER COLOR CHART

N10 A

STARBOARD SIDE PATTERN

N10 A

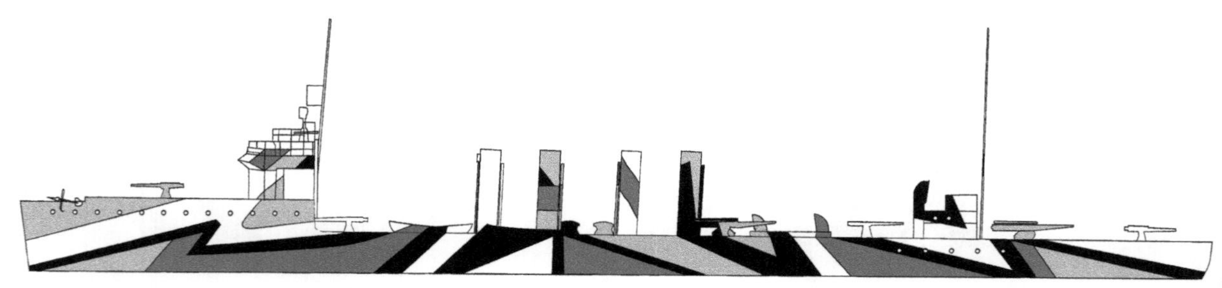

PORT SIDE PATTERN

N10 ADM

Colors used	Ships painted with this pattern
BLACK	DD 37 FANNING
WHITE	
#3 BLUE	
#1 BLUE-GRAY	Pattern adapted from photographs and comparison with a British pattern found on file

N10 ADM

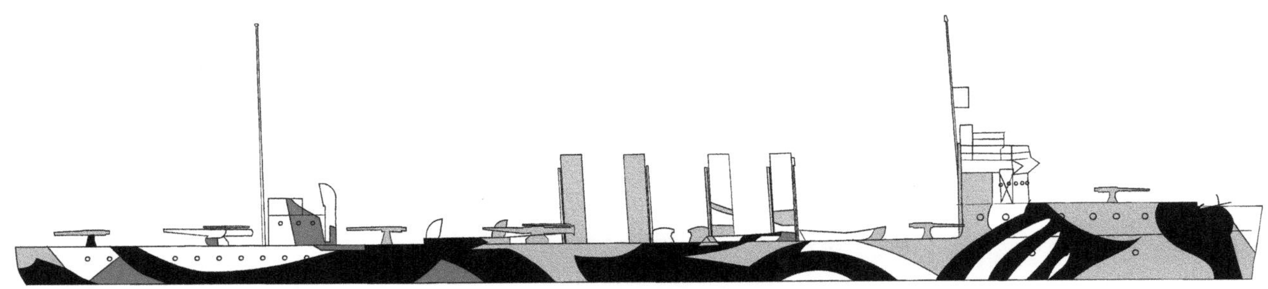

STARBOARD SIDE PATTERN

N10 ADM

PORT SIDE PATTERN

N11 A

Colors used	Ships painted with this pattern
BLACK	AP 1 HENDERSON
WHITE	
#3 BLUE	
#1 BLUE	
#1 BLUE-GRAY	

TYPE·11 N DESIGN·A·

·STARBOARD·SIDE·
SCALE LENGTH 482'-9"
COLORS
NO. 1 BLUE GREY NO. 3 BLUE
BLACK WHITE
NOTE
COLORS·ON·PLAN ARE FOR THE·PURPOSES OF MEASUREMENT ONLY··ACTUAL COLORS AS PER COLOR CHART·

TYPE·11 N· DESIGN·A

·PORT·SIDE·
SCALE LENGTH 482'-9"
COLORS
NO. 1 BLUE GREY NO. 3 BLUE
BLACK WHITE
NO. 1 BLUE
NOTE
COLORS·ON·PLAN ARE FOR THE·PURPOSES OF MEASUREMENT ONLY···ACTUAL·COLORS AS PER COLOR·CHART·

N11 A

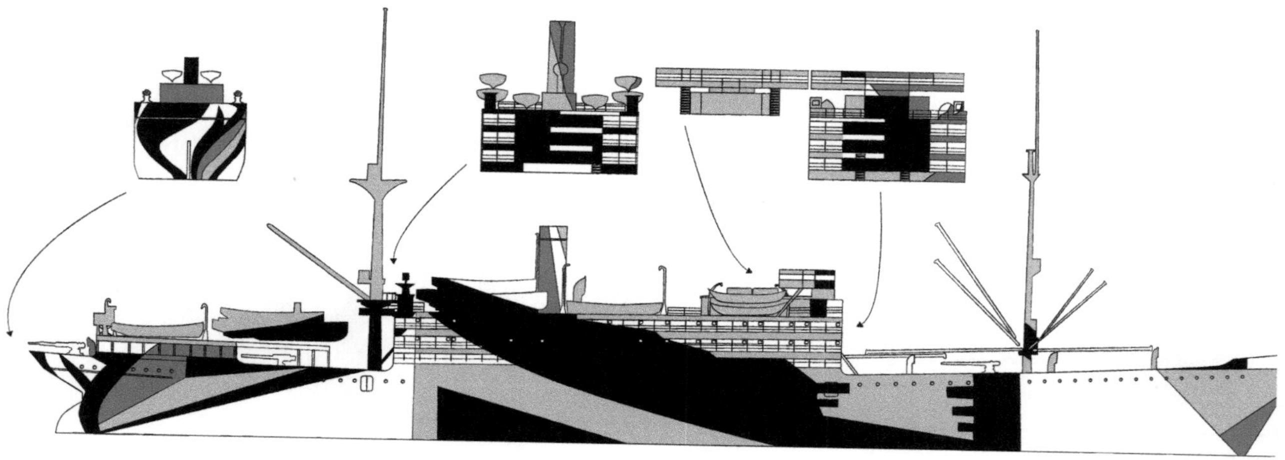

Starboard Side Pattern

N11 A

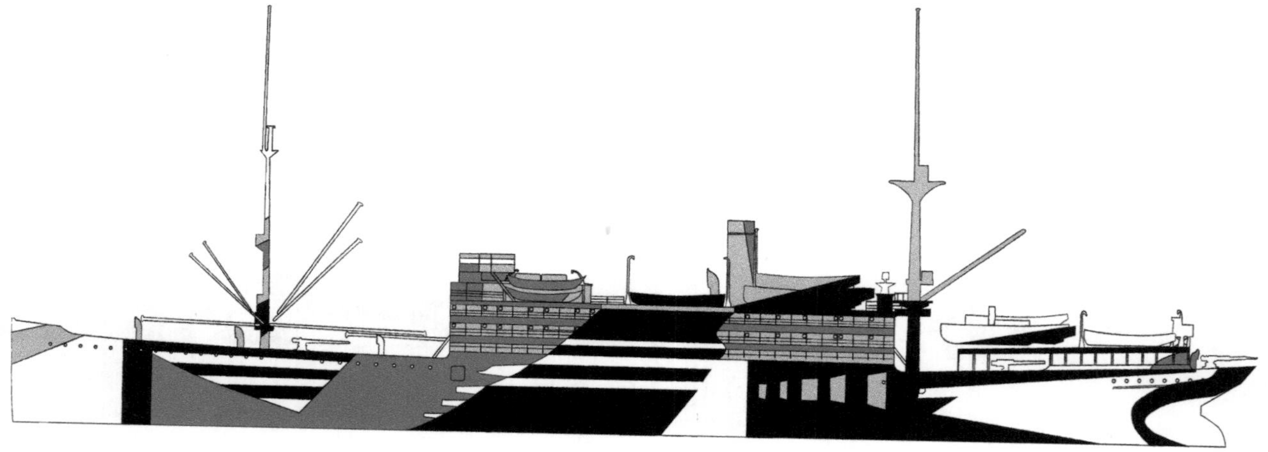

Port Side Pattern

N12 A

Colors used	Ships painted with this pattern
BLACK	DD93 FAIRFAX
WHITE	DD 94 TAYLOR
#3 BLUE	DD 79 LITTLE
#1 BLUE-GRAY	

TYPE · 12 N ·
DESIGN · A ·

∴ PORT SIDE ∴
SCALE 5/64" = 1'-0" LENGTH 310'-0"
COLORS
WHITE N° 1 BLUE GRAY
BLACK N° 3 BLUE
NOTE
COLORS ON PLAN ARE FOR THE PURPOSES OF MEASUREMENT ONLY. ACTUAL COLORS AS PER COLOR CHART.

TYPE · 12 N ·
DESIGN · A ·

STARBOARD SIDE
SCALE 5/64" = 1'-0" LENGTH 310'-0"
COLORS
WHITE N° I BLUE GRAY
BLACK N° 3 BLUE
NOTE
COLORS ON PLAN ARE FOR THE PURPOSES OF MEASUREMENT ONLY. ACTUAL COLORS AS PER COLOR CHART.

N12 A

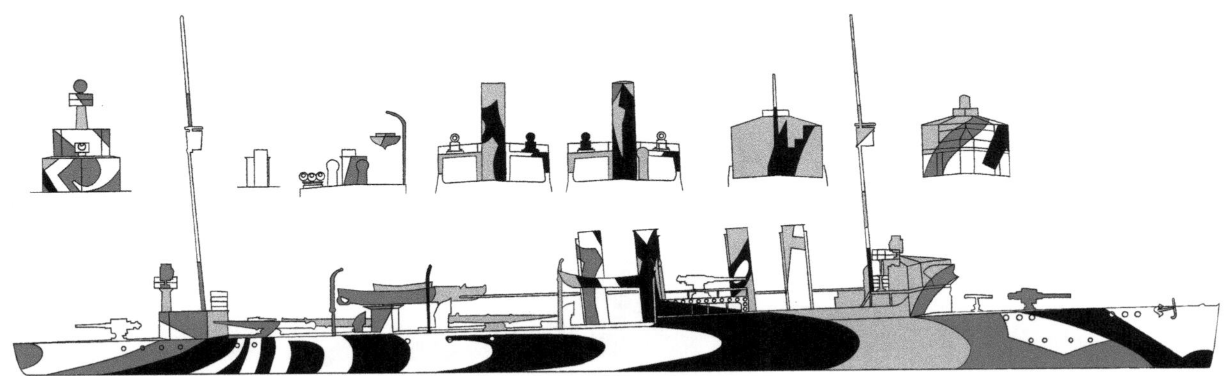

STARBOARD SIDE PATTERN

N12 A

PORT SIDE PATTERN

N12 B

Colors used	Ships painted with this pattern
BLACK	DD 80 KIMBERLEY
WHITE	DD 86 STEVENS
#3 BLUE	DD 113 RATHBURNE
#1 BLUE-GRAY	DD 239 WARD

TYPE N-12
DESIGN B

∴ PORT SIDE ∴
SCALE ⅛"=1'0" LENGTH 310'0"
COLORS
W = WHITE 3B = Nº 3 BLUE
B = BLACK 1BG = Nº 1 BLUE GREY
NOTE
COLORS ON PLAN ARE FOR THE PURPOSES OF MEASUREMENT ONLY. ACTUAL COLORS AS PER COLOR CHART.

TYPE N-12
DESIGN B

STARBOARD SIDE
SCALE ⅛"=1'0" LENGTH 310'0"
COLORS
W = WHITE 3B = Nº 3 BLUE
B = BLACK 1BG = Nº 1 BLUE GREY
NOTE
COLORS ON PLAN ARE FOR THE PURPOSES OF MEASUREMENT ONLY. ACTUAL COLORS AS PER COLOR CHART.

N12 B

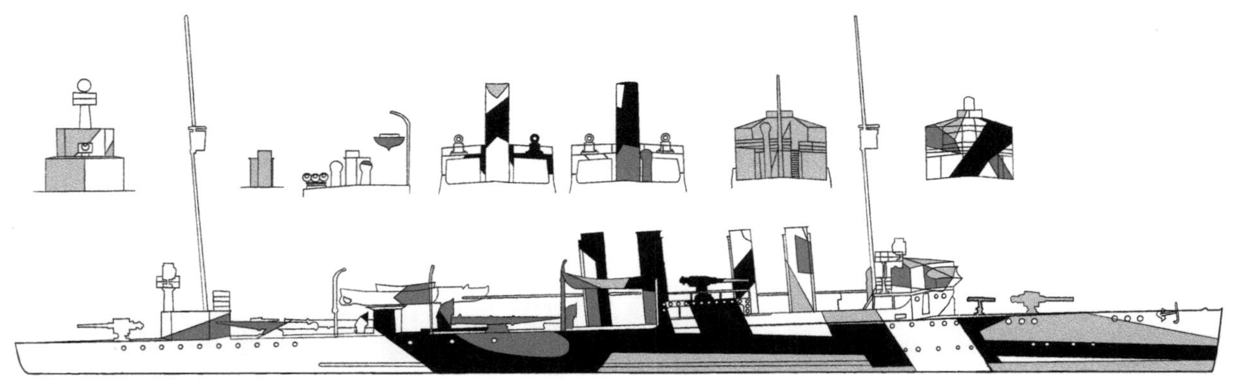

Starboard Side Pattern

N12 B

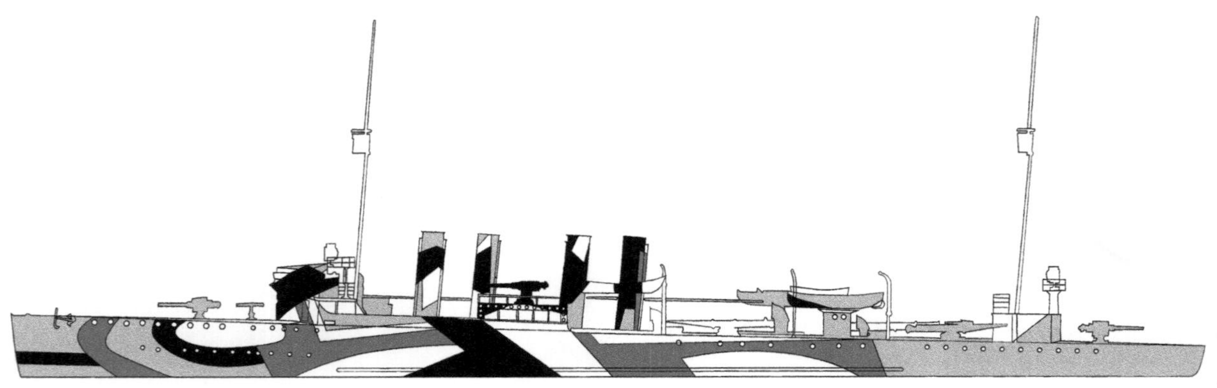

Port Side Pattern

N12 C

Colors used	Ships painted with this pattern
BLACK	DD 84 DYER
WHITE	DD 114 TALBOT
#3 BLUE	DD 82 GREGORY
#1 BLUE-GRAY	

TYPE N-12
DESIGN C

PORT SIDE

SCALE 3/32"=1'-0" LENGTH 310'-0" B.P.

COLORS

WHITE
BLACK
GREYWHITE
NO. 3 BLUE
NO. 1 BLUE GREY

NOTE

COLORS ON PLAN ARE FOR THE PURPOSES OF MEASUREMENT ONLY
ACTUAL COLORS AS PER COLOR CHART

TYPE N-12
DESIGN C

STARBOARD SIDE

SCALE 3/32"=1'-0" LENGTH 310'-0" B.P.

COLORS

BLACK
WHITE
GREYWHITE
NO. 3 BLUE
NO. 1 BLUE GREY

NOTE

COLORS ON PLAN ARE FOR THE PURPOSES OF MEASUREMENT ONLY
ACTUAL COLORS AS PER COLOR CHART

N12 C

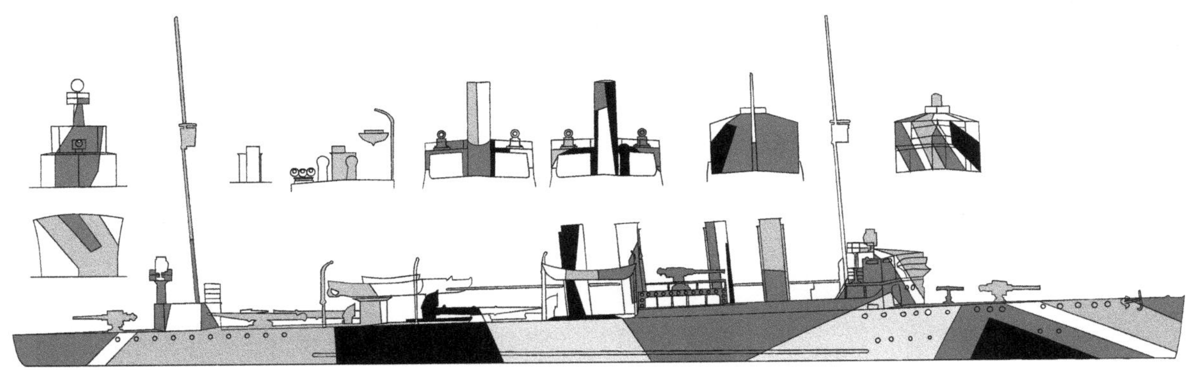

Starboard Side Pattern

N12 C

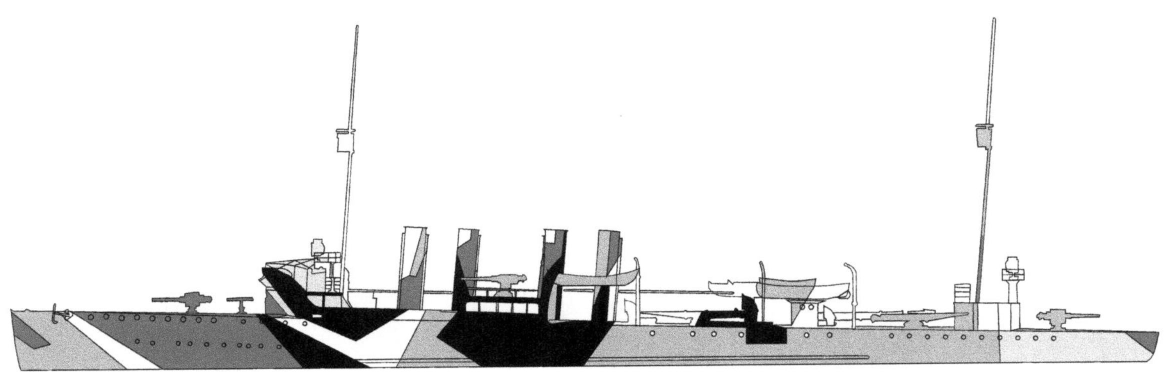

Port Side Pattern

N12 D

Colors used	Ships painted with this pattern
BLACK	DD 116 DENT
WHITE	DD 115 WATERS
#3 BLUE	DD 75 WICKES
#1 BLUE-GRAY	DD 83 STRINGHAM

TYPE N-12
DESIGN D

∴ PORT SIDE ∴
SCALE 5/64"-1'0" LENGTH 310'0"
COLORS
BK = BLACK NBG = No 1 BLUE GREY
W = WHITE 3B = No 3 BLUE
NOTE
COLORS ON PLAN ARE FOR THE PURPOSES OF MEASUREMENT ONLY. ACTUAL COLORS AS PER COLOR CHART.

TYPE N-12
DESIGN D

STARBOARD SIDE
SCALE 5/64"-1'0" LENGTH 310'0"
COLORS
W = WHITE 1BG = No 1 BLUE GREY
BK = BLACK 3B = No 3 BLUE
NOTE
COLORS ON PLAN ARE FOR THE PURPOSES OF MEASUREMENT ONLY. ACTUAL COLORS AS PER COLOR CHART.

N12 D

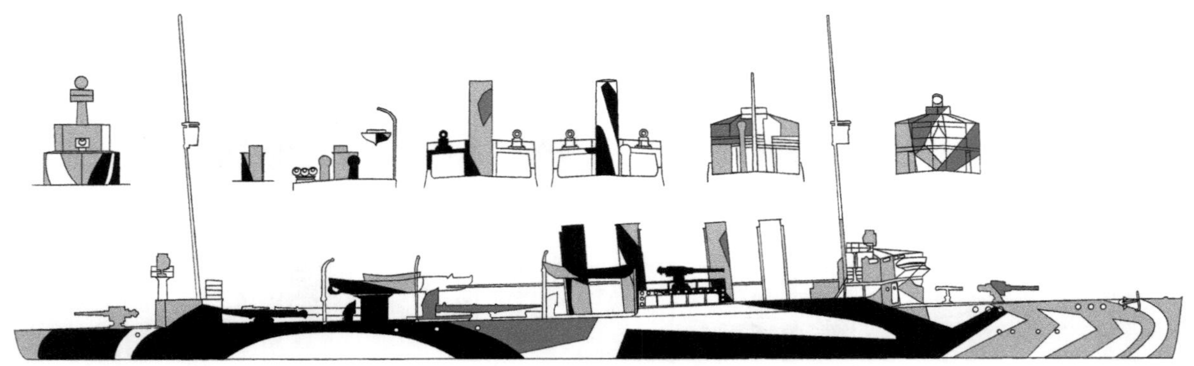

Starboard Side Pattern

N12 D

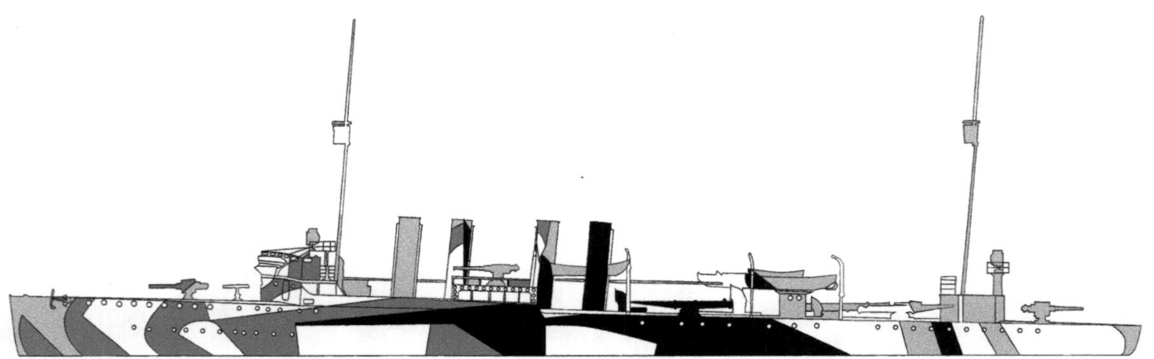

Port Side Pattern

N12 E

Colors used	Ships painted with this pattern
BLACK	DD 103 SCHLEY
WHITE	
GREY-WHITE	
#3 BLUE	

TYPE N-12
DESIGN E
PORT SIDE
COLORS
BLACK WHITE
GREY WHITE
NO. 3 BLUE
NOTE
COLORS ON PLAN ARE FOR THE PURPOSES OF MEASUREMENT ONLY ACTUAL COLORS AS PER COLOR CHART

TYPE N-12
DESIGN E
STARBOARD SIDE
COLORS
GREY WHITE
BLACK
NO. 3 BLUE
NOTE
COLORS ON PLAN ARE FOR THE PURPOSES OF MEASUREMENT ONLY ACTUAL COLORS AS PER COLOR CHART

N12 E

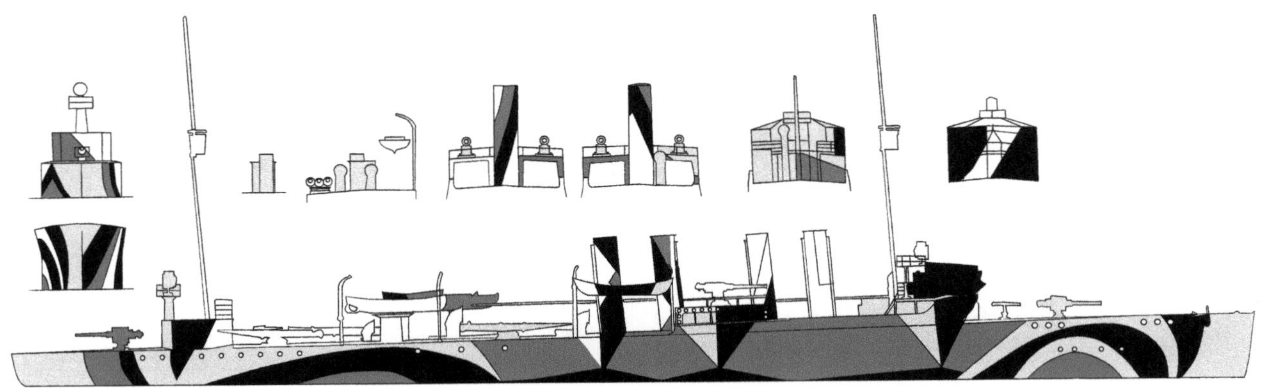

Starboard Side Pattern

N12 E

Port Side Pattern

N12 F

Colors used	Ships painted with this pattern
BLACK	DD 137 KILTY
WHITE	DD 100 MAURY
GREY-WHITE	
#3 BLUE	
#1 BLUE-GRAY	

TYPE N-12
DESIGN F
PORT SIDE
SCALE 3/32" = 1'-0" LENGTH 310' 0" B.P.
COLORS
WHITE
BLACK
GREY-WHITE
NO. 3 BLUE
NO. 1 BLUE GREY
NOTE
COLORS ON PLAN ARE FOR THE PURPOSES OF MEASUREMENT ONLY
ACTUAL COLORS AS PER COLOR CHART

TYPE N-12
DESIGN F
STARBOARD SIDE
SCALE 3/32" = 1'-0" LENGTH 310' 0" B.P.
COLORS
WHITE
BLACK
GREY-WHITE
NO. 3 BLUE
NO. 1 BLUE GREY
NOTE
COLORS ON PLAN ARE FOR THE PURPOSES OF MEASUREMENT ONLY
ACTUAL COLORS AS PER COLOR CHART

N12 F

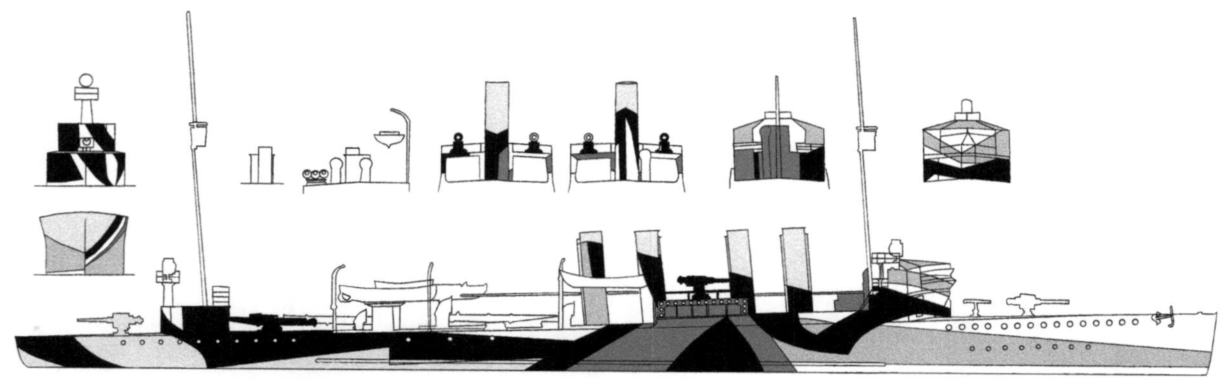

STARBOARD SIDE PATTERN

N12 F

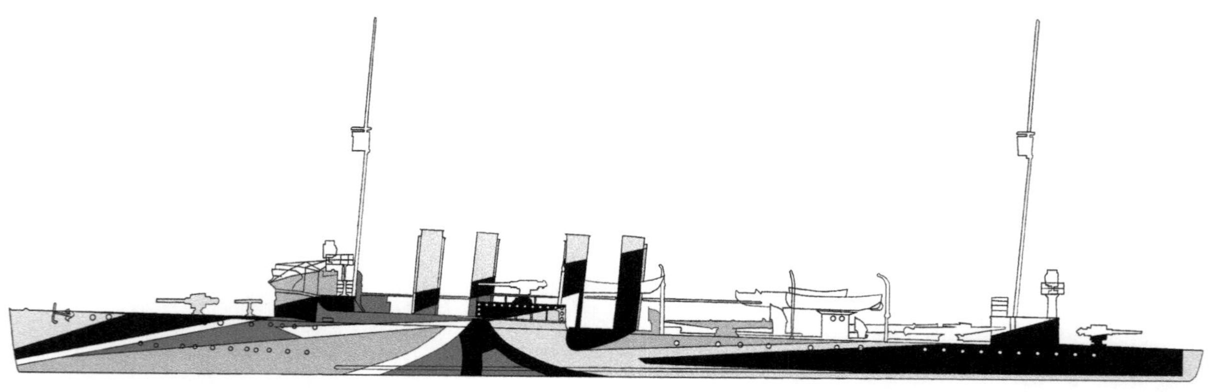

PORT SIDE PATTERN

N12 H

Colors used	Ships painted with this pattern
BLACK	DD 104 CHAMPLIN
WHITE	DD 261 DELPHY
GREY-WHITE	DD 102 MAHAN
#3 BLUE	
#1 BLUE	
#1 GREEN	

TYPE N-12
DESIGN H
PORT SIDE
COLORS
NOTE
COLORS ON PLAN ARE FOR THE PURPOSES OF MEASUREMENT ONLY
ACTUAL COLORS AS PER COLOR CHART

TYPE N-12
DESIGN H
STARBOARD SIDE
COLORS
NOTE
COLORS ON PLAN ARE FOR THE PURPOSES OF MEASUREMENT ONLY
ACTUAL COLORS AS PER COLOR CHART

N12 H

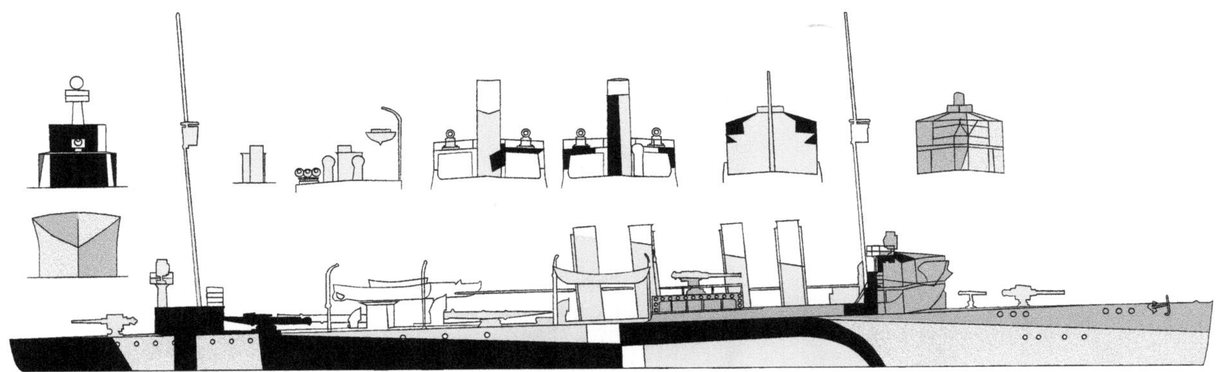

STARBOARD SIDE PATTERN

N12 H

PORT SIDE PATTERN

N12 I

Colors used	Ships painted with this pattern
BLACK	DD 89 RINGGOLD
WHITE	
#3 BLUE	
#1 BLUE	

N12 I

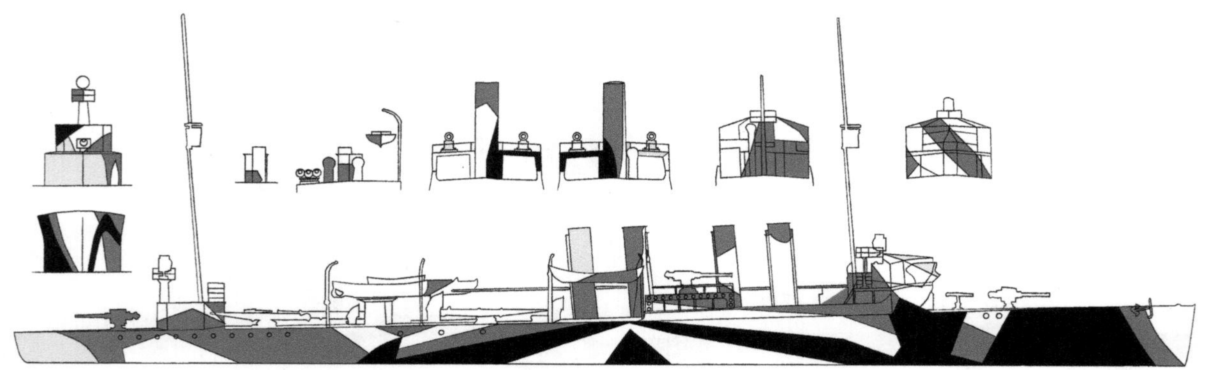

STARBOARD SIDE PATTERN

N12 I

PORT SIDE PATTERN

N12 J

Colors used	Ships painted with this pattern
BLACK	DD 87 MCKEE
WHITE	DD 95 BELL
#3 BLUE	DD 119 LAMBERTON
#1 BLUE	DD 98 ISRAEL
#2 BLUE-GRAY	

TYPE N 12
DESIGN J
PORT SIDE
COLORS
NOTE
COLORS ON PLAN ARE FOR THE PURPOSES OF MEASUREMENT ONLY. ACTUAL COLORS AS PER COLOR CHART.

TYPE N 12
DESIGN J

N12 J

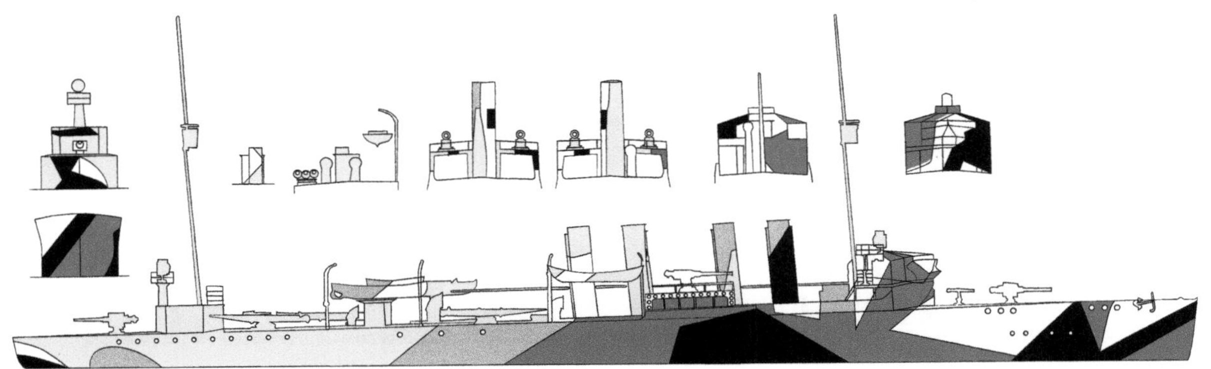

STARBOARD SIDE PATTERN

N12 J

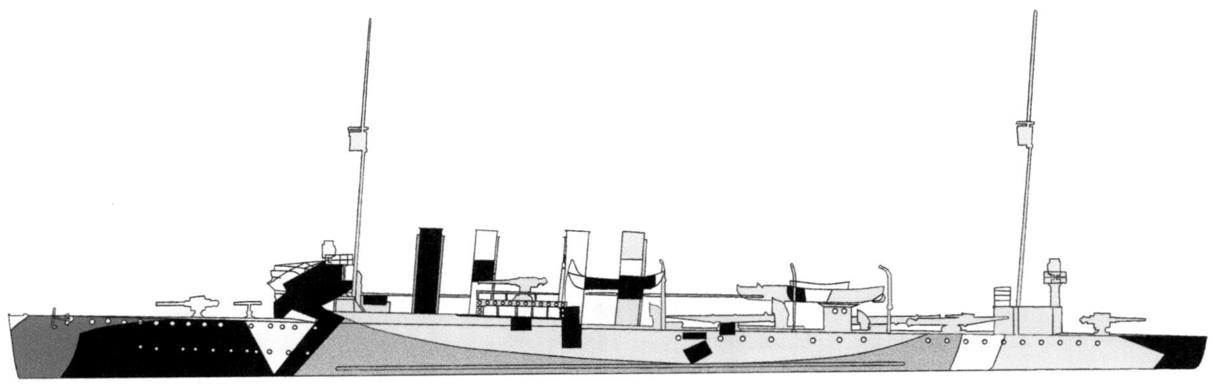

PORT SIDE PATTERN

N12 K

Colors used	Ships painted with this pattern
BLACK	DD 77 WOOLSEY
WHITE	DD 88 ROBINSON
#3 BLUE	DD 85 COLHOUN
#2 BLUE-GRAY	DD 122 BREESE
#1 GREEN	

TYPE N-12
DESIGN K

PORT SIDE

SCALE 3/32"=1'0" LENGTH 310'0"

COLORS

GREY WHITE
NO. 2 BLUE GREY
BLACK
WHITE
NO. 3 BLUE
NO. 1 GREEN

NOTE

COLORS ON PLAN ARE FOR THE PURPOSES OF MEASUREMENT ONLY ACTUAL COLORS AS PER COLOR CHART

TYPE N-12
DESIGN K

STARBOARD SIDE

SCALE 3/32"=1'0" LENGTH 310'0"

COLORS

NO. 1 GREEN
BLACK
NO. 2 BLUE GREY
GREY WHITE
WHITE
NO. 3 BLUE

NOTE

COLORS ON PLAN ARE FOR THE PURPOSES OF MEASUREMENT ONLY ACTUAL COLORS AS PER COLOR CHART

N12 K

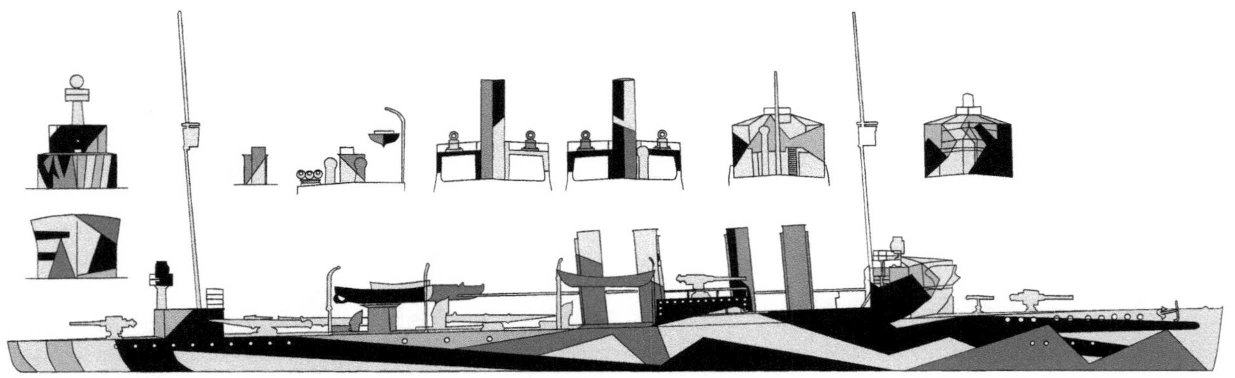

Starboard Side Pattern

N12 K

Port Side Pattern

N12 M

Colors used	Ships painted with this pattern
BLACK	DD 99 LUCE
GREY-WHITE	
#3 BLUE	
#1 BLUE-GRAY	
#1 GREEN	

TYPE N-12
DESIGN M

PORT SIDE

SCALE 3/32"=1'0" LENGTH 310'-0"

COLORS

NO. 3 BLUE BLACK
NO. 1 BLUE GREY
NO. 1 GREEN GREY WHITE

NOTE

COLORS ON PLAN ARE FOR THE PURPOSES OF MEASUREMENT ONLY . . . ACTUAL COLORS AS PER COLOR CHART

TYPE N-12
DESIGN M

STARBOARD SIDE

SCALE 3/32"=1'0" LENGTH 310'0" B.P.

COLORS

NO. 3 BLUE BLACK
NO. 1 BLUE GREY
NO. 1 GREEN GREY WHITE

NOTE

COLORS ON PLAN ARE FOR THE PURPOSES OF MEASUREMENT ONLY . . . ACTUAL COLORS AS PER COLOR CHART

N12 M

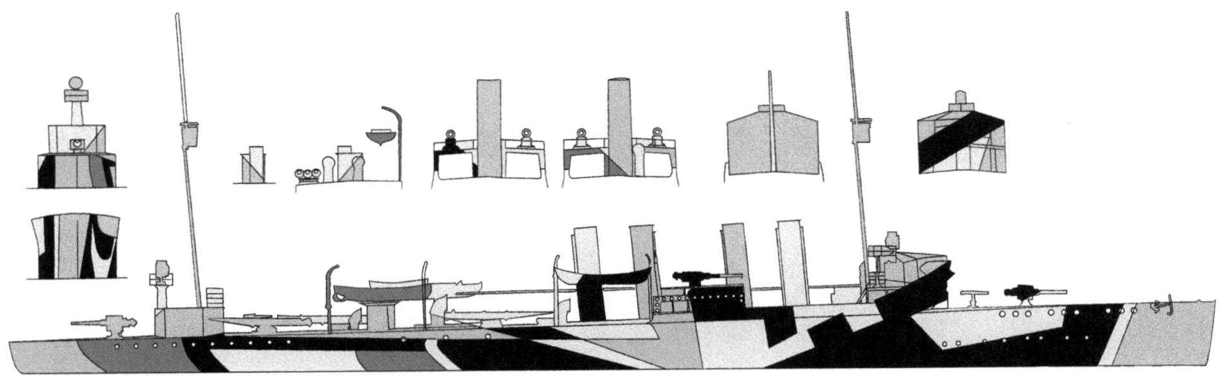

STARBOARD SIDE PATTERN

N12 M

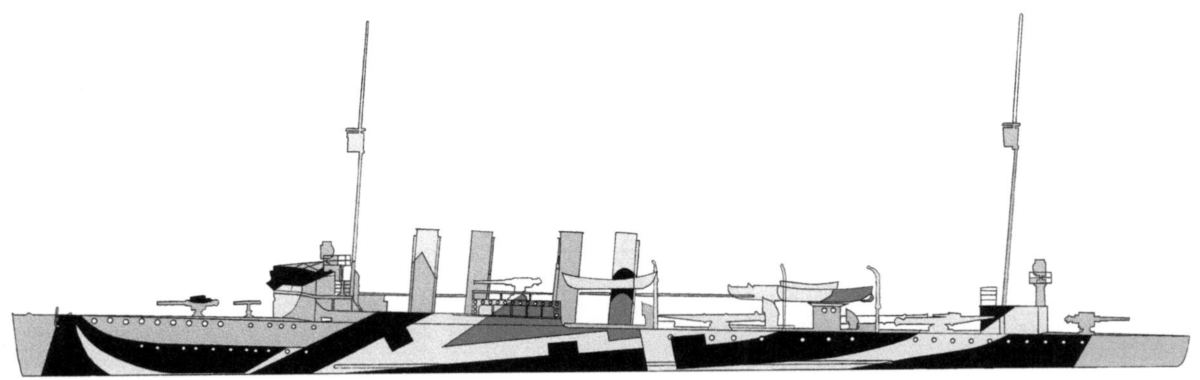

PORT SIDE PATTERN

N12 N

Colors used	Ships painted with this pattern
BLACK	DD 70 CRAVEN
GREY-WHITE	

TYPE N-12
DESIGN N
PORT SIDE
SCALE 3/64
COLORS
gray white
BLACK
NOTE
COLORS ON PLAN ARE FOR THE PURPOSES OF MEASUREMENT ONLY
ACTUAL COLORS AS PER COLOR CHART

TYPE N-12
DESIGN N
STARBOARD SIDE
SCALE 3/64
COLORS
gray white
BLACK
NO. 3 BLUE
NOTE
COLORS ON PLAN ARE FOR THE PURPOSES OF MEASUREMENT ONLY
ACTUAL COLORS AS PER COLOR CHART

N12 N

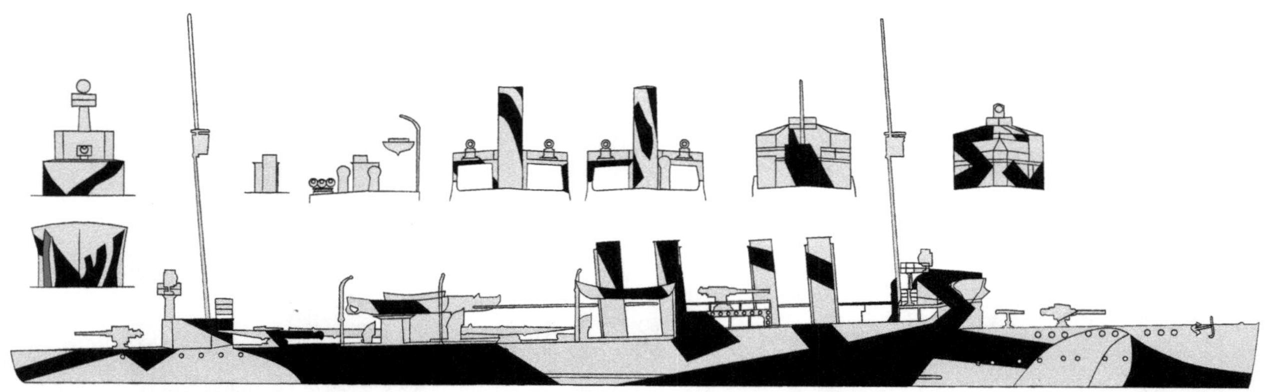

STARBOARD SIDE PATTERN

N12 N

PORT SIDE PATTERN

N12 ADM

Colors used	Ships painted with this pattern
BLACK	DD 69 CALDWELL
WHITE	DD 66 ALLEN
#3 BLUE	
#1 BLUE-GRAY	Pattern adapted from photographs and comparison with a British pattern found on file

N12 ADM

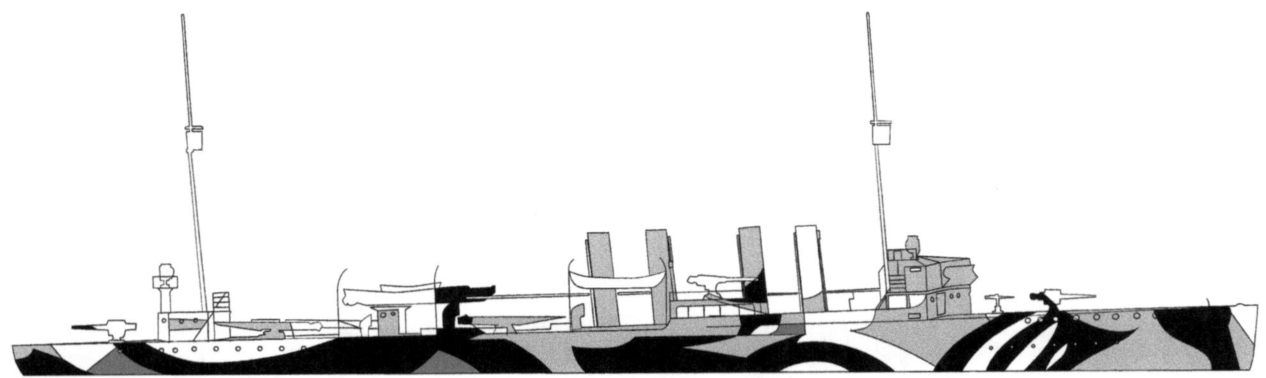

STARBOARD SIDE PATTERN

N12 ADM

PORT SIDE PATTERN

N13 A

Colors used	Ships painted with this pattern
BLACK	ID 4569 GREAT NORTHERN
WHITE	
#3 BLUE	
#1 BLUE-GRAY	

N13 A

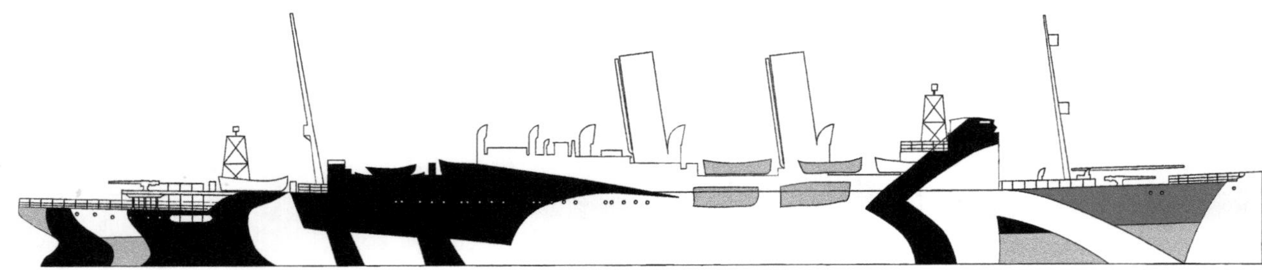

STARBOARD SIDE PATTERN

N13 A

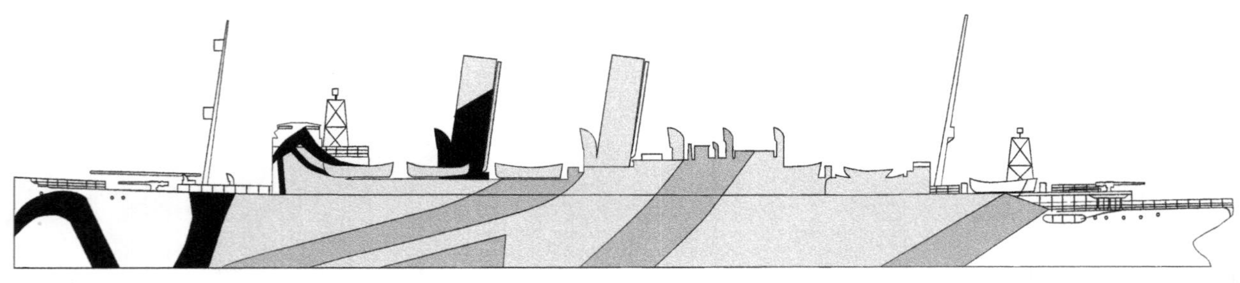

PORT SIDE PATTERN

N13 B

Colors used	Ships painted with this pattern
BLACK	ID NONE NORTHERN PACIFIC
WHITE	
#3 BLUE	
#1 BLUE-GRAY	

TYPE N-13
DESIGN B

∴ PORT SIDE ∴
SCALE 3/64"=1·0" LENGTH 509'-6"
COLORS
NOTE
COLORS ON PLAN ARE FOR THE PURPOSES OF MEASUREMENT ONLY. ACTUAL COLORS AS PER COLOR CHART.

TYPE N-13
DESIGN B

·STARBOARD·SIDE·
SCALE 3/64"=1·0" LENGTH 509'-6"
COLORS
WHITE BLACK
NO. 3 BLUE NO. 1 BLUE GREY
NOTE
COLORS ON PLAN ARE FOR THE PURPOSES OF MEASUREMENT ONLY. ACTUAL COLORS AS PER COLOR CHART.

N13 B

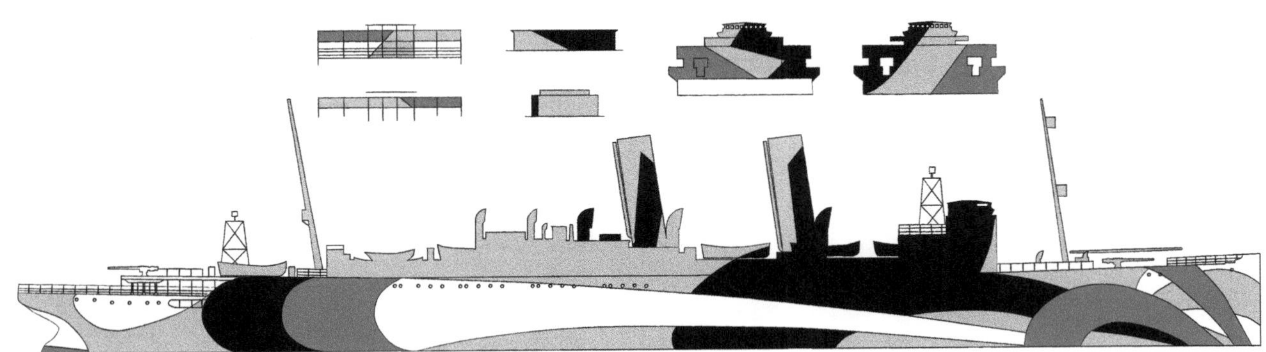

Starboard Side Pattern

N13 B

Port Side Pattern

N14 A

Colors used	Ships painted with this pattern
BLACK	AD 9 BLACKHAWK
WHITE	AK3 NEWPORT NEWS
#3 BLUE	
#1 BLUE-GRAY	

TYPE 14 N
DESIGN A

∴ PORT SIDE ∴
SCALE 1/16"=1'-0" LENGTH 404'-6"
COLORS
WHITE NO. 3 BLUE
BLACK NO. 1 BLUE GREY
NOTE
COLORS ON PLAN ARE FOR THE PURPOSES OF MEASUREMENT ONLY. ACTUAL COLORS AS PER COLOR CHART.

TYPE 14 N
DESIGN A

STARBOARD SIDE
SCALE 1/16"=1'-0" LENGTH 404'-6"
COLORS
WHITE NO. 3 BLUE
BLACK NO. 1 BLUE GREY
NOTE
COLORS ON PLAN ARE FOR THE PURPOSES OF MEASUREMENT ONLY. ACTUAL COLORS AS PER COLOR CHART.

N14 A

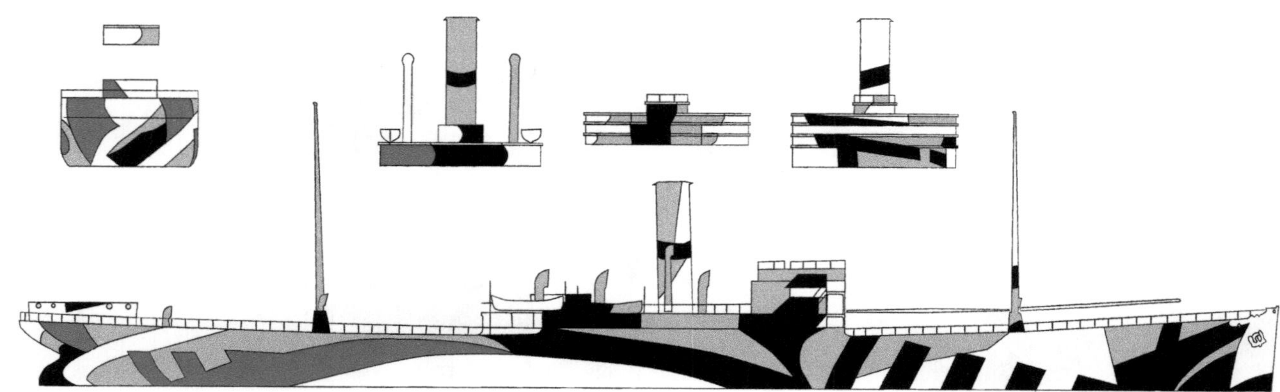

Starboard Side Pattern

N14 A

Port Side Pattern

N15 A

Colors used	Ships painted with this pattern
BLACK	ID 2168 WILHELMINA
WHITE	
#3 BLUE	
#1 BLUE-GRAY	

TYPE N 15
DESIGN A
∴ PORT SIDE ∴
SCALE LENGTH
COLORS
NOTE
COLORS ON PLAN ARE FOR THE PURPOSES OF MEASUREMENT ONLY. ACTUAL COLORS AS PER COLOR CHART.

TYPE N 15
DESIGN A
STARBOARD SIDE
SCALE LENGTH
COLORS
NOTE
COLORS ON PLAN ARE FOR THE PURPOSES OF MEASUREMENT ONLY. ACTUAL COLORS AS PER COLOR CHART.

N15 A

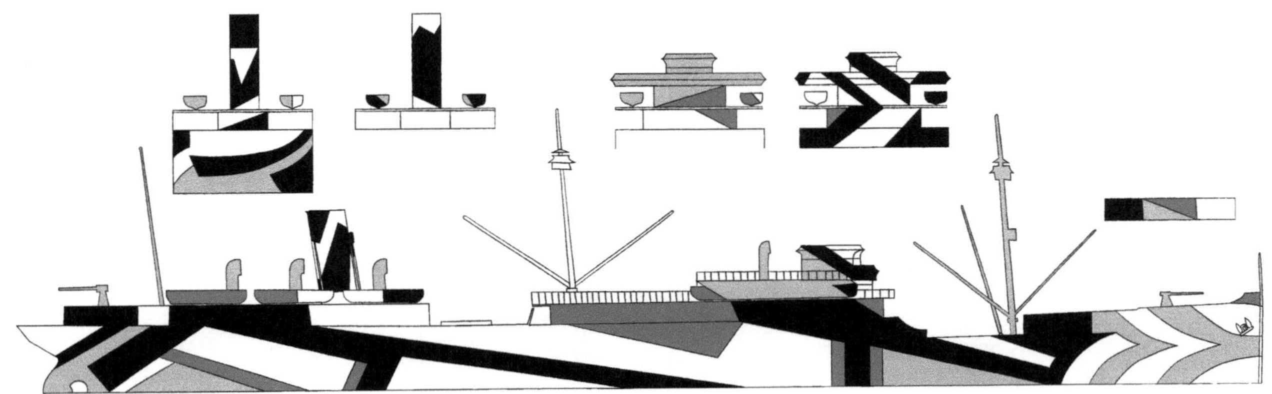

STARBOARD SIDE PATTERN

N15 A

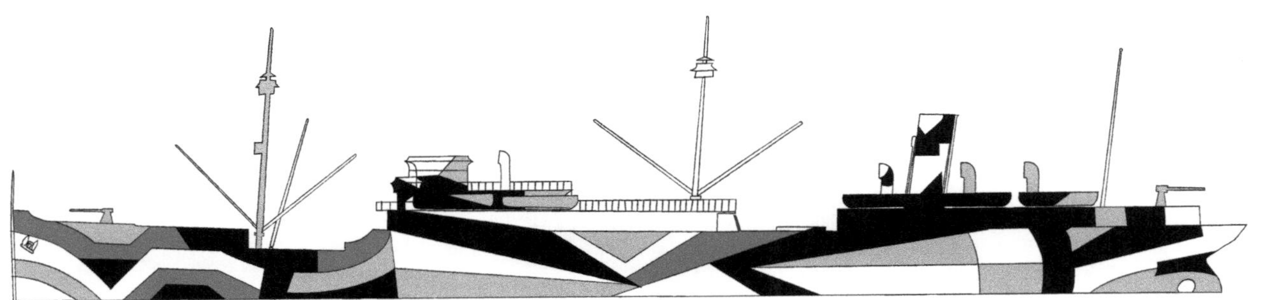

PORT SIDE PATTERN

N15 B

Colors used	Ships painted with this pattern
BLACK	ID 1514 MAUI
WHITE	ID 1589 MATSONIA
#3 BLUE	
#1 BLUE-GRAY	

TYPE N 15
DESIGN B
PORT SIDE
SCALE 3/64=1' LENGTH 501-0"
COLORS
BLACK NO. 1 BLUE GREY
WHITE NO. 3 BLUE
NOTE
COLORS ON PLAN ARE FOR THE PURPOSES OF MEASUREMENT ONLY . . . ACTUAL COLORS AS PER COLOR CHART

TYPE N 15
DESIGN B
STARBOARD SIDE
SCALE 3/64=1' LENGTH 501'-0"
COLORS
BLACK NO. 1 BLUE GREY
WHITE NO. 3 BLUE
NOTE
COLORS ON PLAN ARE FOR THE PURPOSES OF MEASUREMENT ONLY . . . ACTUAL COLORS AS PER COLOR CHART

N15 B

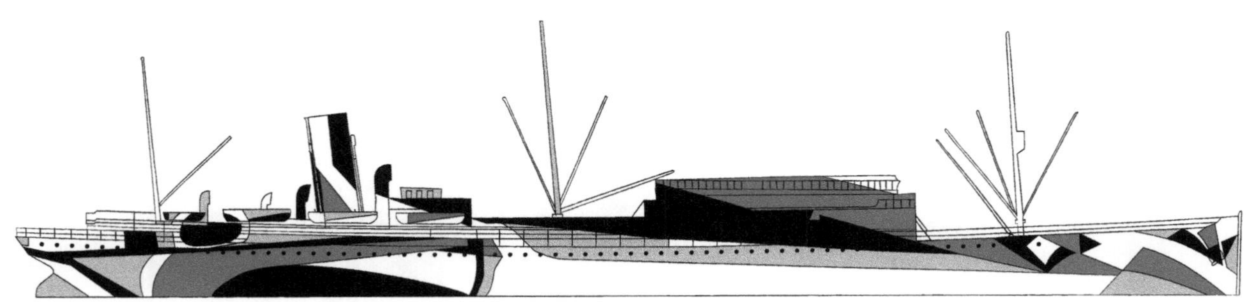

Starboard Side Pattern

N15 B

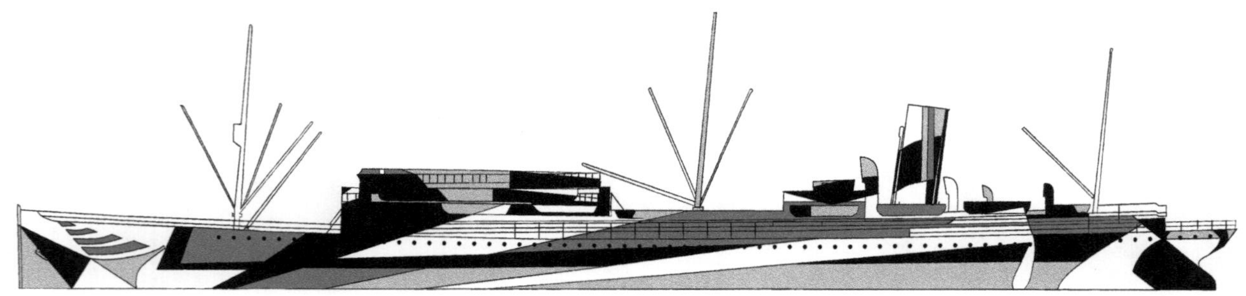

Port Side Pattern

N16 A

Colors used	Ships painted with this pattern
BLACK	NOT USED
WHITE	
#3 BLUE	
#1 BLUE-GRAY	

TYPE N·16
DESIGN A

∴ PORT SIDE ∴
SCALE 1/25=1'-0" LENGTH 599'-0"
COLORS
BLACK NO. 1 BLUE GREY
WHITE NO. 3 BLUE
NOTE
COLORS ON PLAN ARE FOR THE PURPOSES OF MEASUREMENT ONLY. ACTUAL COLORS AS PER COLOR CHART.

TYPE N 16
DESIGN A

STARBOARD SIDE
SCALE 1/25=1'-0" LENGTH 599'-0"
COLORS
BLACK NO. 1 BLUE GREY
WHITE NO. 3 BLUE
NOTE
COLORS ON PLAN ARE FOR THE PURPOSES OF MEASUREMENT ONLY. ACTUAL COLORS AS PER COLOR CHART.

N16 A

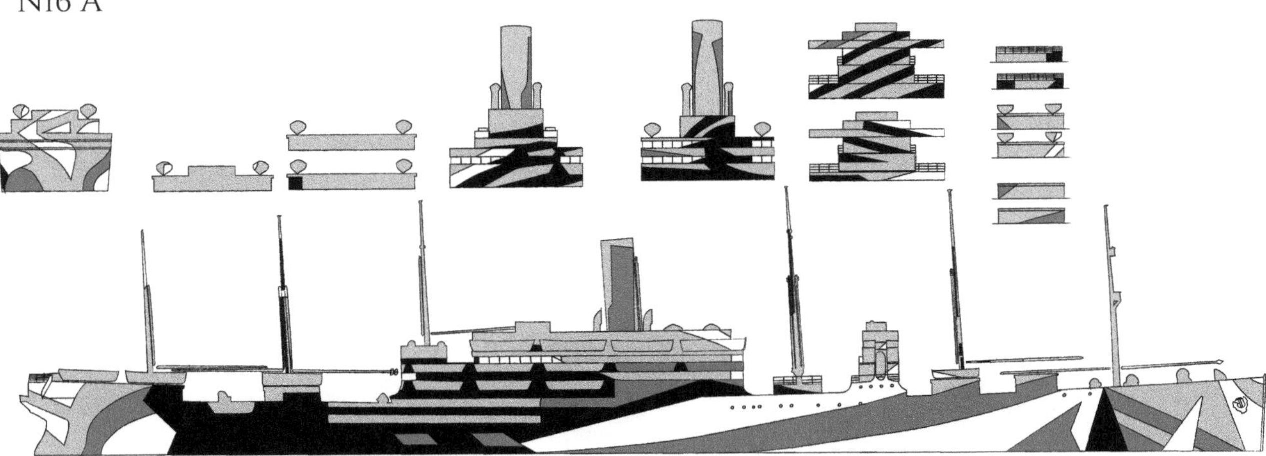

Starboard Side Pattern

N16 A

Port Side Pattern

N16 B

Colors used	Ships painted with this pattern
BLACK	ID 3014 PRESIDENT GRANT
WHITE	
#3 BLUE	
#1 BLUE-GRAY	

TYPE N 16
DESIGN B

∴ PORT SIDE ∴
SCALE LENGTH
COLORS
WHITE NO. 3 BLUE
BLACK NO. 1 BLUE GREY
NOTE
COLORS ON PLAN ARE FOR THE PURPOSES OF MEASUREMENT ONLY. ACTUAL COLORS AS PER COLOR CHART.

TYPE
DESIGN

STARBOARD SIDE
SCALE LENGTH
COLORS
WHITE NO. 3 BLUE
BLACK NO. 1 BLUE GREY
NOTE
COLORS ON PLAN ARE FOR THE PURPOSES OF MEASUREMENT ONLY ACTUAL COLORS AS PER COLOR CHART

N16 B

STARBOARD SIDE PATTERN

N16 B

PORT SIDE PATTERN

N17 A

Colors used	Ships painted with this pattern
BLACK	ID 3044 POCAHONTAS
WHITE	
#3 BLUE	
#1 BLUE-GRAY	

TYPE N-17
DESIGN ·A·

∴ PORT SIDE ∴
SCALE 3/64 = 1·0 LENGTH 523·5"
COLORS
BLACK
WHITE
NO. 1 BLUE GREY
NO. 3 BLUE
NOTE
COLORS ON PLAN ARE FOR THE PURPOSES OF MEASUREMENT ONLY. ACTUAL COLORS AS PER COLOR CHART.

TYPE N-17
DESIGN ·A·

STARBOARD SIDE
SCALE 3/64 = 1·0 LENGTH 523·5"
COLORS
BLACK
WHITE
NO. 1 BLUE GREY
NO. 3 BLUE
NOTE
COLORS ON PLAN ARE FOR THE PURPOSES OF MEASUREMENT ONLY. ACTUAL COLORS AS PER COLOR CHART.

N17 A

Starboard Side Pattern

N17 A

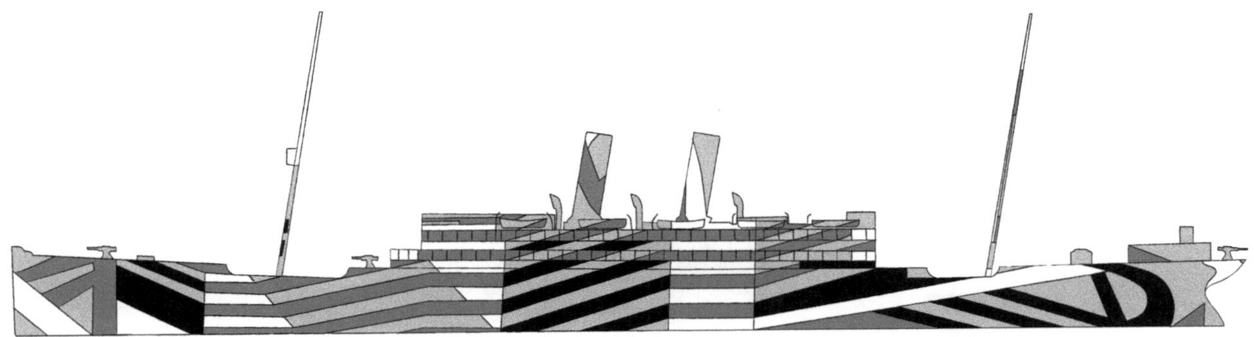

Port Side Pattern

N17 C

Colors used	Ships painted with this pattern
BLACK	ID 3013 POWHATAN
GREY-WHITE	
#3 BLUE	
#1 BLUE-GRAY	

TYPE N-17 DESIGN C	TYPE N-17 DESIGN C
PORT SIDE	STARBOARD SIDE
SCALE [illegible] = 1'-0" LENGTH 523'-0"	SCALE [illegible] = 1'-0" LENGTH 523'-0"
COLORS	COLORS
NO. 1 BLUE GREY, GREY WHITE, NO. 3 BLUE, BLACK	NO. 1 BLUE GREY, GREY WHITE, NO. 3 BLUE, BLACK
NOTE	NOTE
COLORS ON PLAN ARE FOR THE PURPOSES OF MEASUREMENT ONLY ACTUAL COLORS AS PER COLOR CHART	COLORS ON PLAN ARE FOR THE PURPOSES OF MEASUREMENT ONLY ACTUAL COLORS AS PER COLOR CHART

N17 C

Starboard Side Pattern

N17 C

Port Side Pattern

N18 A

Colors used	Ships painted with this pattern
BLACK	ID 3011 MADAWASKA
WHITE	
#3 BLUE	
#1 BLUE-GRAY	

TYPE N-18
DESIGN A

∴ PORT SIDE ∴
SCALE 3/64"=1'0" LENGTH 490'0"
COLORS
WHITE NO. 3 BLUE
NO. 1 BLUE GREY
BLACK
NOTE
COLORS ON PLAN ARE FOR THE PURPOSES OF MEASUREMENT ONLY. ACTUAL COLORS AS PER COLOR CHART.

TYPE N-18
DESIGN A

STARBOARD SIDE
SCALE 3/64"=1'0" LENGTH 490'0"
COLORS
WHITE NO. 1 BLUE GREY
BLACK
NO. 3 BLUE
NOTE
COLORS ON PLAN ARE FOR THE PURPOSES OF MEASUREMENT ONLY. ACTUAL COLORS AS PER COLOR CHART.

N18 A

Starboard Side Pattern

N18 A

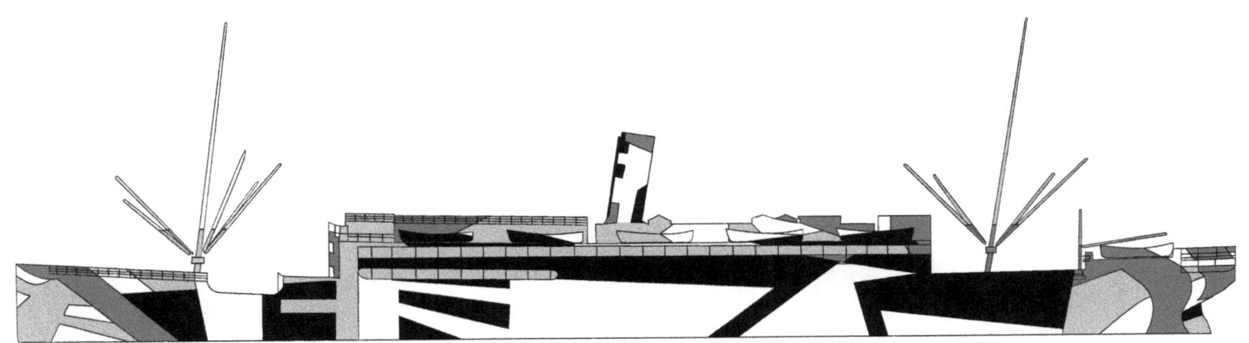

Port Side Pattern

N19 A

Colors used	Ships painted with this pattern
BLACK	ID 3004 AGAMEMNON
WHITE	
#3 BLUE	
#1 BLUE-GRAY	

TYPE N19
DESIGN A

∴ PORT SIDE ∴
SCALE LENGTH
COLORS
WHITE NO. 3 BLUE
BLACK NO. 1 BLUE GREY
NOTE
COLORS ON PLAN ARE FOR THE PURPOSES OF MEASUREMENT ONLY. ACTUAL COLORS AS PER COLOR CHART.

TYPE N19
DESIGN A

STARBOARD SIDE
SCALE LENGTH
COLORS
NO. 3 BLUE WHITE
NO. 1 BLUE GREY BLACK
NOTE
COLORS ON PLAN ARE FOR THE PURPOSES OF MEASUREMENT ONLY. ACTUAL COLORS AS PER COLOR CHART.

N19 A

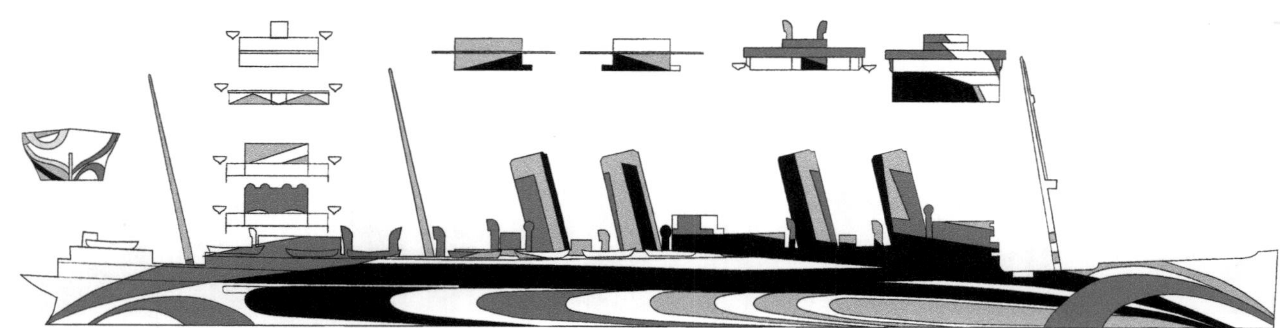

Starboard Side Pattern

N19 A

Port Side Pattern

N19 B

Colors used	Ships painted with this pattern
BLACK	ID 4508 MOUNT VERNON
WHITE	
#3 BLUE	
#1 BLUE-GRAY	

TYPE
DESIGN

∴ PORT SIDE ∴
SCALE LENGTH
COLORS
BLACK
WHITE
NO. 3 BLUE
NO. 1 BLUE GRAY
NOTE
COLORS ON PLAN ARE FOR THE PURPOSES OF MEASUREMENT ONLY. ACTUAL COLORS AS PER COLOR CHART.

TYPE
DESIGN

STARBOARD SIDE
SCALE LENGTH
COLORS
WHITE
BLACK
NO. 3 BLUE
NO. 1 BLUE GREY
NOTE
COLORS ON PLAN ARE FOR THE PURPOSES OF MEASUREMENT ONLY ACTUAL COLORS AS PER COLOR CHART.

N19 B

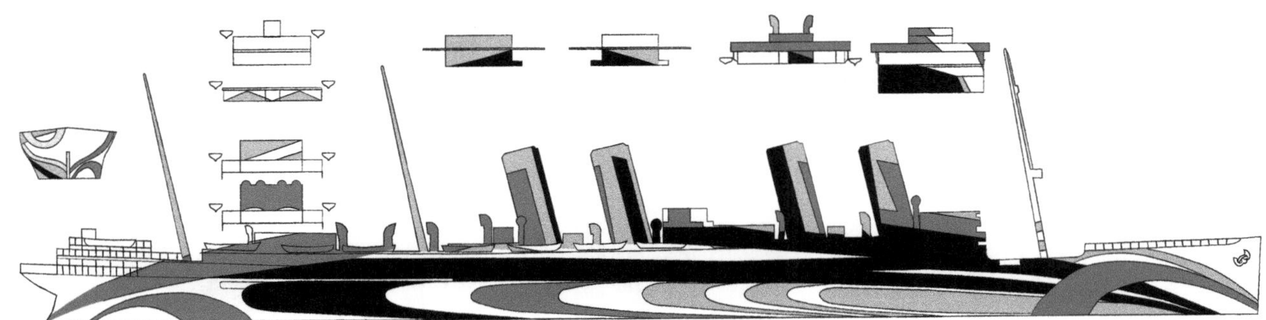

STARBOARD SIDE PATTERN

N19 B

PORT SIDE PATTERN

N20 A

Colors used	Ships painted with this pattern
BLACK	ID 2507 ZEELANDIA
WHITE	ID 2800 OPHIR {T}
#3 BLUE	
#1 BLUE-GRAY	

TYPE N 20
DESIGN A
∴ PORT SIDE ∴
COLORS
NOTE
COLORS ON PLAN ARE FOR THE PURPOSES OF MEASUREMENT ONLY. ACTUAL COLORS AS PER COLOR CHART

TYPE N 20
DESIGN A
STARBOARD SIDE
COLORS
NOTE
COLORS ON PLAN ARE FOR THE PURPOSES OF MEASUREMENT ONLY. ACTUAL COLORS AS PER COLOR CHART.

N20 A

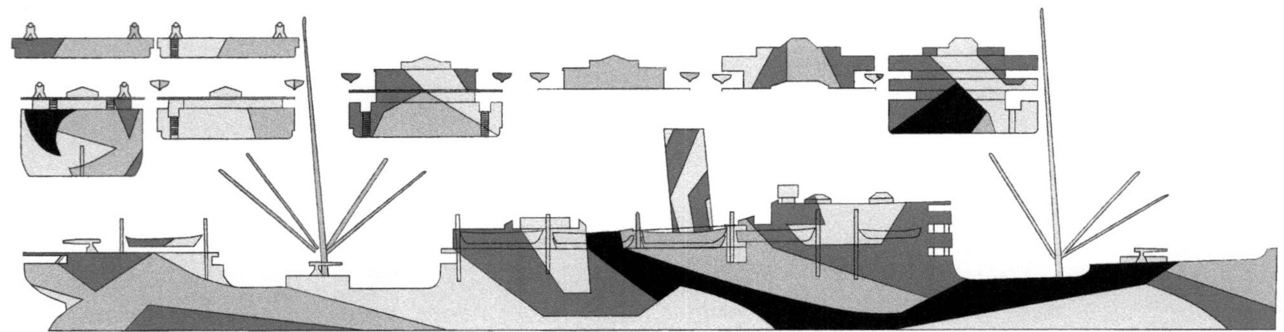

Starboard Side Pattern

N20 A

Port Side Pattern

N21 A

Colors used	Ships painted with this pattern
BLACK	ID 3006 AMERICA
WHITE	
#3 BLUE	
#1 BLUE-GRAY	

TYPE 21 N
DESIGN A

∴ PORT SIDE ∴
SCALE 3/64"=10' LENGTH 669'0"
COLORS
WHITE
NOTE
COLORS ON PLAN ARE FOR THE PURPOSES OF MEASUREMENT ONLY. ACTUAL COLORS AS PER COLOR CHART.

TYPE 21 N
DESIGN A

STARBOARD SIDE
SCALE 3/64"=10' LENGTH 669'0"
COLORS
WHITE
NOTE
COLORS ON PLAN ARE FOR THE PURPOSES OF MEASUREMENT ONLY. ACTUAL COLORS AS PER COLOR CHART.

N21 A

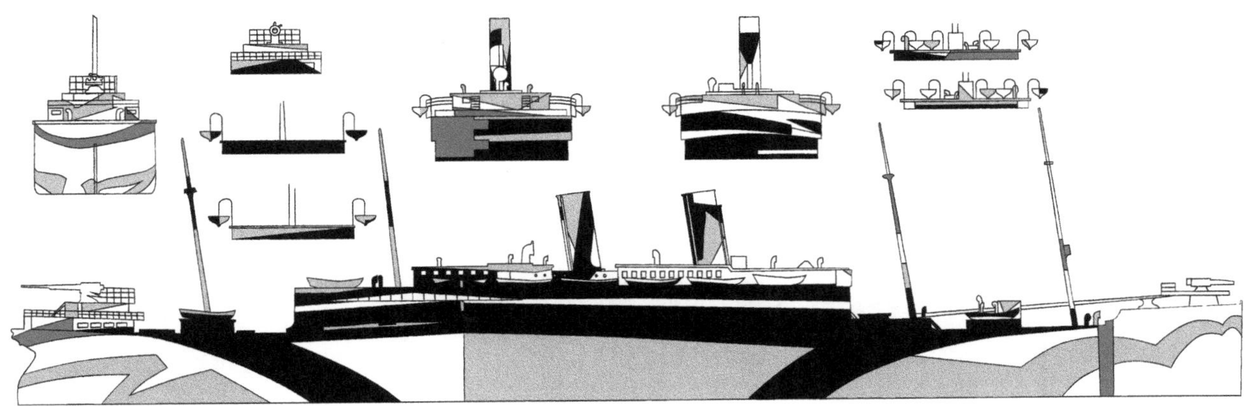

STARBOARD SIDE PATTERN

N21 A

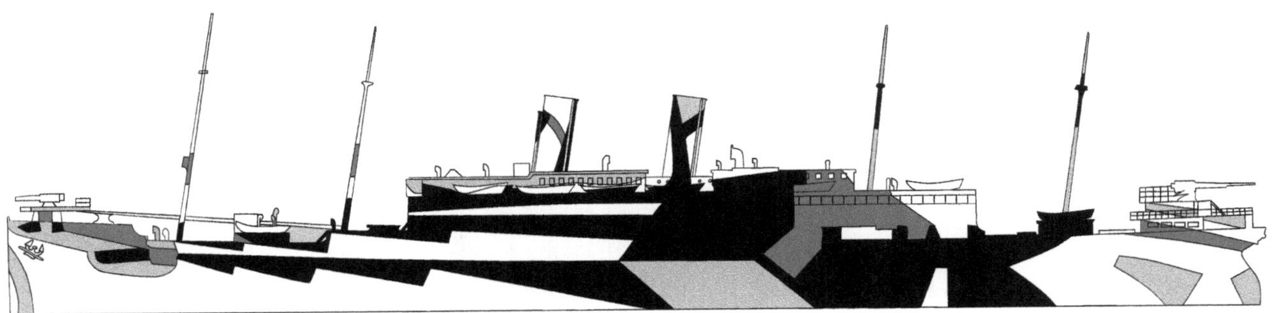

PORT SIDE PATTERN

N22 A

Colors used	Ships painted with this pattern
BLACK	ID 2290 PRINCESS MATOIKA
GREY-WHITE	
#3 BLUE	
#1 BLUE-GRAY	

TYPE N 22
DESIGN A

∴ PORT SIDE ∴
SCALE 3/64"=1'-0" LENGTH 522'-8"
COLORS
GREY WHITE
BLACK
NO. 3 BLUE
NO. 1 BLUE GREY
NOTE
COLORS ON PLAN ARE FOR THE PURPOSES OF MEASUREMENT ONLY. ACTUAL COLORS AS PER COLOR CHART.

TYPE N 22
DESIGN A

STARBOARD SIDE
SCALE 3/64"=1'-0" LENGTH 522'-8"
COLORS
GREYWHITE
BLACK
NO. 1 BLUE GREY
NO. 3 BLUE
NOTE
COLORS ON PLAN ARE FOR THE PURPOSES OF MEASUREMENT ONLY. ACTUAL COLORS AS PER COLOR CHART.

N22 A

Starboard Side Pattern

N22 A

Port Side Pattern

N24 A

Colors used	Ships painted with this pattern
BLACK	DD 36 PATTERSON
WHITE	
#3 BLUE	
#1 BLUE-GRAY	
#1 GREEN	

TYPE N 24
DESIGN A

∴ PORT SIDE ∴
SCALE 3/64"=1'-0" LENGTH 289'-0"
COLORS
BLACK NO. 1 GREEN NO. 1 BLUE GREY
WHITE NO. 3 BLUE
NOTE
COLORS ON PLAN ARE FOR THE PURPOSES OF MEASUREMENT ONLY. ACTUAL COLORS AS PER COLOR CHART.

TYPE N 24
DESIGN A

STARBOARD SIDE
SCALE 3/64"-1'-0" LENGTH 289'-0"
COLORS
WHITE NO. 3 BLUE NO. 1 BLUE GREY
BLACK
NOTE
COLORS ON PLAN ARE FOR THE PURPOSES OF MEASUREMENT ONLY. ACTUAL COLORS AS PER COLOR CHART.

N24 A

STARBOARD SIDE PATTERN

N24 A

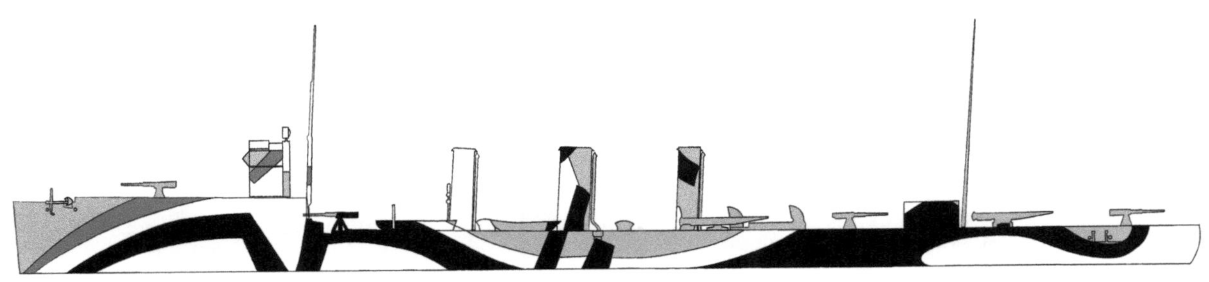

PORT SIDE PATTERN

N24 ADM

Colors used	Ships painted with this pattern
BLACK	DD 45 DOWNES
WHITE	DD 53 WINSLOW
#3 BLUE	
#1 BLUE-GRAY	

N24 ADM

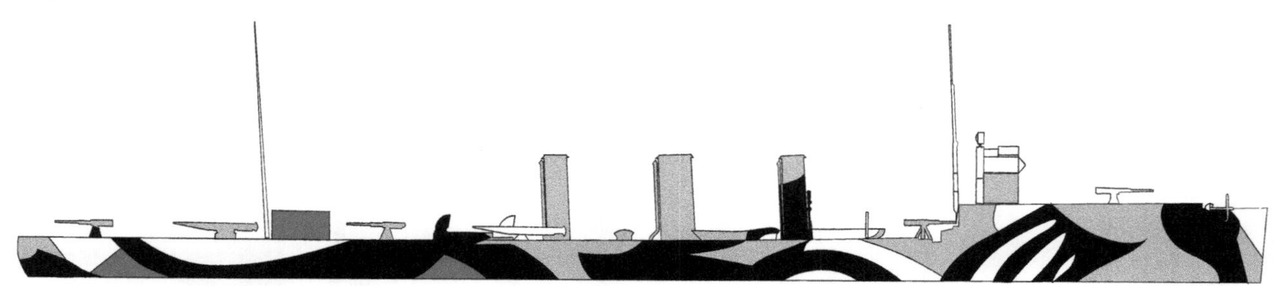

STARBOARD SIDE PATTERN

N24 ADM

PORT SIDE PATTERN

N25 A

Colors used	Ships painted with this pattern
BLACK	DD 8 LAWRENCE
WHITE	
#3 BLUE	
#1 BLUE-GRAY	

TYPE N 25
DESIGN A
PORT SIDE
SCALE 1/8" 1'0" LENGTH 240'7"
COLORS
BLACK 3 BLUE
WHITE 1 BLUE-GREY
NOTE
COLORS ON PLAN ARE FOR THE PURPOSES OF MEASUREMENT ONLY
ACTUAL COLORS AS PER COLOR CHART

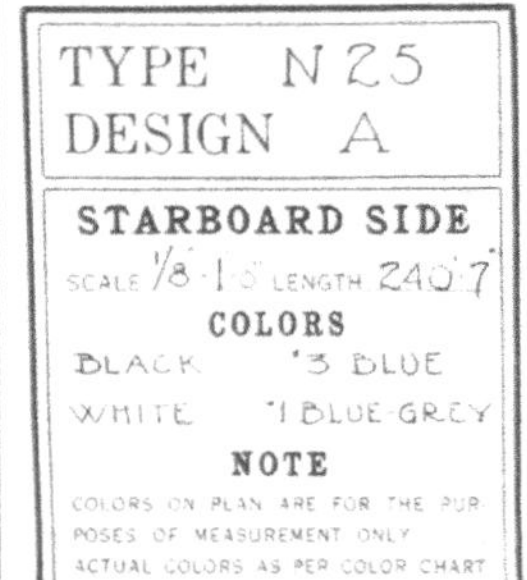

TYPE N 25
DESIGN A
STARBOARD SIDE
SCALE 1/8" 1'0" LENGTH 240'7"
COLORS
BLACK 3 BLUE
WHITE 1 BLUE-GREY
NOTE
COLORS ON PLAN ARE FOR THE PURPOSES OF MEASUREMENT ONLY
ACTUAL COLORS AS PER COLOR CHART

N25 A

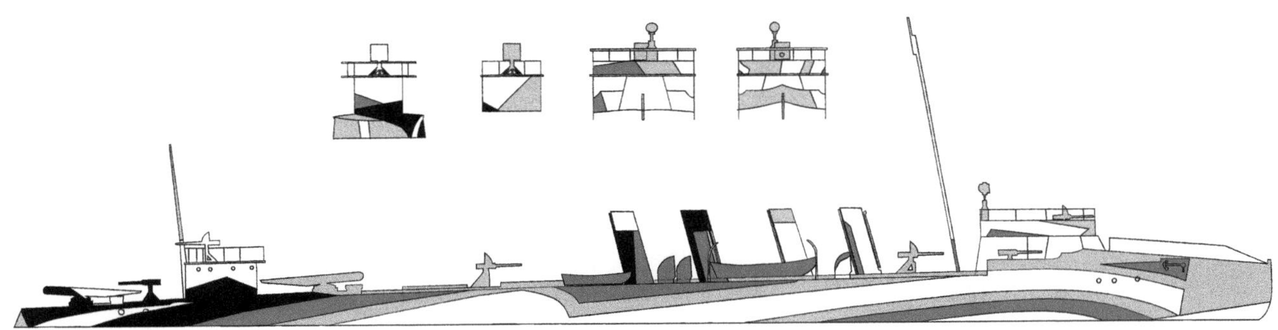

Starboard Side Pattern

N25 A

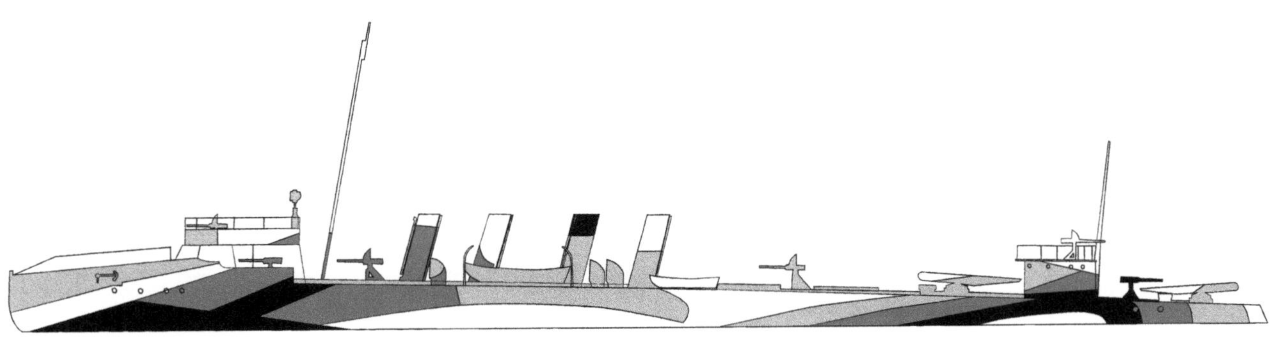

Port Side Pattern

N27 A

Colors used	Ships painted with this pattern
BLACK	AF - SUPPLY
WHITE	
#3 BLUE	
#1 BLUE-GRAY	

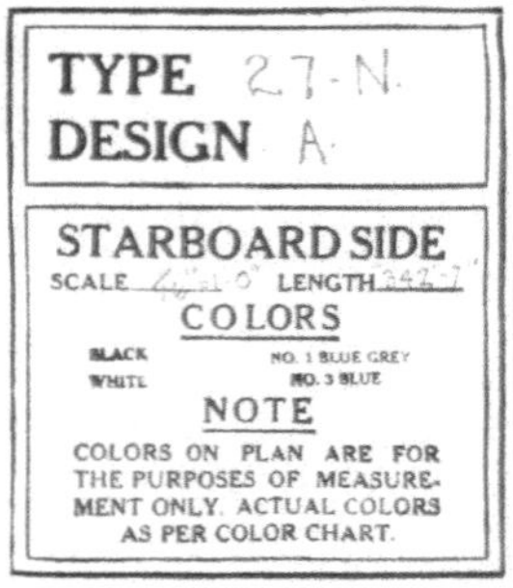

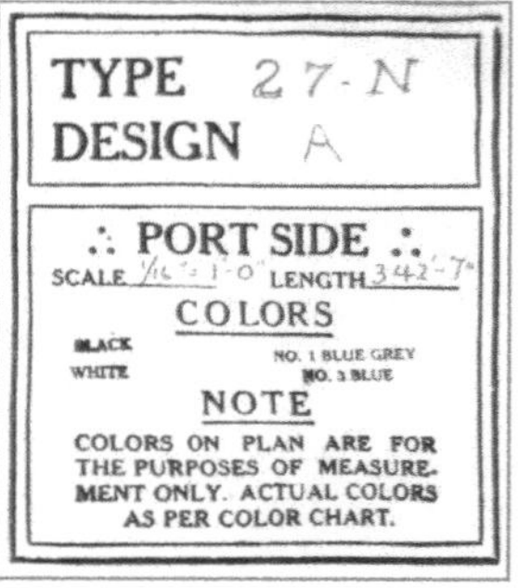

TYPE 27-N
DESIGN A

STARBOARD SIDE
SCALE ¼"=1'-0" LENGTH 342'-7"
COLORS
BLACK NO. 1 BLUE GREY
WHITE NO. 3 BLUE
NOTE
COLORS ON PLAN ARE FOR THE PURPOSES OF MEASUREMENT ONLY. ACTUAL COLORS AS PER COLOR CHART.

TYPE 27-N
DESIGN A

∴ PORT SIDE ∴
SCALE 1/16"=1'-0" LENGTH 342'-7"
COLORS
BLACK NO. 1 BLUE GREY
WHITE NO. 3 BLUE
NOTE
COLORS ON PLAN ARE FOR THE PURPOSES OF MEASUREMENT ONLY. ACTUAL COLORS AS PER COLOR CHART.

N27 A

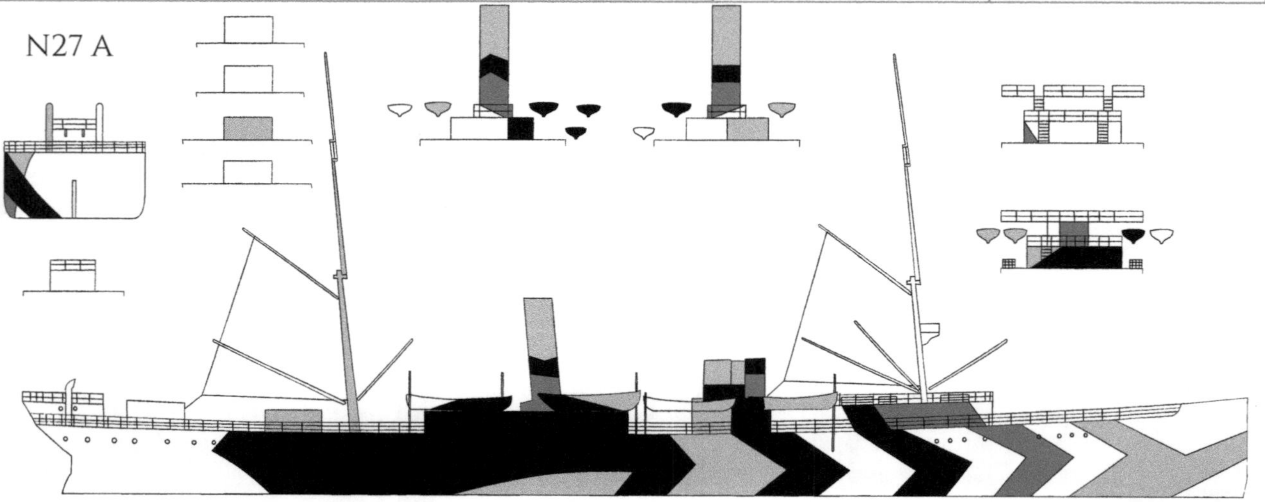

STARBOARD SIDE PATTERN

N27 A

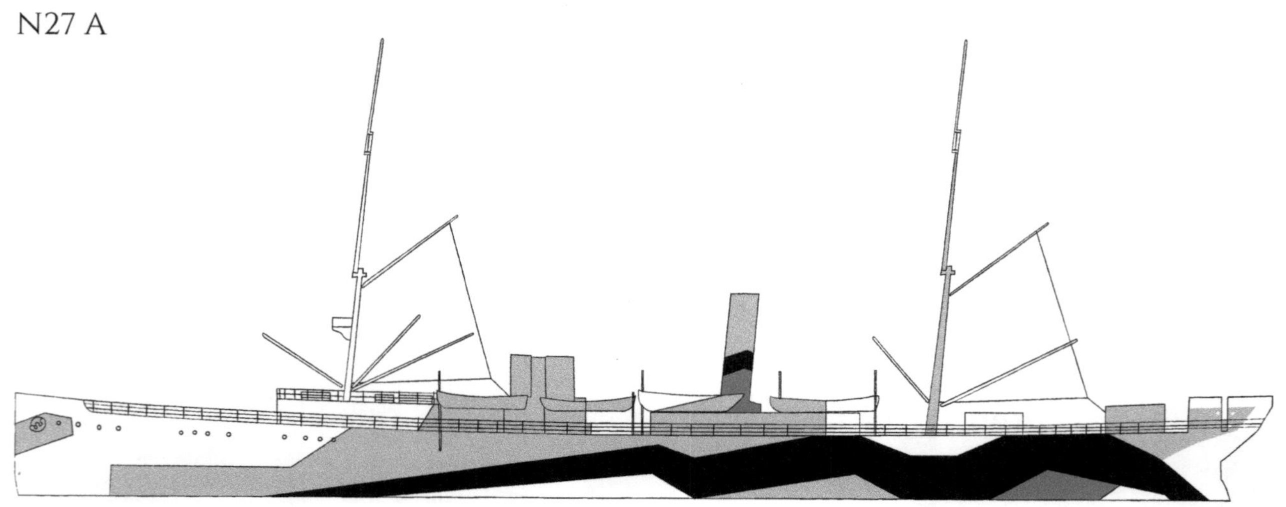

PORT SIDE PATTERN

N28 A

Colors used	Ships painted with this pattern
BLACK	ID 2195 NOPATIN
WHITE	
#3 BLUE	
#1 BLUE-GRAY	

TYPE N-28
DESIGN A

STARBOARD SIDE
SCALE LENGTH 330'-2"
COLORS
NO. 3 BLUE
WHITE
BLACK
NO. 1 BLUE GREY
NOTE
COLORS ON PLAN ARE FOR THE PURPOSES OF MEASUREMENT ONLY. ACTUAL COLORS AS PER COLOR CHART.

TYPE N 28
DESIGN A

STARBOARD SIDE
SCALE LENGTH 330'-2"
COLORS
NO. 3 BLUE
NO. 1 BLUE GREY
BLACK
WHITE
NOTE
COLORS ON PLAN ARE FOR THE PURPOSES OF MEASUREMENT ONLY. ACTUAL COLORS AS PER COLOR CHART.

N28 A

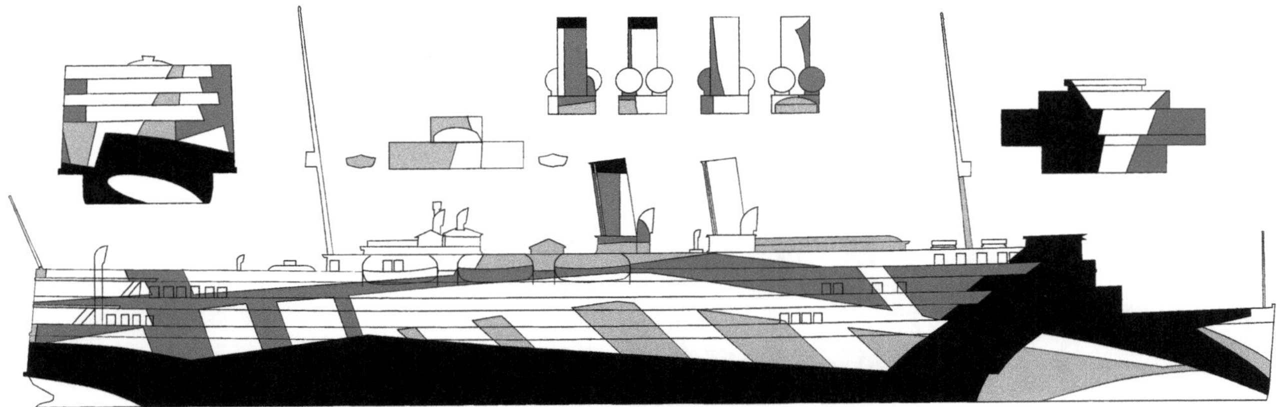

Starboard Side Pattern

N28 A

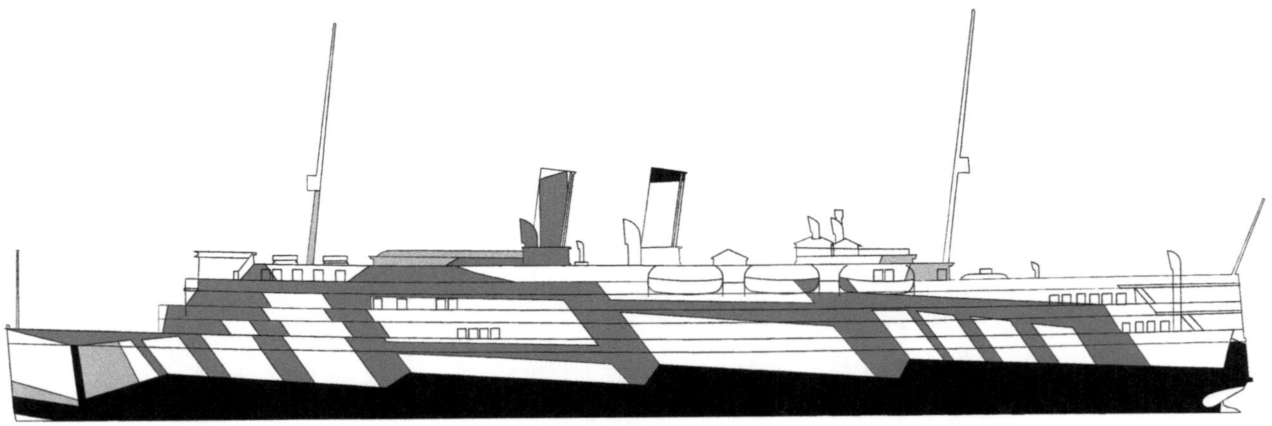

Port Side Pattern

N28 B

Colors used	Ships painted with this pattern
BLACK	ID 2196 NARRAGANSETT
WHITE	
#3 BLUE	
#1 BLUE-GRAY	

TYPE N-28
DESIGN B
PORT SIDE
SCALE 1/16"-1'-0" LENGTH 330'-0"
COLORS
BLACK NO. 1 BLUE GREY NO. 3 BLUE
WHITE
NOTE
COLORS ON PLAN ARE FOR THE PURPOSES OF MEASUREMENT ONLY. ACTUAL COLORS AS PER COLOR CHART.

TYPE N-28
DESIGN B
STARBOARD SIDE
SCALE 1/16"-1'-0" LENGTH 330'-2"
COLORS
BLACK NO. 1 BLUE GREY
WHITE NO. 3 BLUE
NOTE
COLORS ON PLAN ARE FOR THE PURPOSES OF MEASUREMENT ONLY. ACTUAL COLORS AS PER COLOR CHART.

N28 B

STARBOARD SIDE PATTERN

N28 B

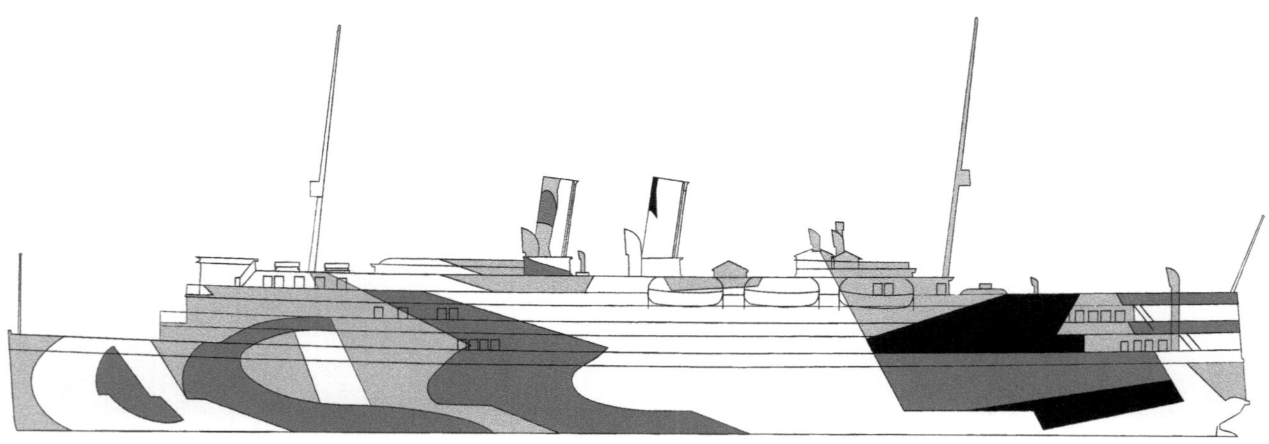

PORT SIDE PATTERN

N34 A

Colors used	Ships painted with this pattern
BLACK	ID 1385 FAVORITE
WHITE	
#3 BLUE	
#1 BLUE-GRAY	

TYPE N·34
DESIGN A

STARBOARD SIDE
SCALE 1/8"=1'-0" LENGTH 195'-0"
COLORS
BLACK NO. 1 BLUE GREY
WHITE NO. 3 BLUE
NOTE
COLORS ON PLAN ARE FOR THE PURPOSES OF MEASUREMENT ONLY. ACTUAL COLORS AS PER COLOR CHART.

TYPE N 34
DESIGN A

∴ PORT SIDE ∴
SCALE 1/8"=1'-0" LENGTH 195'0"
COLORS
BLACK NO. 1 BLUE GREY
WHITE NO. 3 BLUE
NOTE
COLORS ON PLAN ARE FOR THE PURPOSES OF MEASUREMENT ONLY. ACTUAL COLORS AS PER COLOR CHART.

Starboard Side Pattern

Starboard Side Pattern

N35 A

Colors used	Ships painted with this pattern
BLACK	ID 3017 VON STEUBEN
WHITE	
#3 BLUE	
#1 BLUE-GRAY	

TYPE N 35
DESIGN A

STARBOARD SIDE
SCALE 3/64 LENGTH 635'-0"
COLORS

NOTE
COLORS ON PLAN ARE FOR THE PURPOSES OF MEASUREMENT ONLY. ACTUAL COLORS AS PER COLOR CHART.

TYPE N 35
DESIGN A

∴ PORT SIDE ∴
SCALE 3/64 LENGTH 635'-0"
COLORS
BLACK NO. 1 BLUE GREY
WHITE NO. 3 BLUE

NOTE
COLORS ON PLAN ARE FOR THE PURPOSES OF MEASUREMENT ONLY. ACTUAL COLORS AS PER COLOR CHART.

N35 A

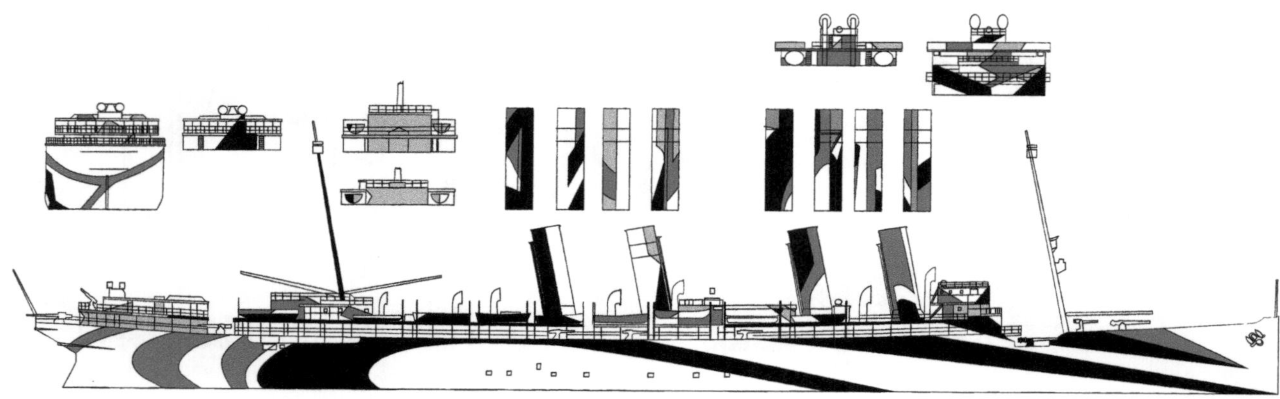

STARBOARD SIDE PATTERN

N35 A

PORT SIDE PATTERN

N36 A

Colors used	Ships painted with this pattern
BLACK	ID 1298 CHARLES
WHITE	
#3 BLUE	
#1 BLUE-GRAY	

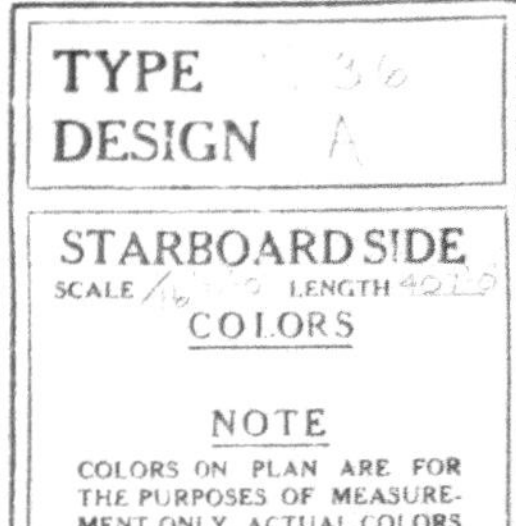

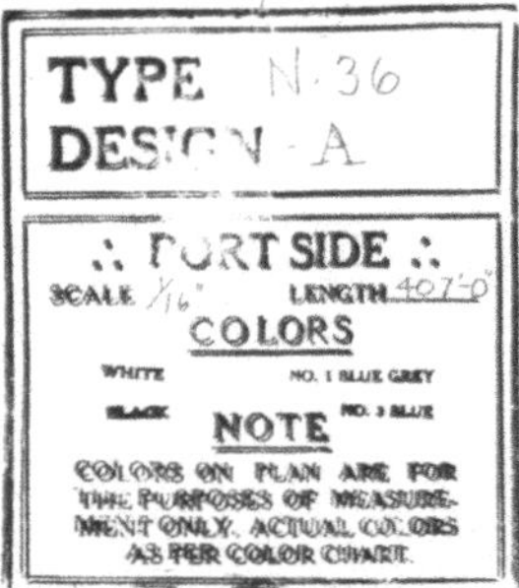

N36 A

Starboard Side Pattern

N36 A

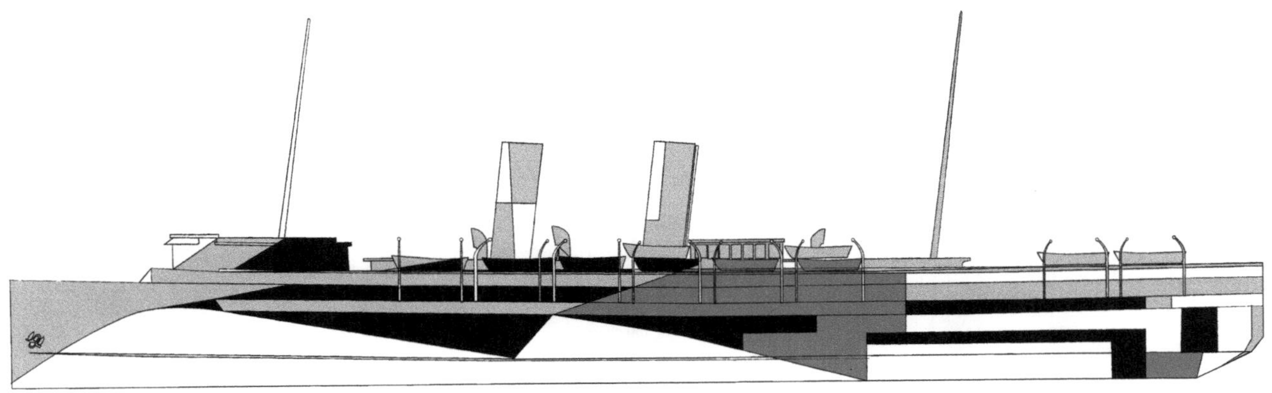

Port Side Pattern

N36 B

Colors used	Ships painted with this pattern
BLACK	ID 1672 YALE
WHITE	
#3 BLUE	
#1 BLUE-GRAY	

TYPE N 36
DESIGN B
STARBOARD SIDE
SCALE LENGTH 407
COLORS
NO. 1 BLUE GREY BLACK WHITE
NO. 3 BLUE
NOTE
COLORS ON PLAN ARE FOR THE PURPOSES OF MEASUREMENT ONLY. ACTUAL COLORS AS PER COLOR CHART.

TYPE N 36
DESIGN B
∴ PORT SIDE ∴
SCALE LENGTH 407
COLORS
NO. 3 BLUE BLACK
NO. 1 BLUE GREY WHITE
NOTE
COLORS ON PLAN ARE FOR THE PURPOSES OF MEASUREMENT ONLY. ACTUAL COLORS AS PER COLOR CHART.

N36 B

STARBOARD SIDE PATTERN

N36 B

PORT SIDE PATTERN

N37 A

Colors used	Ships painted with this pattern
BLACK	ID 3005 AEOLUS
WHITE	
#3 BLUE	
#1 BLUE-GRAY	

TYPE N-37-
DESIGN -A-

STARBOARD SIDE
SCALE 3/64"=1'-0" LENGTH 560'-6"
COLORS
BLACK NO. 1 BLUE GREY
WHITE NO. 3 BLUE
NOTE
COLORS ON PLAN ARE FOR THE PURPOSES OF MEASUREMENT ONLY. ACTUAL COLORS AS PER COLOR CHART.

TYPE N-37-
DESIGN A

∴ PORT SIDE ∴
SCALE 3/64"=1'-0" LENGTH 560'-6"
COLORS
BLACK NO. 1 BLUE GREY
WHITE NO. 3 BLUE
NOTE
COLORS ON PLAN ARE FOR THE PURPOSES OF MEASUREMENT ONLY. ACTUAL COLORS AS PER COLOR CHART.

N37 A

STARBOARD SIDE PATTERN

N37 A

PORT SIDE PATTERN

N38 A

Colors used	Ships painted with this pattern
BLACK	ID 1408 HURON
GREY-WHITE	
#3 BLUE	
#2 BLUE-GRAY	Port side pattern not found

TYPE N-38.
DESIGN A

STARBOARD SIDE
SCALE LENGTH
COLORS
NOTE
COLORS ON PLAN ARE FOR THE PURPOSES OF MEASUREMENT ONLY. ACTUAL COLORS AS PER COLOR CHART

N38 A

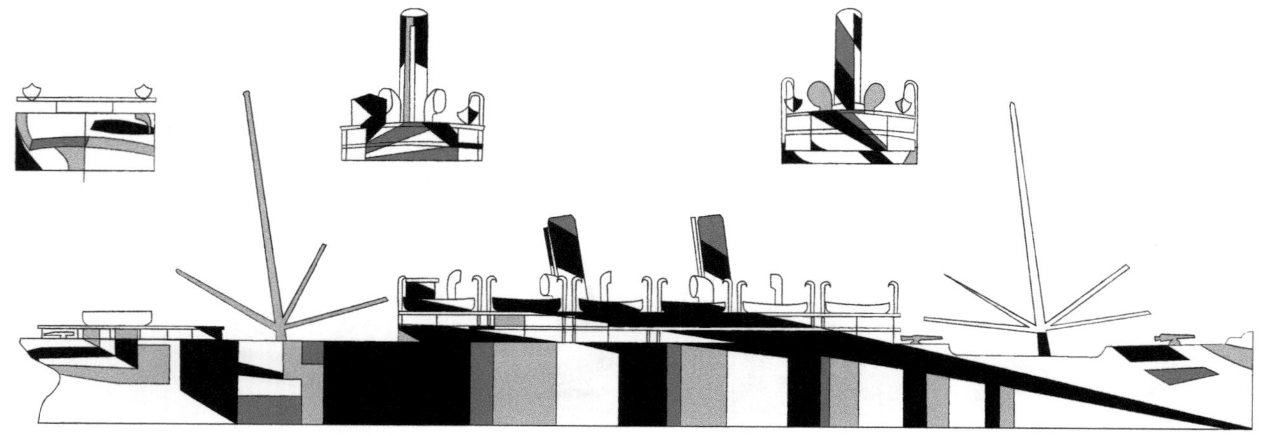

STARBOARD SIDE PATTERN

N39 A

Colors used	Ships painted with this pattern
BLACK	AC 9 PROTEUS
WHITE	
#3 BLUE	

N39 A

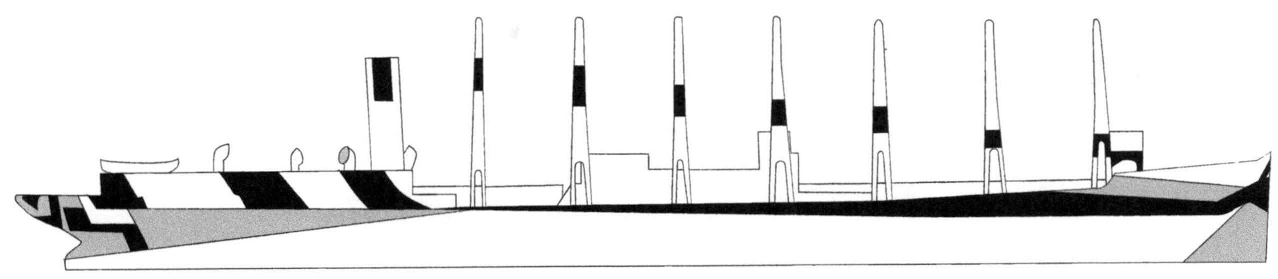

Starboard Side Pattern

N39 A

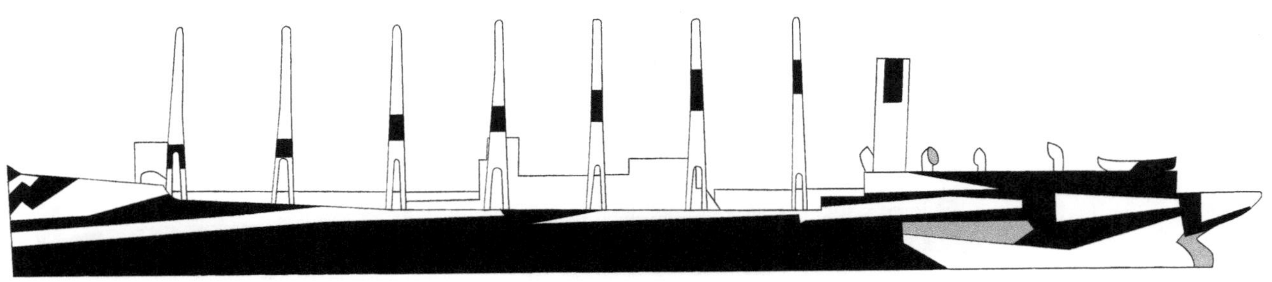

Port Side Pattern

N40 A

Colors used	Ships painted with this pattern
BLACK	ID NONE TENEDORES
WHITE	ID 3662 CALAMARES
#3 BLUE	ID 4540 PASTORES
#1 BLUE-GRAY	

TYPE N 40
DESIGN A
PORT SIDE
SCALE 1/16"-1'0" LENGTH 485'0"
COLORS
NO. 3 BLUE NO. 1 BLUE GREY
WHITE BLACK
NOTE
COLORS ON PLAN ARE FOR THE PURPOSES OF MEASUREMENT ONLY
ACTUAL COLORS AS PER COLOR CHART

TYPE N 40
DESIGN A
STARBOARD SIDE
SCALE 1/16"-1'0" LENGTH 485'0"
COLORS
NO. 3 BLUE NO. 1 BLUE GREY
BLACK WHITE
NOTE
COLORS ON PLAN ARE FOR THE PURPOSES OF MEASUREMENT ONLY . . .
ACTUAL COLORS AS PER COLOR CHART

N40 A

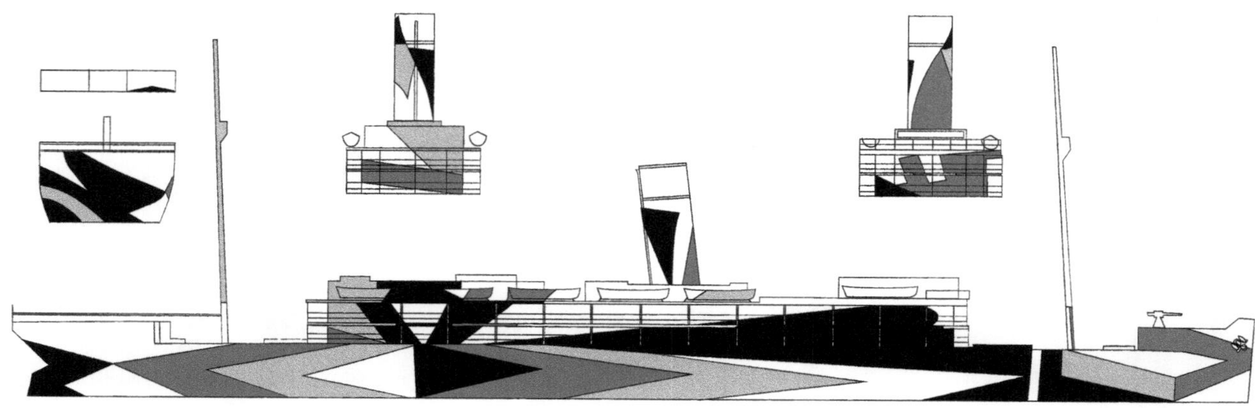

Starboard Side Pattern

N40 A

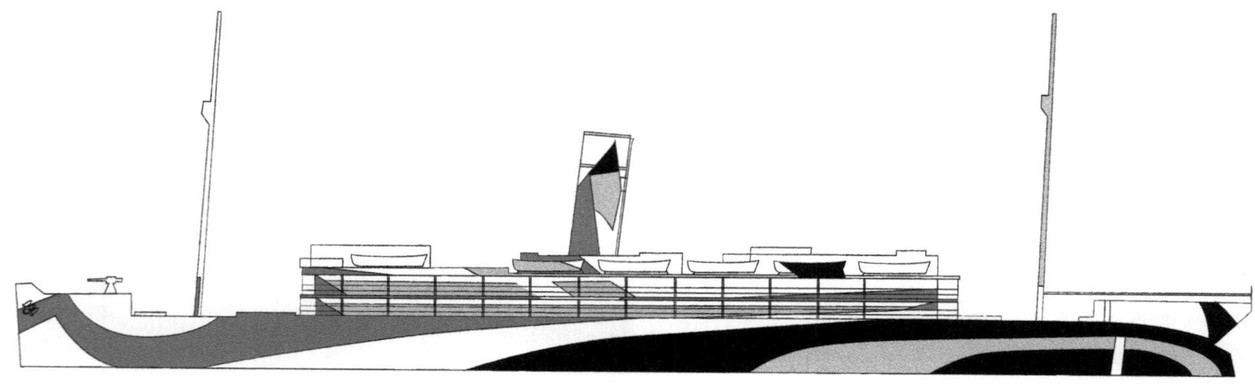

Port Side Pattern

N40 B

Colors used	Ships painted with this pattern
TOCH DARK GRAY	ID 1634 SIERRA
AERIAL GRAY	
PINK	
WHITE	
DARK OLIVE	

TYPE N40
DESIGN B

STARBOARD SIDE
SCALE LENGTH
COLORS
TOCHS DARK GRAY TOCH'S PINK
AERIAL " WHITE
DARK OLIVE
NOTE
COLORS ON PLAN ARE FOR THE PURPOSES OF MEASUREMENT ONLY. ACTUAL COLORS AS PER COLOR CHART.

TYPE N40
DESIGN B

PORT SIDE
SCALE LENGTH
COLORS
TOCHS DARK GRAY TOCHS PINK
AERIAL " WHITE
DARK OLIVE
NOTE
COLORS ON PLAN ARE FOR THE PURPOSES OF MEASUREMENT ONLY. ACTUAL COLORS AS PER COLOR CHART.

N40 B

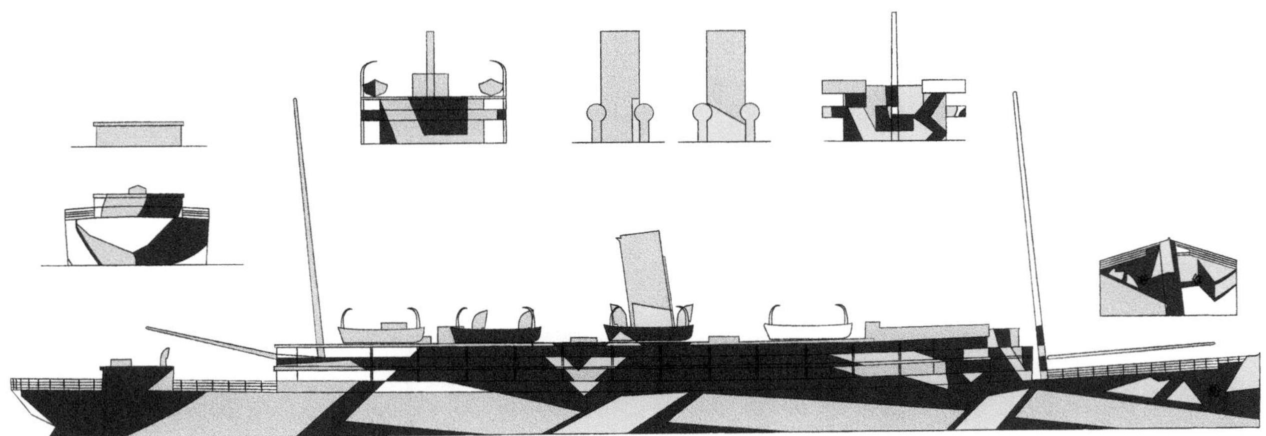

Starboard Side Pattern

N40 B

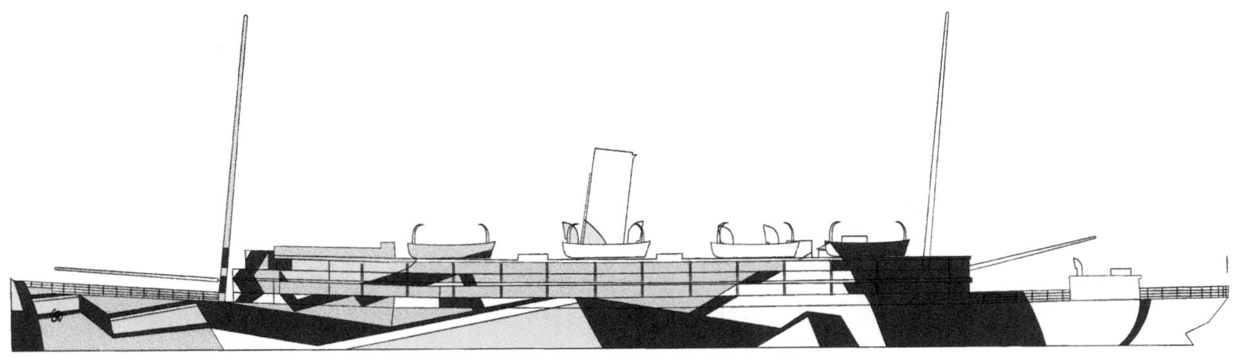

Port Side Pattern

N41 A

Colors used	Ships painted with this pattern
BLACK	ID NONE COROZAL
GREY-WHITE	
#3 BLUE-GRAY	

TYPE N-41
DESIGN A

STARBOARD SIDE
SCALE 1/16"=1'0" LENGTH 335'0"
COLORS
NO. 2 BLUE GREY WHITE
NO. 1 BLUE BLACK
NOTE
COLORS ON PLAN ARE FOR THE PURPOSES OF MEASUREMENT ONLY. ACTUAL COLORS AS PER COLOR CHART.

TYPE N-41
DESIGN A

∴ PORT SIDE ∴
SCALE 1/16"=1'0" LENGTH 335
COLORS
NO. 2 BLUE GREY WHITE
NO. 1 BLUE BLACK
NOTE
COLORS ON PLAN ARE FOR THE PURPOSES OF MEASUREMENT ONLY. ACTUAL COLORS AS PER COLOR CHART.

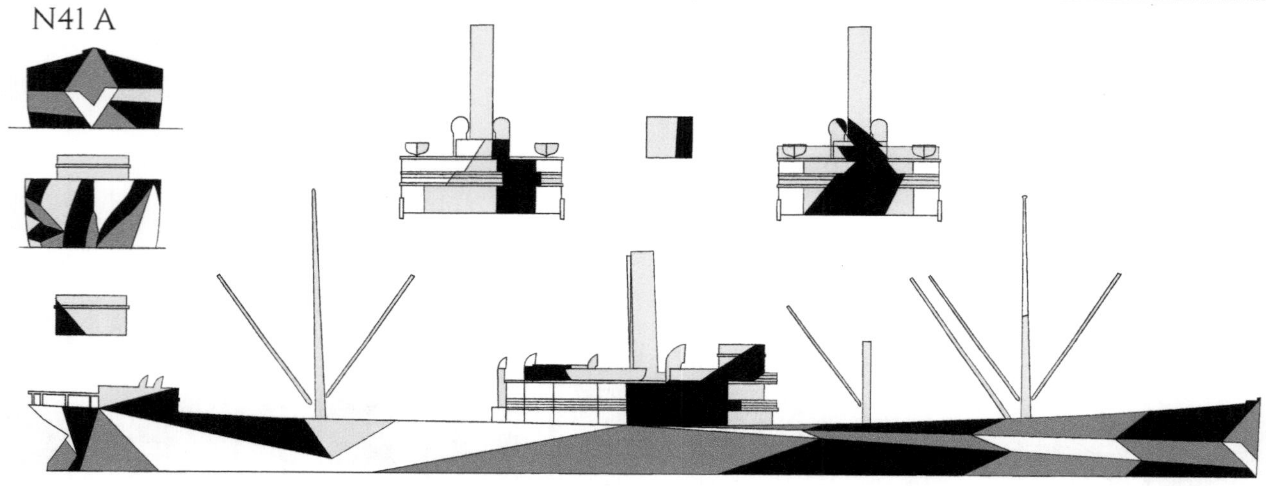

STARBOARD SIDE PATTERN

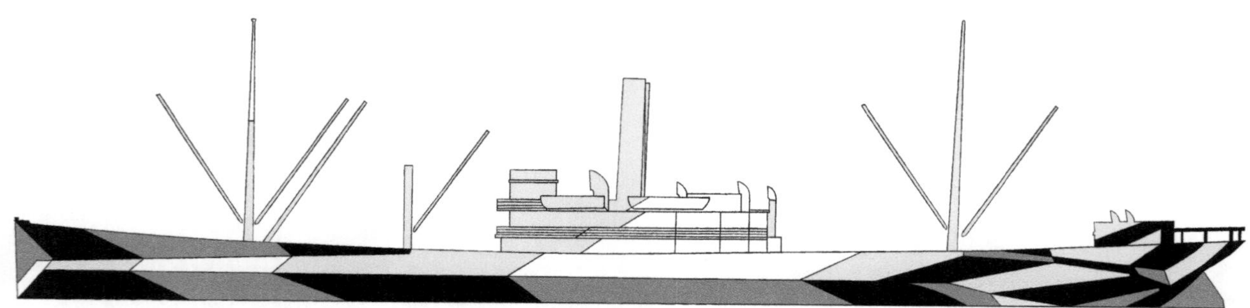

PORT SIDE PATTERN

N41 A

Colors used	Ships painted with this pattern
BLACK	ID NONE ISABELA
WHITE	NONE MONTOSO
#3 BLUE-GRAY	
#1 BLUE	

TYPE N41
DESIGN A
STARBOARD SIDE
SCALE 1/16"=1'-0" LENGTH 347'-7"
COLORS
NO. 3 BLUE GREY gray white
BLACK
NOTE
COLORS ON PLAN ARE FOR THE PURPOSES OF MEASUREMENT ONLY. ACTUAL COLORS AS PER COLOR CHART

TYPE N41
DESIGN A
PORT SIDE
SCALE 1/16"=1'-0" LENGTH 347'-7"
COLORS
NO. 3 BLUE GREY gray white
BLACK
NOTE
COLORS ON PLAN ARE FOR THE PURPOSES OF MEASUREMENT ONLY ACTUAL COLORS AS PER COLOR CHART

N41 A

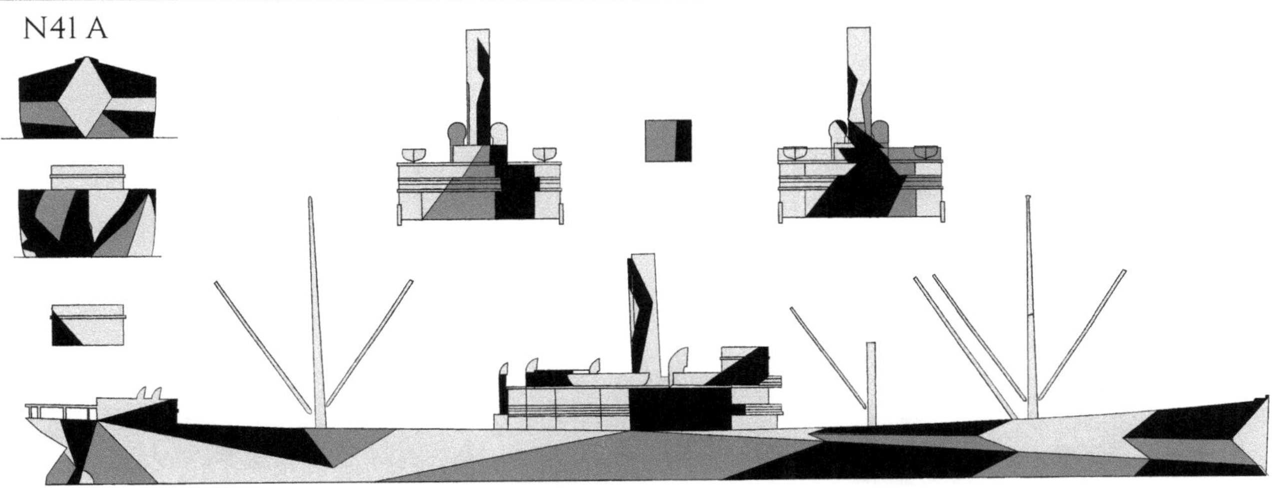

Starboard Side Pattern

N41 A

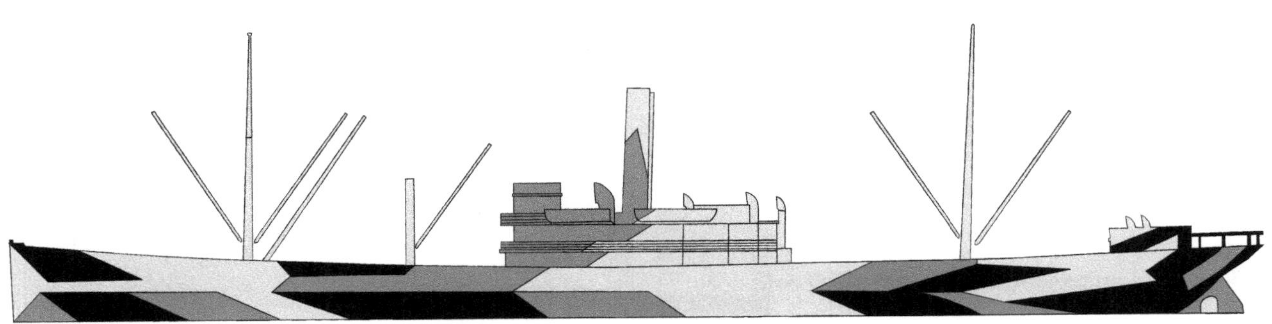

Port Side Pattern

N42 A

Colors used	Ships painted with this pattern
BLACK	AO 1 KANAWHA
WHITE	AO 3 CUYAMA
#3 BLUE	AO 2 MAUMEE (T)
#1 BLUE-GRAY	

TYPE N·42
DESIGN ·A·

STARBOARD SIDE
SCALE 3/64"=1'0" LENGTH 455'0"
COLORS
WHITE NO. 1 BLUE GREY
BLACK NO. 3 BLUE
NOTE
COLORS ON PLAN ARE FOR THE PURPOSES OF MEASUREMENT ONLY. ACTUAL COLORS AS PER COLOR CHART.

TYPE N·42
DESIGN ·A·

∴ PORT SIDE ∴
SCALE 3/64"=1'0" LENGTH 455'0"
COLORS
WHITE NO. 1 BLUE GREY
BLACK NO. 3 BLUE
NOTE
COLORS ON PLAN ARE FOR THE PURPOSES OF MEASUREMENT ONLY. ACTUAL COLORS AS PER COLOR CHART.

N42 A

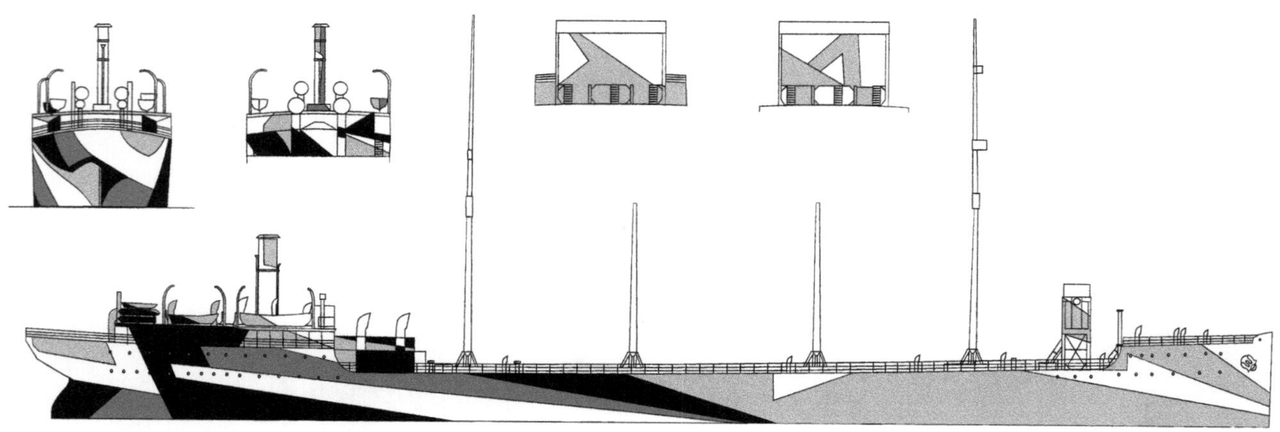

Starboard Side Pattern

N42 A

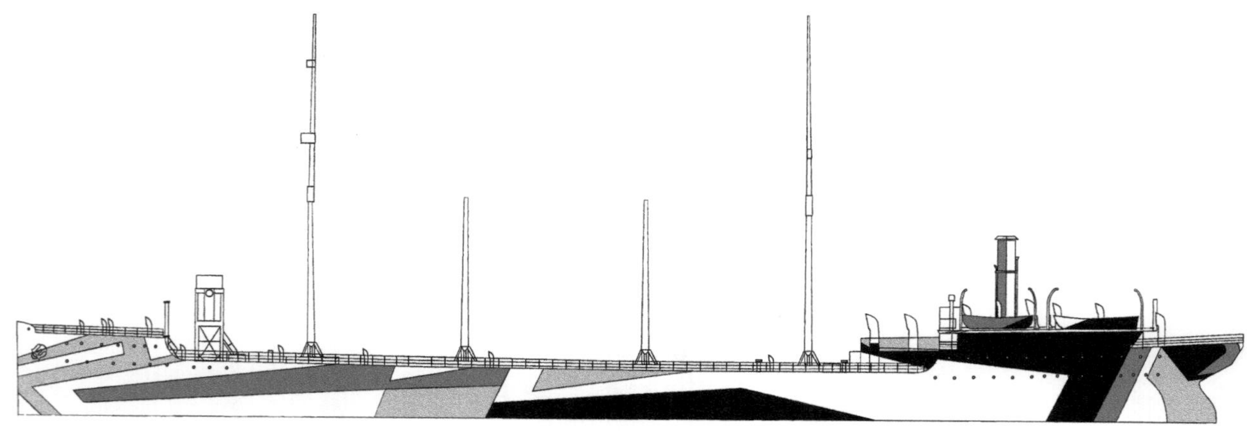

Port Side Pattern

N43 A

Colors used	Ships painted with this pattern
BLACK	ID 3018 GEORGE WASHINGTON
WHITE	
#3 BLUE	
#2 BLUE-GREY	
	No original patterns, colors assumed
	Design recreated from photographs

N43 A

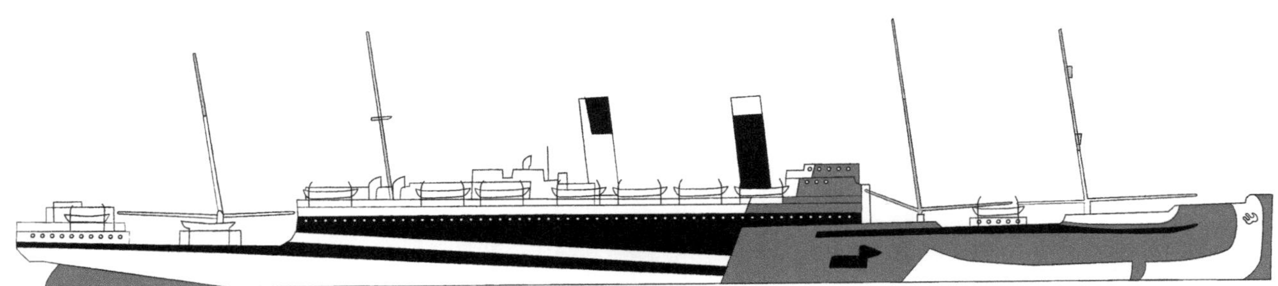

STARBOARD SIDE PATTERN

N43 A

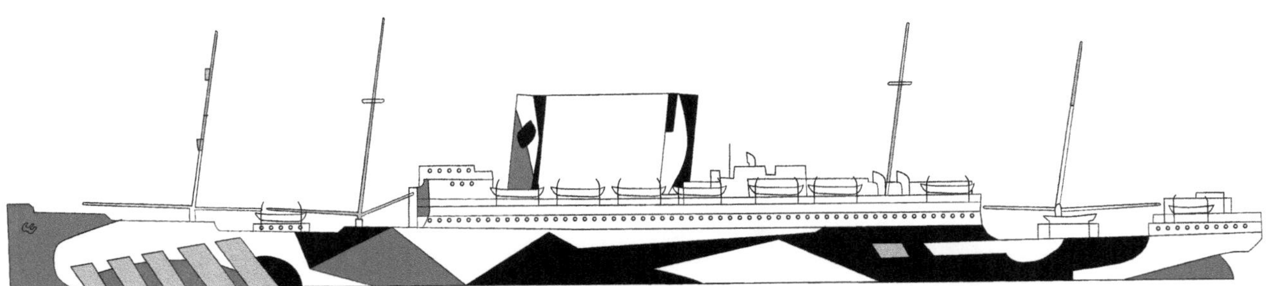

PORT SIDE PATTERN

N44 A

Colors used	Ships painted with this pattern
BLACK	ID 1615 MONGOLIA
WHITE	ID 1633 MANCHURIA
#3 BLUE	
#1 BLUE-GRAY	

TYPE N:44
DESIGN A
∴ PORT SIDE ∴
SCALE 3/32" = 1'0" LENGTH 615'-8"
COLORS
WHITE BLACK
NO. 3 BLUE NO. 1 BLUE GREY
NOTE
COLORS ON PLAN ARE FOR THE PURPOSES OF MEASUREMENT ONLY. ACTUAL COLORS AS PER COLOR CHART.

TYPE N:44
DESIGN A
STARBOARD SIDE
SCALE 3/64" = 1'0" LENGTH 615'-8"
COLORS
BLACK NO. 3 BLUE NO. 1 BLUE GREY
WHITE
NOTE
COLORS ON PLAN ARE FOR THE PURPOSES OF MEASUREMENT ONLY. ACTUAL COLORS AS PER COLOR CHART.

N44 A

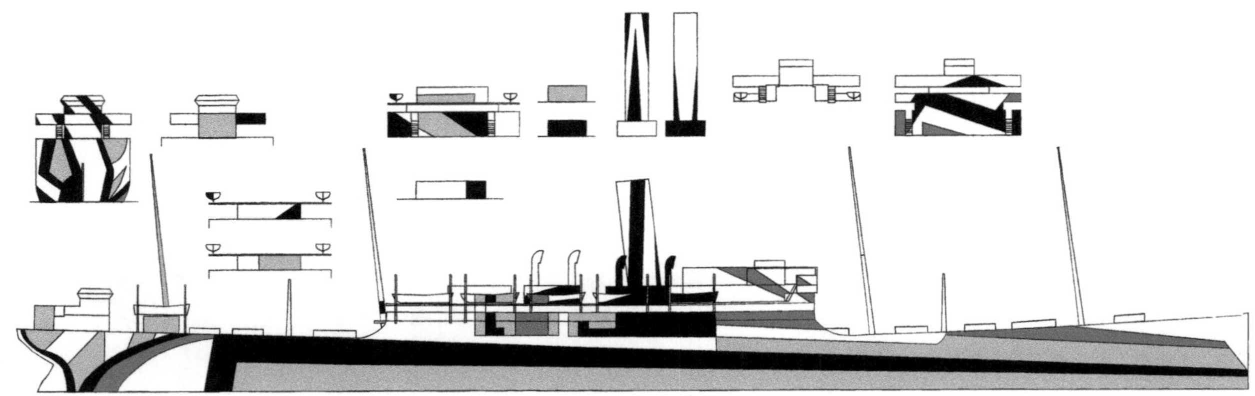

STARBOARD SIDE PATTERN

N44 A

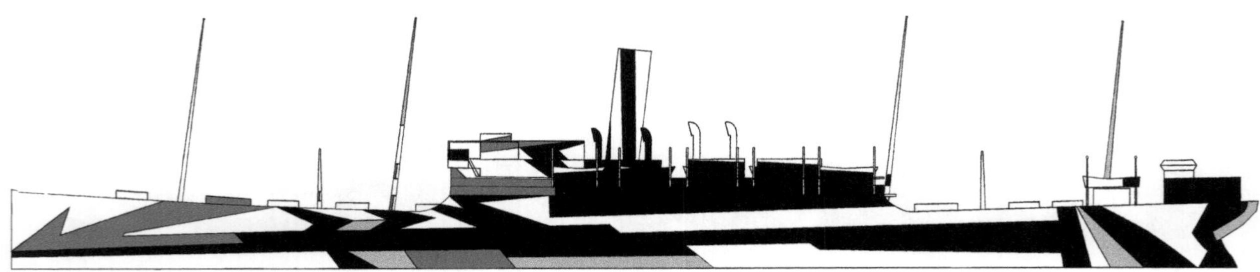

PORT SIDE PATTERN

N45 A

Colors used	Ships painted with this pattern
BLACK	ID 3007 ANTIGONE
WHITE	
#3 BLUE	
#1 BLUE-GRAY	

TYPE
DESIGN
∴ PORT SIDE ∴
SCALE LENGTH
COLORS
NOTE
COLORS ON PLAN ARE FOR THE PURPOSES OF MEASUREMENT ONLY. ACTUAL COLORS AS PER COLOR CHART.

TYPE
DESIGN
STARBOARD SIDE
SCALE LENGTH
COLORS
NOTE
COLORS ON PLAN ARE FOR THE PURPOSES OF MEASUREMENT ONLY. ACTUAL COLORS AS PER COLOR CHART.

N45 A

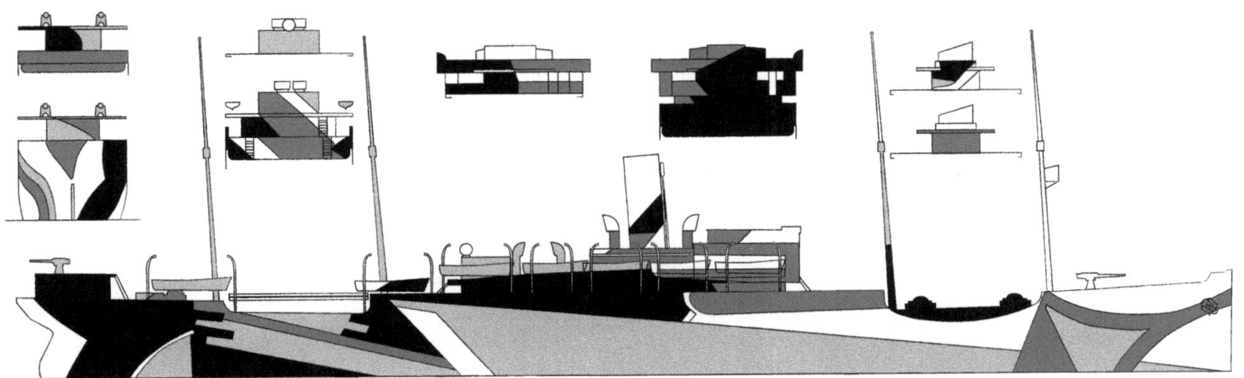

Starboard Side Pattern

N45 A

Port Side Pattern

N46 A

Colors used	Ships painted with this pattern
BLACK	ID 3010 DE KALB
WHITE	ID NONE COLON
#3 BLUE	ID 1635 ALLIANCA
#1 BLUE-GRAY	ID2276 ANDALUSIA

TYPE N·46·
DESIGN ·A·

∴ PORT SIDE ∴
SCALE 3/64"=1'-0" LENGTH 488'-3"
COLORS
BLACK · No 1 BLUE GRAY
WHITE · No 1 BLUE
NOTE
COLORS ON PLAN ARE FOR THE PURPOSES OF MEASUREMENT ONLY. ACTUAL COLORS AS PER COLOR CHART.

TYPE N·46·
DESIGN ·A·

STARBOARD SIDE
SCALE 3/64"=1'-0" LENGTH 488'-3"
COLORS
BLACK No 1 BLUE GRAY
WHITE No 3 BLUE
NOTE
COLORS ON PLAN ARE FOR THE PURPOSES OF MEASUREMENT ONLY. ACTUAL COLORS AS PER COLOR CHART.

N46 A

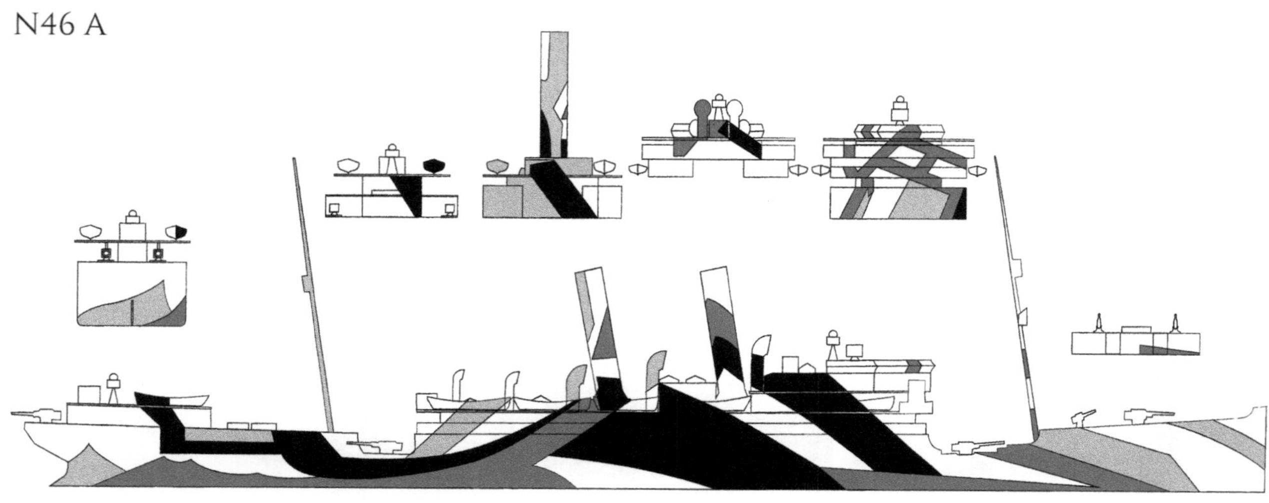

Starboard Side Pattern

N46 A

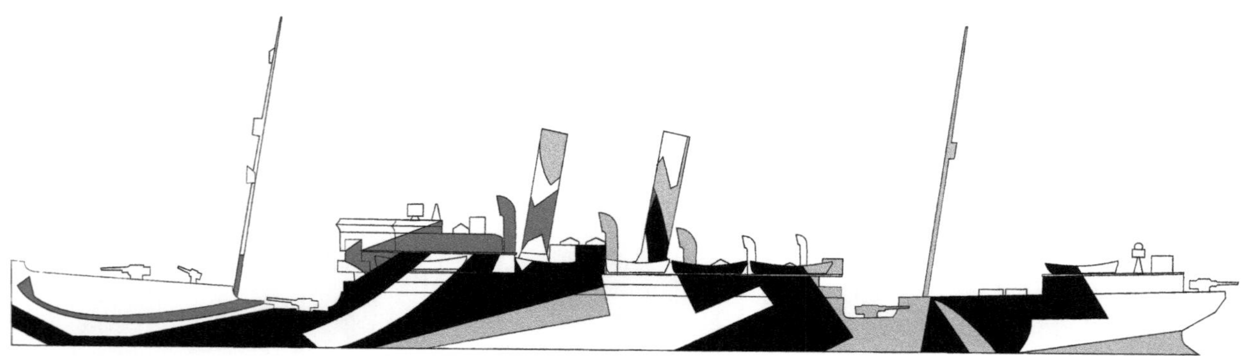

Port Side Pattern

N48 A

Colors used	Ships painted with this pattern
BLACK	ID 3012 MERCURY
WHITE	
#3 BLUE	
#1 BLUE-GRAY	

TYPE N 48
DESIGN A
∴ PORT SIDE ∴
SCALE LENGTH
COLORS
WHITE NO 1 BLUE GRE
BLACK NO 3 BLUE
NOTE
COLORS ON PLAN ARE FOR THE PURPOSES OF MEASUREMENT ONLY. ACTUAL COLORS AS PER COLOR CHART.

TYPE N 48
DESIGN A
STARBOARD SIDE
SCALE LENGTH
COLORS
WHITE NO 1 BLUE GREY
BLACK NO 3 BLUE
NOTE
COLORS ON PLAN ARE FOR THE PURPOSES OF MEASUREMENT ONLY. ACTUAL COLORS AS PER COLOR CHART.

N48 A

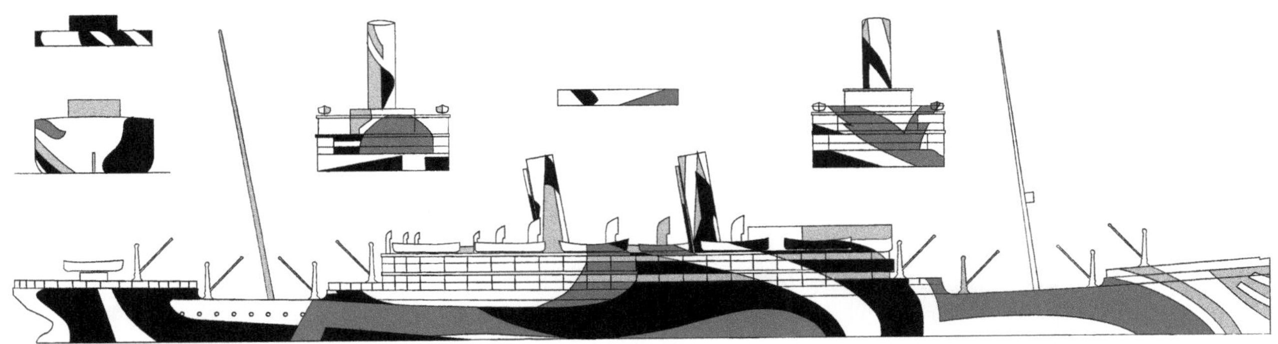

STARBOARD SIDE PATTERN

N48 A

PORT SIDE PATTERN

N49 A

Colors used	Ships painted with this pattern
BLACK	ID NONE MONTOSO
WHITE	
#3 BLUE	
#1 BLUE-GRAY	

TYPE N49
DESIGN A + B

∴ PORT SIDE ∴
SCALE 3/64 LENGTH 556
COLORS
WHITE
NO. 1 BLUE GREY
NO. 3 BLUE
BLACK
NOTE
COLORS ON PLAN ARE FOR THE PURPOSES OF MEASUREMENT ONLY. ACTUAL COLORS AS PER COLOR CHART.

TYPE N49
DESIGN A

STARBOARD SIDE
SCALE 3/64 LENGTH
COLORS
WHITE
NO. 1 BLUE GREY
BLACK
NO. 3 BLUE
NOTE
COLORS ON PLAN ARE FOR THE PURPOSES OF MEASUREMENT ONLY. ACTUAL COLORS AS PER COLOR CHART.

N49 A

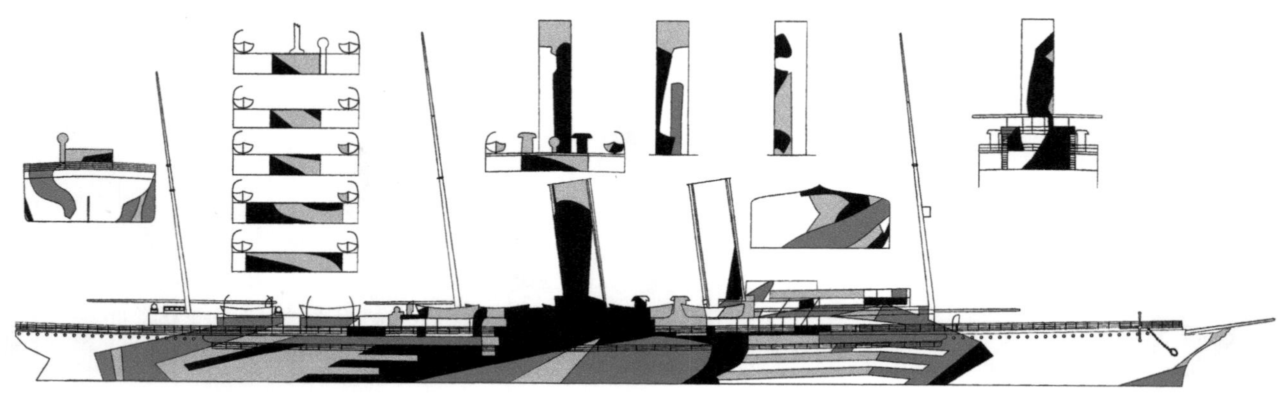

STARBOARD SIDE PATTERN

N49 A

PORT SIDE PATTERN

N49 B

Colors used	Ships painted with this pattern
BLACK	ID 1663 HARRISBURG
WHITE	
#3 BLUE	
#1 BLUE-GRAY	

TYPE N49
DESIGN A+B
∴ PORT SIDE ∴
SCALE 1/64 LENGTH 556
COLORS
WHITE NO. 1 BLUE GREY
BLACK NO. 3 BLUE
NOTE
COLORS ON PLAN ARE FOR THE PURPOSES OF MEASUREMENT ONLY ACTUAL COLORS AS PER COLOR CHART.

TYPE N 49
DESIGN B
STARBOARD SIDE
COLORS
NOTE
COLORS ON PLAN ARE FOR THE PURPOSES OF MEASUREMENT ONLY ACTUAL COLORS AS PER COLOR CHART

N49 B

STARBOARD SIDE PATTERN

N49 B

PORT SIDE PATTERN

N49 C

Colors used	Ships painted with this pattern
BLACK	ID 1645 PLATTSBURG
GREY-WHITE	ID 4514 CITY OF SAVANNAH {T}
#1 GREEN	
#1 GRAY-GREEN	

TYPE N·49 C

SIDE

SCALE 3/64"=1' LENGTH 565'0"

COLORS

gray white NO. 1 BLUE GREY NO. 1 GREEN BLACK

NOTE

COLORS ON PLAN ARE FOR THE PURPOSES OF MEASUREMENT ONLY. ACTUAL COLORS AS PER COLOR CHART.

N·49 C

SCALE 3/64"=1' LENGTH 565'0"

gray white NO. 1 GREY GREEN BLACK NO. 1 BLUE GREY NO. 1 GREEN

NOTE

COLORS ON PLAN ARE FOR THE PURPOSES OF MEASUREMENT ONLY. ACTUAL COLORS AS PER COLOR CHART.

N49 C

Starboard Side Pattern

N49 C

Port Side Pattern

N50 B

Colors used	Ships painted with this pattern
BLACK	ID 1644 LOUISVILLE
WHITE	
#3 BLUE	
#1 BLUE-GRAY	

TYPE N 50
DESIGN B
PORT SIDE
SCALE LENGTH 553'-2"
COLORS
NOTE
COLORS ON PLAN ARE FOR THE PURPOSES OF MEASUREMENT ONLY. ACTUAL COLORS AS PER COLOR CHART.

TYPE N-50
DESIGN B
STARBOARD SIDE
SCALE LENGTH 553'-2"
COLORS
NOTE
COLORS ON PLAN ARE FOR THE PURPOSES OF MEASUREMENT ONLY. ACTUAL COLORS AS PER COLOR CHART.

N50 B

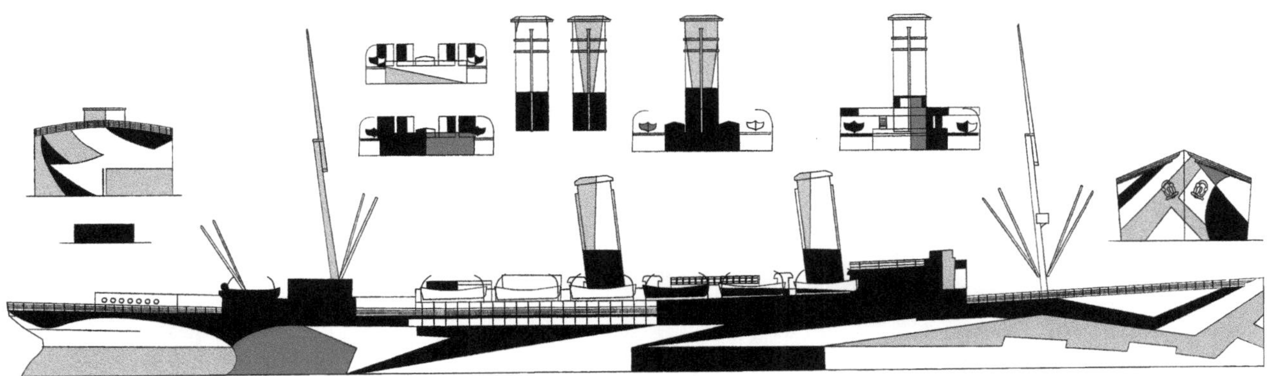

Starboard Side Pattern

N50 B

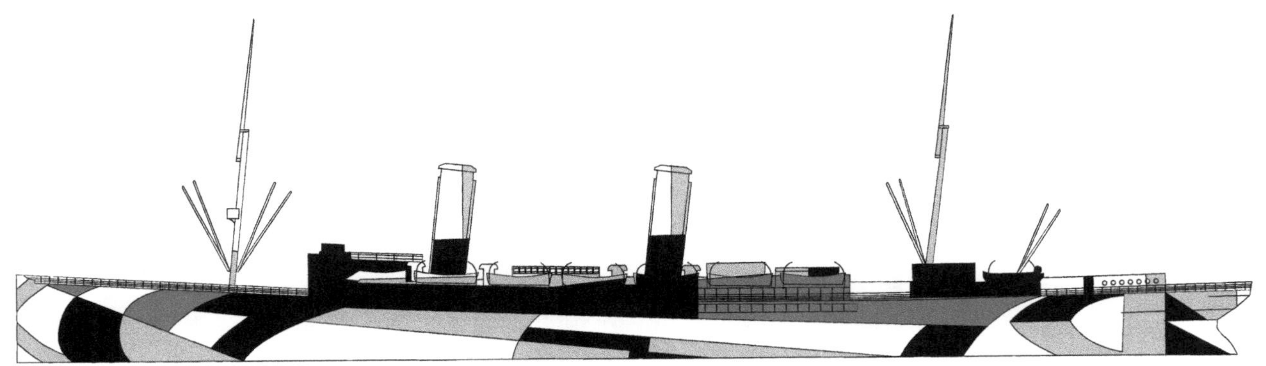

Port Side Pattern

N51 A

Colors used	Ships painted with this pattern
BLACK	ID 3019 MARTHA WASHINGTON
WHITE	
#3 BLUE	
#1 BLUE-GRAY	

TYPE N 51
DESIGN A
∴ PORT SIDE ∴
SCALE 1/16"=1'-0" LENGTH 460'-0"
COLORS
WHITE NO. 1 BLUE GREY
BLACK NO. 3 BLUE
NOTE

TYPE N 51
DESIGN A
STARBOARD SIDE
SCALE 1/16"=1'-0" LENGTH 460'-0"
COLORS
WHITE NO. 1 BLUE GREY
BLACK NO. 3 BLUE
NOTE

N51 A

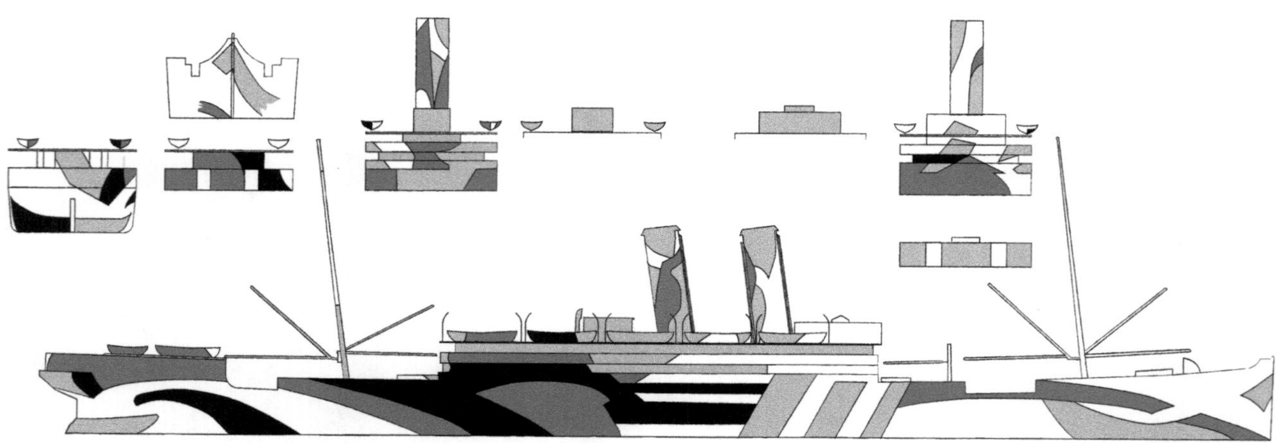

STARBOARD SIDE PATTERN

N51 A

PORT SIDE PATTERN

N53 A

Colors used	Ships painted with this pattern
BLACK	ID 2505 RYNDAM
WHITE	
#3 BLUE	
#1 BLUE-GRAY	

TYPE N 53
DESIGN A

∴ PORT SIDE ∴
SCALE 3/64" = 1'0" LENGTH 560'0"
COLORS
BLACK *3 BLUE
WHITE *1 BLUE-GREY
NOTE
COLORS ON PLAN ARE FOR THE PURPOSES OF MEASUREMENT ONLY. ACTUAL COLORS AS PER COLOR CHART.

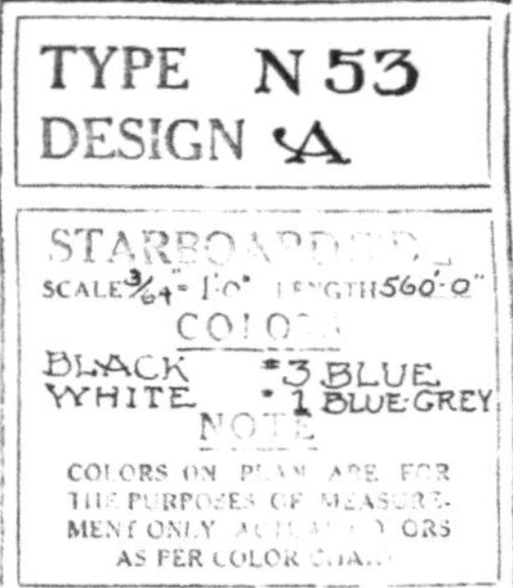

N53 A

Starboard Side Pattern

N53 A

Port Side Pattern

N54 A

Colors used	Ships painted with this pattern
BLACK	ID 3016 SUSQUEHANNA
WHITE	
#3 BLUE	
#1 BLUE-GRAY	

TYPE N·54
DESIGN A·
∴ PORT SIDE ∴
SCALE 3/64"=1'-0" LENGTH 501-0"
COLORS
WHITE NO. 1 BLUE GRAY
BLACK NO. 3 BLUE
NOTE
COLORS ON PLAN ARE FOR THE PURPOSES OF MEASUREMENT ONLY. ACTUAL COLORS AS PER COLOR CHART

TYPE N·54
DESIGN A·
STARBOARD SIDE
SCALE 3/64"=1'-0" LENGTH 501-0"
COLORS
WHITE NO. 1 BLUE GRAY
BLACK NO. 3 BLUE
NOTE
COLORS ON PLAN ARE FOR THE PURPOSES OF MEASUREMENT ONLY. ACTUAL COLORS AS PER COLOR CHART

N54 A

Starboard Side Pattern

N54 A

Port Side Pattern

N55 A

Colors used	Ships painted with this pattern
BLACK	ID 1407 EL CAPITAN
GREY-WHITE	
#3 BLUE	
#2 BLUE-GRAY	

TYPE N 55
DESIGN A
∴ PORT SIDE ∴
SCALE LENGTH
COLORS
NOTE
COLORS ON PLAN ARE FOR THE PURPOSES OF MEASUREMENT ONLY. ACTUAL COLORS AS PER COLOR CHART.

TYPE N 55
DESIGN A
STARBOARD SIDE
SCALE LENGTH
COLORS
NOTE
COLORS ON PLAN ARE FOR THE PURPOSES OF MEASUREMENT ONLY. ACTUAL COLORS AS PER COLOR CHART.

N55 A

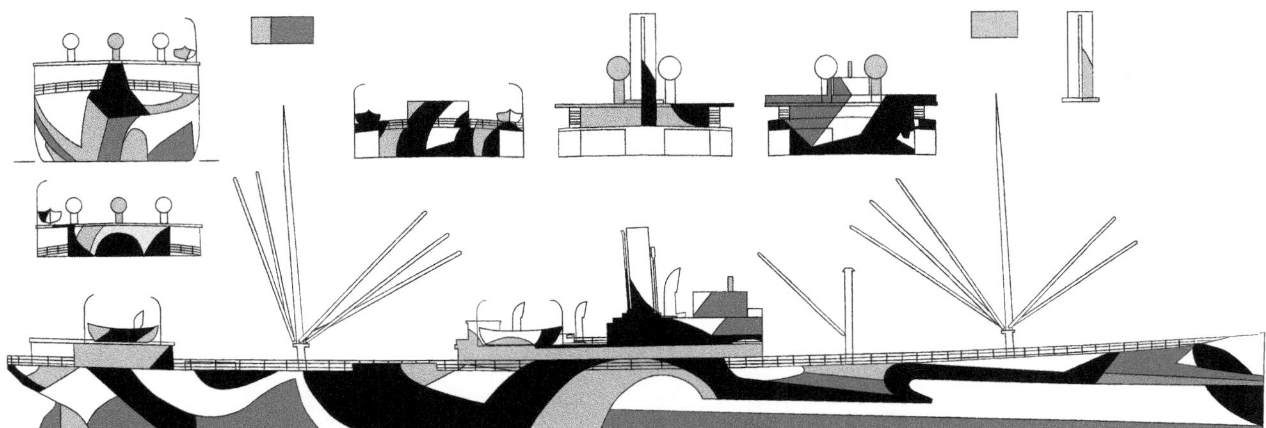

Starboard Side Pattern

N55 A

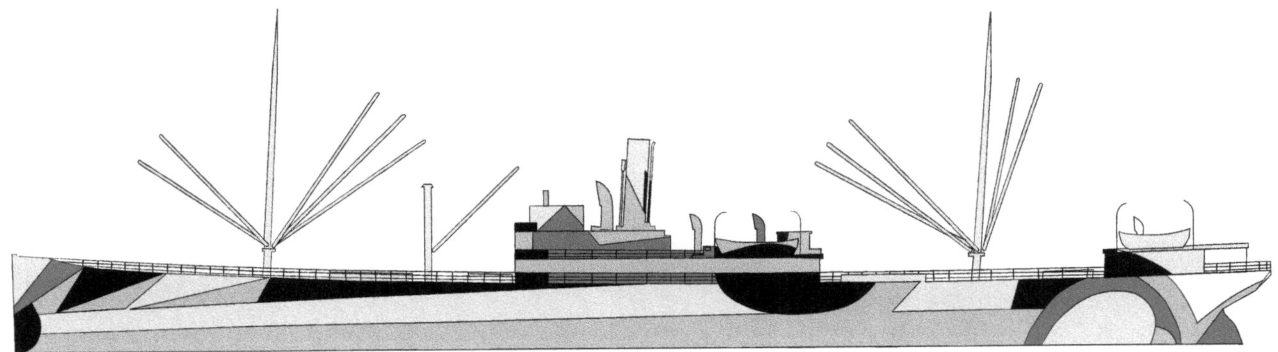

Port Side Pattern

N55 A

Colors used	Ships painted with this pattern
BLACK	ID 2680 CELEBES
WHITE	
#3 BLUE	
#1 BLUE-GRAY	

TYPE N 55
DESIGN A
∴ PORT SIDE ∴
SCALE LENGTH
COLORS
BLACK NO. 1 BLUE GREY
WHITE NO. 3 BLUE
NOTE
COLORS ON PLAN ARE FOR THE PURPOSES OF MEASUREMENT ONLY. ACTUAL COLORS AS PER COLOR CHART.

TYPE N 55
DESIGN A
STARBOARD SIDE
SCALE LENGTH
COLORS
BLACK NO. 1 BLUE GREY
WHITE NO. 3 BLUE
NOTE
COLORS ON PLAN ARE FOR THE PURPOSES OF MEASUREMENT ONLY. ACTUAL COLORS AS PER COLOR CHART.

N55 A

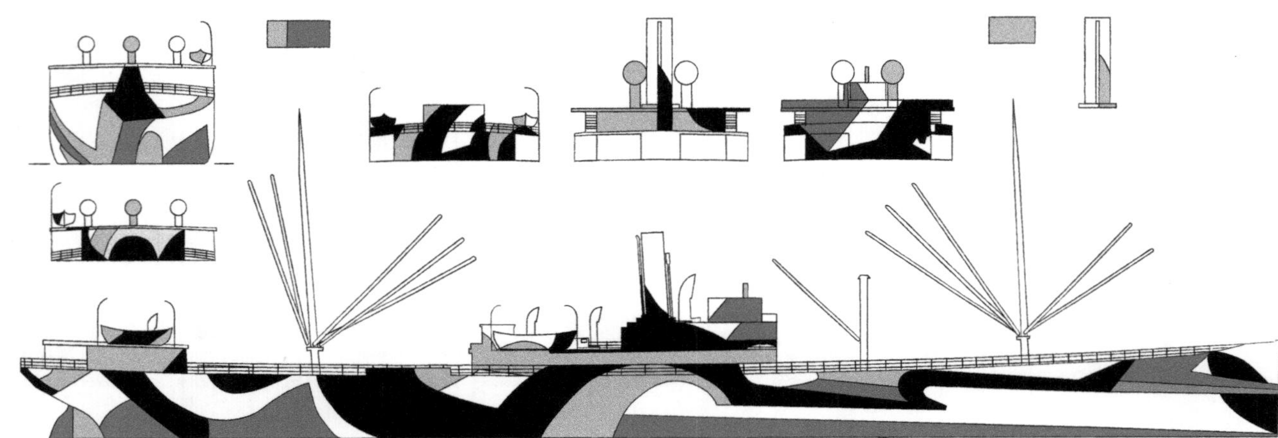

Starboard Side Pattern

N55 A

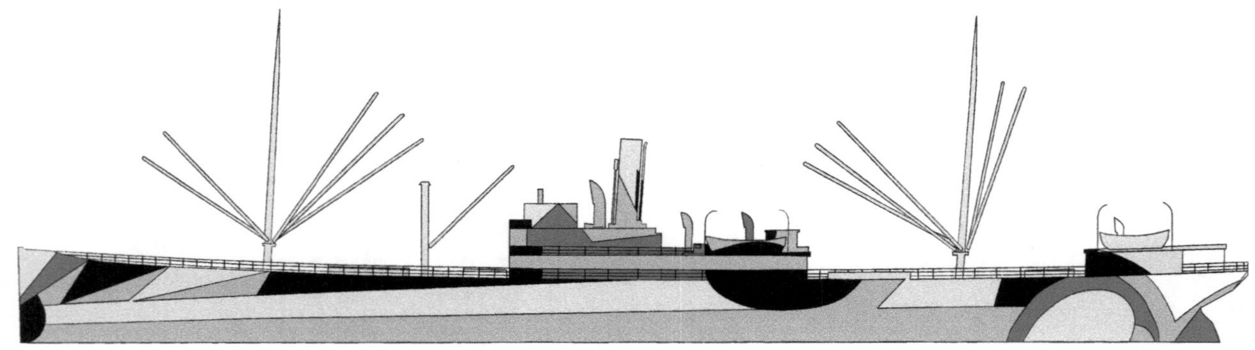

Port Side Pattern

N56 A

Colors used	Ships painted with this pattern
BLACK	ID 4553 FINLAND
WHITE	
#3 BLUE	
#1 BLUE-GRAY	

TYPE N56
DESIGN A
∴ PORT SIDE ∴
SCALE LENGTH
COLORS
BLACK
WHITE
NO. 3 BLUE
NOTE
COLORS ON PLAN ARE FOR THE PURPOSES OF MEASUREMENT ONLY. ACTUAL COLORS AS PER COLOR CHART.

TYPE N56
DESIGN A
STARBOARD SIDE
SCALE LENGTH
COLORS
WHITE
NO. 3 BLUE
NO. 1 BLUE GREY
BLACK
NOTE
COLORS ON PLAN ARE FOR THE PURPOSES OF MEASUREMENT ONLY. ACTUAL COLORS AS PER COLOR CHART.

N56 A

STARBOARD SIDE PATTERN

N56 A

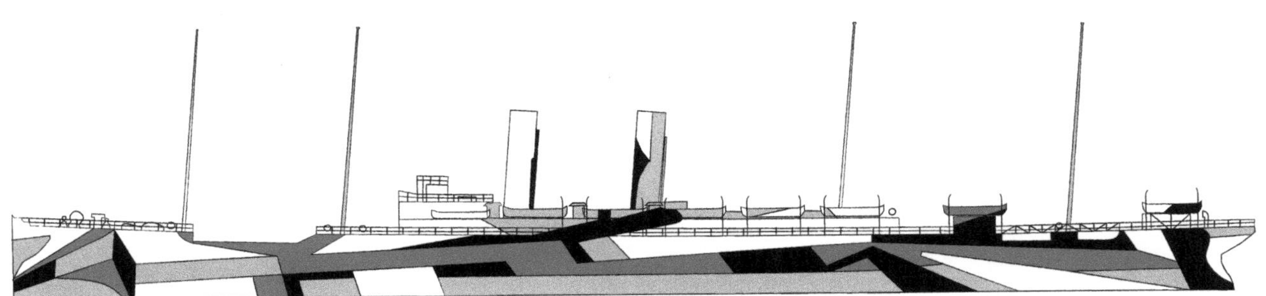

PORT SIDE PATTERN

N56 B

Colors used	Ships painted with this pattern
BLACK	ID 1541 KROONLAND
WHITE	
#3 BLUE	
#1 BLUE-GRAY	

TYPE N 56
DESIGN B
PORT SIDE
SCALE 3/64"=1'-0" LENGTH 560'-0"
COLORS
BLACK No 1 BLUE GREY
WHITE No 3 BLUE
NOTE
COLORS ON PLAN ARE FOR THE PURPOSES OF MEASUREMENT ONLY . . . ACTUAL COLORS AS PER COLOR CHART

N56 B

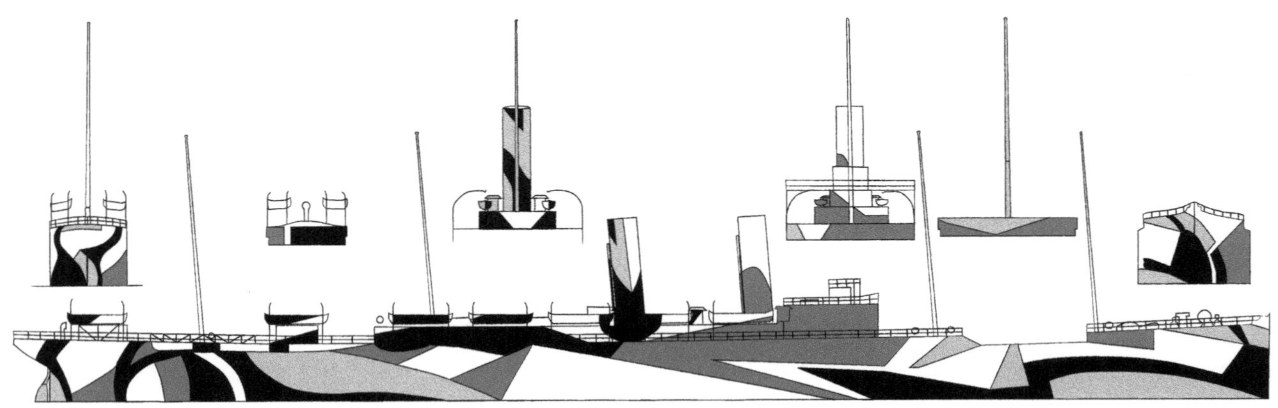

STARBOARD SIDE PATTERN

N56 B

PORT SIDE PATTERN

N57 A

Colors used	Ships painted with this pattern	TYPE N 57 DESIGN A ∴ PORT SIDE ∴ SCALE LENGTH COLORS NOTE COLORS ON PLAN ARE FOR THE PURPOSES OF MEASUREMENT ONLY. ACTUAL COLORS AS PER COLOR CHART.	TYPE N 57 DESIGN A STARBOARD SIDE SCALE LENGTH 381'-2" COLORS NO. 1 BLUE GREY BLACK NOTE COLORS ON PLAN ARE FOR THE PURPOSES OF MEASUREMENT ONLY. AS PER COLOR CHART
BLACK	ID 2700 LENAPE		
WHITE			
#3 BLUE			
#1 BLUE-GRAY			

N57 A

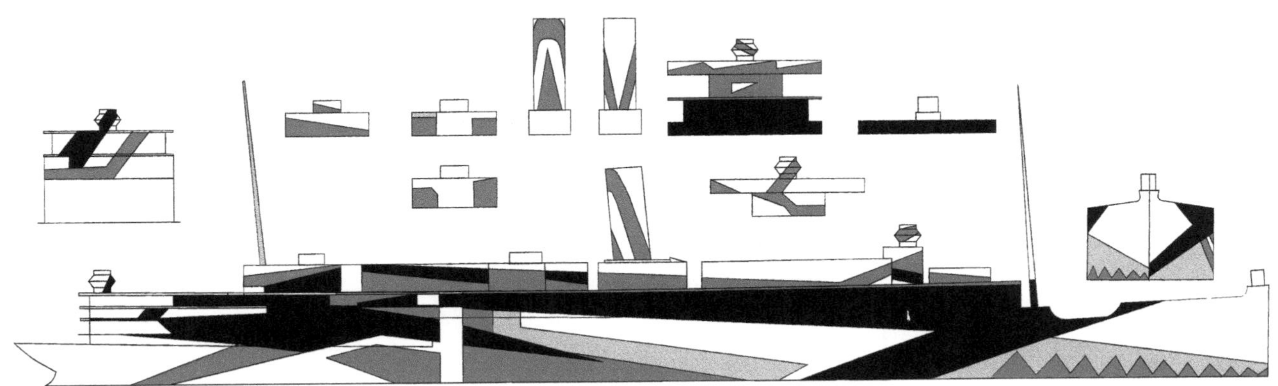

Starboard Side Pattern

N57 A

Port Side Pattern

N58 A

Colors used	Ships painted with this pattern
BLACK	ID 2179 BAVARIA
WHITE	
#3 BLUE	
#1 BLUE-GRAY	

TYPE N-58
DESIGN A

∴ PORT SIDE ∴
SCALE 1/16"=1'-0" LENGTH 371'-4"
COLORS
BLACK NO. 1 BLUE GREY
WHITE NO. 3 BLUE
NOTE
COLORS ON PLAN ARE FOR THE PURPOSES OF MEASUREMENT ONLY. ACTUAL COLORS AS PER COLOR CHART.

TYPE N-58
DESIGN A

STARBOARD SIDE
SCALE 1/16"=1'-0" LENGTH 371'-4"
COLORS
BLACK NO. 1 BLUE GREY
WHITE NO. 3 BLUE
NOTE
COLORS ON PLAN ARE FOR THE PURPOSES OF MEASUREMENT ONLY. ACTUAL COLORS AS PER COLOR CHART.

N58 A

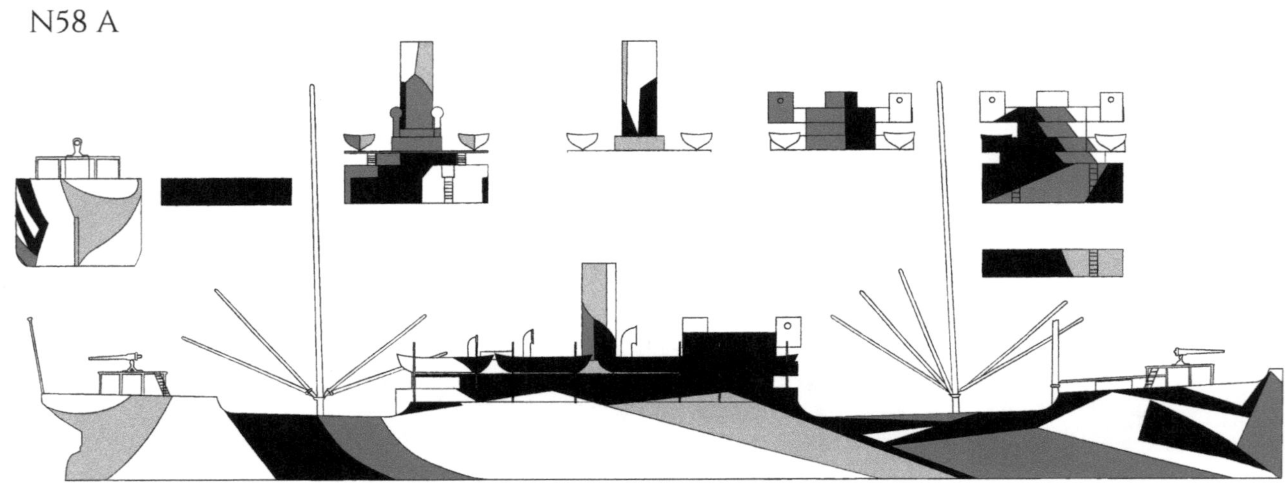

Starboard Side Pattern

N58 A

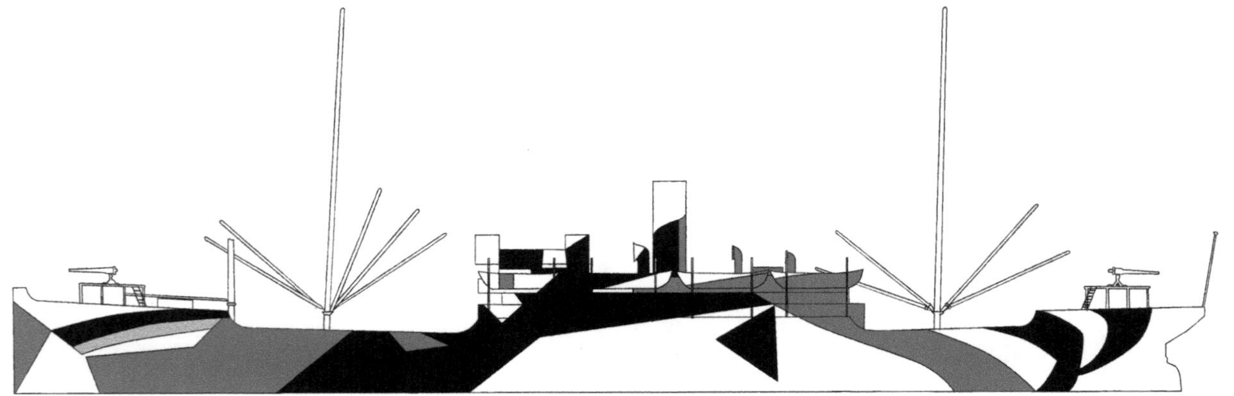

Port Side Pattern

N59 A

Colors used	Ships painted with this pattern
BLACK	AP 3 HANCOCK {T}
WHITE	
#3 BLUE	
#1 BLUE-GRAY	

TYPE N-59
DESIGN A

∴ PORT SIDE ∴
SCALE 1/64"=1'0" LENGTH 465' 0"
COLORS
BLACK NO 1 BLUE GREY
WHITE NO 3 BLUE
NOTE
COLORS ON PLAN ARE FOR THE PURPOSES OF MEASUREMENT ONLY ACTUAL COLORS AS PER COLOR CHART

TYPE N-59
DESIGN A

STARBOARD SIDE
SCALE 1/64"=1'0" LENGTH 465' 6"
COLORS
BLACK NO 1 BLUE GREY
WHITE NO 3 BLUE
NOTE
COLORS ON PLAN ARE FOR THE PURPOSES OF MEASUREMENT ONLY ACTUAL COLORS AS PER COLOR CHART

N59 A

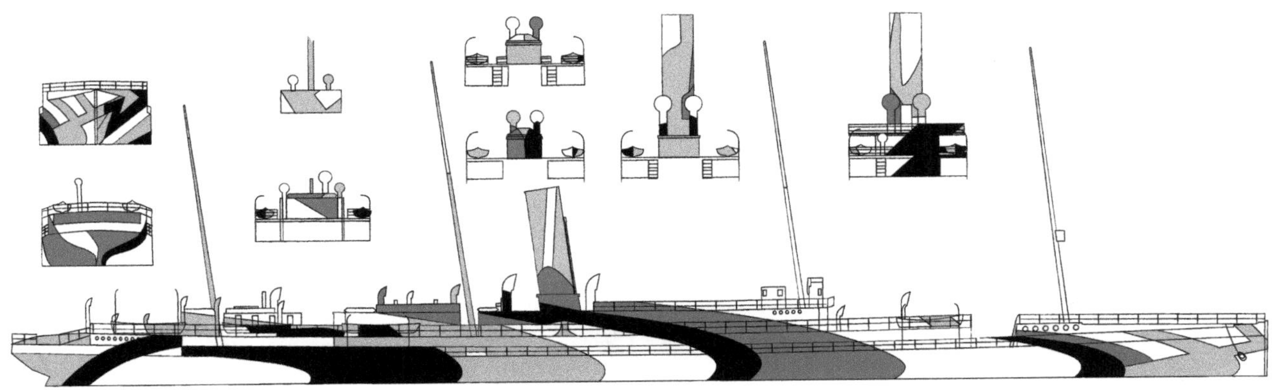

STARBOARD SIDE PATTERN

N59 A

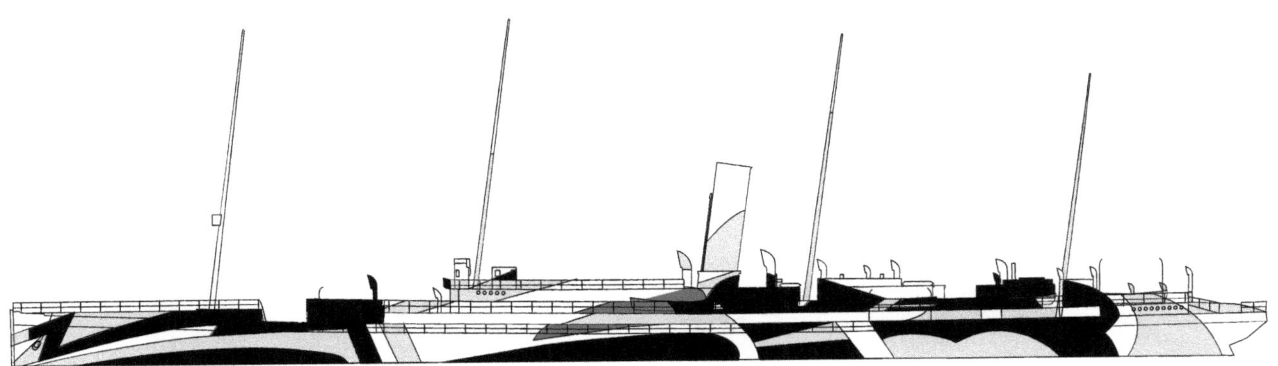

PORT SIDE PATTERN

N60 A

Colors used	Ships painted with this pattern
BLACK	C 20 ST LOUIS
WHITE	
#3 BLUE	
#1 BLUE	

TYPE N-60
DESIGN A

∴ PORT SIDE ∴
SCALE 1/16"=1'0" LENGTH 426 0"
COLORS
BLACK
WHITE
NO. 3 BLUE
NOTE
COLORS ON [illegible] FOR THE PURPOSES OF [illegible] MENT ONLY. [illegible] AS PER COLOR [illegible]

TYPE N-60
DESIGN A

STARBOARD SIDE
SCALE 1/16"=1'0" LENGTH 426 0"
COLORS
NO. 1 BLUE
BLACK
NOTE
COLORS ON PLAN ARE FOR THE PURPOSES OF MEASUREMENT ONLY. ACTUAL COLORS AS PER COLOR CHART

N60 A

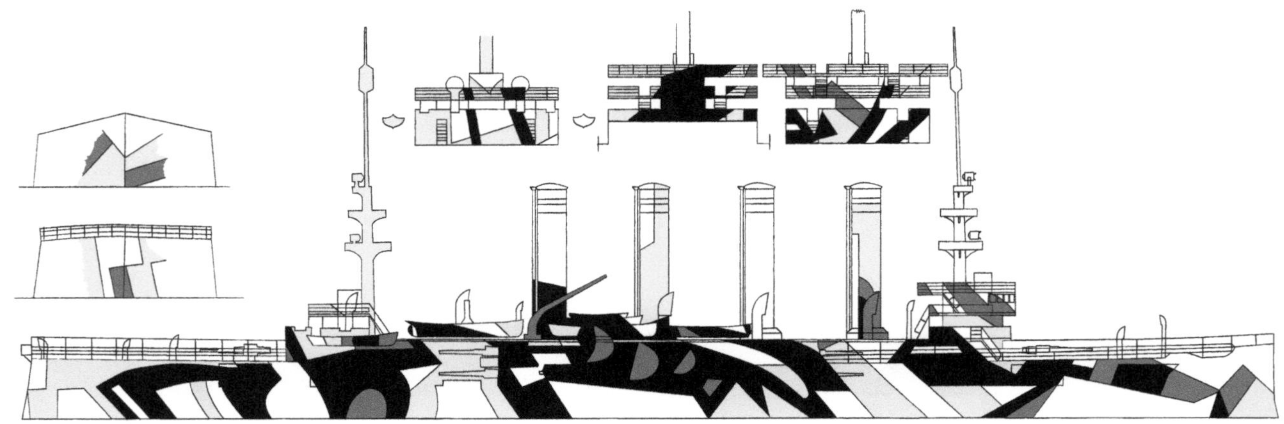

Starboard Side Pattern

N60 A

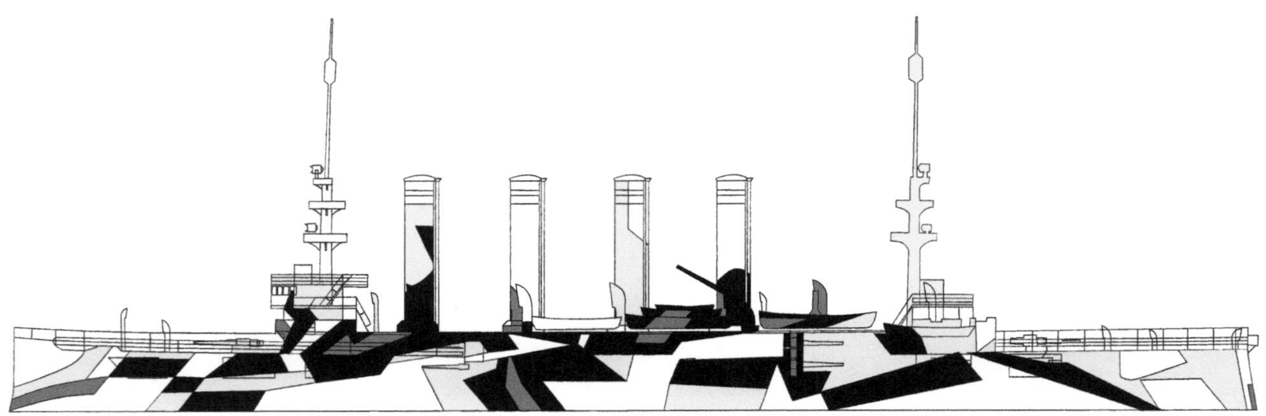

Port Side Pattern

N61 A

Colors used	Ships painted with this pattern
BLACK	ID 1280 HENRY R MALLORY
WHITE	
#3 BLUE	
#1 BLUE	
#1 GREEN	

TYPE N-61
DESIGN A
∴ PORT SIDE ∴
SCALE 1/16"=1'0" LENGTH 440' 7"
COLORS
BLACK NO 1 BLUE NO 3 BLUE
WHITE NO 1 GREEN
NOTE
COLORS ON PLAN ARE FOR THE PURPOSES OF MEASUREMENT ONLY. ACTUAL COLORS AS PER COLOR CHART.

TYPE N-61
DESIGN A
STARBOARD SIDE
SCALE 1/16"=1'-0" LENGTH 440-7"
COLORS
BLACK NO 1 BLUE #3 BLUE
WHITE #1 GREEN
NOTE
COLORS ON PLAN ARE FOR THE PURPOSES OF MEASUREMENT ONLY. ACTUAL COLORS AS PER COLOR CHART.

N61 A

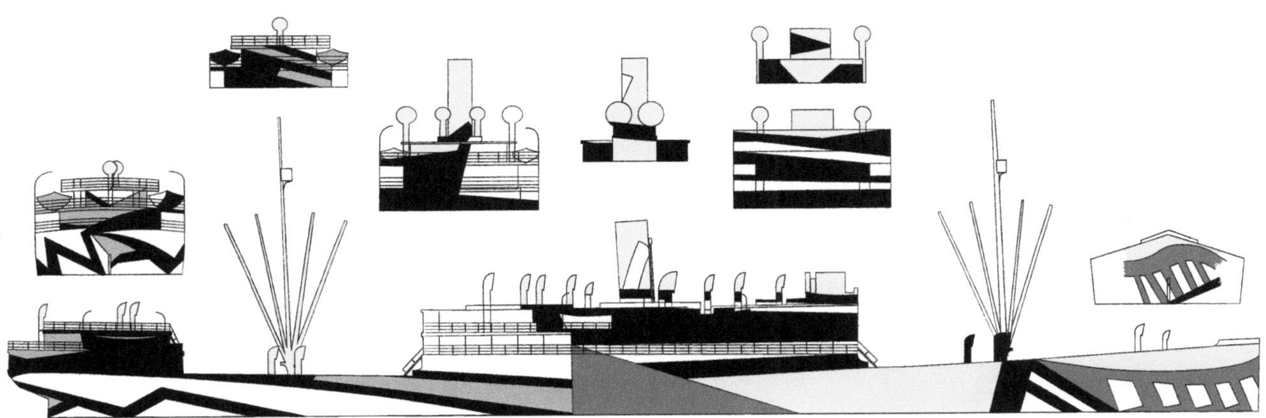

STARBOARD SIDE PATTERN

N61 A

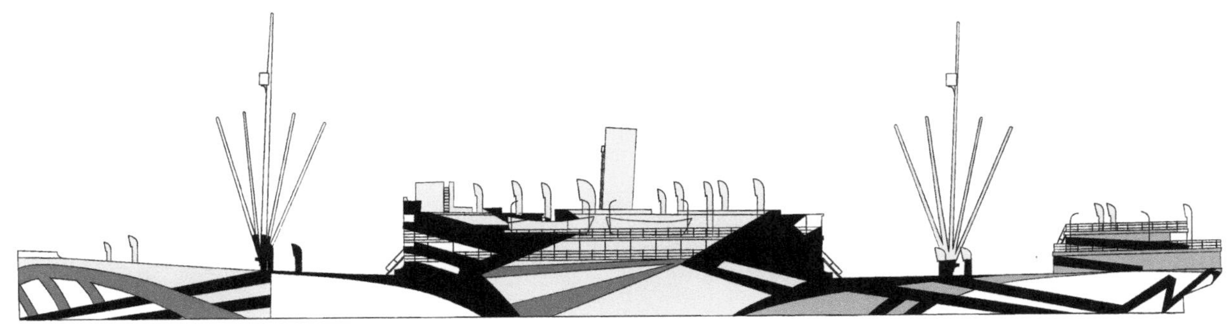

PORT SIDE PATTERN

N62 A

Colors used	Ships painted with this pattern
BLACK	ID 3002 IOWAN
WHITE	ID 3382 DAKOTAN
#3 BLUE	ID 3511 PENNSYLVANIAN (T)
#1 BLUE	
#2 BLUE-GRAY	

TYPE N 62
DESIGN A
∴ PORT SIDE ∴
SCALE 1/16"-1'-0" LENGTH 429'-2"
COLORS
BLACK NO. 2 BLUE GREY NO. 1 BLUE NO. 3 BLUE
NOTE
COLORS ON PLAN ARE FOR THE PURPOSES OF MEASUREMENT ONLY. ACTUAL COLORS AS PER COLOR CHART.

TYPE N 62
DESIGN A
STARBOARD SIDE
SCALE 1/16"-1'-0" LENGTH 429'-2"
COLORS
NO. 2 BLUE GREY NO. 1 BLUE BLACK NO. 3 BLUE
NOTE
COLORS ON PLAN ARE FOR THE PURPOSES OF MEASUREMENT ONLY. ACTUAL COLORS AS PER COLOR CHART.

N62 A

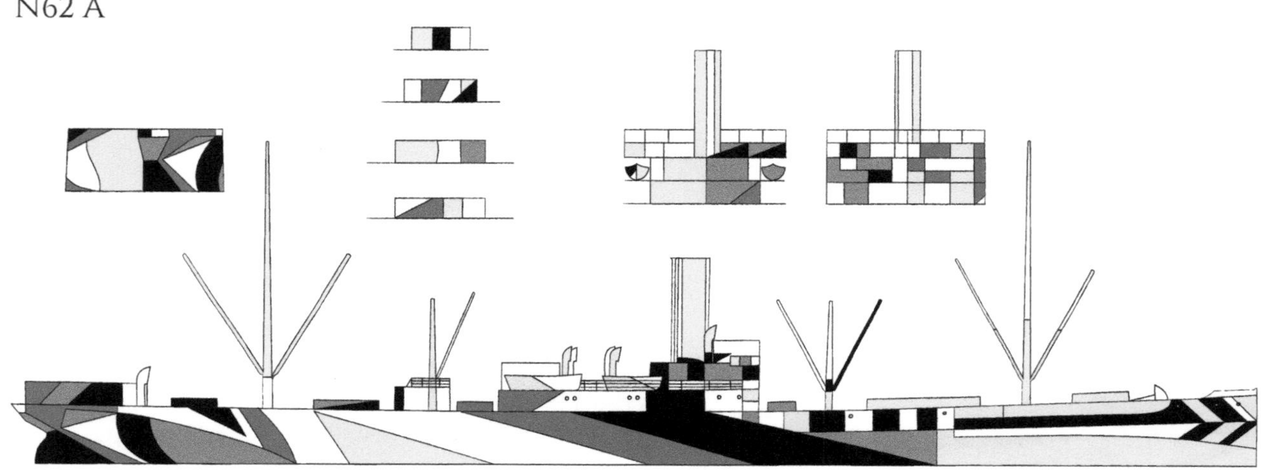

Starboard Side Pattern

N62 A

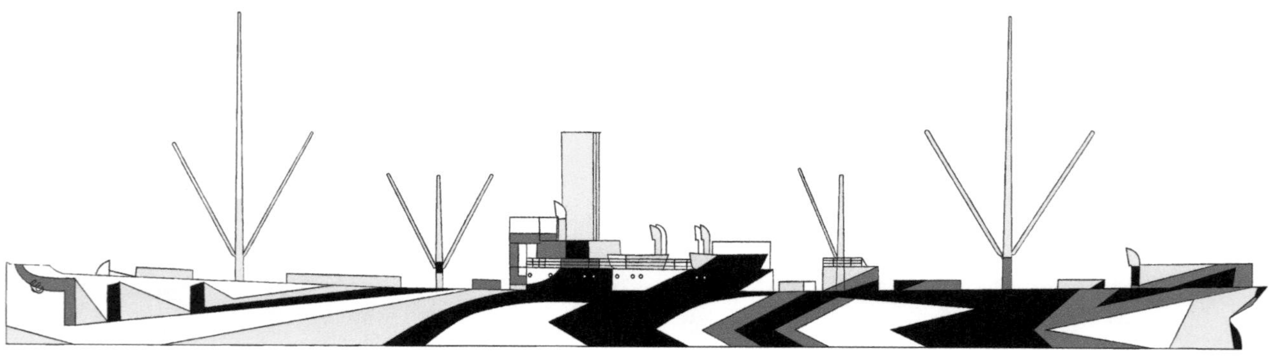

Port Side Pattern

N62 B

Colors used	Ships painted with this pattern
BLACK	ID 1655 MEXICAN
WHITE	ID 4542 ALASKAN
#3 BLUE	
#2 BLUE-GRAY	

TYPE N 62
DESIGN B

∴ PORT SIDE ∴
SCALE 3/64"=1'-0" LENGTH 490'0"
COLORS
NO. 2 BLUE GREY — WHITE
NO. 1 BLUE — BLACK
NOTE
COLORS ON PLAN ARE FOR THE PURPOSES OF MEASUREMENT ONLY. ACTUAL COLORS AS PER COLOR CHART.

TYPE ·N 62·
DESIGN ·B·

STARBOARD SIDE
SCALE 3/64"=1'-0" LENGTH 490'-0"
COLORS
NO. 2 BLUE GREY — BLACK
NO. 1 BLUE — WHITE
NOTE
COLORS ON PLAN ARE FOR THE PURPOSES OF MEASUREMENT ONLY. ACTUAL COLORS AS PER COLOR CHART.

N62 B

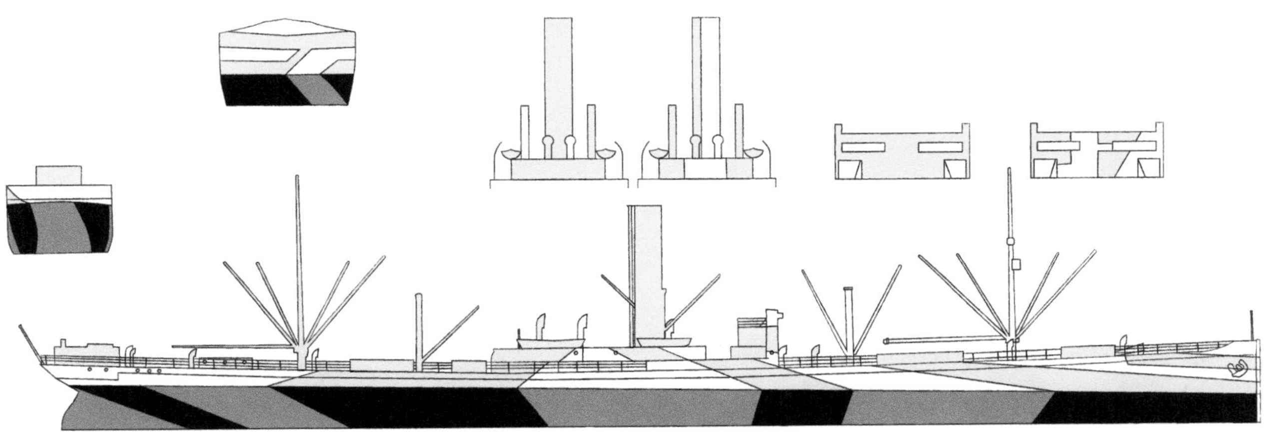

STARBOARD SIDE PATTERN

N62 B

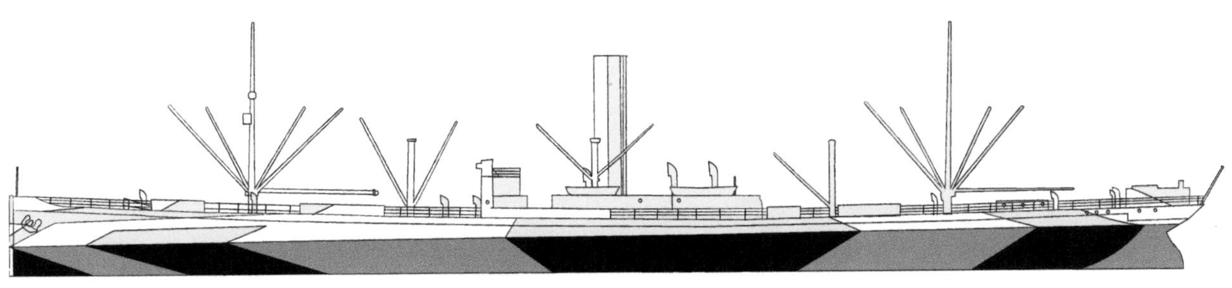

PORT SIDE PATTERN

N63 A

Colors used	Ships painted with this pattern
BLACK	ID 1349 CHARLTON HALL
WHITE	
#3 BLUE	
#1 BLUE	
#1 GREEN	

TYPE·N 63·
DESIGN A
∴ PORT SIDE ∴
SCALE 1/16"=1'-0" LENGTH 412'-0"
COLORS
NO. 1 GREEN NO. 1 BLUE BLACK WHITE
NO. 3 BLUE
NOTE
COLORS ON PLAN ARE FOR THE PURPOSES OF MEASUREMENT ONLY. ACTUAL COLORS AS PER COLOR CHART.

TYPE·N 63·
DESIGN A
STARBOARD SIDE
SCALE 1/16"=1'-0" LENGTH 412'-6"
COLORS
NO. 1 GREEN NO. 1 BLUE WHITE BLACK
NO. 3 BLUE
NOTE
COLORS ON PLAN ARE FOR THE PURPOSES OF MEASUREMENT ONLY. ACTUAL COLORS AS PER COLOR CHART.

N63 A

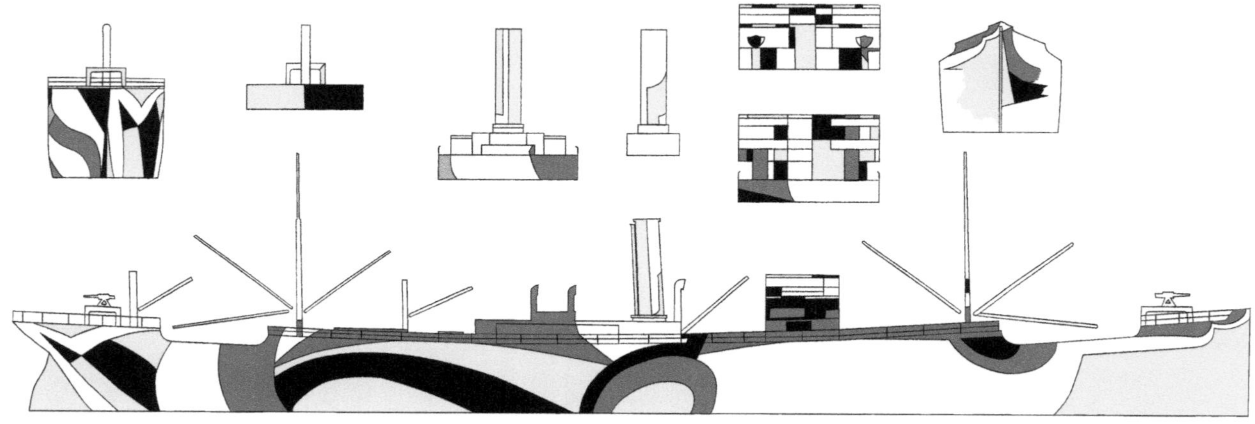

Starboard Side Pattern

N63 A

Port Side Pattern

N64 A

Colors used	Ships painted with this pattern
BLACK	AF 1 BRIDGE
#2 GRAY	
#4 GRAY	
#1 BLUE	
#3 BLUE	

TYPE 64
DESIGN A
∴ PORT SIDE ∴
COLORS
NOTE
COLORS ON PLAN ARE FOR THE PURPOSES OF MEASUREMENT ONLY. ACTUAL COLORS AS PER COLOR CHART

TYPE 64
DESIGN A
STARBOARD SIDE
SCALE 3/64"=1'0 LENGTH 165'-0"
COLORS
WHITE NO. 1 BLUE NO. 1 BLUE GREY NO. 3 BLUE BLACK
NOTE
COLORS ON PLAN ARE FOR THE PURPOSES OF MEASUREMENT ONLY. ACTUAL COLORS AS PER COLOR CHART.

N64 A

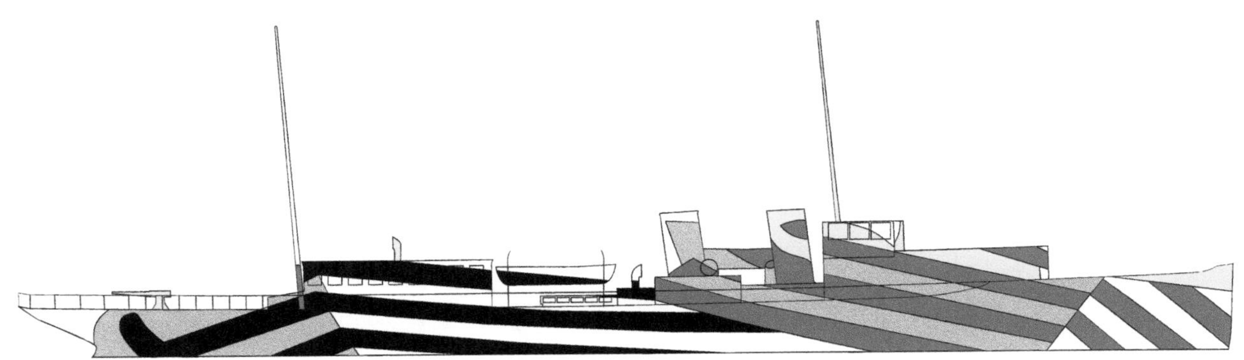

STARBOARD SIDE PATTERN

N64 A

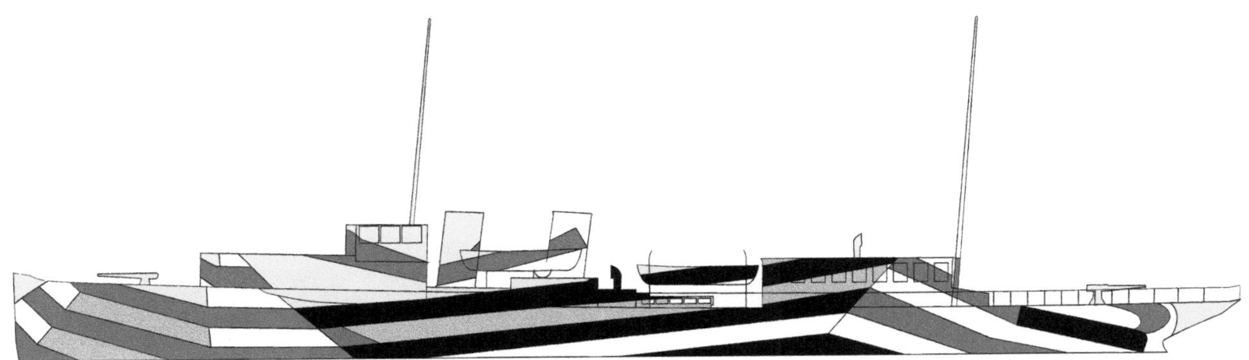

PORT SIDE PATTERN

N65 A

Colors used	Ships painted with this pattern
BLACK	AF 3 CULGOA (T)
GREY-WHITE	
#3 BLUE	
#2 BLUE-GRAY	

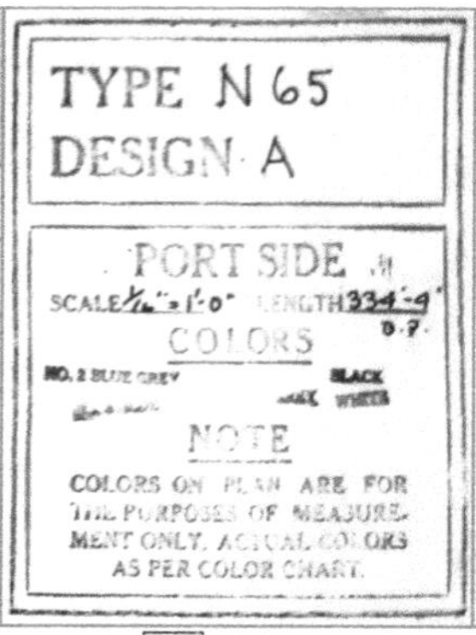

TYPE N 65
DESIGN A

PORT SIDE
SCALE 1/16" = 1'-0" LENGTH 334'-9" B.P.
COLORS
NO. 2 BLUE GREY — BLACK — WHITE
NOTE
COLORS ON PLAN ARE FOR THE PURPOSES OF MEASUREMENT ONLY. ACTUAL COLORS AS PER COLOR CHART.

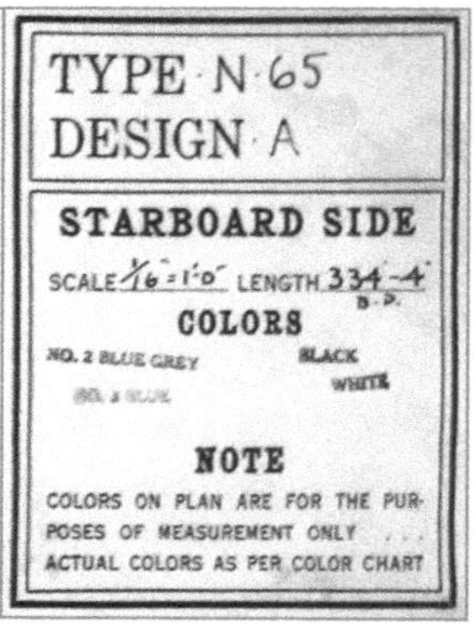

TYPE N 65
DESIGN A

STARBOARD SIDE
SCALE 1/16" = 1'-0" LENGTH 334'-4" B.P.
COLORS
NO. 2 BLUE GREY — BLACK — WHITE
NOTE
COLORS ON PLAN ARE FOR THE PURPOSES OF MEASUREMENT ONLY . . . ACTUAL COLORS AS PER COLOR CHART

N65 A

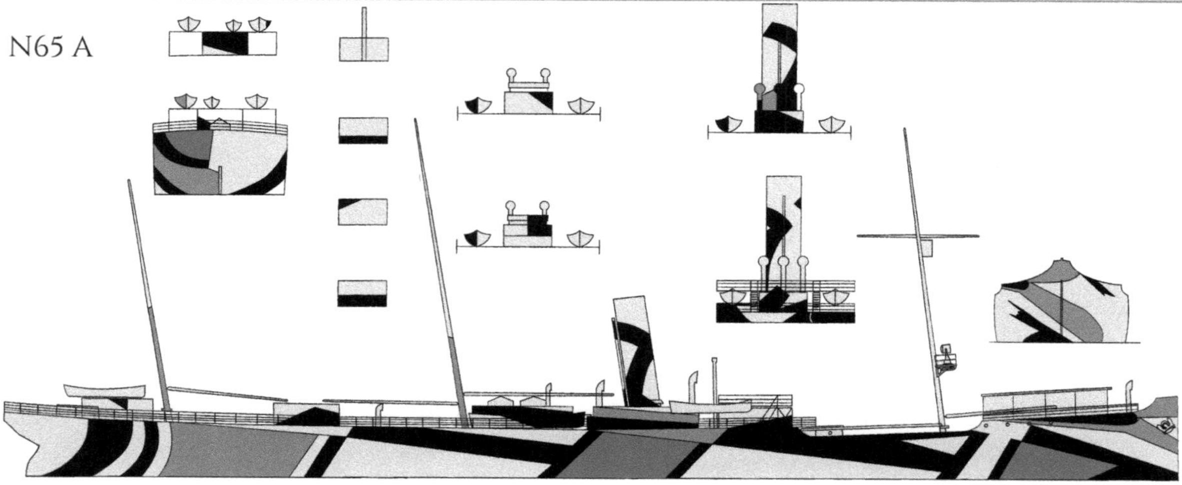

Starboard Side Pattern

N65 A

Port Side Pattern

N66 A

Colors used	Ships painted with this pattern
BLACK	AC 8 NEPTUNE (T)
GREY-WHITE	
#3 BLUE	
#2 BLUE-GRAY	

TYPE N 66
DESIGN A
PORT SIDE
SCALE 3/64"=1'-0" LENGTH 520'-0"
COLORS
NO. 3 BLUE NO. 2 BLUE GREY GREY WHITE BLACK
NOTE
COLORS ON PLAN ARE FOR THE PURPOSES OF MEASUREMENT ONLY. ACTUAL COLORS AS PER COLOR CHART.

TYPE N 66
DESIGN A
PORT SIDE
SCALE 3/64"=1'-0" LENGTH 520'-0"
COLORS
NO. 3 BLUE NO. 2 BLUE GREY GREY WHITE BLACK
NOTE
COLORS ON PLAN ARE FOR THE PURPOSES OF MEASUREMENT ONLY. ACTUAL COLORS AS PER COLOR CHART.

N66 A

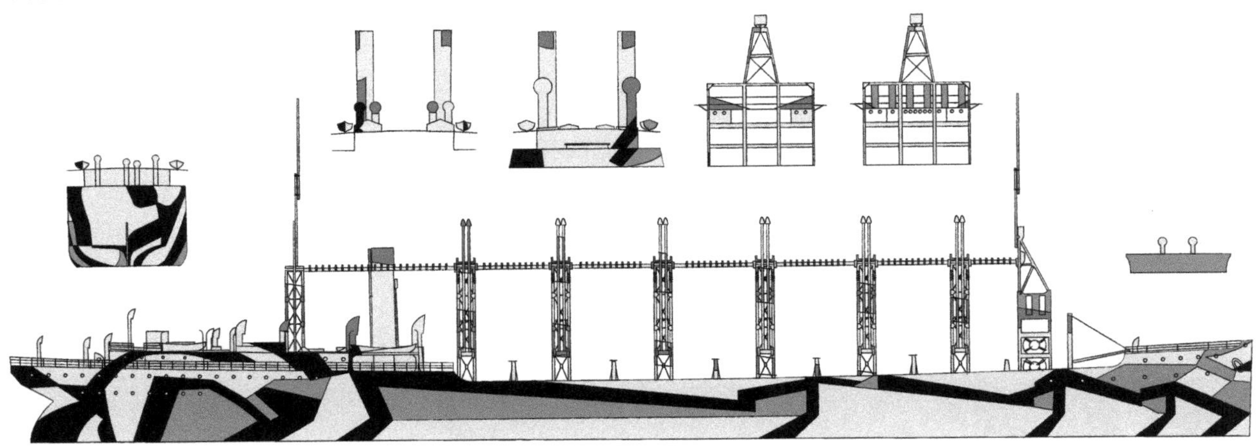

Starboard Side Pattern

N66 A

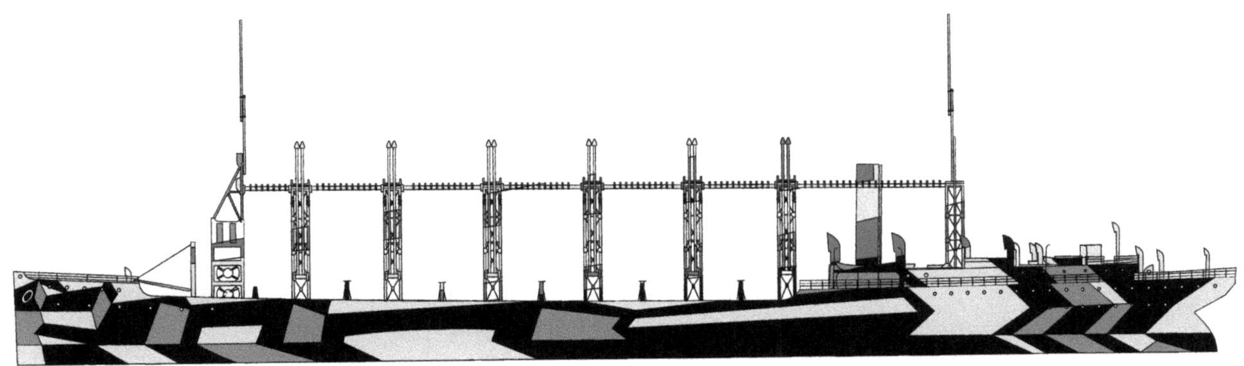

Port Side Pattern

N66 B

Colors used	Ships painted with this pattern
BLACK	AC 4 CYCLOPS
WHITE	AC 3 JUPITER (T)
GREY-WHITE	AC 12 JASON (T)
#2 BLUE-GRAY	

TYPE N66
DESIGN B
PORT SIDE
SCALE 3/64"=1'-0" LENGTH 542'-0"
COLORS
BLACK WHITE
GREY WHITE NO. 2 BLUE GREY
NOTE
COLORS ON PLAN ARE FOR THE PURPOSES OF MEASUREMENT ONLY. ACTUAL COLORS AS PER COLOR CHART.

TYPE N66
DESIGN B
STARBOARD
SCALE 3/64"=1'-0" LENGTH 541'-0"
COLORS
WHITE GREY WHITE
NO. 2 BLUE GREY
NOTE
COLORS ON PLAN ARE FOR THE PURPOSES OF MEASUREMENT ONLY.

N66 B

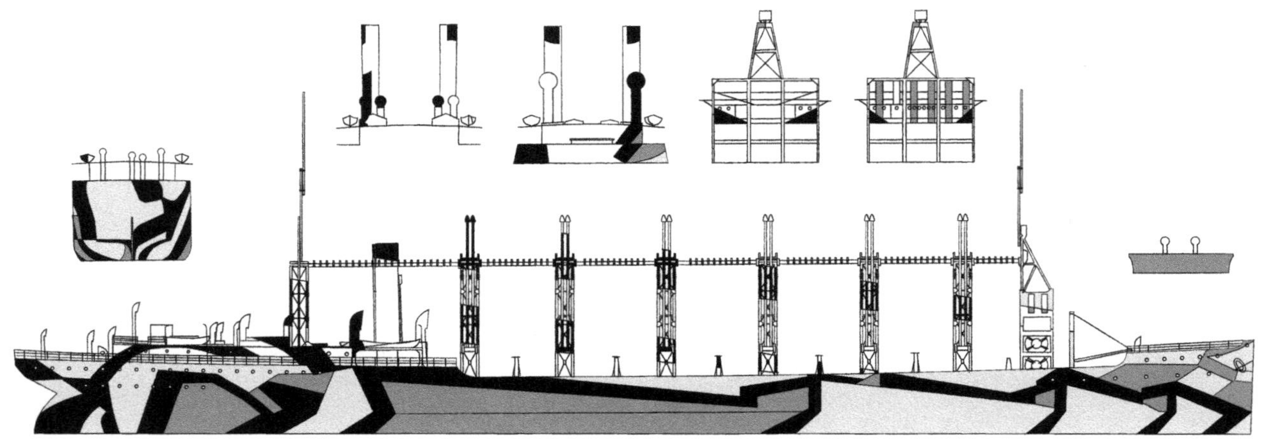

Starboard Side Pattern

N66 B

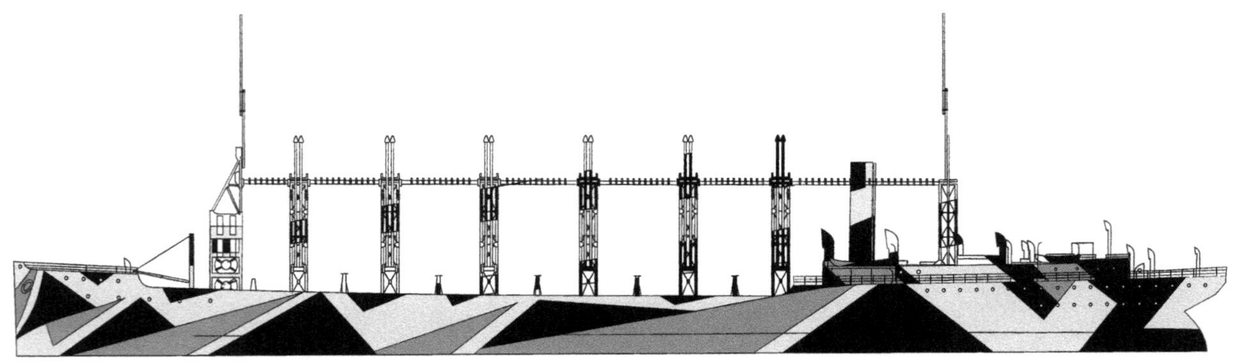

Port Side Pattern

N67 A

Colors used	Ships painted with this pattern
BLACK	ID 2302 BEAVER
GREY-WHITE	
#3 BLUE	
#1 BLUE-GRAY	
#1 GREEN	
#3 BLUE-GRAY	

TYPE N 67
DESIGN A
PORT SIDE
SCALE 3/64"=1'0 LENGTH 580'0"
COLORS
BLACK
GRAY WHITE
NO 1 GREEN
NO 1 BLUE GRAY
NO 2 BLUE GRAY
NO 3 BLUE
NOTE
COLORS ON PLAN ARE FOR THE PURPOSES OF MEASUREMENT ONLY. ACTUAL COLORS AS PER COLOR CHART.

TYPE N-67
DESIGN A
STARBOARD SIDE
SCALE 3/64"=1'0" LENGTH 580'0"
COLORS
BLACK
GRAY WHITE
NO.3 BLUE
NO 1 BLUE GRAY
NO 2
NO 1 GREEN
NOTE

N67 A

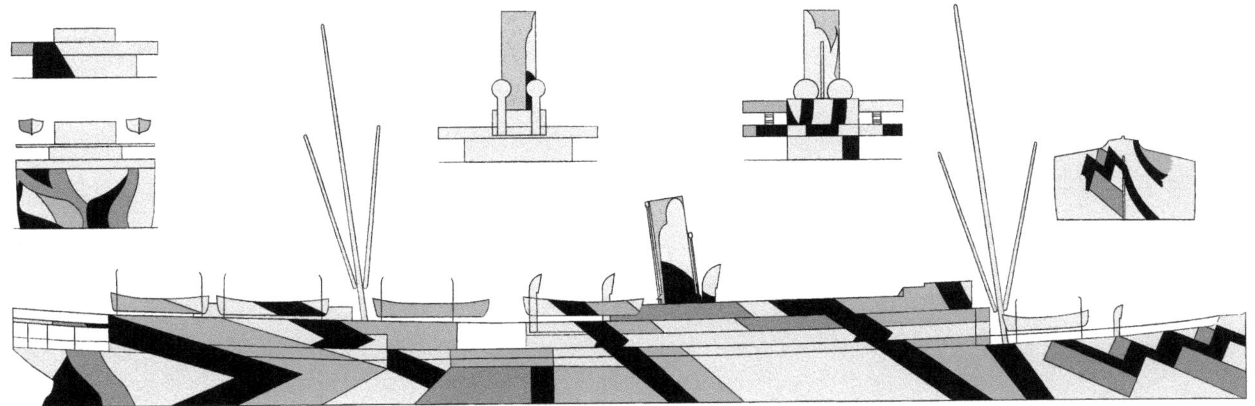

Starboard Side Pattern

N67 A

Port Side Pattern

N68 A

Colors used	Ships painted with this pattern
BLACK	ID 2708 KONINGEN DER NEDERLANDEN
GREY-WHITE	
#3 BLUE	
#2 BLUE-GRAY	

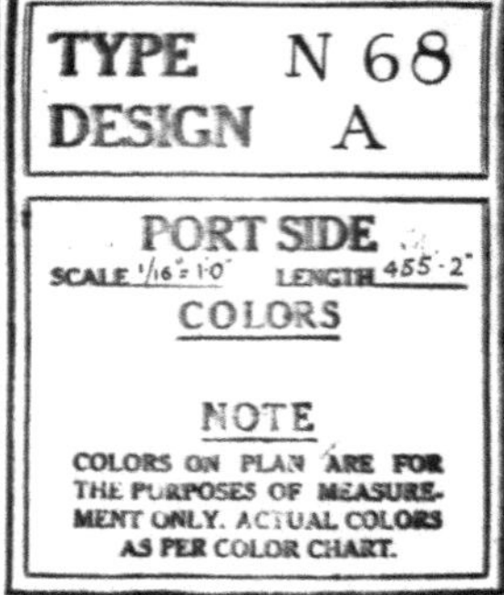

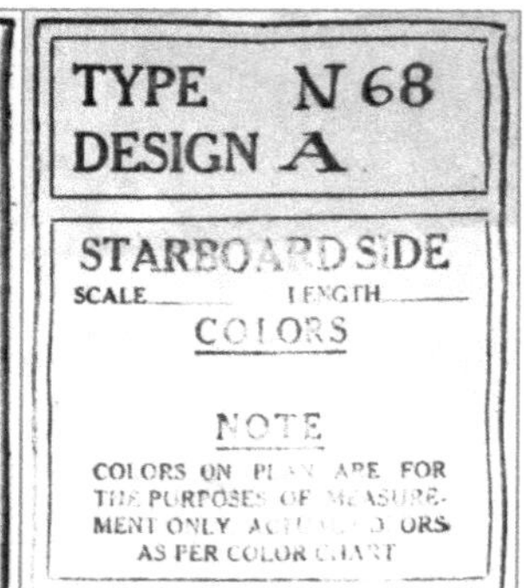

N68 A

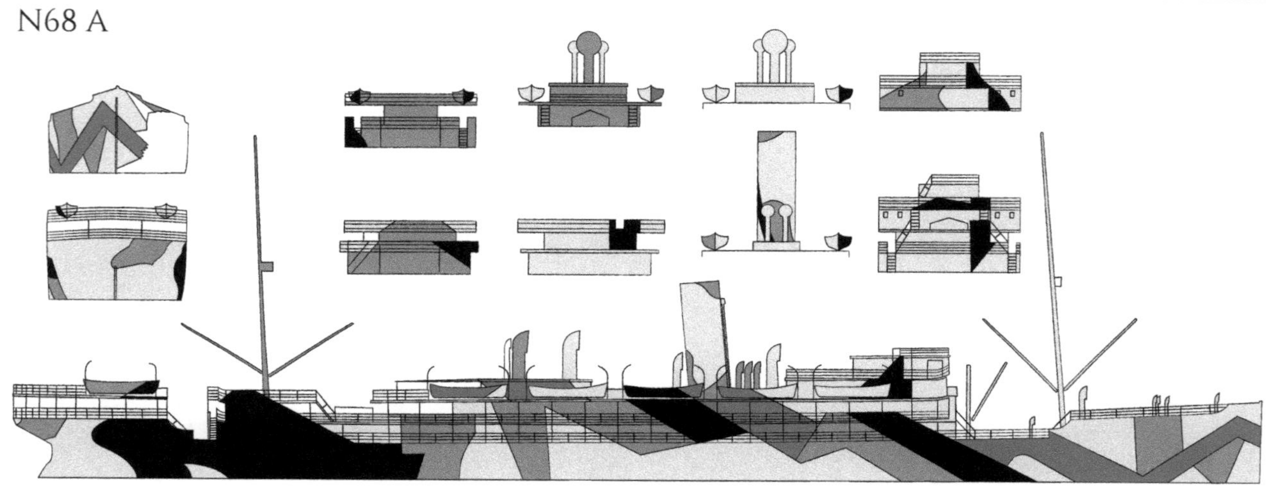

Starboard Side Pattern

N68 A

Port Side Pattern

N69 A

Colors used	Ships painted with this pattern
BLACK	AK 2 KITTERY
GREY-WHITE	
#1 BLUE-GRAY	
#1 GRAY-PINK	

TYPE N69
DESIGN A

PORT SIDE
SCALE 5/64" = 1'-0" LENGTH 295.8'-0"
COLORS
NO. 1 BLUE GREY BLACK
NO. 1 GREY PINK GREY WHITE
NOTE
COLORS ON PLAN ARE FOR THE PURPOSES OF MEASUREMENT ONLY. ACTUAL COLORS AS PER COLOR CHART.

TYPE N69
DESIGN A

SCALE 5/64" = 1'-0" LENGTH 295.8'-0"
COLORS
NO. 1 BLUE GREY BLACK
NO. 1 GREY PINK GREY WHITE
NOTE
COLORS ON PLAN ARE FOR THE PURPOSES OF MEASUREMENT ONLY. ACTUAL COLORS AS PER COLOR CHART.

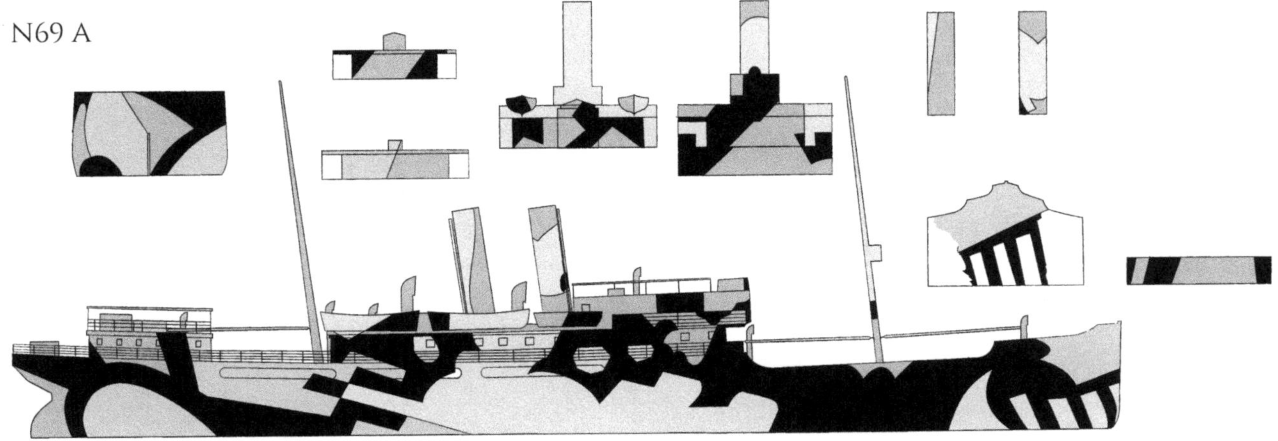

Starboard Side Pattern

N69 A

Port Side Pattern

N70 A

Colors used	Ships painted with this pattern
BLACK	AR 4 VESTAL
GREY-WHITE	ID 2682 GORONTALO {T}
#3 BLUE	
#1 BLUE-GRAY	
#1 GRAY-GREEN	

TYPE N70
DESIGN A
PORT SIDE
SCALE 1/16" = 1'-0" LENGTH 465'-10" B.P.
COLORS
BLACK
GREY WHITE
NO. 3 BLUE
NO. 1 GREY GREEN
NO. 1 BLUE GREY
NOTE
COLORS ON PLAN ARE FOR THE PURPOSES OF MEASUREMENT ONLY. ACTUAL COLORS AS PER COLOR CHART.

TYPE N 70
DESIGN A
STARBOARD SIDE
SCALE 1/16" = 1'-0" LENGTH 465'-10" B.P.
COLORS
BLACK
GREY WHITE
NO. 1 BLUE GREY
NO. 1 GREY GREEN
NO. 3 BLUE
NOTE
COLORS ON PLAN ARE FOR THE PURPOSES OF MEASUREMENT ONLY. ACTUAL COLORS AS PER COLOR CHART.

N70 A

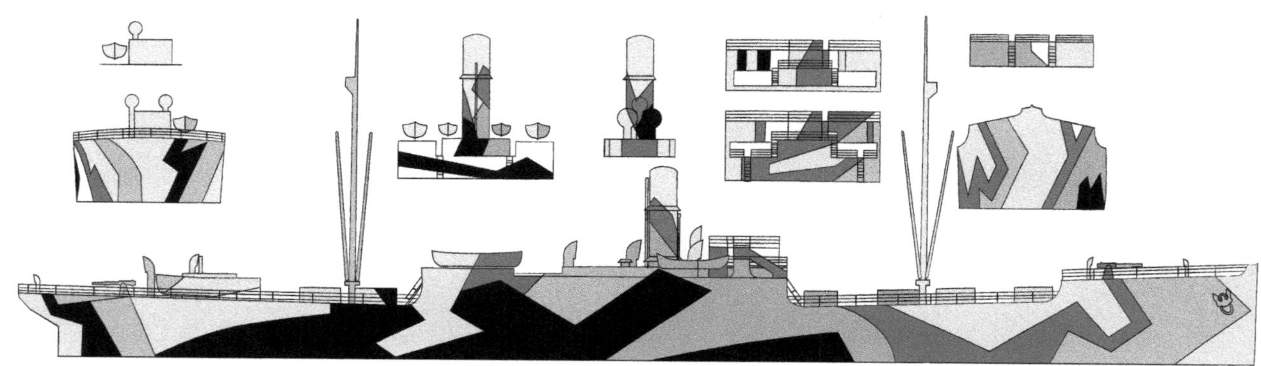

Starboard Side Pattern

N70 A

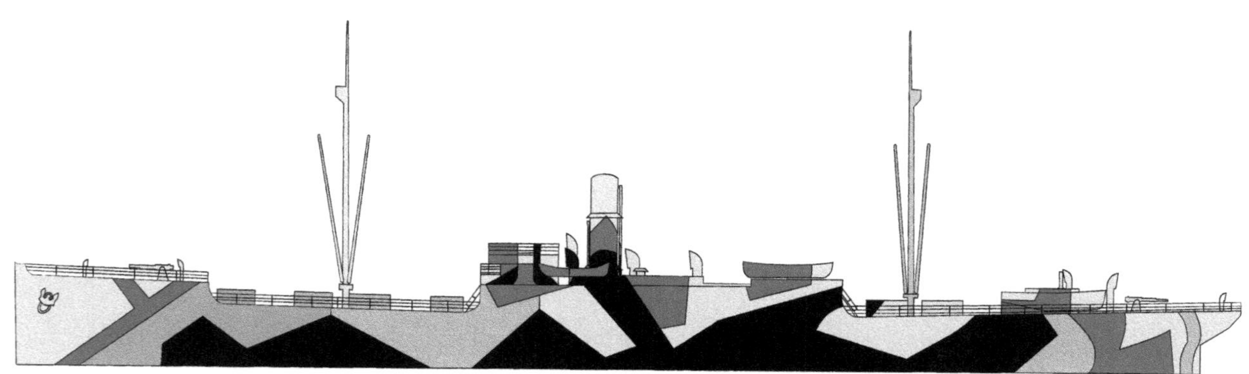

Port Side Pattern

N72 A

Colors used	Ships painted with this pattern
BLACK	ACR 2 ROCHESTER
GREY-WHITE	
#1 GRAY-GREEN	

TYPE N72
DESIGN A

PORT SIDE
SCALE 1/16" = 1'0" LENGTH 384'0"
COLORS
BLACK NO. 1 GREY GREEN
GREY WHITE NO. 3 BLUE
NOTE
COLORS ON PLAN ARE FOR THE PURPOSES OF MEASUREMENT ONLY. ACTUAL COLORS AS PER COLOR CHART.

TYPE N72
DESIGN A

STARBOARD SIDE
SCALE 1/16" = 1'0" LENGTH 384'0"
COLORS
BLACK NO. 1 GREY GREEN
GREY WHITE NO. 3 BLUE
NOTE
COLORS ON PLAN ARE FOR THE PURPOSES OF MEASUREMENT ONLY. ACTUAL COLORS AS PER COLOR CHART.

N72 A

STARBOARD SIDE PATTERN

N72 A

PORT SIDE PATTERN

N73 A

Colors used	Ships painted with this pattern
BLACK	ACR 12 CHARLOTTE
GREY-WHITE	
#4 GRAY	
#3 BLUE	
#1 BLUE	

TYPE N 73
DESIGN A
PORT SIDE
SCALE 3/64"=1'-0" LENGTH 504'-6"
COLORS
NO. 1 BLUE
NO. 3 BLUE
BLACK
NO. 4 GREY
GREYWHITE
NOTE
COLORS ON PLAN ARE FOR THE PURPOSES OF MEASUREMENT ONLY. ACTUAL COLORS AS PER COLOR CHART.

TYPE N-73
DESIGN A
STARBOARD SIDE
SCALE 3/64"=1'-0" LENGTH 504'-6"
COLORS
NO. 1 BLUE
NO. 3 BLUE
BLACK
NO. 4 GREY
GREYWHITE
NOTE
COLORS ON PLAN ARE FOR THE PURPOSES OF MEASUREMENT ONLY. ACTUAL COLORS AS PER COLOR CHART.

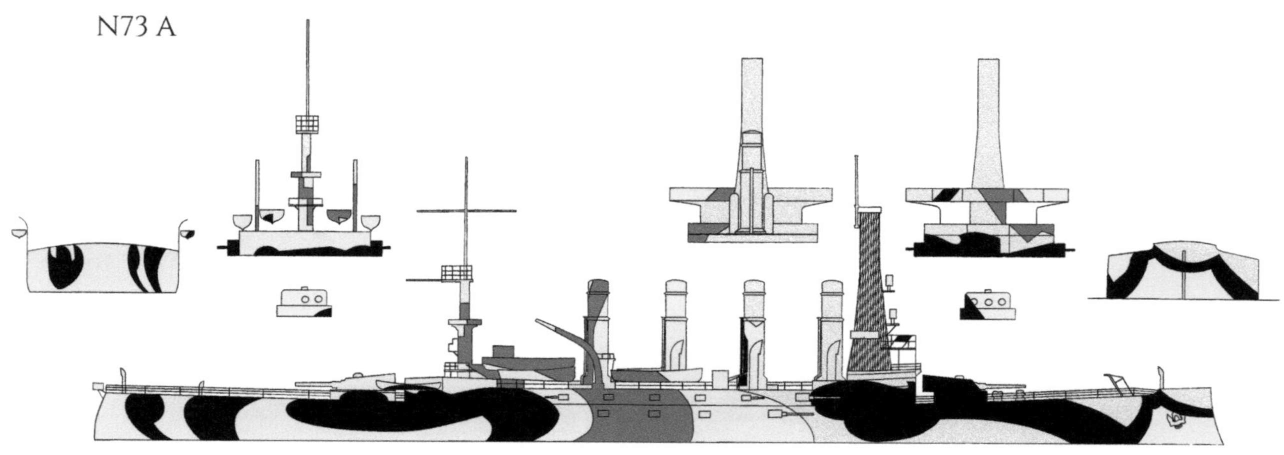

Starboard Side Pattern

N73 A

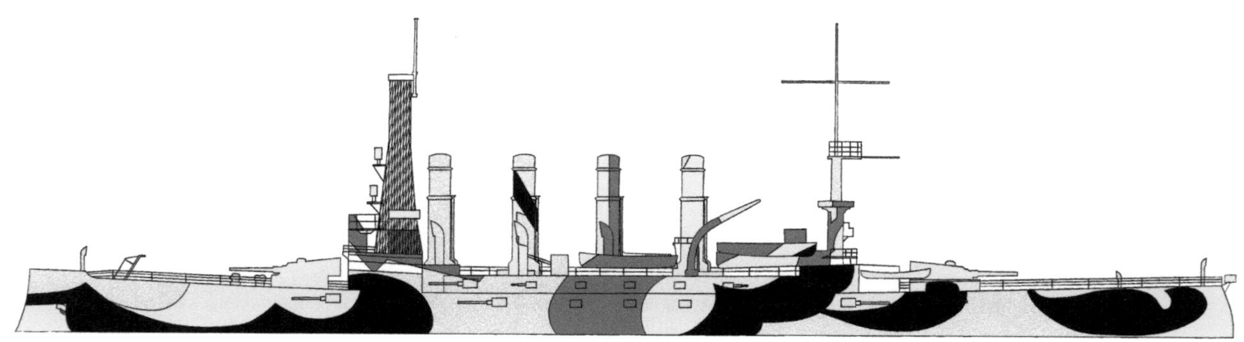

Port Side Pattern

N73 B

Colors used	Ships painted with this pattern
BLACK	ACR 13 MONTANA
GREY-WHITE	
#1 BLUE-GRAY	
#4 GRAY	
#1 GRAY-GREEN	

TYPE N-73
DESIGN B

PORT SIDE

COLORS

NOTE

COLORS ON PLAN ARE FOR THE PURPOSES OF MEASUREMENT ONLY ACTUAL COLORS AS PER COLOR CHART

TYPE · N 73 ·
DESIGN · B ·

STARBOARD SIDE

COLORS

NOTE

N73 B

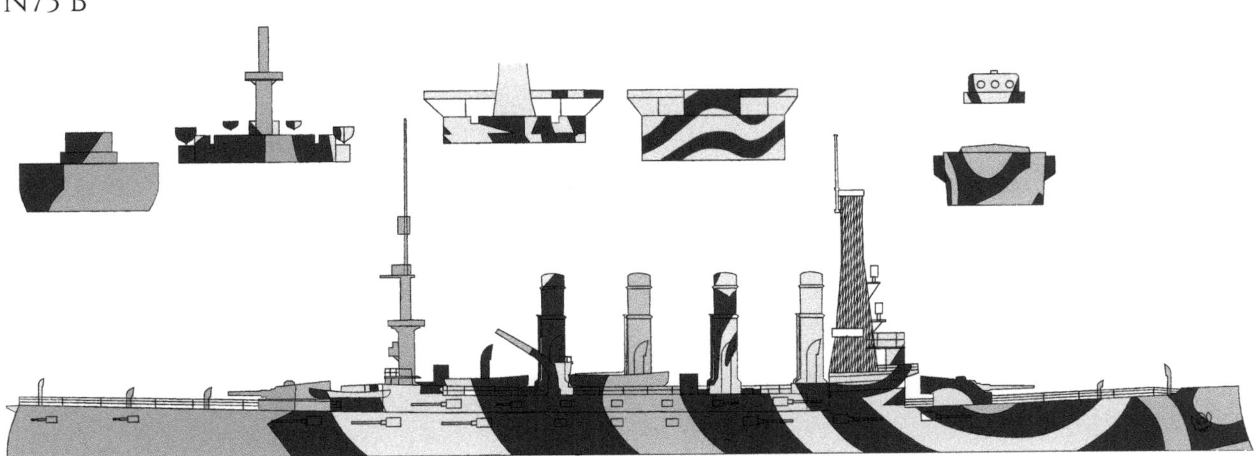

STARBOARD SIDE PATTERN

N73 B

PORT SIDE PATTERN

N73

Colors used	Ships painted with this pattern
BLACK	ACR 5 USS HUNTINGTON
OLIVE	
#1 GREY	
#2 GREY	This is an Admiralty design. The ship was later repainted in US design N73E

NARA *RG38*

N73 D

Colors used	Ships painted with this pattern
BLACK	ACR 8 FREDERICK
#1 GRAY-GREEN	
#4 GRAY	
#1 BLUE	
#3 BLUE	

TYPE N73
DESIGN D
PORT SIDE
SCALE 1/64" = 1-0 LENGTH 504'-6"
COLORS
BLACK No 4 GRAY
No 1 GRAY GREEN No 1 BLUE
No 3 BLUE
NOTE
COLORS ON PLAN ARE FOR THE PURPOSES OF MEASUREMENT ONLY. ACTUAL COLORS AS PER COLOR CHART.
U.S.S. NORTH CAROLINA

TYPE N73
DESIGN D
STARBOARD SIDE
COLORS
NOTE

N73 D

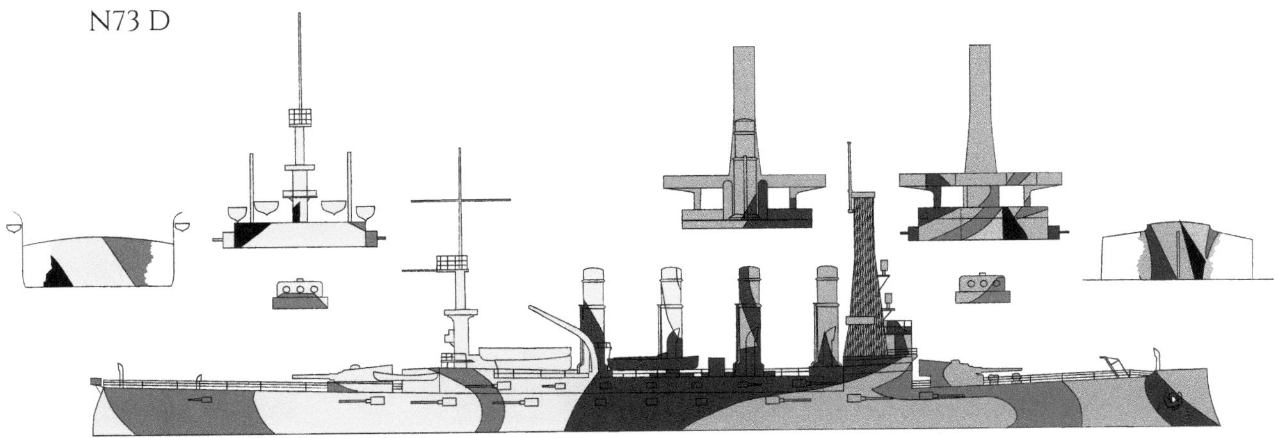

STARBOARD SIDE PATTERN

N73 D

PORT SIDE PATTERN

N 73 E

Colors used	Ships painted with this pattern
BLACK	ACR 5 HUNTINGTON
WHITE	
GREY-WHITE	
#3 BLUE	
#1 GREEN	

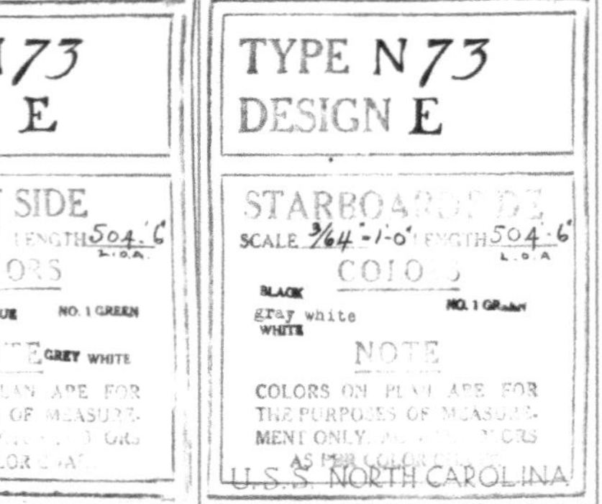

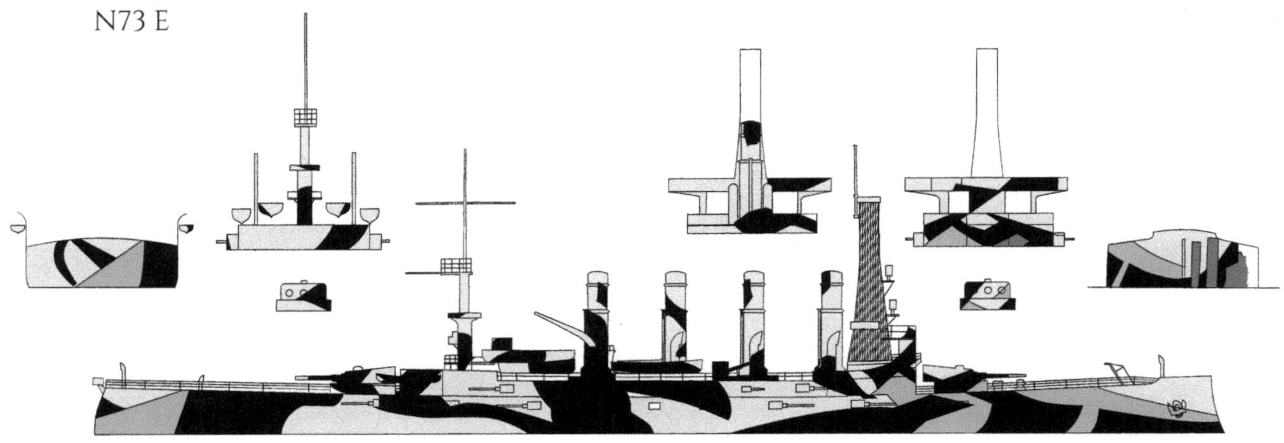

Starboard Side Pattern

N73 E

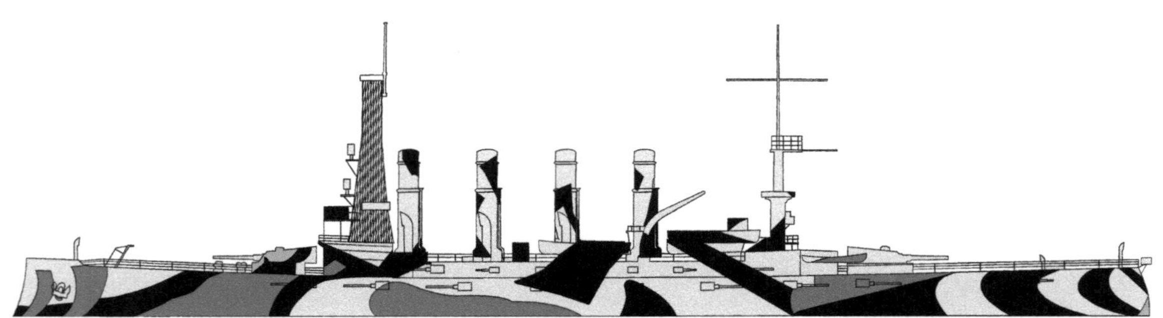

Port Side Pattern

N73 F

Colors used	Ships painted with this pattern
BLACK	ACR 11 SEATTLE
GREY-WHITE	
WHITE	
#3 BLUE	
#1 GRAY-PINK	

TYPE N 73
DESIGN F

PORT SIDE
SCALE 3/64" = 1'0" LENGTH 504' 6"
COLORS
BLACK WHITE NO. 1 GREY PINK
gray white NO. 3 BLUE
NOTE
COLORS ON PLAN ARE FOR THE PURPOSES OF MEASUREMENT ONLY. ACTUAL COLORS AS PER COLOR CHART.

TYPE N 73
DESIGN F

STARBOARD SIDE
SCALE 3/64" = 1'0" LENGTH 504' 6"
COLORS
BLACK WHITE NO. 1 GREY PINK
gray white NO. 3 BLUE
NOTE
COLORS ON PLAN ARE FOR THE PURPOSES OF MEASUREMENT ONLY. ACTUAL COLORS AS PER COLOR CHART.

N73 F

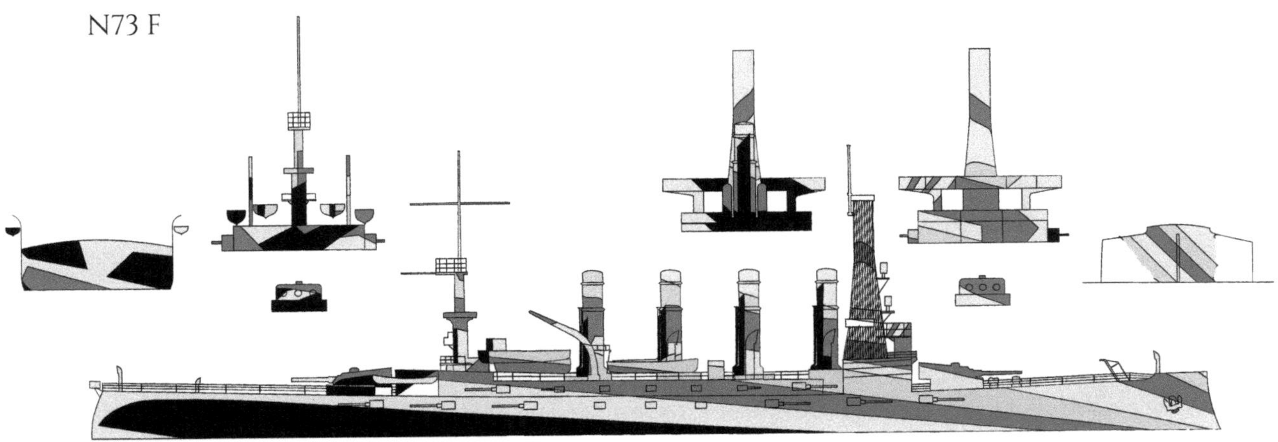

STARBOARD SIDE PATTERN

N73 F

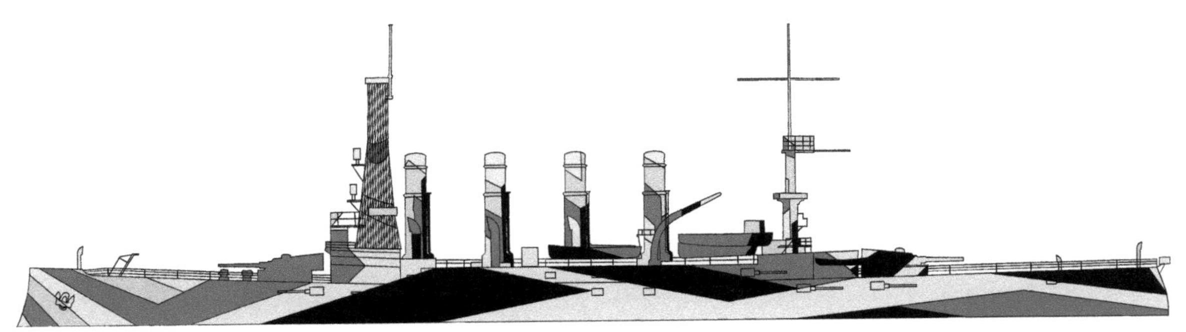

PORT SIDE PATTERN

N74 A

Colors used	Ships painted with this pattern
BLACK	AS 7 RAINBOW
WHITE	
GREY-WHITE	
#3 BLUE	
#1 BLUE	
#4 GRAY	

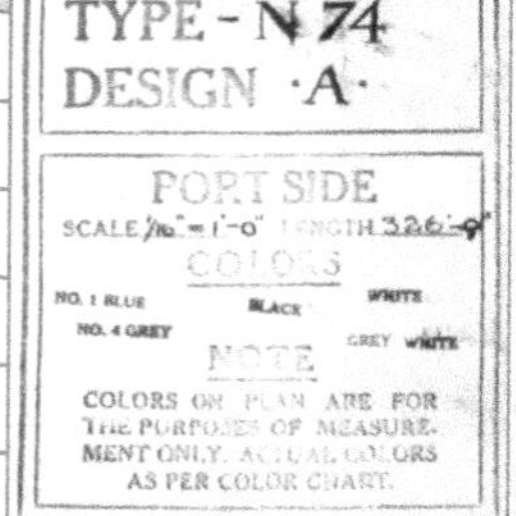

TYPE - N 74
DESIGN ·A·

PORT SIDE
SCALE 1/16" = 1'-0" LENGTH 326'-0"
COLORS
NO. 1 BLUE BLACK WHITE
NO. 4 GREY GREY WHITE
NOTE
COLORS ON PLAN ARE FOR THE PURPOSES OF MEASUREMENT ONLY. ACTUAL COLORS AS PER COLOR CHART.

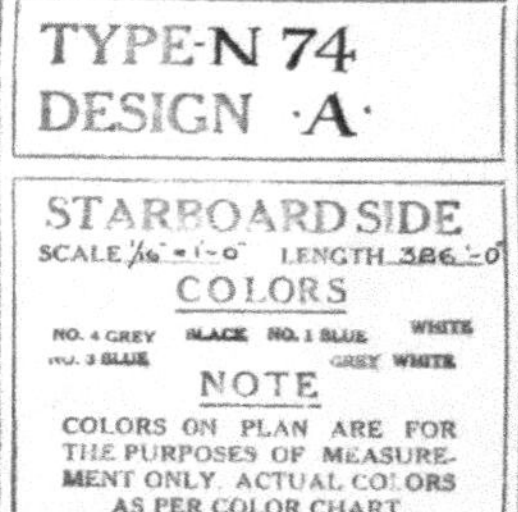

TYPE-N 74
DESIGN ·A·

STARBOARD SIDE
SCALE 1/16" = 1'-0" LENGTH 326'-0"
COLORS
NO. 4 GREY BLACK NO. 1 BLUE WHITE
NO. 3 BLUE GREY WHITE
NOTE
COLORS ON PLAN ARE FOR THE PURPOSES OF MEASUREMENT ONLY. ACTUAL COLORS AS PER COLOR CHART.

N74 A

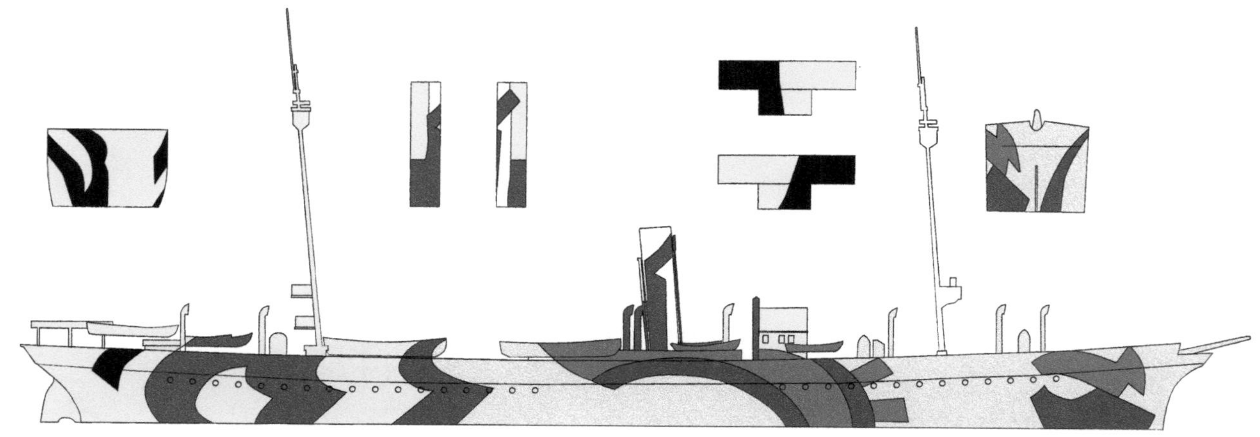

Starboard Side Pattern

N74 A

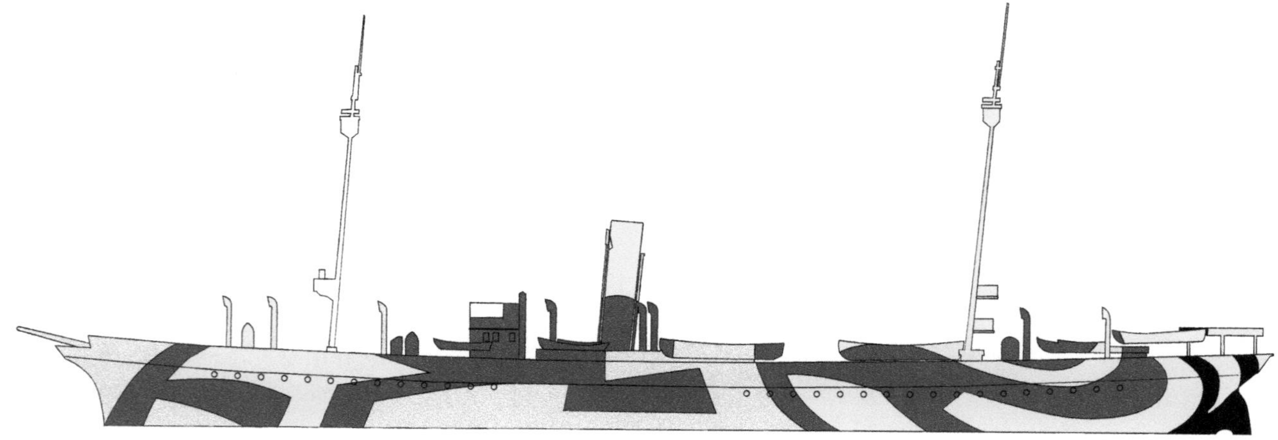

Port Side Pattern

N75 A

Colors used	Ships painted with this pattern
BLACK	C 13 MINNEAPOLIS
GREY-WHITE	
#1 BLUE	
#3 BLUE	
#4 GRAY	

TYPE N 75
DESIGN A

PORT SIDE
SCALE 1/16" = 1'0" LENGTH 415'0" LOA
COLORS
NO. 4 GREY · BLACK · NO. 1 BLUE · GREY WHITE
NOTE
COLORS ON PLAN ARE FOR THE PURPOSES OF MEASUREMENT ONLY. ACTUAL COLORS AS PER COLOR CHART.

TYPE N 75
DESIGN A

STARBOARD SIDE
SCALE 1/16" = 1'0" LENGTH 415'0" LOA
COLORS
WHITE · BLACK · NO. 4 GREY · NO. 3 BLUE · NO. 1 BLUE
NOTE
COLORS ON PLAN ARE FOR THE PURPOSES OF MEASUREMENT ONLY. ACTUAL COLORS AS PER COLOR CHART.

N75 A

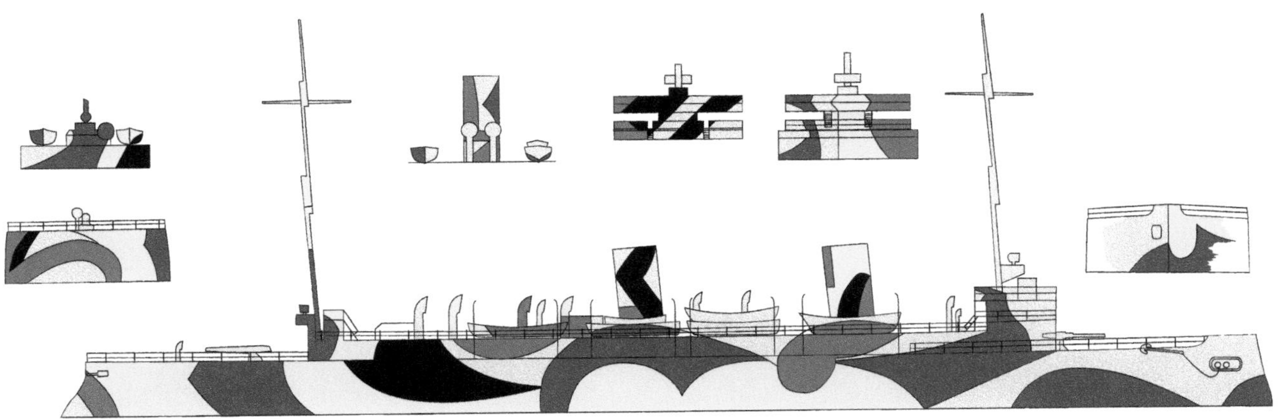

STARBOARD SIDE PATTERN

N75 A

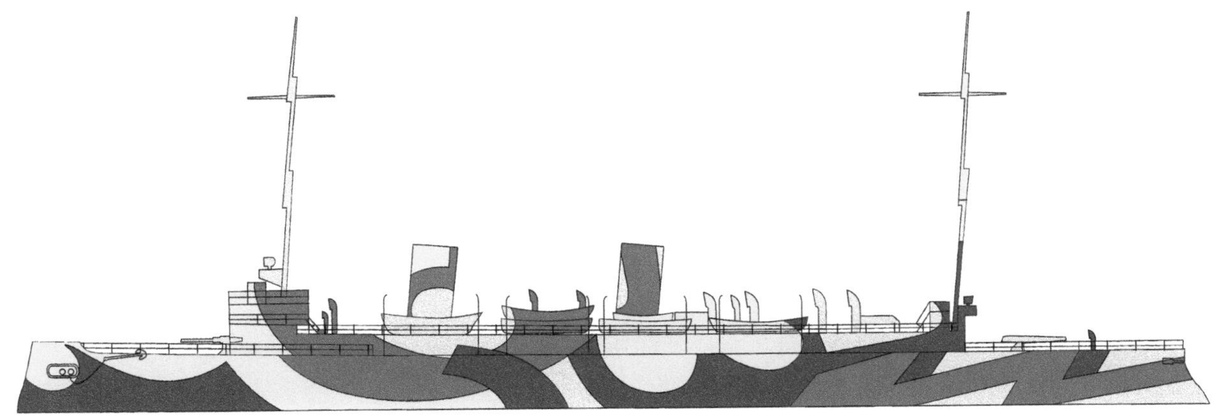

PORT SIDE PATTERN

N76-ADM

Colors used	Ships painted with this pattern
BLACK	CL 2 BIRMINGHAM
#3 BLUE	
#1 GRAY-GREEN	
#2 GRAY	This is an Admiralty design, a copy of which was found in American files
#0 BLUE-GRAY	

N76 D

STARBOARD SIDE PATTERN

N76 D

PORT SIDE PATTERN

N77 A

Colors used	Ships painted with this pattern
BLACK	IX 49 WILMETTE
#1 BLUE	
#3 BLUE	
#1 GREEN	

TYPE N77
DESIGN A
PORT SIDE
SCALE LENGTH
COLORS
BLACK NO. 1 GREEN
NO. 1 BLUE NO. 3 BLUE
NOTE
COLORS ON PLAN ARE FOR THE PURPOSES OF MEASUREMENT ONLY. ACTUAL COLORS AS PER COLOR CHART.

TYPE N77
DESIGN A
STARBOARD SIDE
SCALE LENGTH
COLORS
NO. 1 GREEN BLACK
NO. 1 BLUE NO. 3 BLUE
NOTE
COLORS ON PLAN ARE FOR THE PURPOSES OF MEASUREMENT ONLY. ACTUAL COLORS AS PER COLOR CHART.

N77 A

STARBOARD SIDE PATTERN

N77 A

PORT SIDE PATTERN

N8o A

Colors used	Ships painted with this pattern
BLACK	C 8 RALEIGH
GREY-WHITE	
#3 BLUE	
#1 GRAY-GREEN	

TYPE N 80
DESIGN A

PORT SIDE
SCALE $\frac{1}{16}$"=1'-0" LENGTH 306'-0" (B P)
COLORS
gray white NO. 1 GREY GREEN
NO. 3 BLUE BLACK
NOTE
COLORS ON PLAN ARE FOR
MEASUREMENT ONLY.
AS PER COLOR CHART.

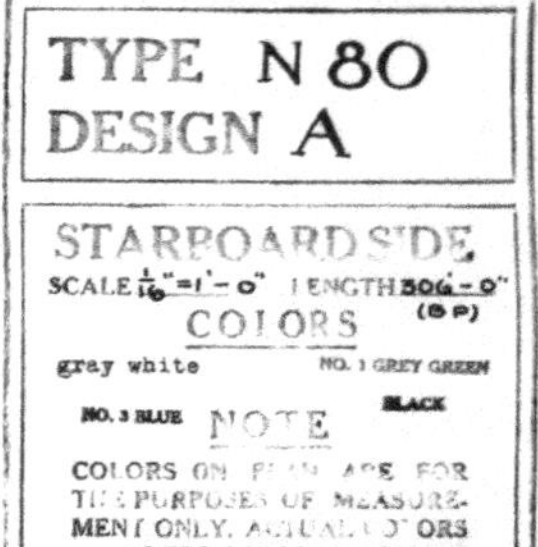

N80 A

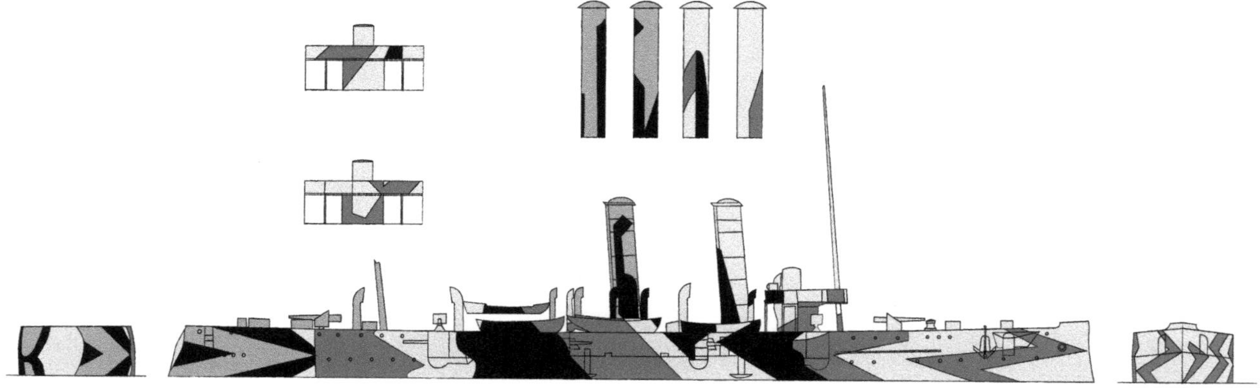

STARBOARD SIDE PATTERN

N80 A

PORT SIDE PATTERN

N8o B

Colors used	Ships painted with this pattern
BLACK	C 7 CINCINNATI
GREY-WHITE	
#4 GRAY	
#1 GREEN	

TYPE N·80
DESIGN ·B·

PORT SIDE
SCALE 1/16"-1'-0" LENGTH 306'-0"
COLORS
BLACK
gray white
NO. 1 GREEN
NO. 4 GREY
NOTE
COLORS ON PLAN ARE FOR THE PURPOSES OF MEASURE- MENT [illegible] ORS [illegible]

TYPE N80
DESIGN B

STARBOARD SIDE
SCALE 1/16"-1'0" LENGTH 306'-0"
COLORS
gray white
GREEN
NO. 4 [illegible]
BLACK
NOTE
COLORS ON PLAN ARE FOR THE PURPOSES OF MEASURE- MENT ONLY. ACTUAL COLORS AS PER COLOR CHART.

N80 B

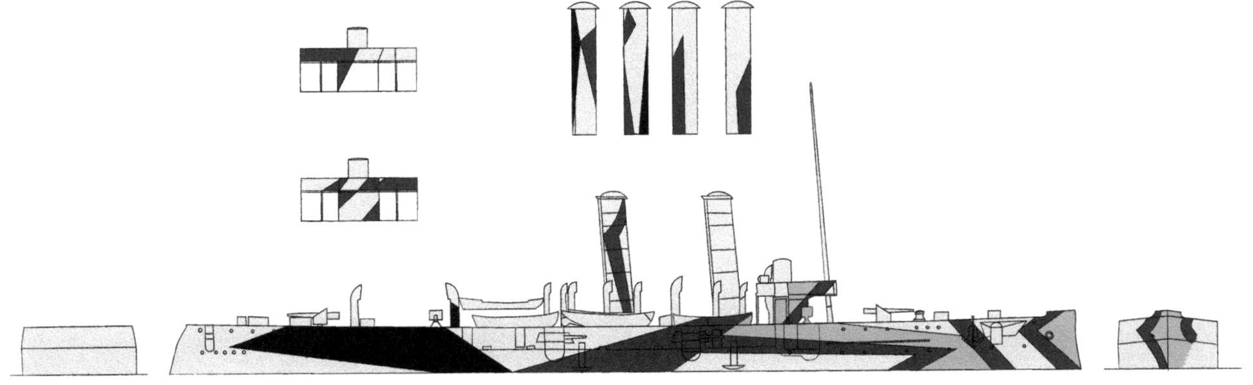

Starboard Side Pattern

N80 B

Port Side Pattern

N86 A

Colors used	Ships painted with this pattern
BLACK	PG 24 DOLPHIN
GREY-WHITE	
#1 GREEN	

TYPE N·86
DESIGN A

PORT SIDE
SCALE 3/32"=1'0" LENGTH 240'0"
COLORS
NOTE
COLORS ON PLAN ARE FOR THE PURPOSES OF MEASUREMENT ONLY. ACTUAL COLORS AS PER COLOR CHART.

TYPE N·86
DESIGN A

STARBOARD SIDE
SCALE 3/32"=1'0" LENGTH 240'0"
COLORS
gray white NO. 1 GREEN BLACK
NOTE
COLORS ON PLAN ARE FOR THE PURPOSES OF MEASUREMENT ONLY. ACTUAL COLORS AS PER COLOR CHART.

N86 A

Starboard Side Pattern

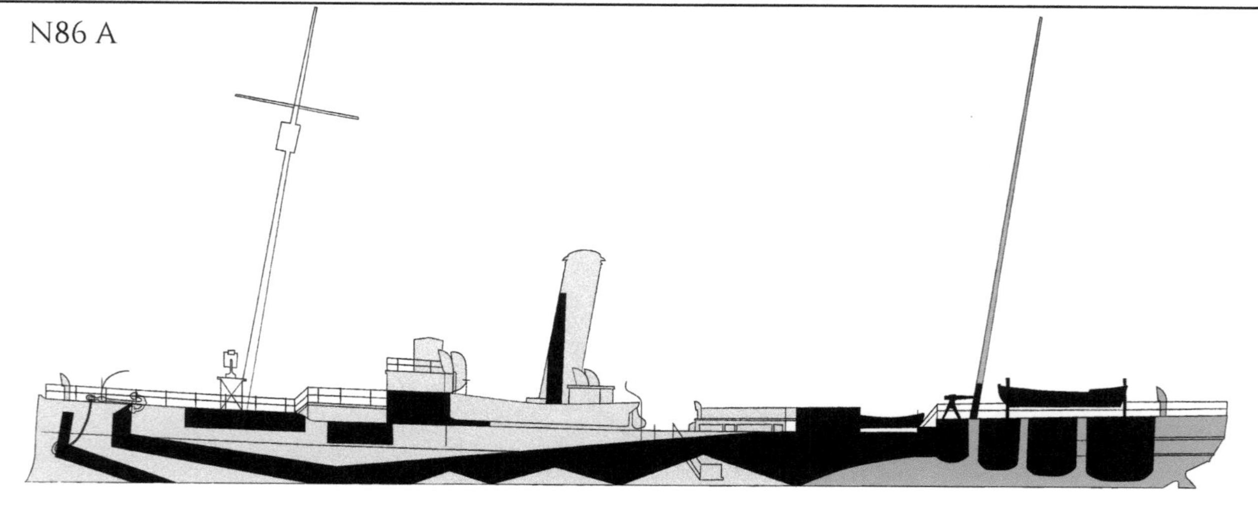

Port Side Pattern

N87 A

Colors used	Ships painted with this pattern
BLACK	ID 2527 CITY OF SOUTH HAVEN
GREY-WHITE	
#1 BLUE-GRAY	

TYPE N87
DESIGN A
PORT SIDE
SCALE [illegible] 1'-0" LENGTH 256'-0"
COLORS
NO. 1 BLUE GREY gray white
BLACK
NOTE
COLORS ON PLAN ARE FOR THE PURPOSES OF MEASUREMENT ONLY. ACTUAL COLORS AS PER COLOR CHART

TYPE N87
DESIGN A
STARBOARD SIDE
SCALE [illegible] 1'-0" LENGTH 256'-0"
COLORS
gray white NO. 1 BLUE GREY
BLACK
NOTE
COLORS ON PLAN ARE FOR THE PURPOSES OF MEASUREMENT ONLY. ACTUAL COLORS AS PER COLOR CHART

N87 A

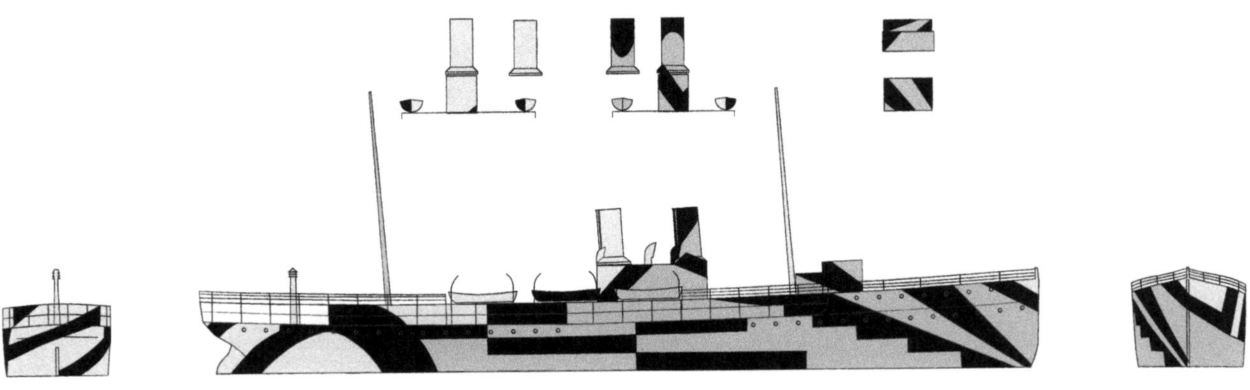

Starboard Side Pattern

N87 A

Port Side Pattern

N88 A

Colors used	Ships painted with this pattern
BLACK	ID 2432 BLUE RIDGE
GREY-WHITE	
#3 BLUE	
#1 BLUE-GRAY	

TYPE N·88
DESIGN A
PORT SIDE
SCALE 1/16"=1'0" LENGTH 270'0"
COLORS
NO. 3 BLUE BLACK
NO. 1 BLUE GREY gray white
NOTE
COLORS ON PLAN ARE FOR THE PURPOSES OF MEASUREMENT ONLY. ACTUAL COLORS AS PER COLOR CHART.

TYPE N·88
DESIGN A
STARBOARD SIDE
SCALE 1/16"=1'0" LENGTH 270'0"
COLORS
NO. 3 BLUE BLACK
gray white NO. 1 BLUE GREY
NOTE
COLORS ON PLAN ARE FOR THE PURPOSES OF MEASUREMENT ONLY. ACTUAL COLORS AS PER COLOR CHART.

N88 A

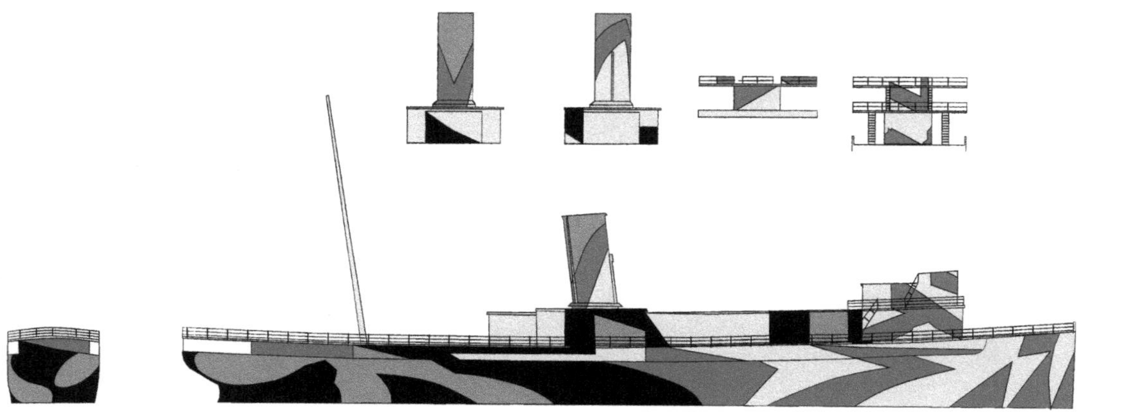

Starboard Side Pattern

N88 A

Port Side Pattern

N96 A

Colors used	Ships painted with this pattern
BLACK	AS 1 FULTON
GREY-WHITE	
#3 BLUE	
#1 BLUE-GRAY	

TYPE N. 96
DESIGN A.
PORT SIDE
SCALE 1/8":1'-0" LENGTH 226'-6"
COLORS
NOTE
COLORS ON PLAN ARE FOR THE PURPOSES OF MEASUREMENT ONLY. ACTUAL COLORS AS PER COLOR CHART.

TYPE N 96
DESIGN A
NO. 3 BLUE BLACK
NO. 1 BLUE GREY gray white

N96 A

Starboard Side Pattern

N96 A

Port Side Pattern

N UNKNOWN

Colors used	Ships painted with this pattern
BLACK	AM-26 USS RAIL
GREY-WHITE	
#1 BLUE-GRAY	
#3 BLUE	

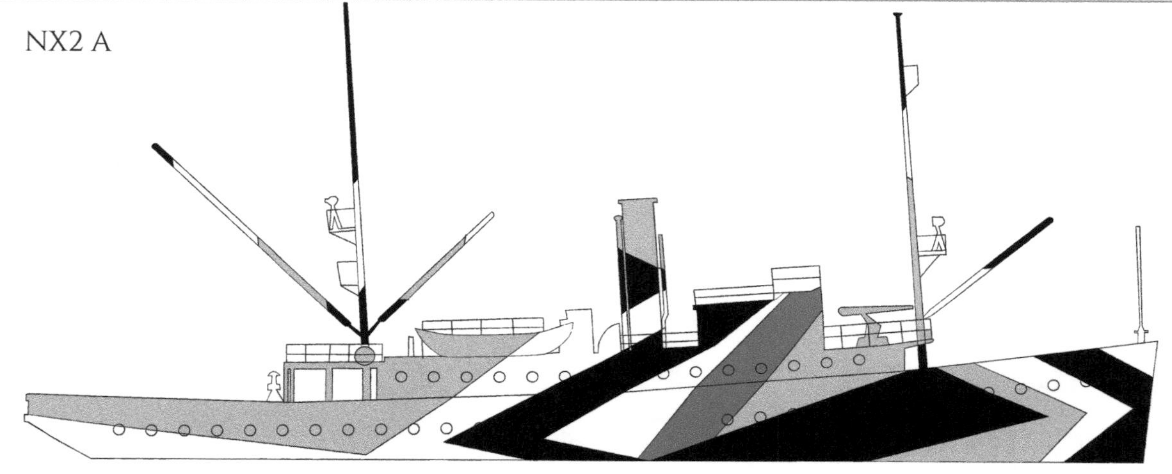

STARBOARD SIDE PATTERN

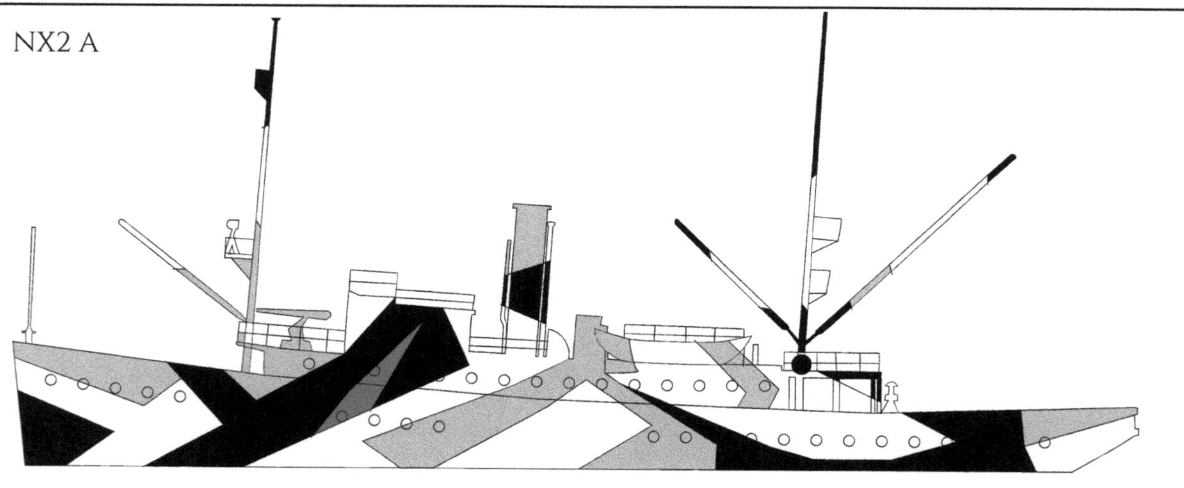

PORT SIDE PATTERN

NORFOLK-WATSON

Colors used	Ships painted with this pattern
BLACK	BB 14 NEBRASKA
WHITE	C 9 ANNISTON
GRAY	No patterns in Bureau files

NORFOLK-WATSON 2

GEOMETRIC DESIGNS COULD BE APLIED TO EITHER PORT OR STARBOARD

NORFOLK-WATSON 3

Nebraska port USNIP *Jul 1971* *Anniston port* *NH100399*

Nebraska starboard *NH101208*

Anniston starboard *NH57227"*

RN DESIGNS

Colors used	Ships painted with this pattern
BLACK	ID NONE SANTEE
#3 BLUE	SP 575 CYTHERA
#1 BLUE	SP 130 PIQUA
#1 GREY	ID 1326 LEVIATHAN

The ships listed are just some of the ones that received admiralty Patterns when serving overseas. The colors listed are for LEVIATHAN only. Other ships are shown in photographs or ina picture of a model (SANTEE). RN colors varied considerably. The only ones I've listed are ones for which I found documentation

Leviathan

Santee model

Leviathan

Santee model

Perkins model

Walke model

T1 A

Colors used	Ships painted with this pattern
BLACK	ID 2925 AMPETCO
WHITE	NONE GEORGE W BARNES
#3 BLUE	ID 1532 STANDARD ARROW
#1 BLUE-GRAY	ID 2703 JOHN M CONNOLEY

TYPE 1
DESIGN A
PORT SIDE
SCALE 1/16" 1'-0 LENGTH 500-0
COLORS
WHITE NO. 3 BLUE
BLACK NO. 1 BLUE GREY
NOTE
COLORS ON PLAN ARE FOR THE PURPOSES OF MEASUREMENT ONLY — ACTUAL COLORS AS PER COLOR CHART

TYPE 1
DESIGN A
STARBOARD SIDE
SCALE 1/16" 1'-0 LENGTH 500-0
COLORS
WHITE NO. 3 BLUE
BLACK NO. 1 BLUE GREY
NOTE
COLORS ON PLAN ARE FOR THE PURPOSES OF MEASUREMENT ONLY — ACTUAL COLORS AS PER COLOR CHART

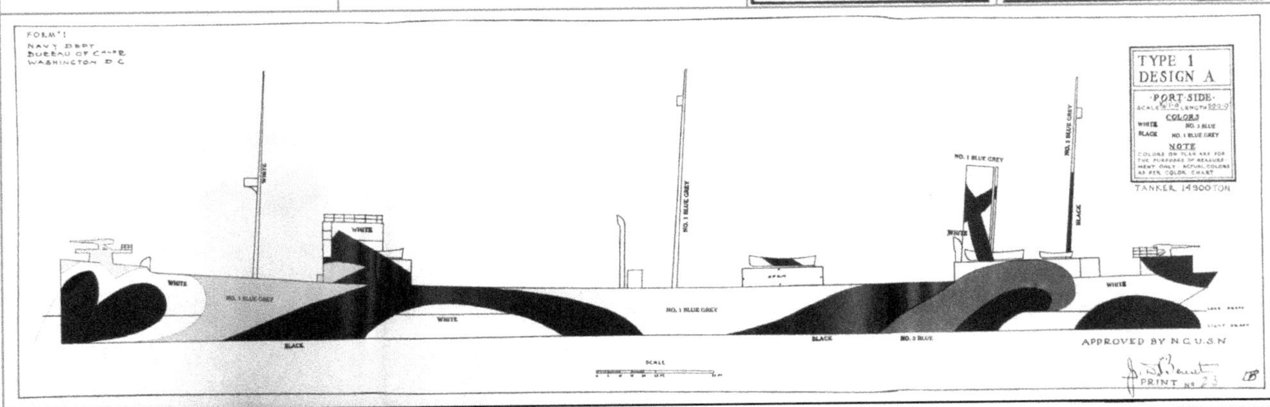

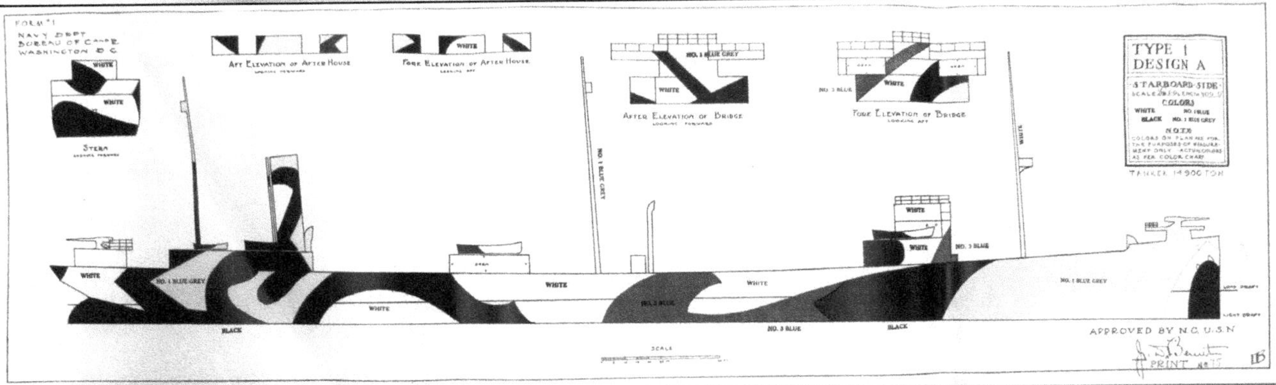

T1 B

Colors used	Ships painted with this pattern
BLACK	ID 3131 ABSECON
#1 BLUE-GRAY	ID 3344 CALALA

TYPE 1
DESIGN · B
·PORT·SIDE·
SCALE ——— LENGTH 435'
COLORS
WHITE NO. 1 BLUE GREY
BLACK
NOTE
COLORS ON PLAN ARE FOR THE PURPOSES OF MEASUREMENT ONLY · ACTUAL COLORS AS PER COLOR CHART

TYPE 1
DESIGN · B
·STARBOARD·SIDE·
SCALE ——— LENGTH 435'
COLORS
WHITE NO. 1 BLUE GREY
BLACK
NOTE
COLORS ON PLAN ARE FOR THE PURPOSES OF MEASUREMENT ONLY · ACTUAL COLORS AS PER COLOR CHART

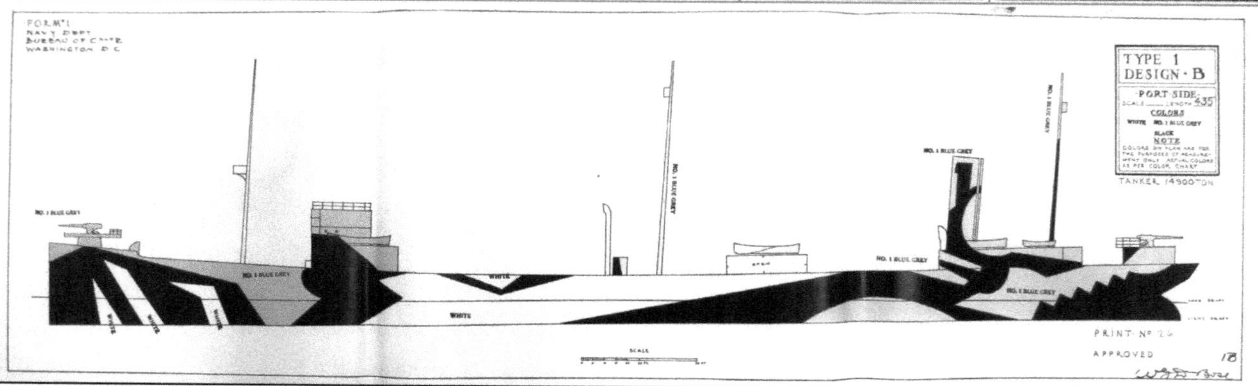

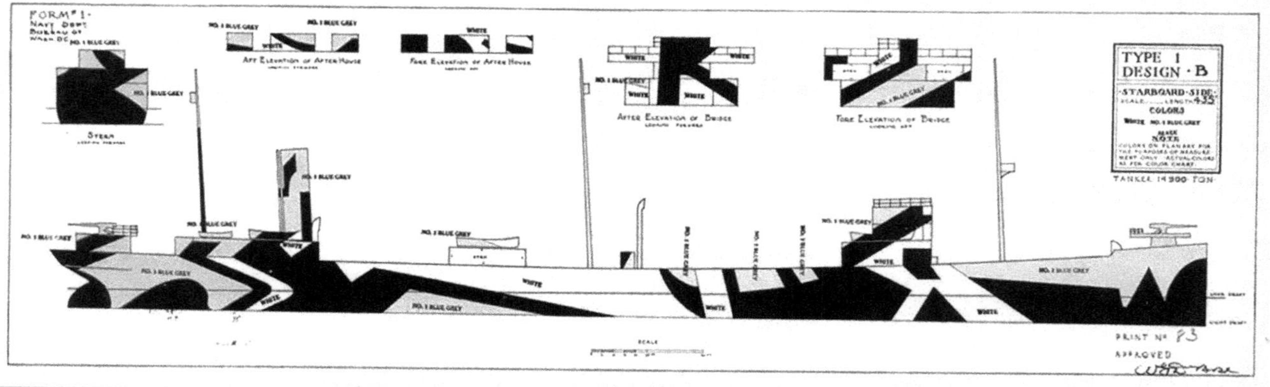

T1 D

Colors used	Ships painted with this pattern
BLACK	ID 1543 ARDMORE
GREY-WHITE	
#3 BLUE	
#2 BLUE-GRAY	

TYPE 1
DESIGN D

PORT SIDE
SCALE 3/64"=1'0" LENGTH 500-0
COLORS
GRAY WHITE NO. 3 BLUE
NO. 2 BLUE GRAY BLACK
NOTE
COLORS ON PLAN ARE FOR THE PURPOSES OF MEASUREMENT ONLY — ACTUAL COLORS AS PER COLOR CHART

TYPE 1
DESIGN D

STARBOARD SIDE
SCALE 3/64"=1'0" LENGTH 500-0
COLORS
BLACK NO. 2 BLUE GRAY
GRAY WHITE NO. 3 BLUE
NOTE
COLORS ON PLAN ARE FOR THE PURPOSES OF MEASUREMENT ONLY — ACTUAL COLORS AS PER COLOR CHART

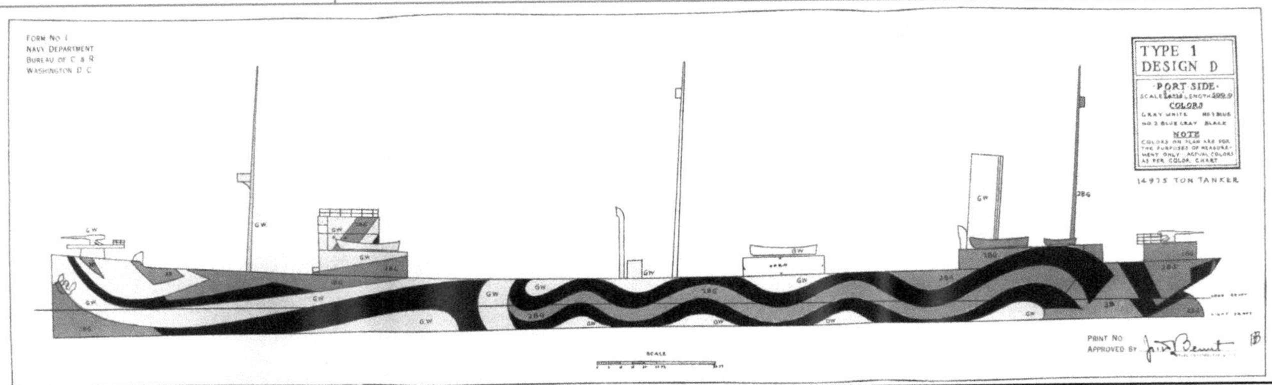

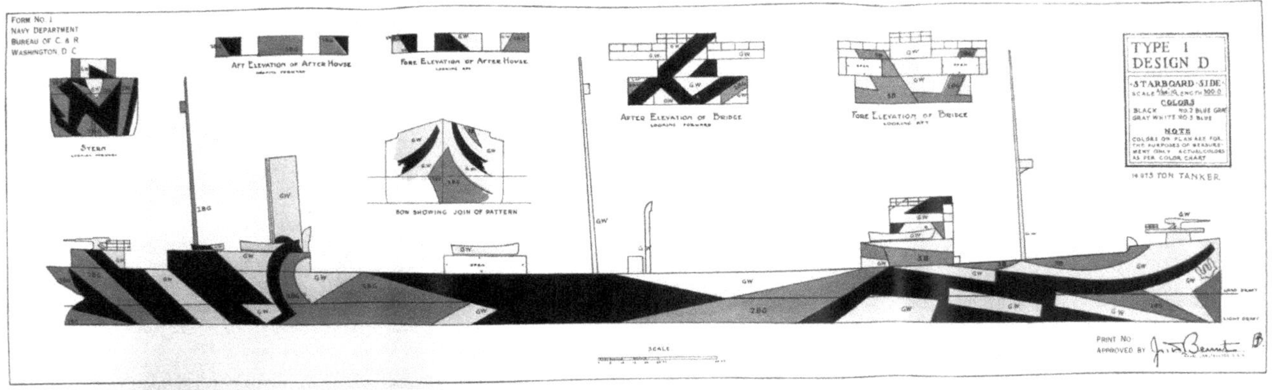

T2 A

Colors used	Ships painted with this pattern
BLACK	ID 1791 LAKE CHAMPLAIN
WHITE	ID 3597 LAKE CLEAR
#3 BLUE	ID 2915 LAKE ARTHUR
#1 BLUE-GRAY	ID 1792 LAKE SHORE (T)

TYPE 2
DESIGN·A
·PORT·SIDE·
SCALE [illegible] LENGTH [illegible]
COLORS
WHITE NO. 1 BLUE GREY
NO. 3 BLUE BLACK
NOTE
COLORS ON PLAN ARE FOR THE PURPOSES OF MEASUREMENT ONLY – ACTUAL COLORS AS PER COLOR CHART

TYPE 2
DESIGN·A
·STARBOARD·SIDE·
SCALE [illegible] LENGTH [illegible]
COLORS
BLACK NO. 1 BLUE GREY
NO. 3 BLUE WHITE
NOTE
COLORS ON PLAN ARE FOR THE PURPOSES OF MEASUREMENT ONLY ACTUAL COLORS AS PER COLOR CHART

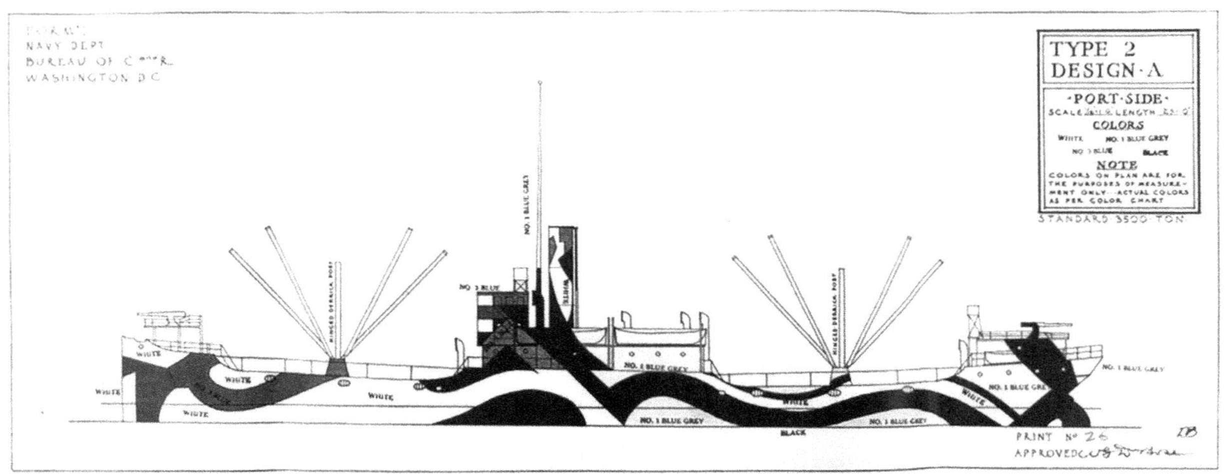

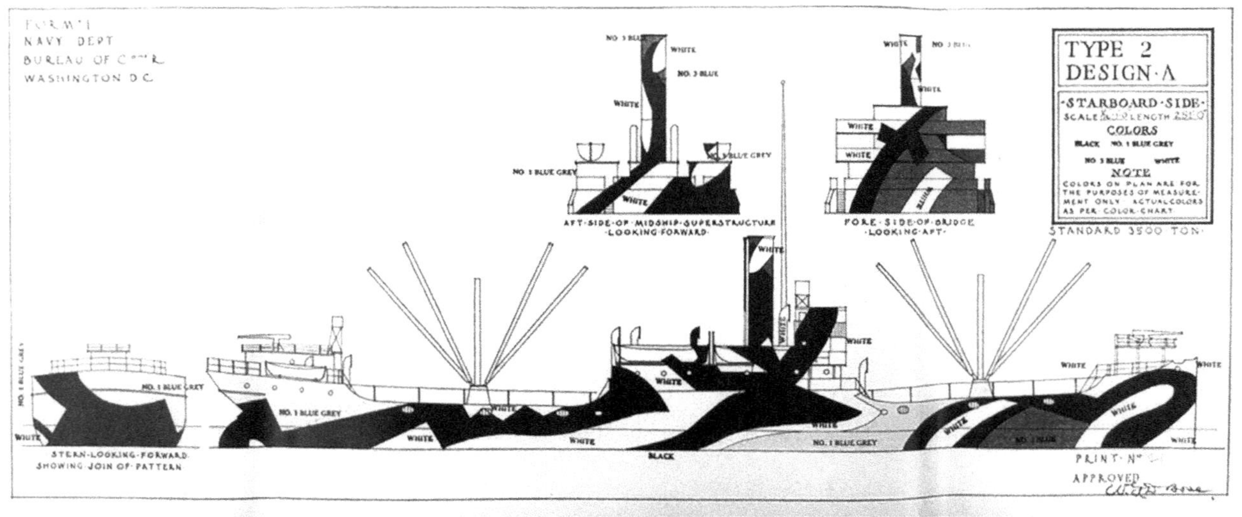

T2 B

Colors used	Ships painted with this pattern
BLACK	ID NONE LAKE PORTAGE
WHITE	ID 2211 BELLA
#3 BLUE	ID 2906 LAKE PEWAUKEE
#1 BLUE-GRAY	ID 2997 LAKE WORTH

TYPE 2
DESIGN·B

·PORT·SIDE·
SCALE LENGTH 251
COLORS
WHITE NO. 1 BLUE GREY
NO. 3 BLUE BLACK
NOTE
COLORS ON PLAN ARE FOR THE PURPOSES OF MEASUREMENT ONLY···ACTUAL COLORS AS PER COLOR CHART·

TYPE 2
DESIGN·B

·STARBOARD·SIDE·
SCALE LENGTH 251
COLORS
WHITE NO. 1 BLUE GREY
NO. 3 BLUE BLACK
NOTE
COLORS ON PLAN ARE FOR THE PURPOSES OF MEASUREMENT ONLY ACTUAL COLORS AS PER COLOR CHART·

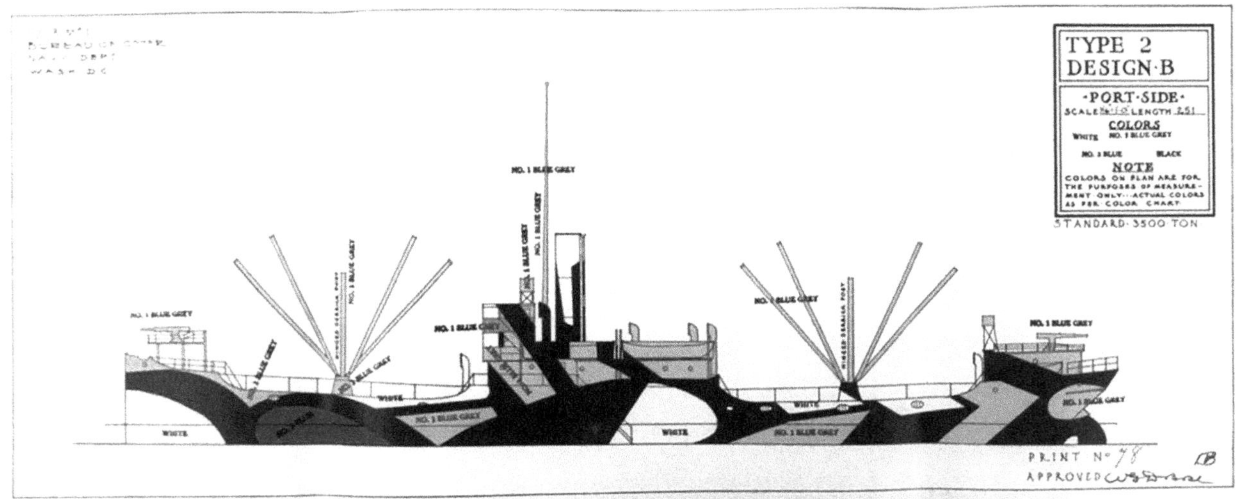

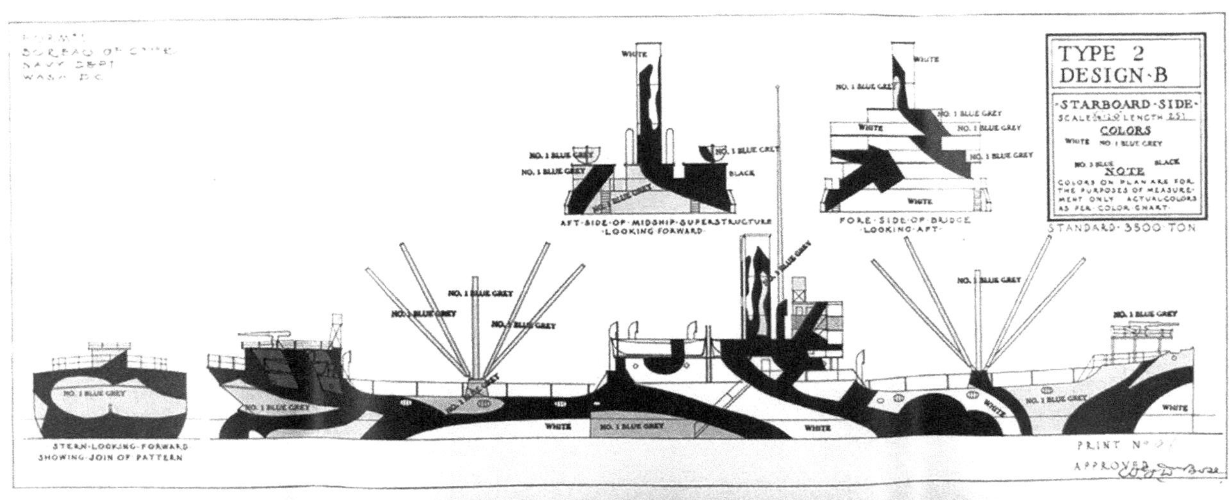

T2 C

Colors used	Ships painted with this pattern
BLACK	ID 3765A LAKE LARGA
WHITE	NONE LAKE WOOD
#3 BLUE	NONE NICKERIE
#1 BLUE-GRAY	ID 1616 PLIEDES (T)

TYPE 2 DESIGN·C
·PORT·SIDE·
SCALE 1/8"-1'-0" LENGTH 251
COLORS
NO. 3 BLUE, WHITE, NO. 1 BLUE GREY, BLACK
NOTE
COLORS ON PLAN ARE FOR THE PURPOSES OF MEASUREMENT ONLY...ACTUAL COLORS AS PER COLOR CHART.

TYPE 2 DESIGN·C
·STARBOARD·SIDE·
SCALE 1/8"-1'-0" LENGTH 251
COLORS
BLACK, NO. 1 BLUE GREY, NO. 3 BLUE, WHITE
NOTE
COLORS ON PLAN ARE FOR THE PURPOSES OF MEASUREMENT ONLY. ACTUAL COLORS AS PER COLOR CHART.

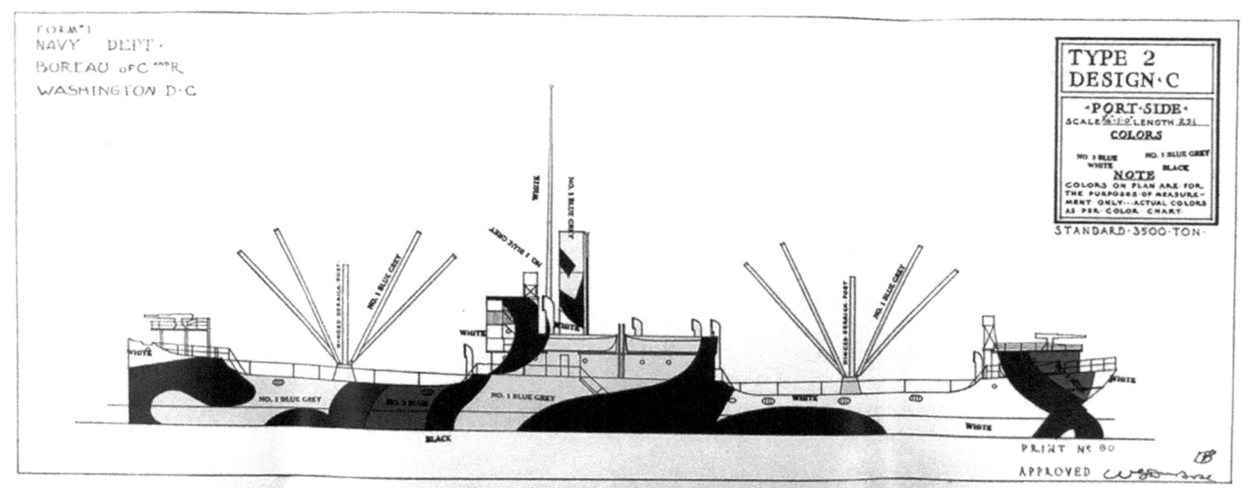

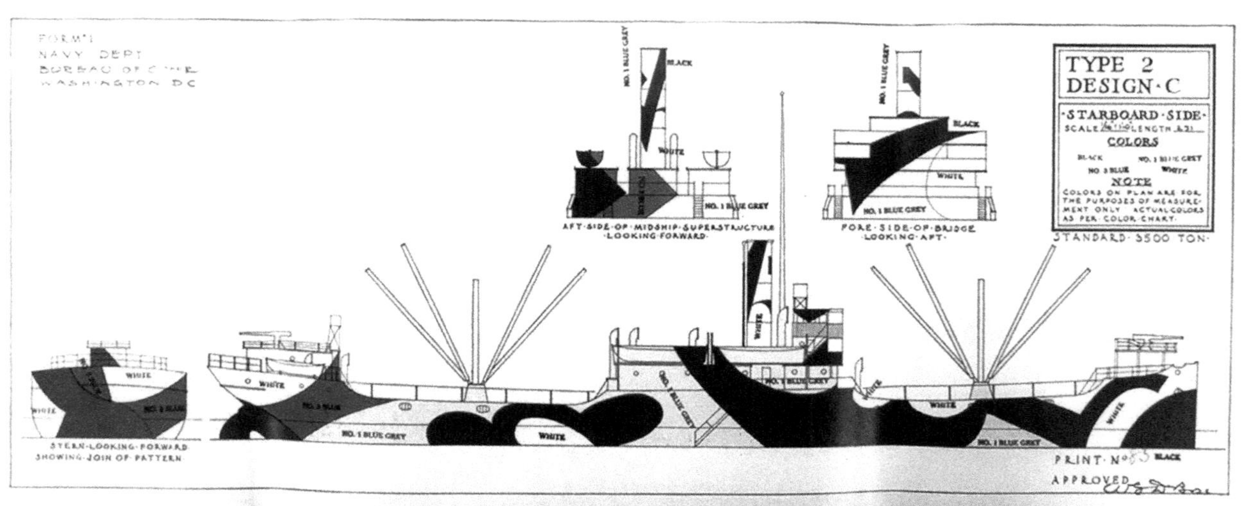

T2 D

Colors used	Ships painted with this pattern
BLACK	ID 4099 LAKE LESA
WHITE	ID 4410C LAKE HARNEY
#3 BLUE	ID 2036 MANTA
#1 BLUE-GRAY	ID 4358 LAKE CAPENS

TYPE - 2
DESIGN - D
PORT SIDE
SCALE 1/16"=1'0" LENGTH 251'0"
COLORS
BLACK NO 1 BLUE GREY
WHITE NO 3 BLUE
NOTE
COLORS ON PLAN ARE FOR THE PURPOSES OF MEASUREMENT ONLY
ACTUAL COLORS AS PER COLOR CHART

TYPE - 2
DESIGN - D
STARBOARD SIDE
SCALE 1/16"=1'0" LENGTH 251'0"
COLORS
BLACK NO 1 BLUE GREY
WHITE NO 3 BLUE
NOTE
COLORS ON PLAN ARE FOR THE PURPOSES OF MEASUREMENT ONLY
ACTUAL COLORS AS PER COLOR CHART

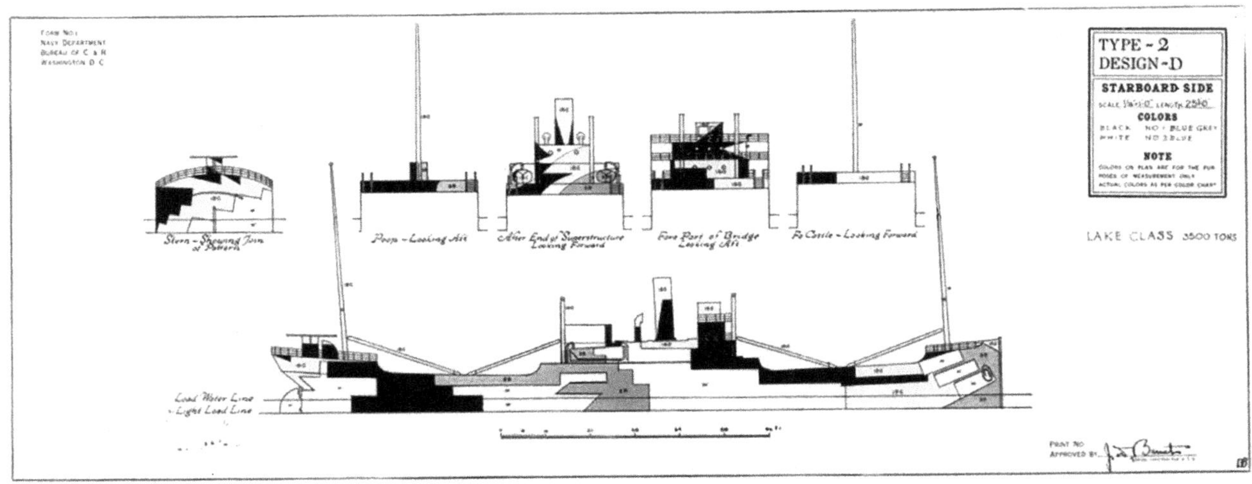

T2 E

Colors used	Ships painted with this pattern
BLACK	ID 2521 KRALINGEN
WHITE	ID 3230 WESTGAMBO
#3 BLUE	ID 4210 WESTERN STAR
#1 BLUE-GRAY	ID 4267 LAKE PACHUTA
	ID 1648 CHOCTAW (T)

TYPE 2
DESIGN E
PORT SIDE
SCALE 1/16"=1'0" LENGTH 251'0"
COLORS
BLACK NO 1 BLUE GREY
WHITE NO 3 BLUE
NOTE
COLORS ON PLAN ARE FOR THE PURPOSES OF MEASUREMENT ONLY
ACTUAL COLORS AS PER COLOR CHART

TYPE 2
DESIGN E
STARBOARD SIDE
SCALE 1/16"=1'0" LENGTH 251'0"
COLORS
BLACK NO 1 BLUE GREY
WHITE NO 3 BLUE
NOTE
COLORS ON PLAN ARE FOR THE PURPOSES OF MEASUREMENT ONLY
ACTUAL COLORS AS PER COLOR CHART

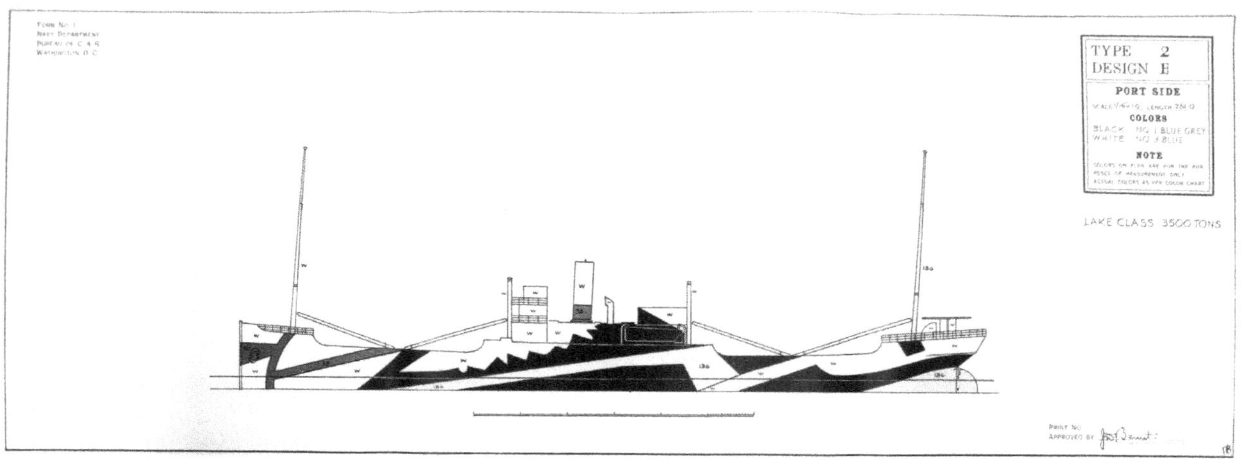

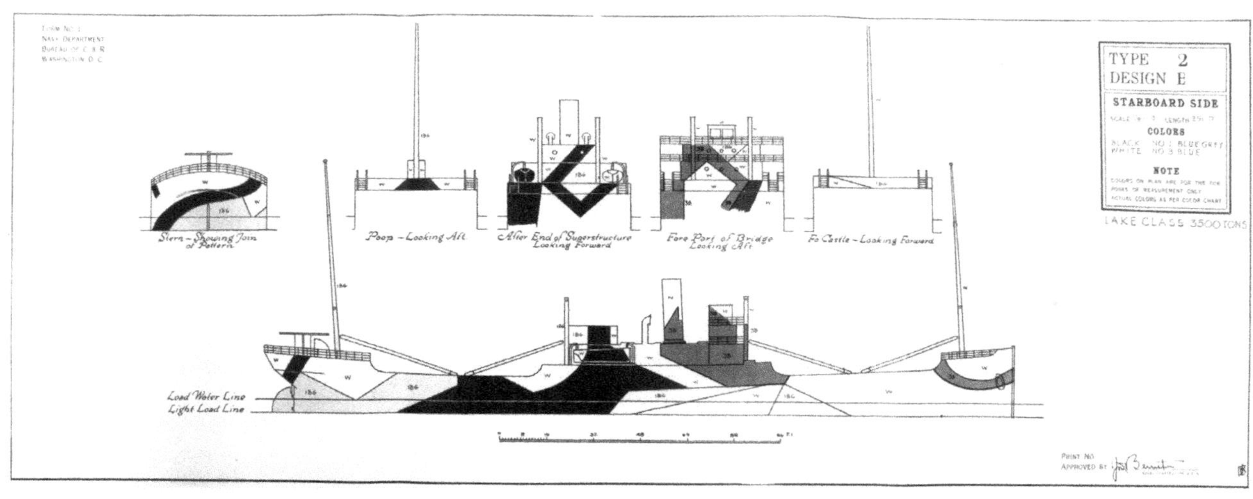

T2 F

Colors used	Ships painted with this pattern
BLACK	ID 2467 TRITON
WHITE	ID 2190 LAKE ERIE
#3 BLUE	ID 2995 LAKE SUPERIOR
#1 BLUE-GRAY	ID 4428 LAKE DARAGA

TYPE 2
DESIGN F
·PORT·SIDE·
SCALE 1/16"=1'-0" LENGTH 251'-0"
COLORS
BLACK NO. 1 BLUE GREY
WHITE NO. 3 BLUE
NOTE
COLORS ON PLAN ARE FOR THE PURPOSES OF MEASUREMENT ONLY... ACTUAL COLORS AS PER COLOR CHART

TYPE 2
DESIGN F
·STARBOARD·SIDE·
SCALE 1/16"=1'-0" LENGTH 251'-0"
COLORS
BLACK NO. 1 BLUE GREY
WHITE NO. 3 BLUE
NOTE
COLORS ON PLAN ARE FOR THE PURPOSES OF MEASUREMENT ONLY... ACTUAL COLORS AS PER COLOR CHART

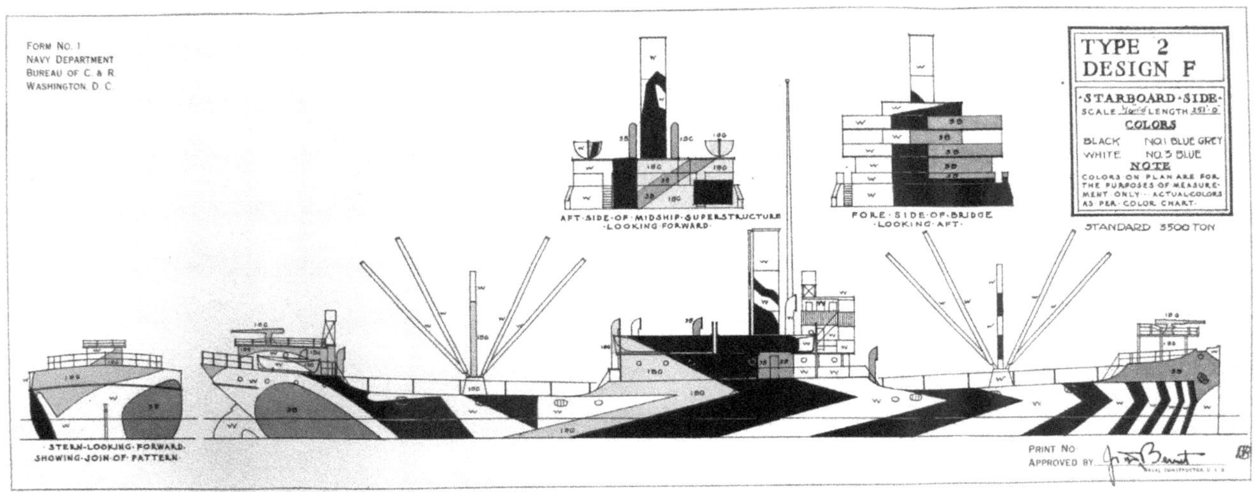

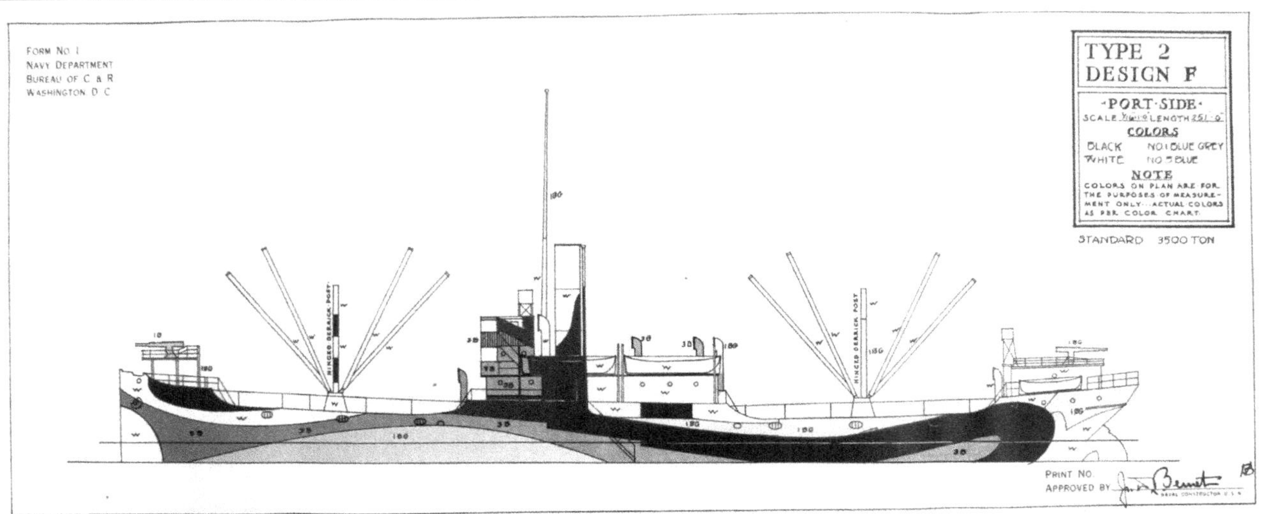

T2 G

Colors used	Ships painted with this pattern
BLACK	ID NONE ANDRA
WHITE	ID 4094A LAKE BLEDSOE
#3 BLUE	ID NONE LAKE BORGNE
#1 BLUE-GRAY	ID 4410G LAKE WIMICO

TYPE 2
DESIGN G

·PORT·SIDE·
SCALE 1/16"=1'0" LENGTH 251'-0"
COLORS
BLACK NO 1 BLUE GREY
WHITE NO 3 BLUE
NOTE
COLORS ON PLAN ARE FOR THE PURPOSES OF MEASUREMENT ONLY···ACTUAL COLORS AS PER COLOR CHART·

TYPE 2
DESIGN G

·STARBOARD·SIDE·
SCALE 1/16"=1'0" LENGTH 251'-0"
COLORS
BLACK NO 1 BLUE GREY
WHITE NO 3 BLUE
NOTE
COLORS ON PLAN ARE FOR THE PURPOSES OF MEASUREMENT ONLY · ACTUAL COLORS AS PER COLOR CHART·

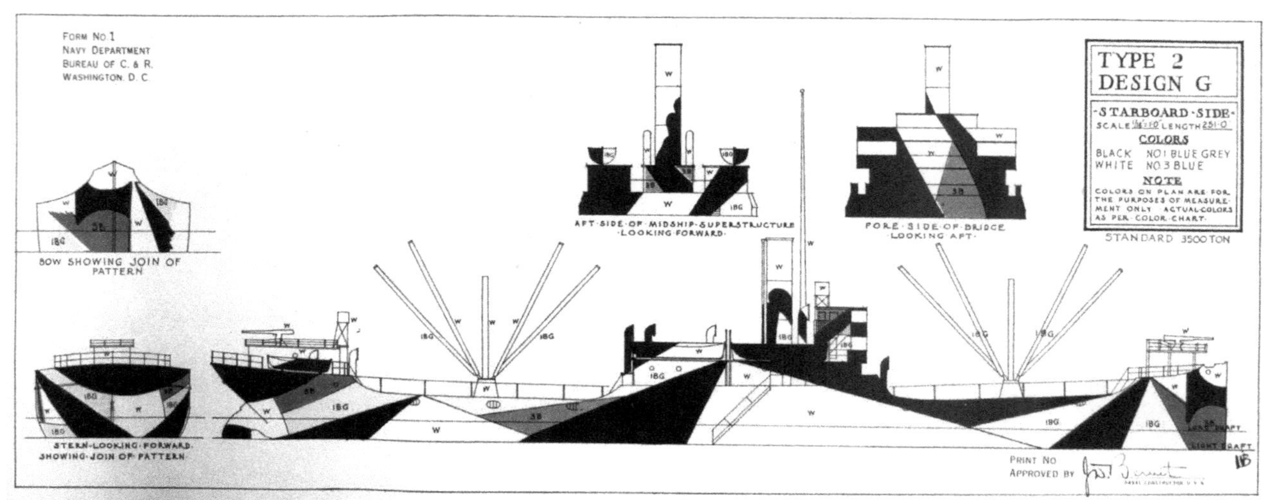

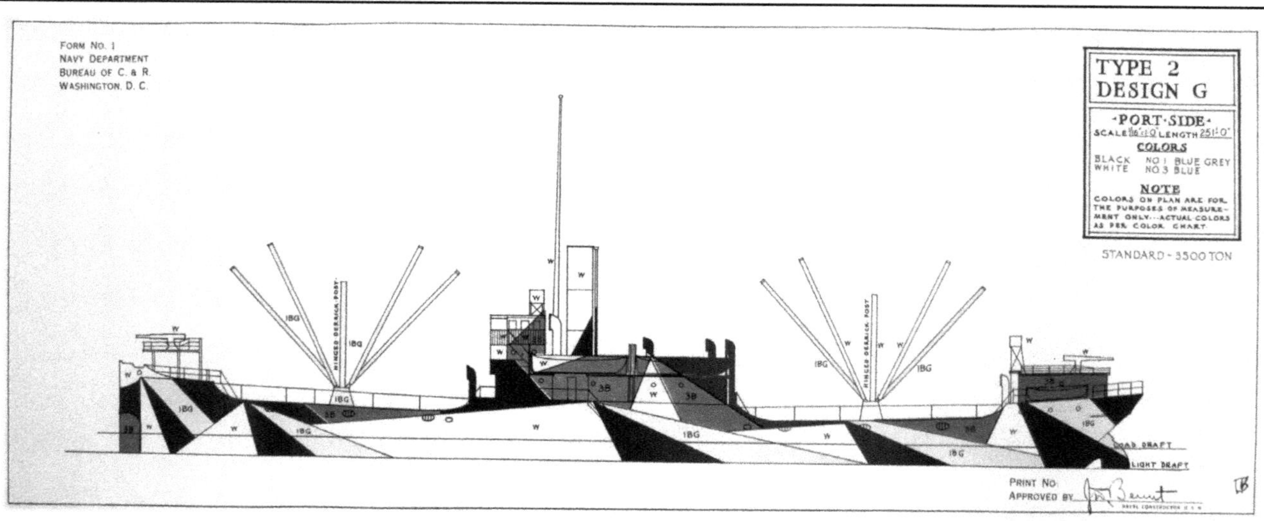

T2 H

Colors used	Ships painted with this pattern
BLACK	ID NONE BEDMINSTIR
WHITE	ID3369 ALVADO
#3 BLUE	ID 4311G LAKE OSWEYO
#1 GRAY	ID 2125 LAKE PEPIN (T)

TYPE 2
DESIGN H

·PORT·SIDE·
SCALE 1/16"=1'0" LENGTH 251'0"
COLORS
BLACK NO. 1 BLUE GREY
WHITE NO. 3 BLUE
NOTE
COLORS ON PLAN ARE FOR THE PURPOSES OF MEASUREMENT ONLY ... ACTUAL COLORS AS PER COLOR CHART.

TYPE 2
DESIGN H

·STARBOARD·SIDE·
SCALE 1/16"=1'0" LENGTH 251'0"
COLORS
BLACK NO 1 BLUE GREY
WHITE NO 3 BLUE
NOTE
COLORS ON PLAN ARE FOR THE PURPOSES OF MEASUREMENT ONLY · ACTUAL COLORS AS PER COLOR CHART.

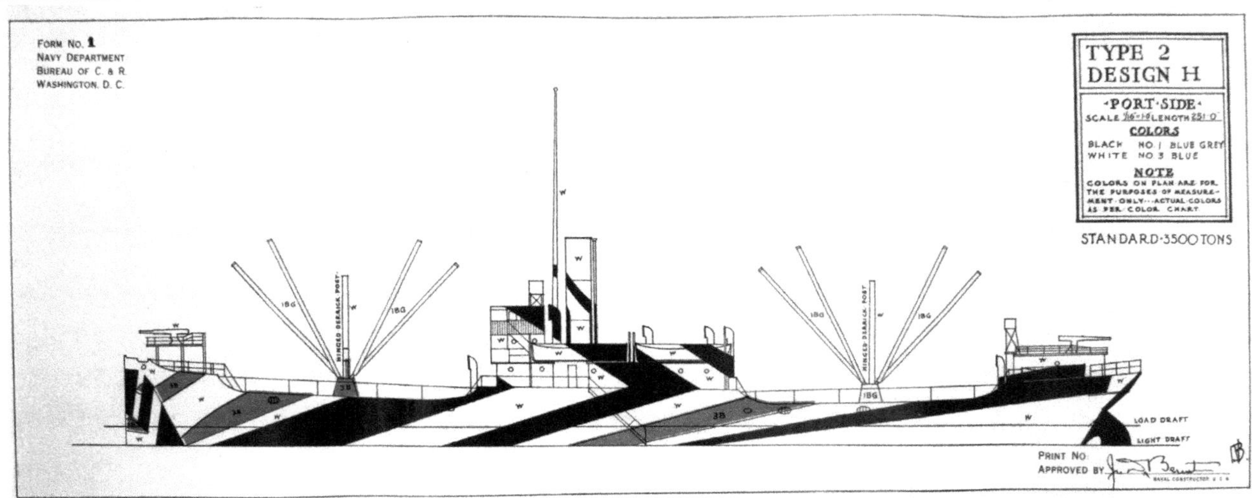

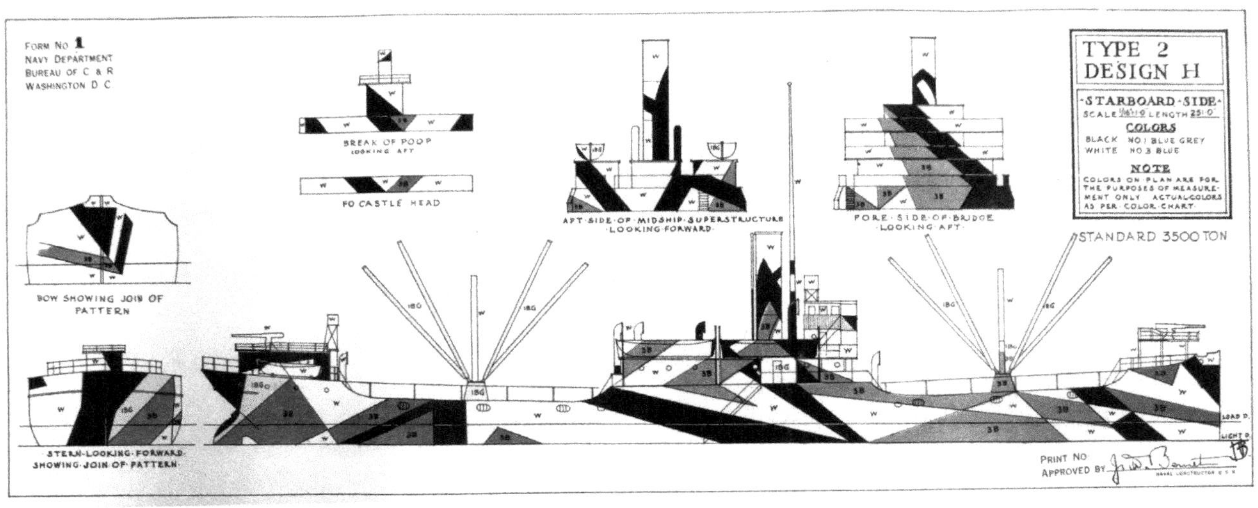

T2 I

Colors used	Ships painted with this pattern
BLACK	ID NONE EVERGLADES
WHITE	ID 1785A LAKE PLEASANT
#3 BLUE	ID 3974 LAKE YAHARA
#1 BLUE-GRAY	ID 4117 LAKE GARDNER

TYPE 2
DESIGN I
·PORT·SIDE·
SCALE 1/16"=1'0" LENGTH 251'0"
COLORS
BLACK NO 1 BLUE GRAY
WHITE NO 3 BLUE
NOTE
COLORS ON PLAN ARE FOR THE PURPOSES OF MEASUREMENT ONLY ... ACTUAL COLORS AS PER COLOR CHART

TYPE 2
DESIGN I
·STARBOARD·SIDE·
SCALE 1/16"=1'0" LENGTH 251'0"
COLORS
BLACK NO 1 BLUE GRAY
WHITE NO 3 BLUE
NOTE
COLORS ON PLAN ARE FOR THE PURPOSES OF MEASUREMENT ONLY · ACTUAL COLORS AS PER COLOR CHART

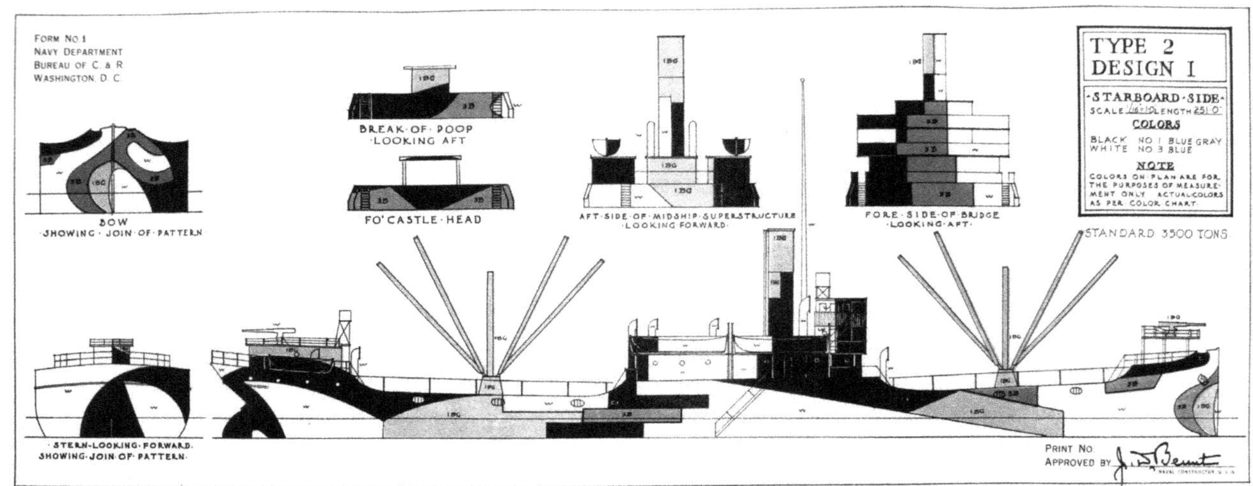

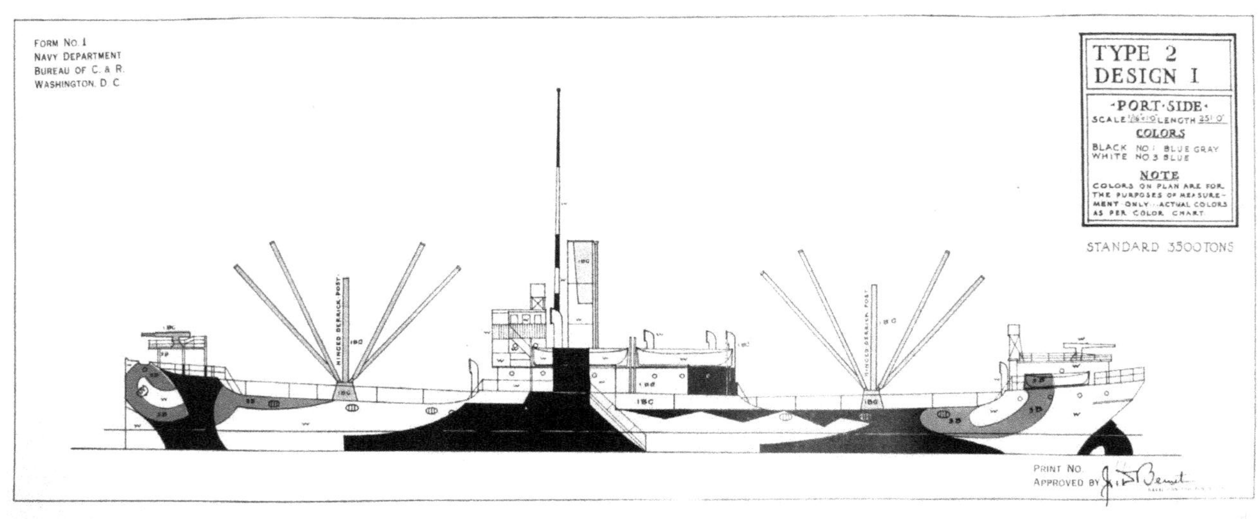

T2 J

Colors used	Ships painted with this pattern
BLACK	ID 3789A CRAWL KEYS
GREY-WHITE	ID 3394 ALPAHA
#2 BLUE-GRAY	ID 2454 SASSENHEIM (T)

TYPE 2
DESIGN J
·PORT·SIDE·
SCALE 1/16"·1'0 LENGTH 251'0" BP
COLORS
BLACK
GRAY·WHITE NO.2 BLUE·GRAY
NOTE
COLORS ON PLAN ARE FOR THE PURPOSES OF MEASUREMENT ONLY···ACTUAL COLORS AS PER COLOR CHART

TYPE 2
DESIGN J
·STARBOARD·SIDE·
SCALE 1/16"·1'0 LENGTH 251'0" BP
COLORS
BLACK
GRAY·WHITE· NO.2 BLUE·GRAY·
NOTE
COLORS ON PLAN ARE FOR THE PURPOSES OF MEASUREMENT ONLY ACTUAL COLORS AS PER COLOR CHART·

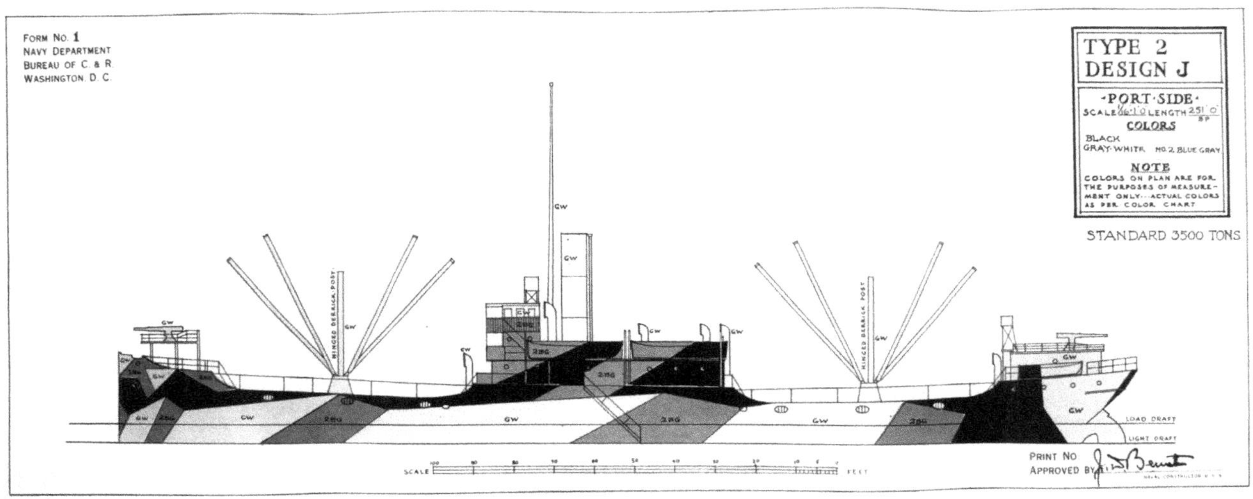

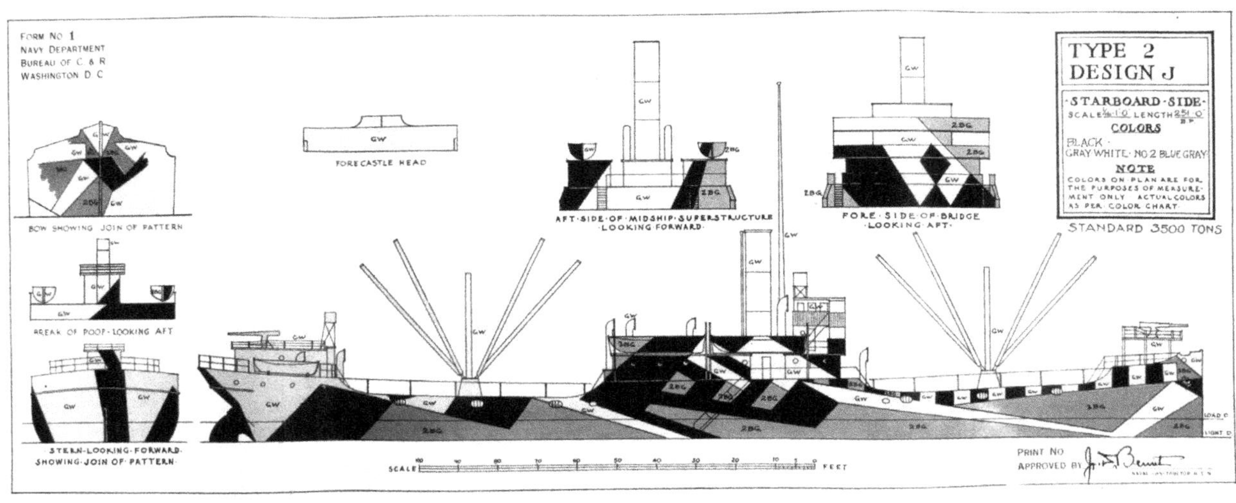

T2 K

Colors used	Ships painted with this pattern
BLACK	ID 3593 ALANTHUS
GREY-WHITE	ID 4131 LAKE DYMER
#3 BLUE	ID 3765C LAKE GEDNEY (T)
#1 BLUE-GRAY	
#1 GREEN	

TYPE 2
DESIGN K
·PORT·SIDE·
SCALE 1/16"-1'0 LENGTH 251' 0" BP
COLORS
BLACK NO 1 BLUE GRAY
GRAY WHITE NO 3 BLUE
NO 1 GREEN
NOTE
COLORS ON PLAN ARE FOR THE PURPOSES OF MEASUREMENT ONLY - ACTUAL COLORS AS PER COLOR CHART

TYPE 2
DESIGN K
·STARBOARD·SIDE·
SCALE 1/16"-1'0 LENGTH 251' 0" BP
COLORS
BLACK NO 1 BLUE GRAY
GRAY WHITE NO 3 BLUE
NO 1 GREEN
NOTE
COLORS ON PLAN ARE FOR THE PURPOSES OF MEASUREMENT ONLY ACTUAL COLORS AS PER COLOR CHART

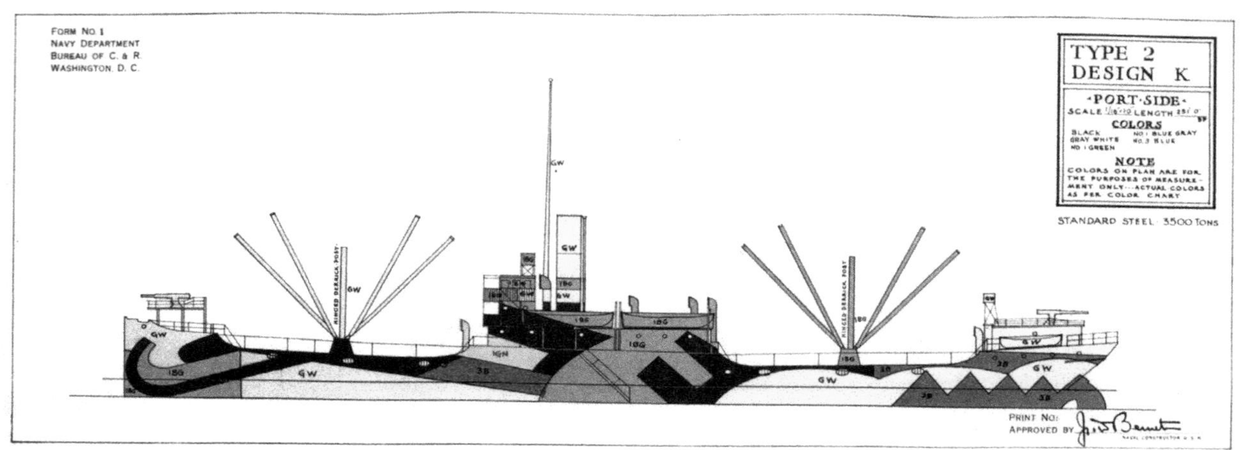

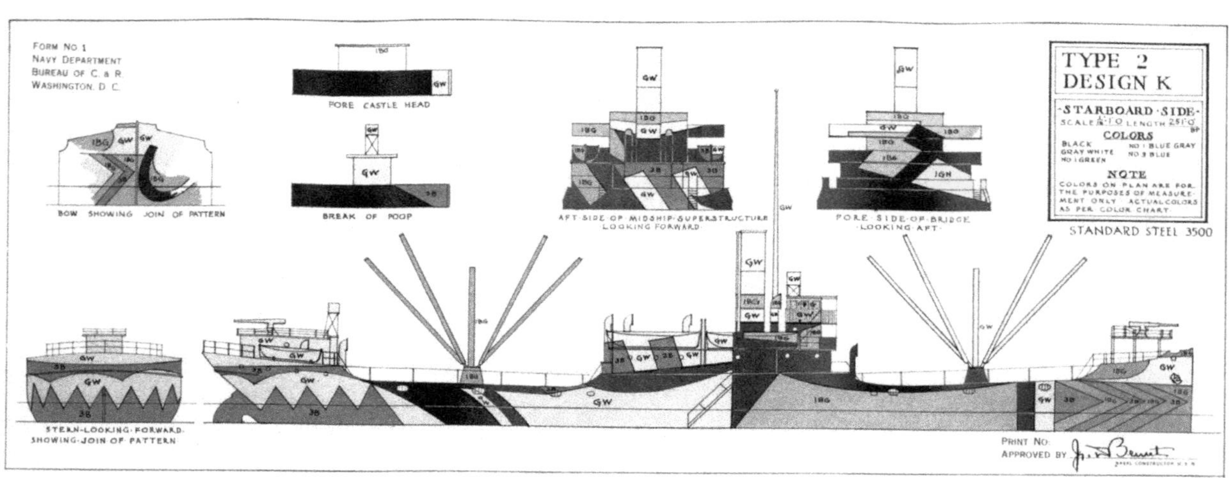

T2 L

Colors used	Ships painted with this pattern
BLACK	ID 4353AA LAKE ELIKO
WHITE	
#3 BLUE	
#2 BLUE-GRAY	
#1 GRAY-GREEN	

TYPE 2
DESIGN L
·PORT·SIDE·
SCALE 1/16"=1'0 LENGTH 261' 0"
COLORS
BLACK NO. 2 BLUE GRAY
WHITE NO. 3 BLUE
NO. 1 GRAY GREEN
NOTE
COLORS ON PLAN ARE FOR THE PURPOSES OF MEASUREMENT ONLY... ACTUAL COLORS AS PER COLOR CHART

TYPE 2
DESIGN L
·STARBOARD·SIDE·
SCALE 1/16"=1'0 LENGTH 261' 0"
COLORS
BLACK NO. 2 BLUE GRAY
WHITE NO. 3 BLUE
NO. 1 GRAY GREEN
NOTE
COLORS ON PLAN ARE FOR THE PURPOSES OF MEASUREMENT ONLY · ACTUAL COLORS AS PER COLOR CHART

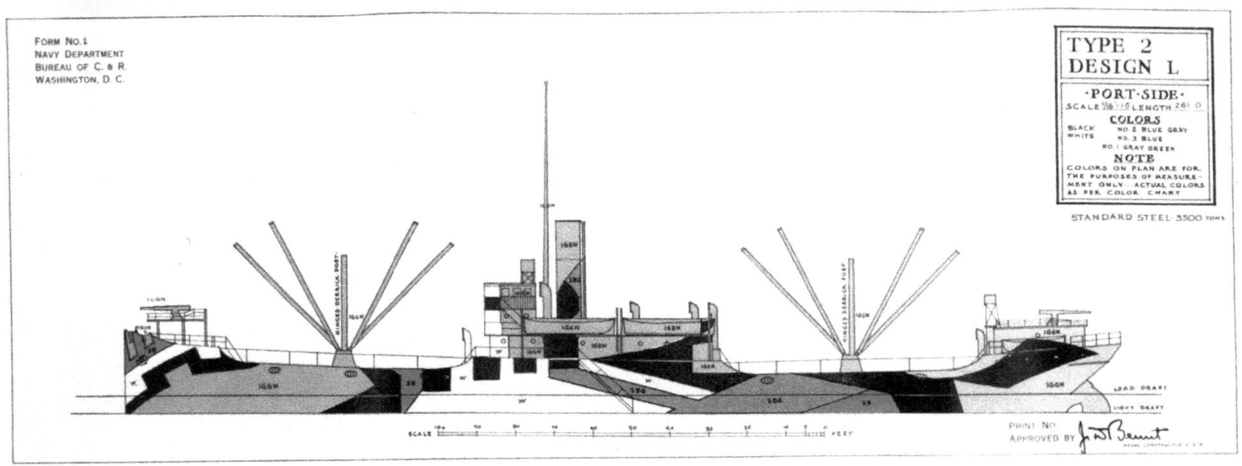

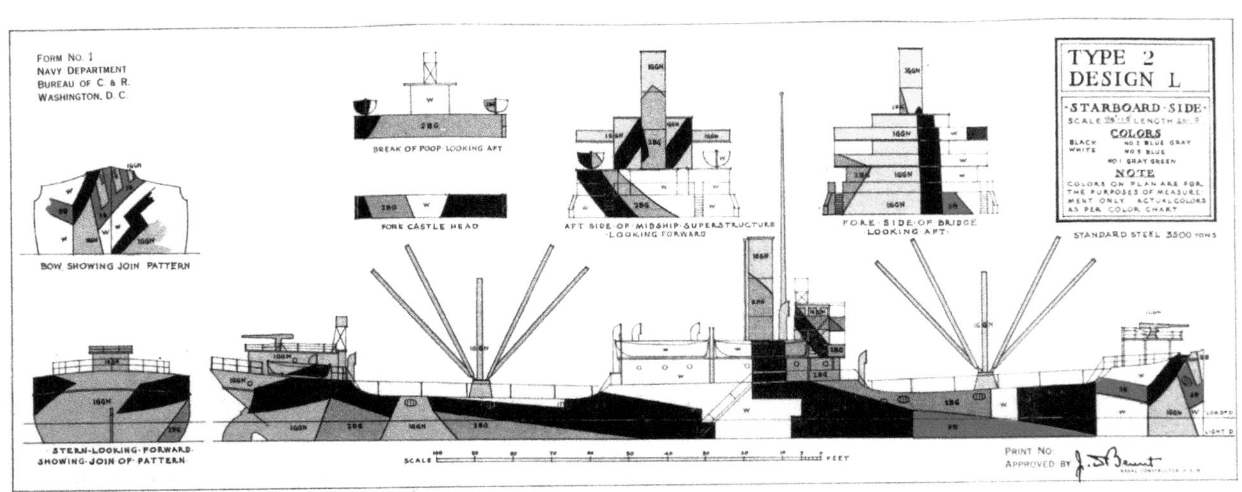

T2 N

Colors used	Ships painted with this pattern
BLACK	ID 3765B LAKE ELSINORE
#3 BLUE	ID 2993 LAKE MICHIGAN
#2 GRAY-GREEN	

TYPE · 2 · DESIGN · N ·

· PORT · SIDE ·
SCALE 1/16" 1'0" LENGTH 251'0"
COLORS
NO · 1 GRAY-GREEN
NO · 3 BLUE
BLACK
NOTE
COLORS ON PLAN ARE FOR THE PURPOSES OF MEASUREMENT ONLY · · · ACTUAL COLORS AS PER COLOR CHART

TYPE · 2 · DESIGN · N ·

· STARBOARD · SIDE ·
SCALE 1/16" 1'0" LENGTH 251'0"
COLORS
NO · 1 GRAY-GREEN
NO · 3 BLUE
BLACK
NOTE
COLORS ON PLAN ARE FOR THE PURPOSES OF MEASUREMENT ONLY · · · ACTUAL COLORS AS PER COLOR CHART

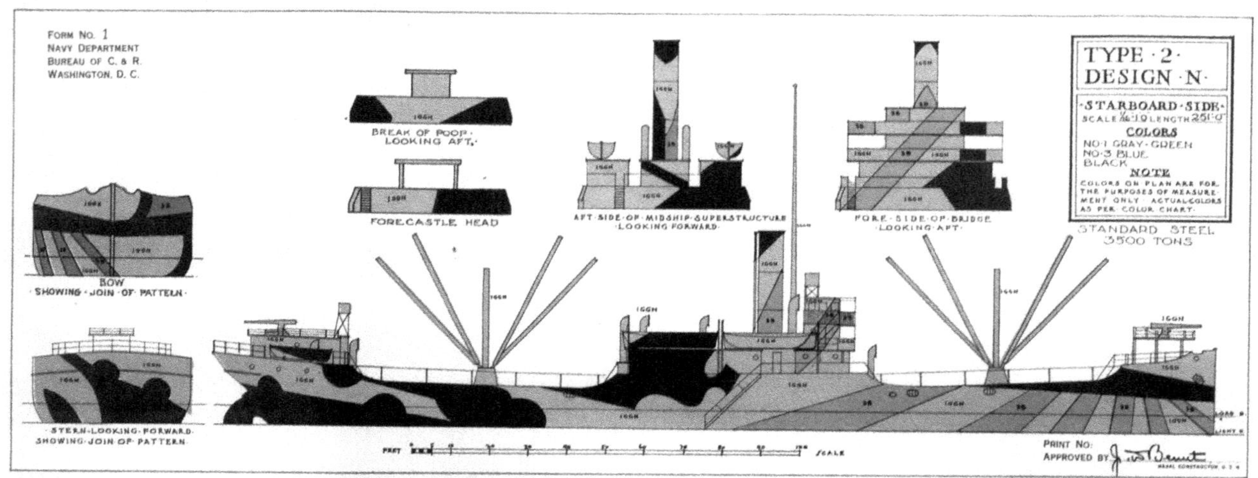

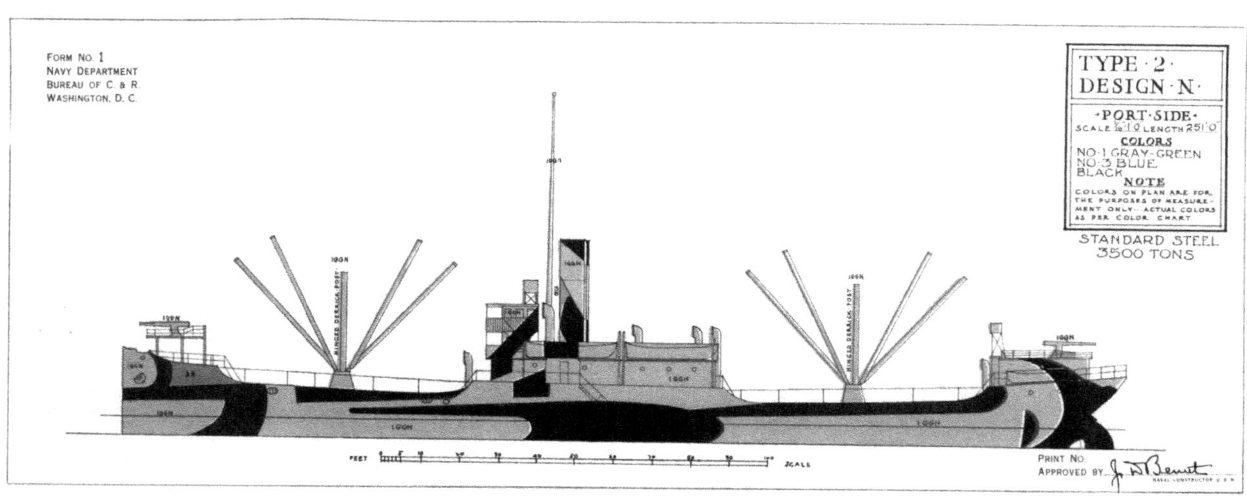

T2 O

Colors used	Ships painted with this pattern
BLACK	
GREY-WHITE	
#1 GRAY-GREEN	

TYPE 2
DESIGN O
·PORT·SIDE·
SCALE LENGTH 251'-0" B.P.
COLORS
BLACK 1 GRAY GREEN
GRAY WHITE
NOTE
COLORS ON PLAN ARE FOR THE PURPOSES OF MEASUREMENT ONLY — ACTUAL COLORS AS PER COLOR CHART

TYPE 2
DESIGN O
·STARBOARD·SIDE·
SCALE LENGTH 251'-0" B.P.
COLORS
BLACK 1 GRAY GREEN
GRAY WHITE
NOTE
COLORS ON PLAN ARE FOR THE PURPOSES OF MEASUREMENT ONLY — ACTUAL COLORS AS PER COLOR CHART

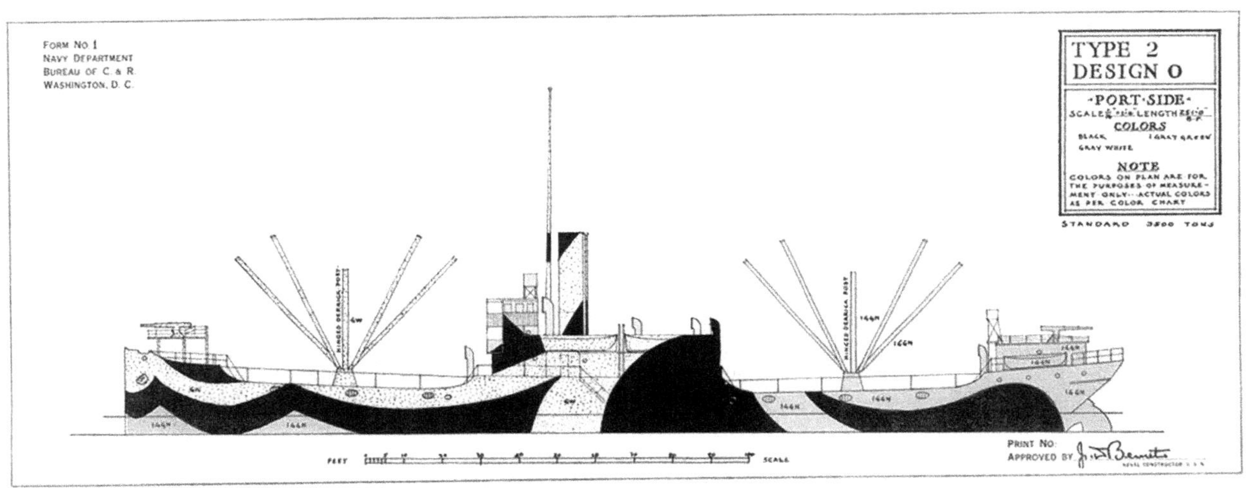

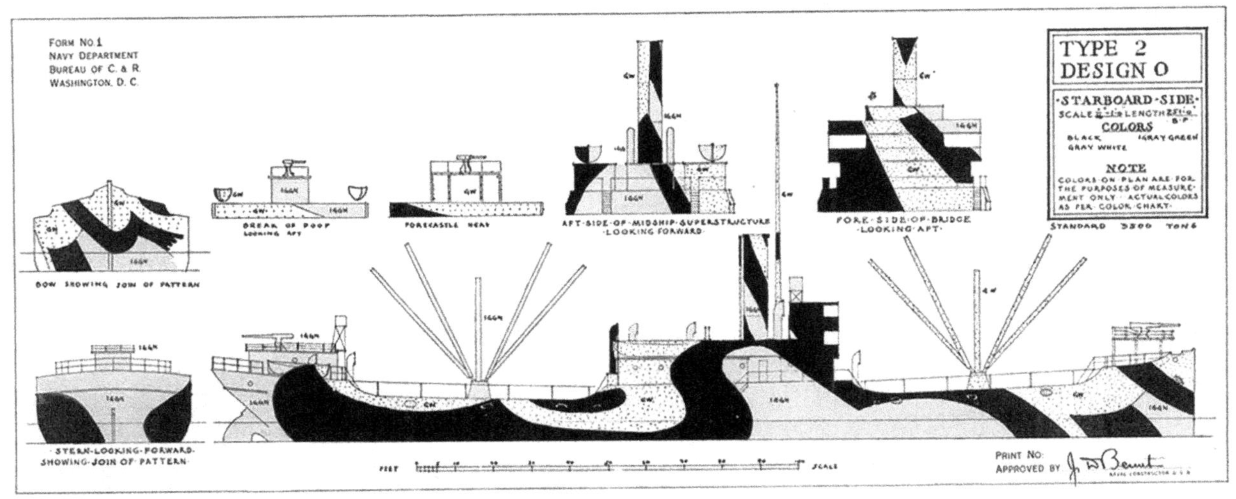

T2-P

Colors used	Ships painted with this pattern
BLACK	CHERON
BLUE #1	
GREEN #1	
BLUE #3	

TYPE · 2 · DESIGN · P ·
·PORT·SIDE·
SCALE 1/16=1'-0 LENGTH 251'-0" B.P.
COLORS
BLACK · NO. 1 · GREEN
NO. 1 · BLUE · NO. 3 · BLUE
NOTE
COLORS ON PLAN ARE FOR THE PURPOSES OF MEASUREMENT ONLY... ACTUAL COLORS AS PER COLOR CHART.

TYPE 2 DESIGN P
·STARBOARD·SIDE·
SCALE 1/16=1'-0 LENGTH 251'-0" BP
COLORS
BLACK NO 1 GREEN
NO 1 BLUE NO 3 BLUE
NOTE
COLORS·ON·PLAN·ARE·FOR THE·PURPOSES·OF·MEASUREMENT·ONLY···ACTUAL·COLORS AS·PER·COLOR·CHART·

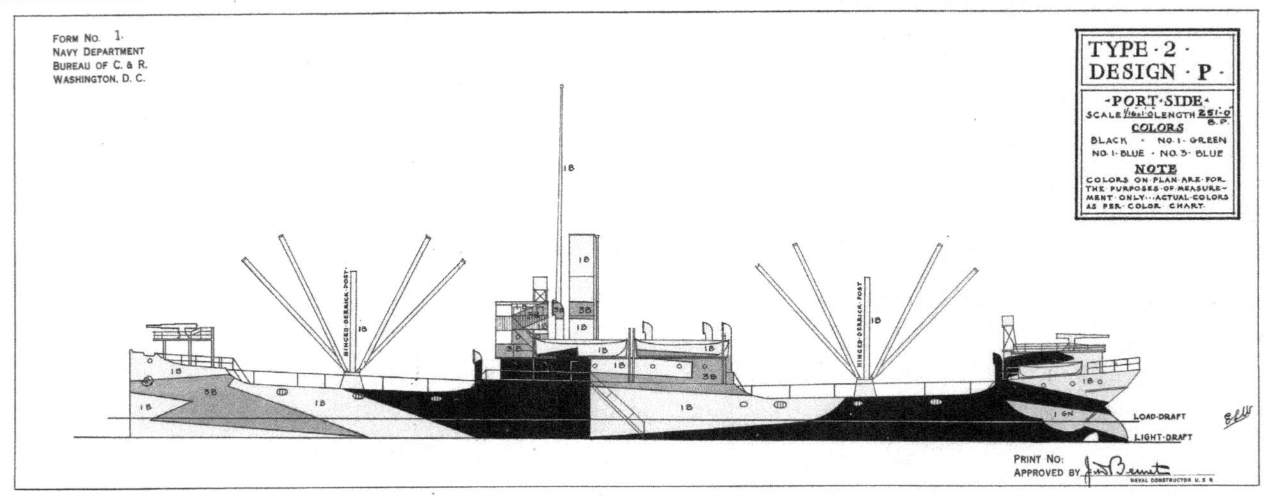

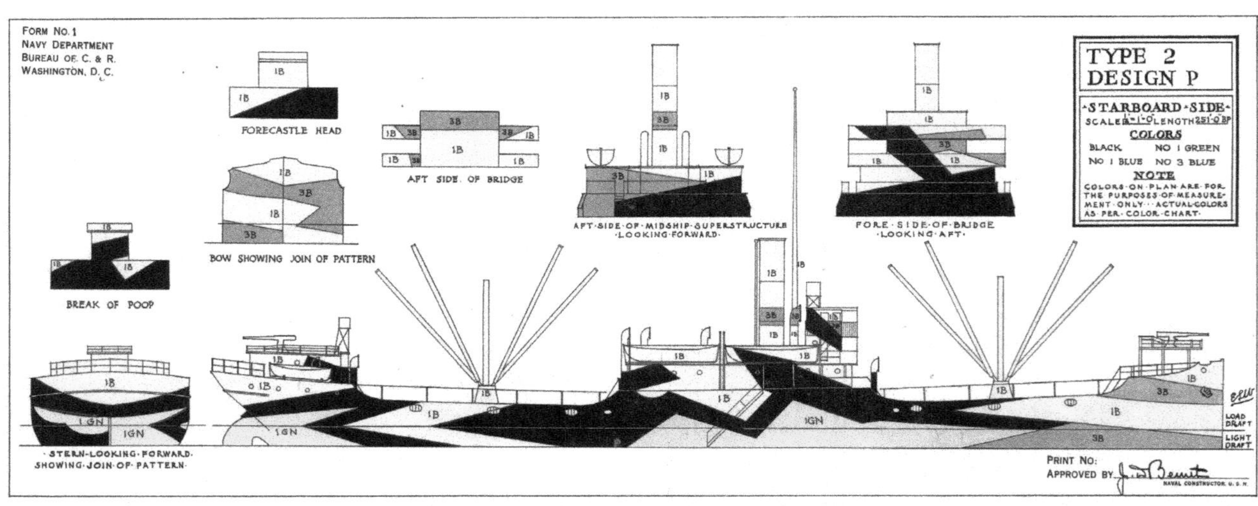

T2 Q

Colors used	Ships painted with this pattern
BLACK	ID NONE ANOKA
GREY-WHITE	
#3 BLUE	
#1 BLUE-GRAY	

TYPE 2
DESIGN Q
PORT SIDE
SCALE 1/16"=1'0" LENGTH 251'-0"
COLORS
BLACK NO 1 BLUE GRAY
GRAY WHITE NO 3 BLUE
NOTE
COLORS ON PLAN ARE FOR THE PURPOSES OF MEASUREMENT ONLY
ACTUAL COLORS AS PER COLOR CHART

TYPE 2
DESIGN Q
STARBOARD SIDE
SCALE 1/16"=1'0" LENGTH 251'0
COLORS
BLACK NO 1 BLUE GRAY
GRAY WHITE NO 3 BLUE
NOTE
COLORS ON PLAN ARE FOR THE PURPOSES OF MEASUREMENT ONLY
ACTUAL COLORS AS PER COLOR CHART

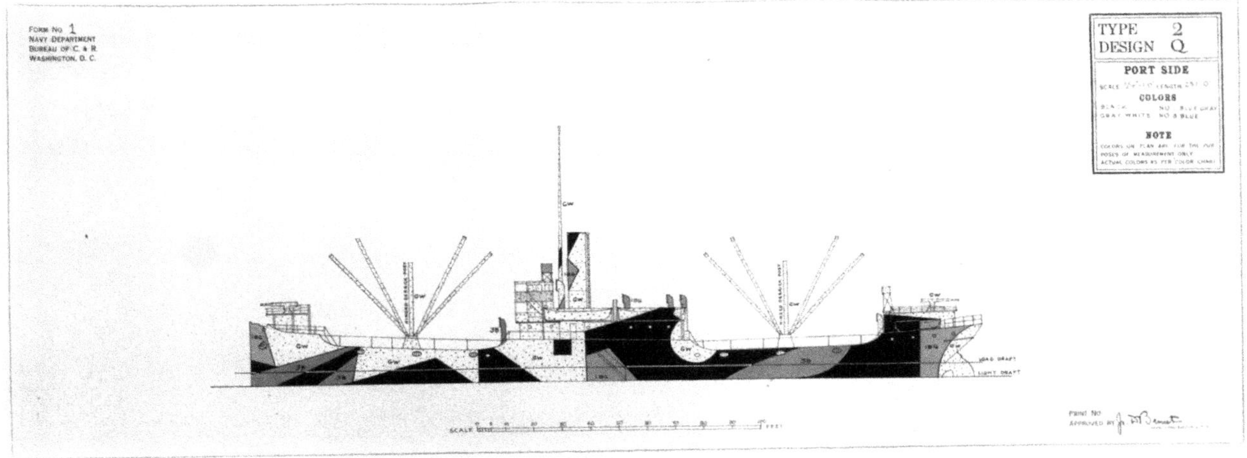

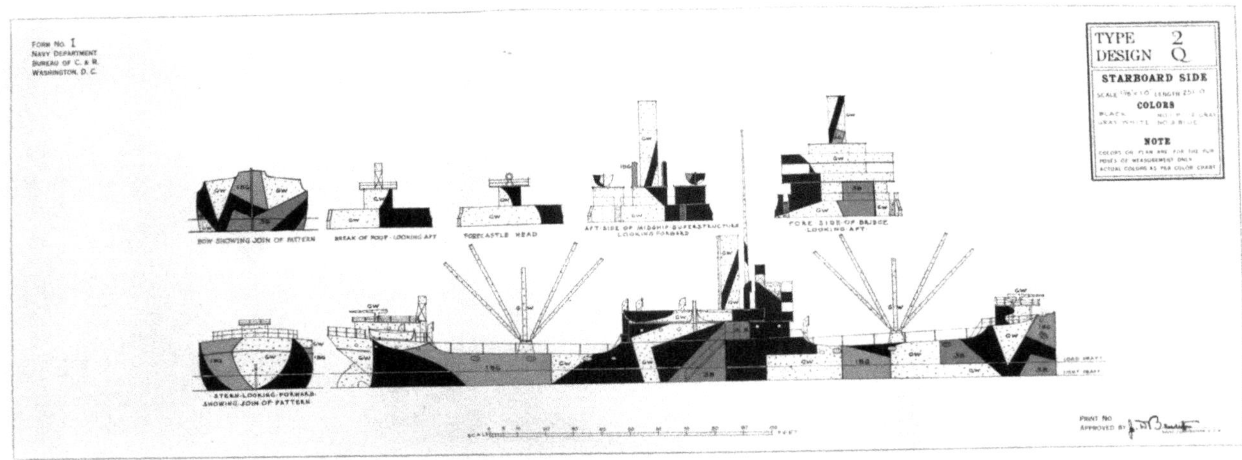

T2 R

Colors used	Ships painted with this pattern
BLACK	
GREY-WHITE	
#3 BLUE	

TYPE 2
DESIGN R

PORT SIDE

SCALE 1/16" = 1'-0" LENGTH 251'-0"

COLORS

GRAY WHITE · NO 3 BLUE · BLACK ·

NOTE

COLORS ON PLAN ARE FOR THE PURPOSES OF MEASUREMENT ONLY
ACTUAL COLORS AS PER COLOR CHART

TYPE 2
DESIGN R

STARBOARD SIDE

SCALE 1/16" = 1'-0 LENGTH 251'-0"

COLORS

GRAY WHITE · NO 3 BLUE · BLACK ·

NOTE

COLORS ON PLAN ARE FOR THE PURPOSES OF MEASUREMENT ONLY
ACTUAL COLORS AS PER COLOR CHART

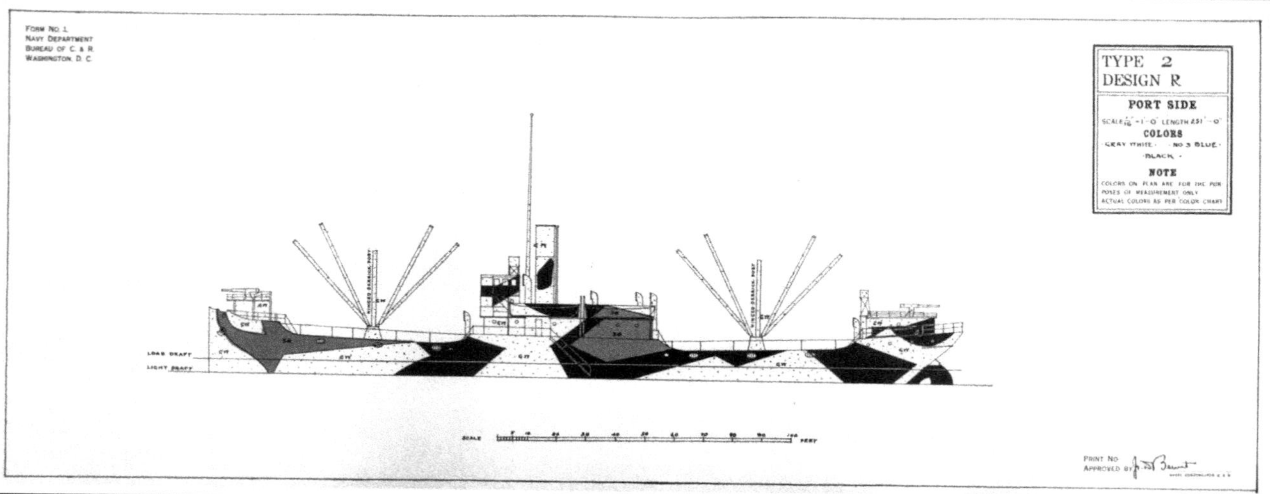

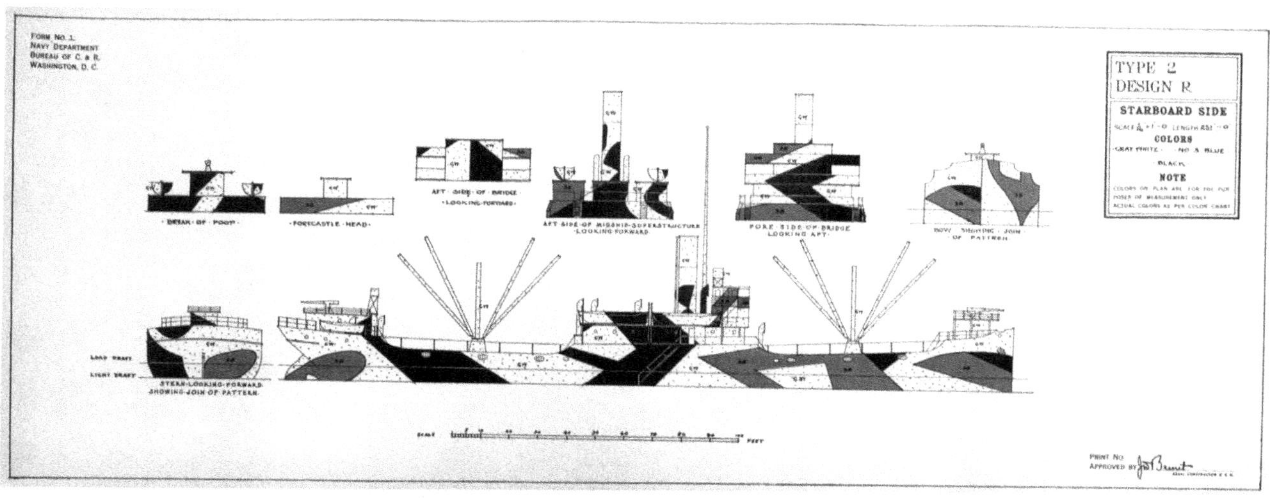

T2 S

Colors used	Ships painted with this pattern
BLACK	NONE LAKE AGOMAK
GREY-WHITE	
#3 BLUE	
#1 GREEN	

TYPE 2
DESIGN 5

PORT SIDE

SCALE ______ LENGTH 251'-0" BP

COLORS

NO 1 GREEN — BLACK
NO 3 BLUE — GRAY WHITE

NOTE

COLORS ON PLAN ARE FOR THE PURPOSES OF MEASUREMENT ONLY
ACTUAL COLORS AS PER COLOR CHART

TYPE 2
DESIGN 5

STARBOARD SIDE

SCALE ______ LENGTH 251'-0" BP

COLORS

NO 1 GREEN — BLACK
NO 3 BLUE — GRAY WHITE

NOTE

COLORS ON PLAN ARE FOR THE PURPOSES OF MEASUREMENT ONLY
ACTUAL COLORS AS PER COLOR CHART

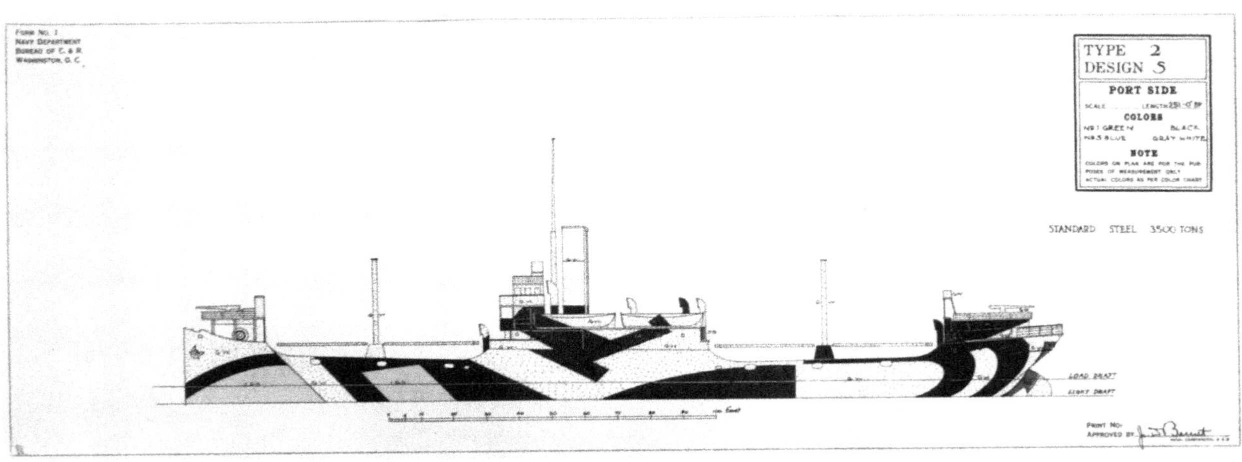

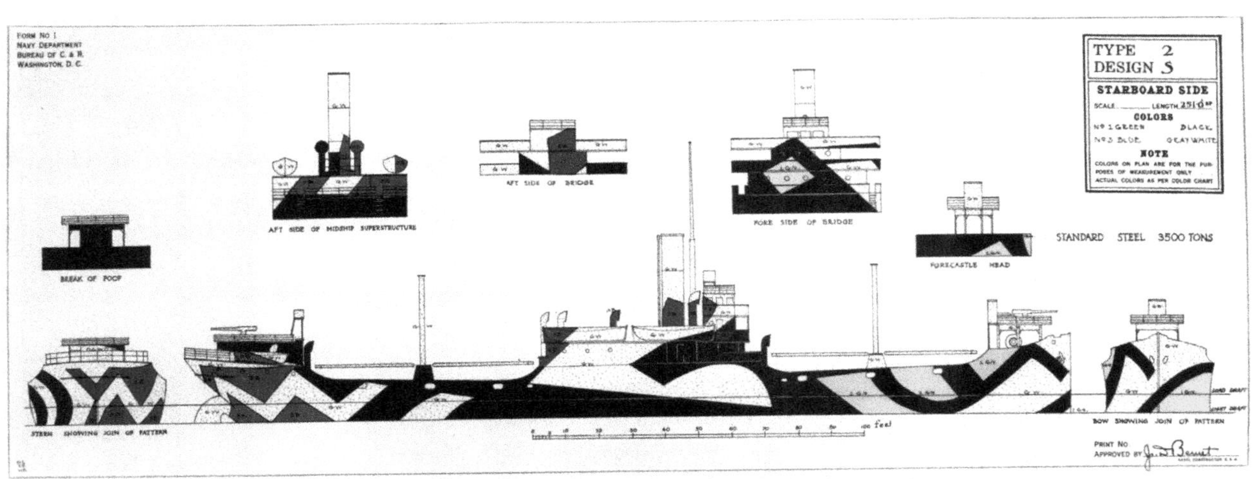

T2 T

Colors used	Ships painted with this pattern
BLACK	ID NONE LAKE EDON
GREY-WHITE	
#3 BLUE	
#1 GREEN	

TYPE 2
DESIGN T
PORT SIDE
SCALE ¼" = 1'-0" LENGTH 251'-0" BP
COLORS
NO 1 GREEN NO 3 BLUE
GRAY WHITE BLACK
NOTE
COLORS ON PLAN ARE FOR THE PURPOSES OF MEASUREMENT ONLY
ACTUAL COLORS AS PER COLOR CHART

TYPE 2
DESIGN T
STARBOARD SIDE
SCALE ¼" = 1'-0" LENGTH 251'-0" BP
COLORS
NO 1 GREEN NO 3 BLUE
GRAY WHITE BLACK
NOTE
COLORS ON PLAN ARE FOR THE PURPOSES OF MEASUREMENT ONLY
ACTUAL COLORS AS PER COLOR CHART

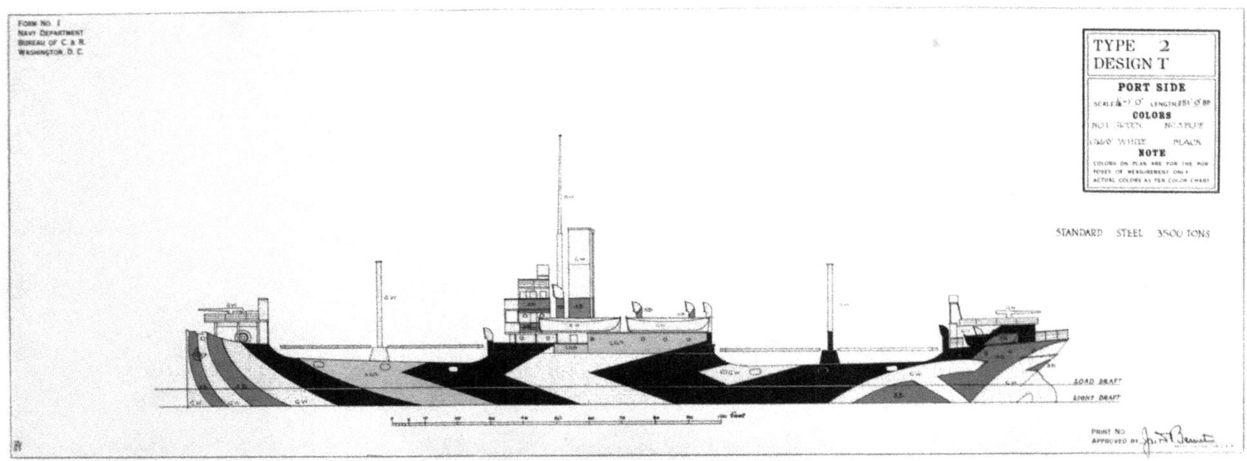

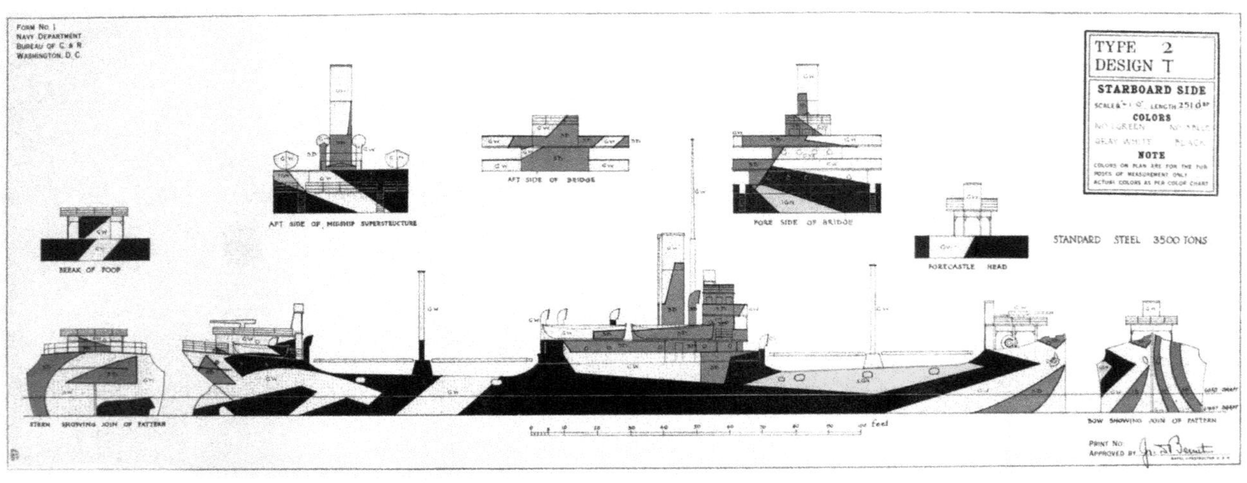

T2 X

Colors used	Ships painted with this pattern
BLACK	ID 4276E LAKE MATTATO
GREY-WHITE	
#3 BLUE	

TYPE 2
DESIGN X

PORT SIDE

SCALE ¼" = 1' 0" LENGTH 251' 0" BP

COLORS

GRAY WHITE 3 BLUE BLACK

NOTE

COLORS ON PLAN ARE FOR THE PURPOSES OF MEASUREMENT ONLY ACTUAL COLORS AS PER COLOR CHART

TYPE 2
DESIGN X

STARBOARD SIDE

SCALE ¼" = 1' 0" LENGTH 251' 0" BP

COLORS

GRAY WHITE 3 BLUE BLACK

NOTE

COLORS ON PLAN ARE FOR THE PURPOSES OF MEASUREMENT ONLY ACTUAL COLORS AS PER COLOR CHART

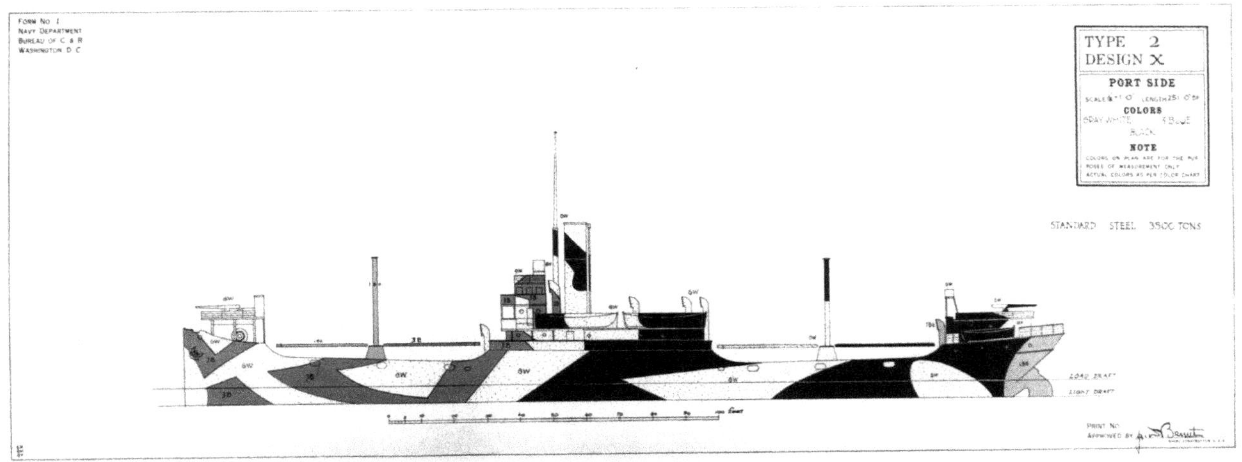

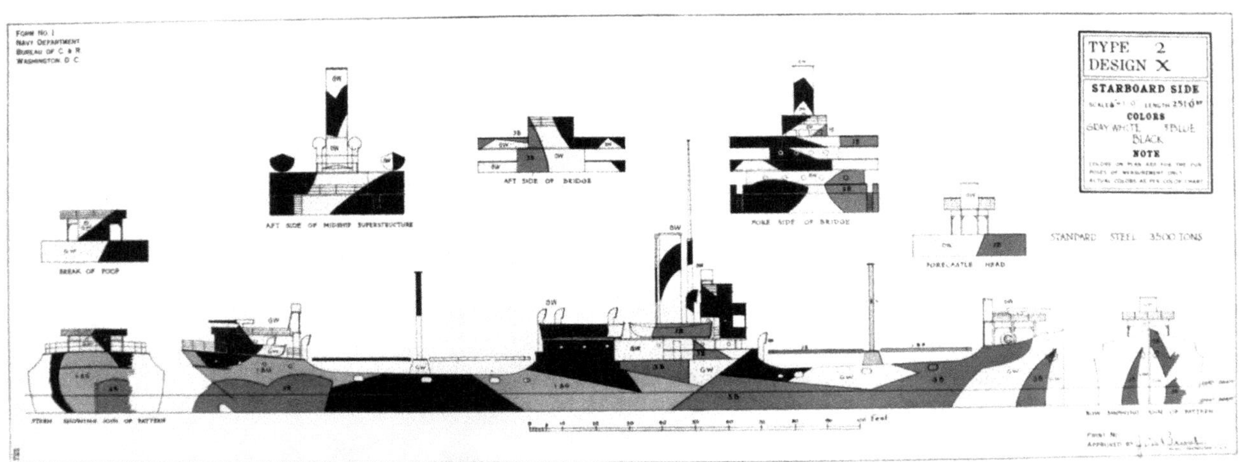

T3 A

Colors used	Ships painted with this pattern
BLACK	ID 2486 HATTIE LUCHENBACK (T)
WHITE	ID 2667 PLUTO (T)
#3 BLUE	ID 2292 AMERICAN (T)
#1 BLUE-GRAY	ID 2429 FAIRMONT(T)
	ID 3944 MARIANNA

TYPE 3
DESIGN A
·PORT·SIDE·
COLORS
NOTE
COLORS ON PLAN ARE FOR THE PURPOSES OF MEASUREMENT ONLY ACTUAL COLORS AS PER COLOR CHART

TYPE 3
DESIGN A
·STARBOARD·SIDE·
COLORS
NOTE
COLORS ON PLAN ARE FOR THE PURPOSES OF MEASUREMENT ONLY ACTUAL COLORS AS PER COLOR CHART.

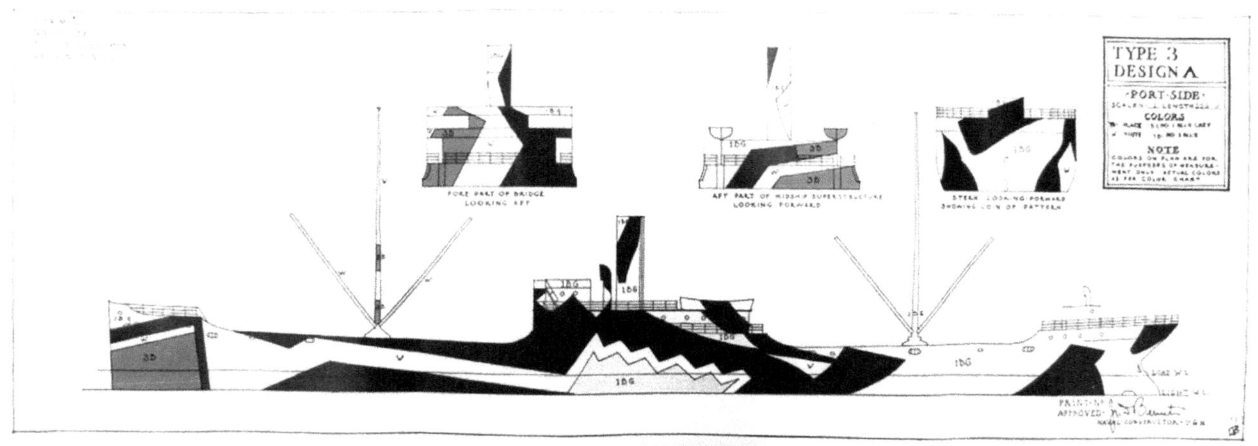

T3 B

Colors used	Ships painted with this pattern
BLACK	ID 2691 LUELLA
WHITE	ID 2508 CANTON (T)
#3 BLUE	ID 1619 ERNY
#1 BLUE-GRAY	ID 1637 GUANTANAMO (T)
	ID 3253 WESTCOHAS (T)

TYPE 3
DESIGN B
·PORT·SIDE·
COLORS
BLACK 3B=NO 3 BLUE
WHITE 1BG=NO 1 BLUBGREY
NOTE
COLORS ON PLAN ARE FOR THE PURPOSES OF MEASUREMENT ONLY. ACTUAL COLORS AS PER COLOR CHART

TYPE 3
DESIGN B
·STARBOARD·SIDE·
COLORS
BLACK 3B=NO.3 BLUE
WHITE 1BG=NO.1 BLUE GREY
NOTE
COLORS ON PLAN ARE FOR THE PURPOSES OF MEASUREMENT ONLY ACTUAL COLORS AS PER COLOR CHART

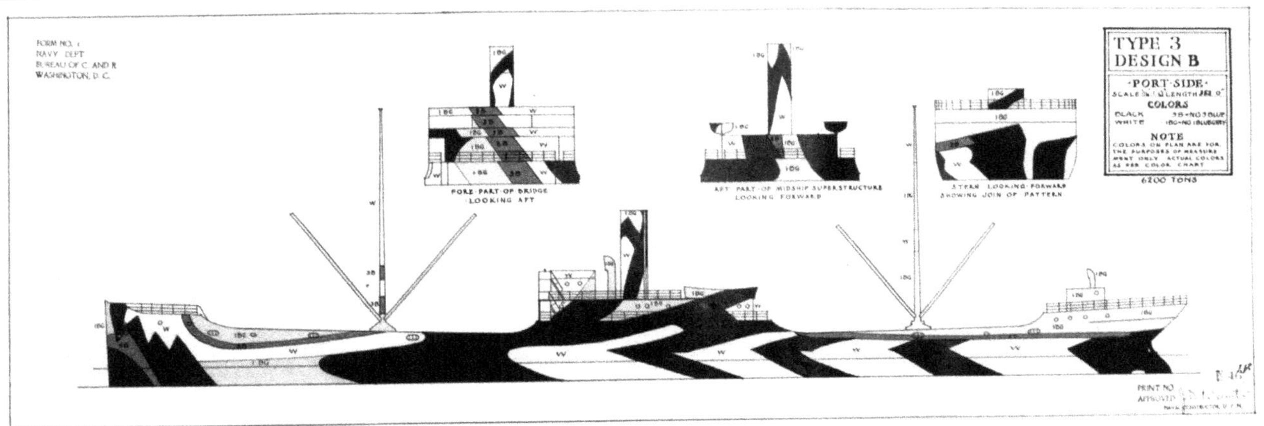

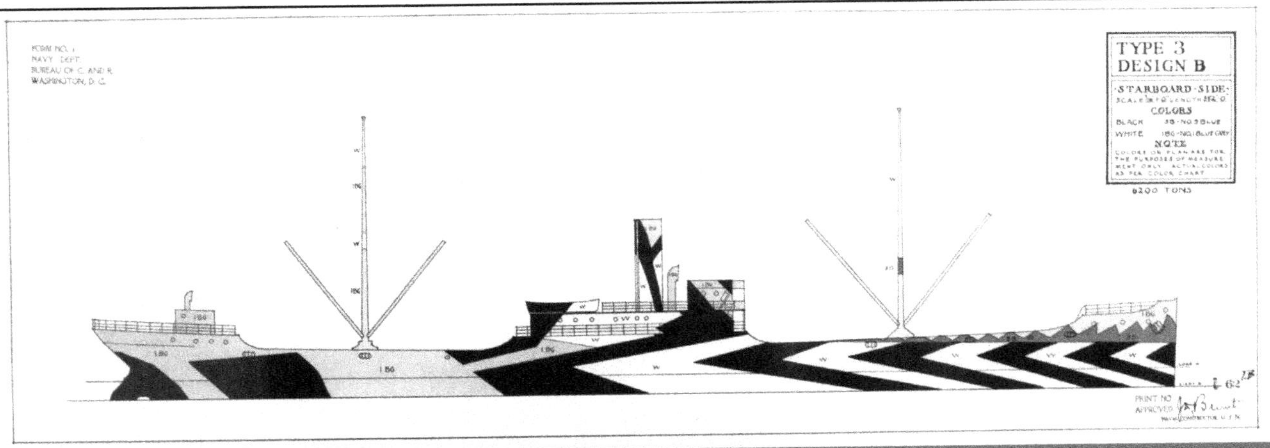

T3 C

Colors used	Ships painted with this pattern
BLACK	ID 2005 ASTORIA ((T)
WHITE	ID2465 ELINOR (T)
#3 BLUE	ID 2485 JOBSHAVEN
#1 BLUE-GRAY	NONE WYANDOTTE (T)
	ID NONE MATILDA WEEMS

TYPE 3
DESIGN·C·

·PORT·SIDE·
SCALE ⅛"=1'-0" LENGTH 352'-0"
COLORS
WHITE NO. 3 BLUE
BLACK NO. 1 BLUE GREY
NOTE
COLORS ON PLAN ARE FOR THE PURPOSES OF MEASUREMENT ONLY···ACTUAL COLORS AS PER COLOR CHART

TYPE 3
DESIGN·C·

·STARBOARD·SIDE·
SCALE ⅛"=1'-0" LENGTH 352'-0"
COLORS
BLACK NO. 3 BLUE
WHITE NO. 1 BLUE GREY
NOTE
COLORS·ON·PLAN ARE FOR THE PURPOSES OF MEASUREMENT ONLY ACTUAL·COLORS AS PER·COLOR·CHART·

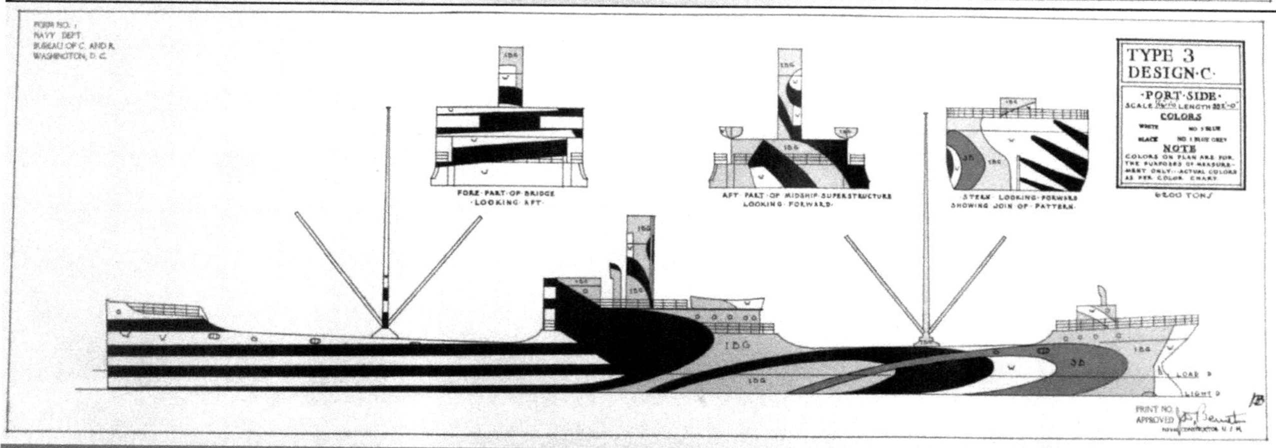

T3 D

Colors used	Ships painted with this pattern
BLACK	ID 4688 ARETHUSA
WHITE	ID 4522 SANTA BARBARA
#3 BLUE	ID 2529 NEPTUNUS
#1 BLUE-GRAY	ID 2514 WESTERDIJK

TYPE 3
DESIGN D

·PORT·SIDE·
SCALE 1/16"=1'0 LENGTH 352'0
COLORS
BLACK NO 1 BLUE GREY
WHITE NO 3 BLUE
NOTE
COLORS ON PLAN ARE FOR THE PURPOSES OF MEASUREMENT ONLY ACTUAL COLORS AS PER COLOR CHART

TYPE 3
DESIGN D

·STARBOARD·SIDE·
SCALE 1/16"=1'0 LENGTH 352'0
COLORS
BLACK NO 1 BLUE GREY
WHITE NO 3 BLUE
NOTE
COLORS ON PLAN ARE FOR THE PURPOSES OF MEASUREMENT ONLY ACTUAL COLORS AS PER COLOR CHART

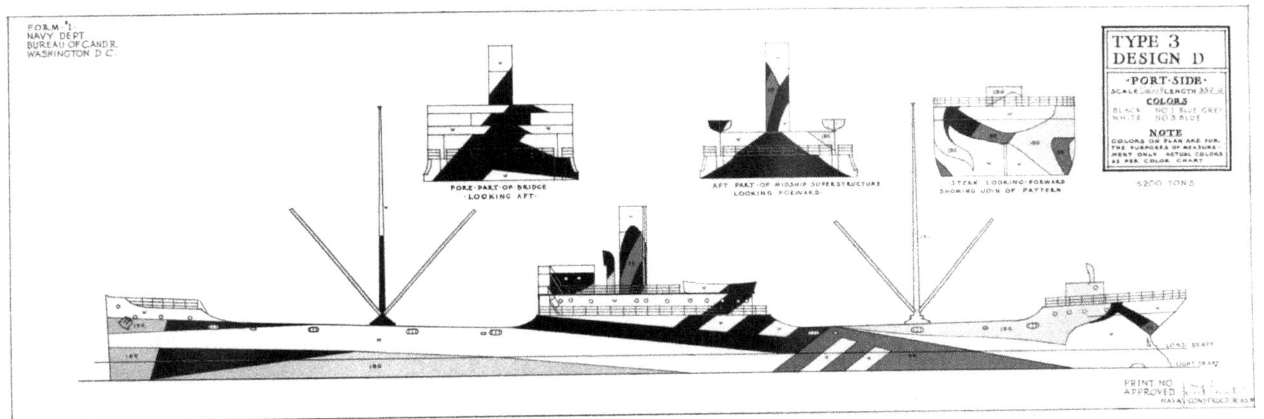

T3 E

Colors used	Ships painted with this pattern
BLACK	ID 2510 MARGARET
WHITE	ID NONE MERCURINE
#3 BLUE	
#1 BLUE-GRAY	

TYPE 3
DESIGN E
·PORT·SIDE·
SCALE 1/16"=1'0" LENGTH 352'-0"
COLORS
BLACK #1 BLUE-GRAY
WHITE #1 GREEN
#3 BLUE
NOTE
COLORS ON PLAN ARE FOR THE PURPOSES OF MEASUREMENT ONLY···ACTUAL COLORS AS PER COLOR CHART

TYPE 3
DESIGN E
·STARBOARD·SIDE·
COLORS
NOTE

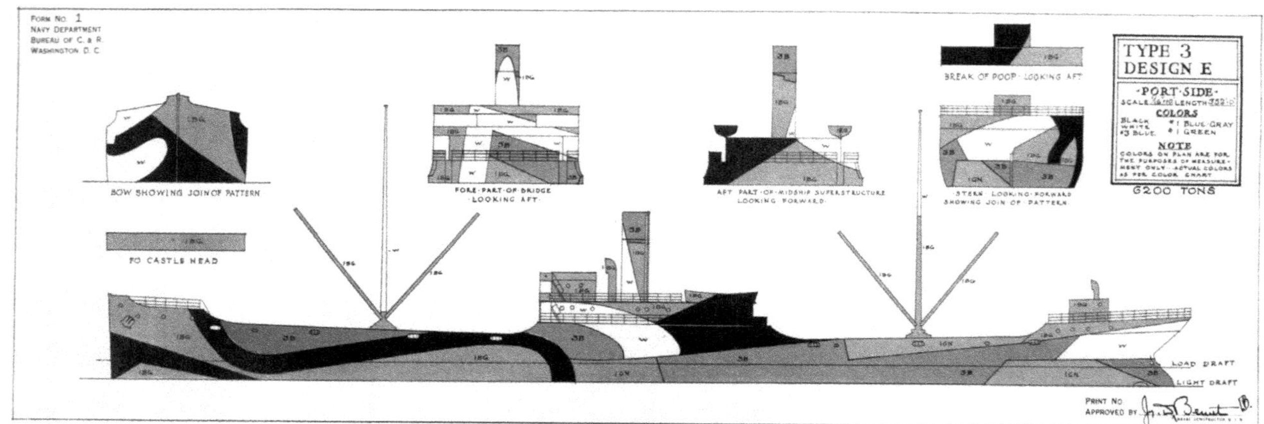

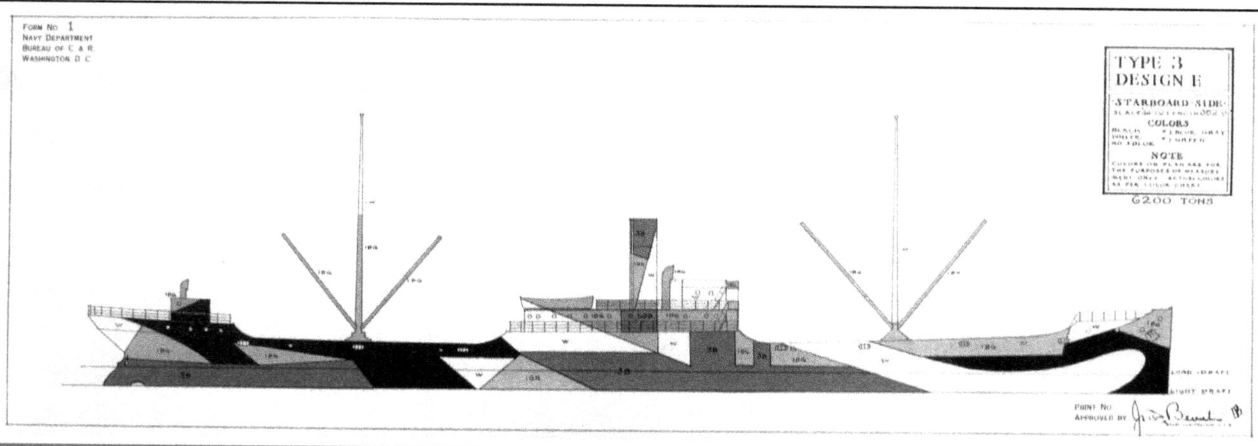

T3 F

Colors used	Ships painted with this pattern
BLACK	ID 1655 MEXICAN
WHITE	
#3 BLUE	
#1 BLUE-GRAY	

TYPE 3
DESIGN F

·PORT·SIDE·
SCALE 1/16" 1'0" LENGTH 352' 0"

COLORS

WHITE NO 1 BLUE
BLACK NO 2 BLUE GRAY

NOTE

COLORS ON PLAN ARE FOR THE PURPOSES OF MEASUREMENT ONLY · · ACTUAL COLORS AS PER COLOR CHART

TYPE 3
DESIGN F

·STARBOARD·SIDE·
SCALE 1/16" 1'0" LENGTH 352' 0"

COLORS

WHITE NO 1 BLUE
BLACK NO 2 BLUE GRAY

NOTE

COLORS ON PLAN ARE FOR THE PURPOSES OF MEASUREMENT ONLY ACTUAL COLORS AS PER COLOR CHART

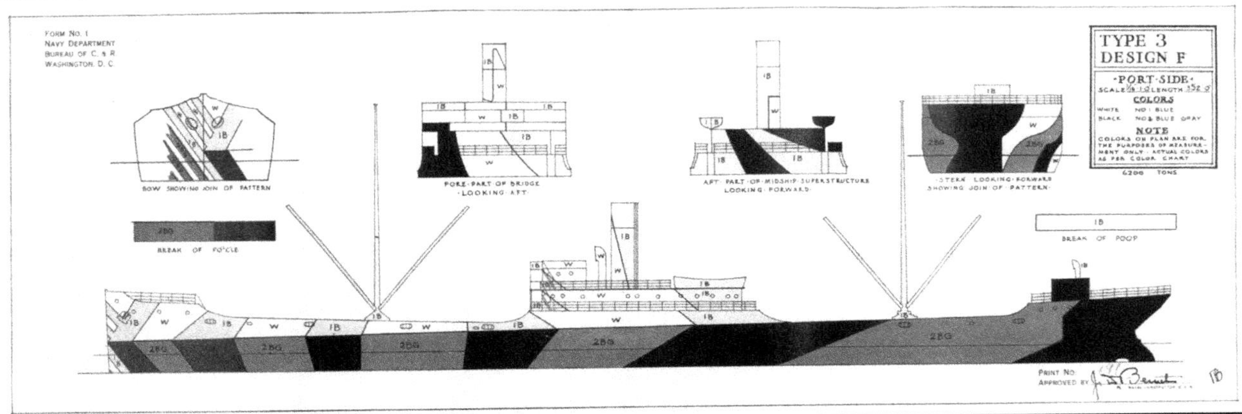

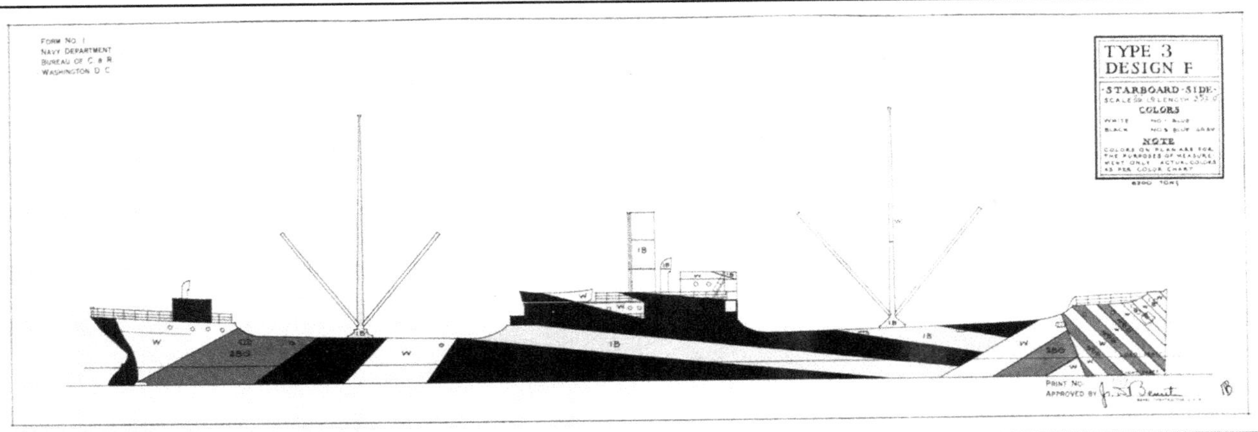

T3 G

Colors used	Ships painted with this pattern
BLACK	ID3439 OZAUKEE
WHITE	ID 2545 MIRACH (T)
#3 BLUE	ID 2793 DRECHTERLAND (T)
#1 BLUE	

TYPE 3
DESIGN G

·PORT·SIDE·
SCALE 1/16"=1'0" LENGTH 352'0"
COLORS
BLACK NO 1 BLUE
WHITE NO 3 BLUE
NOTE
COLORS ON PLAN ARE FOR THE PURPOSES OF MEASUREMENT ONLY... ACTUAL COLORS AS PER COLOR CHART

TYPE 3
DESIGN · G

·STARBOARD·SIDE·
SCALE 1/16"=1'0" LENGTH 352'0"
COLORS
BLACK NO. 1 BLUE
WHITE NO. 3 BLUE
NOTE
COLORS ON PLAN ARE FOR THE PURPOSES OF MEASUREMENT ONLY · ACTUAL COLORS AS PER · COLOR · CHART ·

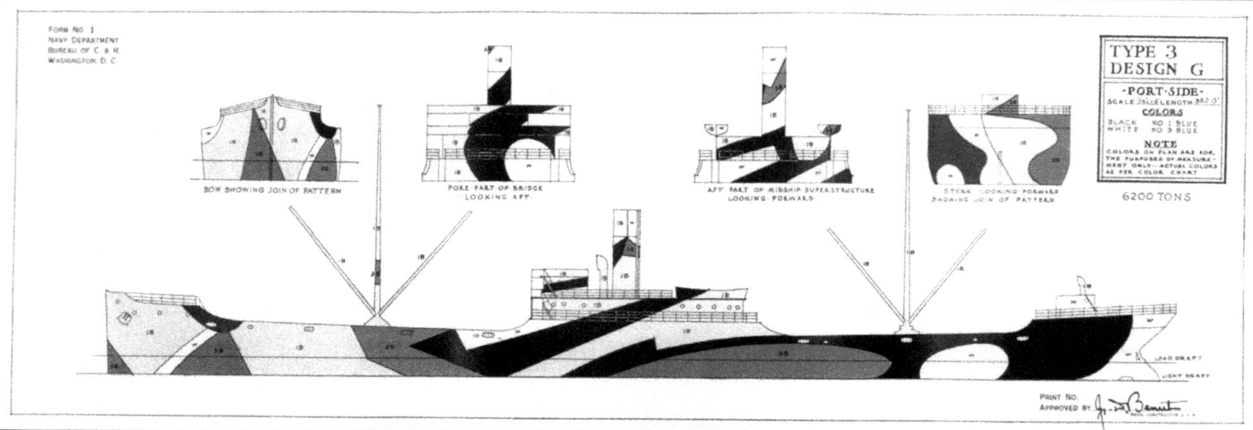

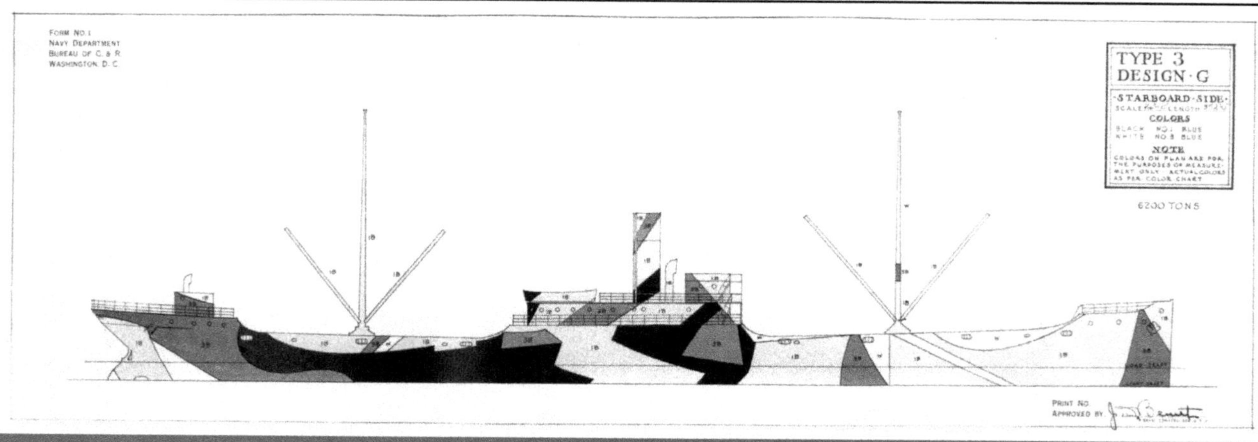

T3 I

Colors used	Ships painted with this pattern
BLACK	ID 2224 ARAKAN
GREY-WHITE	
#3 BLUE	
#2 BLUE-GRAY	
#1 GREEN	

TYPE 3
DESIGN I

·PORT·SIDE·
SCALE 1/16"=1'0" LENGTH 352'0" B.P.

COLORS
BLACK — NO 2 BLUE GRAY
GRAY WHITE — NO 3 BLUE
NO 1 GRAY PINK

NOTE
COLORS ON PLAN ARE FOR THE PURPOSES OF MEASUREMENT ONLY... ACTUAL COLORS AS PER COLOR CHART.

TYPE 3
DESIGN I

·STARBOARD·SIDE·
SCALE 1/16"=1'0" LENGTH 352'0" B.P.

COLORS
BLACK — NO 2 BLUE GRAY
GRAY WHITE — NO 3 BLUE
NO 1 GRAY PINK

NOTE
COLORS ON PLAN ARE FOR THE PURPOSES OF MEASUREMENT ONLY · ACTUAL COLORS AS PER COLOR CHART.

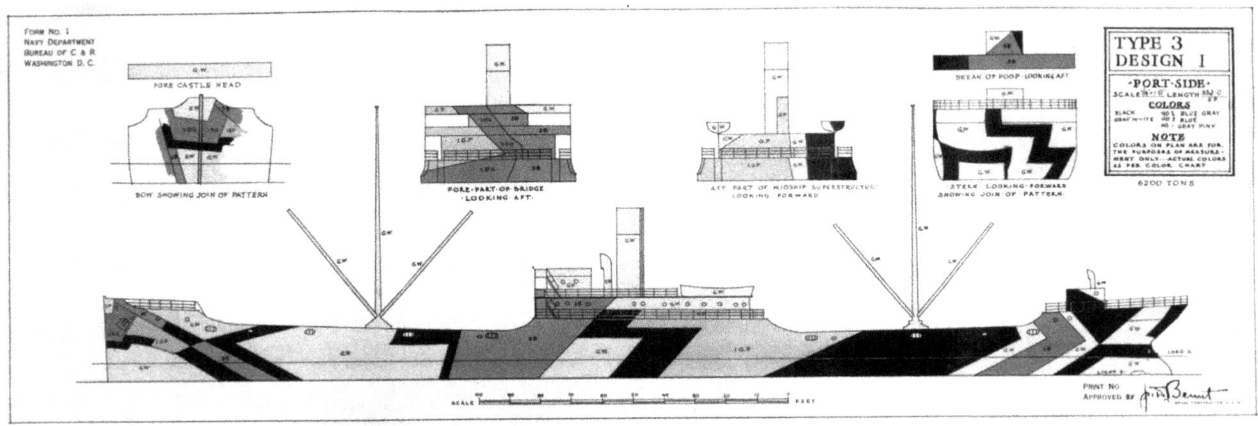

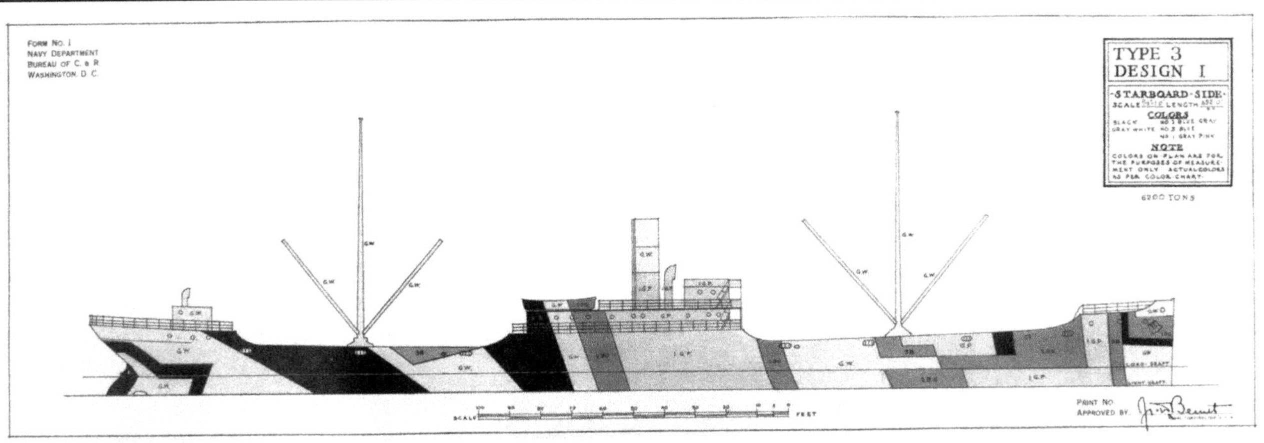

T3 J

Colors used	Ships painted with this pattern
BLACK	ID 2534 BESOEKI
GREY-WHITE	
#3 BLUE	
#1 BLUE-GRAY	
#1 GREEN	

TYPE 3
DESIGN J
·PORT·SIDE·
SCALE 1/16"=1'0" LENGTH 353' 3"
COLORS
GRAY WHITE NO.1 GREEN
NO.1 BLUE GRAY NO.3 BLUE
NOTE BLACK
COLORS ON PLAN ARE FOR THE PURPOSES OF MEASUREMENT ONLY···ACTUAL COLORS AS PER COLOR CHART·

TYPE 3
DESIGN J
·STARBOARD·SIDE·
SCALE 1/16"=1'0" LENGTH 353' 3"
COLORS
GRAY WHITE NO.1 GREEN
NO.1 BLUE GRAY NO.3 BLUE
BLACK
NOTE
COLORS ON PLAN ARE FOR THE PURPOSES OF MEASUREMENT ONLY··ACTUAL COLORS AS PER COLOR CHART·

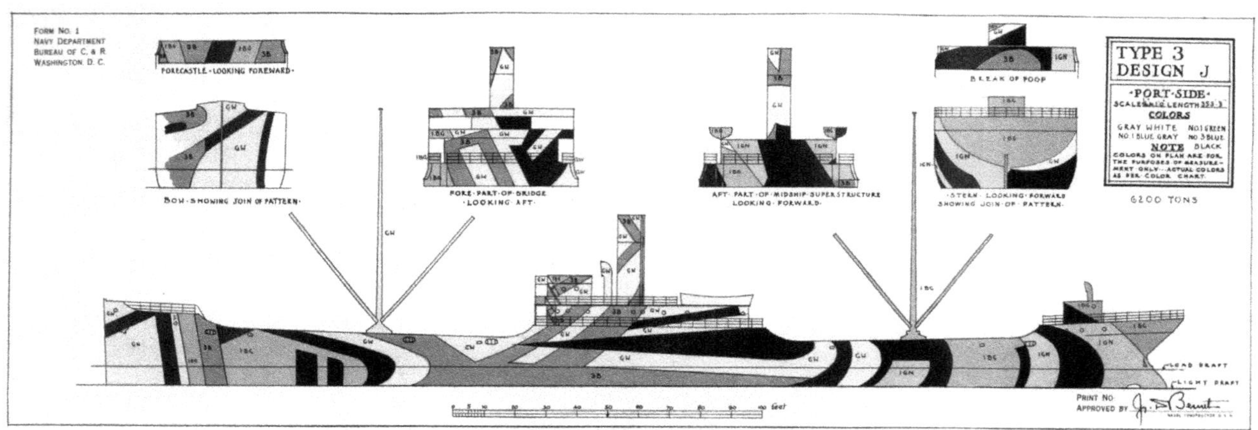

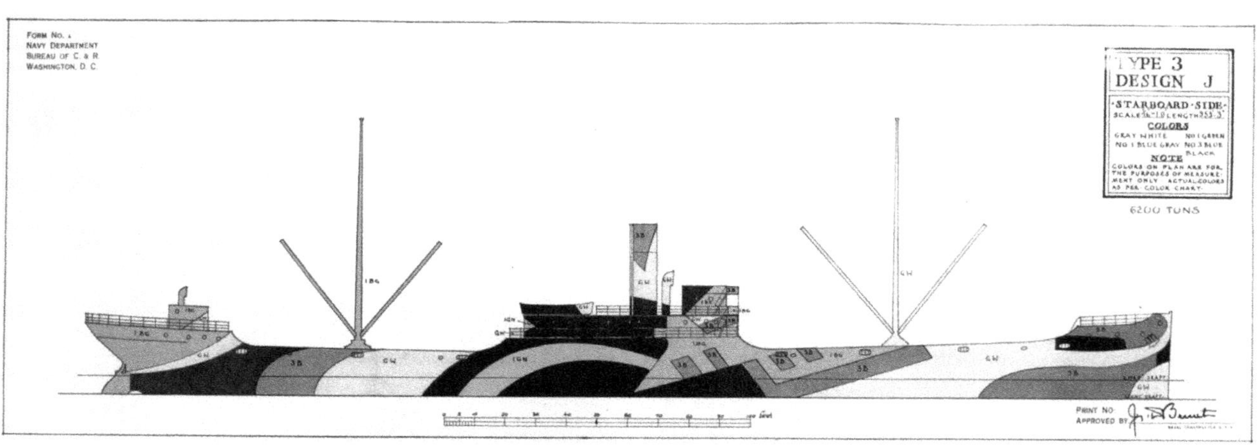

T3 K

Colors used	Ships painted with this pattern
BLACK	ID 3325 AURORA
GREY-WHITE	ID 3693 CRUSO
#2 BLUE-GRAY	
#1 GRAY-GREEN	

TYPE 3
DESIGN K

·PORT·SIDE·
SCALE 1/4"=1'0" LENGTH 352'0"
COLORS
BLACK 2 BLUE GRAY
GRAY WHITE 1 GRAY GREEN
NOTE
COLORS ON PLAN ARE FOR THE PURPOSES OF MEASUREMENT ONLY... ACTUAL COLORS AS PER COLOR CHART

TYPE 3
DESIGN K

·STARBOARD·SIDE·
SCALE 1/4"=1'0" LENGTH 352'0"
COLORS
BLACK 2 BLUE GRAY
GRAY WHITE 1 GRAY GREEN
NOTE
COLORS ON PLAN ARE FOR THE PURPOSES OF MEASUREMENT ONLY ACTUAL COLORS AS PER COLOR CHART

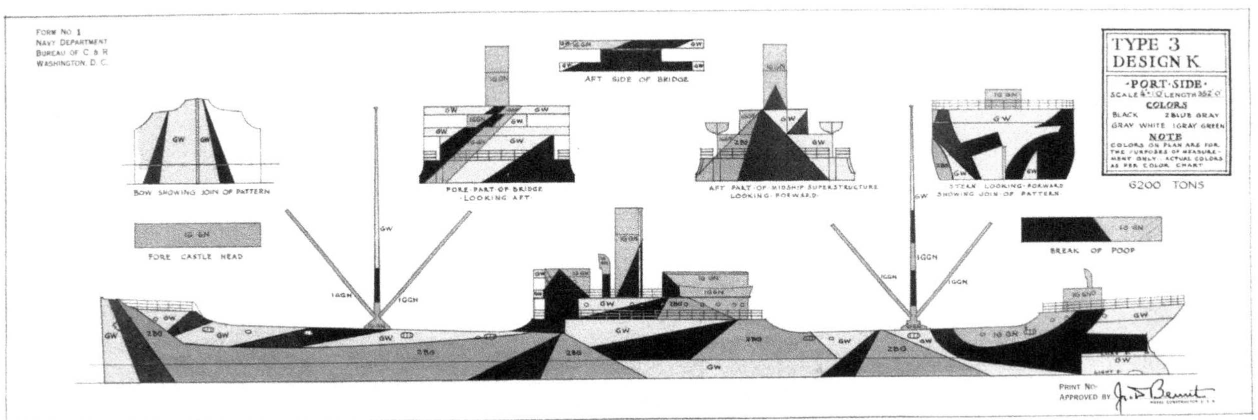

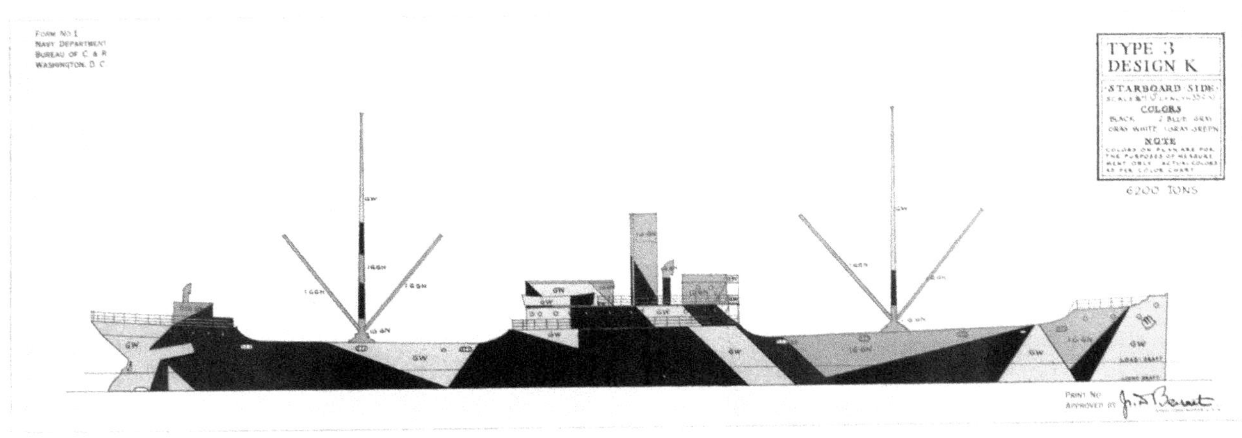

T3 R

Colors used	Ships painted with this pattern
BLACK	ID 3651 POLAR LAND
GREY-WHITE	
#1 BLUE-GRAY	

TYPE 3
DESIGN R
PORT SIDE
SCALE LENGTH 352-0" BP
COLORS
BLACK BLUE GRAY
GRAY WHITE
NOTE
COLORS ON PLAN ARE FOR THE PURPOSES OF MEASUREMENT ONLY
ACTUAL COLORS AS PER COLOR CHART

TYPE 3
DESIGN R
STARBOARD SIDE
COLORS
NOTE
COLORS ON PLAN ARE FOR THE PURPOSES OF MEASUREMENT ONLY
ACTUAL COLORS AS PER COLOR CHART

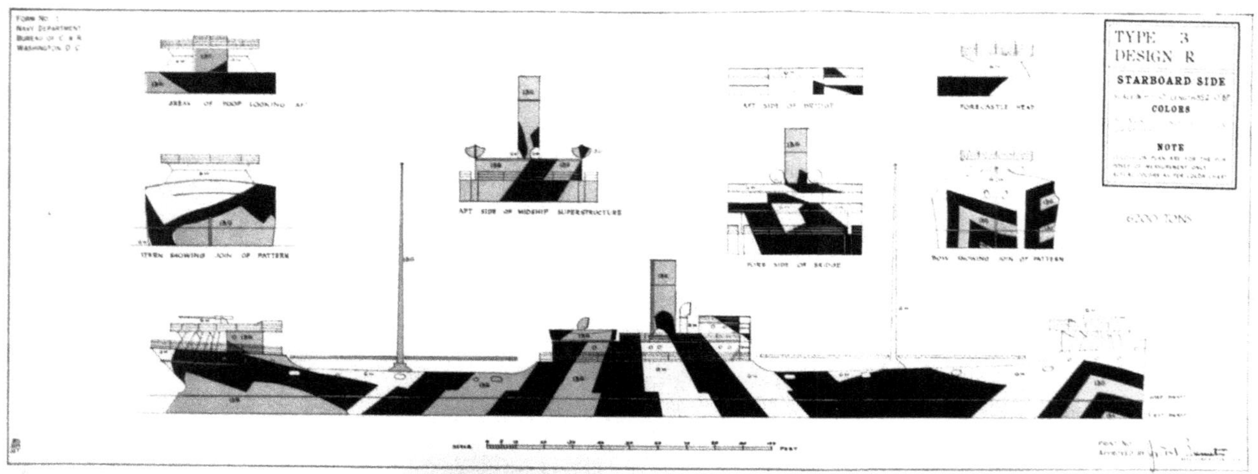

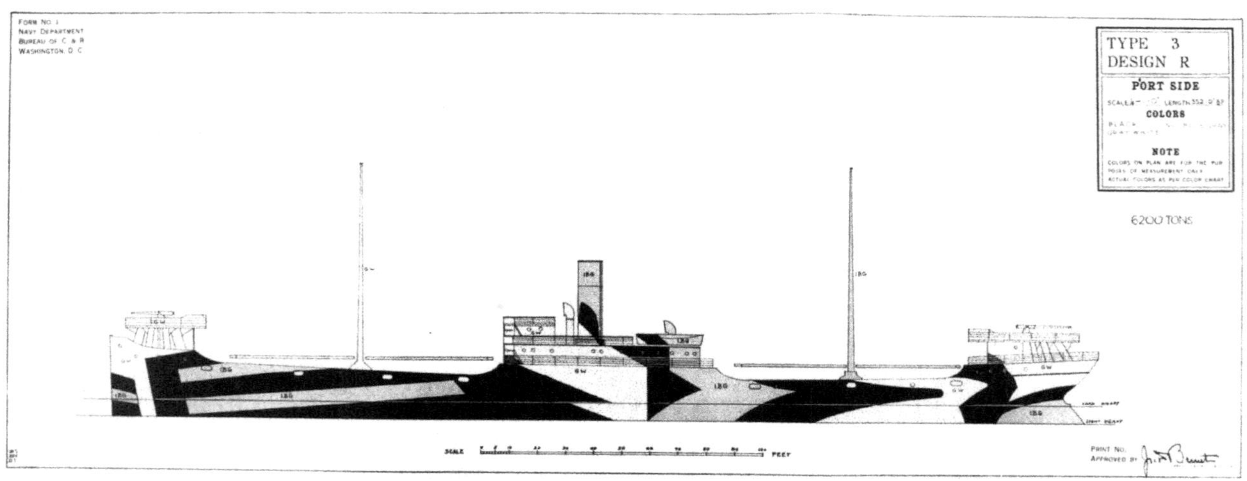

T4 A

Colors used	Ships painted with this pattern
BLACK	ID NONE ALCOR
WHITE	ID 3308 PLYMOUTH
#3 BLUE	ID 1320 SUWANEE (T)
#1 BLUE-GRAY	ID 2126 MUSCATINE (T)

TYPE 4
DESIGN A
PORT SIDE
COLORS
NOTE
COLORS ON PLAN ARE FOR THE PURPOSES OF MEASUREMENT ONLY ACTUAL COLORS AS PER COLOR CHART

TYPE 4
DESIGN A
STARBOARD SIDE
COLORS
1BG-N°1 BLUE GRAY W-WHITE
3B-N°3 BLUE B BLACK
NOTE
COLORS ON PLAN ARE FOR THE PURPOSES OF MEASUREMENT ONLY ACTUAL COLORS AS PER COLOR CHART

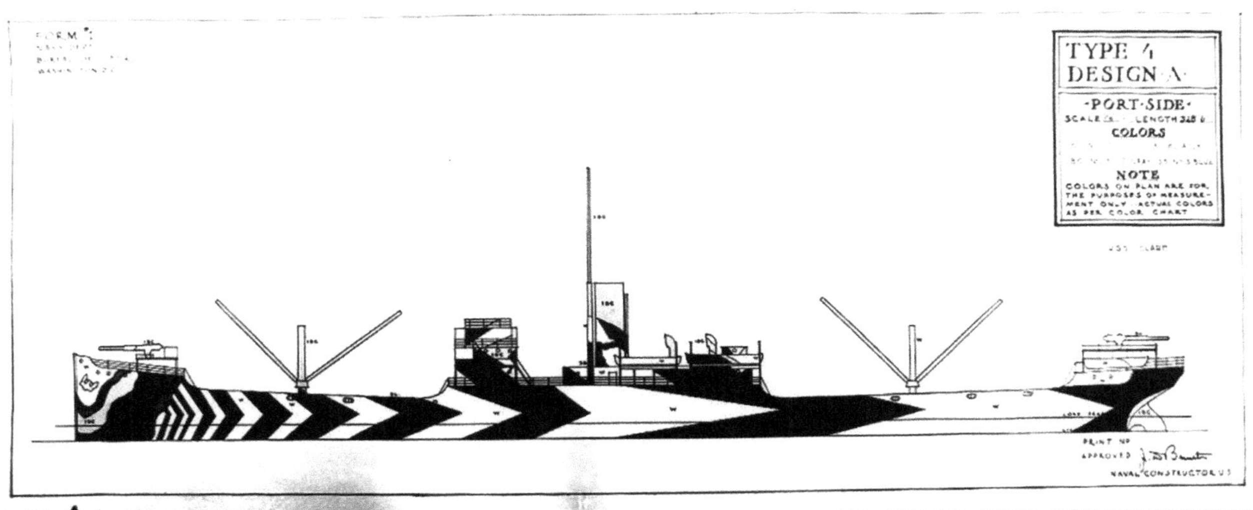

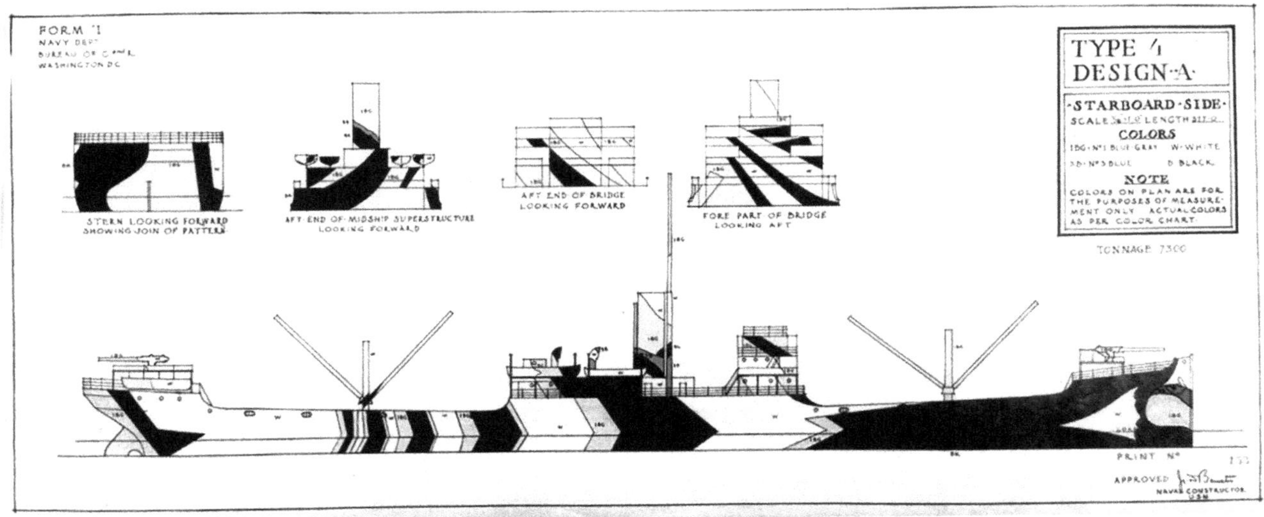

T4 B

Colors used	Ships painted with this pattern
BLACK	ID 3833 LAKE LEDAN
WHITE	2197 ARTEMIS (T)
#3 BLUE	AF 2 CELTIC
#1 BLUE-GRAY	ID 1758 DOCHRA (T)

TYPE 4
DESIGN·B·

·PORT·SIDE·
SCALE 1/16"=1'0" LENGTH 377'0"
COLORS
WHITE No1 BLUE·GREY
BLACK No3 BLUE
NOTE
COLORS ON PLAN ARE FOR THE PURPOSES OF MEASUREMENT ONLY···ACTUAL COLORS AS PER COLOR CHART

TYPE 4
DESIGN·B·

·STARBOARD·SIDE·
SCALE 1/16"=1'0" LENGTH 377'0"
COLORS
WHITE No1 BLUE·GREY
BLACK No3 BLUE
NOTE
COLORS ON·PLAN ARE FOR THE PURPOSES OF MEASUREMENT ONLY ··ACTUAL·COLORS AS PER·COLOR·CHART·

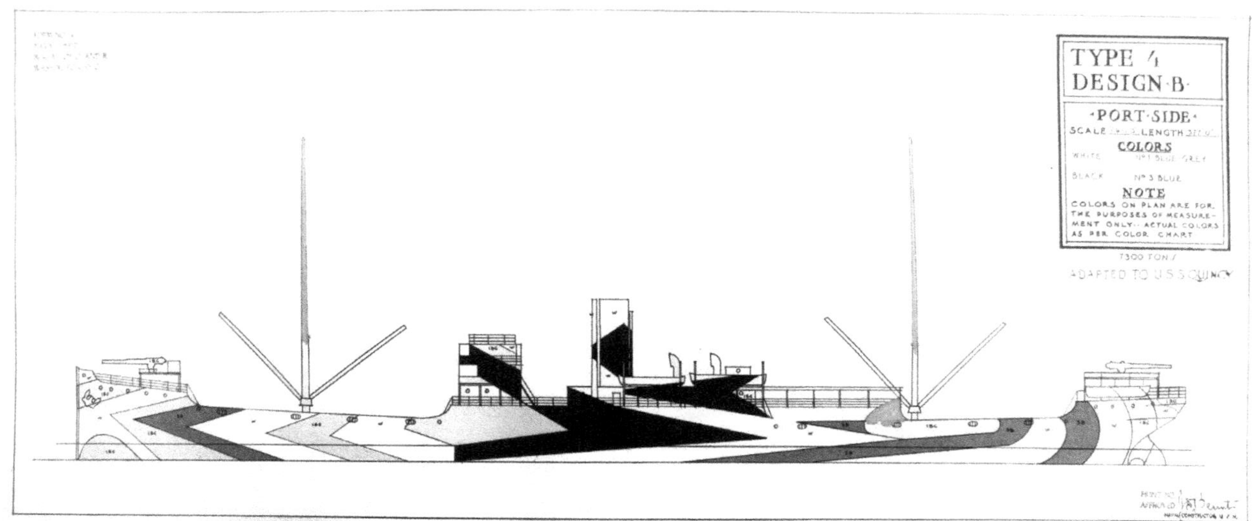

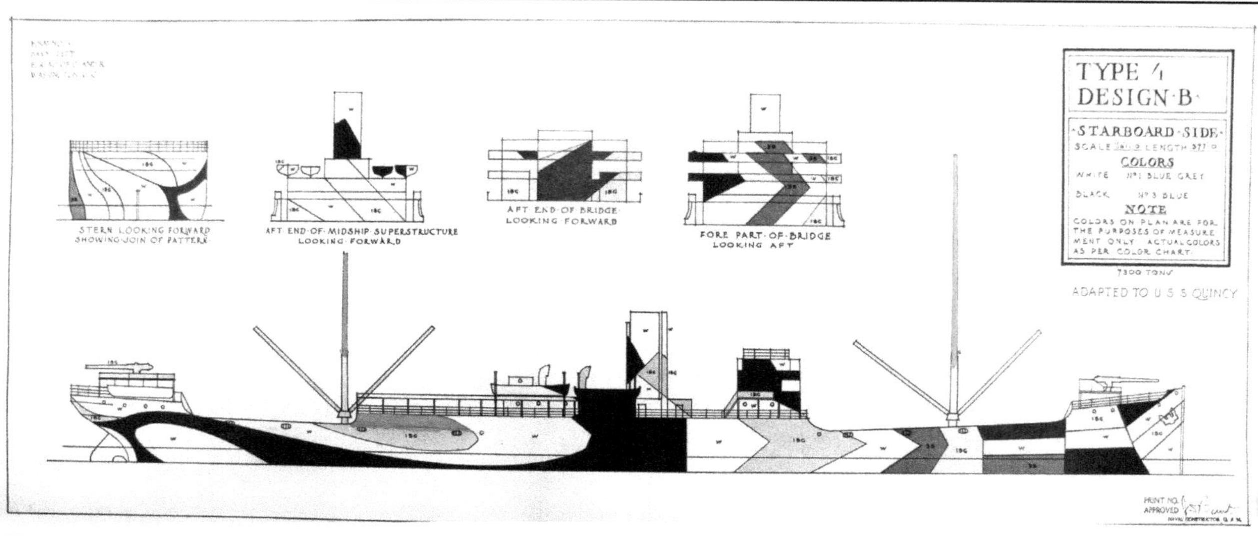

T4 C

Colors used	Ships painted with this pattern
BLACK	ID 3568 LAKE CATHERINE
WHITE	ID 1806 KERESAN
#3 BLUE	ID NONE ALFENOS
#1 BLUE-GRAY	ID 2970 CAPE ROMAIN

TYPE 4
DESIGN C
PORT·SIDE
SCALE ____ LENGTH 328'-6"
COLORS
BLACK NO 1 BLUE GREY
WHITE NO 3 BLUE
NOTE
COLORS ON PLAN ARE FOR THE PURPOSES OF MEASUREMENT ONLY... ACTUAL COLORS AS PER COLOR CHART

TYPE 4
DESIGN C
STARBOARD·SIDE
SCALE ____ LENGTH 328'-6"
COLORS
BLACK NO 1 BLUE GREY
WHITE NO 3 BLUE
NOTE
COLORS ON PLAN ARE FOR THE PURPOSES OF MEASUREMENT ONLY. ACTUAL COLORS AS PER COLOR CHART

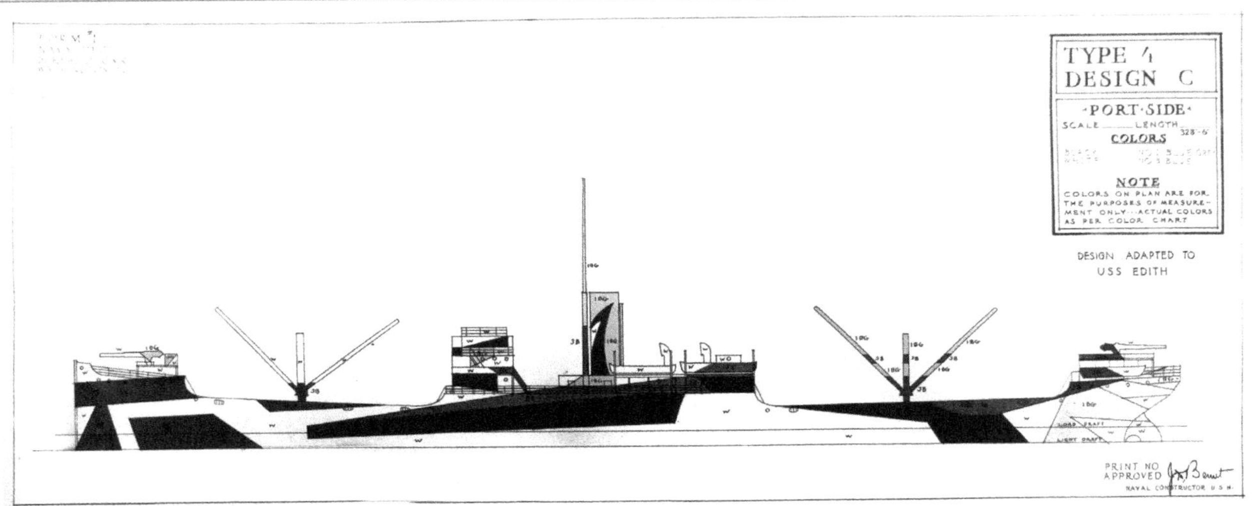

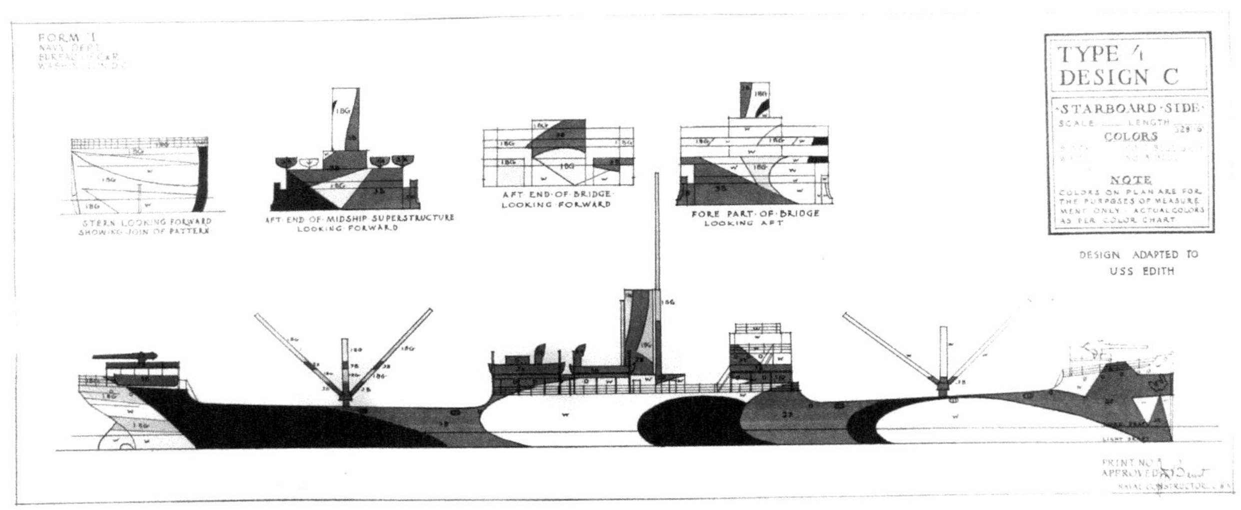

T4 D

Colors used	Ships painted with this pattern
BLACK	ID 4054A LAKE JANET
WHITE	
#3 BLUE	
#1 BLUE-GRAY	

TYPE 4
DESIGN D

·PORT·SIDE·
SCALE 1/16"=1'0" LENGTH 377'0"
COLORS
BLACK NO 1 BLUE GREY
WHITE NO 3 BLUE

NOTE
COLORS ON PLAN ARE FOR THE PURPOSES OF MEASUREMENT ONLY··· ACTUAL COLORS AS PER COLOR CHART

TYPE 4
DESIGN D

·STARBOARD·SIDE·
SCALE 1/16"=1'0" LENGTH 377'0"
COLORS
BLACK NO 1 BLUE GREY
WHITE NO 3 BLUE

NOTE
COLORS ON PLAN ARE FOR THE PURPOSES OF MEASUREMENT ONLY ACTUAL COLORS AS PER COLOR CHART

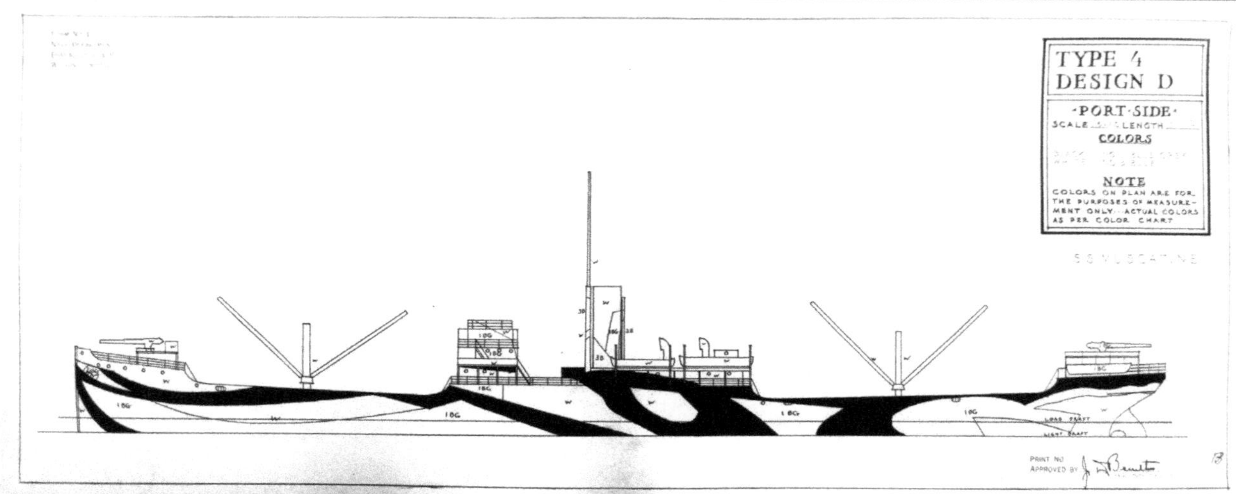

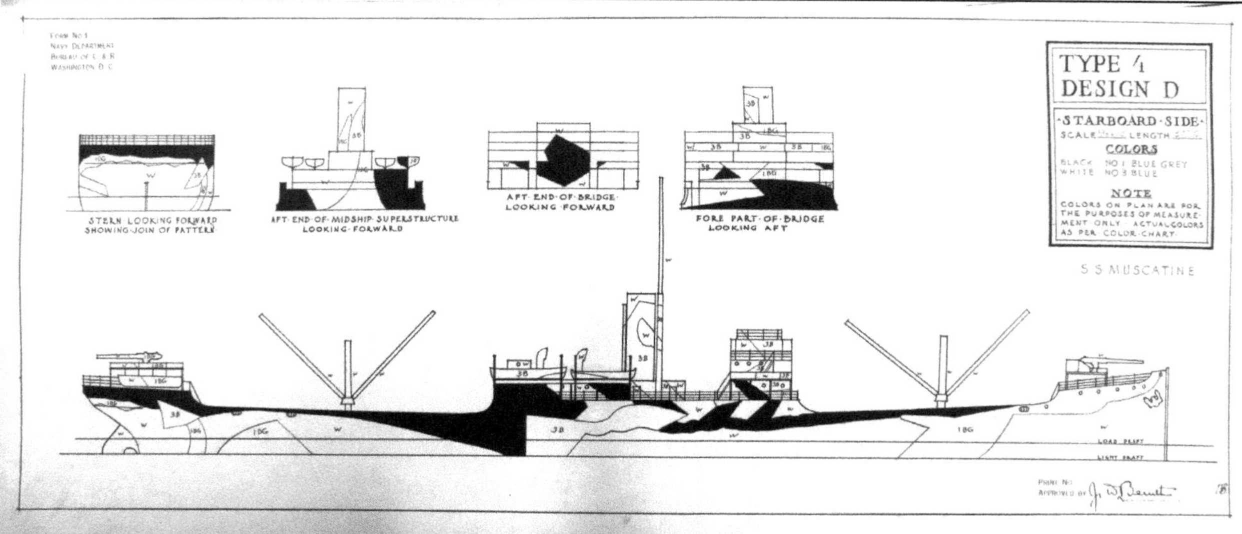

T4 E

Colors used	Ships painted with this pattern
BLACK	ID 1341 EL ALMIRANTE
WHITE	2805 JAN VAN NASSAU (T)
#3 BLUE	ID 3547C LAKE BLANCHESTER (T)
#1 BLUE-GRAY	ID 1597 NORLINA (T)

TYPE 4
DESIGN E
-PORT-SIDE-
SCALE 1/16"=1'0 LENGTH 377' 0"
COLORS
BLACK NO 1 BLUE GREY
WHITE NO 3 BLUE
NOTE
COLORS ON PLAN ARE FOR THE PURPOSES OF MEASUREMENT ONLY ... ACTUAL COLORS AS PER COLOR CHART

TYPE 4
DESIGN E
-STARBOARD-SIDE-
SCALE 1/16"=1'0 LENGTH 377' 0"
COLORS
BLACK NO 1 BLUE GREY
WHITE NO 3 BLUE
NOTE
COLORS ON PLAN ARE FOR THE PURPOSES OF MEASUREMENT ONLY ... ACTUAL COLORS AS PER COLOR CHART

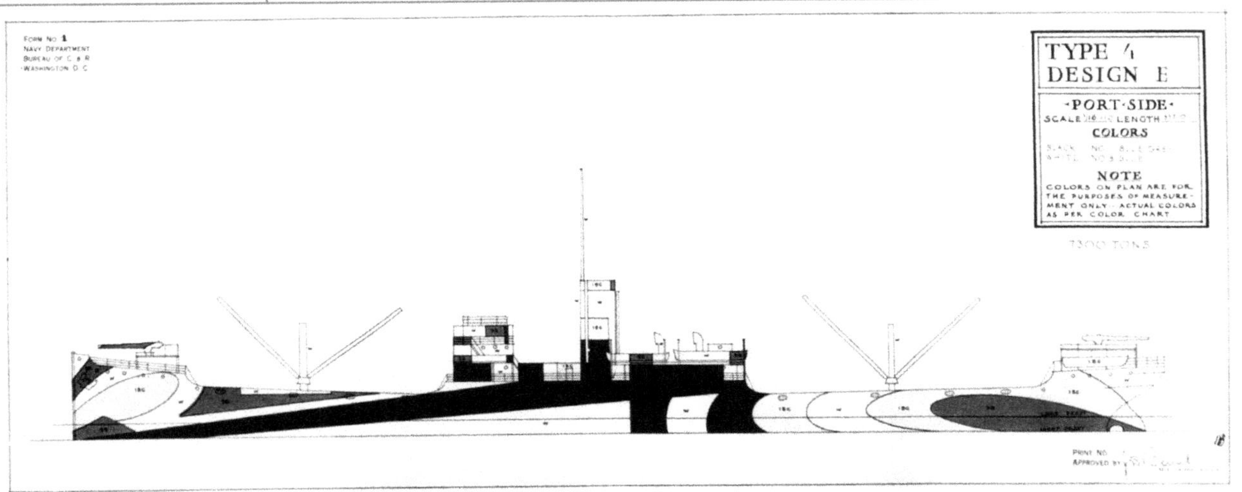

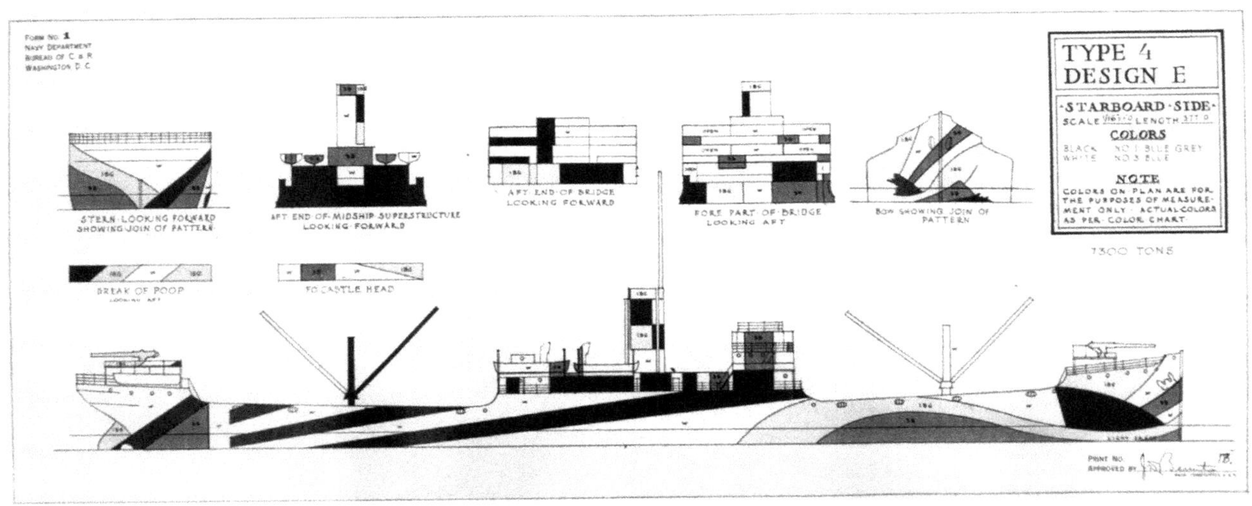

T4 F

Colors used	Ships painted with this pattern
BLACK	ID3322 WESTGOTOMSKA
WHITE	
#3 BLUE	
#1 BLUE-GRAY	

TYPE 4
DESIGN F
·PORT·SIDE·
SCALE 1/16"=1'0" LENGTH 377'-0"
COLORS
BLACK NO 1 BLUE GREY
WHITE NO 3 BLUE
NOTE
COLORS ON PLAN ARE FOR THE PURPOSES OF MEASUREMENT ONLY···ACTUAL COLORS AS PER COLOR CHART

TYPE 4
DESIGN F
·STARBOARD·SIDE·
SCALE 1/16"=1'0" LENGTH 377'-0"
COLORS
BLACK NO 1 BLUE GREY
WHITE NO 3 BLUE
NOTE
COLORS ON PLAN ARE FOR THE PURPOSES OF MEASUREMENT ONLY···ACTUAL COLORS AS PER COLOR CHART

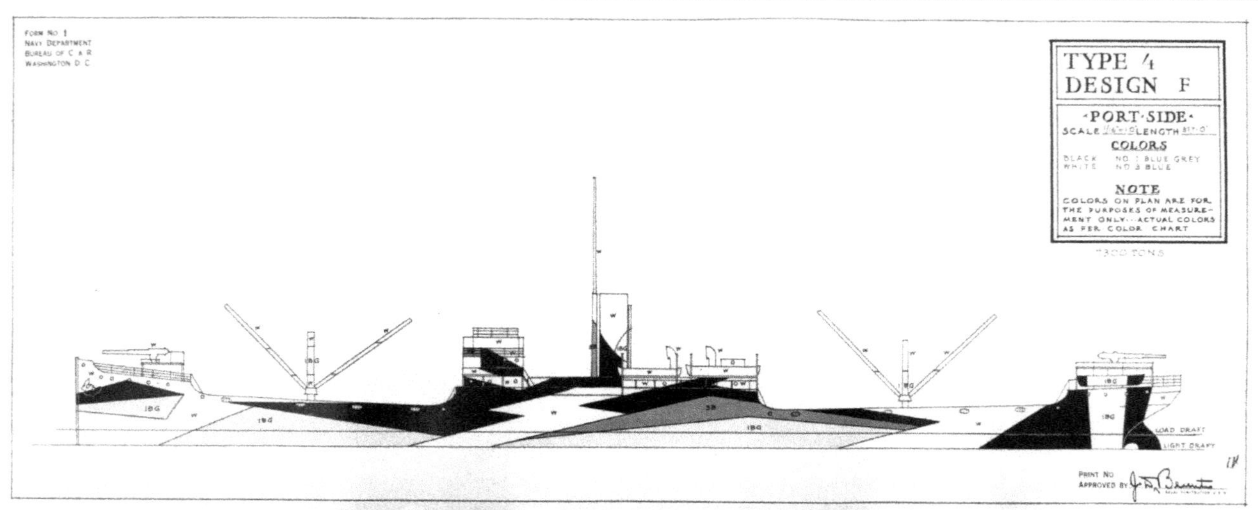

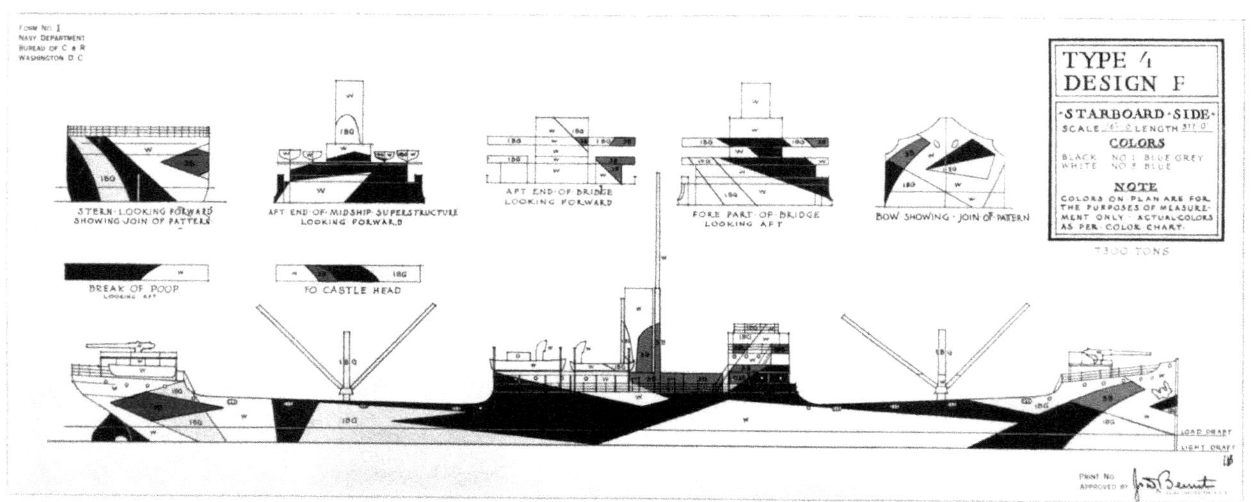

T4 G

Colors used	Ships painted with this pattern
BLACK	ID 3461 LIBERTY
WHITE	ID 3565 BERWYN
#3 BLUE	CLARK (T)
#1 BLUE	

TYPE 4
DESIGN G

·PORT·SIDE·
SCALE 1/16=1'0" LENGTH 377'0"
COLORS
WHITE NO 3 BLUE
NO 1 BLUE GRAY BLACK
NO 1 BLUE
NOTE
COLORS ON PLAN ARE FOR THE PURPOSES OF MEASUREMENT ONLY···ACTUAL COLORS AS PER COLOR CHART

TYPE 4
DESIGN G

·STARBOARD·SIDE·
SCALE 1/16=1'0" LENGTH 377'0"
COLORS
WHITE NO 3 BLUE
NO 1 BLUE GRAY BLACK
NO 1 BLUE
NOTE
COLORS ON PLAN ARE FOR THE PURPOSES OF MEASUREMENT ONLY · ACTUAL COLORS AS PER COLOR CHART

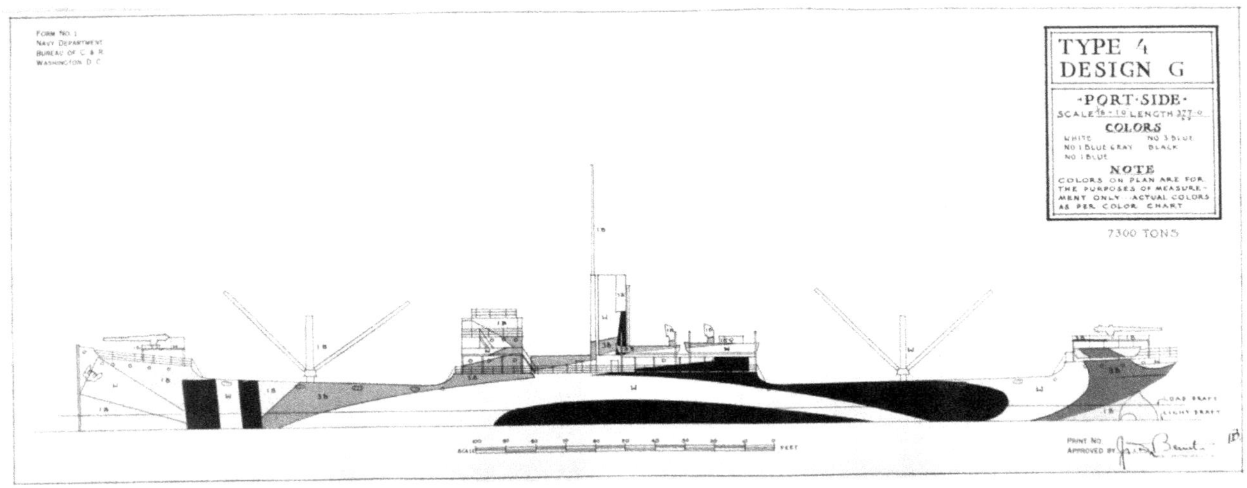

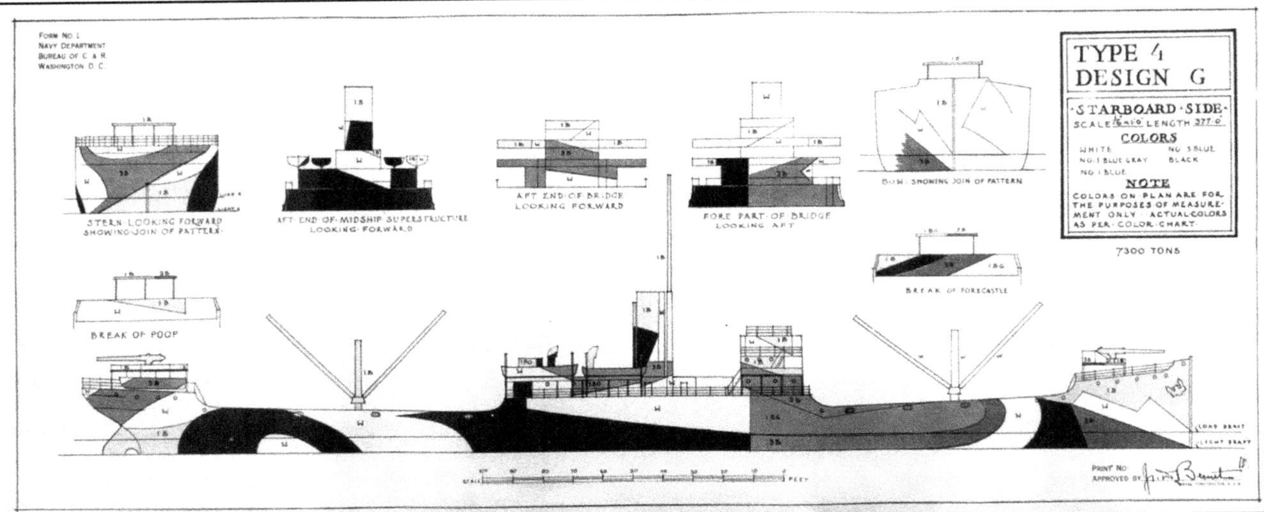

T4 H

Colors used	Ships painted with this pattern
BLACK	ID 3401 CANIBAS
GREY-WHITE	
#3 BLUE	
#1 BLUE	
#1 GREEN	

TYPE 4
DESIGN H

PORT·SIDE
SCALE 1/16"=1'-0" LENGTH 377'-0"
COLORS
NO 1 BLUE · NO 1 GREEN · BLACK
NO 3 BLUE GRAY WHITE
NOTE
COLORS ON PLAN ARE FOR THE PURPOSES OF MEASUREMENT ONLY... ACTUAL COLORS AS PER COLOR CHART

TYPE 4
DESIGN H

STARBOARD·SIDE
SCALE 1/16"=1'-0" LENGTH 377'-0"
COLORS
NO. 3 BLUE GRAY WHITE
NO. 1 BLUE · NO 1 GREEN · BLACK
NOTE
COLORS ON PLAN ARE FOR THE PURPOSES OF MEASUREMENT ONLY... ACTUAL COLORS AS PER COLOR CHART

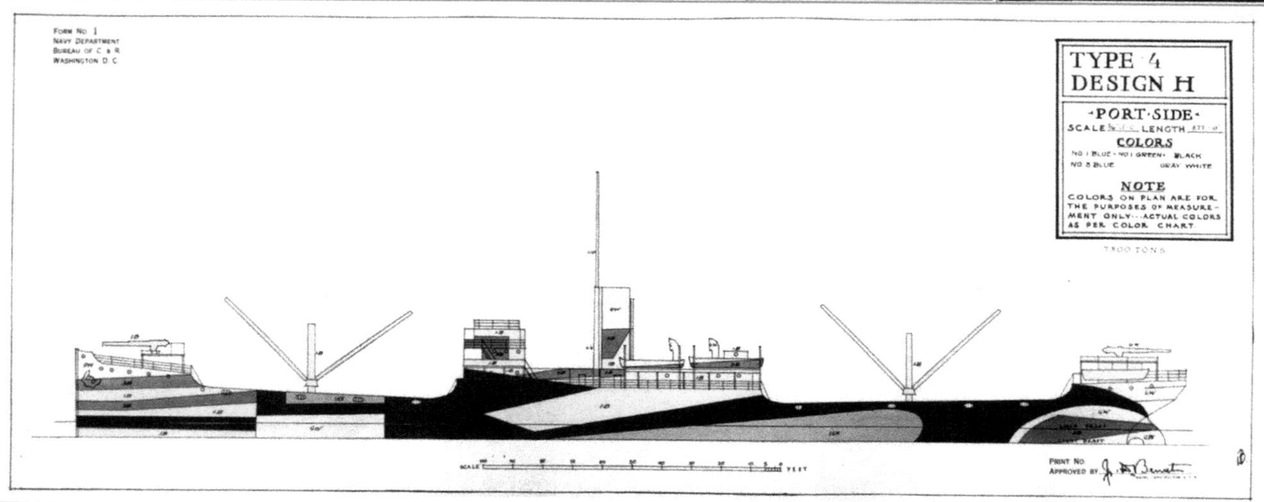

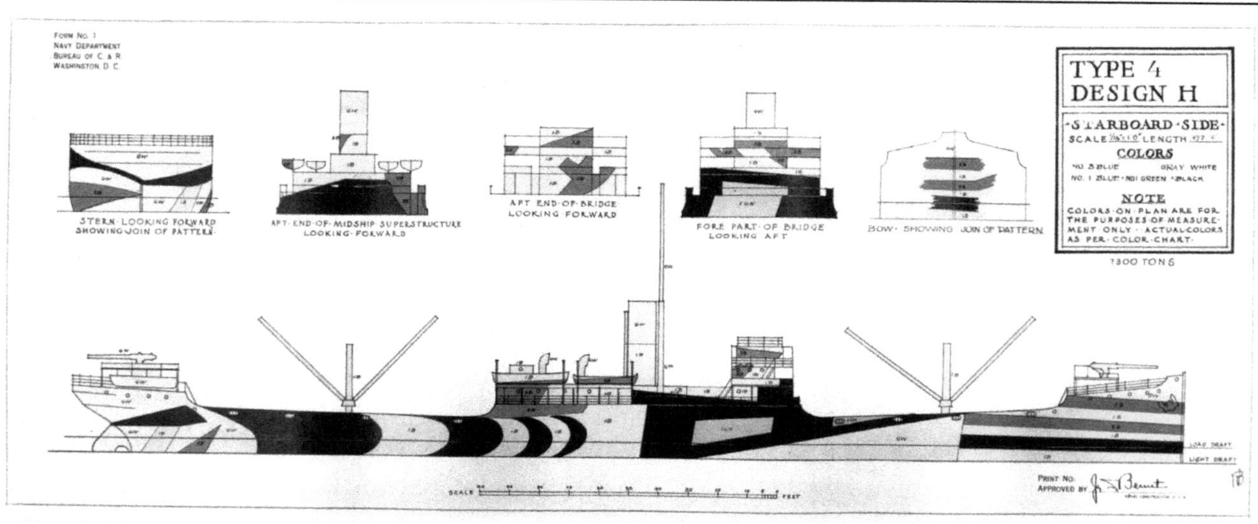

T4 I

Colors used	Ships painted with this pattern
BLACK	ID 3657 FEDERAL
GREY-WHITE	
#1 BLUE-GRAY	

TYPE 4
DESIGN I
·PORT·SIDE·
SCALE 1/16"·1'·0" LENGTH 377'·0"
COLORS
NO 1 BLUE GRAY
GRAY WHITE
BLACK
NOTE
COLORS ON PLAN ARE FOR THE PURPOSES OF MEASUREMENT ONLY···ACTUAL COLORS AS PER COLOR CHART

TYPE 4
DESIGN I
·STARBOARD·SIDE·
SCALE 1/16"·1'·0" LENGTH 377'·0"
COLORS
NO 1 BLUE GRAY
GRAY WHITE
BLACK
NOTE
COLORS ON PLAN ARE FOR THE PURPOSES OF MEASUREMENT ONLY · ACTUAL COLORS AS PER COLOR CHART

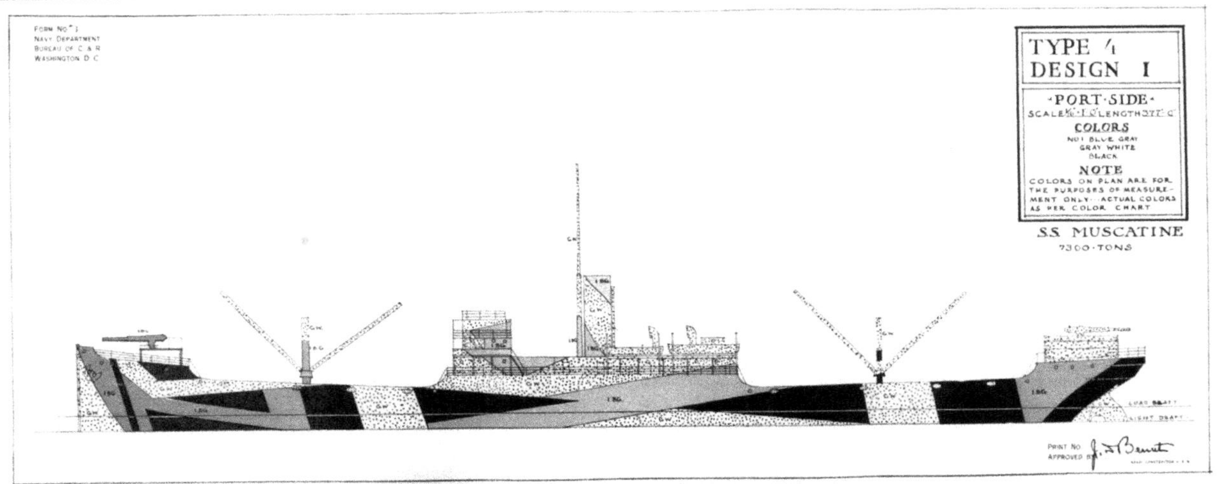

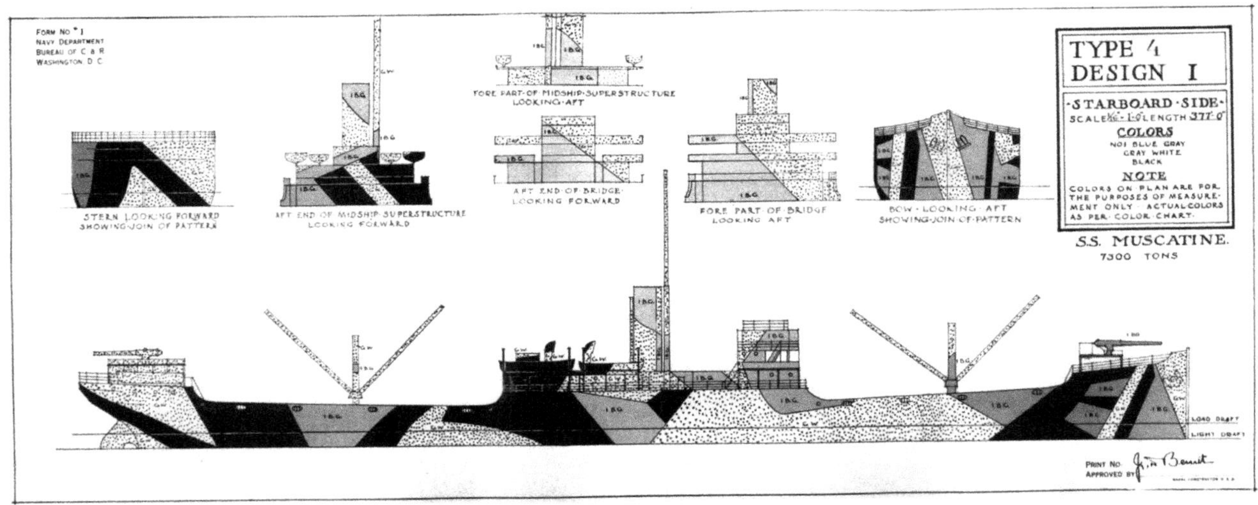

T4 J

Colors used	Ships painted with this pattern
BLACK	ID 3554 HICKMAN
GREY-WHITE	ID 2515 VEENDIJK
#3 BLUE	
#1 BLUE-GRAY	

TYPE 4
DESIGN J
·PORT·SIDE·
SCALE 1/16"=1'0" LENGTH 377'0"
COLORS
BLACK NO 1 BLUE GRAY
GRAY WHITE NO 3 BLUE
NOTE
COLORS ON PLAN ARE FOR THE PURPOSES OF MEASUREMENT ONLY···ACTUAL COLORS AS PER COLOR CHART

TYPE 4
DESIGN J
·STARBOARD·SIDE·
SCALE 1/16"=1'0" LENGTH 377'0"
COLORS
BLACK NO 1 BLUE GRAY
GRAY WHITE NO 3 BLUE
NOTE
COLORS·ON·PLAN ARE FOR THE PURPOSES OF MEASUREMENT ONLY ··ACTUAL·COLORS AS PER·COLOR·CHART·

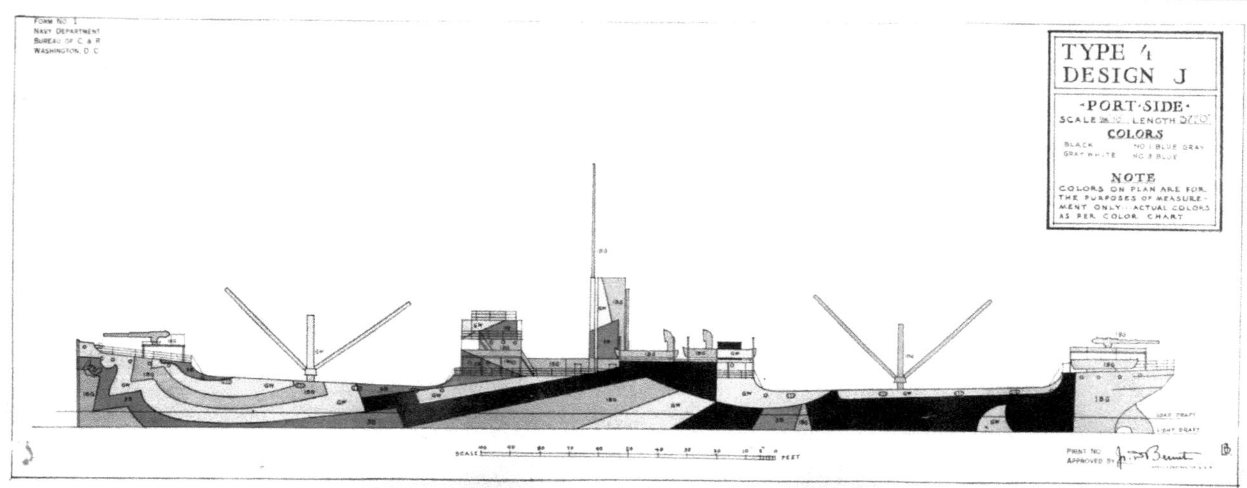

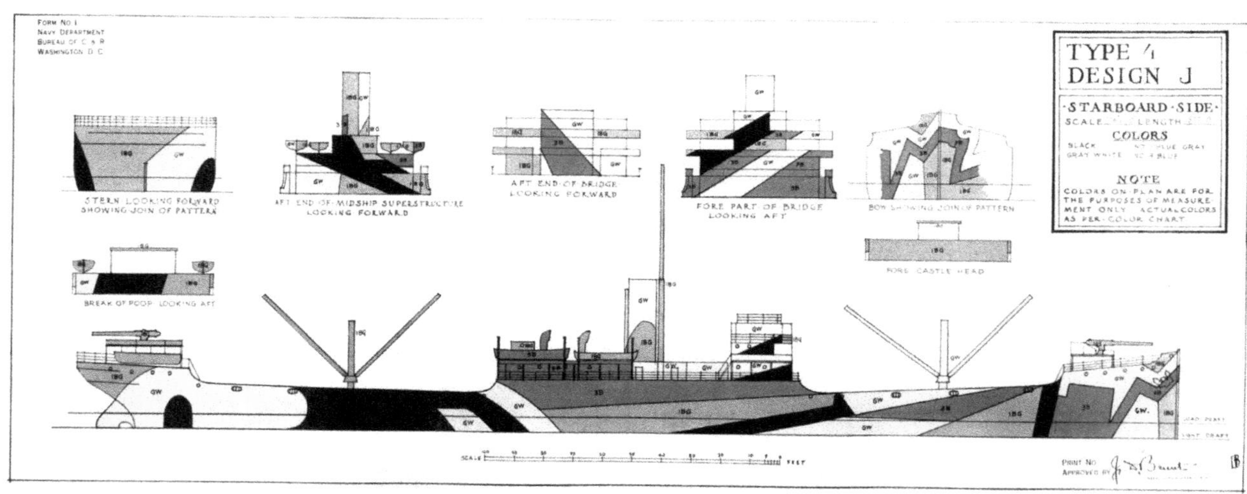

T4 M

Colors used	Ships painted with this pattern
BLACK	ID 3700 WEST LASHAWAY
GREY-WHITE	
#3 BLUE	

TYPE 4
DESIGN ·M·
PORT SIDE
SCALE 1/16 "–1'-0" LENGTH 377'-0"
COLORS
BLACK·
GW· GRAY-WHITE·
3B· NO·3 BLUE·
NOTE
COLORS ON PLAN ARE FOR THE PURPOSES OF MEASUREMENT ONLY . . . ACTUAL COLORS AS PER COLOR CHART

TYPE 4
DESIGN M
STARBOARD SIDE
SCALE 1/16 "–1'-0" LENGTH 377'-0"
COLORS
BLACK·
GW· GRAY-WHITE·
NO·3 BLUE ·3B·
NOTE
COLORS ON PLAN ARE FOR THE PURPOSES OF MEASUREMENT ONLY . . . ACTUAL COLORS AS PER COLOR CHART

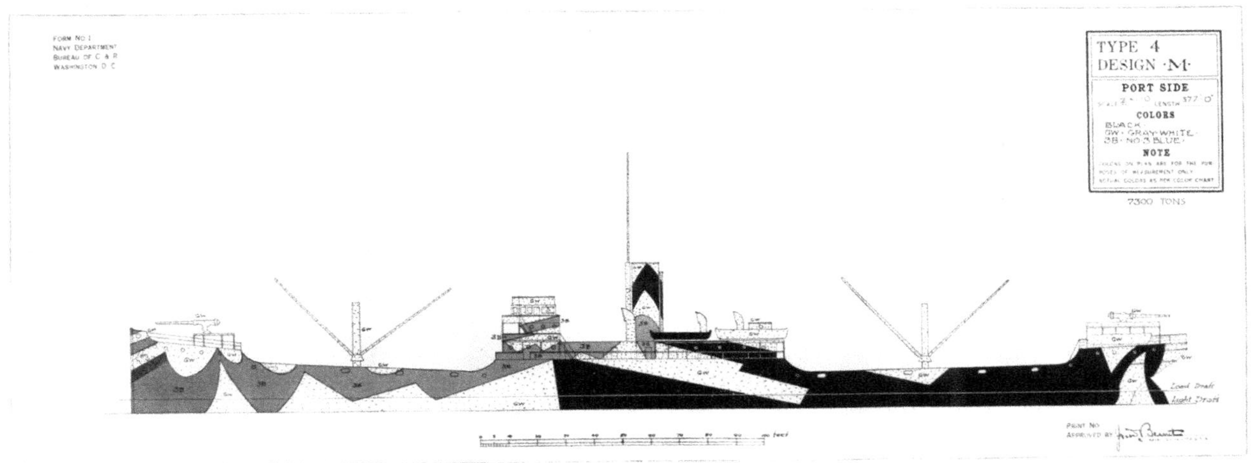

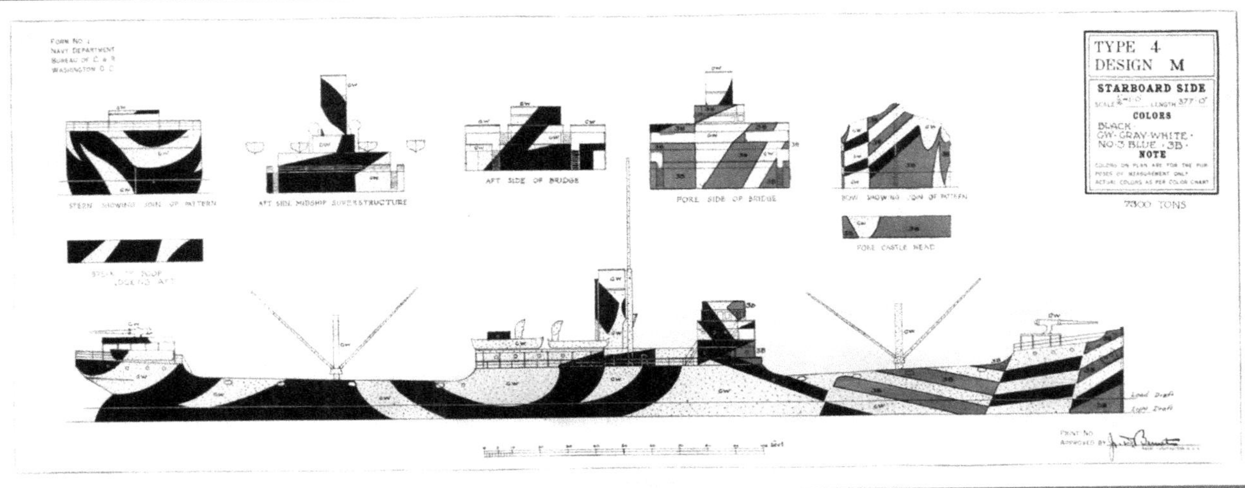

T5 A

Colors used	Ships painted with this pattern
BLACK	ID 3023 RADNOR
WHITE	ID 3020 KATRINA LUCKENBACH
#3 BLUE	ID 3171 WALTER A LUCKENBACH
#1 BLUE-GRAY	ID 1954 MONTPELIER (T)

TYPE 5
DESIGN A

·PORT·SIDE·
SCALE 1/16"=1'0 LENGTH 447'0
COLORS
WHITE BLACK
NO. 3 BLUE NO. 1 BLUE GREY
NOTE
COLORS ON PLAN ARE FOR THE PURPOSES OF MEASUREMENT ONLY. ACTUAL COLORS AS PER COLOR CHART

TYPE 5
DESIGN A

·STARBOARD·SIDE·
SCALE 1/16"=1'0 LENGTH 447'0
COLORS
WHITE BLACK
NO. 3 BLUE NO. 1 BLUE GREY
NOTE
COLORS ON PLAN ARE FOR THE PURPOSES OF MEASUREMENT ONLY. ACTUAL COLORS AS PER COLOR CHART

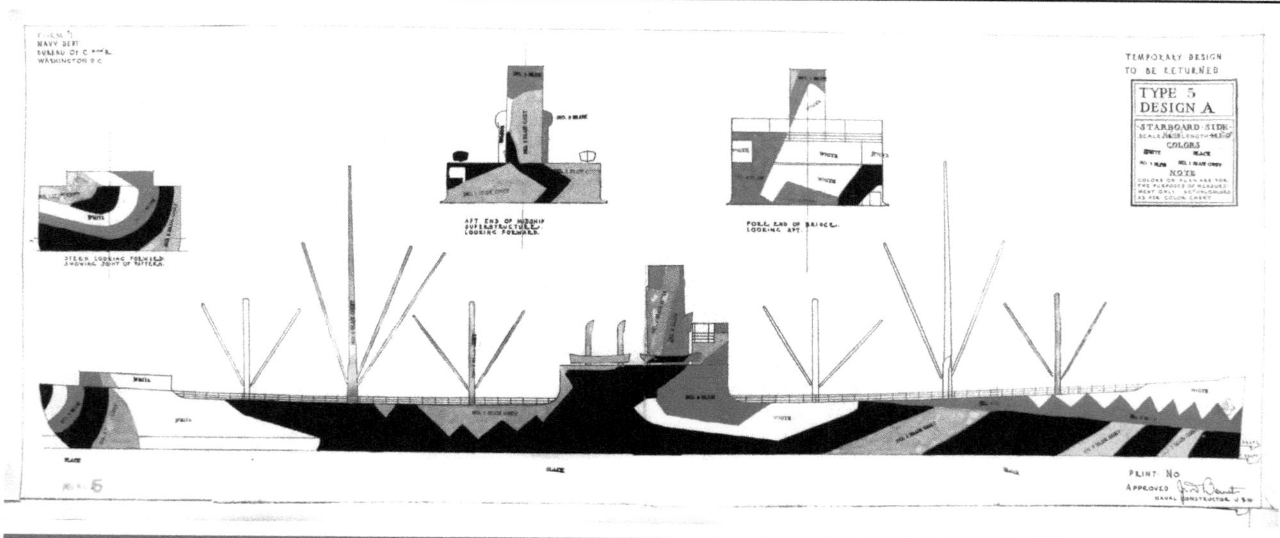

T5 B

Colors used	Ships painted with this pattern
BLACK	ID 3134 LIBERATOR
WHITE	ID 2160 F J LUCKENBACH
#3 BLUE	ID 2890 WESTERNER (T)
#1 BLUE-GRAY	ID 3122 WESTCHESTER (T)

TYPE 5
DESIGN B

·PORT·SIDE·
SCALE LENGTH 441'0"
COLORS
BLACK NO. 1 BLUE GREY
WHITE NO. 3 BLUE
NOTE
COLORS ON PLAN ARE FOR THE PURPOSES OF MEASUREMENT ONLY···ACTUAL COLORS AS PER COLOR CHART

TYPE 5
DESIGN B

·STARBOARD·SIDE·
SCALE LENGTH 441'0"
COLORS
WHITE NO. 3 BLUE
BLACK NO. 1 BLUE GREY
NOTE
COLORS ON PLAN ARE FOR THE PURPOSES OF MEASUREMENT ONLY ACTUAL COLORS AS PER COLOR CHART

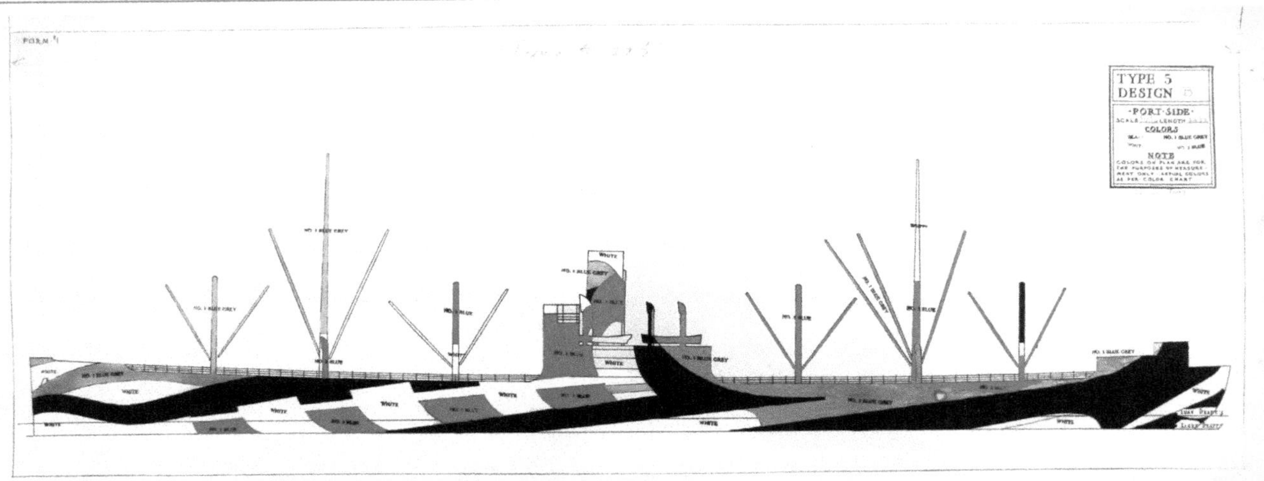

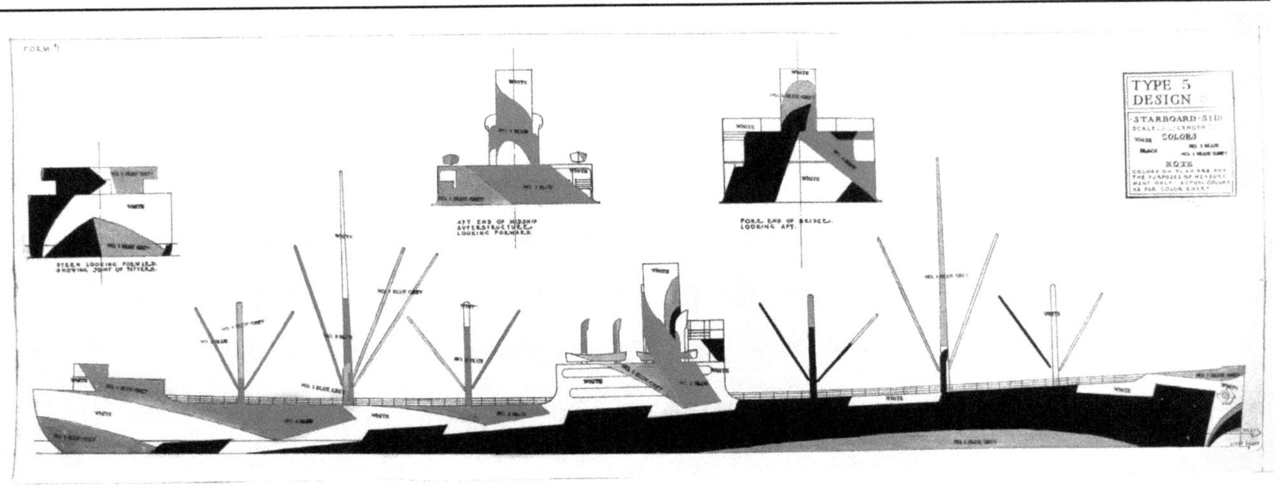

T5 C

Colors used	Ships painted with this pattern
BLACK	ID 3390 EASTERN CHIEF
WHITE	ID 1662 EDWARD LUCKENBACH
#3 BLUE	ID 4410 LAKE FERNWOOD
#1 BLUE-GRAY	ID 4587 EDGAR F LUCKENBACH

TYPE 5
DESIGN C

PORT SIDE

SCALE 1/16"=1'0" LENGTH 447'0"

COLORS

BLACK NO 1 BLUE GREY
WHITE NO 3 BLUE

NOTE

COLORS ON PLAN ARE FOR THE PURPOSES OF MEASUREMENT ONLY ... ACTUAL COLORS AS PER COLOR CHART

TYPE 5
DESIGN C

STARBOARD SIDE

SCALE 1/16"=1'0" LENGTH 447'0"

COLORS

BLACK NO 1 BLUE GREY
WHITE NO 3 BLUE

NOTE

COLORS ON PLAN ARE FOR THE PURPOSES OF MEASUREMENT ONLY ... ACTUAL COLORS AS PER COLOR CHART

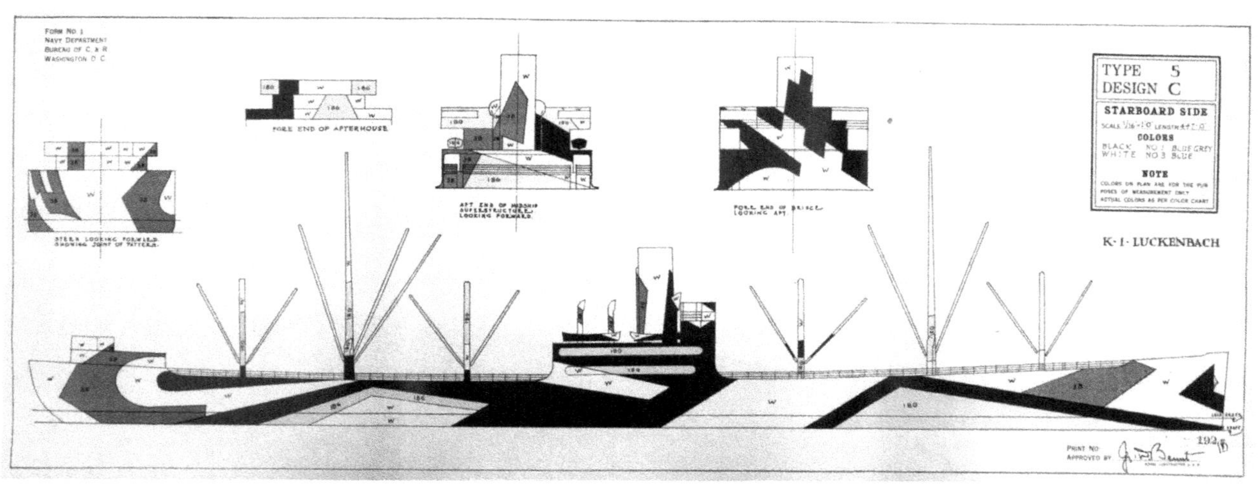

T5 D

Colors used	Ships painted with this pattern
BLACK	ID 2407 JULIA LUCKENBACH
WHITE	
#3 BLUE	
#1 BLUE-GRAY	
#1 GREEN	

TYPE 5
DESIGN D
·PORT·SIDE·
SCALE 1/16"=1'0 LENGTH 447'0 BP
COLORS
BLACK 3 BLUE
WHITE 1 BLUE-GRAY
1 GREEN
NOTE
COLORS ON PLAN ARE FOR THE PURPOSES OF MEASUREMENT ONLY. ACTUAL COLORS AS PER COLOR CHART

TYPE 5
DESIGN D
·STARBOARD·SIDE·
SCALE 1/16"=1'0 LENGTH 447'0 BP
COLORS
BLACK 3 BLUE
WHITE 1 BLUE-GRAY
1 GREEN
NOTE
COLORS ON PLAN ARE FOR THE PURPOSES OF MEASUREMENT ONLY. ACTUAL COLORS AS PER COLOR CHART.

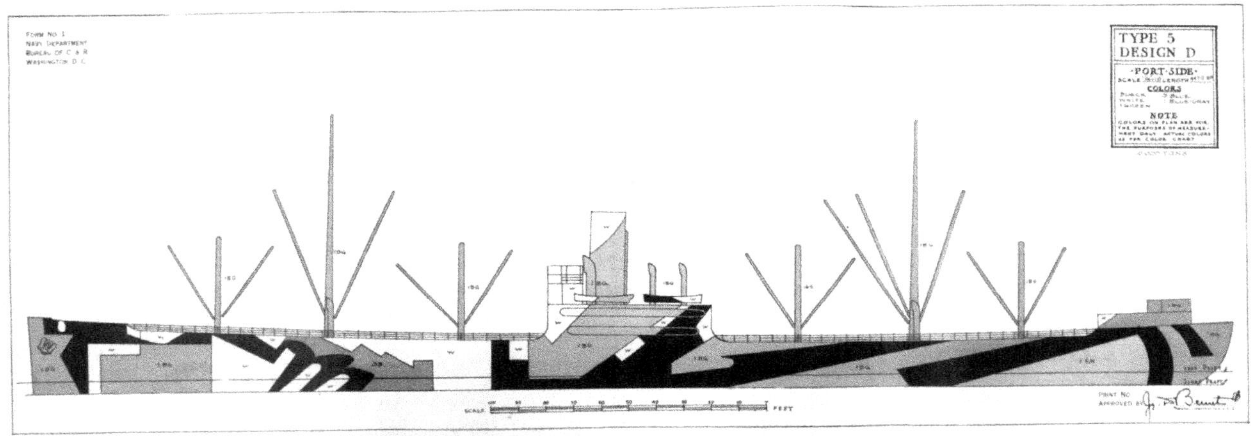

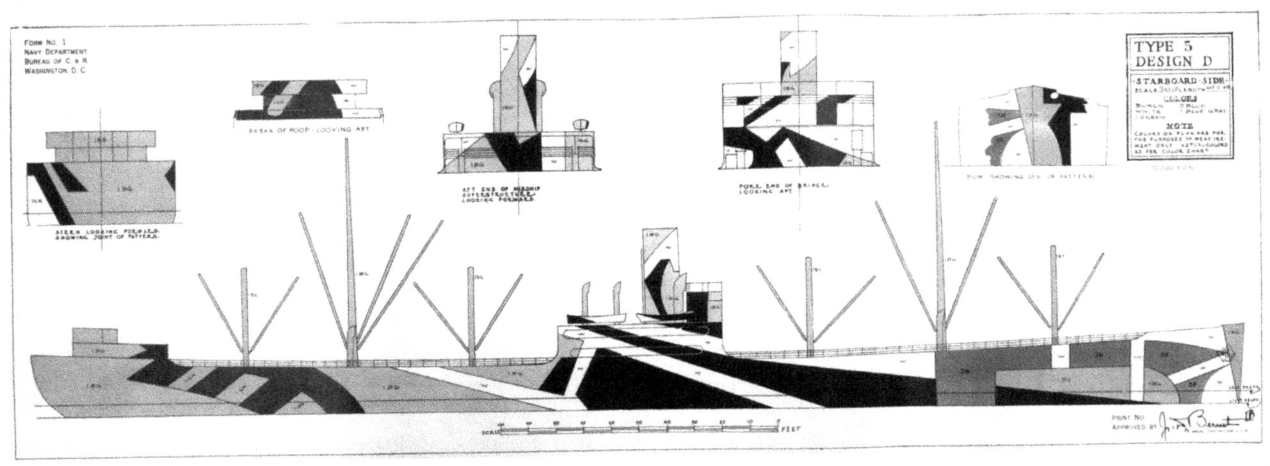

T6 A

Colors used	Ships painted with this pattern
BLACK	ID 2902 WILLIAM A MCKENNEY
WHITE	
#3 BLUE	
#1 BLUE-GRAY	

TYPE 6
DESIGN · A
· PORT · SIDE ·
SCALE ⅛"=1'0" LENGTH 324'0"
COLORS
WHITE NO. 3 BLUE NO. 1 BLUE GREY
BLACK
NOTE
COLORS ON PLAN ARE FOR THE PURPOSES OF MEASUREMENT ONLY · · · ACTUAL COLORS AS PER COLOR CHART

TYPE 6
DESIGN · A
· STARBOARD · SIDE ·
SCALE ⅛"=1'0" LENGTH 324'0"
COLORS
WHITE NO. 3 BLUE NO. 1 BLUE GREY
BLACK
NOTE
COLORS ON PLAN ARE FOR THE PURPOSES OF MEASUREMENT ONLY · · · ACTUAL COLORS AS PER COLOR CHART

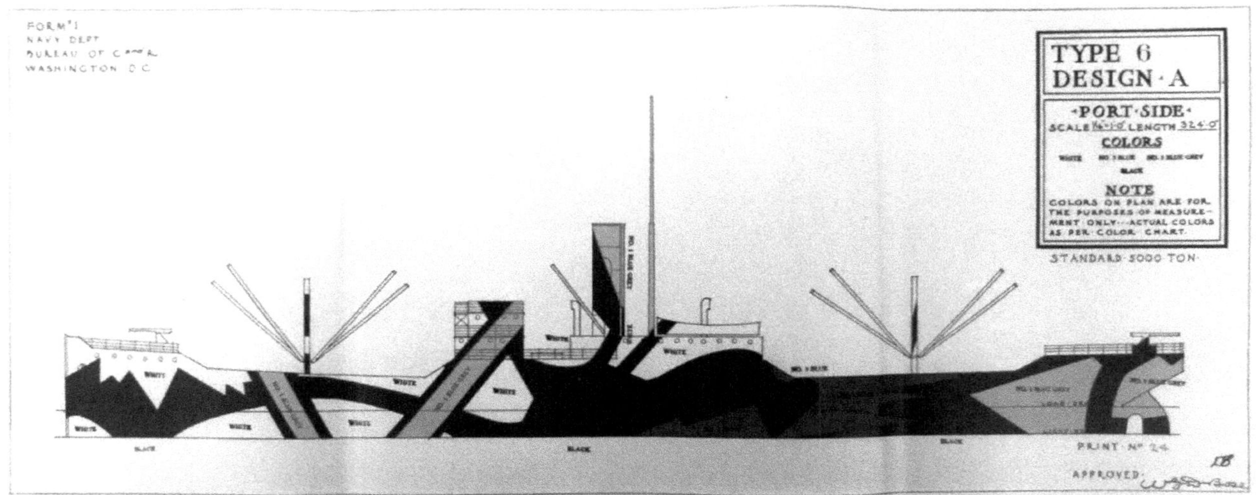

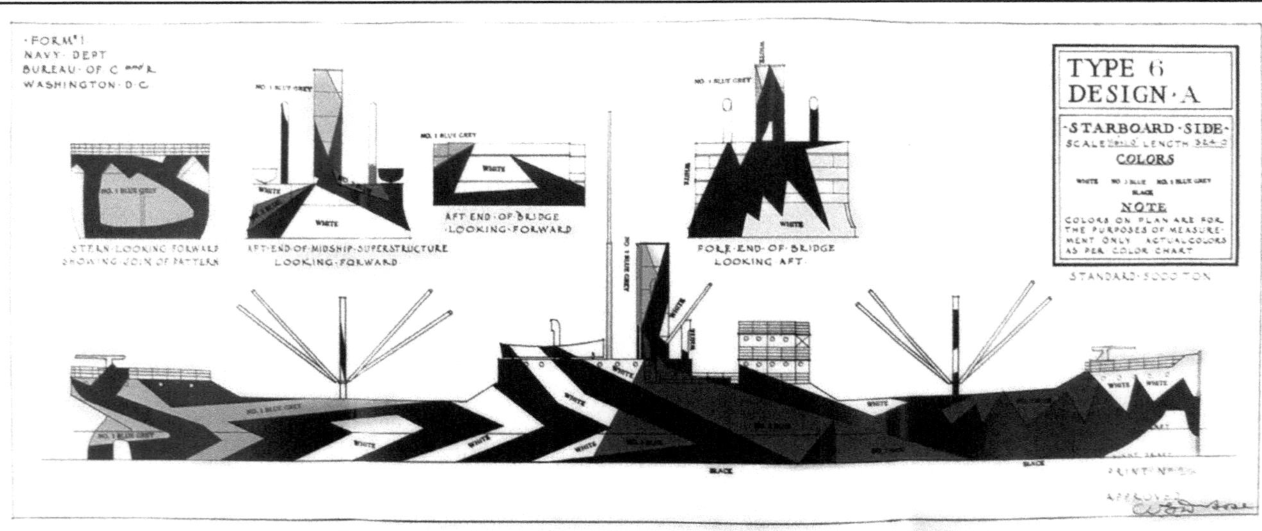

T6 B

Colors used	Ships painted with this pattern
BLACK	ID 2228 EVELYN
WHITE	ID 3120 WESTINDIAN
#3 BLUE	ID 2078 PENSACOLA
#1 BLUE-GRAY	ID 3459 EDITH (T)

TYPE 6
DESIGN B
·PORT·SIDE·
SCALE LENGTH 324'-0"
COLORS
NO. 3 BLUE NO. 1 BLUE GREY WHITE
BLACK
NOTE
COLORS ON PLAN ARE FOR THE PURPOSES OF MEASUREMENT ONLY···ACTUAL COLORS AS PER COLOR CHART·

TYPE 6
DESIGN·B
·STARBOARD·SIDE·
SCALE LENGTH 324'-0"
COLORS
NO. 3 BLUE NO. 1 BLUE GREY WHITE
BLACK
NOTE
COLORS·ON·PLAN·ARE·FOR THE·PURPOSES·OF·MEASUREMENT·ONLY· ACTUAL·COLORS AS·PER·COLOR·CHART·

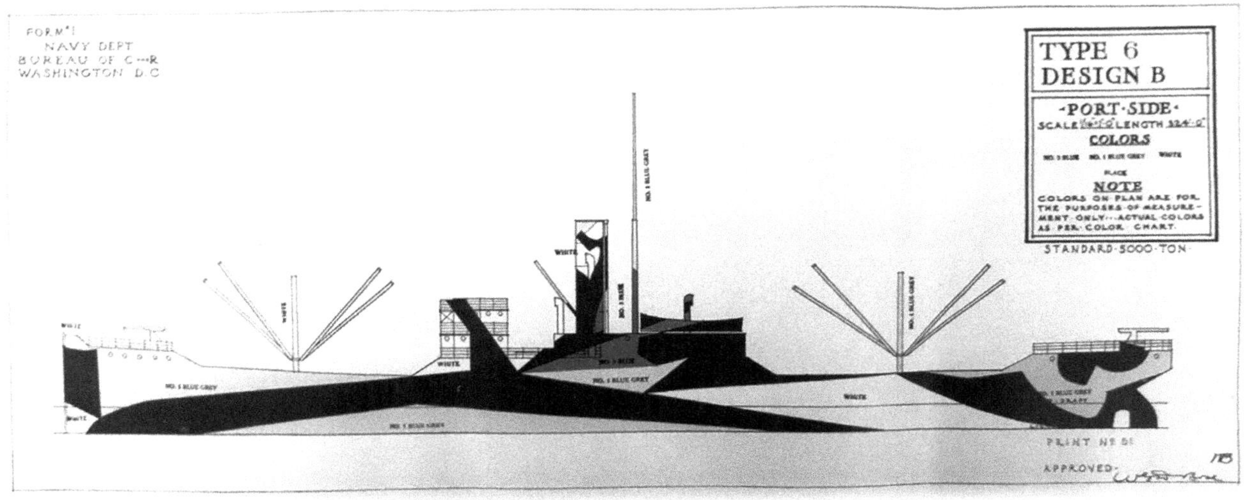

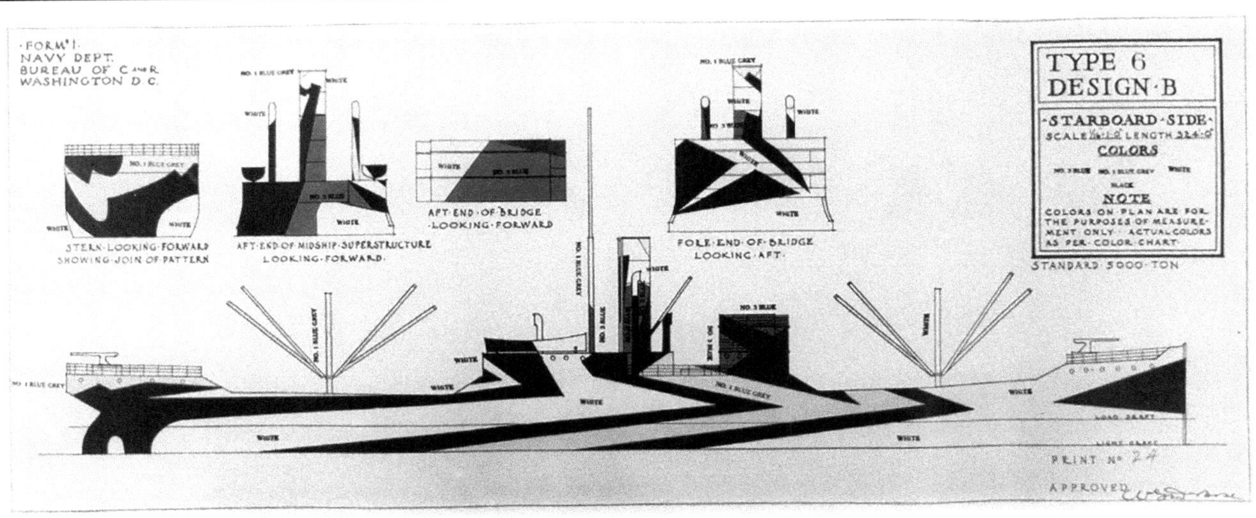

T6 C

Colors used	Ships painted with this pattern
BLACK	ID 3056 CAPE HENRY
WHITE	ID 1301 MUNDELTA (T)
#3 BLUE	ID 2093 MUNINDIES (T)
#1 BLUE-GRAY	ID 1510 WALTER D MUNSON (T)

TYPE 6 DESIGN·C
·PORT·SIDE·
COLORS
NOTE
COLORS ON PLAN ARE FOR THE PURPOSES OF MEASUREMENT ONLY...ACTUAL COLORS AS PER COLOR CHART

TYPE 6 DESIGN·C
·STARBOARD·SIDE·
COLORS
NOTE
COLORS ON PLAN ARE FOR THE PURPOSES OF MEASUREMENT ONLY...ACTUAL COLORS AS PER COLOR CHART

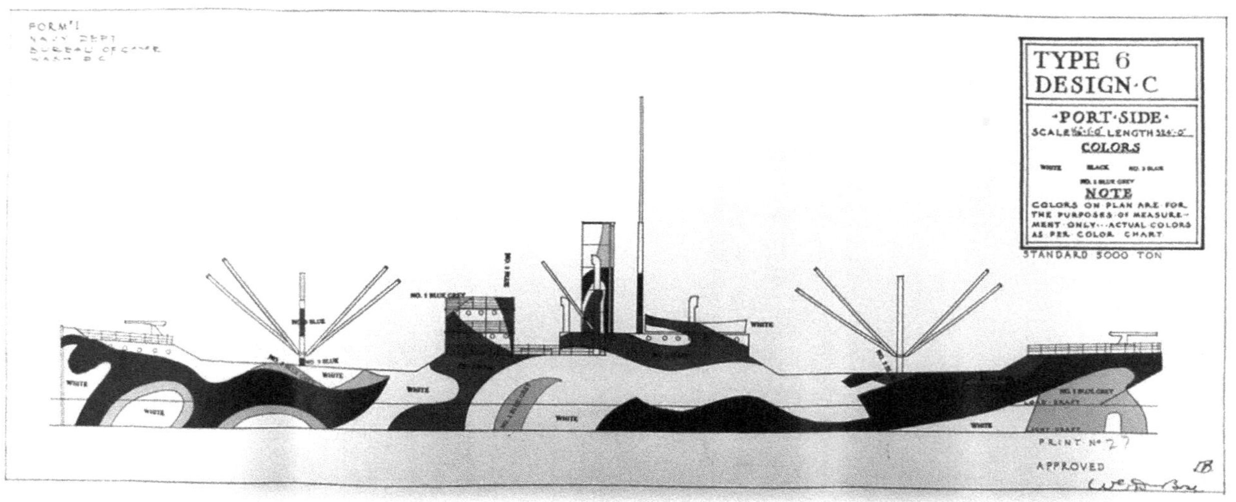

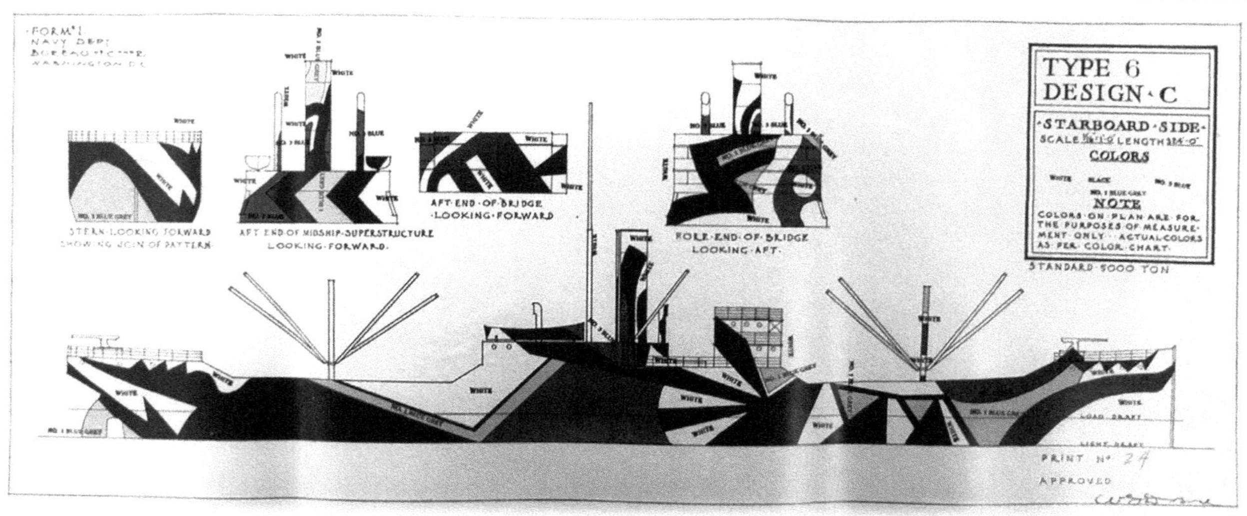

T6 D

Colors used	Ships painted with this pattern
BLACK	ID 3125 SANTA OLIVIA
WHITE	ID 1650 ORION (T)
#3 BLUE	NONE VEELHAVEN (T)
#1 BLUE-GRAY	NONE YSELHAVEN (T)

TYPE 6
DESIGN D
·PORT·SIDE·
SCALE 1/16"=1'-0" LENGTH 324'-0"
COLORS
WHITE Nº 1 BLUE GRAY
BLACK Nº 3 BLUE
NOTE
COLORS ON PLAN ARE FOR THE PURPOSES OF MEASUREMENT ONLY... ACTUAL COLORS AS PER COLOR CHART

TYPE 6
DESIGN D
·PORT·SIDE·
SCALE 1/16"=1'-0" LENGTH 324'-0"
COLORS
WHITE Nº 1 BLUE GRAY
BLACK Nº 3 BLUE
NOTE
COLORS ON PLAN ARE FOR THE PURPOSES OF MEASUREMENT ONLY... ACTUAL COLORS AS PER COLOR CHART

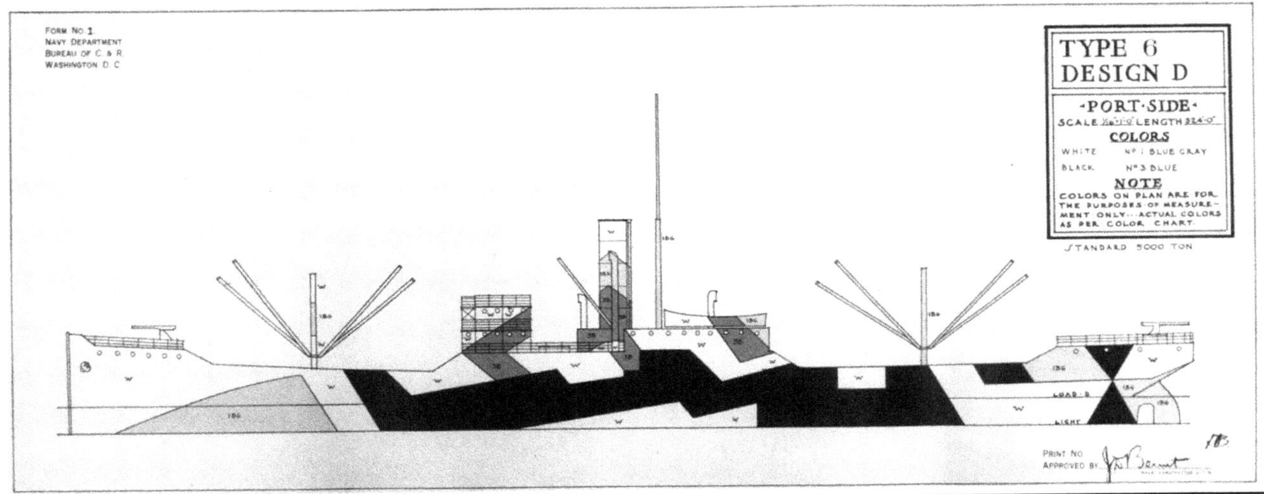

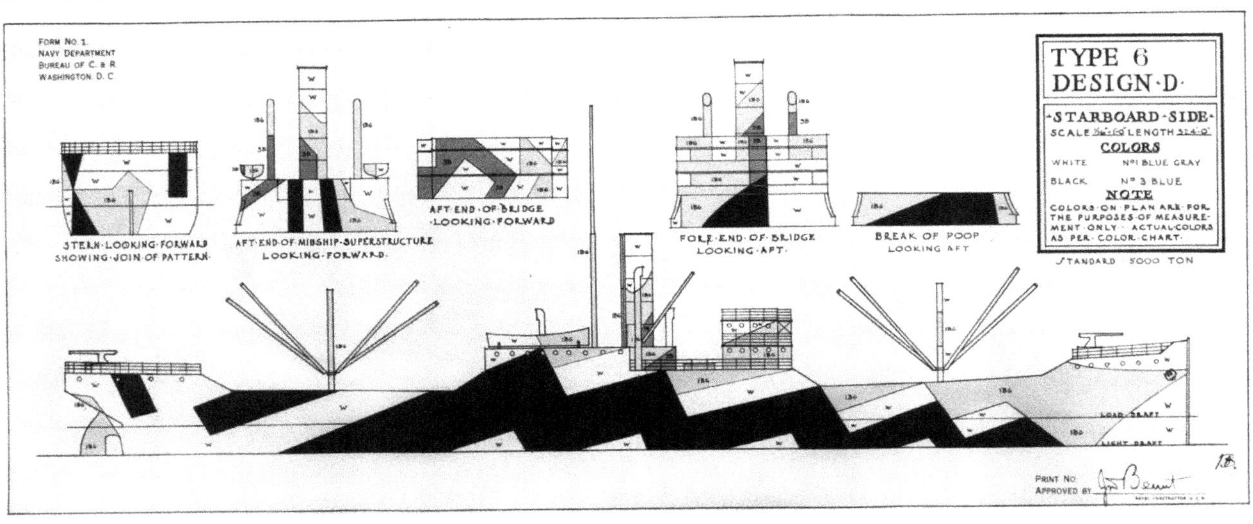

T6 E

Colors used	Ships painted with this pattern
BLACK	ID 2497 MAARTENSDIJK
WHITE	ID 3164 WESTERN SPIRIT
#3 BLUE	ID 4406 LAKE FRANCIS (T)
#1 BLUE-GRAY	

TYPE 6
DESIGN E
·PORT·SIDE·
SCALE 1/16"-1'-0" LENGTH 324'-0"
COLORS
BLACK 1 BLUE-GREY
WHITE 3 BLUE
NOTE
COLORS ON PLAN ARE FOR THE PURPOSES OF MEASUREMENT ONLY···ACTUAL COLORS AS PER COLOR CHART

TYPE 6
DESIGN E
·STARBOARD·SIDE·
SCALE 1/16"-1'-0" LENGTH 324'-0"
COLORS
BLACK 1 BLUE-GREY
WHITE 3 BLUE
NOTE
COLORS·ON·PLAN ARE FOR THE PURPOSES OF MEASUREMENT ONLY · ACTUAL·COLORS AS PER·COLOR·CHART·

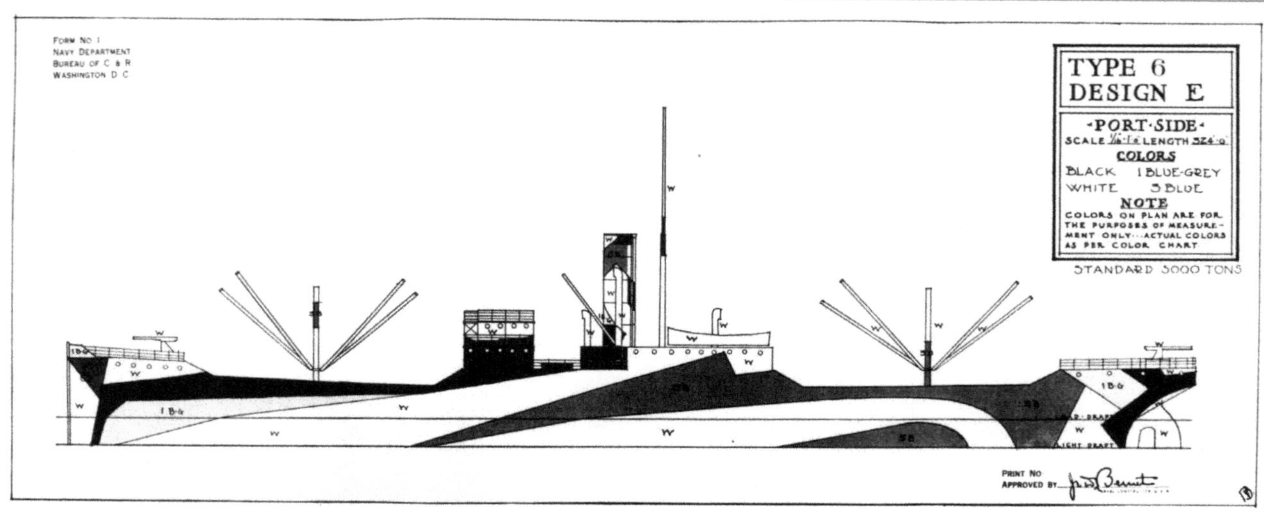

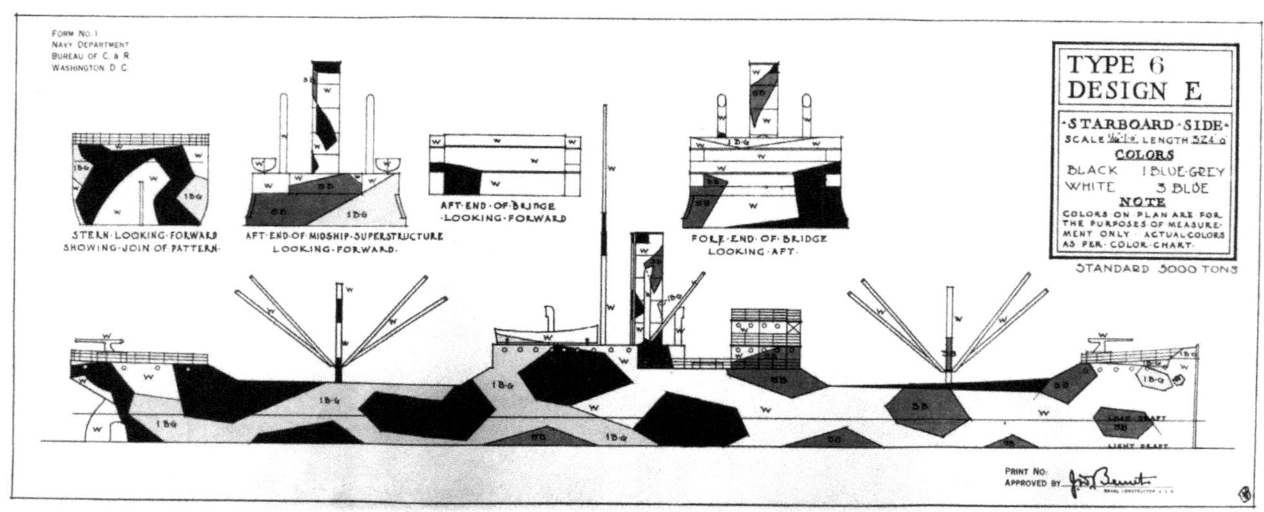

T6 F

Colors used	Ships painted with this pattern
BLACK	ID 2784 BACCHUS
WHITE	
#3 BLUE	
#1 BLUE-GRAY	
#4 GRAY	

TYPE 6
DESIGN F
·PORT·SIDE·
SCALE 1/16"=1'0" LENGTH 324'0"
COLORS
BLACK NO 1 BLUE GREY
WHITE NO 3 BLUE
NOTE
COLORS ON PLAN ARE FOR THE PURPOSES OF MEASUREMENT ONLY... ACTUAL COLORS AS PER COLOR CHART

TYPE 6
DESIGN F
·STARBOARD·SIDE·
SCALE 1/16"=1'0" LENGTH 324'0"
COLORS
BLACK NO 1 BLUE GREY
WHITE NO 3 BLUE
NOTE
COLORS·ON·PLAN·ARE·FOR THE·PURPOSES·OF·MEASUREMENT·ONLY··ACTUAL·COLORS AS·PER·COLOR·CHART·

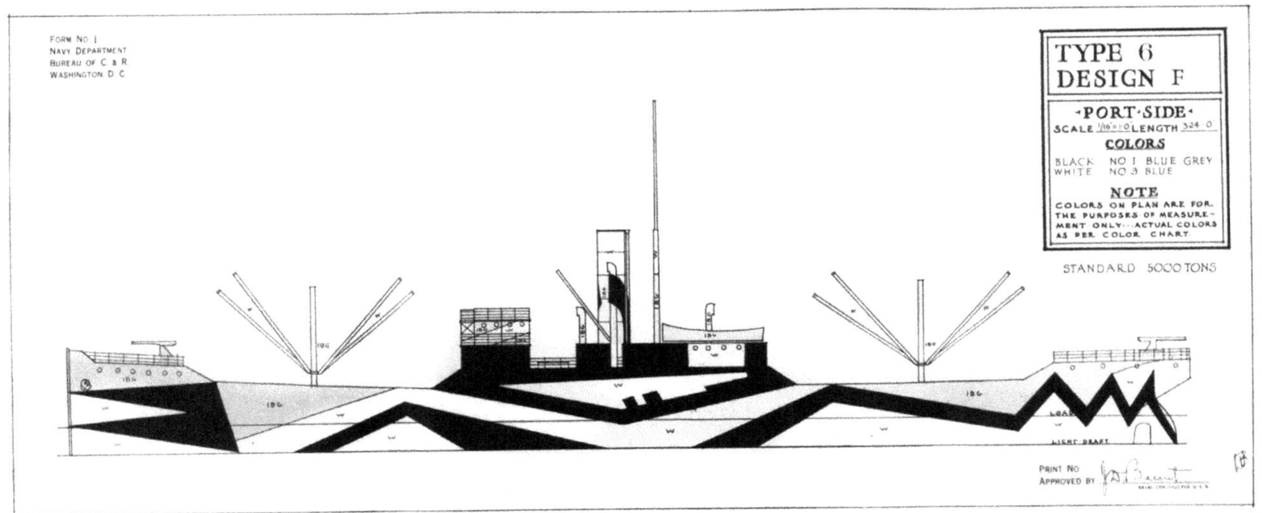

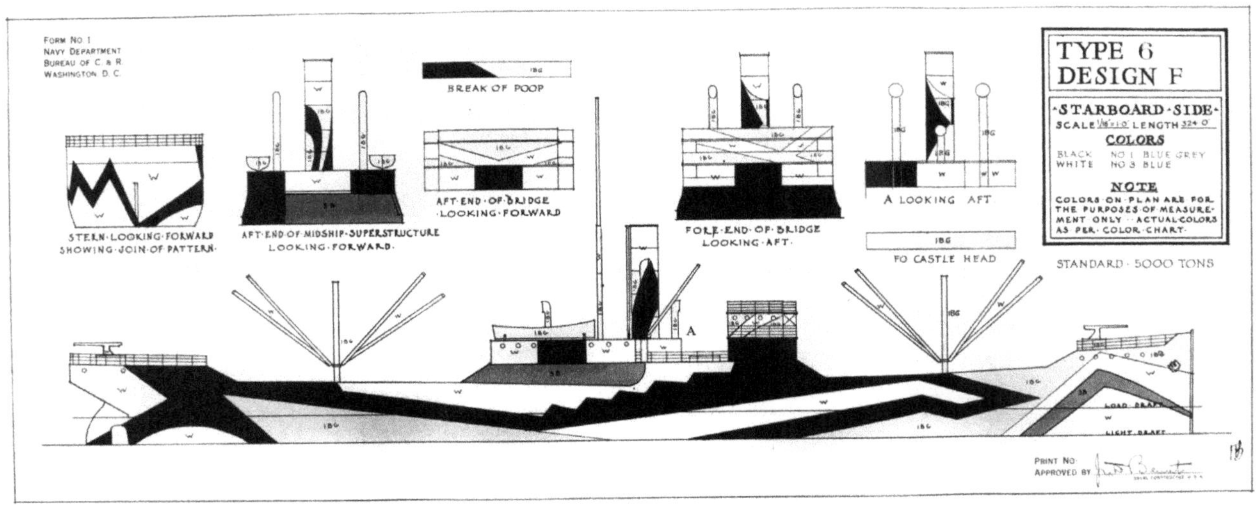

T6 G

Colors used	Ships painted with this pattern
BLACK	ID 3335 WESTHOBOMAC
WHITE	ID 3325 AGAWAM
#3 BLUE	ID 3826 QUISTCONCK
#1 BLUE	ID 2792 PIQUA

TYPE 6 DESIGN G
·PORT·SIDE·
SCALE 1/16"=1'-0" LENGTH 324'-0"
COLORS
BLACK NO 1 BLUE
WHITE NO 3 BLUE
NOTE
COLORS ON PLAN ARE FOR THE PURPOSES OF MEASUREMENT ONLY... ACTUAL COLORS AS PER COLOR CHART

TYPE 6 DESIGN G
·STARBOARD·SIDE·
SCALE 1/16"=1'-0" LENGTH 324'-0"
COLORS
BLACK NO 1 BLUE
WHITE NO 3 BLUE
NOTE
COLORS ON PLAN ARE FOR THE PURPOSES OF MEASUREMENT ONLY... ACTUAL COLORS AS PER COLOR CHART

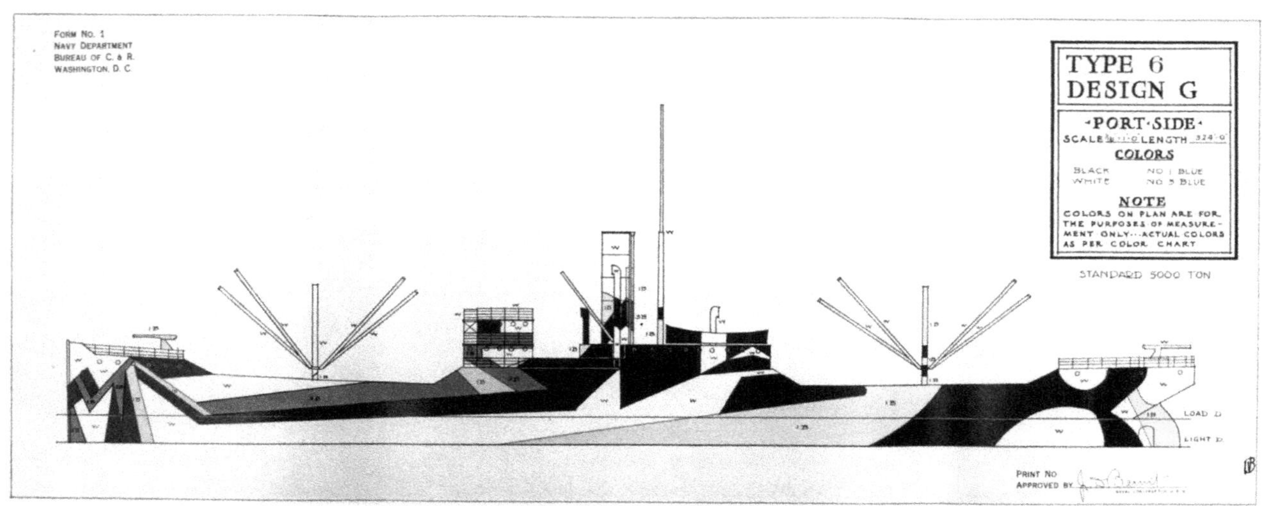

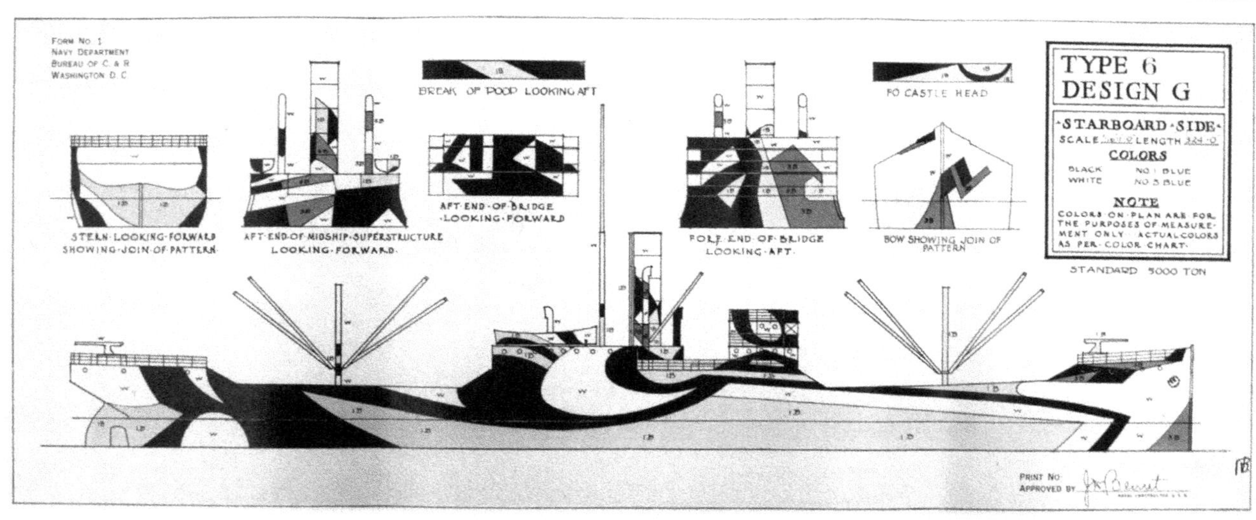

T6 H

Colors used	Ships painted with this pattern
BLACK	ID 2197 MUNAIRES
WHITE	
#3 BLUE	
#1 BLUE-GRAY	

TYPE 6
DESIGN H

·PORT·SIDE·
SCALE 1/16"=1 FT LENGTH 324'0"
COLORS
BLACK NO 1 BLUE GRAY
WHITE NO 3 BLUE
NOTE
COLORS ON PLAN ARE FOR THE PURPOSES OF MEASUREMENT ONLY···ACTUAL COLORS AS PER COLOR CHART.

TYPE 6
DESIGN H

·STARBOARD·SIDE·
SCALE 1/16"=1 FT LENGTH 324'0"
COLORS
BLACK NO 1 BLUE GRAY
WHITE NO 3 BLUE
NOTE
COLORS ON PLAN ARE FOR THE PURPOSES OF MEASUREMENT ONLY··ACTUAL COLORS AS PER COLOR CHART.

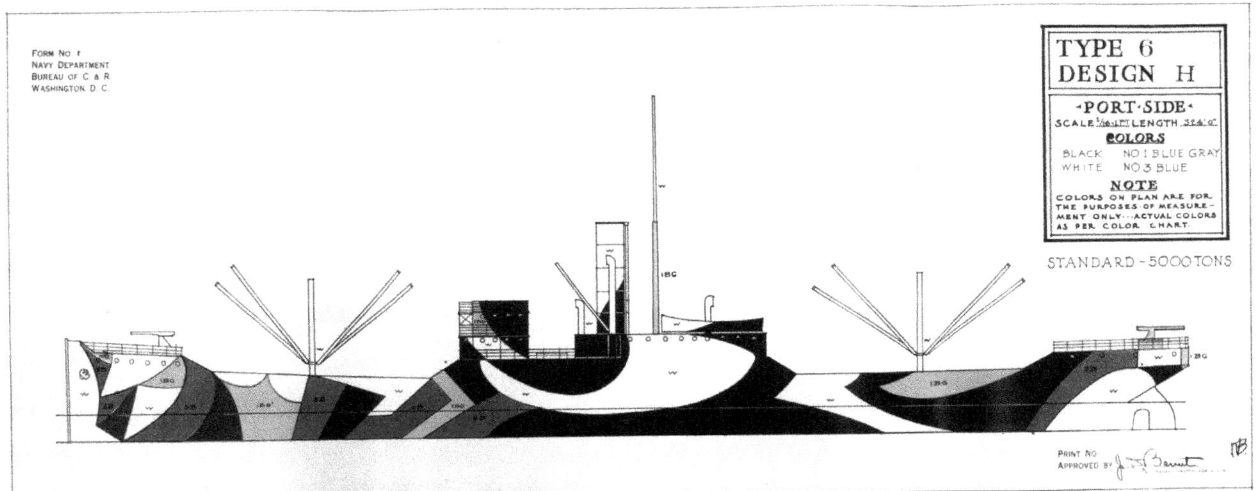

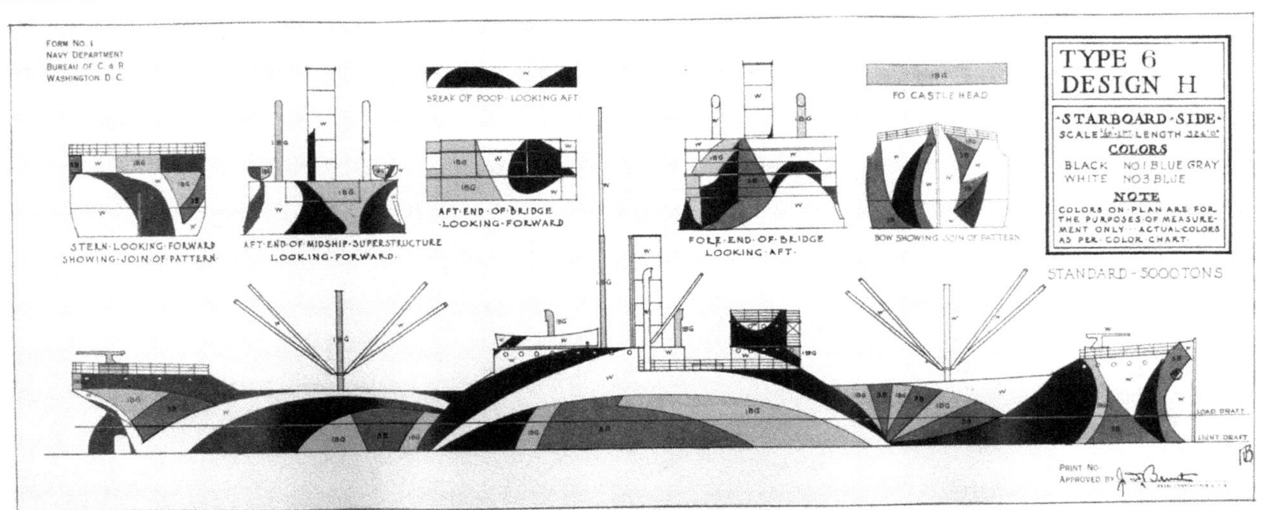

T6 I

Colors used	Ships painted with this pattern
BLACK	ID 2518 ALKAID
WHITE	
#3 BLUE	
#1 BLUE-GRAY	

TYPE 6
DESIGN I
·PORT·SIDE·
SCALE 1/16-1-0 LENGTH 324'-0
COLORS
WHITE NO 1 BLUE GRAY
BLACK NO 3 BLUE
NOTE
COLORS ON PLAN ARE FOR THE PURPOSES OF MEASUREMENT ONLY...ACTUAL COLORS AS PER COLOR CHART

TYPE 6
DESIGN I
·STARBOARD·SIDE·
SCALE 1/16-1-0 LENGTH 324'-0
COLORS
WHITE NO 1 BLUE GRAY
BLACK NO 3 BLUE
NOTE
COLORS ON PLAN ARE FOR THE PURPOSES OF MEASUREMENT ONLY...ACTUAL COLORS AS PER COLOR CHART

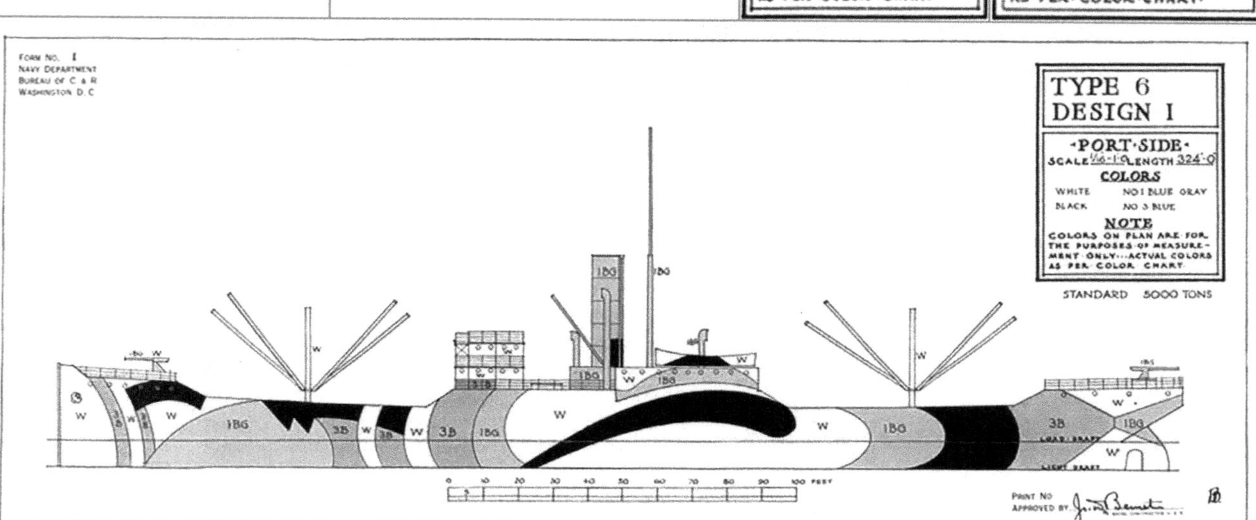

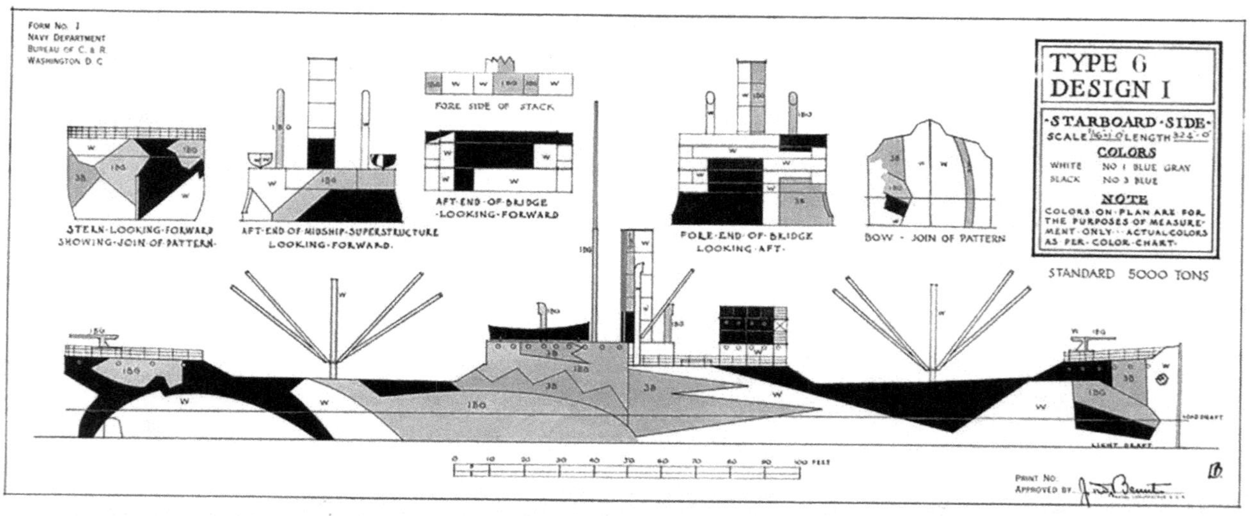

T6 J

Colors used	Ships painted with this pattern
BLACK	ID 3637 MAJOR WHEELER
GREY-WHITE	
#3 BLUE	
#1 BLUE	
#2 BLUE-GRAY	

TYPE 6
DESIGN J
·STARBOARD·SIDE·
SCALE 6·1·0 LENGTH 324·0
COLORS
BLACK· NO·1 BLUE
GRAY·WHITE· NO·3 BLUE
NO·2 BLUE-GRAY·
NOTE
COLORS·ON·PLAN ARE·FOR·THE·PURPOSES·OF·MEASUREMENT·ONLY···ACTUAL·COLORS AS·PER·COLOR·CHART·

TYPE 6
DESIGN J
·PORT·SIDE·
SCALE 6·1·0 LENGTH 324·0
COLORS
BLACK· NO·1 BLUE
GRAY·WHITE· NO·3 BLUE
NO·2 BLUE-GRAY·
NOTE
COLORS ON PLAN ARE FOR THE PURPOSES OF MEASUREMENT ONLY···ACTUAL COLORS AS PER COLOR CHART

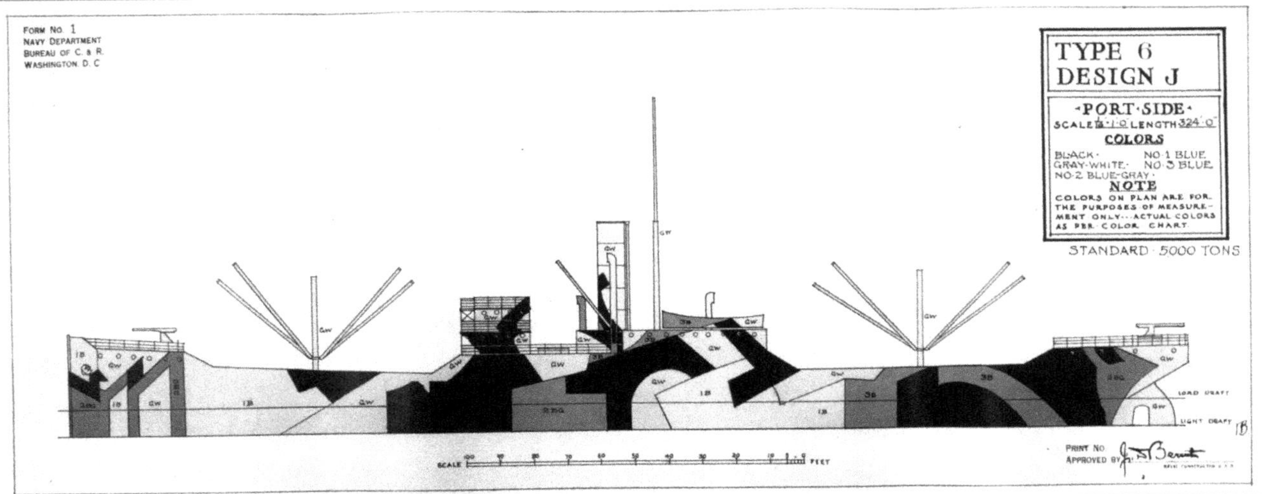

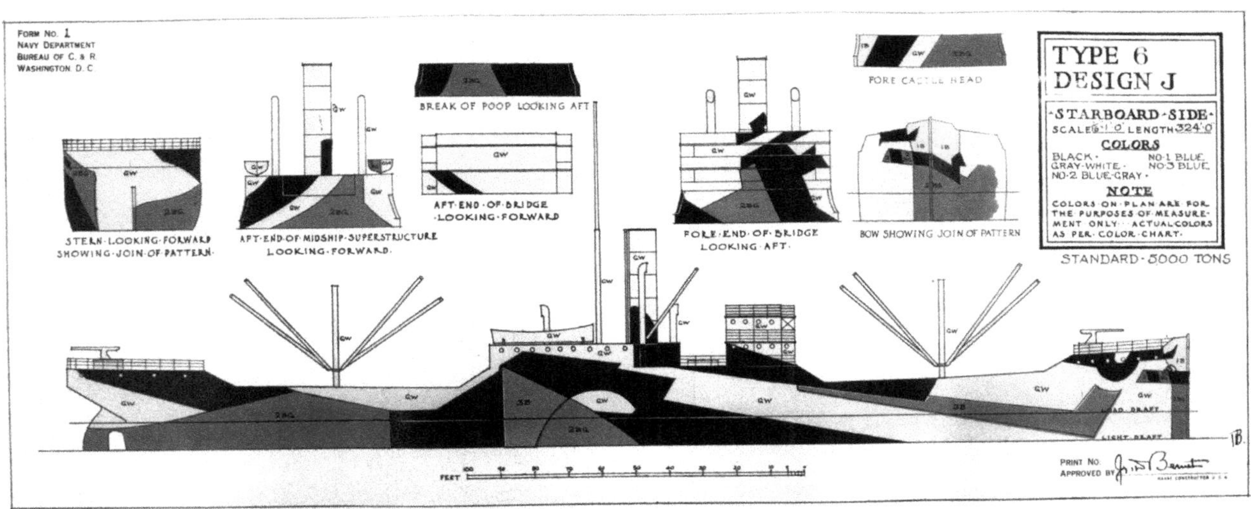

T6 K

Colors used	Ships painted with this pattern
BLACK	ID 2493 RIJNDIJK (T)
GREY-WHITE	
#3 BLUE	
#1 GREEN	

TYPE 6
DESIGN K
-PORT-SIDE-
SCALE 1/16"=1'-0" LENGTH 324'-0" B.P.
COLORS
BLACK Nº 3 BLUE
GRAY WHITE Nº 1 GREEN
NOTE
COLORS ON PLAN ARE FOR THE PURPOSES OF MEASUREMENT ONLY... ACTUAL COLORS AS PER COLOR CHART

TYPE 6
DESIGN K
-STARBOARD-SIDE-
SCALE 1/16"=1'-0" LENGTH 324'-0" B.P.
COLORS
BLACK Nº 3 BLUE
GRAY WHITE Nº 1 GREEN
NOTE
COLORS ON PLAN ARE FOR THE PURPOSES OF MEASUREMENT ONLY... ACTUAL COLORS AS PER COLOR CHART

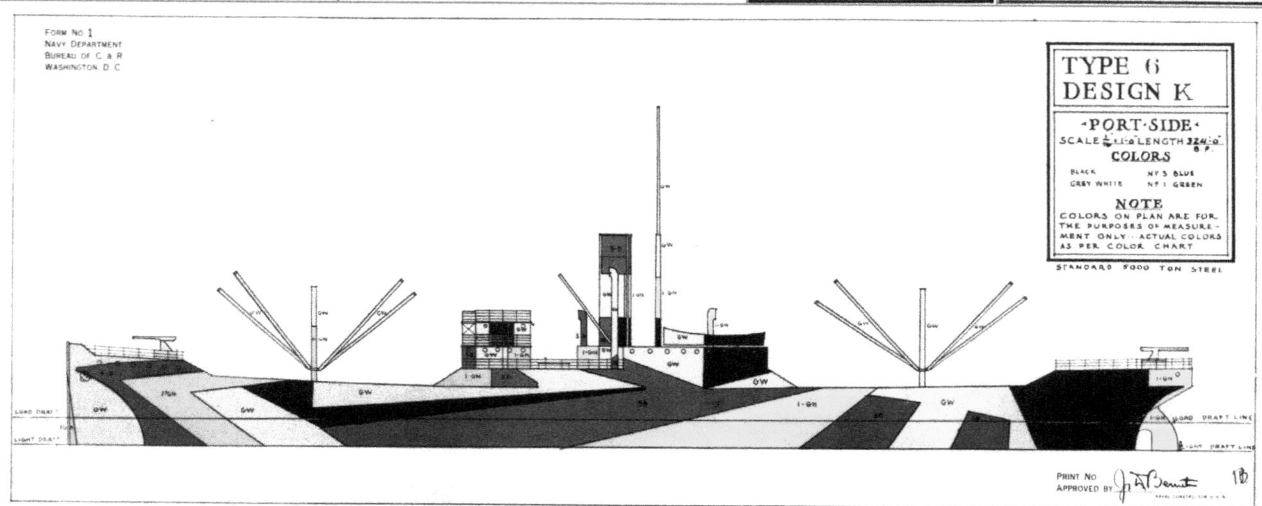

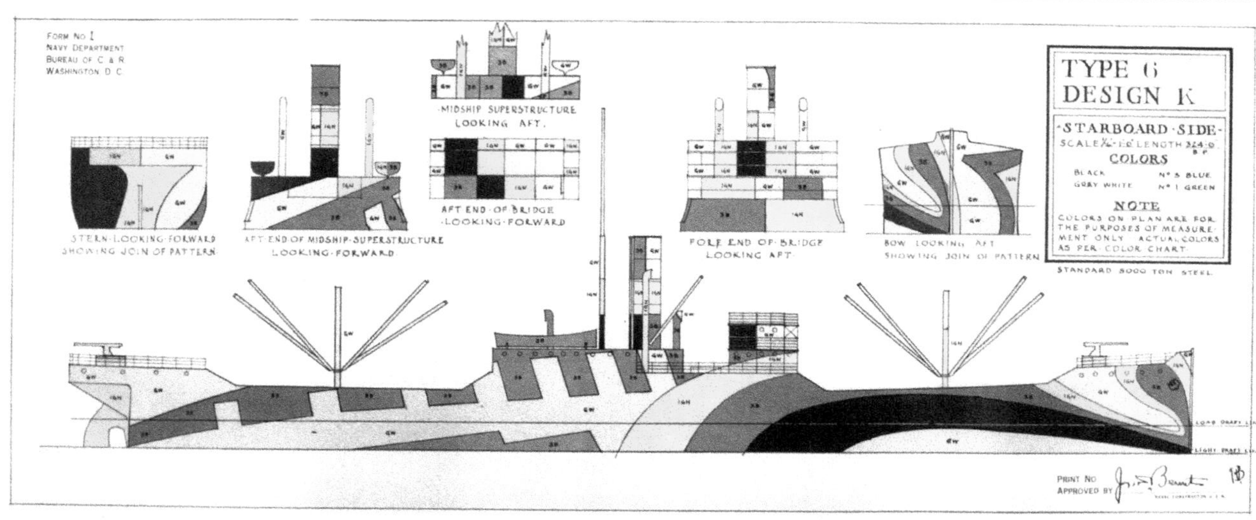

T6 U

Colors used	Ships painted with this pattern
BLACK	ID 4464 AGWIDALE
#3 BLUE	
#1 BLUE-GRAY	

TYPE 6
DESIGN U

PORT SIDE
SCALE 1/16" = 1'-0" LENGTH 324'-0"
COLORS
BLACK NO 1 BLUE GRAY
GRAY-WHITE NO 3 BLUE
NOTE
COLORS ON PLAN ARE FOR THE PURPOSES OF MEASUREMENT ONLY
ACTUAL COLORS AS PER COLOR CHART

TYPE 6
DESIGN U

STARBOARD SIDE
SCALE 1/16" = 1'-0" LENGTH 324'-0"
COLORS
BLACK NO 1 BLUE GRAY
GRAY WHITE NO 3 BLUE
NOTE
COLORS ON PLAN ARE FOR THE PURPOSES OF MEASUREMENT ONLY
ACTUAL COLORS AS PER COLOR CHART

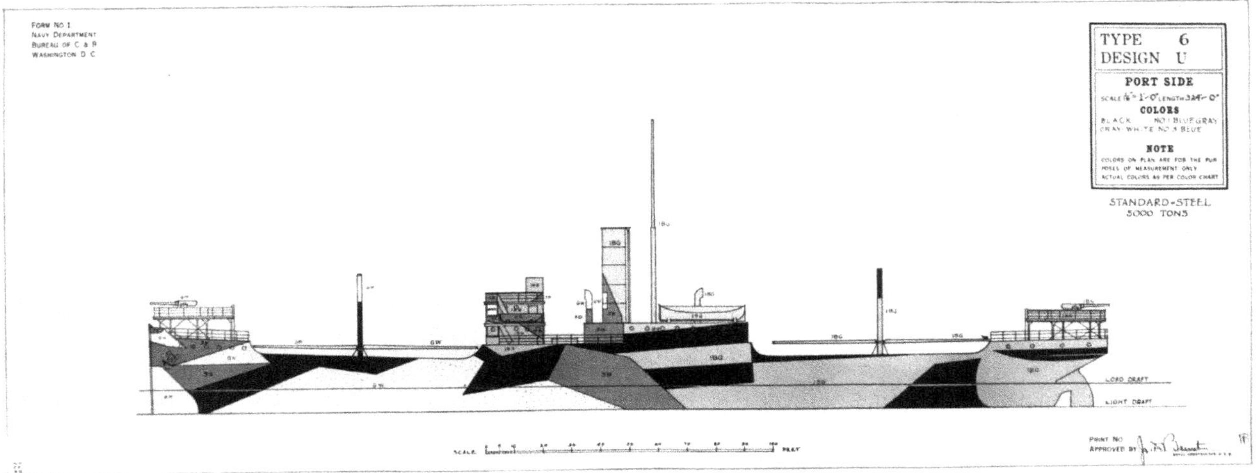

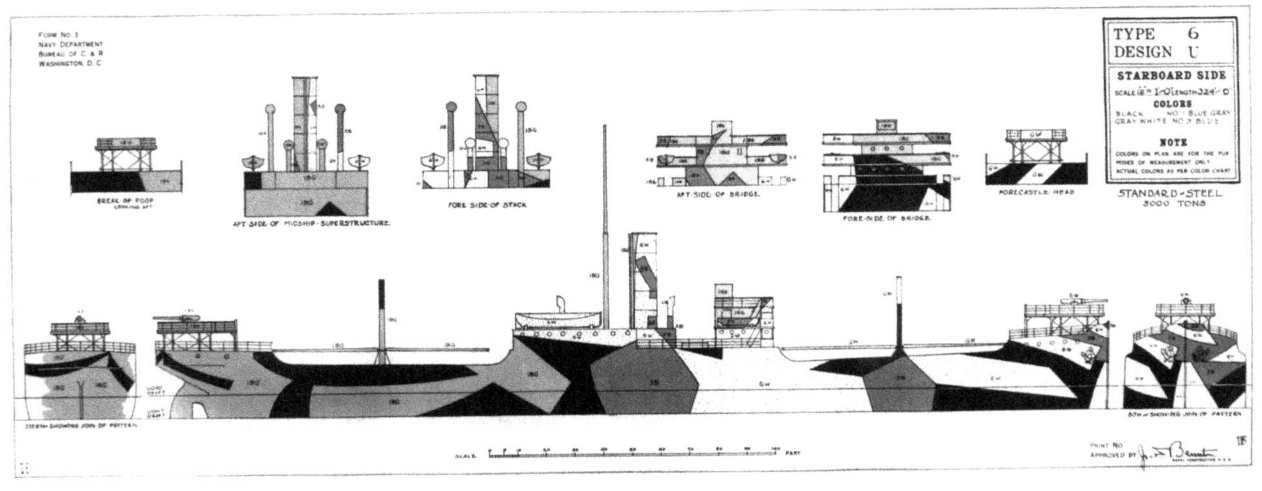

T7 A

Colors used	Ships painted with this pattern
BLACK	ID 1470 LOS ANGELES
WHITE	ID NONE W M BURTON
#3 BLUE	ID NONE PEARL SHELL
#1 BLUE-GRAY	ID 3345 SHERMAN (T)

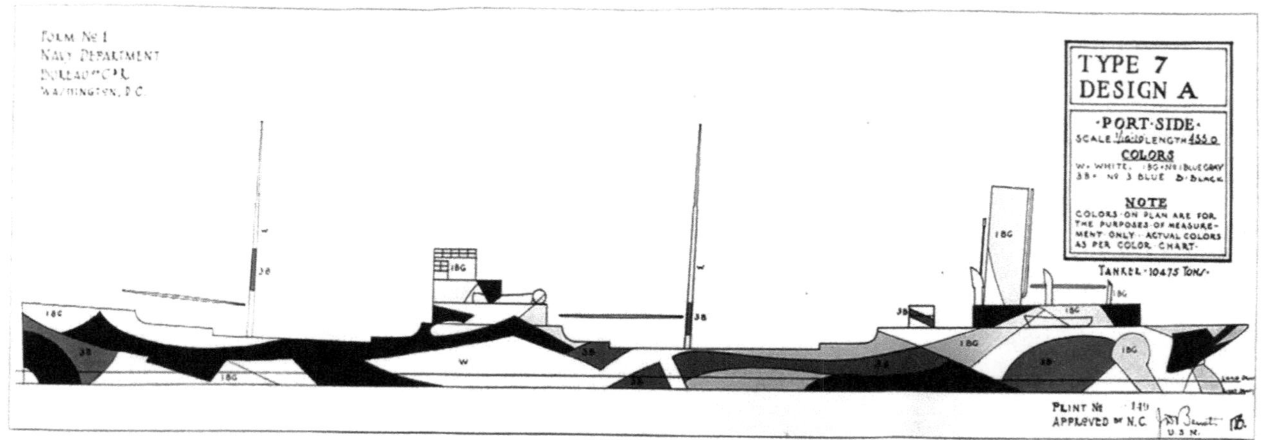

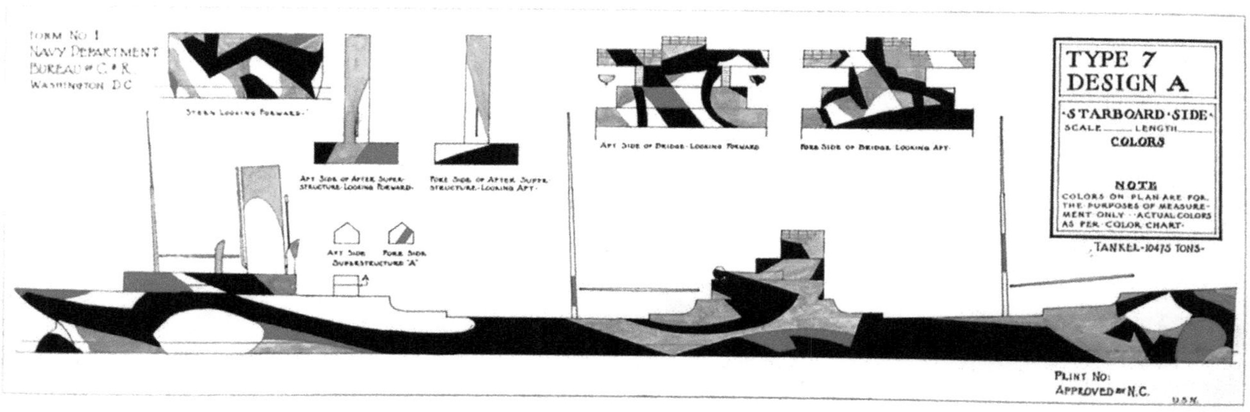

T7 B

Colors used	Ships painted with this pattern
BLACK	ID 1953 HISKO
WHITE	ID 2339 HERBERTL PRATT
#3 BLUE	ID 4712 H M FLAGLER
#1 BLUE-GRAY	VIRGINIA (T)

TYPE 7
DESIGN B
·PORT·SIDE·
SCALE 1/16"=1'0" LENGTH 435'0"
COLORS
BLACK NO 1 BLUE GREY
WHITE NO 3 BLUE
NOTE
COLORS ON PLAN ARE FOR THE PURPOSES OF MEASUREMENT ONLY ACTUAL COLORS AS PER COLOR CHART

TYPE 7
DESIGN B
·STARBOARD·SIDE·
SCALE 1/16"=1'0" LENGTH 435'0"
COLORS
BLACK NO 1 BLUE GREY
WHITE NO 3 BLUE
NOTE
COLORS ON PLAN ARE FOR THE PURPOSES OF MEASUREMENT ONLY ACTUAL COLORS AS PER COLOR CHART

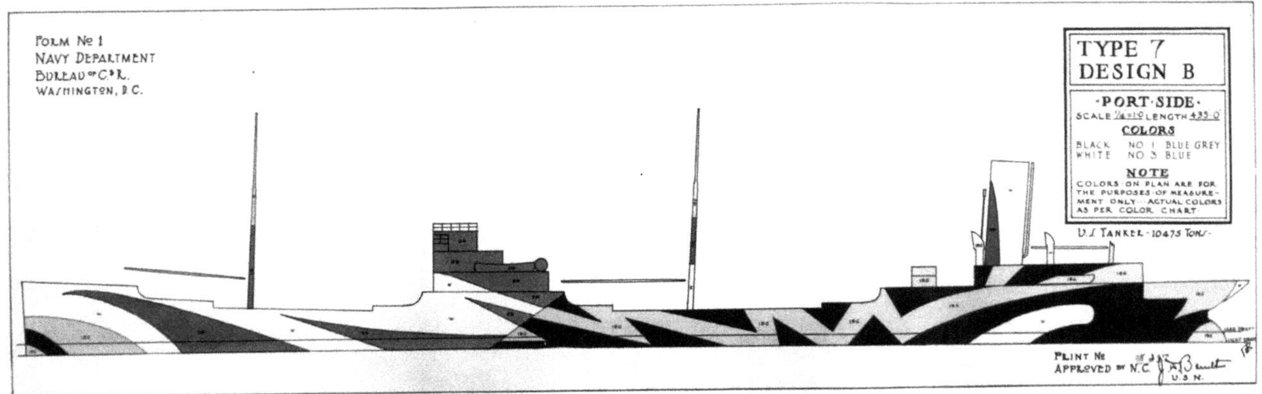

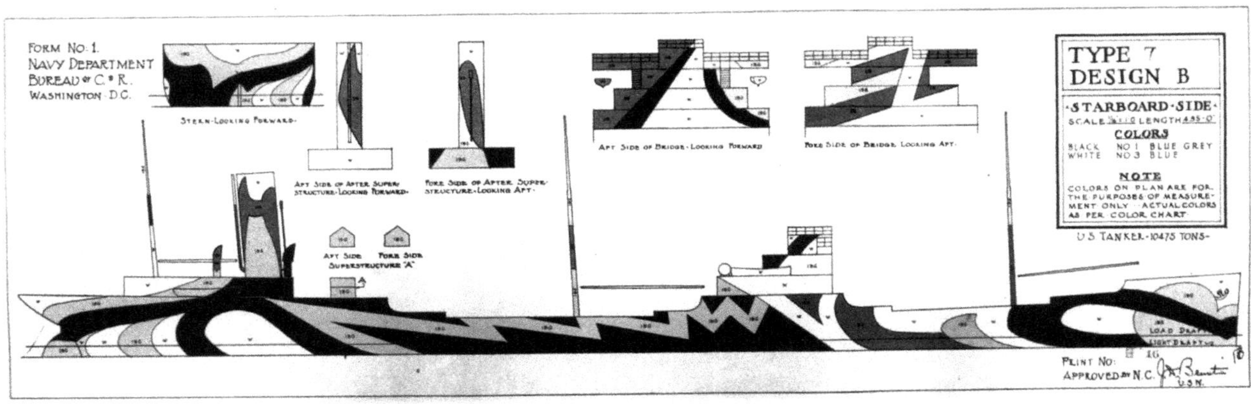

T7 C

Colors used	Ships painted with this pattern
BLACK	ID NONE BAYWAY
WHITE	NONE MARE (T)
#3 BLUE	
#1 BLUE-GRAY	

TYPE 7
DESIGN C

∴ PORT SIDE ∴
SCALE 1/16"=1'0" LENGTH 435'0"
COLORS
BLACK NO 1 BLUE GREY
WHITE NO 3 BLUE
NOTE
COLORS ON PLAN ARE FOR THE PURPOSES OF MEASUREMENT ONLY. ACTUAL COLORS AS PER COLOR CHART.

TYPE 7
DESIGN C

STARBOARD SIDE
SCALE 1/16"=1'0" LENGTH 435'0"
COLORS
BLACK NO 1 BLUE GREY
WHITE NO 3 BLUE
NOTE
COLORS ON PLAN ARE FOR THE PURPOSES OF MEASUREMENT ONLY. ACTUAL COLORS AS PER COLOR CHART.

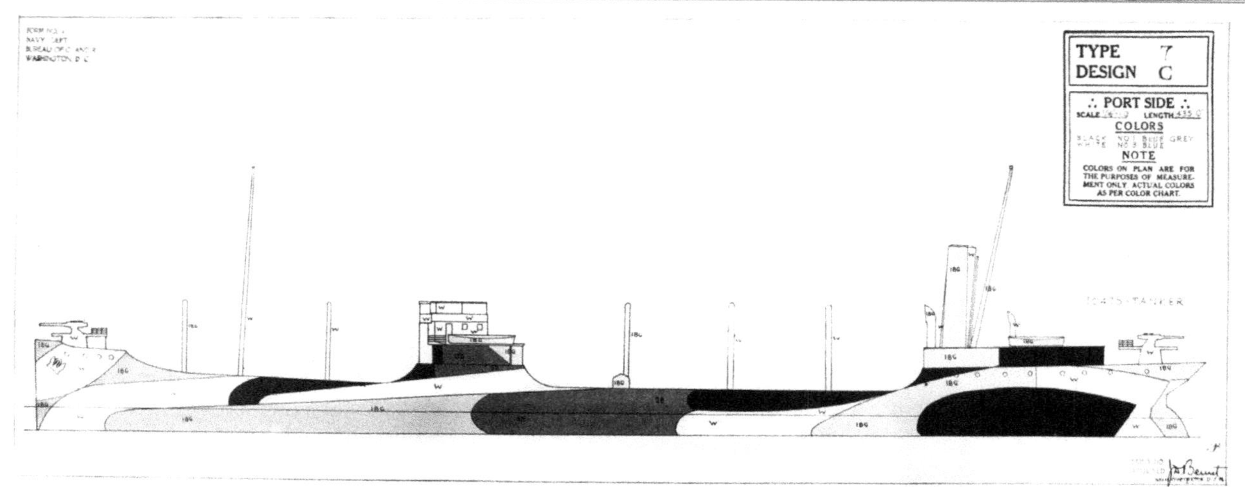

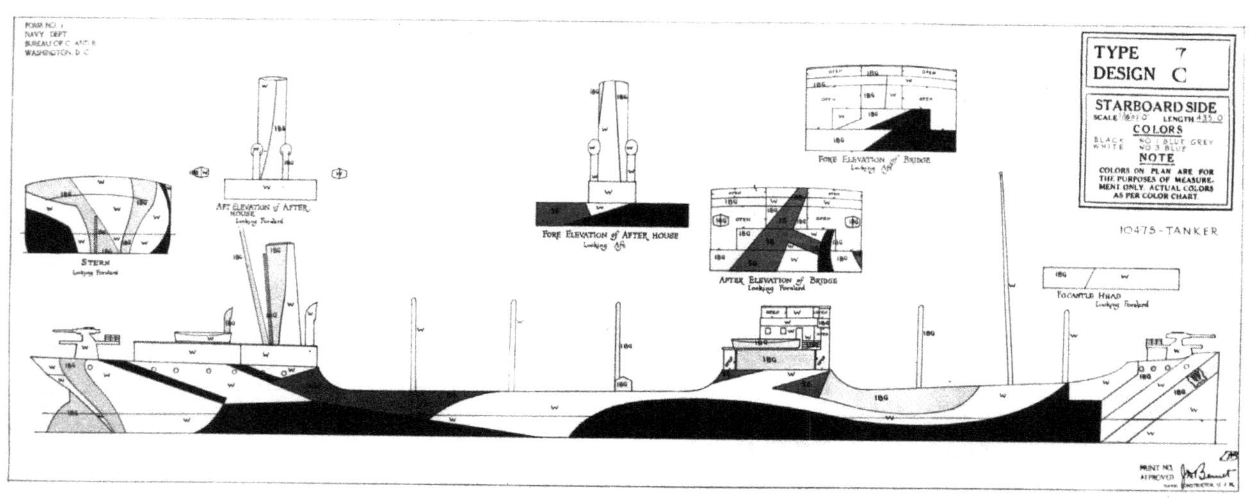

T7 D

Colors used	Ships painted with this pattern
BLACK	IX 27 STURGEON BAY
WHITE	
#3 BLUE	
#1 BLUE-GRAY	

TYPE 7
DESIGN ·D·
PORT SIDE
SCALE 1/16" = 1'0 LENGTH 385'7
COLORS
WHITE No 1 BLUE GREY
BLACK No 3 BLUE
NOTE
COLORS ON PLAN ARE FOR THE PURPOSES OF MEASUREMENT ONLY
ACTUAL COLORS AS PER COLOR CHART

TYPE 7
DESIGN D
STARBOARD SIDE
SCALE 1/16" = 1'0 LENGTH 385 7
COLORS
WHITE No 1 BLUE GREY
BLACK No 3 BLUE
NOTE
COLORS ON PLAN ARE FOR THE PURPOSES OF MEASUREMENT ONLY
ACTUAL COLORS AS PER COLOR CHART

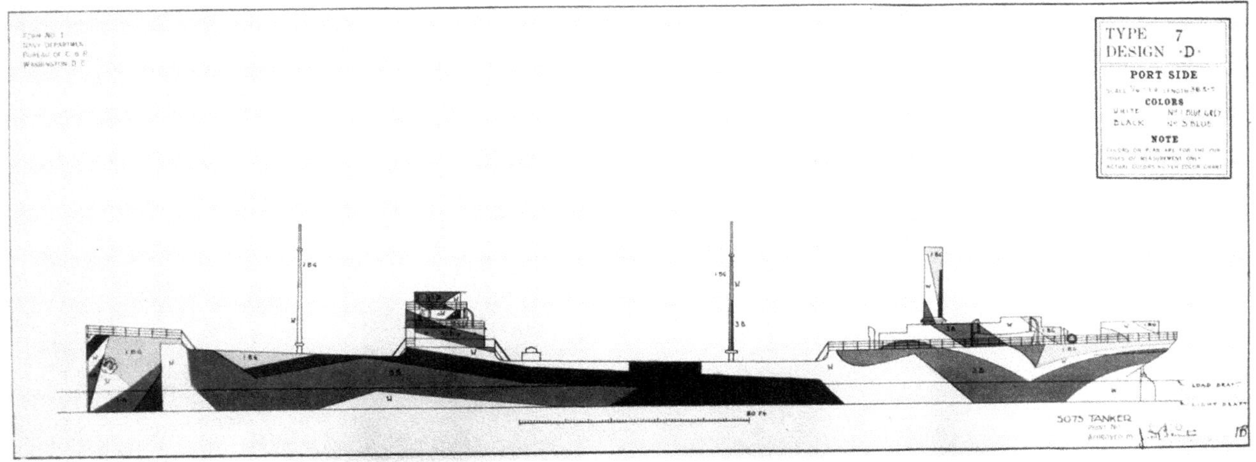

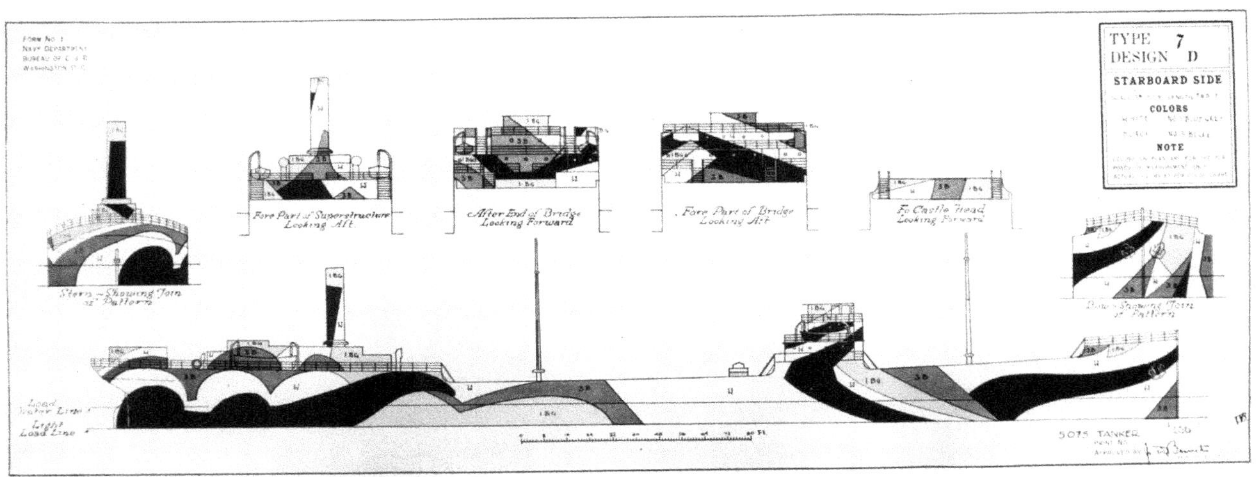

T7 E

Colors used	Ships painted with this pattern
BLACK	ID 3835 EDWARD L DOHENEY III
WHITE	ID NONE FREDERICK R KELLOG
#3 BLUE	ID 4526 STEPHEN R JONES (T)
#1 BLUE-GRAY	ID 3001 TOPLA (T)

TYPE 7
DESIGN E

PORT SIDE

SCALE 1/16"=1'-0" LENGTH 435'-0"

COLORS

BLACK NO 1 BLUE GREY
WHITE NO 3 BLUE

NOTE

COLORS ON PLAN ARE FOR THE PURPOSES OF MEASUREMENT ONLY
ACTUAL COLORS AS PER COLOR CHART

TYPE 7
DESIGN E

STARBOARD SIDE

SCALE 1/16"=1'-0" LENGTH 435'-0"

COLORS

BLACK NO 1 BLUE GREY
WHITE NO 1 BLUE

NOTE

COLORS ON PLAN ARE FOR THE PURPOSES OF MEASUREMENT ONLY
ACTUAL COLORS AS PER COLOR CHART

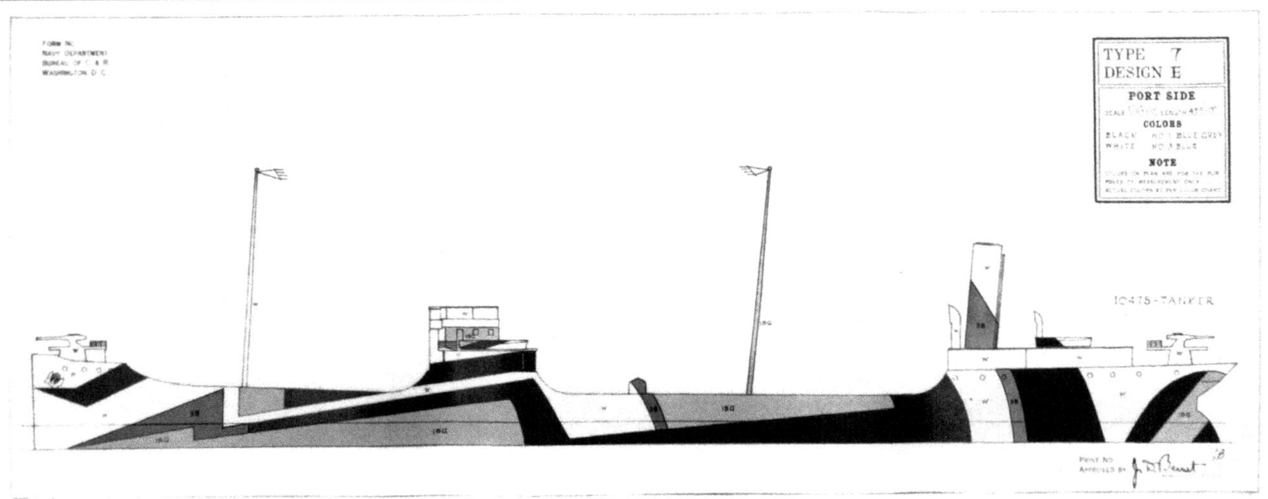

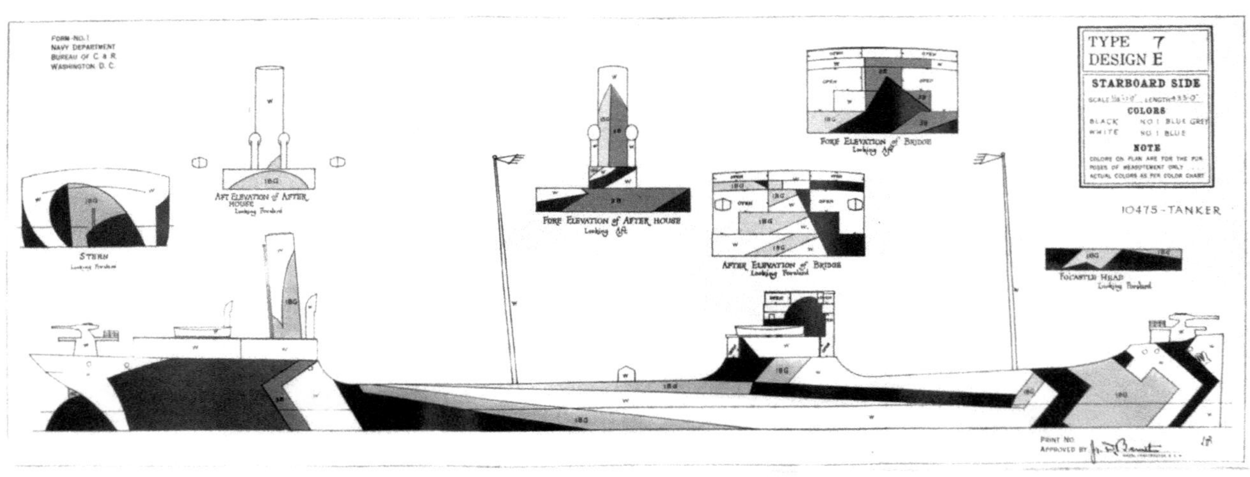

T7 F

Colors used	Ships painted with this pattern
BLACK	ID 3443 ALLENTOWN
WHITE	ID 3148 SARA THOMPSON
#3 BLUE	ID 3846 MIJDRECHT(T)
#1 BLUE	

TYPE 7
DESIGN F
PORT SIDE
SCALE 1/16"=1'0" LENGTH 385'7"
COLORS
BLACK NO 1 BLUE
WHITE NO 3 BLUE
NOTE
COLORS ON PLAN ARE FOR THE PURPOSES OF MEASUREMENT ONLY
ACTUAL COLORS AS PER COLOR CHART

TYPE 7
DESIGN F
STARBOARD SIDE
SCALE 1/16"=1'0" LENGTH 385'-7"
COLORS
BLACK NO 1 BLUE
WHITE NO 3 BLUE
NOTE
COLORS ON PLAN ARE FOR THE PURPOSES OF MEASUREMENT ONLY
ACTUAL COLORS AS PER COLOR CHART

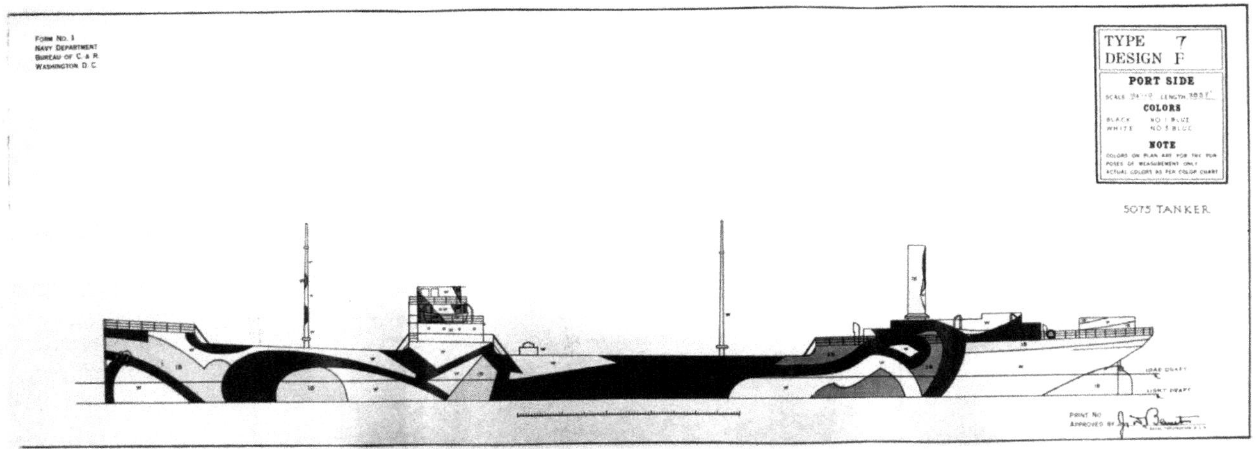

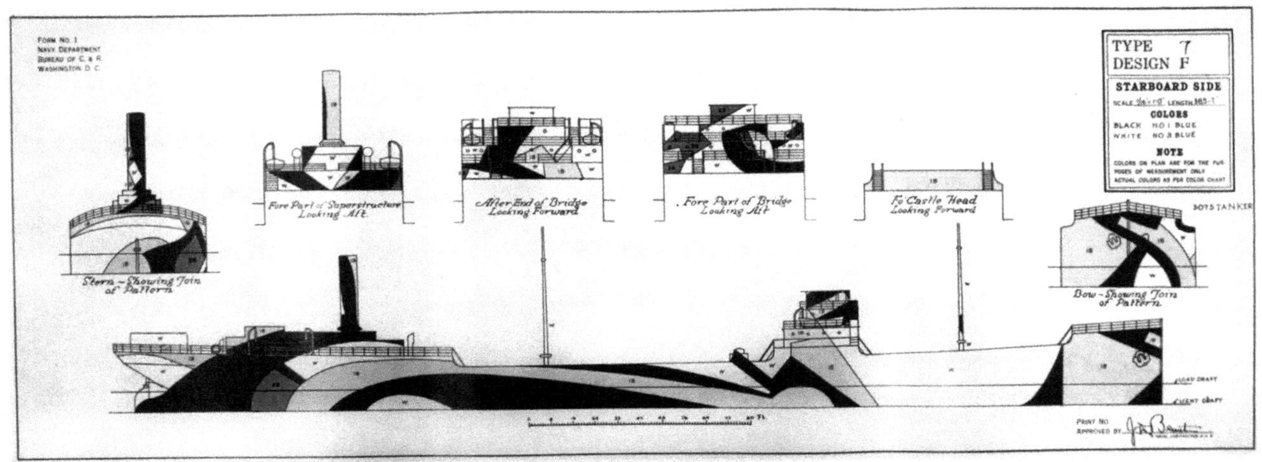

T7 G

Colors used	Ships painted with this pattern
BLACK	ID NONE MIDDLESEX
WHITE	ID NONE S V HARKNESS
#3 BLUE	
#1 BLUE-GRAY	

TYPE 7
DESIGN G
·PORT·SIDE·
SCALE 1/16"=1'0" LENGTH 435'0"
COLORS
BLACK 3 BLUE
WHITE 1 BLUE GREY
NOTE
COLORS·ON·PLAN ARE FOR THE PURPOSES OF MEASUREMENT ONLY··ACTUAL COLORS AS PER·COLOR·CHART·

TYPE 7
DESIGN G
·STARBOARD·SIDE·
SCALE 1/16"=1'0" LENGTH 435'0"
COLORS
BLACK 3 BLUE
WHITE 1 BLUE GREY
NOTE
COLORS·ON·PLAN·ARE·FOR THE·PURPOSES·OF MEASUREMENT·ONLY···ACTUAL·COLORS AS PER·COLOR·CHART·

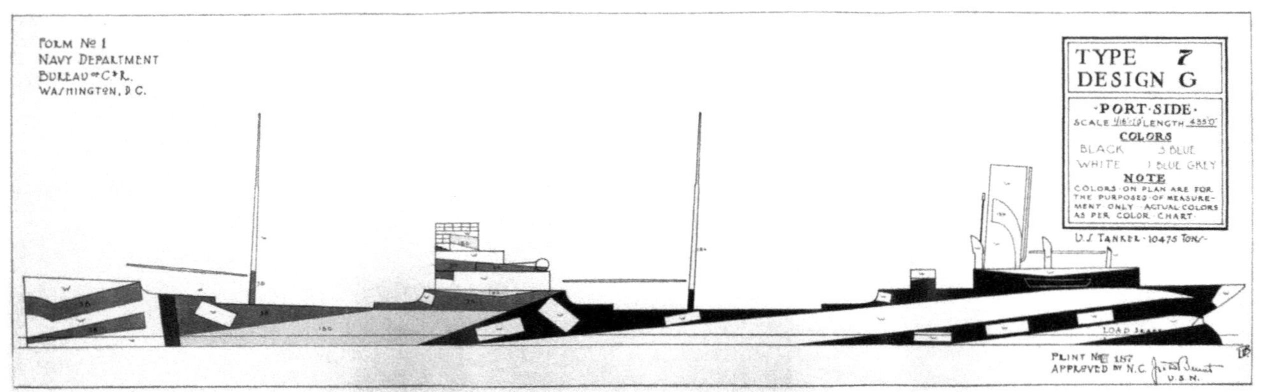

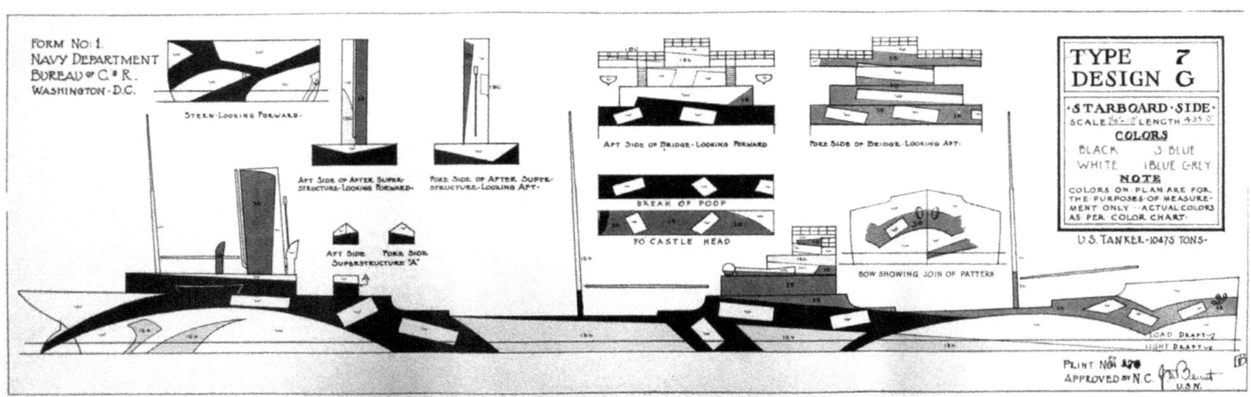

T7 I

Colors used	Ships painted with this pattern
BLACK	ID 2526 CHESTNUTHILL
GREY-WHITE	ID NONE L J DRAKE
#3 BLUE	
#1 BLUE-GRAY	

TYPE 7
DESIGN I
PORT SIDE
SCALE 1/16" = 1'0" LENGTH 435'0"
COLORS
GRAY WHITE BLACK
NO 1 BLUE GRAY NO 3 BLUE
NOTE
COLORS ON PLAN ARE FOR THE PURPOSES OF MEASUREMENT ONLY
ACTUAL COLORS AS PER COLOR CHART

TYPE 7
DESIGN I
STARBOARD SIDE
SCALE 1/16" = 1'0" LENGTH 435'0"
COLORS
GRAY WHITE BLACK
NO 1 BLUE GRAY NO 3 BLUE
NOTE
COLORS ON PLAN ARE FOR THE PURPOSES OF MEASUREMENT ONLY
ACTUAL COLORS AS PER COLOR CHART

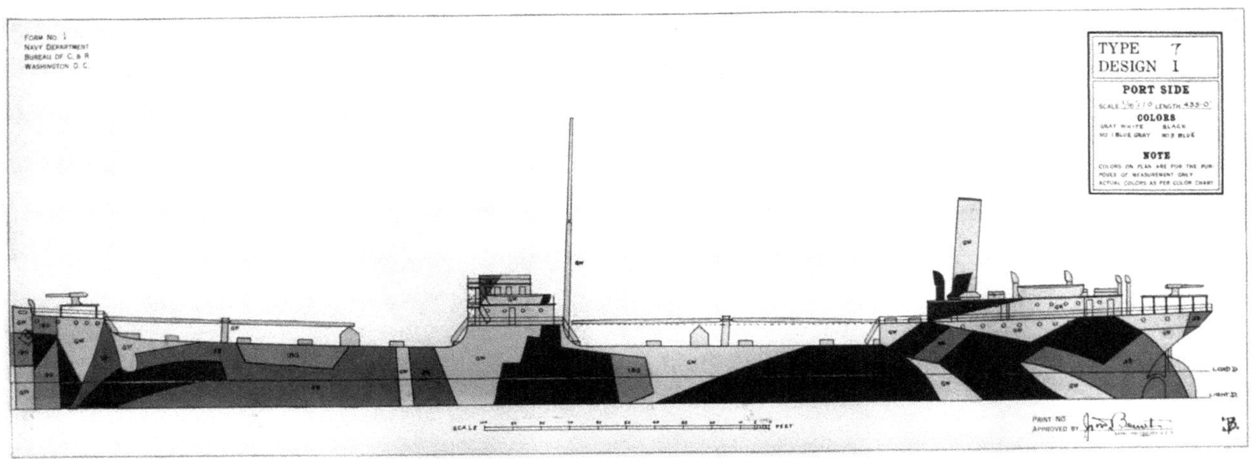

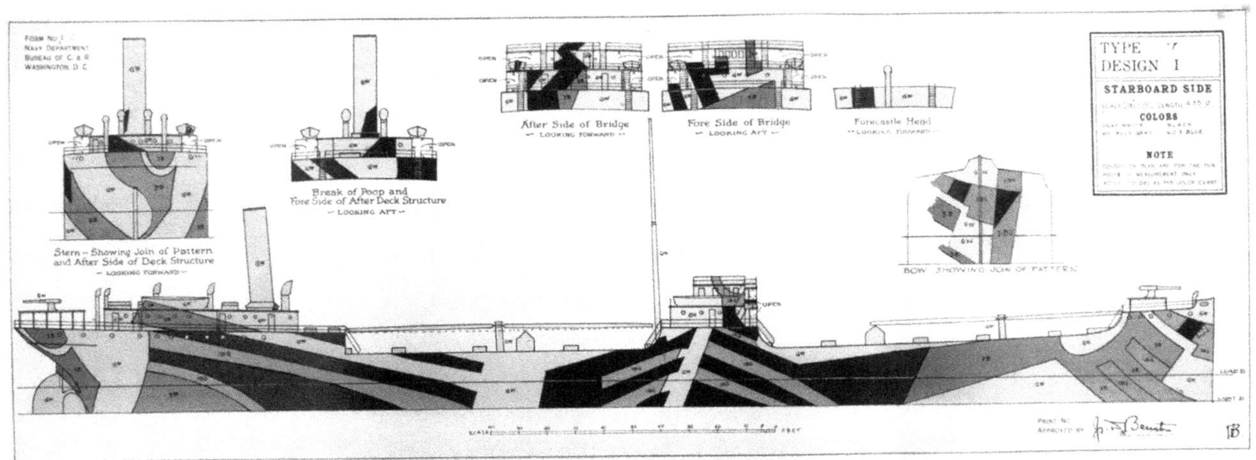

T7 J

Colors used	Ships painted with this pattern
BLACK	ID 3449 W D STEED
GREY-WHITE	ID 3513 M J SCANLON
#3 BLUE	ID 2518 WIELDRECHT(T)
#1 BLUE-GRAY	

TYPE 7
DESIGN J
PORT SIDE
SCALE ⅛" = 1'-0" LENGTH 340'-0" BP
COLORS
GRAY WHITE NO 3 BLUE
BLACK NO 1 BLUE GRAY
NOTE
COLORS ON PLAN ARE FOR THE PURPOSES OF MEASUREMENT ONLY
ACTUAL COLORS AS PER COLOR CHART

TYPE 7
DESIGN J
STARBOARD SIDE
SCALE ⅛" = 1'-0" LENGTH 340'-0" BP
COLORS
GRAY WHITE NO 3 BLUE
BLACK NO 1 BLUE GRAY
NOTE
COLORS ON PLAN ARE FOR THE PURPOSES OF MEASUREMENT ONLY
ACTUAL COLORS AS PER COLOR CHART

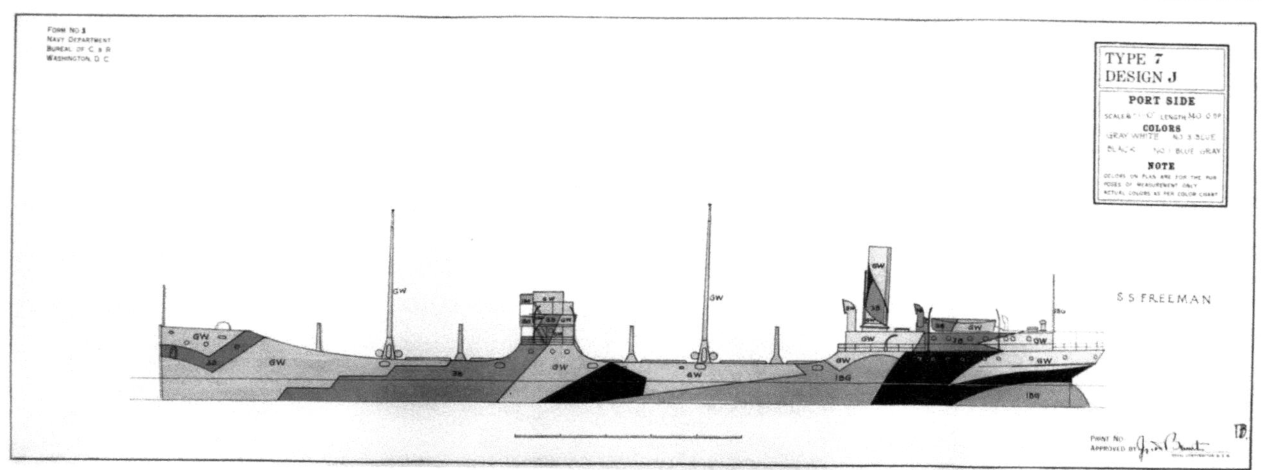

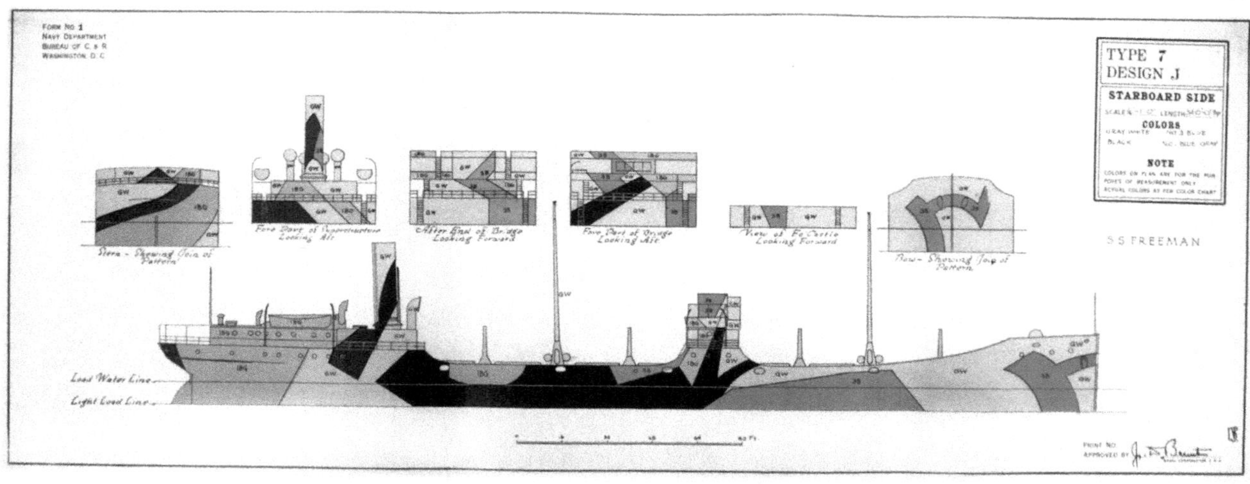

T8 A

Colors used	Ships painted with this pattern
BLACK	ID 1555 WILLIAM ISOM (T)
WHITE	
#1 BLUE-GRAY	

TYPE 8
DESIGN A
PORT SIDE
SCALE 1/16"=1'-0" LENGTH 261'-0"
COLORS
NO. 1 BLUE GREY BLACK
WHITE
NOTE
COLORS ON PLAN ARE FOR THE PURPOSES OF MEASUREMENT ONLY. ACTUAL COLORS AS PER COLOR CHART

TYPE 8
DESIGN A
STARBOARD SIDE
SCALE 1/16"=1'-0" LENGTH 261'-0"
COLORS
WHITE BLACK
NO. 1 BLUE NO. 1 BLUE GREY
NOTE
COLORS ON PLAN ARE FOR THE PURPOSES OF MEASUREMENT ONLY. ACTUAL COLORS AS PER COLOR CHART

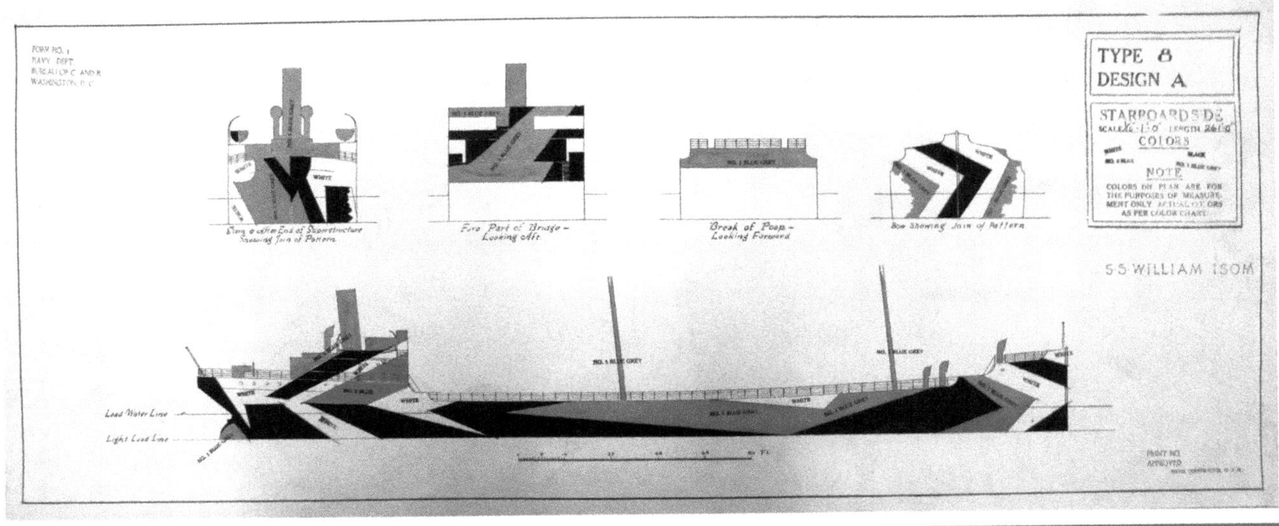

T8 C

Colors used	Ships painted with this pattern
BLACK	ID 4276-D LAKE YEMASSEE
WHITE	ID 3496 POINTBONITA (T)
#3 BLUE	ID 3125 SANTA OLIVIA
#1 BLUE-GRAY	

TYPE 8 DESIGN C
·PORT·SIDE·
SCALE 1/16"=1' LENGTH 260'0"
COLORS
BLACK NO. 3 BLUE
WHITE NO. 1 BLUE GREY
NOTE
COLORS ON PLAN ARE FOR THE PURPOSES OF MEASUREMENT ONLY ··· ACTUAL COLORS AS PER COLOR CHART·

TYPE 8 DESIGN C
·STARBOARD·SIDE·
SCALE 1/16"=1' LENGTH 260'0"
COLORS
BLACK NO. 3 BLUE
WHITE NO. 1 BLUE GREY
NOTE
COLORS ON PLAN ARE FOR THE PURPOSES OF MEASUREMENT ONLY ··· ACTUAL COLORS AS PER COLOR CHART·

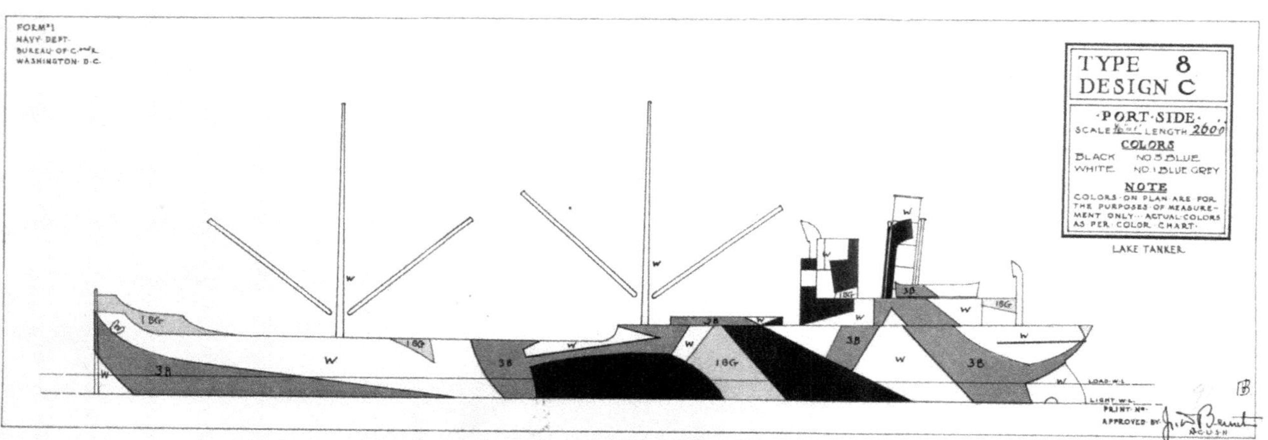

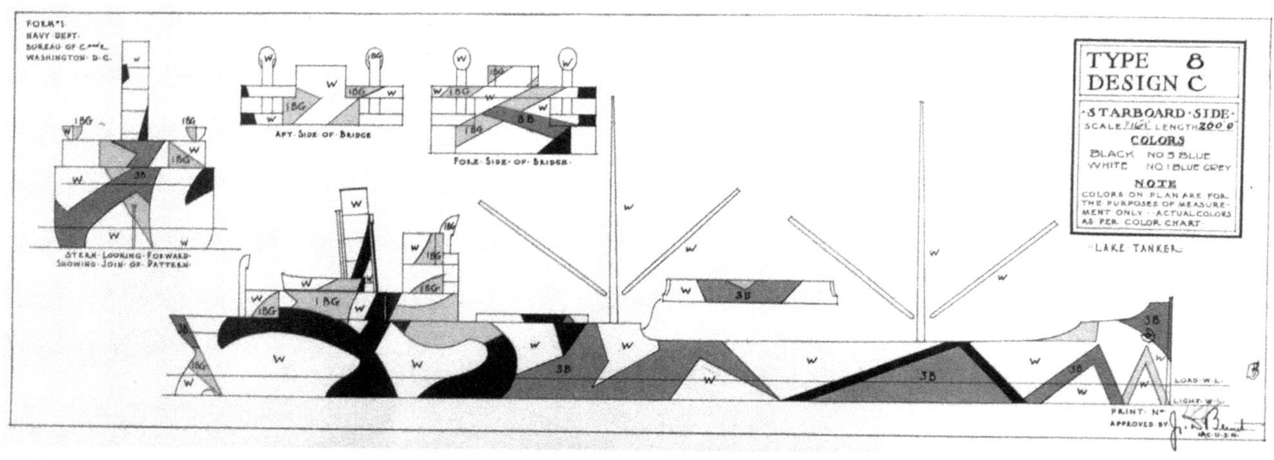

T8 E

Colors used	Ships painted with this pattern
BLACK	ID NONE SILVERADO
WHITE	
#3 BLUE	
#1 BLUE	

TYPE 8
DESIGN E

·PORT·SIDE·
SCALE 1/16"=1'0" LENGTH 261'0" B.P.
COLORS
BLACK NO. 1 BLUE
WHITE NO. 3 BLUE
NOTE
COLORS·ON·PLAN ARE FOR THE PURPOSES·OF MEASURE-MENT·ONLY···ACTUAL·COLORS AS PER·COLOR·CHART·

TYPE 8
DESIGN E

·STARBOARD·SIDE·
SCALE 1/16"=1'0" LENGTH 261'0" B.P.
COLORS
BLACK NO. 1 BLUE
WHITE NO. 3 BLUE
NOTE
COLORS·ON·PLAN·ARE·FOR·THE·PURPOSES·OF·MEASURE-MENT·ONLY···ACTUAL·COLORS AS·PER·COLOR·CHART·

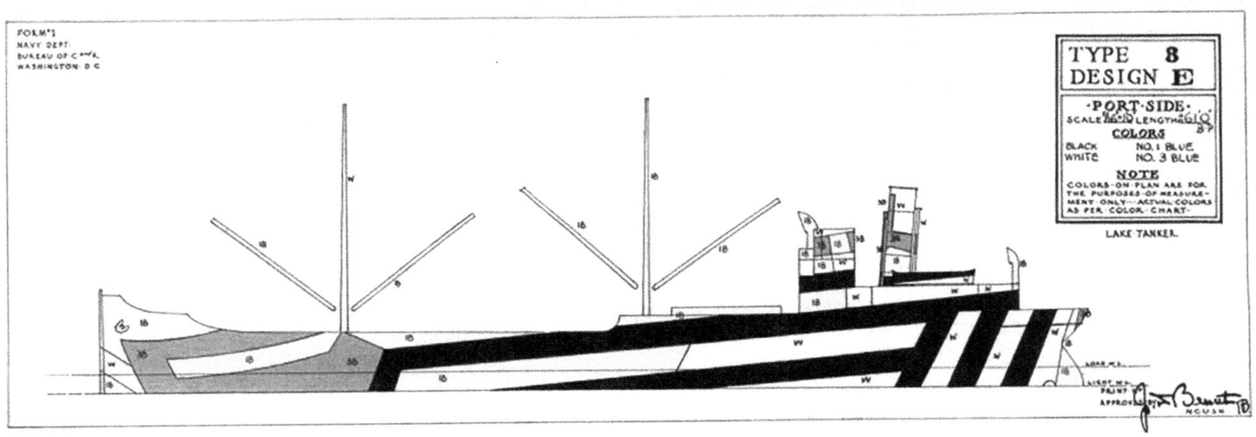

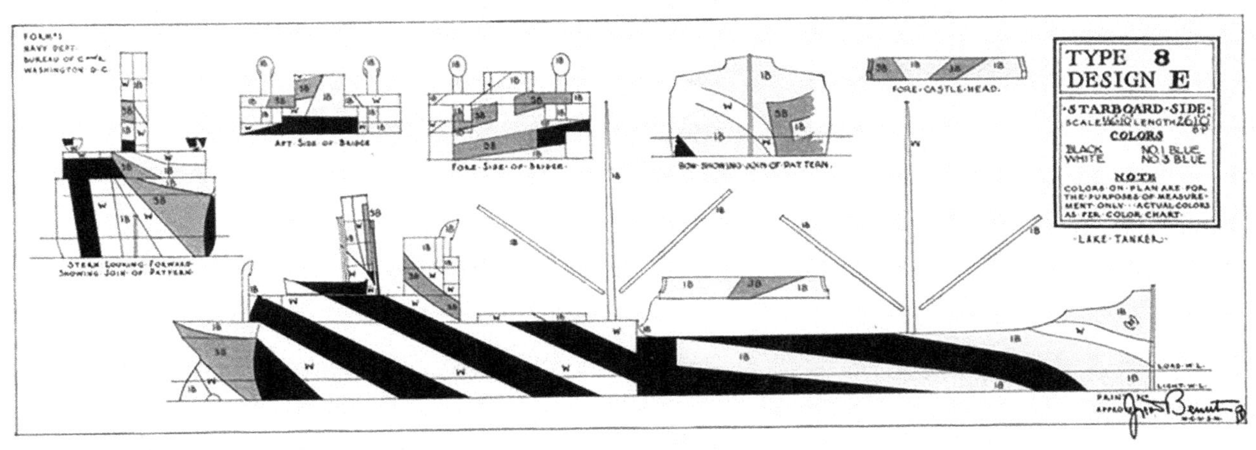

T8 G

Colors used	Ships painted with this pattern
BLACK	LAKE ONEIDA
WHITE	
#3 BLUE	
#1 BLUE-GRAY	

TYPE 8
DESIGN G
PORT SIDE
SCALE 1/4"-1'0" LENGTH 251'0"
COLORS
BLACK 4 GRAY
GRAY WHITE 1 GRAY GREEN
NOTE
COLORS ON PLAN ARE FOR THE PURPOSES OF MEASUREMENT ONLY
ACTUAL COLORS AS PER COLOR CHART

TYPE 8
DESIGN G
STARBOARD SIDE
SCALE 1/4"-1'0" LENGTH 251'0"
COLORS
BLACK 4 GRAY
GRAY WHITE 1 GRAY GREEN
NOTE
COLORS ON PLAN ARE FOR THE PURPOSES OF MEASUREMENT ONLY
ACTUAL COLORS AS PER COLOR CHART

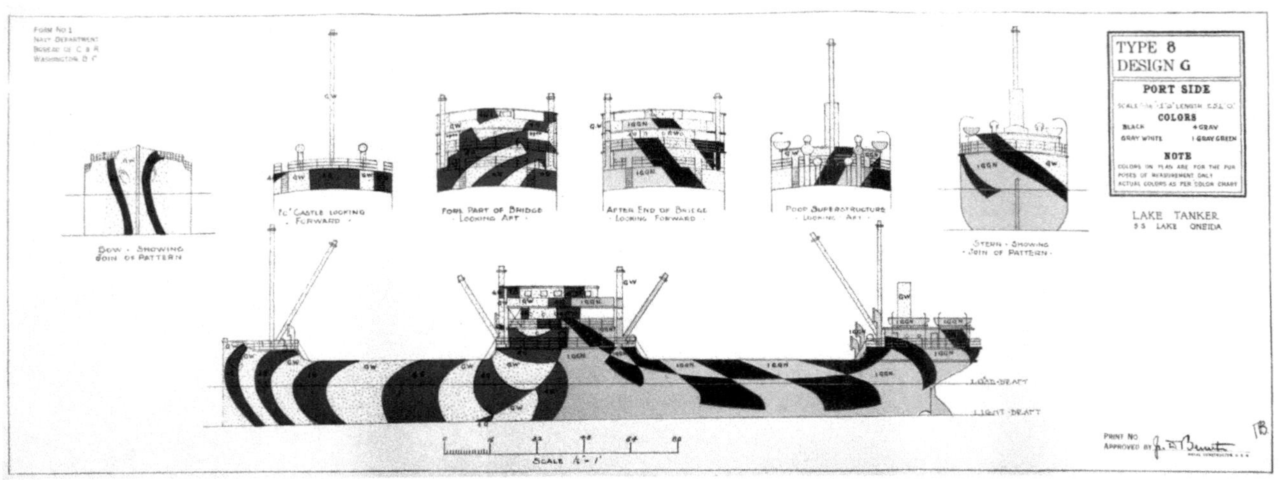

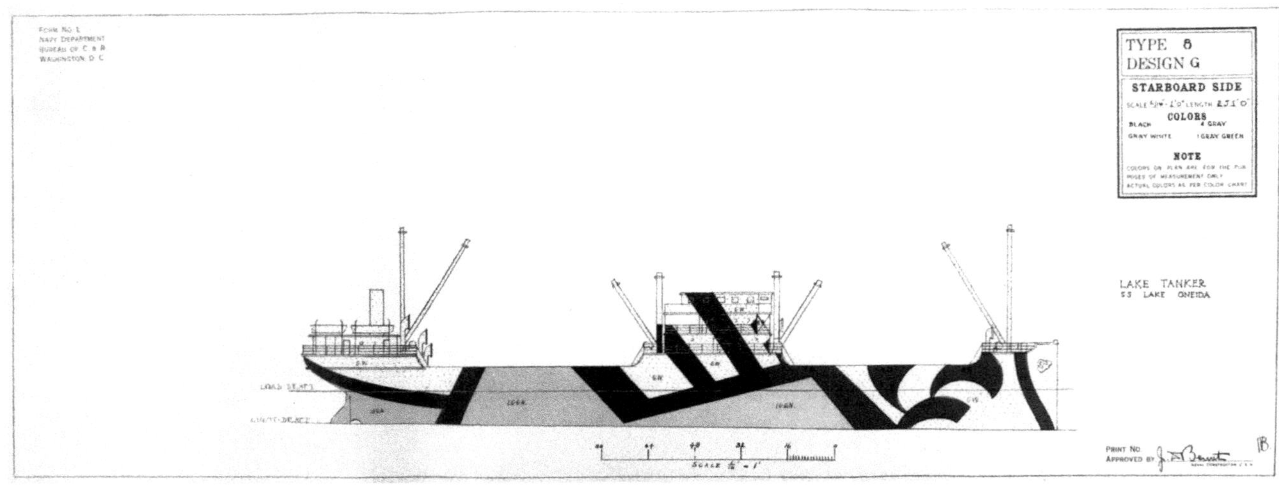

T8 I

Colors used	Ships painted with this pattern
GREY-WHITE	COSTILLA
BLACK	

TYPE 8
DESIGN I
PORT SIDE
SCALE 1/16"-1'0" LENGTH 261'0"
COLORS
GRAYWHITE BLACK
NOTE
COLORS ON PLAN ARE FOR THE PURPOSES OF MEASUREMENT ONLY
ACTUAL COLORS AS PER COLOR CHART

TYPE 8
DESIGN I
STARBOARD SIDE
SCALE 1/16"=1'-0" LENGTH 261'-0"
COLORS
GRAY-WHITE · BLACK
NOTE
COLORS ON PLAN ARE FOR THE PURPOSES OF MEASUREMENT ONLY
ACTUAL COLORS AS PER COLOR CHART

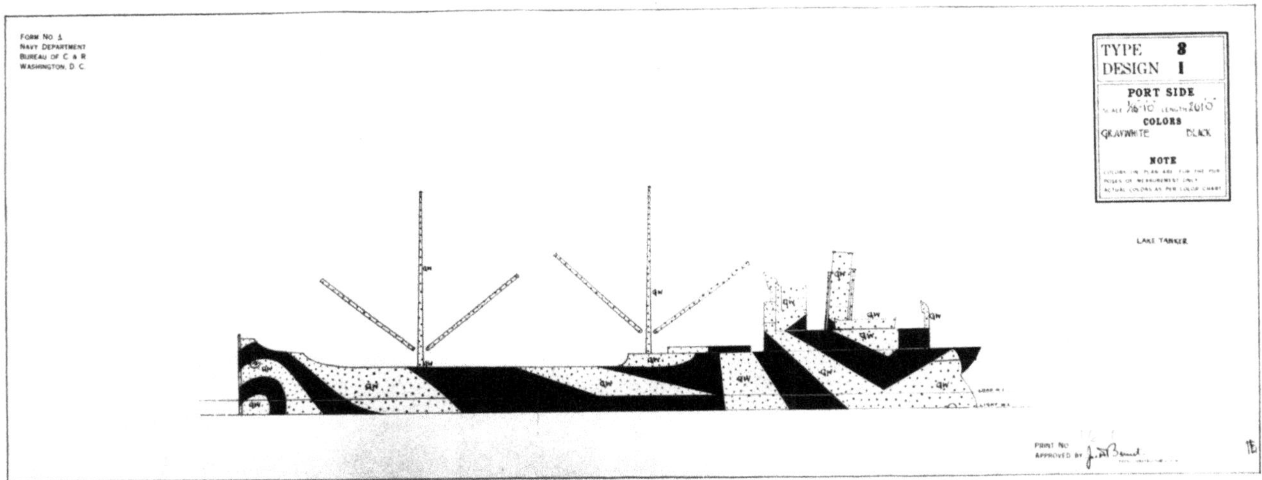

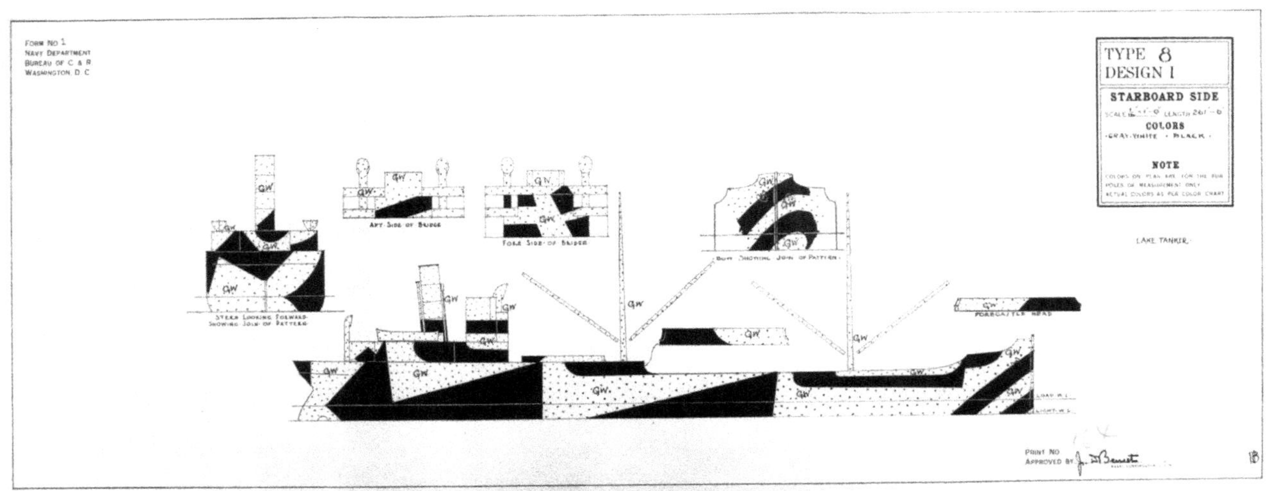

T9 A

Colors used	Ships painted with this pattern
BLACK	ID 2847 OAKLAND
WHITE	ID 2888 WESTBRIDGE
#3 BLUE	ID 3147 WAKULLA
#1 BLUE-GRAY	ID 3041 ACCOMAC
	ID 3202 WESTMOUNT(T)

TYPE 9
DESIGN A
·PORT·SIDE·
SCALE 1/8"-1'-0" LENGTH 410'-0"
COLORS
3B = NO.3 BLUE · · · · BLACK
1 BG = NO.1 BLUE GREY · · · ·
W = WHITE · · · · · · ·
NOTE
COLORS·ON PLAN ARE FOR THE PURPOSES·OF MEASUREMENT ONLY···ACTUAL·COLORS AS PER COLOR·CHART·

TYPE 9
DESIGN A
·STARBOARD·SIDE·
SCALE 1/8" 1'0" LENGTH 410'-0"
COLORS
3 B = NO. 3 BLUE
1 BG = NO. 1 BLUE GREY
W = WHITE
BLACK
NOTE
COLORS ON PLAN ARE FOR THE PURPOSES OF MEASUREMENT ONLY · · ACTUAL COLORS AS PER COLOR CHART·

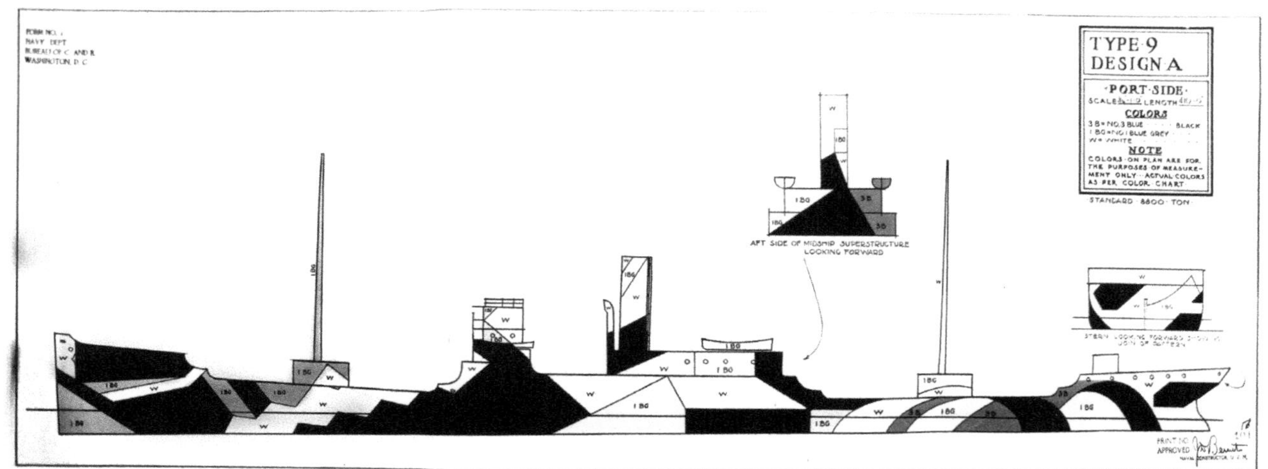

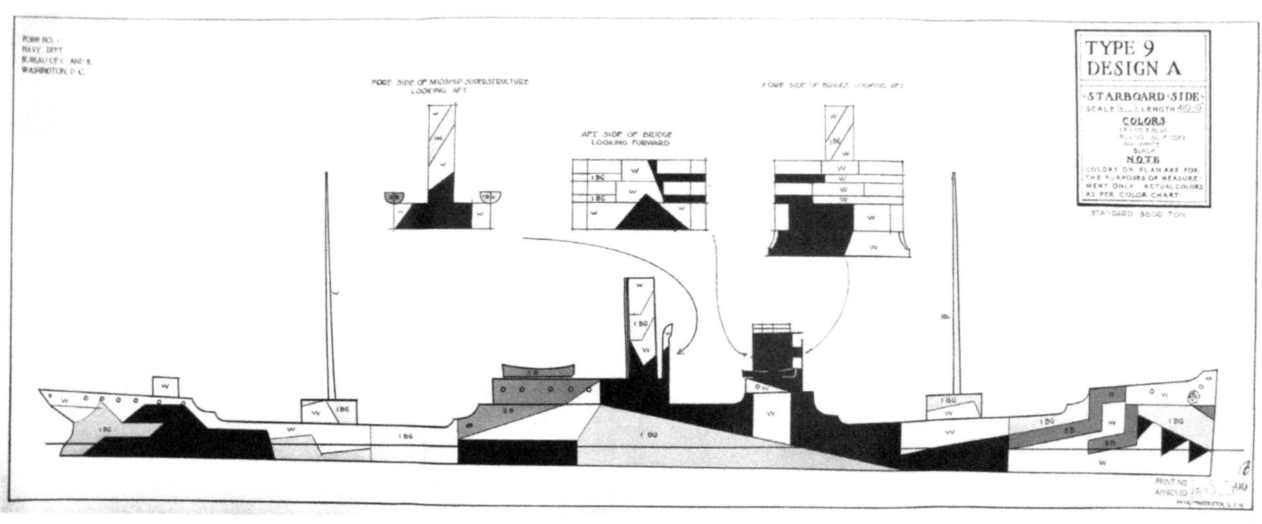

T9 B

Colors used	Ships painted with this pattern
BLACK	ID 2317 SAETIA
WHITE	ID 3063 FRESNO
#3 BLUE	ID 3138 ALLOWAY
#1 BLUE-GRAY	ID 3221 WESTAPAUM
	ID 3818 BUFORD (T)

TYPE 9
DESIGN B
PORT SIDE
SCALE 3/32"=1'0" LENGTH 410'0"
COLORS
BLACK No 1 BLUE GRAY
WHITE No 3 BLUE
NOTE
COLORS ON PLAN ARE FOR THE PURPOSES OF MEASUREMENT ONLY. ACTUAL COLORS AS PER COLOR CHART

TYPE 9
DESIGN B
STARBOARD SIDE
COLORS
BLACK No 1 BLUE GRAY
WHITE No 3 BLUE
NOTE
COLORS ON PLAN ARE FOR THE PURPOSES OF MEASUREMENT ONLY. ACTUAL COLORS AS PER COLOR CHART

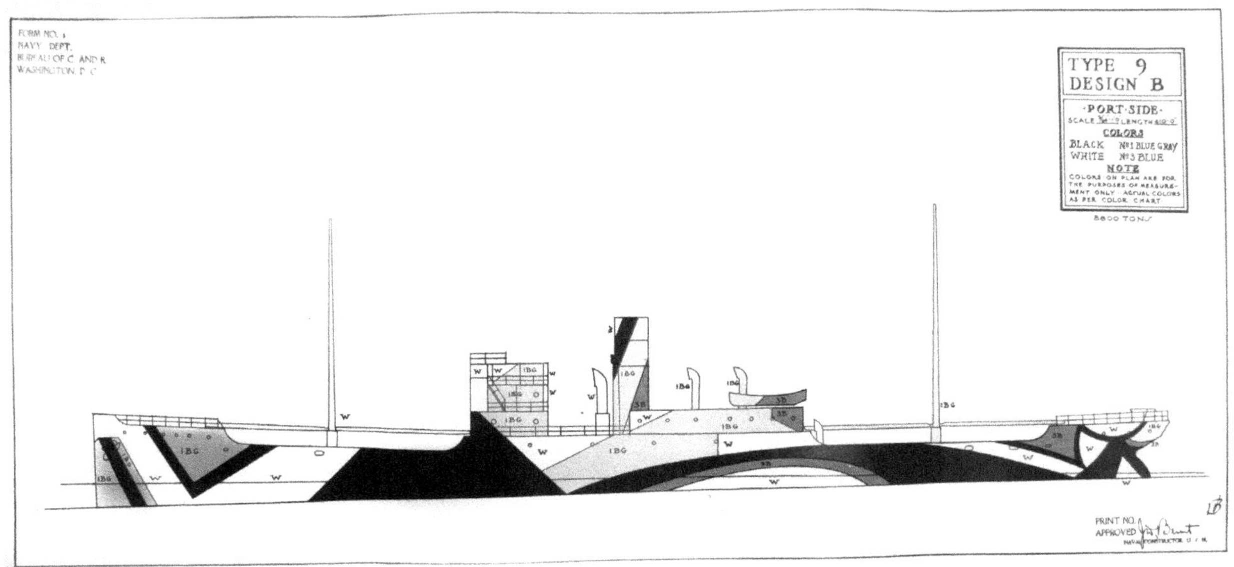

T9 C

Colors used	Ships painted with this pattern
BLACK	ID 3496 POINTBONITA
WHITE	ID 3153 WESTERN SEA
#3 BLUE	ID 4806 IROQUOIS (T)
#1 BLUE-GRAY	

TYPE 9
DESIGN C

∴ PORT SIDE ∴
SCALE LENGTH 410' 0"
COLORS
1 BG = NO 1 BLUE GREY BLACK
3B = NO 3 BLUE WHITE
NOTE
COLORS ON PLAN ARE FOR THE PURPOSES OF MEASUREMENT ONLY. ACTUAL COLORS AS PER COLOR CHART.

TYPE 9
DESIGN C

STARBOARD SIDE
SCALE LENGTH 410' 0"
COLORS
1 BG = NO 1 BLUE GREY BLACK
3B = NO 3 BLUE WHITE
NOTE
COLORS ON PLAN ARE FOR THE PURPOSES OF MEASUREMENT ONLY. ACTUAL COLORS AS PER COLOR CHART.

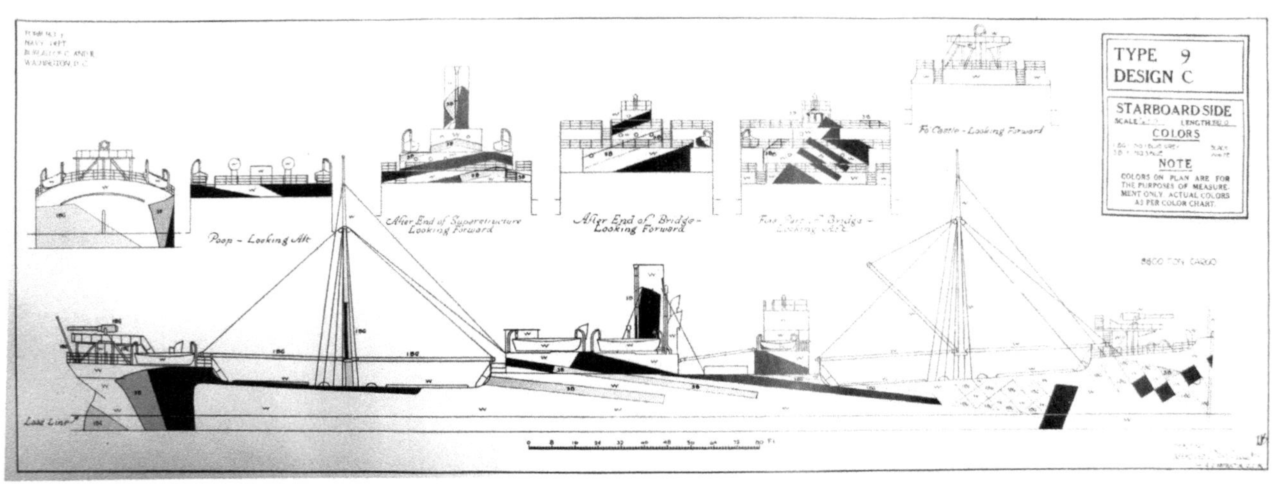

T9 D

Colors used	Ships painted with this pattern
BLACK	ID 2142 MINEOLA
WHITE	ID 2758 WESTLIANGA
#3 BLUE	ID 3146 ANIWA
#1 BLUE-GRAY	ID 3230 WASSAIC

TYPE 9 DESIGN D	TYPE 9 DESIGN D
PORT SIDE SCALE 1/16" = 1'-0" LENGTH 415'-0" COLORS BLACK NO 1 BLUE GREY WHITE NO 3 BLUE NOTE COLORS ON PLAN ARE FOR THE PURPOSES OF MEASUREMENT ONLY ACTUAL COLORS AS PER COLOR CHART	STARBOARD SIDE SCALE 1/16" = 1'-0" LENGTH 415'-0" COLORS BLACK NO 1 BLUE GREY WHITE NO 3 BLUE NOTE COLORS ON PLAN ARE FOR THE PURPOSES OF MEASUREMENT ONLY ACTUAL COLORS AS PER COLOR CHART

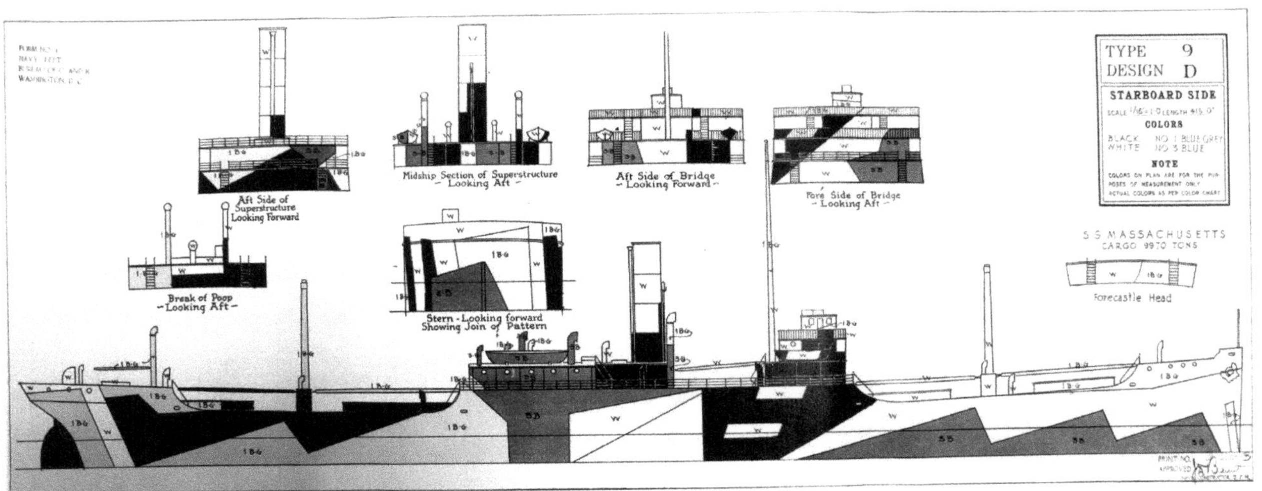

T9 E

Colors used	Ships painted with this pattern
BLACK	ID 3876 WATANOWAN
WHITE	ID 1484 KERESASPA
#3 BLUE	ID 3300 WESTERN LIGHT(T)
#1 BLUE-GRAY	

TYPE 9
DESIGN E
PORT SIDE
SCALE 1/16" = 1'-0" LENGTH 415' 0"
COLORS
BLACK NO 1 BLUE GREY
WHITE NO 3 BLUE
NOTE
COLORS ON PLAN ARE FOR THE PURPOSES OF MEASUREMENT ONLY ... ACTUAL COLORS AS PER COLOR CHART

TYPE 9
DESIGN E
STARBOARD SIDE
SCALE 1/16" = 1'-0" LENGTH 415' 0"
COLORS
BLACK NO 1 BLUE GREY
WHITE NO 3 BLUE
NOTE
COLORS ON PLAN ARE FOR THE PURPOSES OF MEASUREMENT ONLY ... ACTUAL COLORS AS PER COLOR CHART

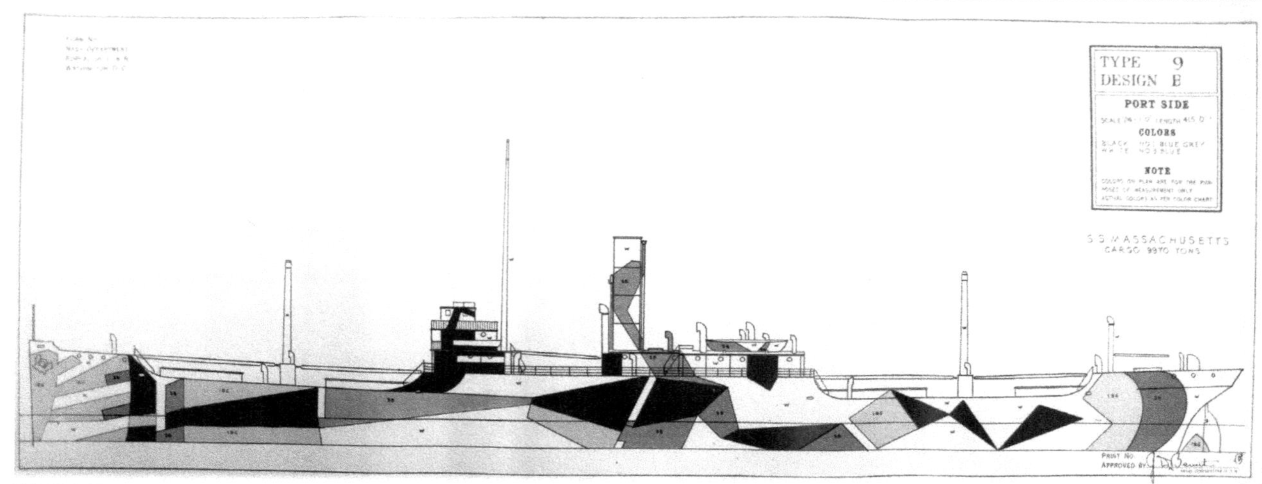

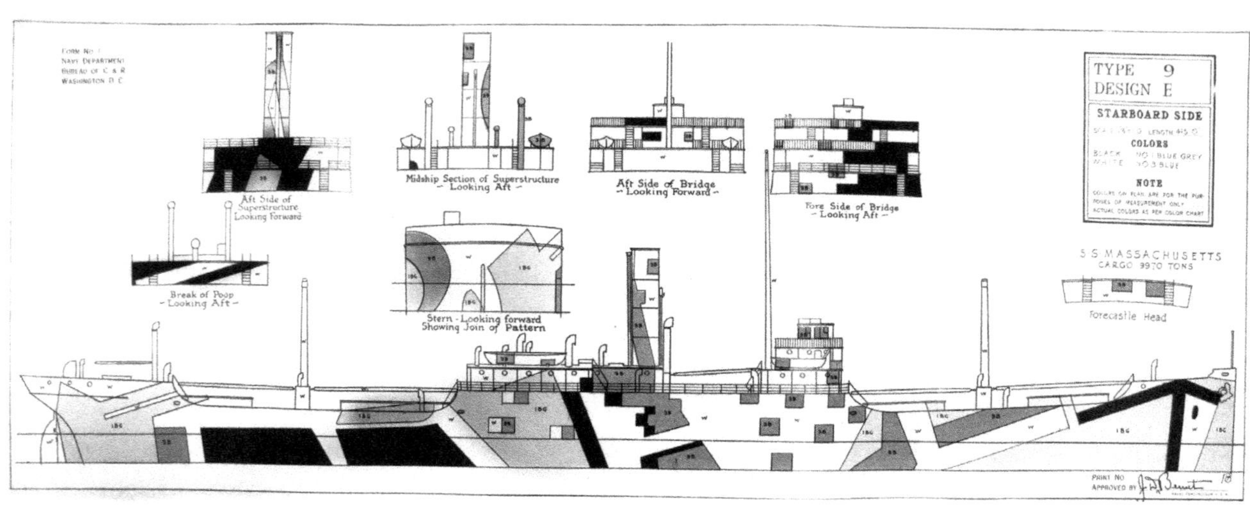

T9 F

Colors used	Ships painted with this pattern
BLACK	ID 1605 ARCADIA
WHITE	ID 3242 VOLUNTEER
#3 BLUE	ID 2482 GORREDIJK
#1 BLUE-GRAY	ID 2511 SAMARINDA

TYPE 9
DESIGN F

PORT SIDE

SCALE 1/16" = 1.0' LENGTH 415.0'

COLORS

BLACK NO 1 BLUE GREY
WHITE NO 3 BLUE

NOTE

COLORS ON PLAN ARE FOR THE PURPOSES OF MEASUREMENT ONLY
ACTUAL COLORS AS PER COLOR CHART

TYPE 9
DESIGN F

STARBOARD SIDE

SCALE LENGTH

COLORS

BLACK NO 1 BLUE GREY
WHITE NO 3 BLUE

NOTE

COLORS ON PLAN ARE FOR THE PURPOSES OF MEASUREMENT ONLY
ACTUAL COLORS AS PER COLOR CHART

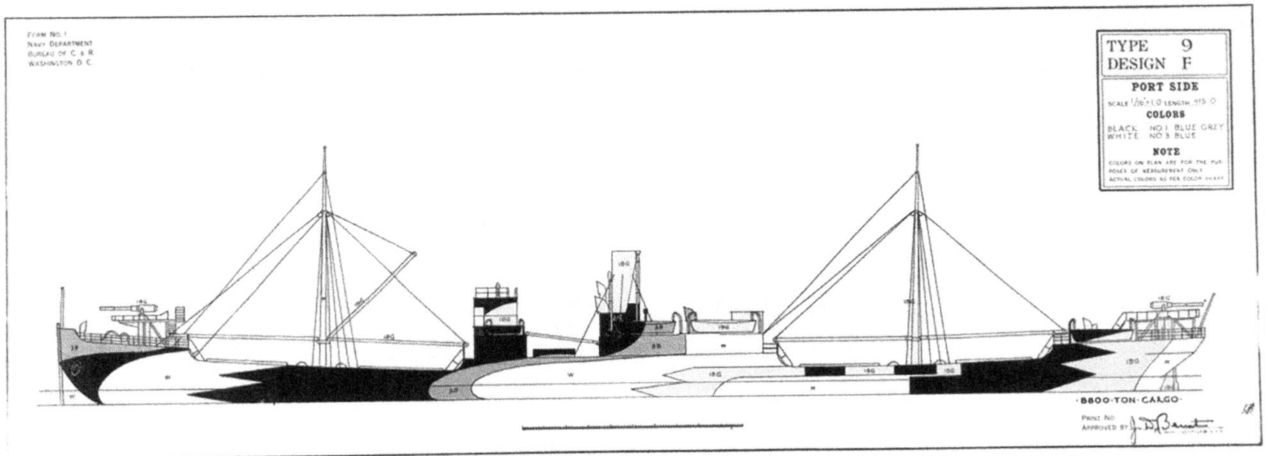

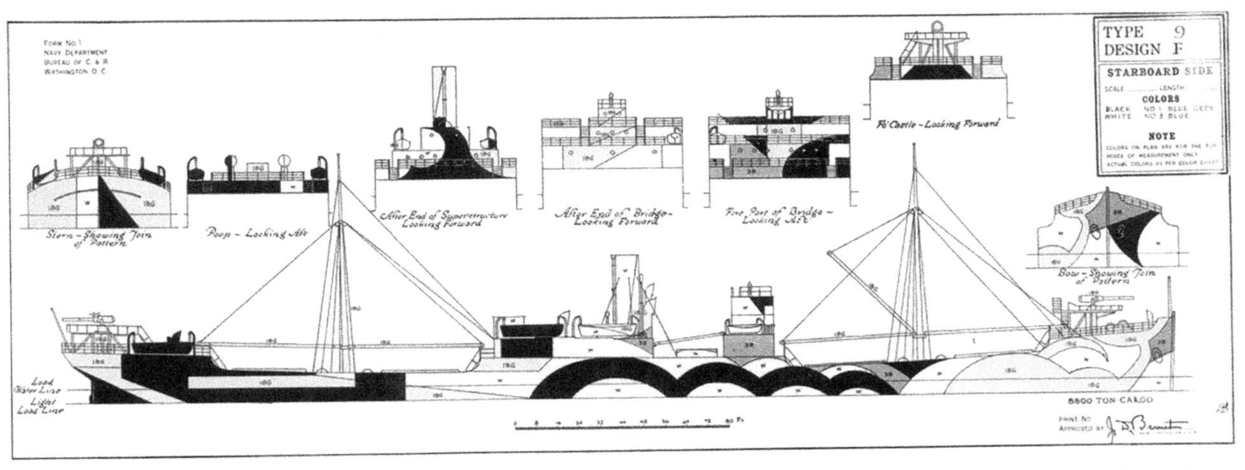

T9 G

Colors used	Ships painted with this pattern
BLACK	ID 3330 WESTGALETA
WHITE	ID 3347 WESTGALOC
#3 BLUE	ID 3214 CAPE LOOKOUT(T)
#1 BLUE-GREEN	ID 3121 WESTWIND (T)

TYPE·9·
DESIGN·G·

PORT SIDE

SCALE 3/16"-1'0" LENGTH 410'0"

COLORS

BLACK NO·3 BLUE
WHITE NO·1 BLUE-GREY

NOTE

COLORS ON PLAN ARE FOR THE PURPOSES OF MEASUREMENT ONLY
ACTUAL COLORS AS PER COLOR CHART

TYPE 9
DESIGN G

STARBOARD SIDE

SCALE 1/16"=1'0" LENGTH 410'0"

COLORS

BLACK NO 1 BLUE GREY
WHITE NO 3 BLUE

NOTE

COLORS ON PLAN ARE FOR THE PURPOSES OF MEASUREMENT ONLY
ACTUAL COLORS AS PER COLOR CHART

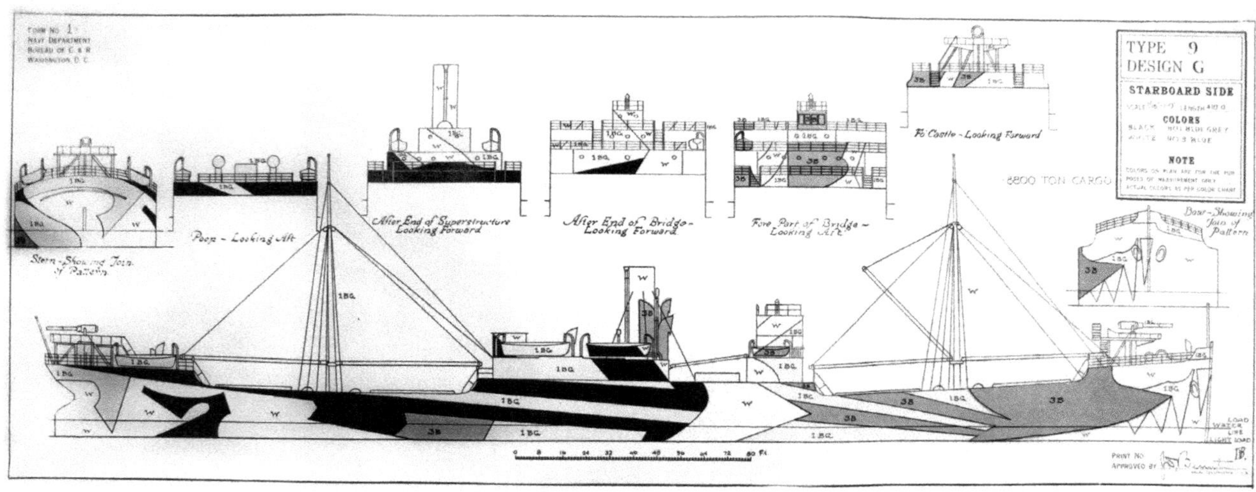

T9 H

Colors used	Ships painted with this pattern
BLACK	ID 3501 WESTZULA
WHITE	
#3 BLUE	
#1 BLUE	

TYPE 9
DESIGN H
·PORT·SIDE·
SCALE 1/16"=1'0" LENGTH 410' 0"
COLORS
BLACK NO 1 BLUE
WHITE NO 3 BLUE
NOTE
COLORS ON PLAN ARE FOR THE PURPOSES OF MEASUREMENT ONLY ··· ACTUAL COLORS AS PER COLOR CHART·

TYPE 9
DESIGN H
·STARBOARD·SIDE·
SCALE 1/16"=1'0" LENGTH 410' 0"
COLORS
BLACK NO 1 BLUE
WHITE NO 3 BLUE
NOTE
COLORS ON PLAN ARE FOR THE PURPOSES OF MEASUREMENT ONLY ··· ACTUAL COLORS AS PER COLOR CHART·

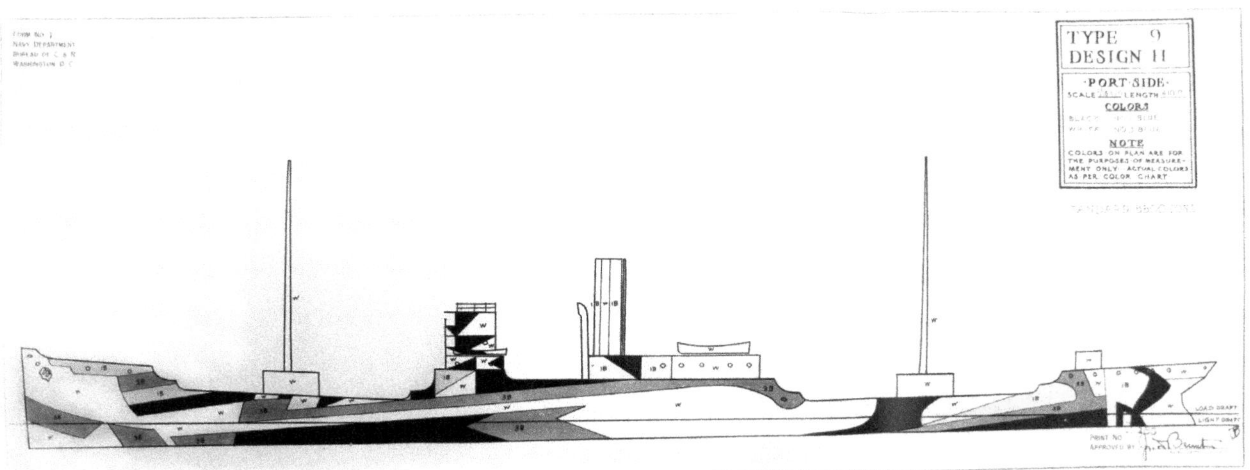

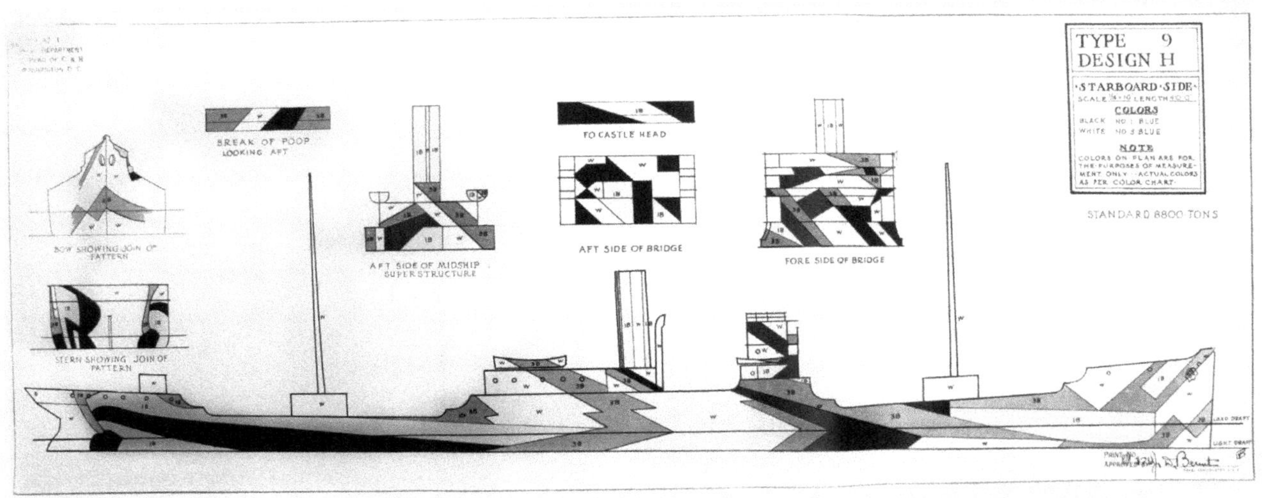

T9 I

Colors used	Ships painted with this pattern
BLACK	ID 3671 INVINCIBLE
GREY-WHITE	
#3 BLUE	
#1 BLUE	
#2 BLUE-GRAY	

TYPE 9
DESIGN 1
PORT SIDE
COLORS
GRAY WHITE NO 3 BLUE
NO 2 BLUE GRAY BLACK
NO 1 BLUE
NOTE
COLORS ON PLAN ARE FOR THE PURPOSES OF MEASUREMENT ONLY. ACTUAL COLORS AS PER COLOR CHART

TYPE 9
DESIGN 1
STARBOARD SIDE
COLORS
GRAY WHITE NO 3 BLUE
NO 2 BLUE GRAY BLACK
NO 1 BLUE
NOTE
COLORS ON PLAN ARE FOR THE PURPOSES OF MEASUREMENT ONLY. ACTUAL COLORS AS PER COLOR CHART

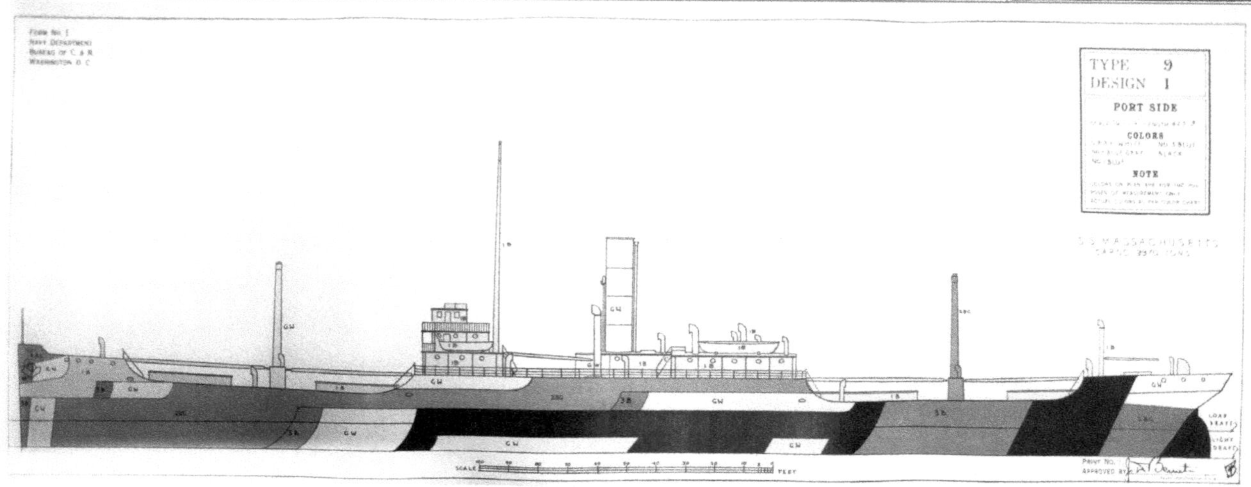

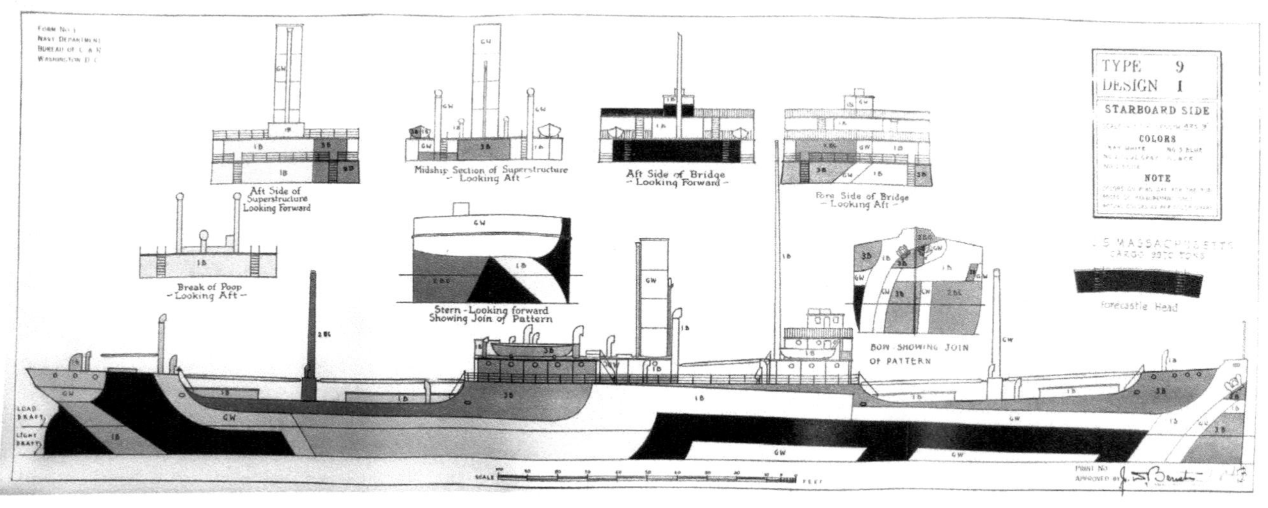

T9 J

Colors used	Ships painted with this pattern
BLACK	ID 1821 NYANZA
GREY-WHITE	ID 3584 WESTZUCKER
#3 BLUE	ID 2550 AMELAND
#1 BLUE-GRAY	

TYPE 9
DESIGN J
·PORT·SIDE·
SCALE 3/64"=1'0" LENGTH 410'-0"
COLORS
GRAY WHITE NO 3 BLUE
NO.1 BLUE GRAY BLACK
NOTE
COLORS ON PLAN ARE FOR THE PURPOSES OF MEASUREMENT ONLY... ACTUAL COLORS AS PER COLOR CHART·

TYPE 9
DESIGN J
·STARBOARD·SIDE·
SCALE 3/64"=1'0" LENGTH 410'0"
COLORS
GRAY WHITE NO. 3 BLUE
NO. 1 BLUE GRAY BLACK
NOTE
COLORS ON PLAN ARE FOR THE PURPOSES OF MEASUREMENT ONLY · ACTUAL COLORS AS PER COLOR CHART·

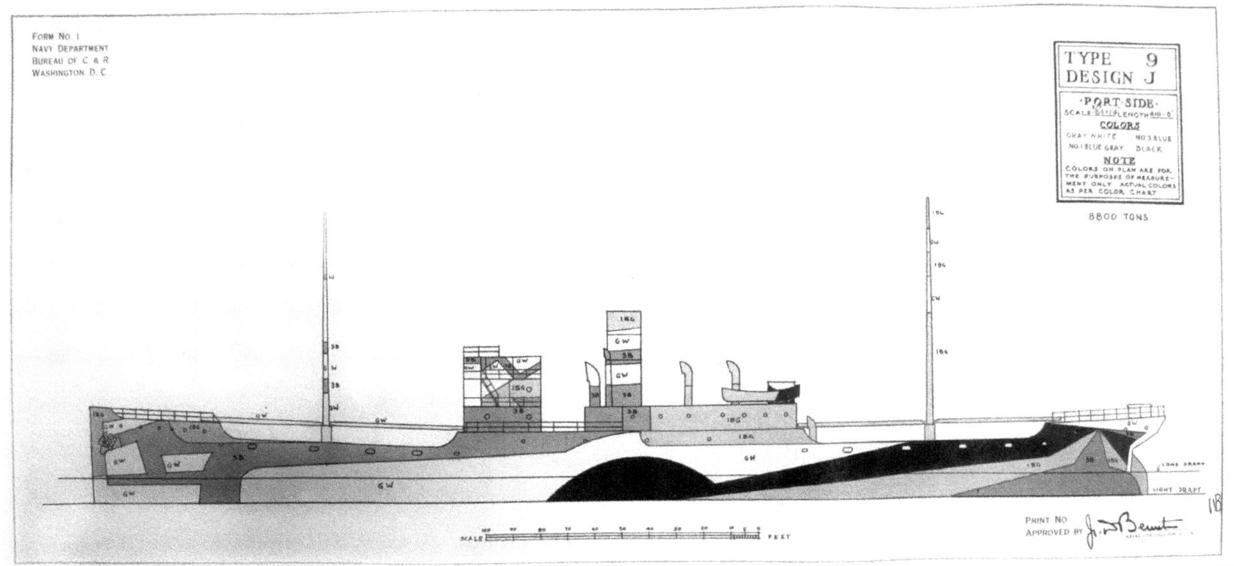

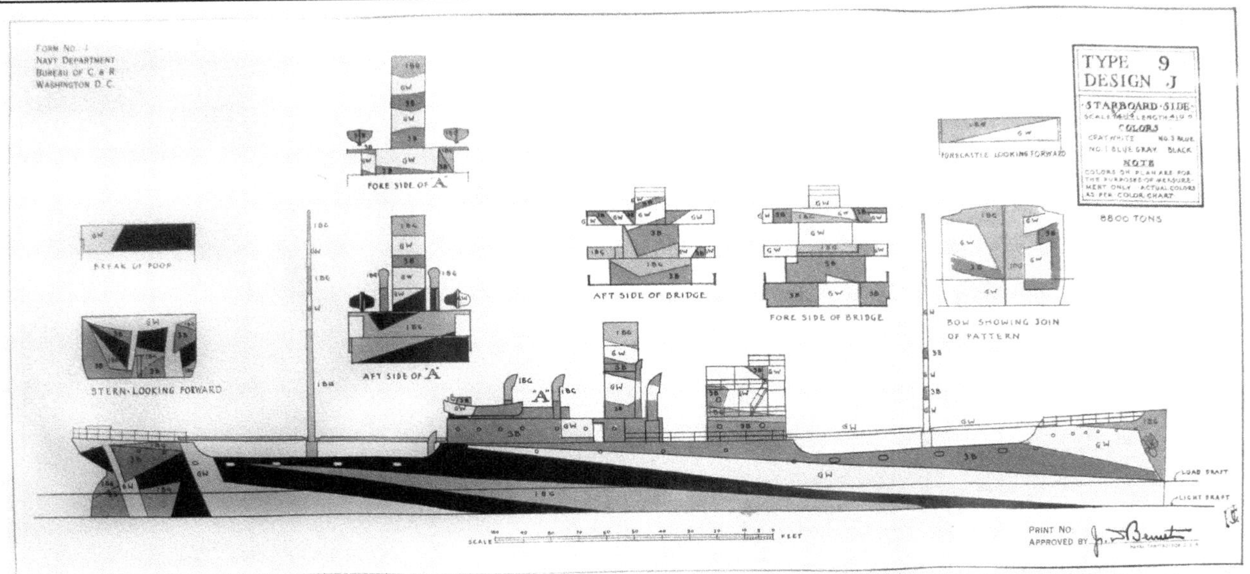

T9 K

Colors used	Ships painted with this pattern
BLACK	ID 3142 MINNEOLA
GREY-WHITE	ID 3569 WESTERN COMET
#1 BLUE	ID 3423 ISANTI
#1 BLUE-GRAY	ID 3170 WESTSHORE
#1 GREEN	

TYPE 9
DESIGN K
PORT SIDE
SCALE 3/64" = 1'-0" LENGTH 410'-0"
COLORS
WHITE NO 1 BLUE NO 1 GREEN
BLACK NO 1 BLUE GRAY
NOTE
COLORS ON PLAN ARE FOR THE PURPOSES OF MEASUREMENT ONLY
ACTUAL COLORS AS PER COLOR CHART

TYPE 9
DESIGN K
STARBOARD SIDE
SCALE 3/64" = 1'-0" LENGTH 410'-0"
COLORS
WHITE NO 1 BLUE NO 1 GREEN
BLACK NO 1 BLUE GRAY
NOTE
COLORS ON PLAN ARE FOR THE PURPOSES OF MEASUREMENT ONLY
ACTUAL COLORS AS PER COLOR CHART

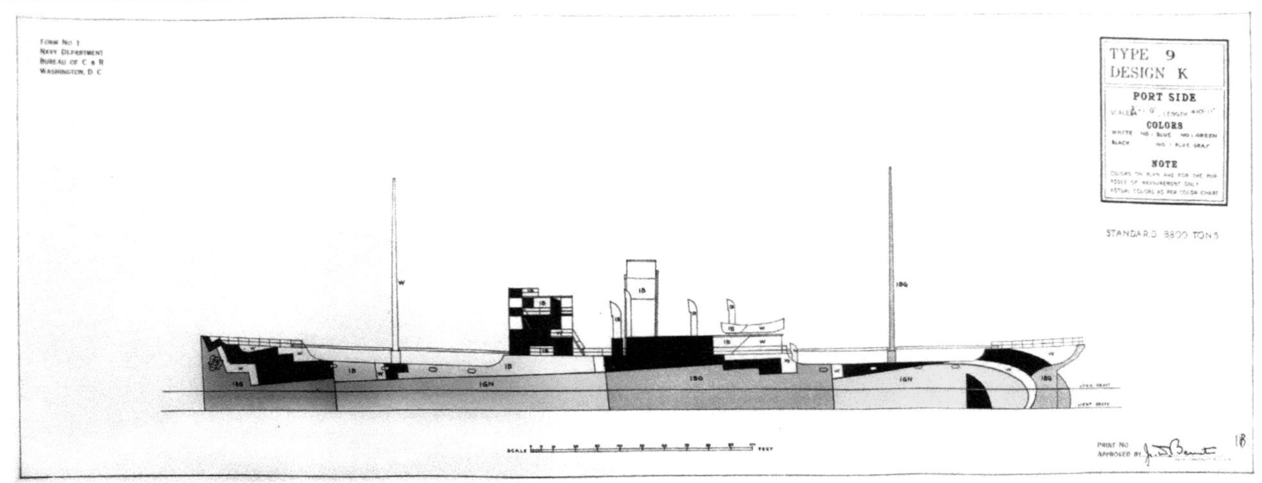

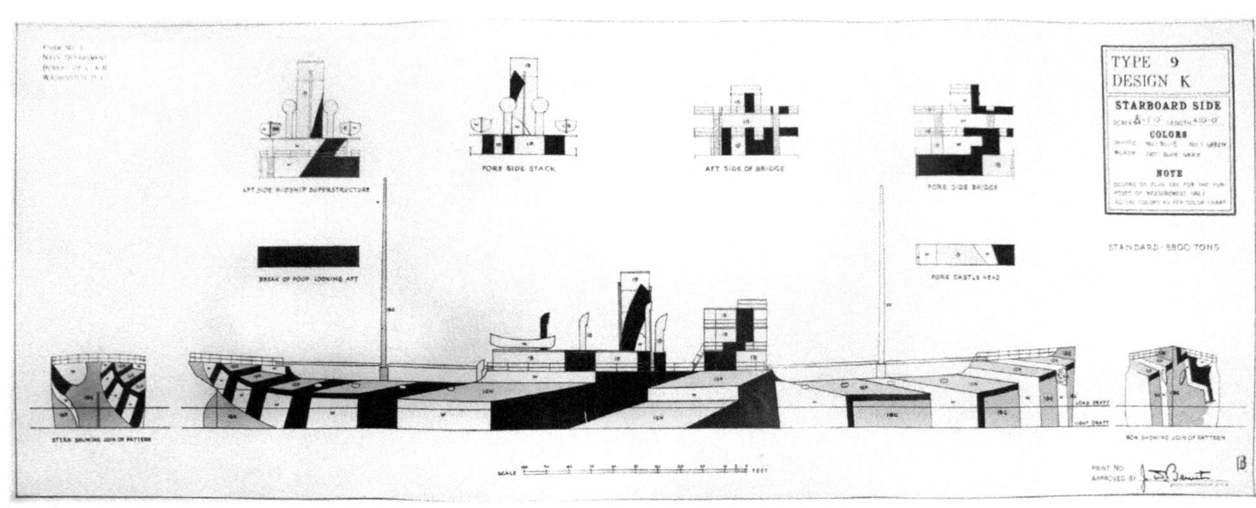

T9 L

Colors used	Ships painted with this pattern
BLACK	ID 3514 VICTORIOUS
GREY-WHITE	BRAZIL ARACAJU
#2 BLUE-GRAY	
#1 GRAY-GREEN	

TYPE 9
DESIGN L

PORT SIDE
SCALE 1/16" = 1'-0" LENGTH 415'-0" BP
COLORS
BLACK · 1 GRAY GREEN
GRAY WHITE · 2 BLUE GRAY
NOTE
COLORS ON PLAN ARE FOR THE PURPOSES OF MEASUREMENT ONLY. ACTUAL COLORS AS PER COLOR CHART.

TYPE 9
DESIGN L

STARBOARD SIDE
SCALE 1/16" = 1'-0" LENGTH 415'-0"
COLORS
BLACK 1 GRAY GREEN
GRAY WHITE 2 BLUE GRAY
NOTE
COLORS ON PLAN ARE FOR THE PURPOSES OF MEASUREMENT ONLY. ACTUAL COLORS AS PER COLOR CHART.

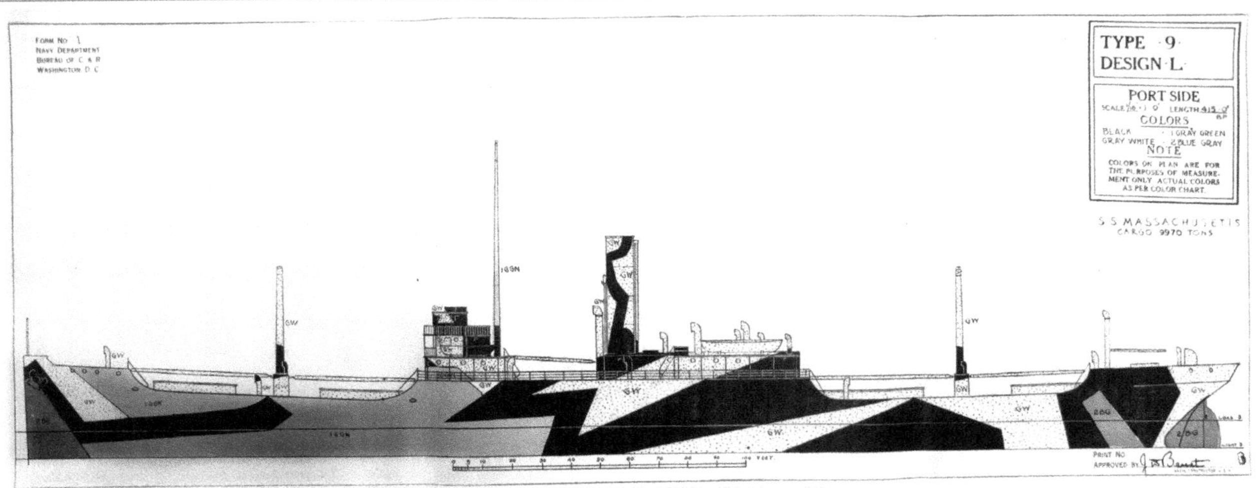

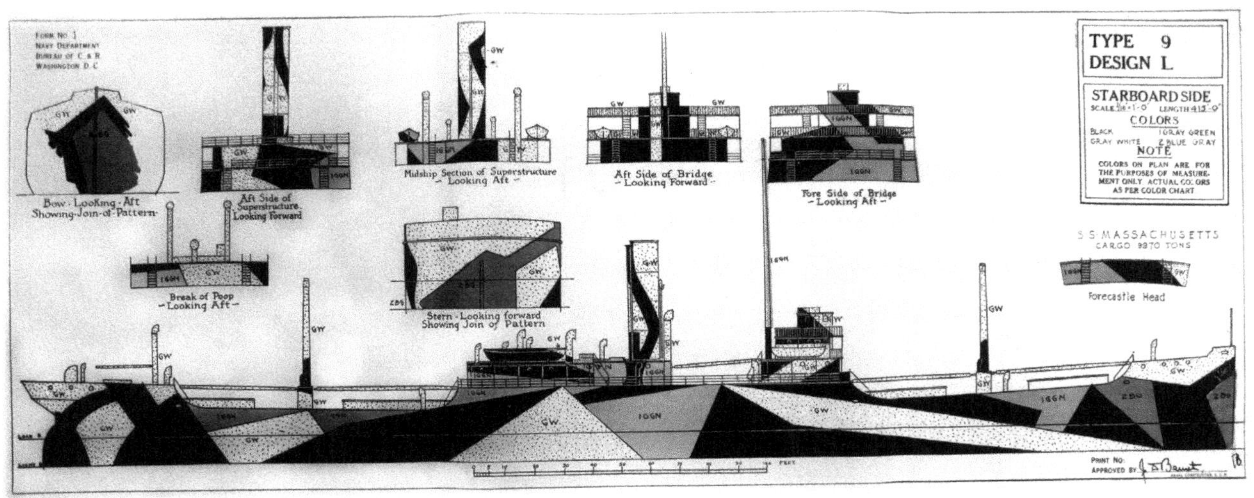

T9 O

Colors used	Ships painted with this pattern
BLACK	ID 3512 NAIWA
GREY-WHITE	ID 3519 NANTAHALA
#3 BLUE	ID 3478 NANTASKET
#4 GRAY	
#1 BLUE-GRAY	

TYPE 9
DESIGN O

PORT SIDE

SCALE 3/64"=1'-0" LENGTH 410'-0"

COLORS

BLACK · NO 4 GRAY
GRAY WHITE · NO 3 BLUE
NO 1 BLUE GRAY

NOTE

COLORS ON PLAN ARE FOR THE PURPOSES OF MEASUREMENT ONLY ACTUAL COLORS AS PER COLOR CHART

TYPE 9
DESIGN O

STARBOARD SIDE

SCALE 3/64"=1'-0" LENGTH 410'-0"

COLORS

BLACK · NO 3 BLUE
GRAY WHITE · NO 1 BLUE GRAY
NO 4 GRAY

NOTE

COLORS ON PLAN ARE FOR THE PURPOSES OF MEASUREMENT ONLY ACTUAL COLORS AS PER COLOR CHART

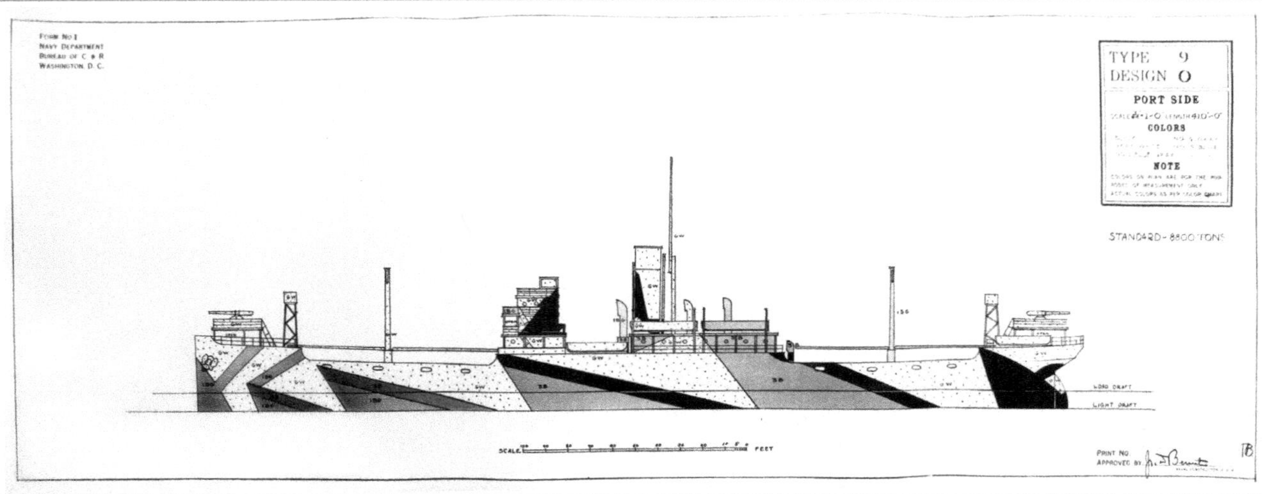

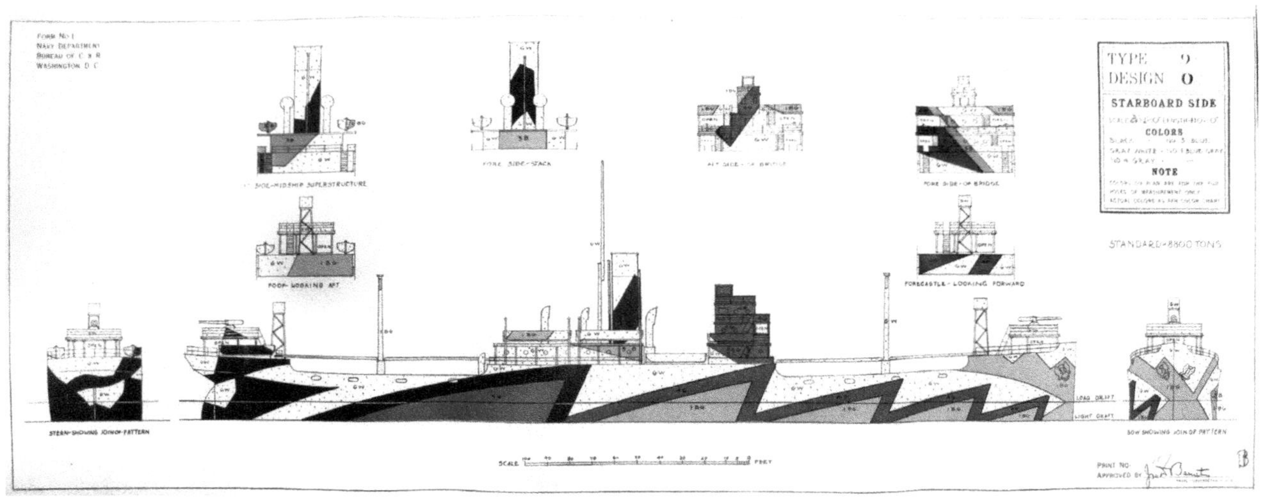

T9 P

Colors used	Ships painted with this pattern
BLACK	ID 3676 INDEPENDENCE
GREY-WHITE	
#3 BLUE	
#1 GRAY-GREEN	

TYPE 9
DESIGN P

PORT SIDE

SCALE 1/8"=1'-0" LENGTH 410'-0"

COLORS

BLACK · NO 3 BLUE
GRAY WHITE NO 1 GRAY GREEN

NOTE

COLORS ON PLAN ARE FOR THE PURPOSES OF MEASUREMENT ONLY ... ACTUAL COLORS AS PER COLOR CHART

TYPE 9
DESIGN P

STARBOARD SIDE

SCALE 1/8"=1'-0" LENGTH 410'-0"

COLORS

BLACK · NO 3 BLUE
GRAY WHITE · NO 1 GRAY GREEN

NOTE

COLORS ON PLAN ARE FOR THE PURPOSES OF MEASUREMENT ONLY ... ACTUAL COLORS AS PER COLOR CHART

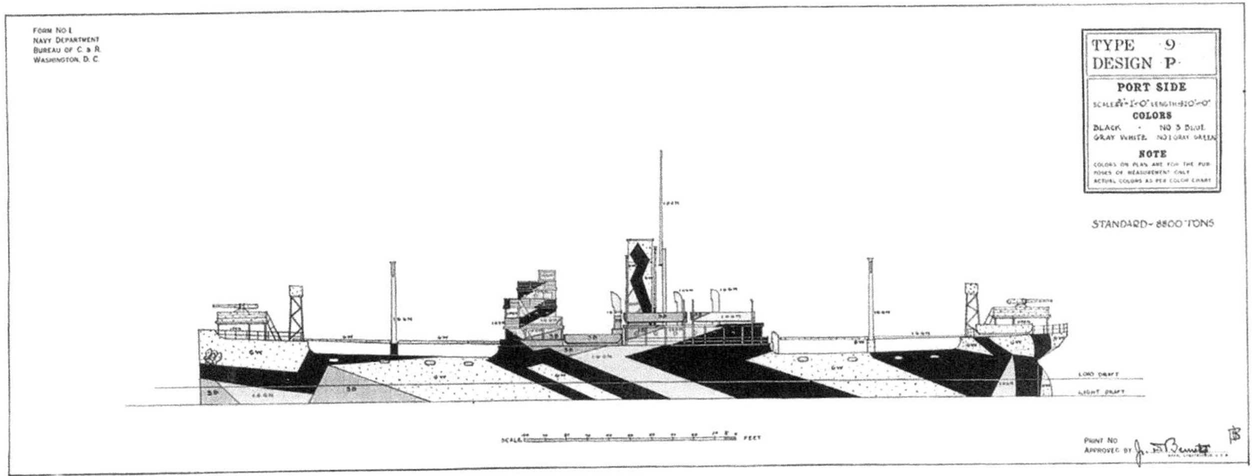

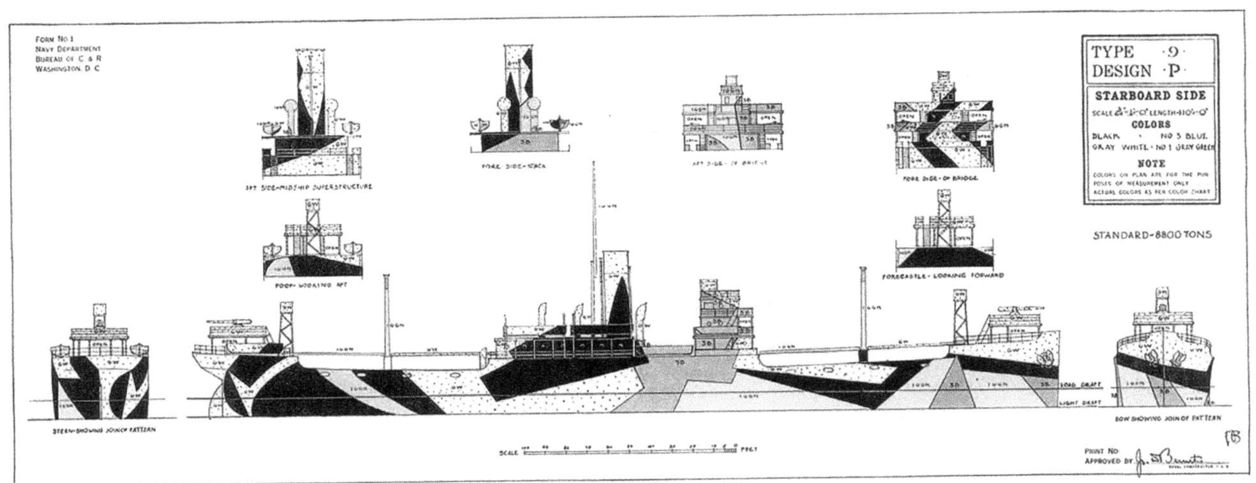

T9 S

Colors used	Ships painted with this pattern
BLACK	ID 3681 WESTMAHOMET
GREY-WHITE	
#3 BLUE	
#1 BLUE	

TYPE 9
DESIGN S

PORT SIDE

SCALE ⅛"=1'-0" LENGTH 410'-0"

COLORS

BLACK N° 1 BLUE

GRAY WHITE N° 3 BLUE

NOTE

COLORS ON PLAN ARE FOR THE PURPOSES OF MEASUREMENT ONLY ACTUAL COLORS AS PER COLOR CHART

TYPE 9
DESIGN S

STARBOARD SIDE

SCALE ⅛"=1'-0" LENGTH 410'-0"

COLORS

BLACK N° 1 BLUE

GRAY WHITE N° 3 BLUE

NOTE

COLORS ON PLAN ARE FOR THE PURPOSES OF MEASUREMENT ONLY ACTUAL COLORS AS PER COLOR CHART

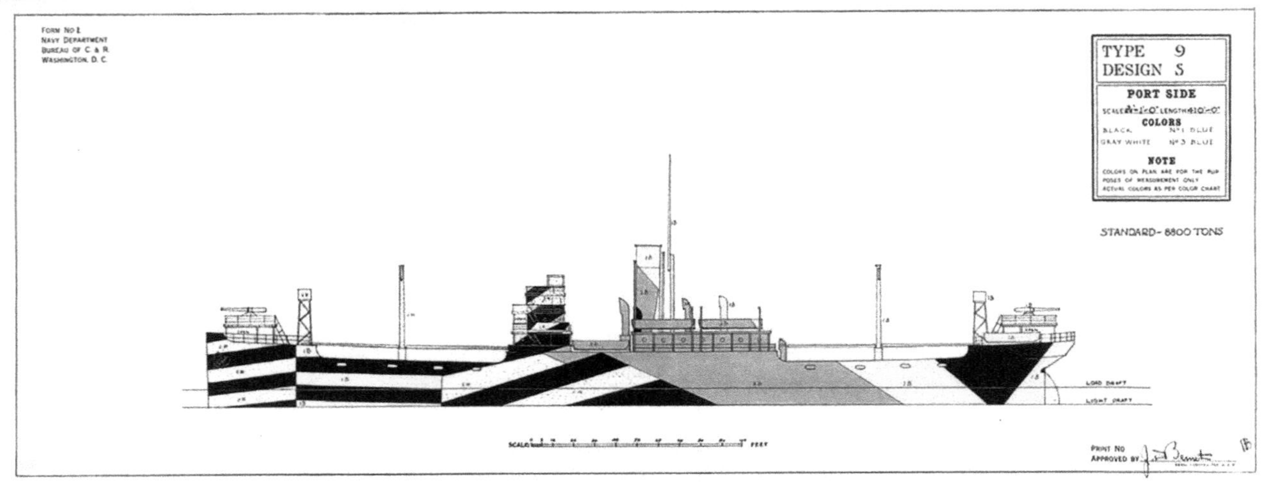

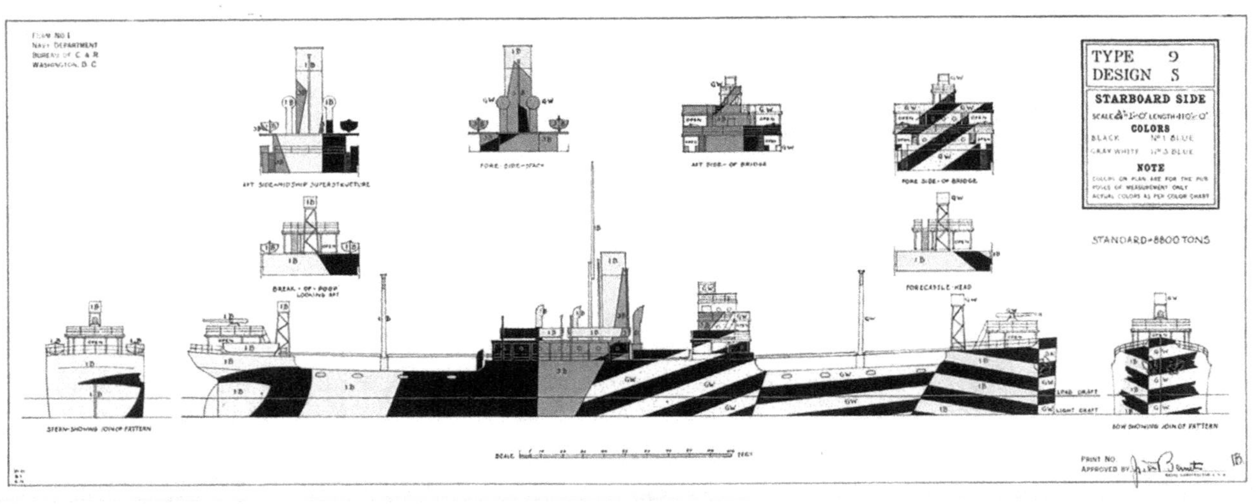

T9 T

Colors used	Ships painted with this pattern
BLACK	ID 3636 WESTMADAKET
GREY-WHITE	
#3 BLUE	

TYPE 9
DESIGN T
PORT SIDE
SCALE 1/8"-1'-0" LENGTH 410'-0"
COLORS
BLACK GRAY WHITE
NO 3 BLUE
NOTE
COLORS ON PLAN ARE FOR THE PURPOSES OF MEASUREMENT ONLY ... ACTUAL COLORS AS PER COLOR CHART

TYPE 9
DESIGN T
STARBOARD SIDE
SCALE 1/8"-1'-0" LENGTH 410'-0"
COLORS
BLACK GRAY WHITE
NO 3 BLUE
NOTE
COLORS ON PLAN ARE FOR THE PURPOSES OF MEASUREMENT ONLY ... ACTUAL COLORS AS PER COLOR CHART

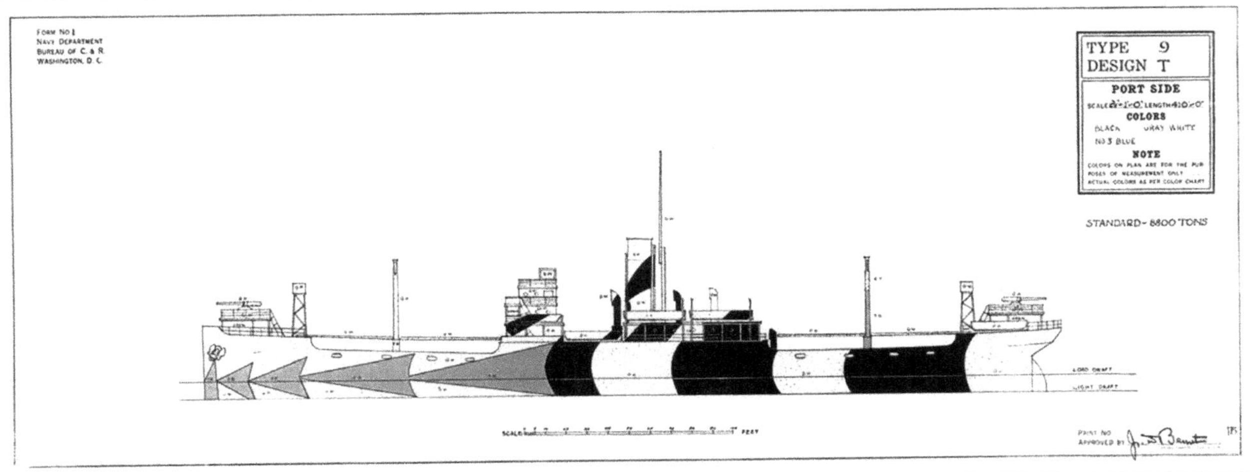

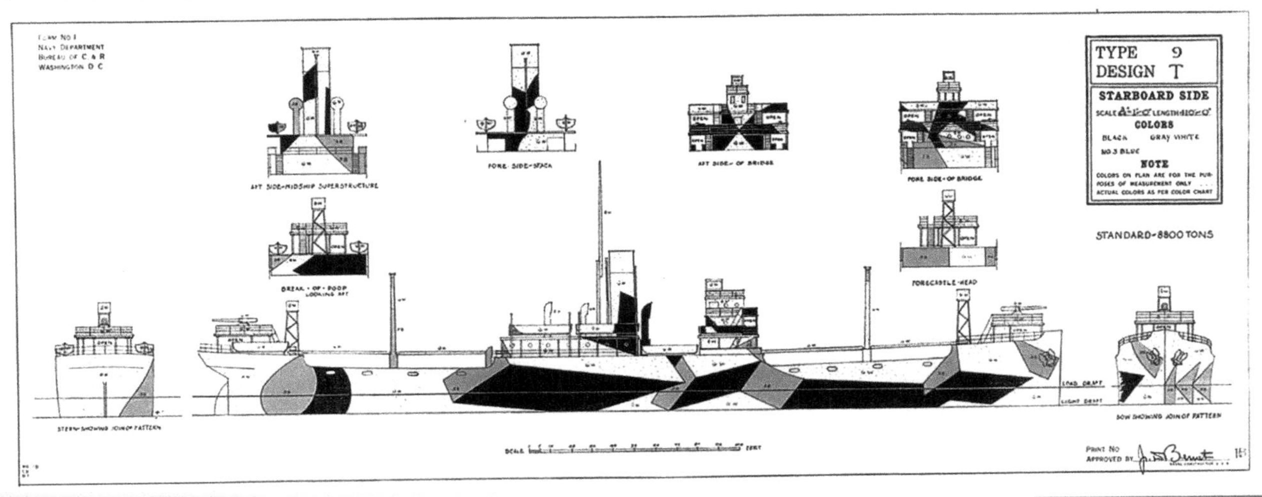

T9 U

Colors used	Ships painted with this pattern
BLACK	ID NONE WESTVIEW
#1 BLUE	ID 3768 NEWBURGH
#3 BLUE	
#1 GREEN	

TYPE · 9 ·
DESIGN · U ·
PORT SIDE
SCALE 1/16" - 1'-0" LENGTH 415'-0" O.A.
COLORS
BLACK ·
NO · 1 · BLUE ·
NO · 3 · BLUE ·
NO · 1 · GREEN ·
NOTE
COLORS ON PLAN ARE FOR THE PURPOSES OF MEASUREMENT ONLY . . . . ACTUAL COLORS AS PER COLOR CHART

TYPE · 9 ·
DESIGN · U ·
STARBOARD SIDE
SCALE 1/16" - 1'-0" LENGTH 415'-0" O.A.
COLORS
BLACK
NO · 1 · BLUE
NO · 3 · BLUE
NO · 1 · GREEN
NOTE
COLORS ON PLAN ARE FOR THE PURPOSES OF MEASUREMENT ONLY . . . . ACTUAL COLORS AS PER COLOR CHART

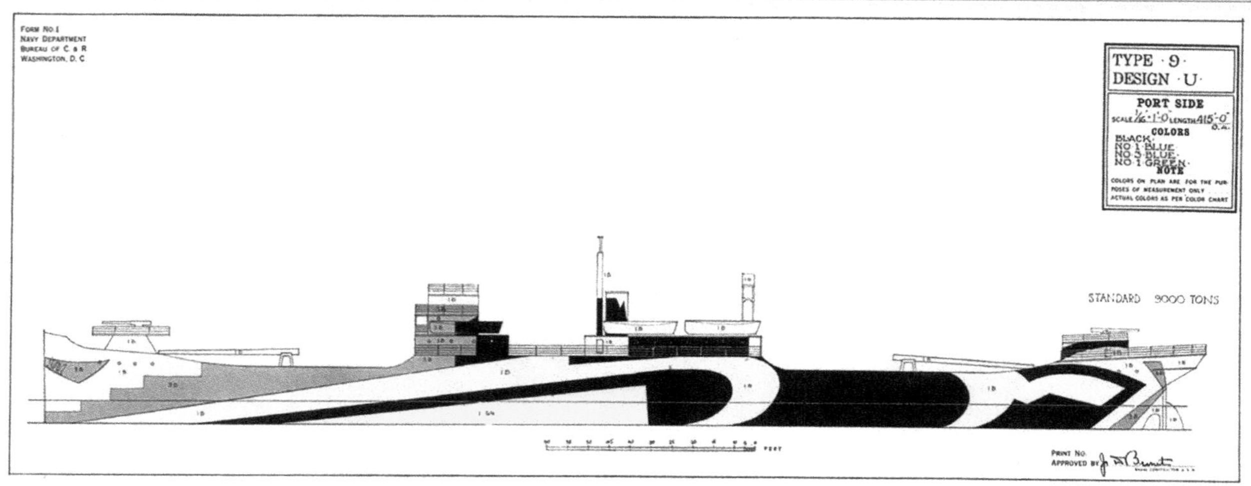

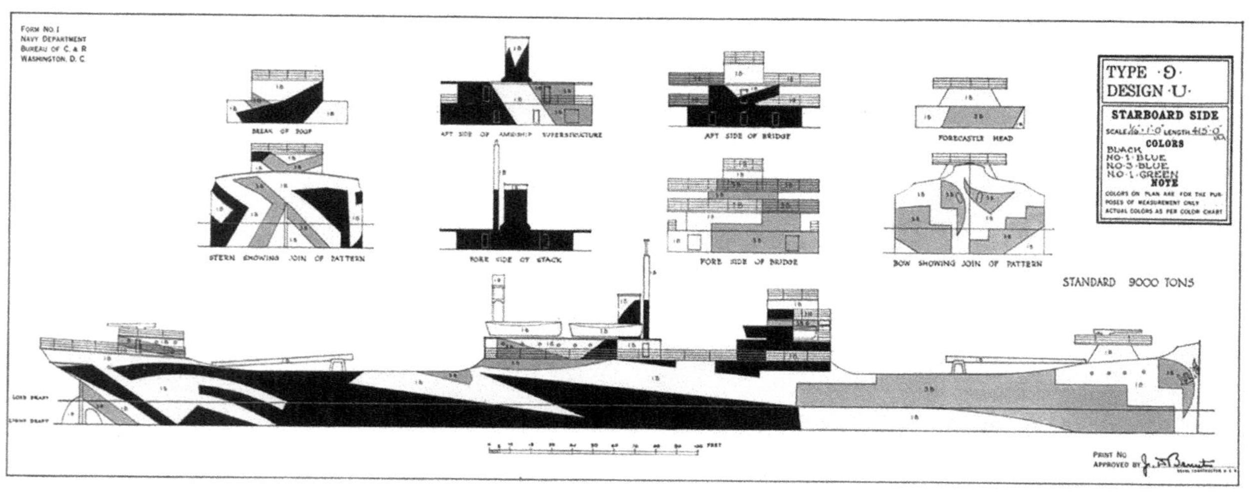

T10 A

Colors used	Ships painted with this pattern
BLACK	ID 3497 MONTCLAIR
WHITE	
#3 BLUE	
#1 BLUE-GRAY	

TYPE ·10· DESIGN · A

∴ PORT SIDE ∴
SCALE 1/16"=1'-0" LENGTH 281'-6"
COLORS
WHITE NO. 3 BLUE
BLACK NO. 1 BLUE GREY
NOTE
COLORS ON PLAN ARE FOR THE PURPOSES OF MEASUREMENT ONLY ACTUAL COLORS AS PER COLOR CHART.

TYPE ·10· DESIGN · A·

STARBOARD SIDE
SCALE 1/16"=1'-0" LENGTH 281'-6"
COLORS
WHITE NO. 3 BLUE
BLACK NO. 1 BLUE GREY
NOTE
COLORS ON PLAN ARE FOR THE PURPOSES OF MEASUREMENT ONLY ACTUAL COLORS AS PER COLOR CHART

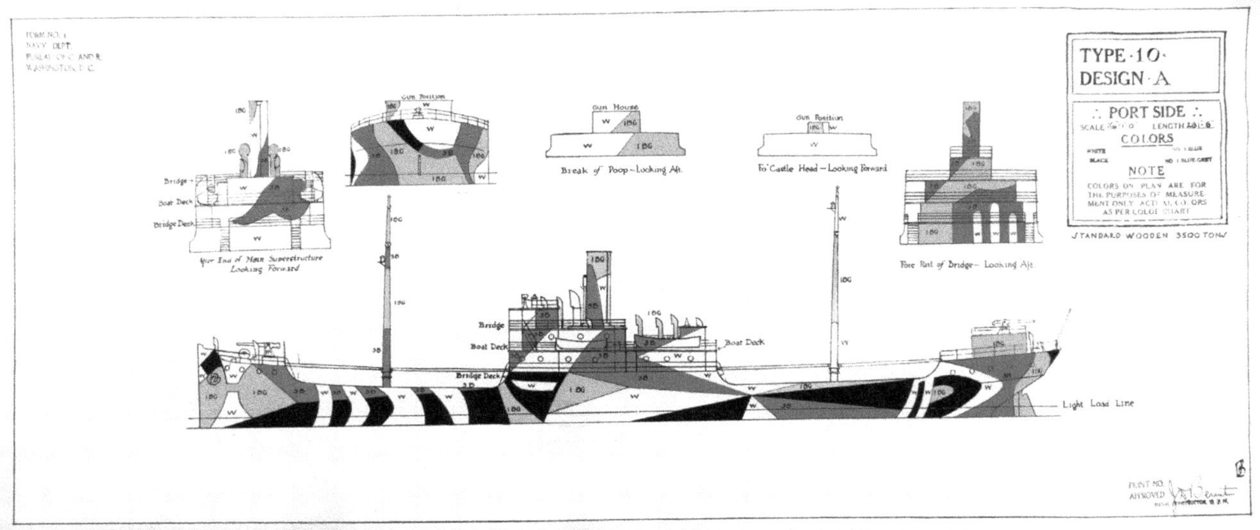

T10 B

Colors used	Ships painted with this pattern
BLACK	ID 3098 WESTWARD HO
WHITE	ID NONE RED CLOUD
#3 BLUE	ID 3313 WESTEEKONK
#1 BLUE-GRAY	ID 2549 MIZAR (T)

TYPE 10
DESIGN B
∴ PORT SIDE ∴
COLORS
WHITE 3 BLUE
BLACK 1 BLUE GREY
NOTE
COLORS ON PLAN ARE FOR THE PURPOSES OF MEASUREMENT ONLY. ACTUAL COLORS AS PER COLOR CHART.

TYPE 10
DESIGN B
STARBOARD SIDE
COLORS
WHITE 3 BLUE
BLACK 1 BLUE GREY
NOTE
COLORS ON PLAN ARE FOR THE PURPOSES OF MEASUREMENT ONLY. ACTUAL COLORS AS PER COLOR CHART.

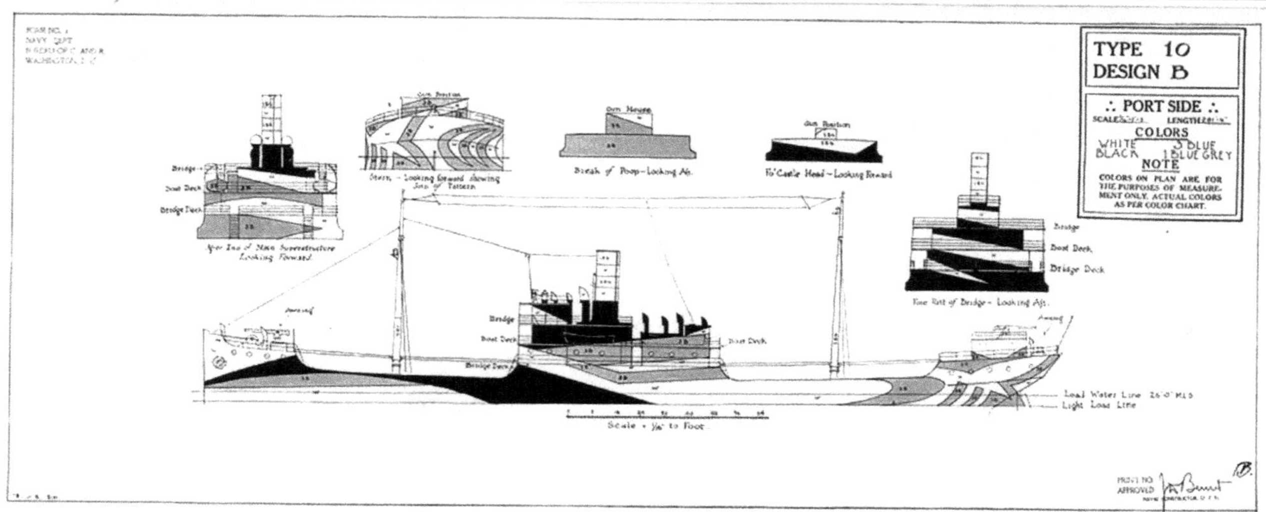

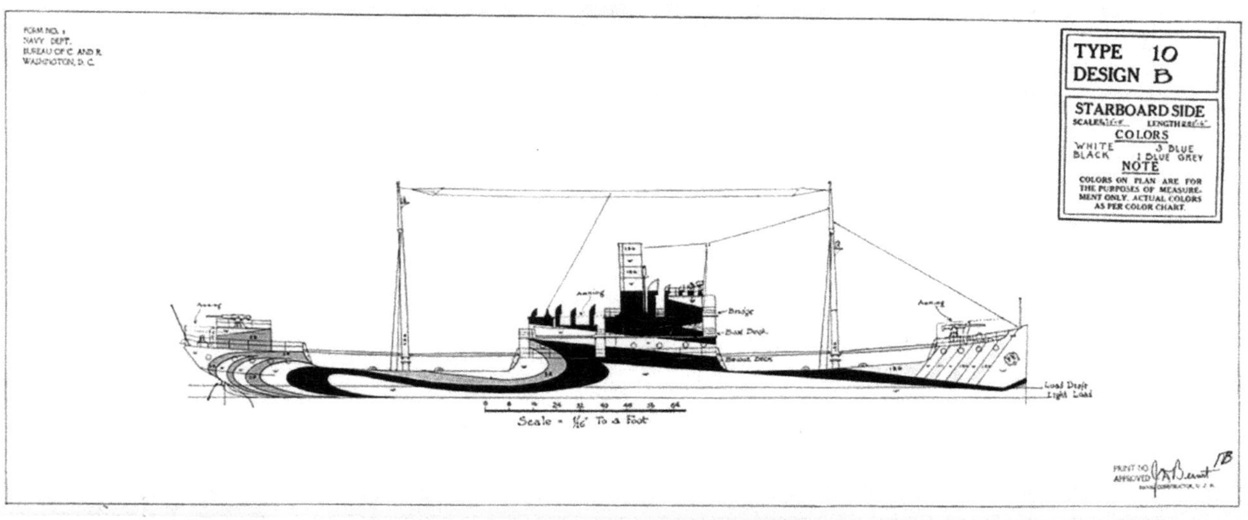

T10 C

Colors used	Ships painted with this pattern
BLACK	ID 4429A LAKE HARRIS
WHITE	ID NONE COOS BAY
#3 BLUE	ID 2223 ALIOTH
#1 BLUE-GRAY	ID 3455 NAMECKI

TYPE 10
DESIGN C
PORT SIDE
SCALE 1/16"=1'0 LENGTH 281' 6"
COLORS
BLACK NO 1 BLUE GREY
WHITE NO 3 BLUE
NOTE
COLORS ON PLAN ARE FOR THE PURPOSES OF MEASUREMENT ONLY
ACTUAL COLORS AS PER COLOR CHART

TYPE 10
DESIGN C
STARBOARD SIDE
SCALE 1/16"=1'0 LENGTH 281' 6"
COLORS
BLACK NO 1 BLUE GREY
WHITE NO 3 BLUE
NOTE
COLORS ON PLAN ARE FOR THE PURPOSES OF MEASUREMENT ONLY
ACTUAL COLORS AS PER COLOR CHART

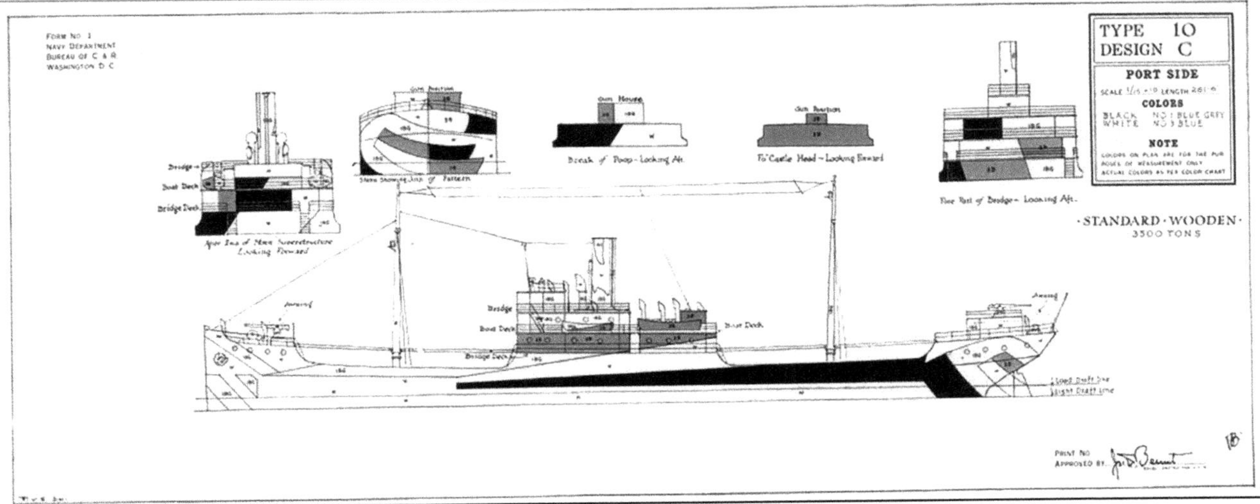

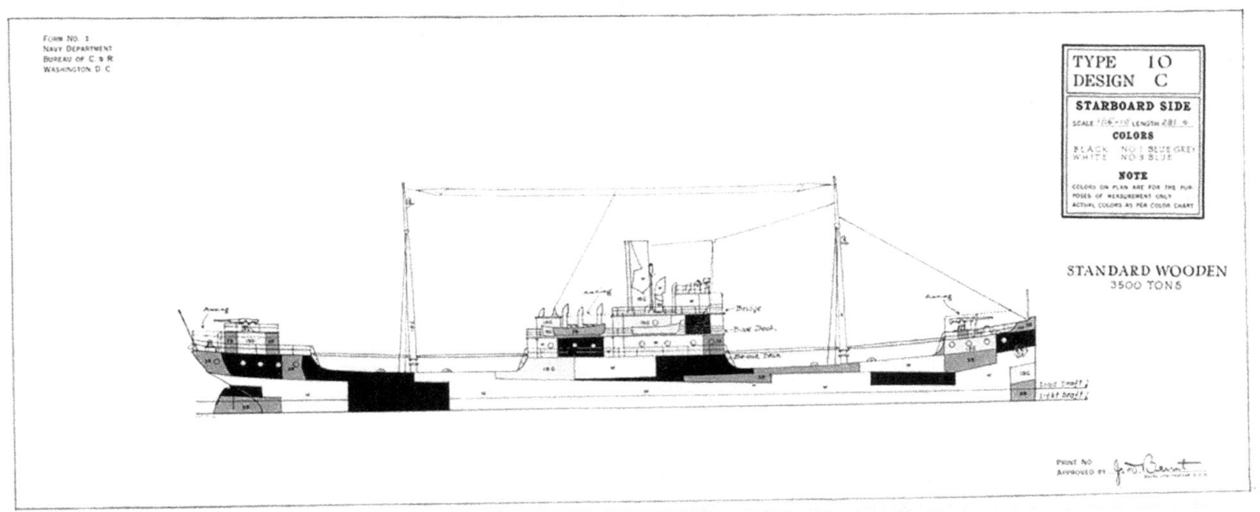

T10 D

Colors used	Ships painted with this pattern
BLACK	ID 2077 MARYANNE
WHITE	ID 4276C LAKE BERDAN
#3 BLUE	ID 2539 VEERHAVEN (T)
#1 BLUE-GRAY	

TYPE 10
DESIGN D
PORT SIDE
SCALE 1/16" = 1'0" LENGTH 281'-6"
COLORS
BLACK NO 1 BLUE GRAY
WHITE NO 3 BLUE
NOTE
COLORS ON PLAN ARE FOR THE PURPOSES OF MEASUREMENT ONLY
ACTUAL COLORS AS PER COLOR CHART

TYPE 10
DESIGN D
STARBOARD SIDE
SCALE 1/16" = 1'0" LENGTH 281'-6"
COLORS
BLACK NO 1 BLUE GRAY
WHITE NO 3 BLUE
NOTE
COLORS ON PLAN ARE FOR THE PURPOSES OF MEASUREMENT ONLY
ACTUAL COLORS AS PER COLOR CHART

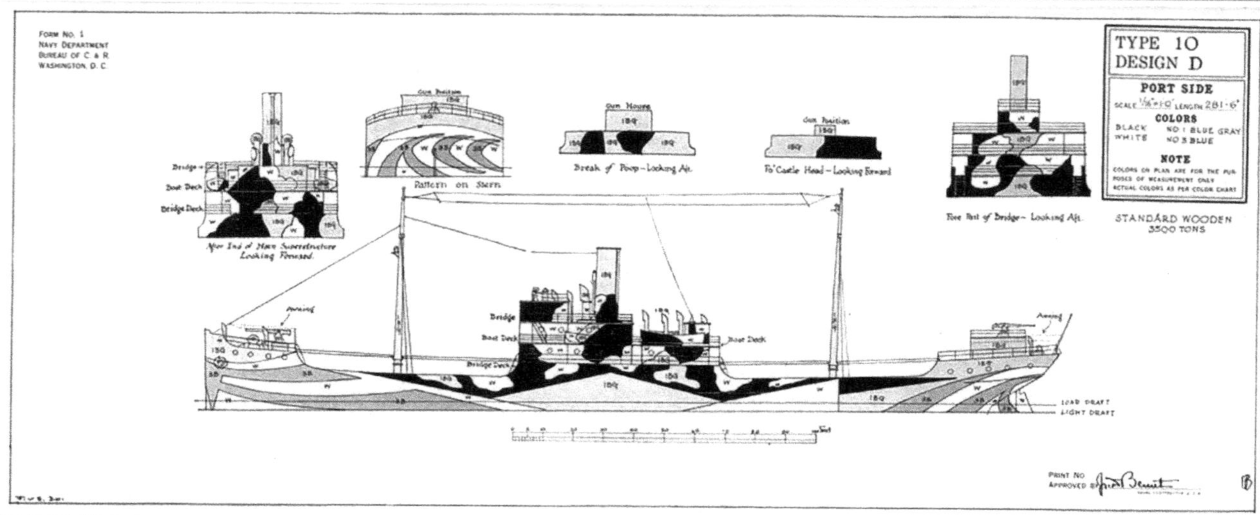

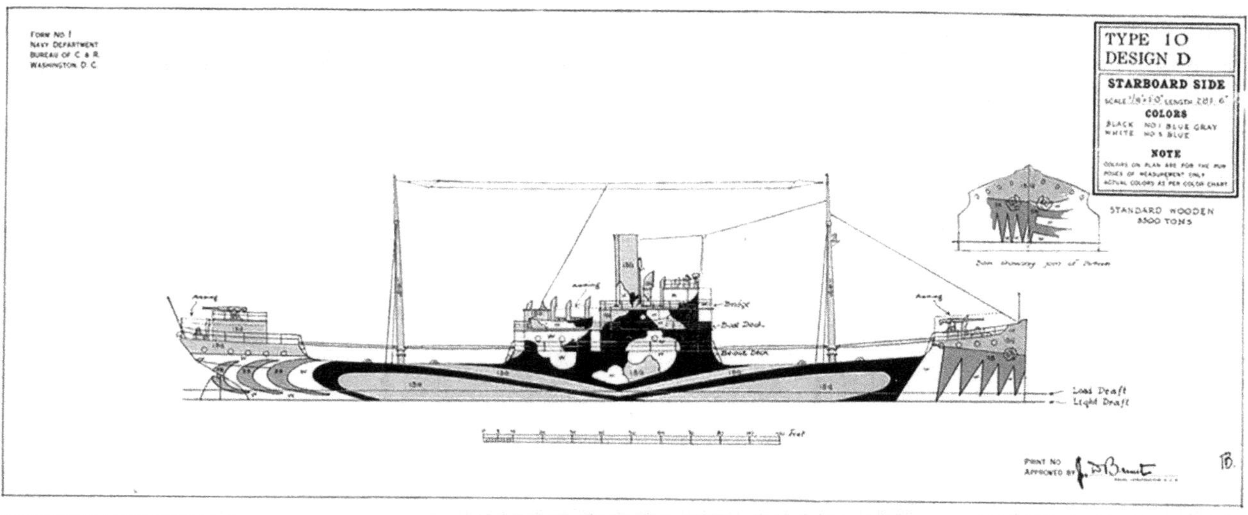

T10 E

Colors used	Ships painted with this pattern
BLACK	ID NONE PASCAGOULA
GREY-WHITE	ID 3490 CHIBIABOS
#3 BLUE	ID 3352 SAG HARBOR
#1 BLUE-GRAY	

TYPE 10
DESIGN E

PORT SIDE

SCALE 1/16" = 1'0" LENGTH 281' 6 B.P.

COLORS

GRAY WHITE BLACK
NO 1 BLUE GRAY NO 4 GRAY

NOTE

COLORS ON PLAN ARE FOR THE PURPOSES OF MEASUREMENT ONLY
ACTUAL COLORS AS PER COLOR CHART

TYPE 10
DESIGN E

STARBOARD SIDE

SCALE 1/16" = 1'0" LENGTH 281' 6 B.P.

COLORS

GRAY WHITE BLACK
NO 1 BLUE GRAY NO 4 GRAY

NOTE

COLORS ON PLAN ARE FOR THE PURPOSES OF MEASUREMENT ONLY
ACTUAL COLORS AS PER COLOR CHART

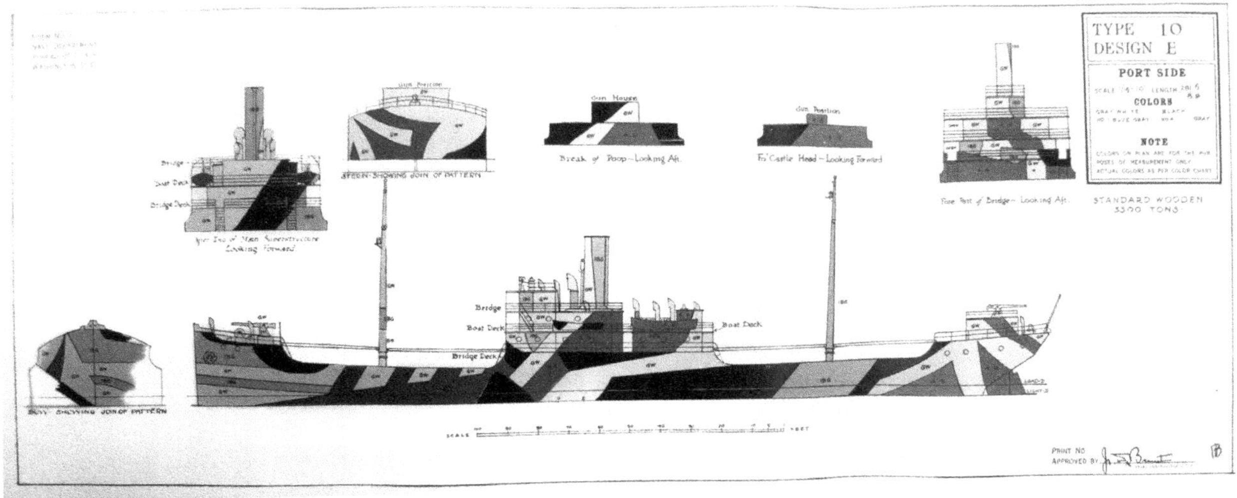

T10 F

Colors used	Ships painted with this pattern
BLACK	ID NONE CUMBERLAND
GREY-WHITE	ID 3470 CATAWBA
#3 BLUE	

TYPE 10
DESIGN F
PORT SIDE
COLORS
BLACK No 3 BLUE
GRAY WHITE
NOTE
COLORS ON PLAN ARE FOR THE PURPOSES OF MEASUREMENT ONLY
ACTUAL COLORS AS PER COLOR CHART

TYPE 10
DESIGN F
STARBOARD SIDE
COLORS
NOTE

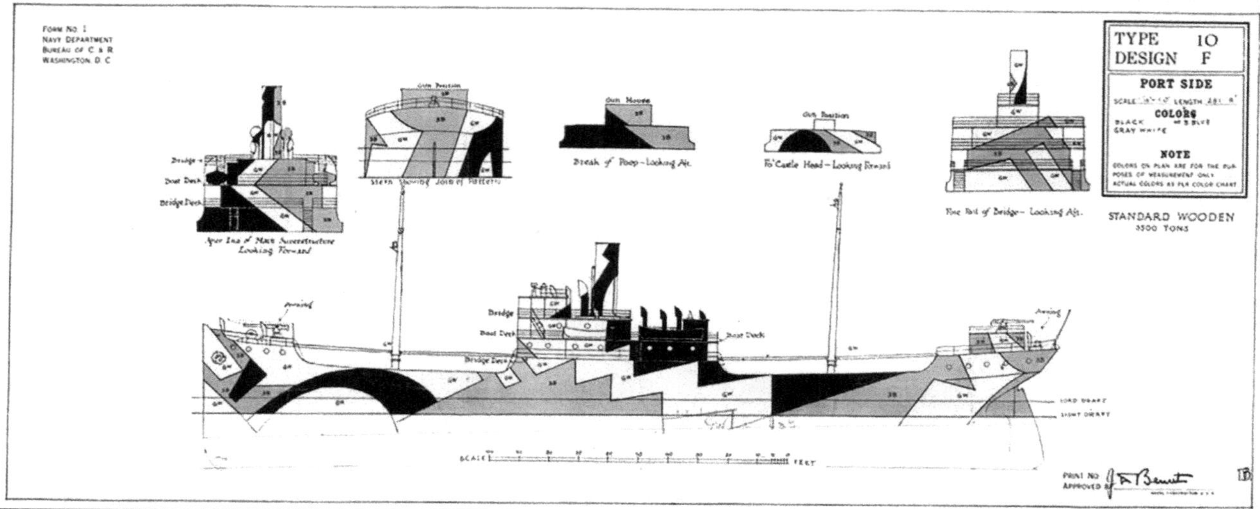

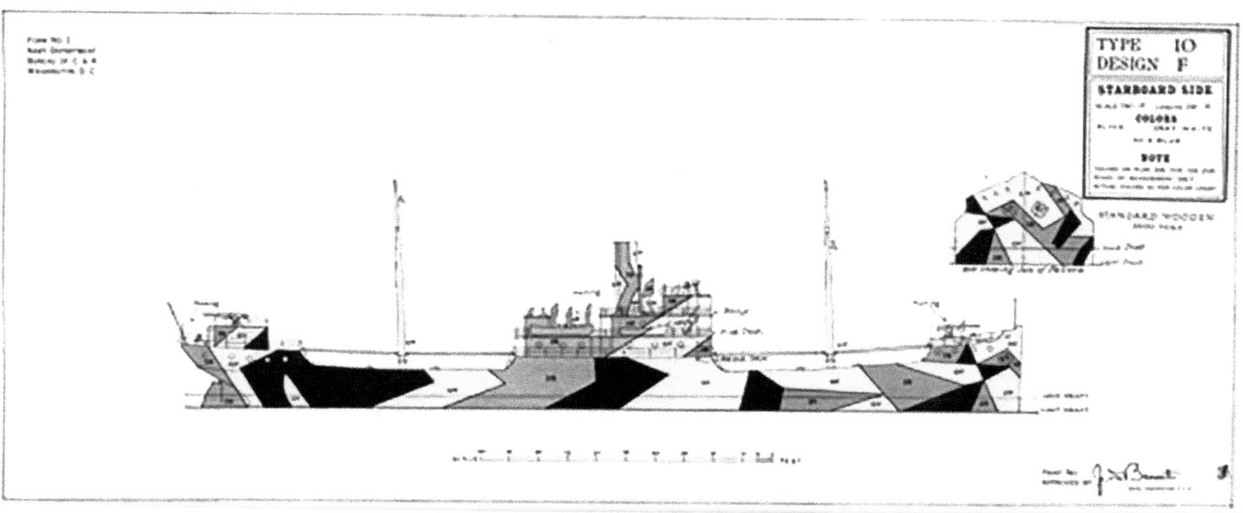

T10 G

Colors used	Ships painted with this pattern
BLACK	ID 3810 BANANGO
GREY-WHITE	ID NONE ADVANCE
#3 BLUE	
#1 GRAY-GREEN	

TYPE 10
DESIGN G

PORT SIDE

COLORS

BLACK NO. 1 GREY GREEN
NO. 3 BLUE
GREY WHITE

NOTE

COLORS ON PLAN ARE FOR THE PURPOSES OF MEASUREMENT ONLY
ACTUAL COLORS AS PER COLOR CHART

TYPE 10
DESIGN G

STARBOARD SIDE

COLORS

GREY WHITE · NO.3 BLUE
NO1 GREY GREEN · BLACK

NOTE

COLORS ON PLAN ARE FOR THE PURPOSES OF MEASUREMENT ONLY
ACTUAL COLORS AS PER COLOR CHART

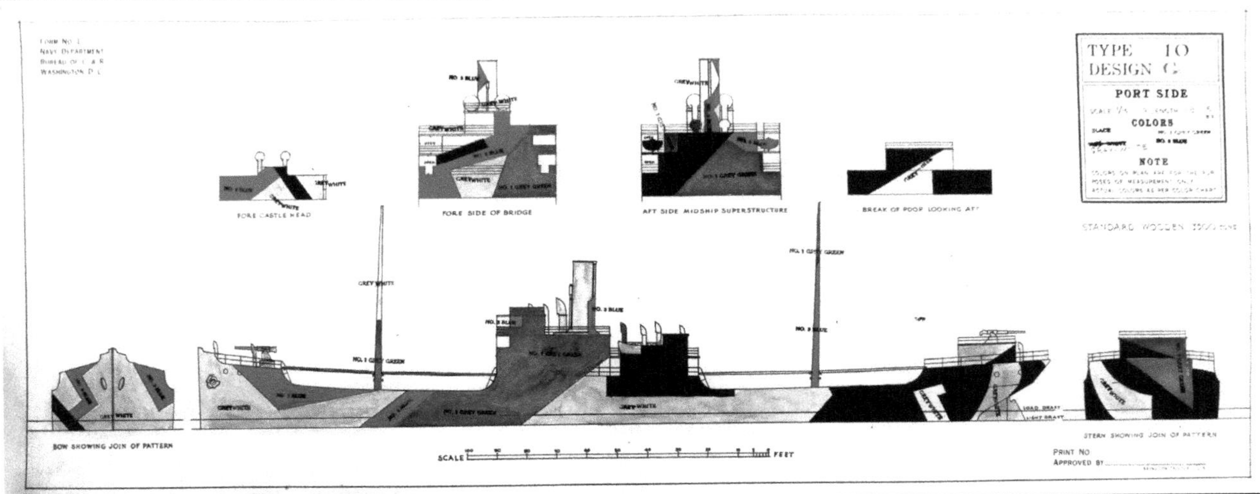

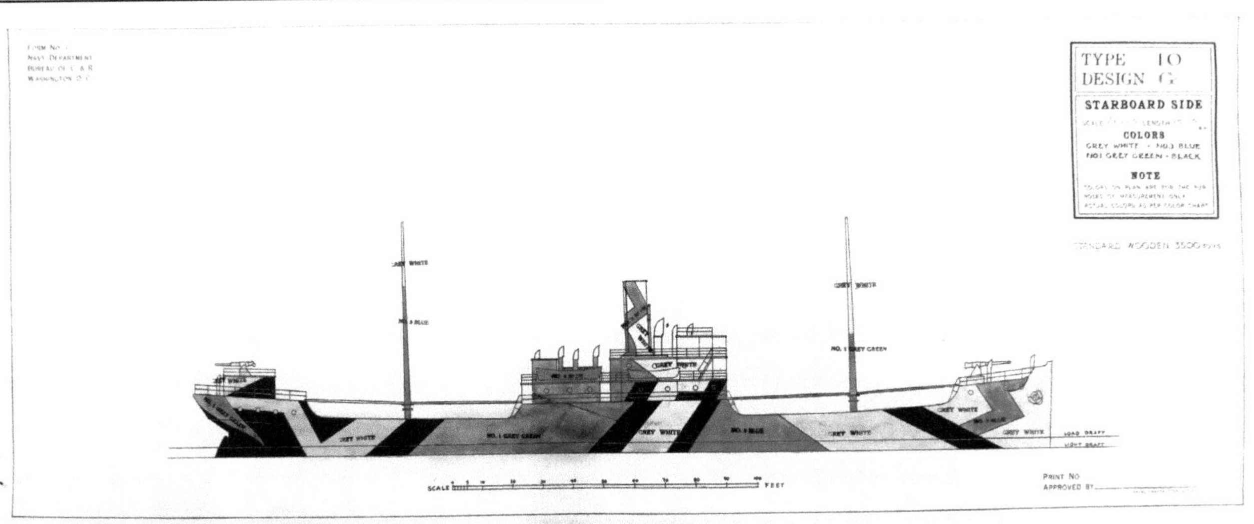

T10 H

Colors used	Ships painted with this pattern
BLACK	ID 3574 ALABET
GREY-WHITE	ID 4407L LAKE DANCEY
#3 BLUE	ID NONE AGRIA
#1 GRAY-GREEN	

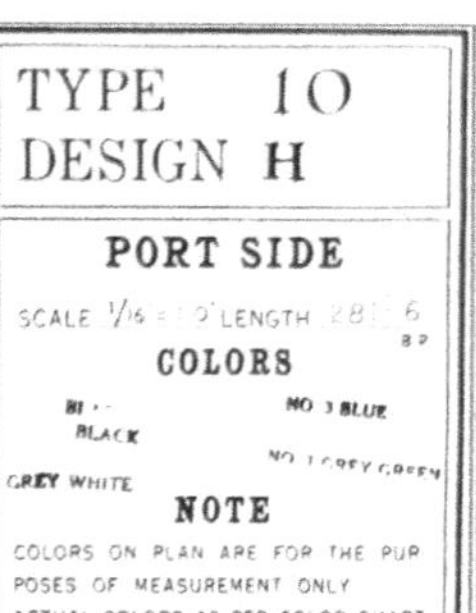

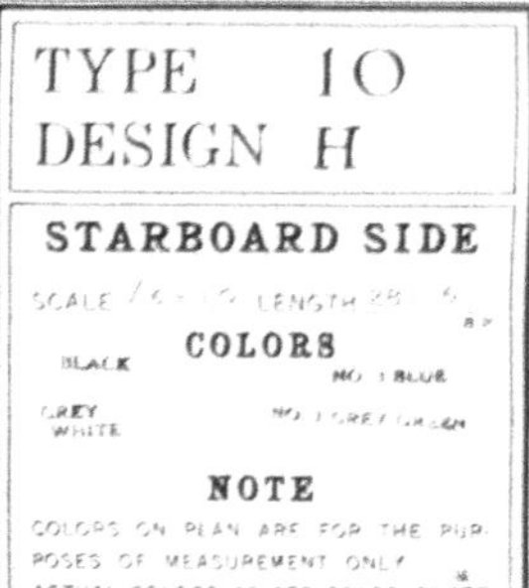

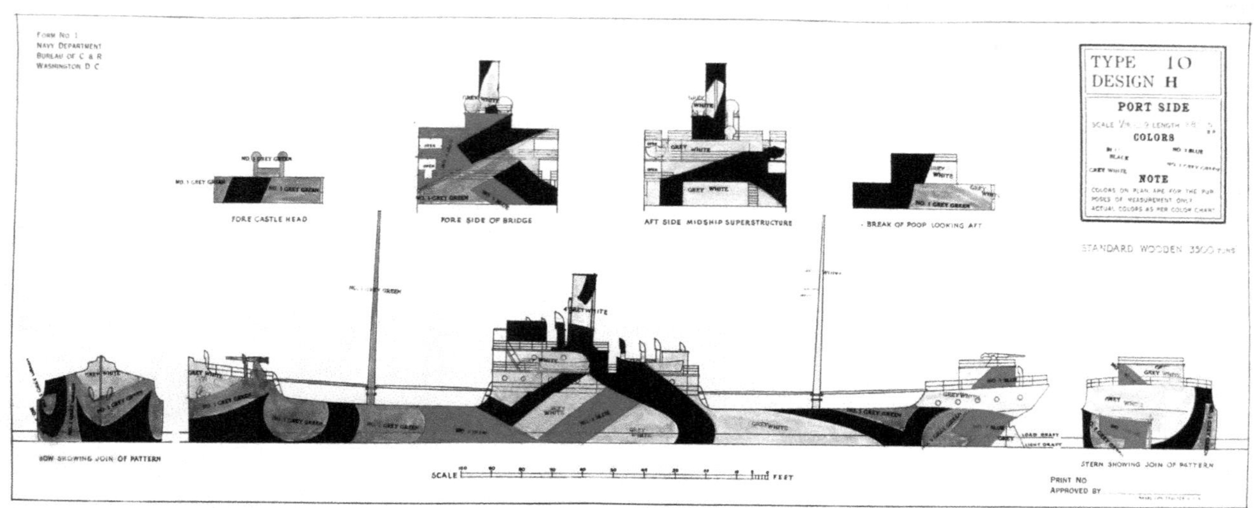

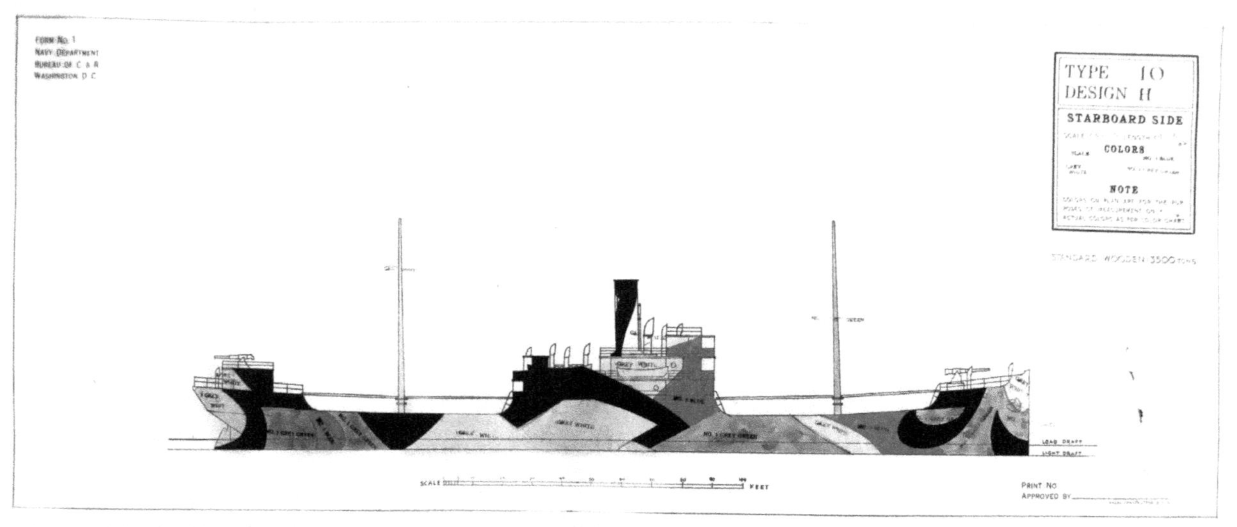

T10 I

Colors used	Ships painted with this pattern
BLACK	ID 3626 CARIBOU
GREY-WHITE	
#3 BLUE	
#1 BLUE-GRAY	

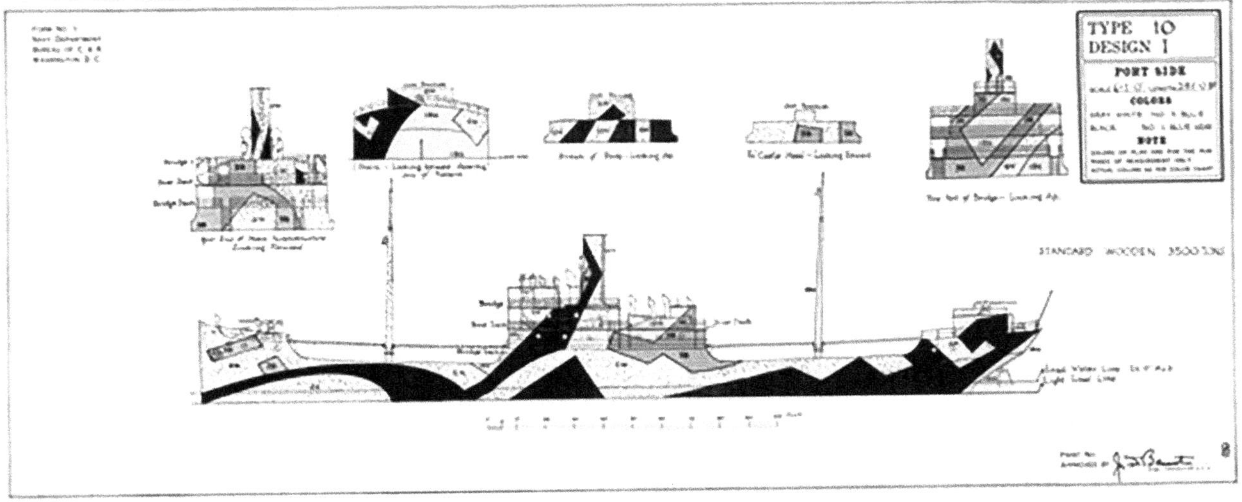

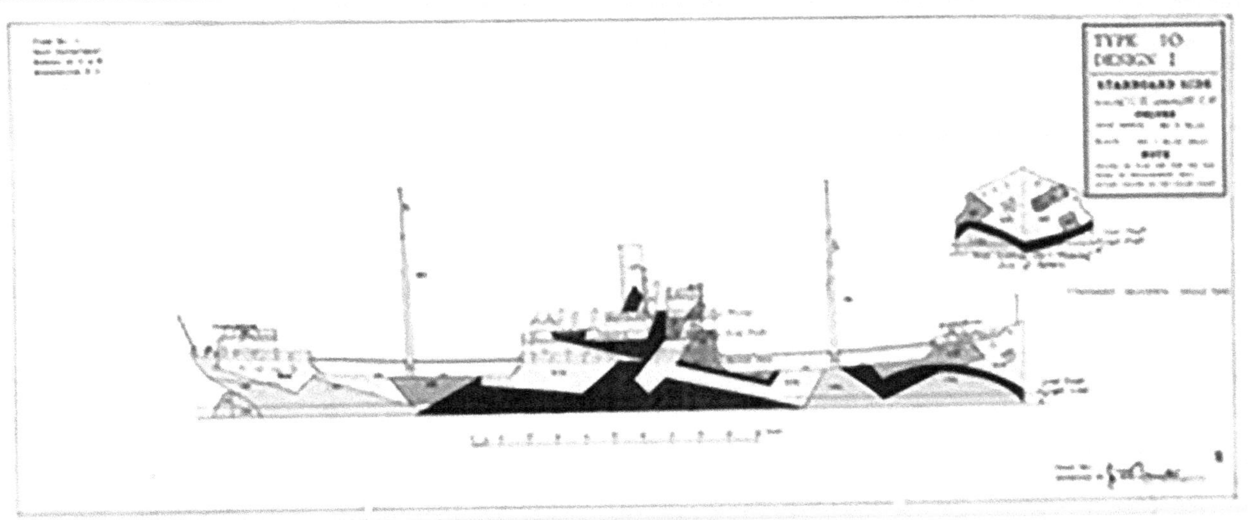

T10 K

Colors used	Ships painted with this pattern
BLACK	ID 4449 BAXLEY
GREY-WHITE	ID 4155 LAKE ARLINE (T)
#3 BLUE	
#1 BLUE-GRAY	

TYPE 10
DESIGN K
PORT SIDE
SCALE 1/16 = 1'0" LENGTH 281' 6" B.P.
COLORS
BLACK NO. 1 BLUE GREY
gray white NO. 3 BLUE
NOTE
COLORS ON PLAN ARE FOR THE PURPOSES OF MEASUREMENT ONLY
ACTUAL COLORS AS PER COLOR CHART

TYPE 10
DESIGN K
STARBOARD SIDE
SCALE 1/16 = 1'0" LENGTH 281' 6" B.P.
COLORS
gray white NO. 1 BLUE GREY
BLACK NO. 3 BLUE
NOTE
COLORS ON PLAN ARE FOR THE PURPOSES OF MEASUREMENT ONLY
ACTUAL COLORS AS PER COLOR CHART

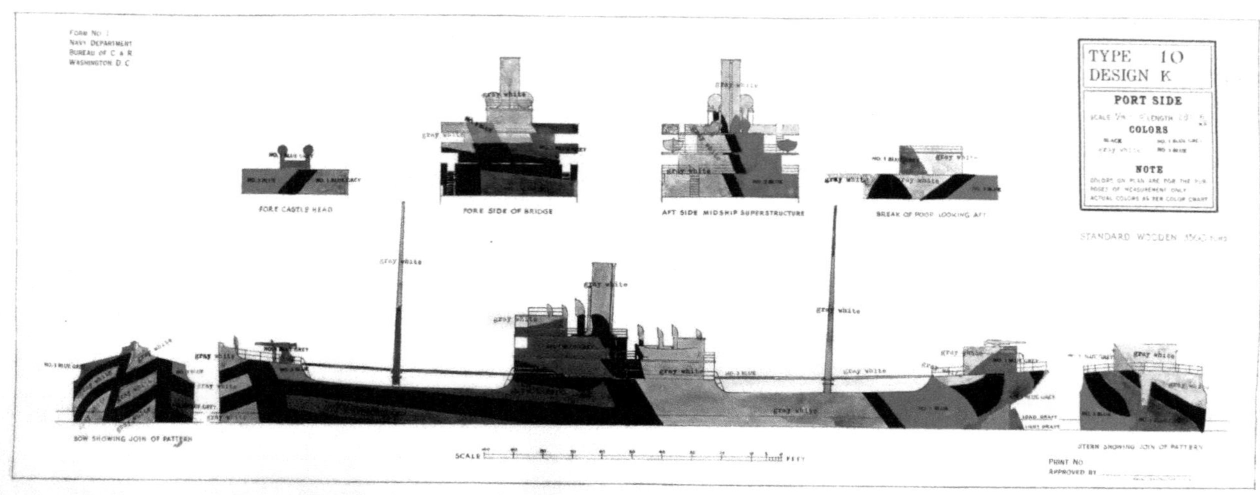

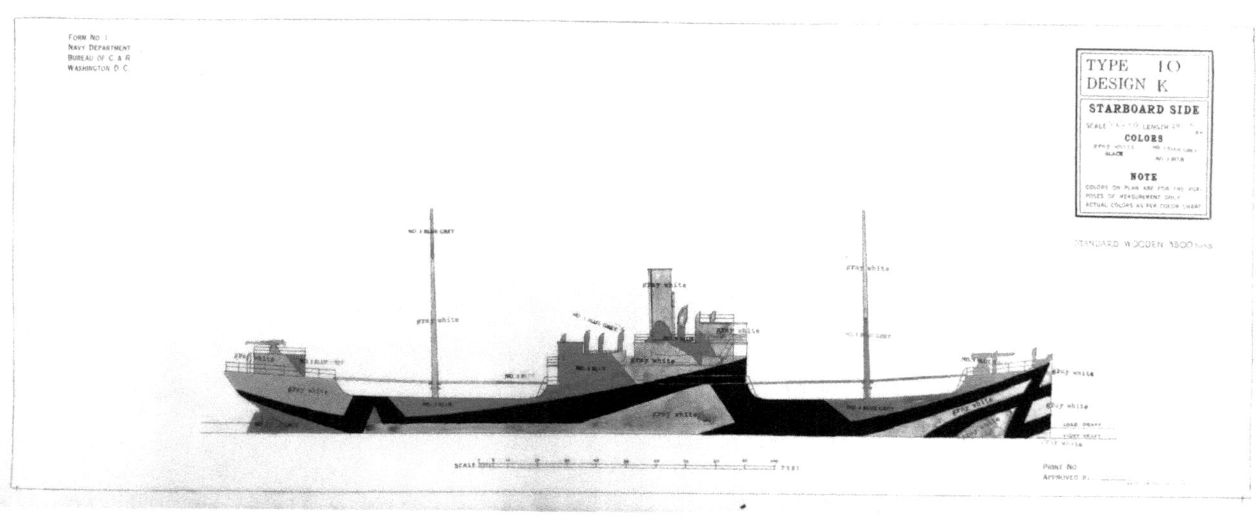

T10 L

Colors used	Ships painted with this pattern
BLACK	ID NONE ALPACO
GREY-WHITE	ID 4449 BAXLEY
#3 BLUE	ID 3546 BOTSFORD (T)
#1 BLUE	

TYPE 10
DESIGN L

PORT SIDE

COLORS

gray white NO 3 BLUE

NO 1 BLUE BLACK NO 4 GREY

NOTE

COLORS ON PLAN ARE FOR THE PURPOSES OF MEASUREMENT ONLY ACTUAL COLORS AS PER COLOR CHART

TYPE 10
DESIGN L

STARBOARD SIDE

COLORS

NO 1 BLUE BLACK

NO 3 BLUE gray white

NOTE

COLORS ON PLAN ARE FOR THE PURPOSES OF MEASUREMENT ONLY ACTUAL COLORS AS PER COLOR CHART

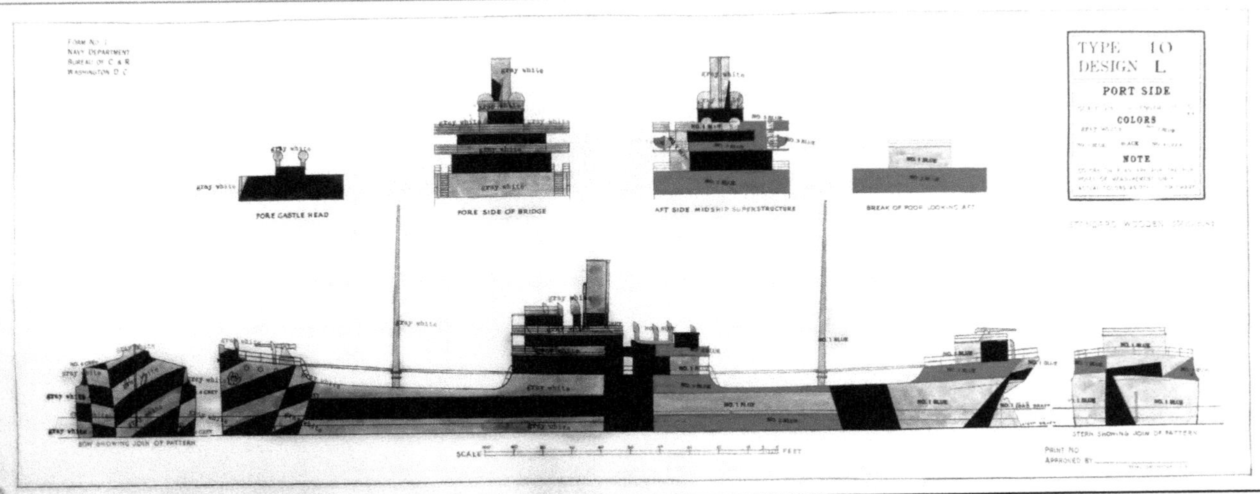

T10 M

Colors used	Ships painted with this pattern
BLACK	ID 4311H LAKE WINOOSKI
GREY-WHITE	
#3 BLUE	
#2 BLUE-GRAY	

TYPE 10
DESIGN M
PORT SIDE
COLORS
NO. 2 BLUE GREY
NO. 3 BLUE
BLACK
NOTE
COLORS ON PLAN ARE FOR THE PURPOSES OF MEASUREMENT ONLY
ACTUAL COLORS AS PER COLOR CHART

TYPE 10
DESIGN M
STARBOARD SIDE
COLORS
GREY WHITE
NO. 2 BLUE GREY
NO. 3 BLUE
BLACK
NOTE
COLORS ON PLAN ARE FOR THE PURPOSES OF MEASUREMENT ONLY
ACTUAL COLORS AS PER COLOR CHART

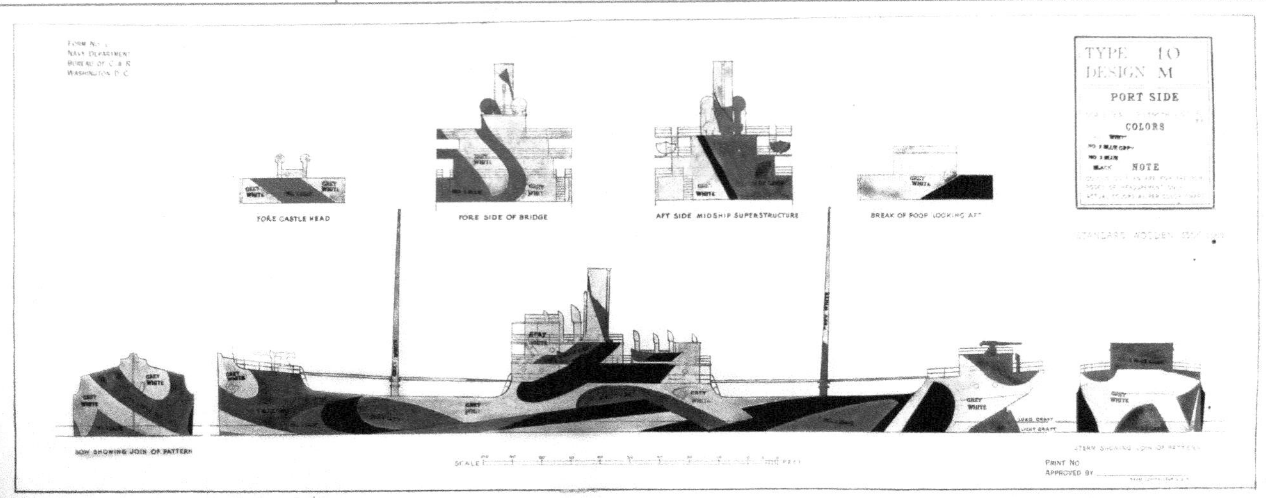

T11 B

Colors used	Ships painted with this pattern
BLACK	ID 2683 LEERSUM
WHITE	
#3 BLUE	
#1 BLUE	
#1 GREEN	

TYPE 11
DESIGN B
PORT SIDE
SCALE 1/16" = 1'-0" LENGTH 418'-7"
COLORS
BLACK *1 BLUE
WHITE *3 BLUE
*1 GREEN
NOTE
COLORS ON PLAN ARE FOR THE PURPOSES OF MEASUREMENT ONLY
ACTUAL COLORS AS PER COLOR CHART

TYPE 11
DESIGN B
STARBOARD SIDE
SCALE 1/16" = 1'-0" LENGTH 418'-7"
COLORS
BLACK *1 BLUE
WHITE *3 BLUE
*1 GREEN
NOTE
COLORS ON PLAN ARE FOR THE PURPOSES OF MEASUREMENT ONLY
ACTUAL COLORS AS PER COLOR CHART

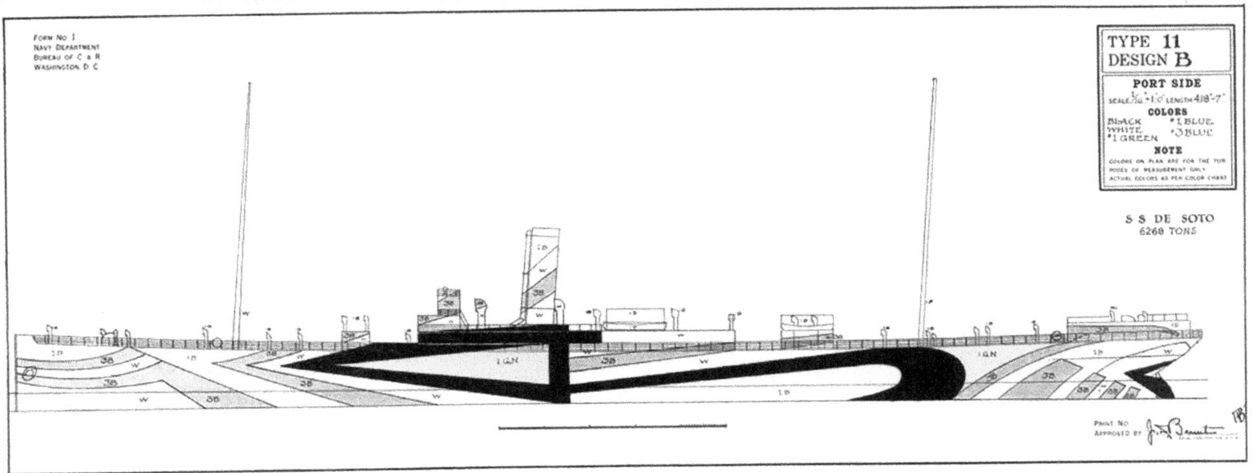

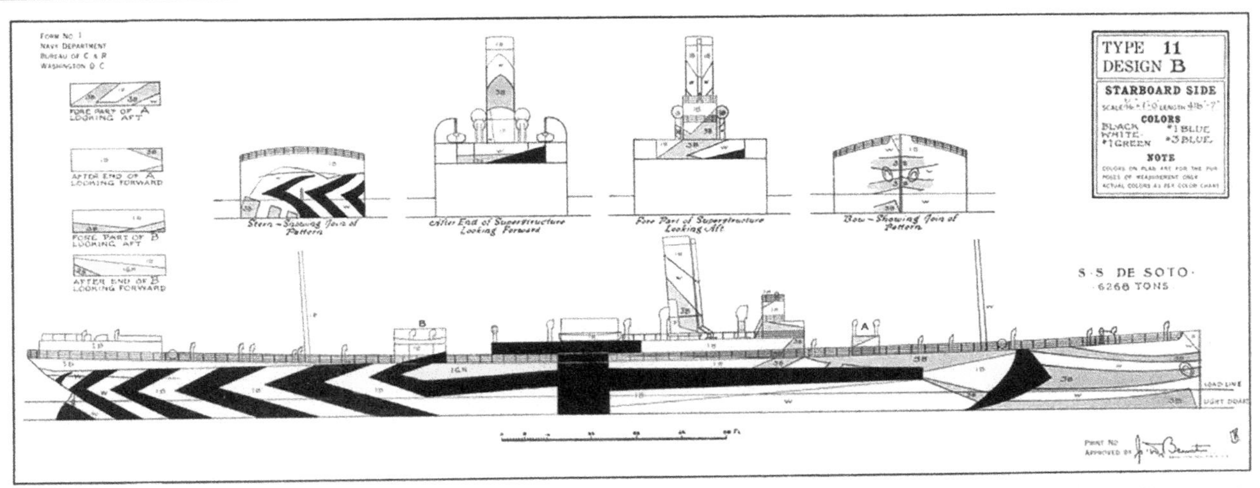

T11 C

Colors used	Ships painted with this pattern
BLACK	ID 3327 DEFIANCE
GREY-WHITE	
#1 BLUE	
#2 BLUE-GRAY	
#1 GREEN	

TYPE 11
DESIGN C

PORT SIDE
SCALE 1/16"=1'0" LENGTH 418' 7"
COLORS
BLACK NO. 1 BLUE
GRAY WHITE NO. 2 BLUE GRAY
NOTE
COLORS ON PLAN ARE FOR THE PURPOSES OF MEASUREMENT ONLY ... ACTUAL COLORS AS PER COLOR CHART

TYPE 11
DESIGN C

STARBOARD SIDE
SCALE 1/16"=1'0" LENGTH 418' 7"
COLORS
BLACK NO. 1 BLUE
GRAY WHITE NO. 2 BLUE GRAY
NO. 1 GREEN
NOTE
COLORS ON PLAN ARE FOR THE PURPOSES OF MEASUREMENT ONLY ... ACTUAL COLORS AS PER COLOR CHART

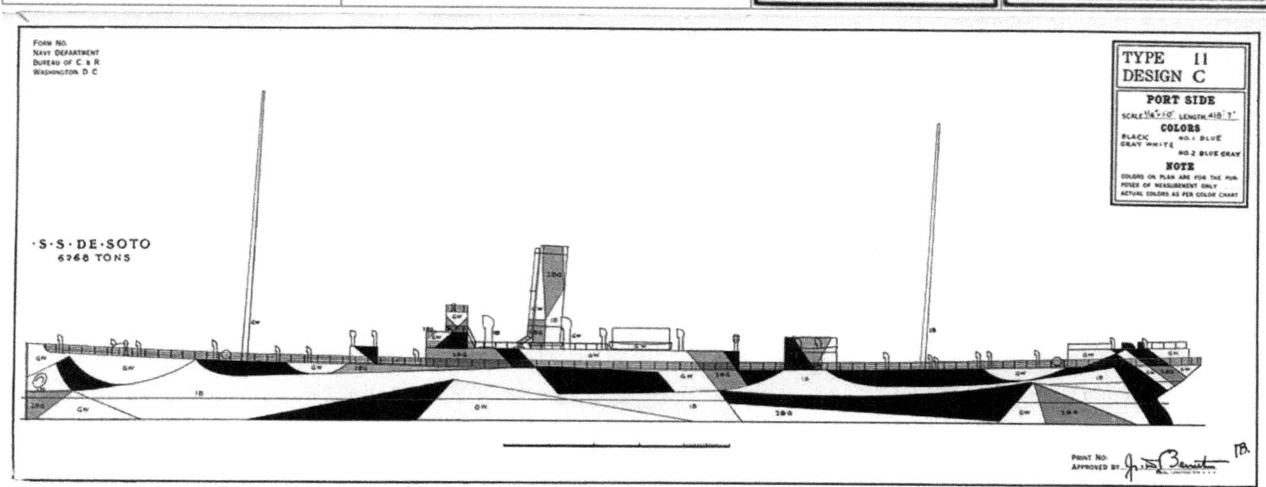

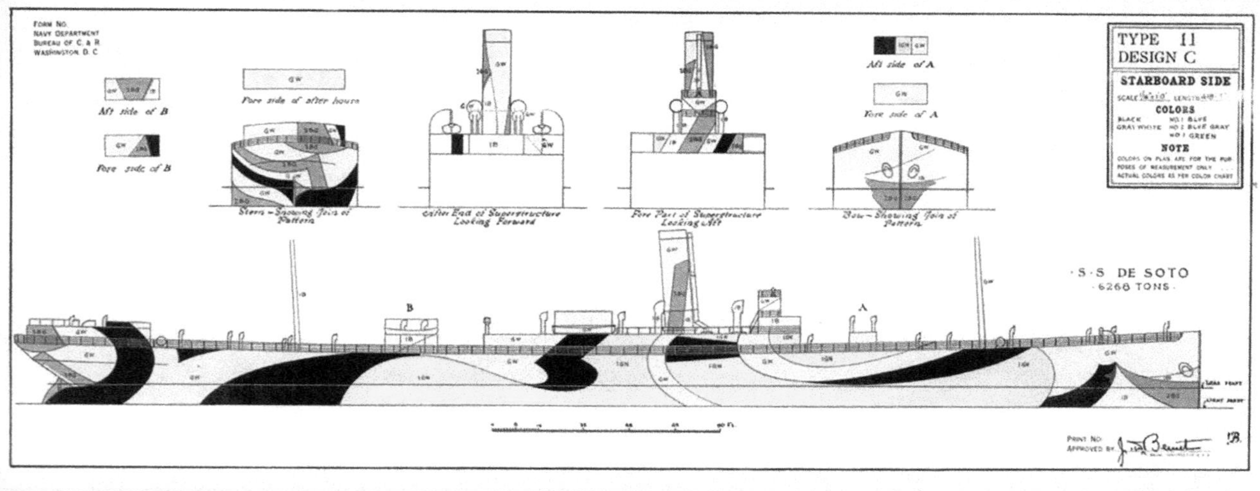

T11 D

Colors used	Ships painted with this pattern	TYPE 11 DESIGN D PORT SIDE SCALE 1/4"=1'0 LENGTH 412 0 COLORS BLACK NO 1 GREEN GRAY WHITE NO 1 GRAY PINK NOTE COLORS ON PLAN ARE FOR THE PURPOSES OF MEASUREMENT ONLY ACTUAL COLORS AS PER COLOR CHART	TYPE 11 DESIGN D STARBOARD SIDE SCALE 1/8"=1'0 LENGTH 412 0" COLORS BLACK NO 1 GREEN GRAY WHITE NO 1 GRAY PINK NOTE COLORS ON PLAN ARE FOR THE PURPOSES OF MEASUREMENT ONLY ACTUAL COLORS AS PER COLOR CHART
BLACK	ID 3331 EASTERNER		
GREY-WHITE			
#1 GREEN			
#1 GRAY-PINK			

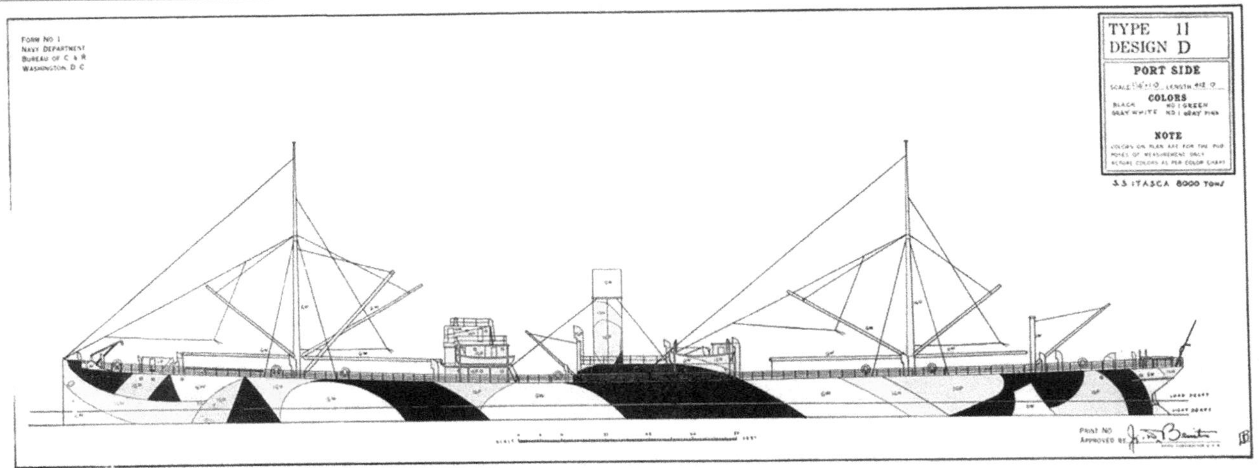

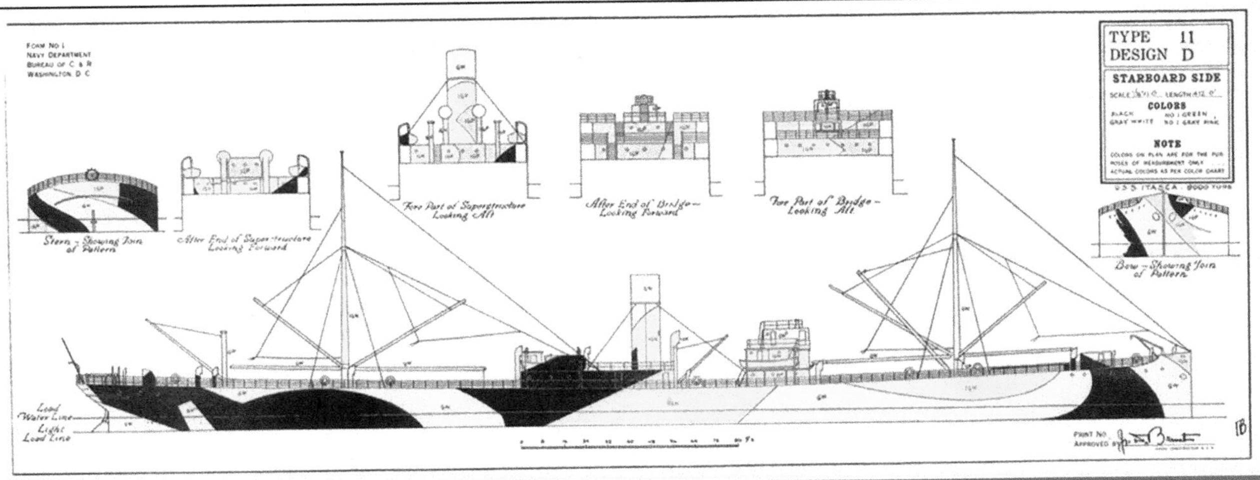

T11 E

Colors used	Ships painted with this pattern
BLACK	ID 1419 CHIPPEWA
GREY-WHITE	
#1 BLUE-GRAY	

TYPE ·11·
DESIGN·E·

PORT SIDE
SCALE 1/16"·1'-0" LENGTH 418'-7" BP
COLORS
BLACK NO. 1 BLUE GRAY
GRAY WHITE
NOTE
COLORS ON PLAN ARE FOR THE PURPOSES OF MEASUREMENT ONLY. ACTUAL COLORS AS PER COLOR CHART.

TYPE ·11·
DESIGN·E·

STARBOARD SIDE
SCALE 1/16"·1'-0" LENGTH 418'-7" BP
COLORS
BLACK · NO. 1 BLUE GRAY
GRAY WHITE
NOTE
COLORS ON PLAN ARE FOR THE PURPOSES OF MEASUREMENT ONLY. ACTUAL COLORS AS PER COLOR CHART

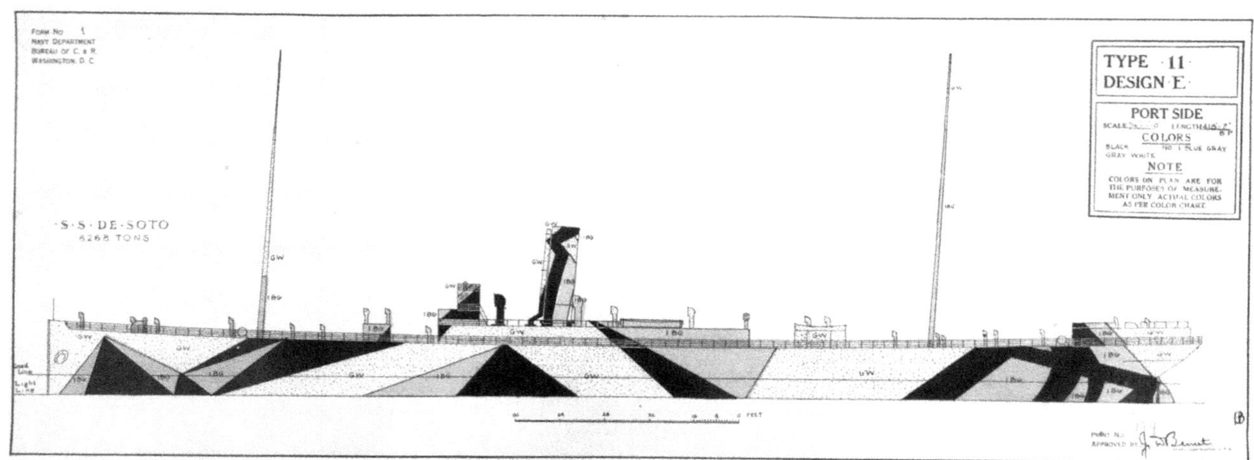

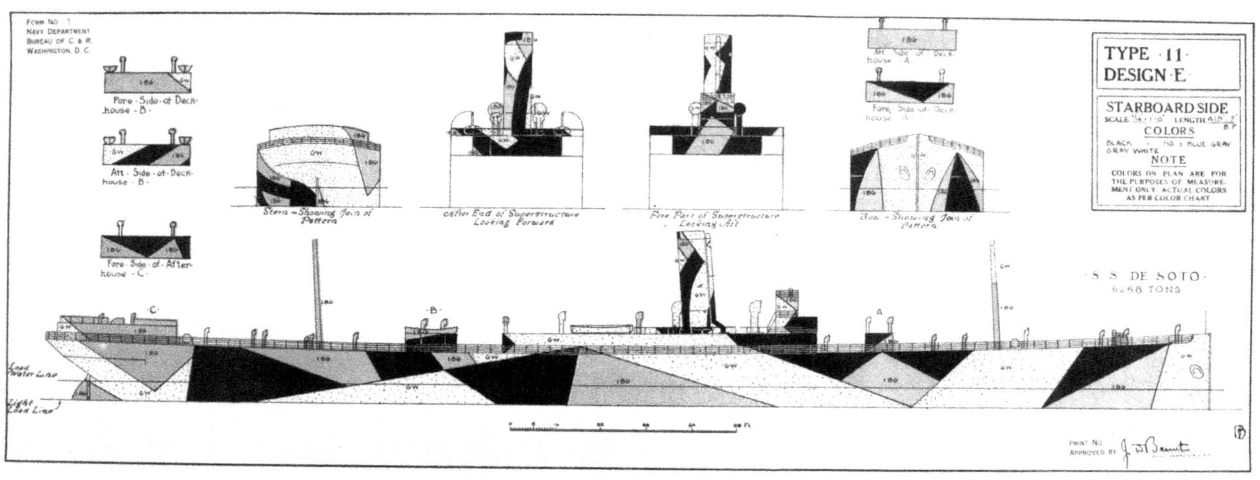

T11 F

Colors used	Ships painted with this pattern
BLACK	ID 3630 CHALLANGER
GREY-WHITE	
#3 BLUE	
#1 BLUE	

TYPE 11
DESIGN F
PORT SIDE
SCALE 1/16" = 1'-0" LENGTH 418'-7"
COLORS
Black 3 Blue
Gray White 1 Blue
NOTE
COLORS ON PLAN ARE FOR THE PURPOSES OF MEASUREMENT ONLY
ACTUAL COLORS AS PER COLOR CHART

TYPE 11
DESIGN F
STARBOARD SIDE
SCALE 1/16" = 1'-0" LENGTH 418'-7"
COLORS
Black 3 Blue
Grey White 1 Blue
NOTE
COLORS ON PLAN ARE FOR THE PURPOSES OF MEASUREMENT ONLY
ACTUAL COLORS AS PER COLOR CHART

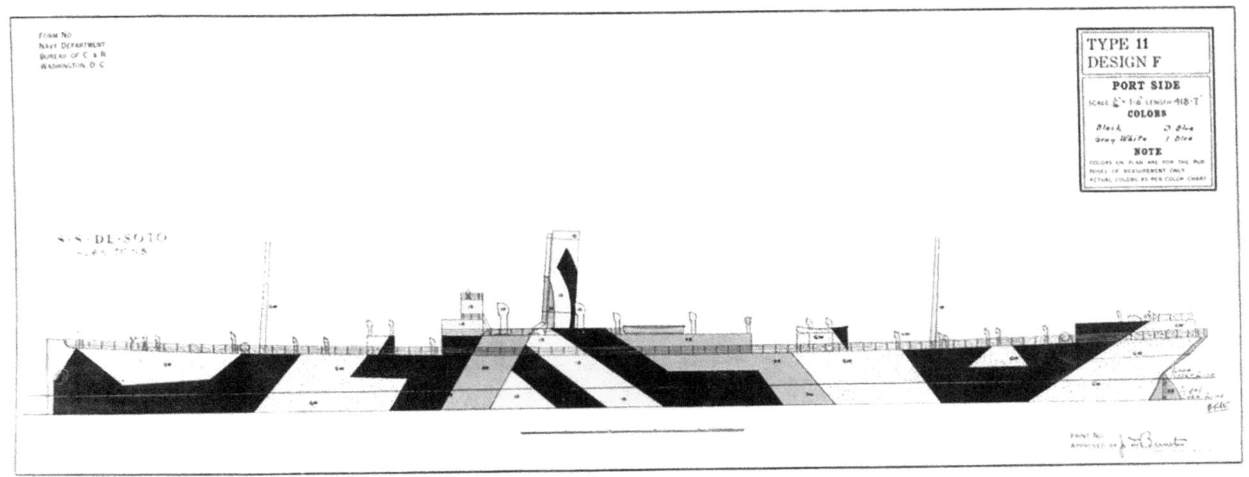

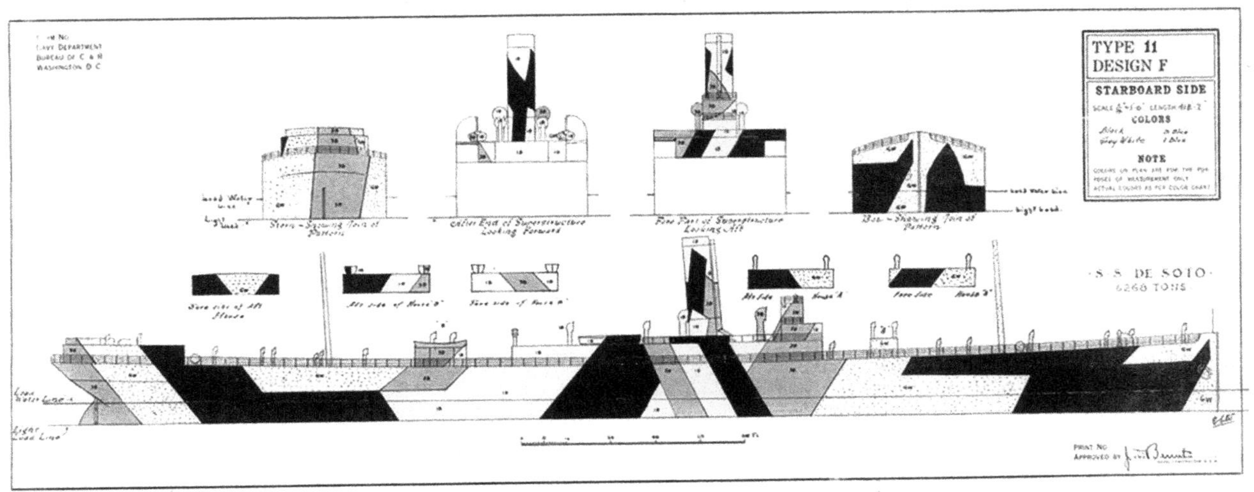

T12 A

Colors used	Ships painted with this pattern
BLACK	ID 1854 RAPPAHANNOCK
WHITE	ID 2689 ADONIS
#3 BLUE	ID 4254 ANACORTES
#1 BLUE-GRAY	ID 4239G LEBANON

TYPE 12
DESIGN A
PORT SIDE
SCALE ¾" 1' 0" LENGTH 471' 2"
COLORS
BLACK 1 BLUE-GREY
WHITE 3 BLUE
NOTE
COLORS ON PLAN ARE FOR THE PURPOSES OF MEASUREMENT ONLY
ACTUAL COLORS AS PER COLOR CHART

TYPE 12
DESIGN A
STARBOARD SIDE
SCALE 3/64" 1' LENGTH 471' 2"
COLORS
BLACK NO 1 BLUE GREY
WHITE NO 3 BLUE
NOTE
COLORS ON PLAN ARE FOR THE PURPOSES OF MEASUREMENT ONLY
ACTUAL COLORS AS PER COLOR CHART

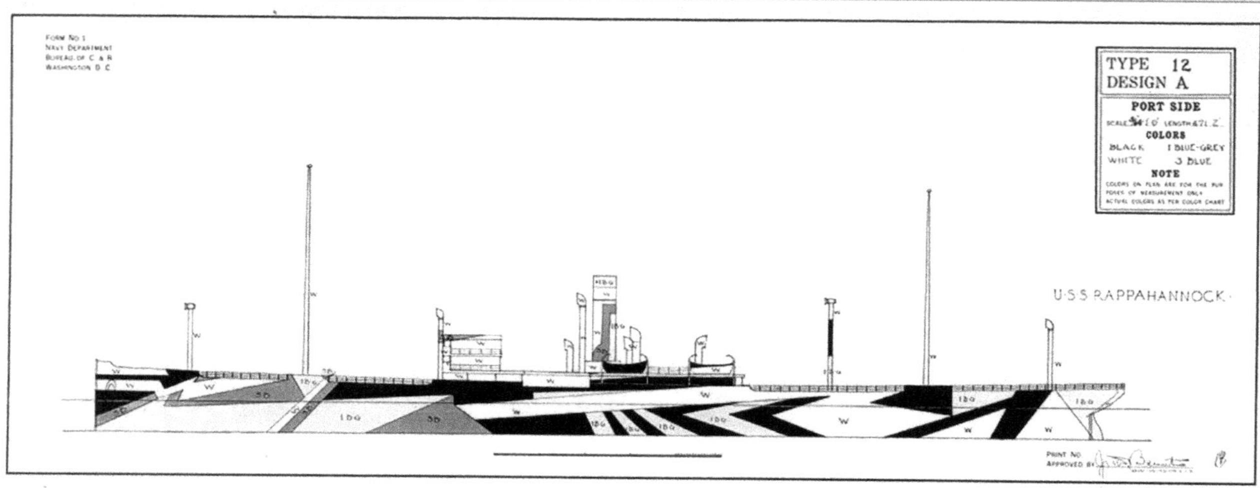

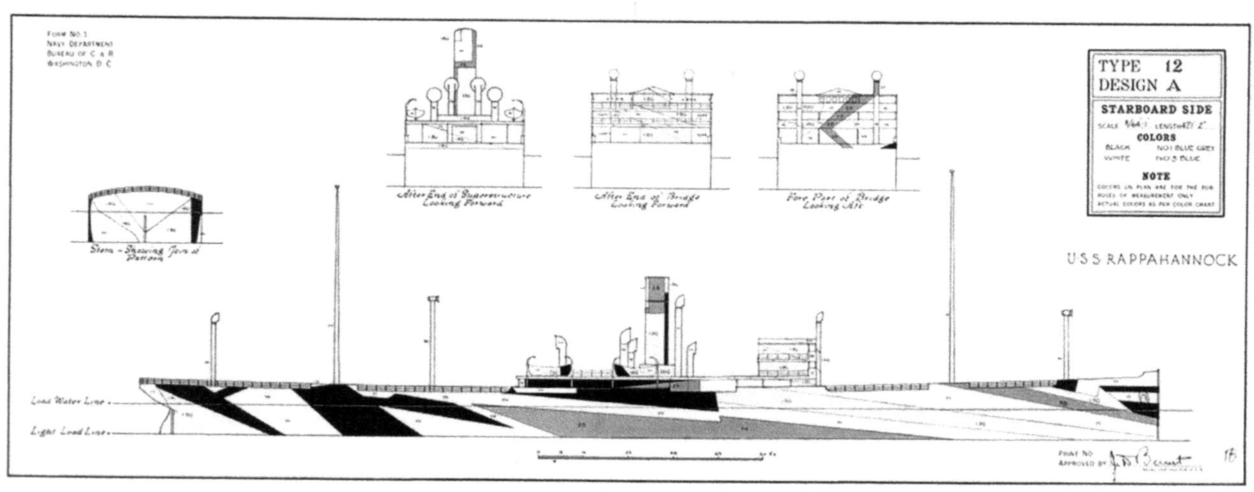

T12 B

Colors used	Ships painted with this pattern
BLACK	ID 3695 WESTHOSOKIE
WHITE	
#3 BLUE	
#1 BLUE-GRAY	
#1 GREEN	

TYPE 12
DESIGN B
PORT SIDE
SCALE 3/64"=1'-0" LENGTH 471'-2"
COLORS
WHITE NO1 BLUE GRAY
BLACK NO 3 BLUE NO 1 GREEN
NOTE
COLORS ON PLAN ARE FOR THE PURPOSES OF MEASUREMENT ONLY
ACTUAL COLORS AS PER COLOR CHART

TYPE 12
DESIGN B
STARBOARD SIDE
SCALE 3/64"=1'-0" LENGTH 471'-2"
COLORS
WHITE NO 1 BLUE GRAY
BLACK NO 3 BLUE NO 1 GREEN
NOTE
COLORS ON PLAN ARE FOR THE PURPOSES OF MEASUREMENT ONLY
ACTUAL COLORS AS PER COLOR CHART

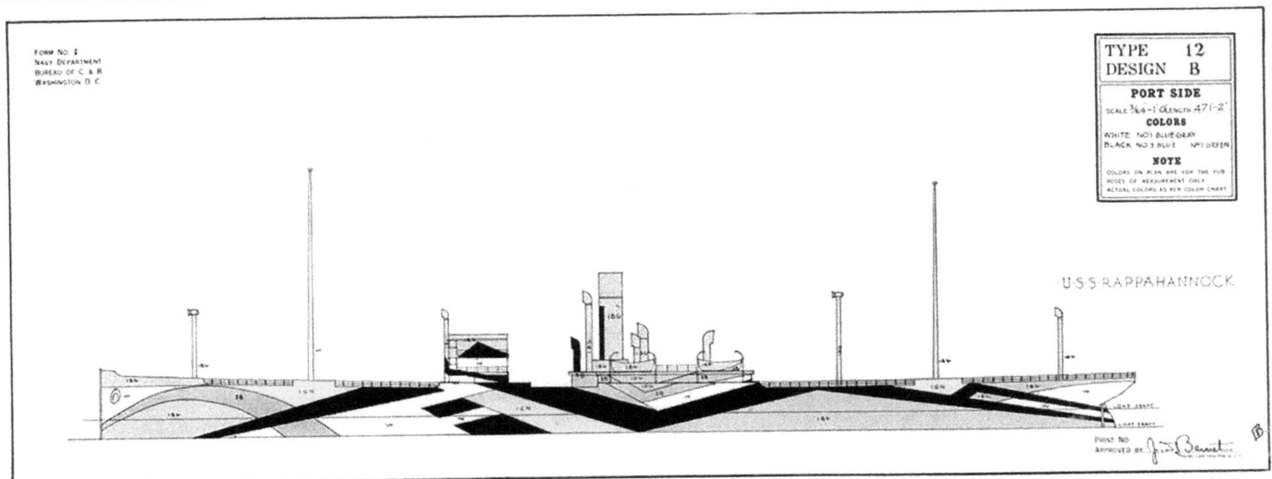

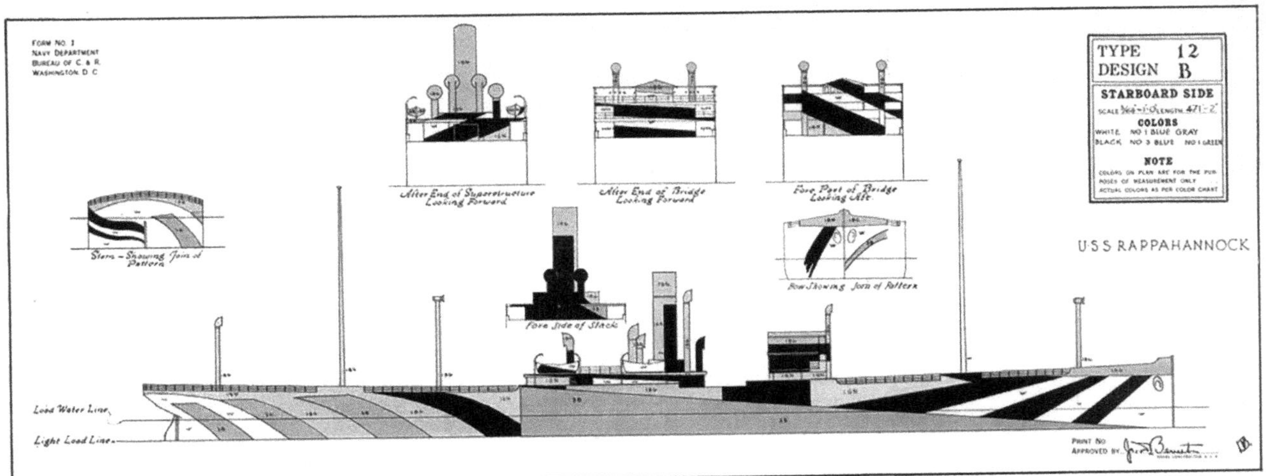

T12 C

Colors used	Ships painted with this pattern
BLACK	ID 3581 NEPONSET
GREY-WHITE	
#3 BLUE	
#2 BLUE-GRAY	

TYPE 12
DESIGN C
PORT SIDE
SCALE 1/16" = 1'0" LENGTH 471'-2" BP
COLORS
BLACK NO 2 BLUE GRAY
GRAY WHITE NO 3 BLUE
NOTE
COLORS ON PLAN ARE FOR THE PURPOSES OF MEASUREMENT ONLY
ACTUAL COLORS AS PER COLOR CHART

TYPE 12
DESIGN C
STARBOARD SIDE
SCALE 1/16" = 1'0" LENGTH 471'-2" BP
COLORS
BLACK NO.2 BLUE GRAY
GRAY WHITE NO 3 BLUE
NOTE
COLORS ON PLAN ARE FOR THE PURPOSES OF MEASUREMENT ONLY
ACTUAL COLORS AS PER COLOR CHART

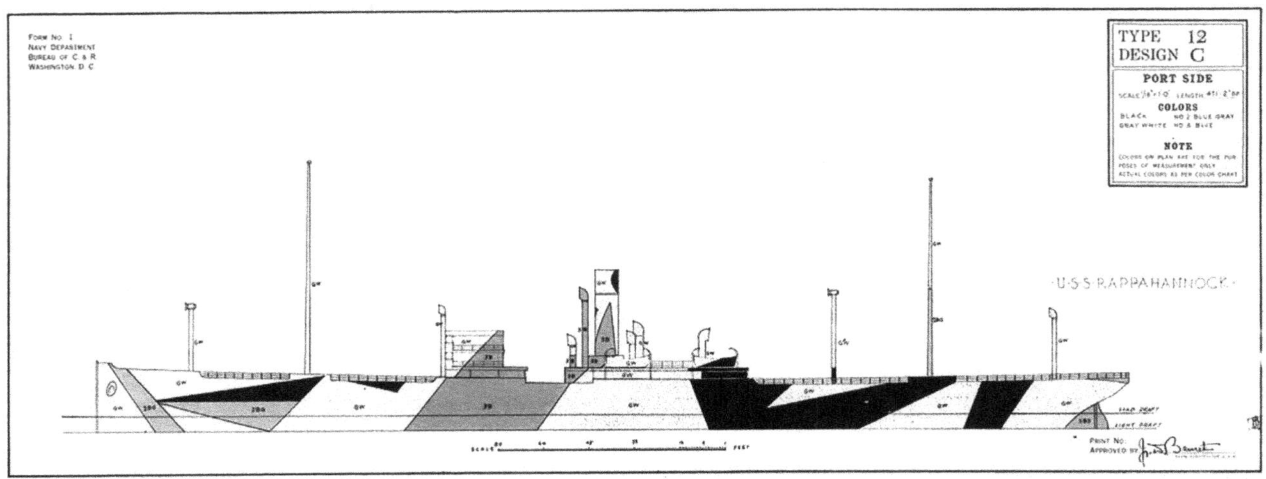

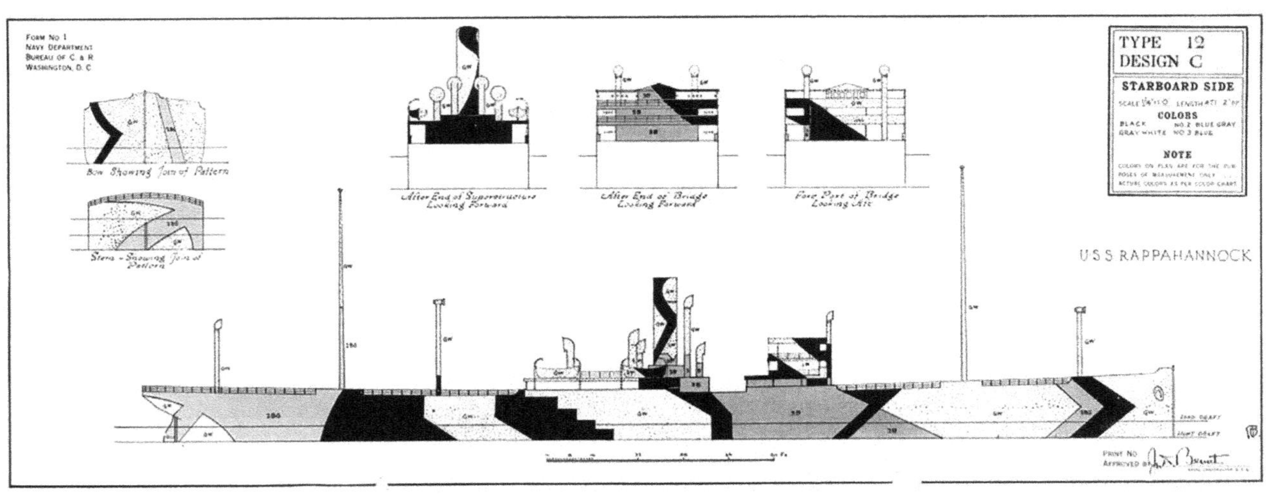

T13 A

Colors used	Ships painted with this pattern
BLACK	NORTHERN WIND
WHITE	
#3 BLUE	
#1 BLUE-GRAY	

TYPE 13
DESIGN A

PORT SIDE

SCALE 1/16" = 1'-0" LENGTH 299'-0"

COLORS

BLACK NO 1 BLUE GREY
WHITE NO 3 BLUE

NOTE

COLORS ON PLAN ARE FOR THE PURPOSES OF MEASUREMENT ONLY ACTUAL COLORS AS PER COLOR CHART

TYPE 13
DESIGN A

STARBOARD SIDE

SCALE 1/16" = 1'-0" LENGTH 299'-0"

COLORS

BLACK NO 1 BLUE GREY
WHITE NO 3 BLUE

NOTE

COLORS ON PLAN ARE FOR THE PURPOSES OF MEASUREMENT ONLY ACTUAL COLORS AS PER COLOR CHART

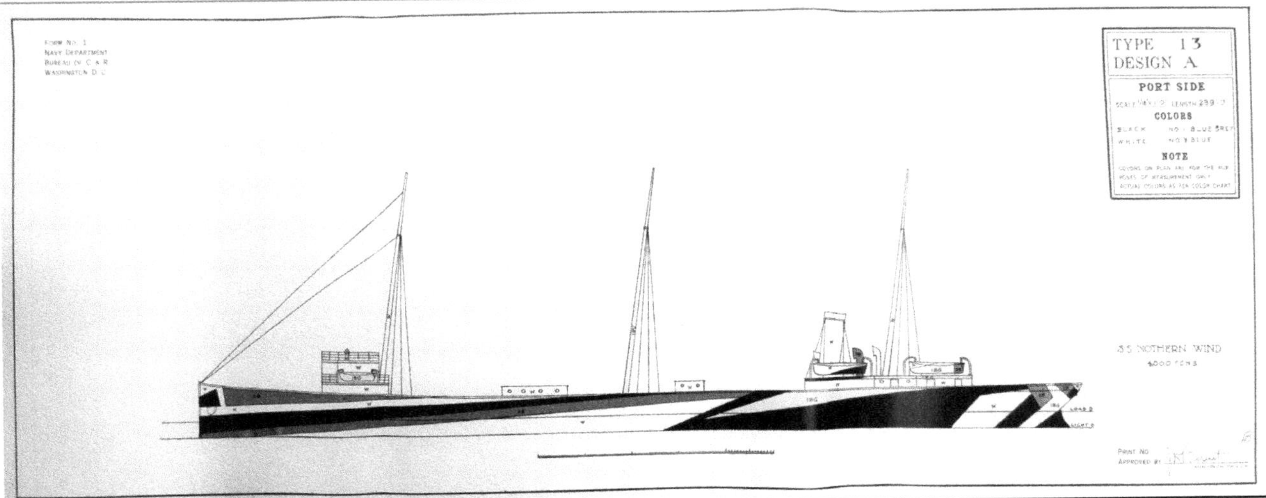

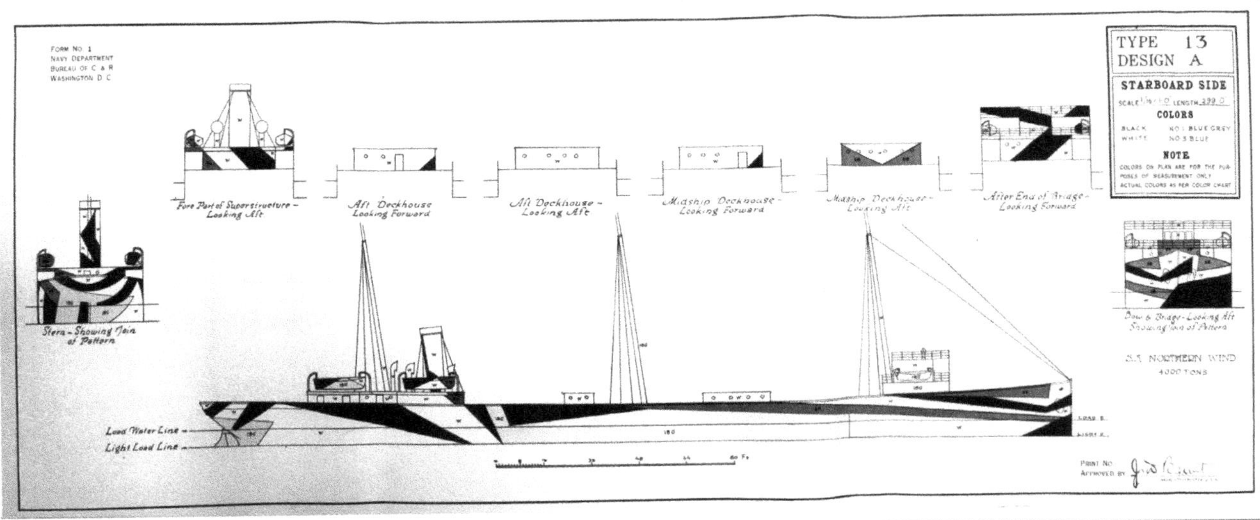

T13 B

Colors used	Ships painted with this pattern
BLACK	ID 3356 MONTROLITE
WHITE	
#1 BLUE	
#2 BLUE-GRAY	

TYPE 13
DESIGN B

PORT SIDE
SCALE 1/16"=1'0" LENGTH 299'0"
COLORS
WHITE NO 1 BLUE
BLACK NO 2 BLUE GRAY
NOTE
COLORS ON PLAN ARE FOR THE PURPOSES OF MEASUREMENT ONLY
ACTUAL COLORS AS PER COLOR CHART

TYPE 13
DESIGN B

STARBOARD SIDE
SCALE 1/16"=1'0" LENGTH 299'0"
COLORS
WHITE NO 1 BLUE
BLACK NO 2 BLUE GRAY
NOTE
COLORS ON PLAN ARE FOR THE PURPOSES OF MEASUREMENT ONLY
ACTUAL COLORS AS PER COLOR CHART

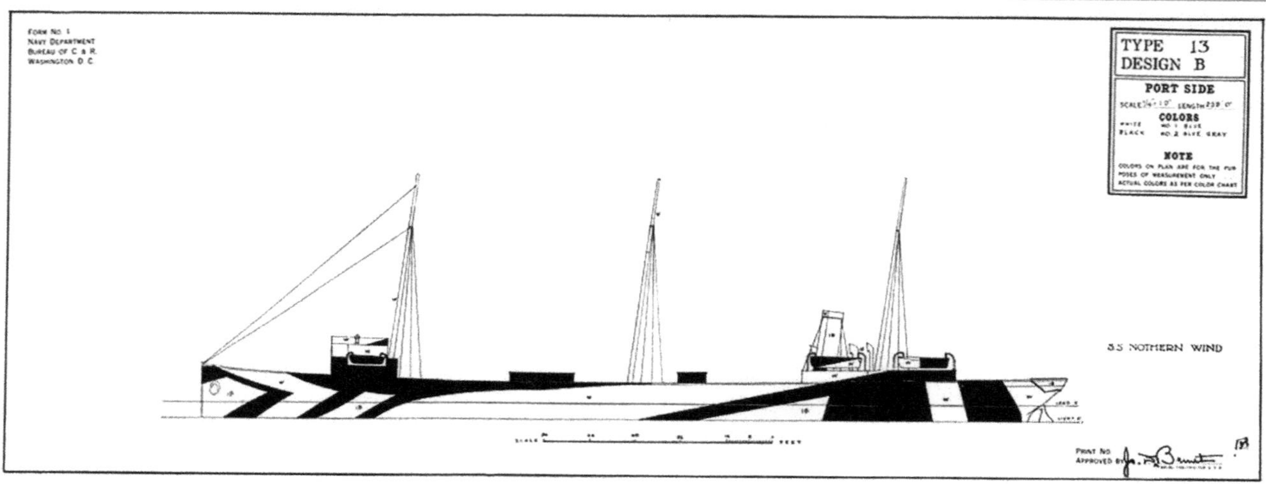

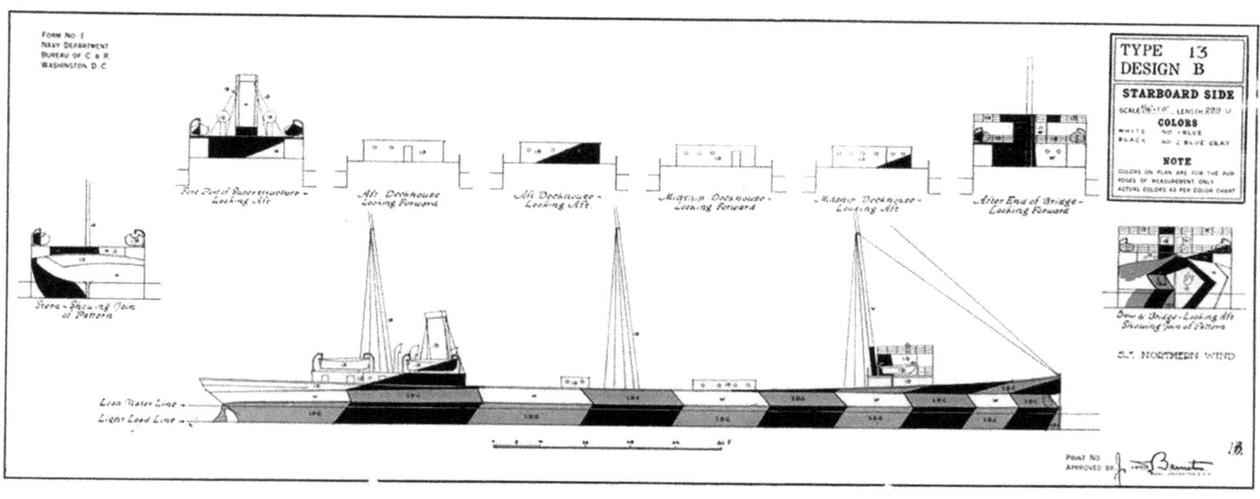

T13 C

Colors used	Ships painted with this pattern
BLACK	
GREY-WHITE	
#3 BLUE	
#1 GRAY-GREEN	

TYPE 13
DESIGN C
PORT SIDE
SCALE 1/8" = 1'-0" LENGTH 299'-0"
COLORS
No 1 GRAY GREEN BLACK
No 3 BLUE GRAY WHITE
NOTE
COLORS ON PLAN ARE FOR THE PURPOSES OF MEASUREMENT ONLY ... ACTUAL COLORS AS PER COLOR CHART

TYPE 13
DESIGN C
STARBOARD SIDE
SCALE 1/8" = 1'-0" LENGTH 299'-0"
COLORS
No 1 GRAY GREEN BLACK
No 3 BLUE GRAY WHITE
NOTE
COLORS ON PLAN ARE FOR THE PURPOSES OF MEASUREMENT ONLY ... ACTUAL COLORS AS PER COLOR CHART

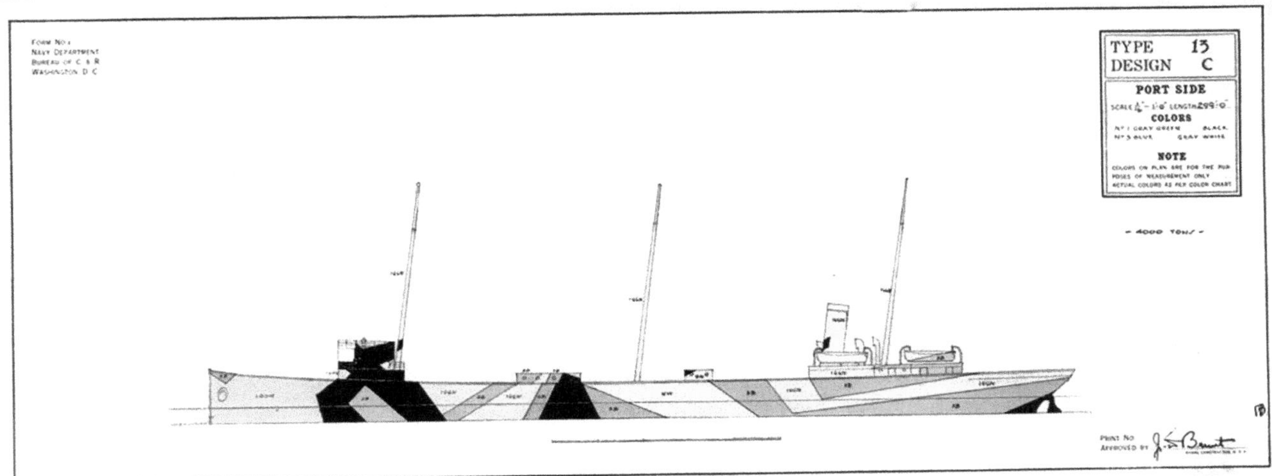

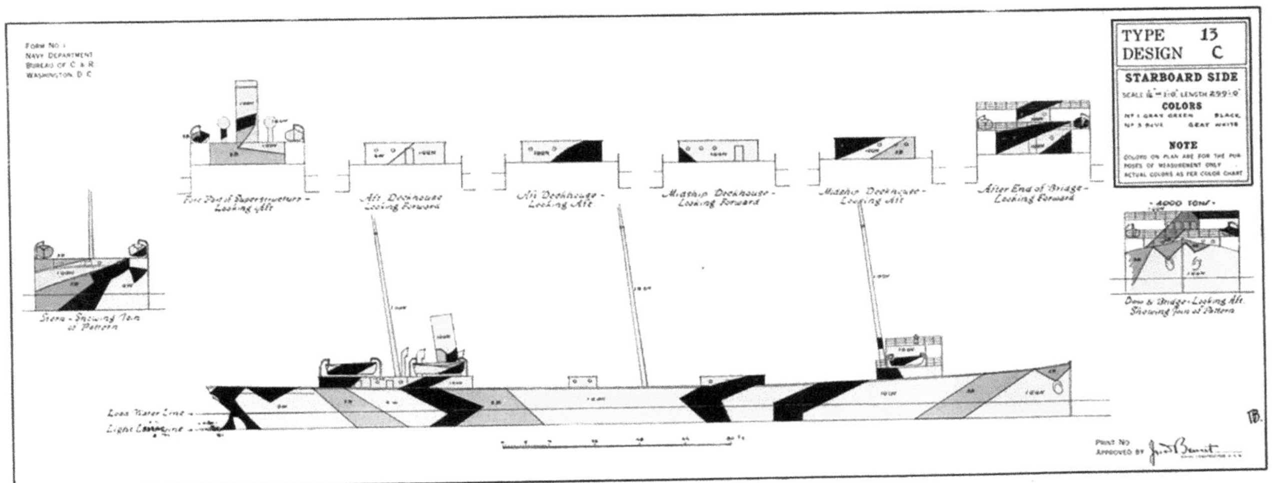

T14 A

Colors used	Ships painted with this pattern
BLACK	ID 2777 SIXAOLA
WHITE	ID NONE MEXICO
#3 BLUE	NONE KILPATRICK
#1 BLUE-GRAY	NONE KIRKPATRICK

TYPE 14
DESIGN A
PORT SIDE
SCALE 1/32"=1'0" LENGTH 364'-0"
COLORS
WHITE NO 1 BLUE GREY
BLACK NO 3 BLUE
NOTE
COLORS ON PLAN ARE FOR THE PURPOSES OF MEASUREMENT ONLY
ACTUAL COLORS AS PER COLOR CHART

TYPE 14
DESIGN A
STARBOARD SIDE
SCALE 1/32"=1'0" LENGTH 364'-0"
COLORS
WHITE NO 1 BLUE GREY
BLACK NO 3 BLUE
NOTE
COLORS ON PLAN ARE FOR THE PURPOSES OF MEASUREMENT ONLY
ACTUAL COLORS AS PER COLOR CHART

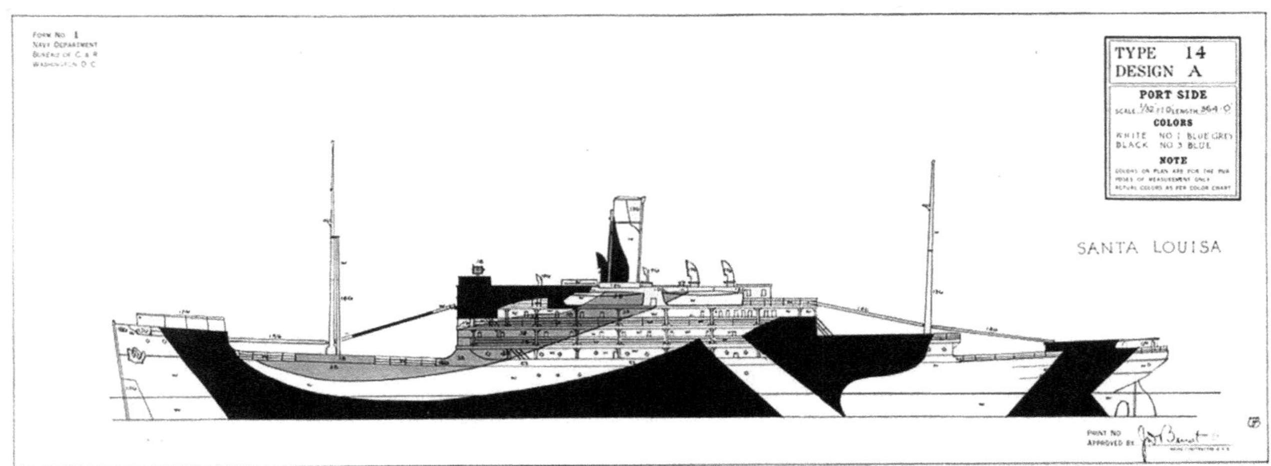

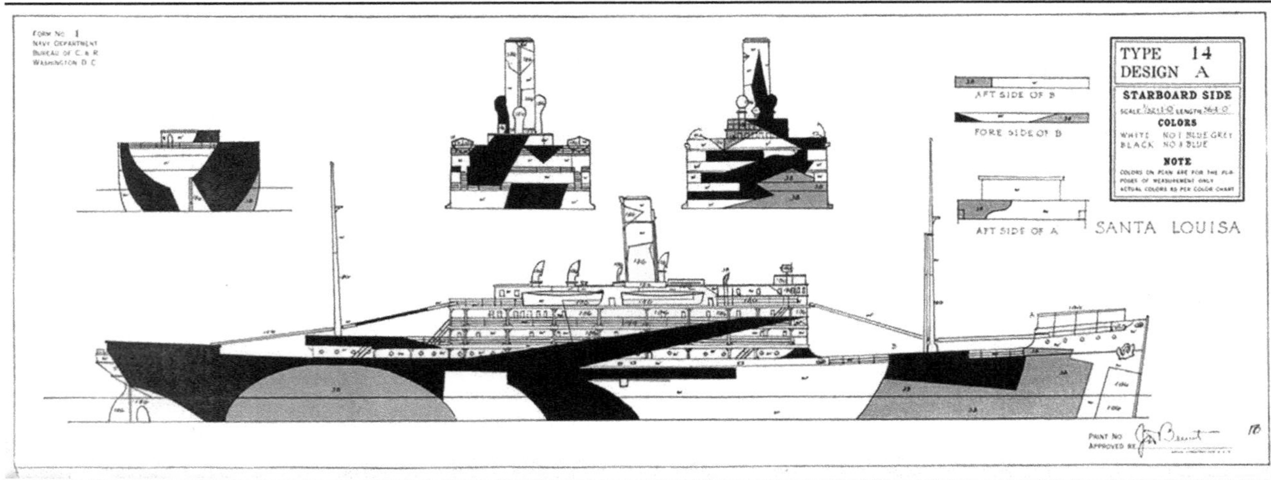

T14 B

Colors used	Ships painted with this pattern
BLACK	ID NONE COMANCHE
WHITE	ID 1406 CARILLO (T)
#3 BLUE	
#1 BLUE	
#1 GREEN	

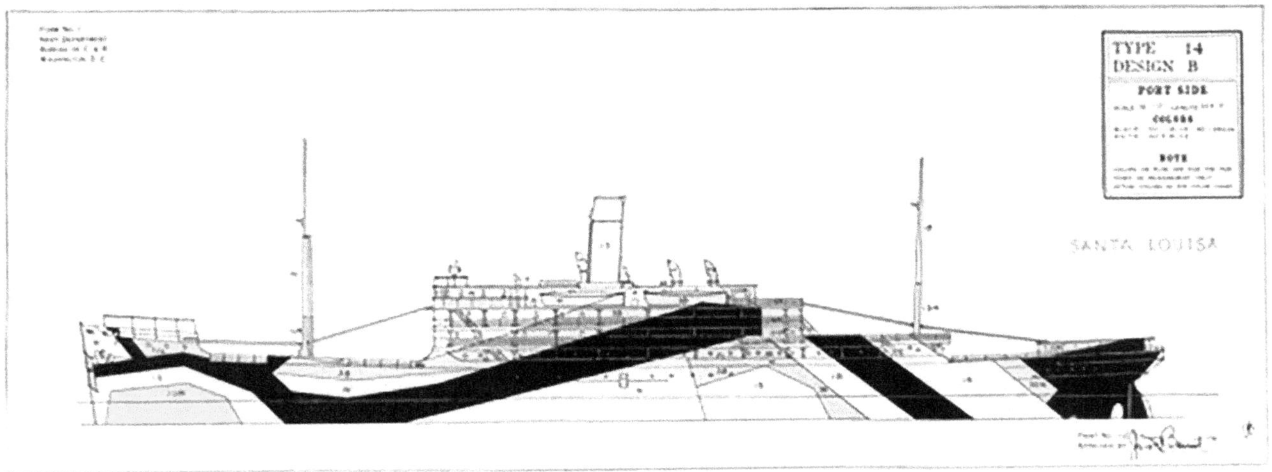

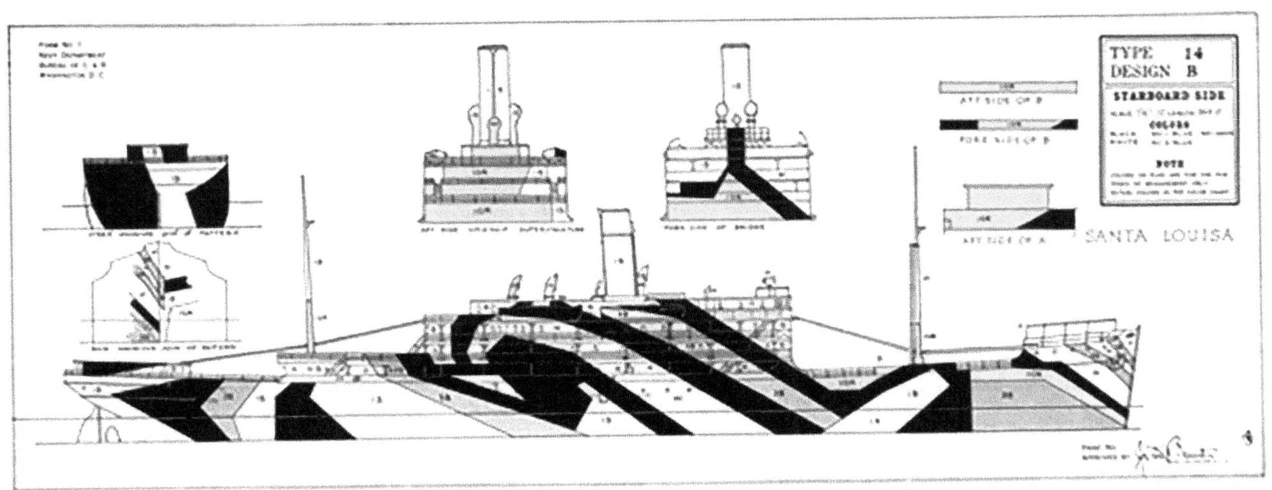

T14 E

Colors used	Ships painted with this pattern
BLACK	ID 3804 SANTA TERESA
GREY-WHITE	ID 2873 SANTA LUISA (T)
#3 BLUE	
#1 BLUE-GRAY	

TYPE 14
DESIGN E

PORT SIDE
SCALE 1/16" 1'0" LENGTH 304'0"
COLORS
GRAYWHITE NO. 3 BLUE
NO. 1 BLUEGRAY BLACK
NOTE
COLORS ON PLAN ARE FOR THE PURPOSES OF MEASUREMENT ONLY ... ACTUAL COLORS AS PER COLOR CHART

TYPE 14
DESIGN E

STARBOARD SIDE
SCALE 1/16" 1'0" LENGTH 364'0"
COLORS
GRAYWHITE NO. 3 BLUE
NO. 1 BLUEGRAY BLACK
NOTE
COLORS ON PLAN ARE FOR THE PURPOSES OF MEASUREMENT ONLY ... ACTUAL COLORS AS PER COLOR CHART

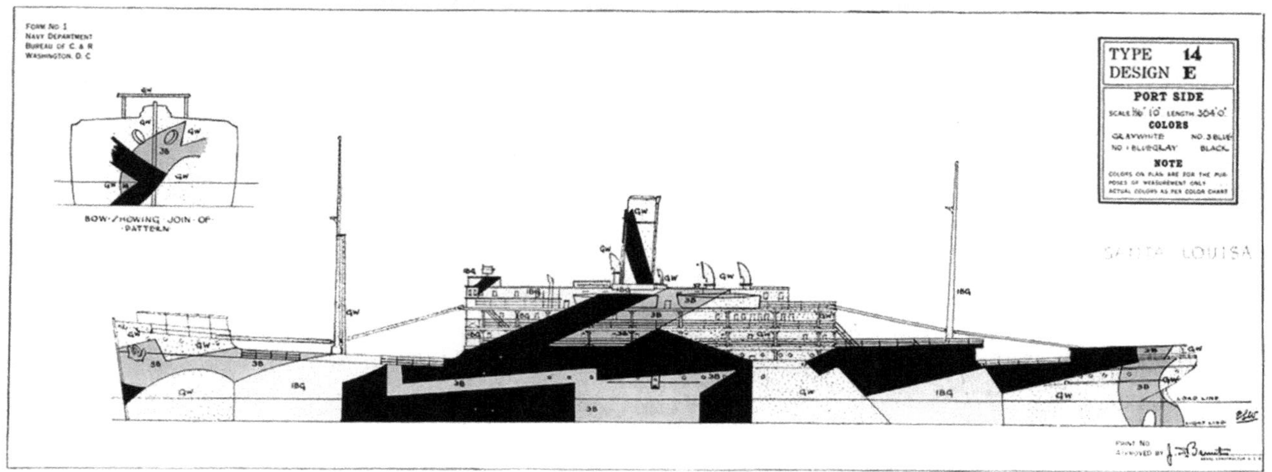

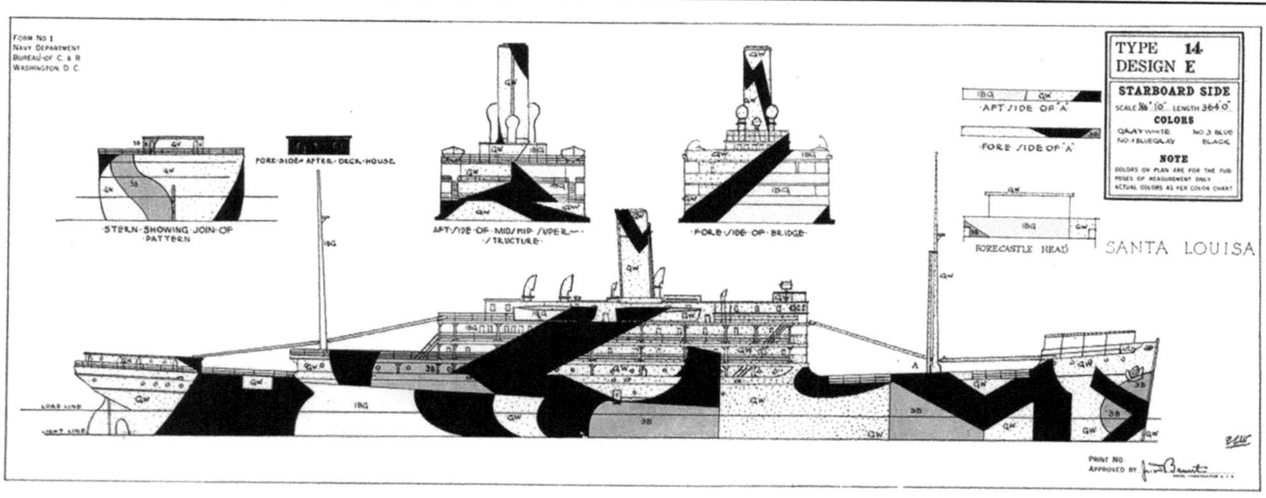

T15 A

Colors used	Ships painted with this pattern
BLACK	ID 1303 HOWICK HALL
GREY-WHITE	
#3 BLUE	
#1 BLUE-GRAY	
#1 GREEN	

TYPE 15
DESIGN A
PORT SIDE
SCALE 1/8"=1'-0" LENGTH 380'-0"
COLORS
BLACK NO 1 BLUE GRAY
GRAY WHITE NO 3 BLUE
NO 1 GREEN
NOTE
COLORS ON PLAN ARE FOR THE PURPOSES OF MEASUREMENT ONLY
ACTUAL COLORS AS PER COLOR CHART

TYPE 15
DESIGN A
STARBOARD SIDE
SCALE 1/8"=1'-0" LENGTH 380'-0"
COLORS
BLACK NO 1 BLUE GRAY
GRAY WHITE NO 3 BLUE
NO 1 GREEN
NOTE
COLORS ON PLAN ARE FOR THE PURPOSES OF MEASUREMENT ONLY
ACTUAL COLORS AS PER COLOR CHART

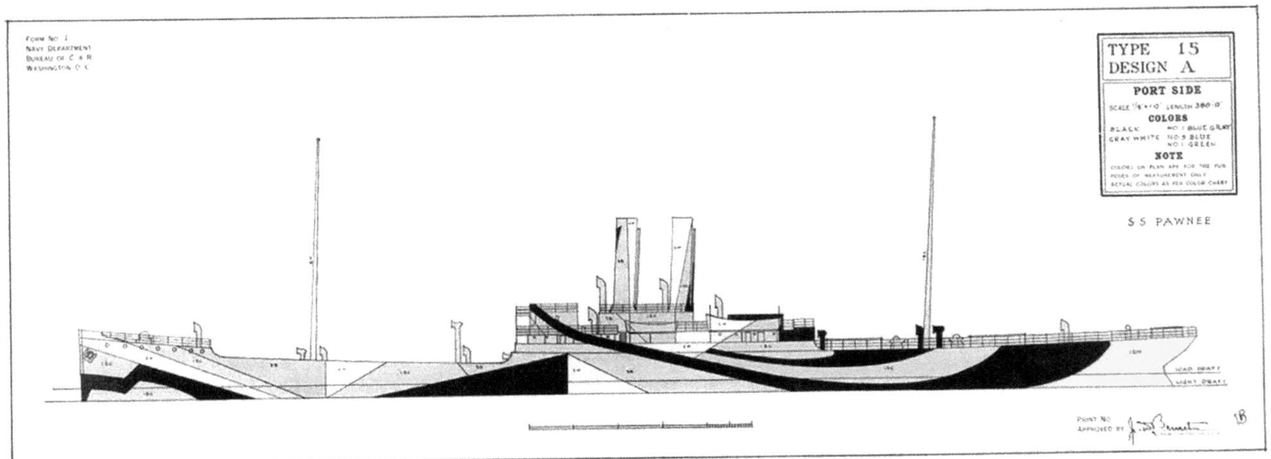

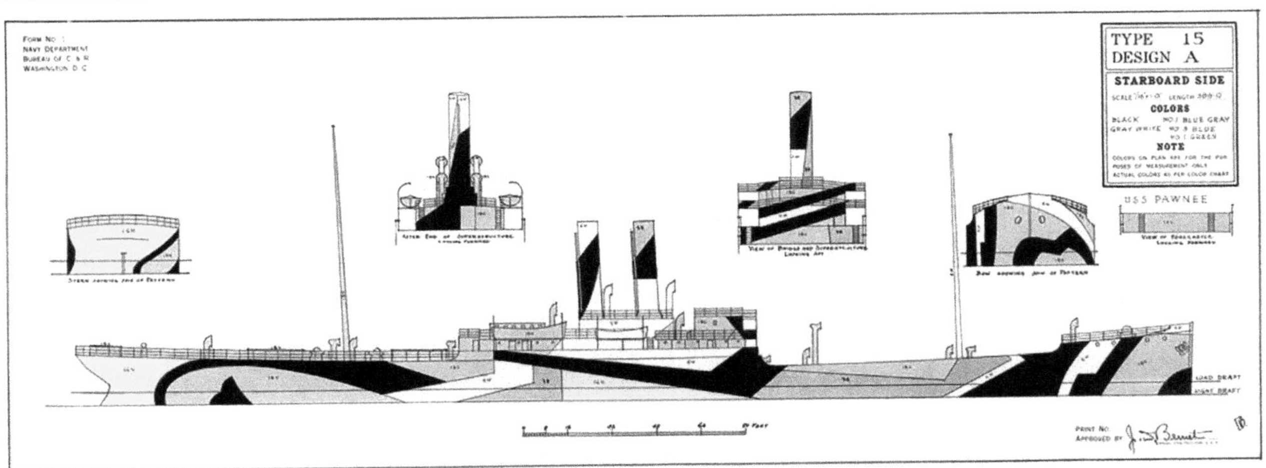

T15 D

Colors used	Ships painted with this pattern
BLACK	ID 3243 CAMDEN
GREY-WHITE	
#3 BLUE	
#1 GRAY-GREEN	

TYPE 15
DESIGN D
PORT SIDE
SCALE 1/16"=1'0 LENGTH 405'-8"
COLORS
Nº 3 BLUE GRAY-WHITE
Nº 1 GRAY-GREEN BLACK
NOTE
COLORS ON PLAN ARE FOR THE PURPOSES OF MEASUREMENT ONLY
ACTUAL COLORS AS PER COLOR CHART

TYPE 15
DESIGN D
STARBOARD SIDE
SCALE 1/16"=1'0 LENGTH 405'-8"
COLORS
Nº 3 BLUE GRAY-WHITE
Nº 1 GRAY-GREEN BLACK
NOTE
COLORS ON PLAN ARE FOR THE PURPOSES OF MEASUREMENT ONLY
ACTUAL COLORS AS PER COLOR CHART

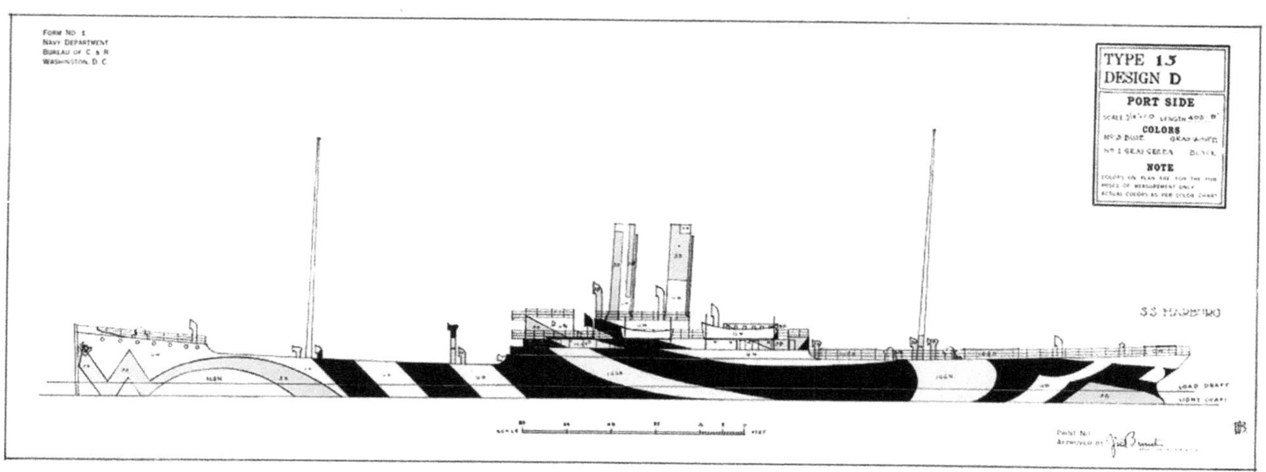

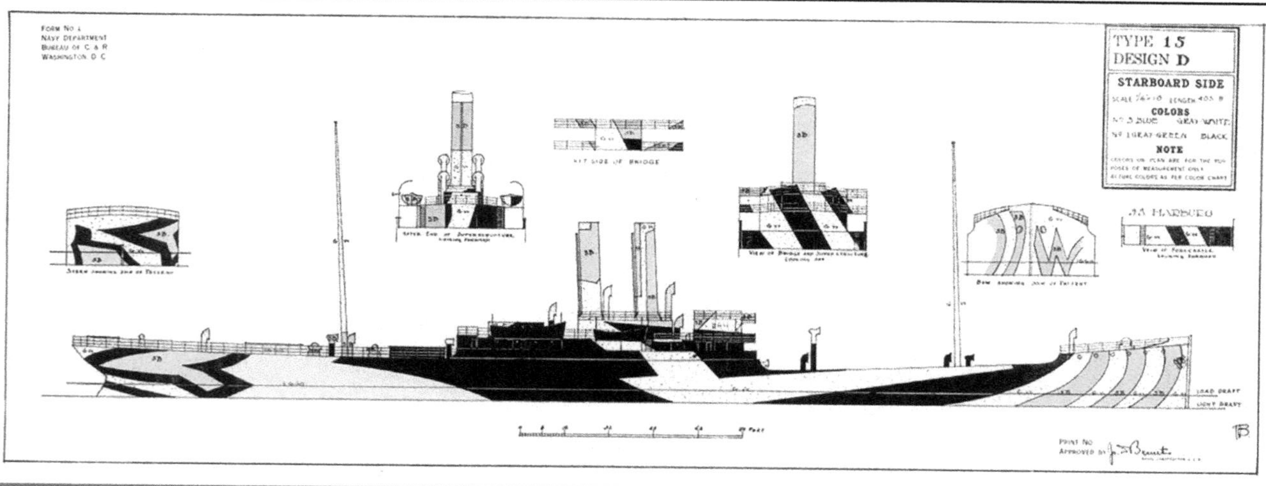

T16 A

Colors used	Ships painted with this pattern
BLACK	ID 1400 PEQUOT
GREY-WHITE	
#3 BLUE	
#1 BLUE-GRAY	
#1 GREEN	

TYPE 16
DESIGN A

PORT SIDE

SCALE 1/22"=1'0" LENGTH 470'0"

COLORS

BLACK — NO 1 GREEN
GRAY WHITE — NO 1 BLUE GRAY
NO 3 BLUE

NOTE

COLORS ON PLAN ARE FOR THE PURPOSES OF MEASUREMENT ONLY
ACTUAL COLORS AS PER COLOR CHART

TYPE 16
DESIGN A

STARBOARD SIDE

SCALE 1/22"=1'0" LENGTH 470'0"

COLORS

BLACK — NO 1 GREEN
GRAY WHITE — NO 1 BLUE GRAY
NO 3 BLUE

NOTE

COLORS ON PLAN ARE FOR THE PURPOSES OF MEASUREMENT ONLY
ACTUAL COLORS AS PER COLOR CHART

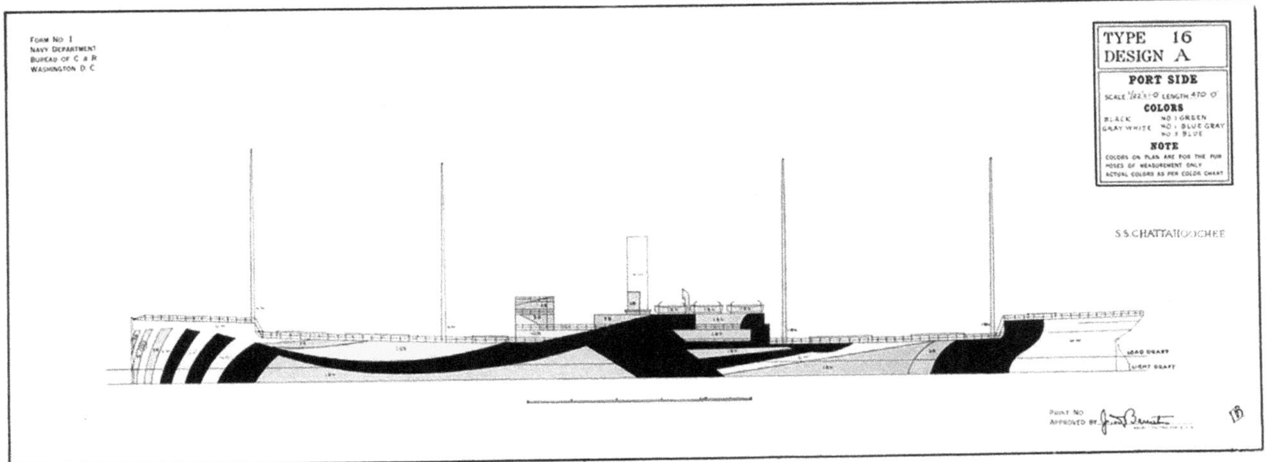

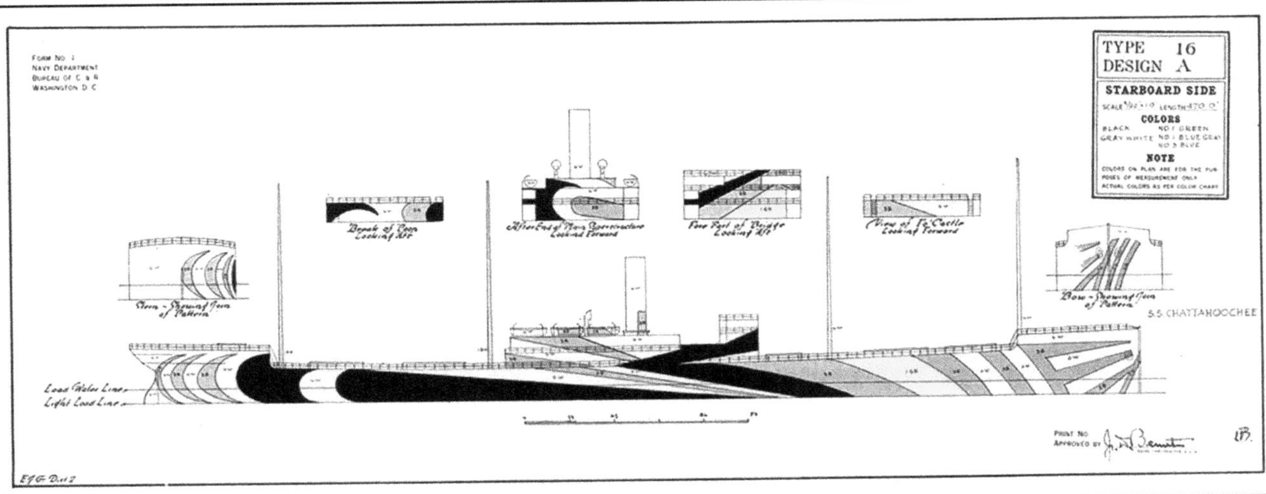

T17 A

Colors used	Ships painted with this pattern
BLACK	ID 1822 MOUNTSHASTA
GREY-WHITE	
#3 BLUE	
#1 BLUE-GRAY	
#2 BLUE-GRAY	

TYPE 17
DESIGN A

PORT SIDE

SCALE 1/16"=1'0" LENGTH 402' 0"

COLORS

BLACK NO 1 BLUE GRAY
GRAY WHITE NO 2 BLUE GRAY
NO 3 BLUE

NOTE

COLORS ON PLAN ARE FOR THE PURPOSES OF MEASUREMENT ONLY
ACTUAL COLORS AS PER COLOR CHART

TYPE 17
DESIGN A

PORT SIDE

SCALE 1/16"=1'0" LENGTH 402' 0"

COLORS

BLACK NO 1 BLUE GRAY
GRAY WHITE NO 2 BLUE GRAY
NO 3 BLUE

NOTE

COLORS ON PLAN ARE FOR THE PURPOSES OF MEASUREMENT ONLY
ACTUAL COLORS AS PER COLOR CHART

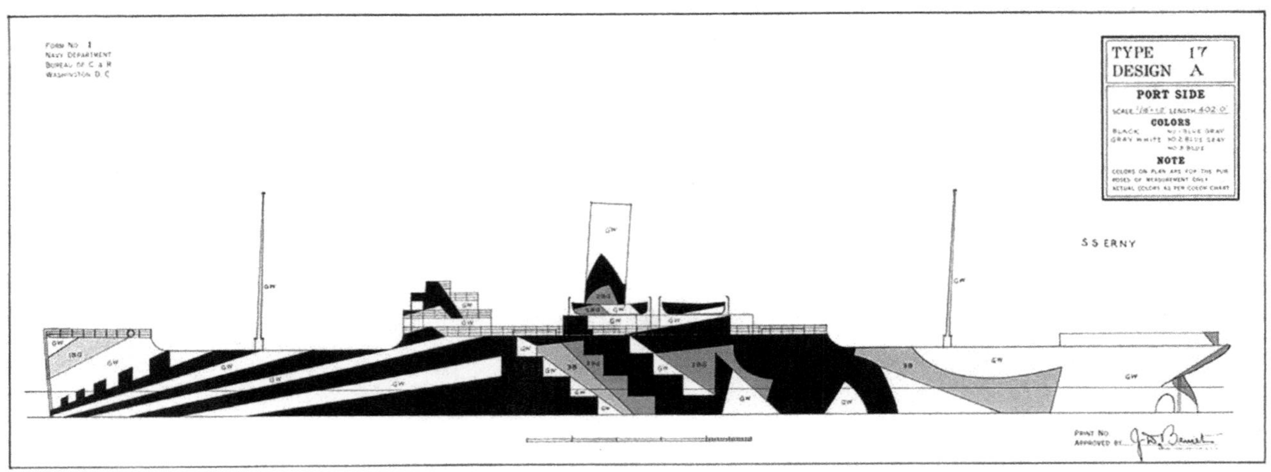

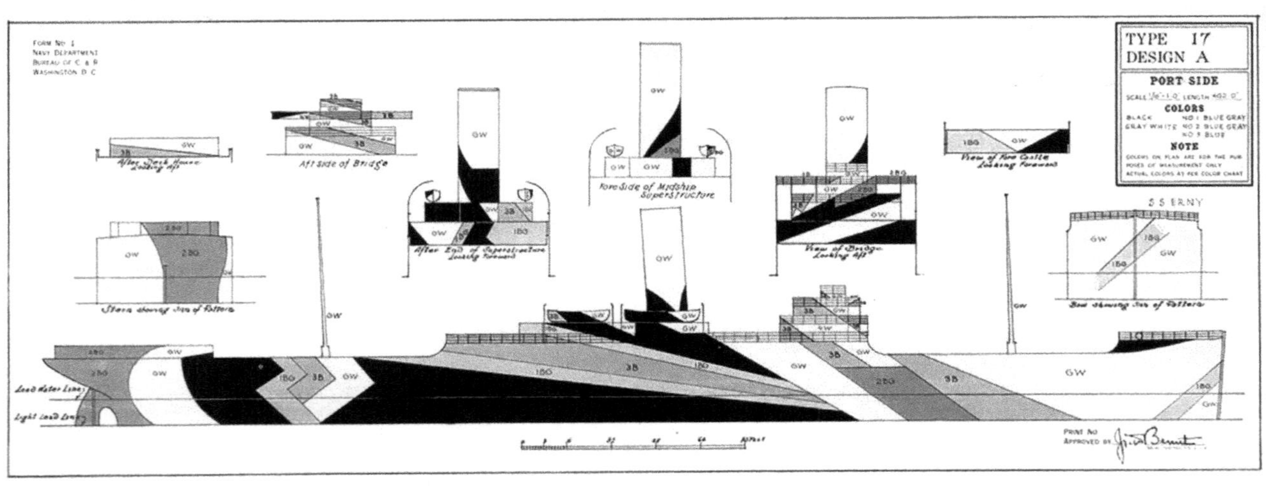

T17 D

Colors used	Ships painted with this pattern
BLACK	ID 3701 WEST KYSKA
GREY-WHITE	
#3 BLUE	
#4 GRAY	
#2 BLUE-GRAY	

TYPE ·17·
DESIGN ·D
PORT SIDE
SCALE ⅛"=1'0" LENGTH 402'0"
COLORS
GRAY-WHITE · BLACK ·
NO 3 BLUE ·
NO 2 BLUE-GRAY ·
NO 4 GRAY ·
NOTE
COLORS ON PLAN ARE FOR THE PURPOSES OF MEASUREMENT ONLY
ACTUAL COLORS AS PER COLOR CHART

TYPE ·17·
DESIGN ·D·
STARBOARD SIDE
SCALE ⅛"=1'0" LENGTH 402'0"
COLORS
GRAY-WHITE · BLACK ·
NO 3 BLUE ·
NO 2 BLUE-GRAY ·
NO 4 GRAY ·
NOTE
COLORS ON PLAN ARE FOR THE PURPOSES OF MEASUREMENT ONLY
ACTUAL COLORS AS PER COLOR CHART

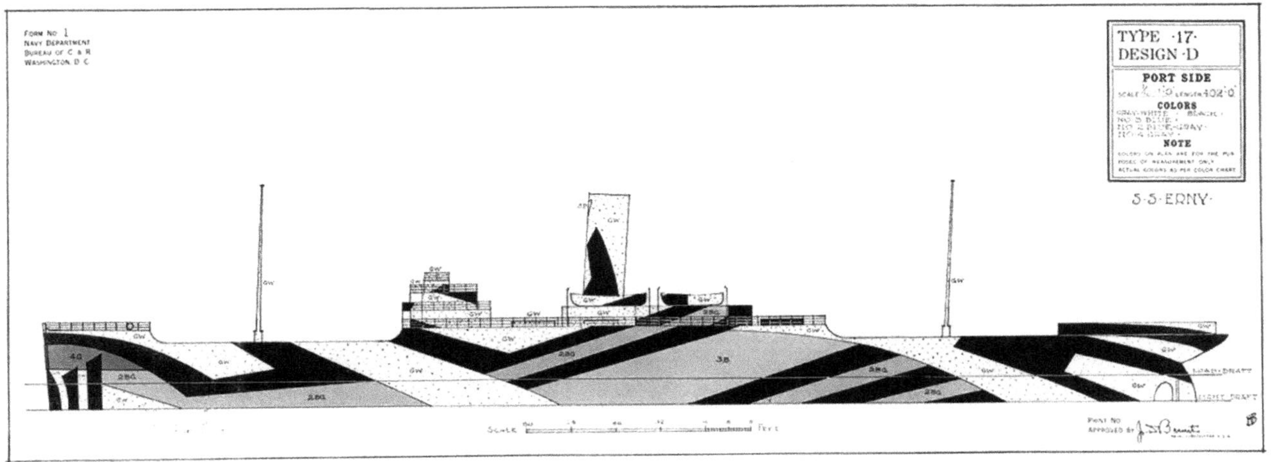

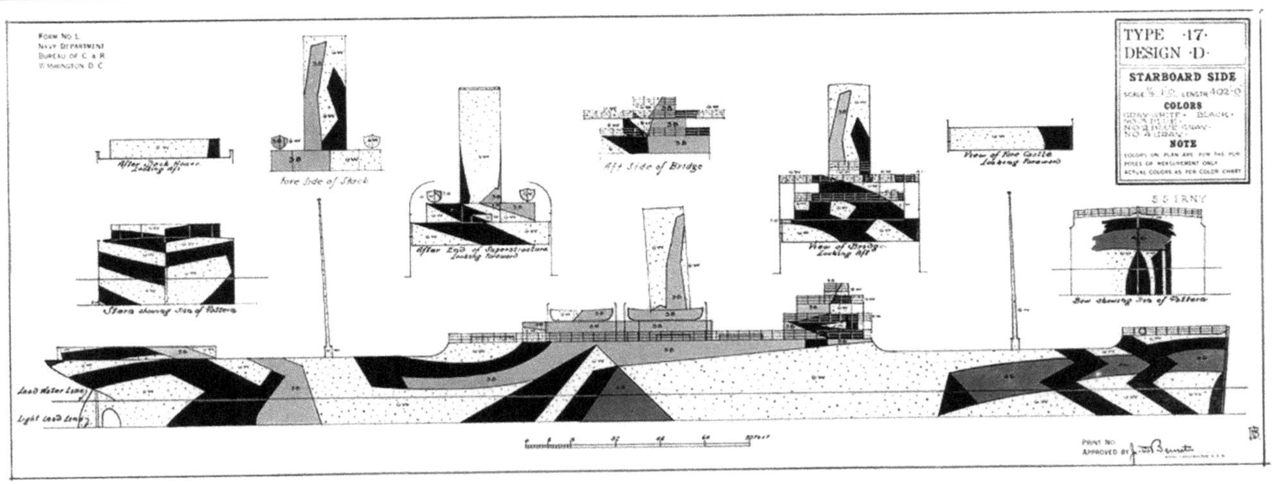

T17 E

Colors used	Ships painted with this pattern
BLACK	ID 2867 WESTOVER
GREY-WHITE	
#3 BLUE	
#1 GREEN	

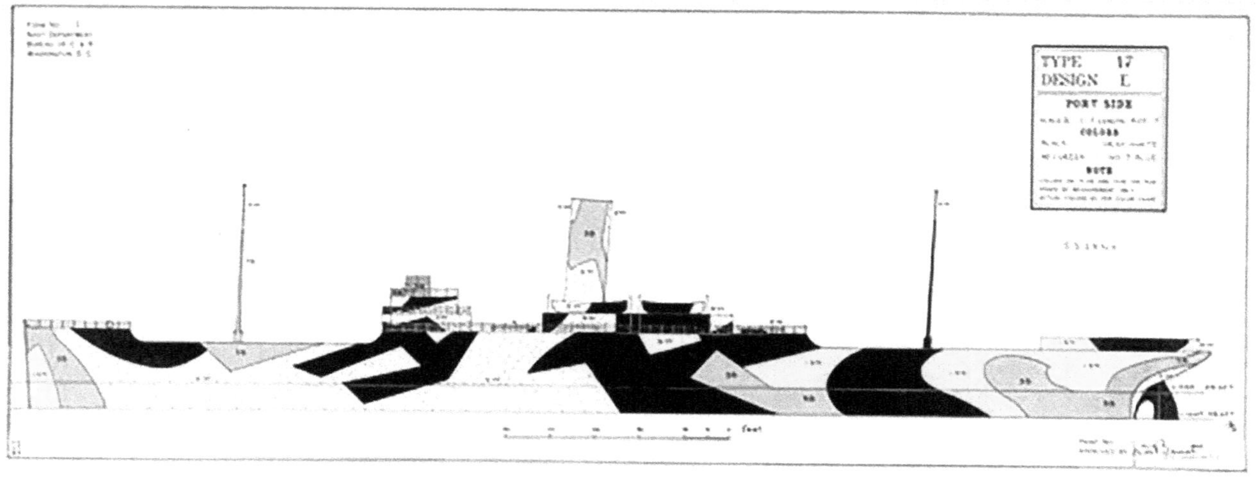

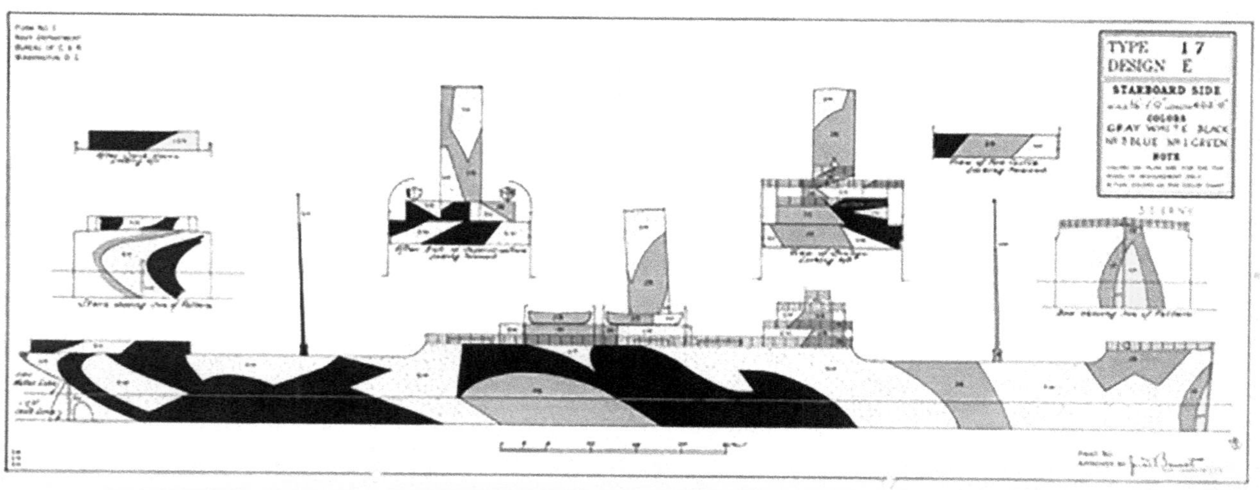

T19 E

Colors used	Ships painted with this pattern
BLACK	WEST KYSKA
GREY-WHITE	
#3 BLUE	
#1 GREEN	

TYPE 19 DESIGN E

PORT SIDE

SCALE ¼" = 1'0" LENGTH 314' 0"

COLORS

Nº 3 BLUE — BLACK

Nº 1 GREEN — GRAY WHITE

NOTE

COLORS ON PLAN ARE FOR THE PURPOSES OF MEASUREMENT ONLY ACTUAL COLORS AS PER COLOR CHART

TYPE 19 DESIGN E

STARBOARD SIDE

SCALE ¼" = 1'0" LENGTH 314' 0"

COLORS

BLACK — Nº 3 BLUE

GRAY WHITE — Nº 1 GREEN

NOTE

COLORS ON PLAN ARE FOR THE PURPOSES OF MEASUREMENT ONLY ACTUAL COLORS AS PER COLOR CHART

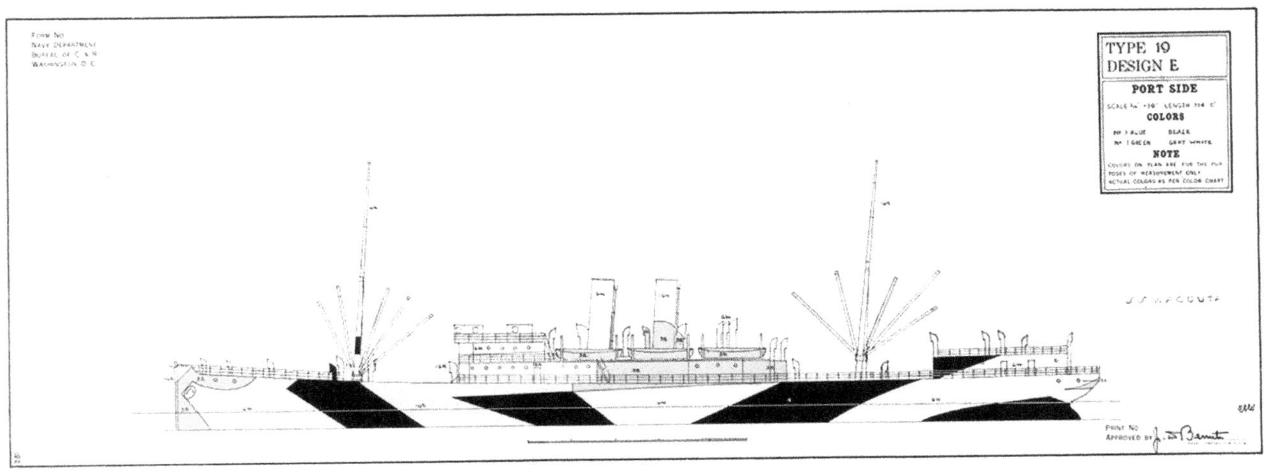

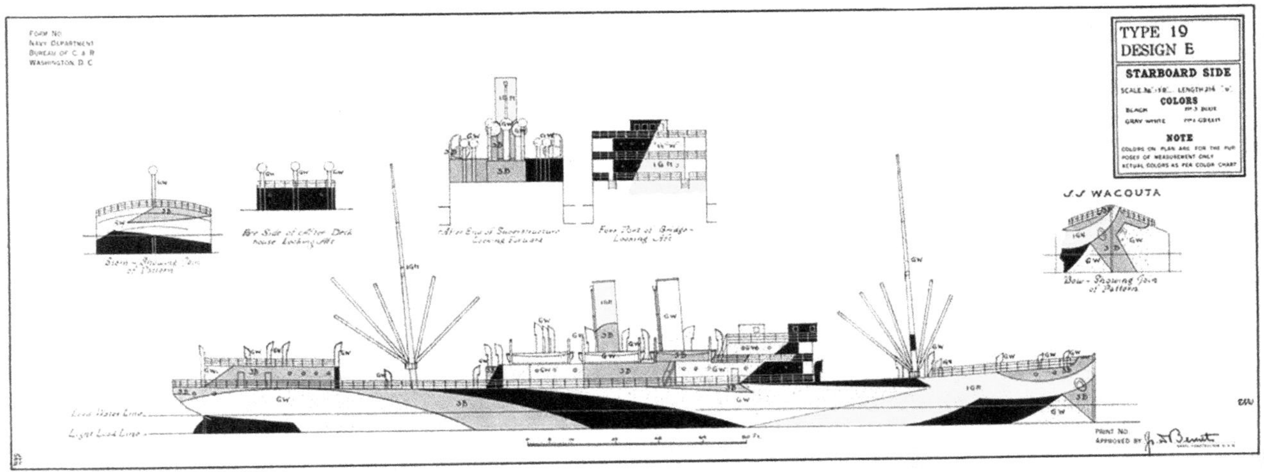

T21 A

Colors used	Ships painted with this pattern
BLACK	ID 3407 ZIRKEL
GREY-WHITE	
#3 BLUE	
#4 GRAY	

TYPE 21
DESIGN A
PORT SIDE
SCALE 1/8"=1'0" LENGTH 402' 0"
COLORS
BLACK NO 3 BLUE
GRAY WHITE NO 4 GRAY
NOTE
COLORS ON PLAN ARE FOR THE PURPOSES OF MEASUREMENT ONLY
ACTUAL COLORS AS PER COLOR CHART

TYPE 21
DESIGN A
STARBOARD SIDE
SCALE 1/8"=1'0" LENGTH 402' 0"
COLORS
BLACK NO 3 BLUE
GRAY WHITE NO 4 GRAY
NOTE
COLORS ON PLAN ARE FOR THE PURPOSES OF MEASUREMENT ONLY
ACTUAL COLORS AS PER COLOR CHART

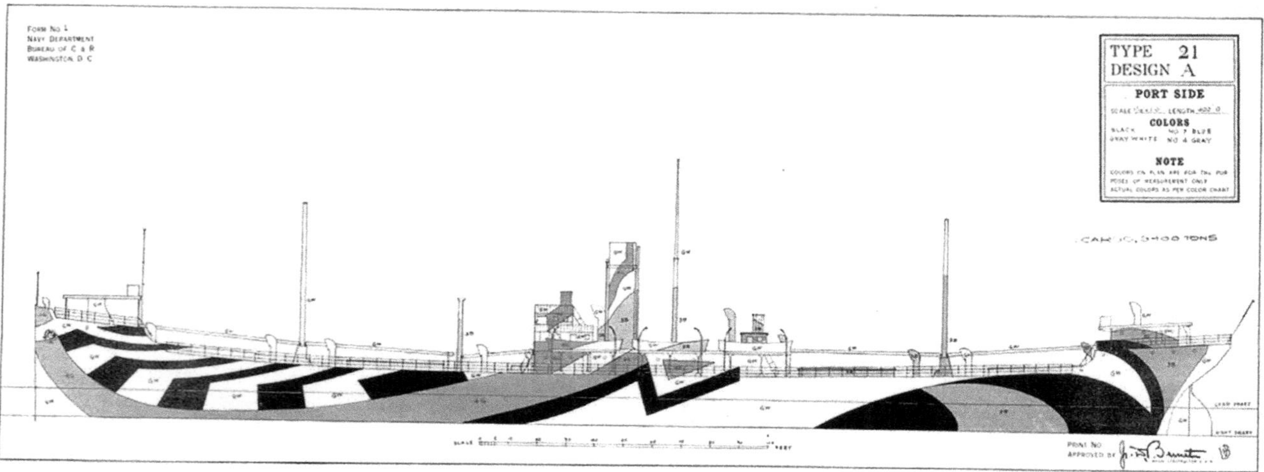

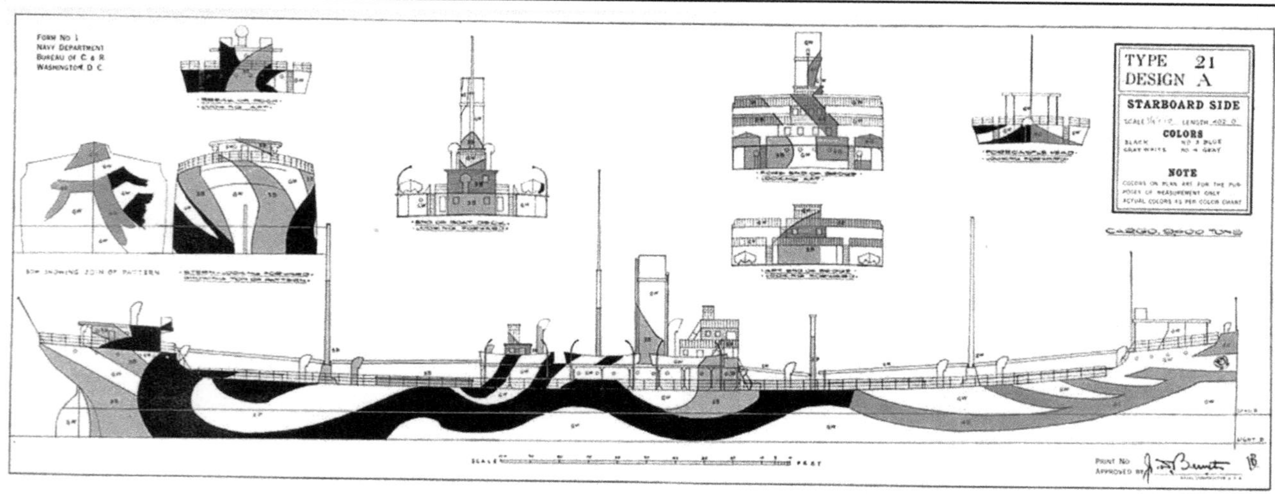

T21 B

Colors used	Ships painted with this pattern
BLACK	ID 3792 ZACA
GREY-WHITE	
#3 BLUE	

TYPE 21
DESIGN B

PORT SIDE

SCALE 1/16"=1'-0" LENGTH 402'-0"

COLORS

GRAY WHITE NO 3 BLUE

BLACK

NOTE

COLORS ON PLAN ARE FOR THE PURPOSES OF MEASUREMENT ONLY ACTUAL COLORS AS PER COLOR CHART

TYPE 21
DESIGN B

STARBOARD SIDE

SCALE LENGTH

COLORS

GRAY WHITE NO 3 BLUE

BLACK

NOTE

COLORS ON PLAN ARE FOR THE PURPOSES OF MEASUREMENT ONLY ACTUAL COLORS AS PER COLOR CHART

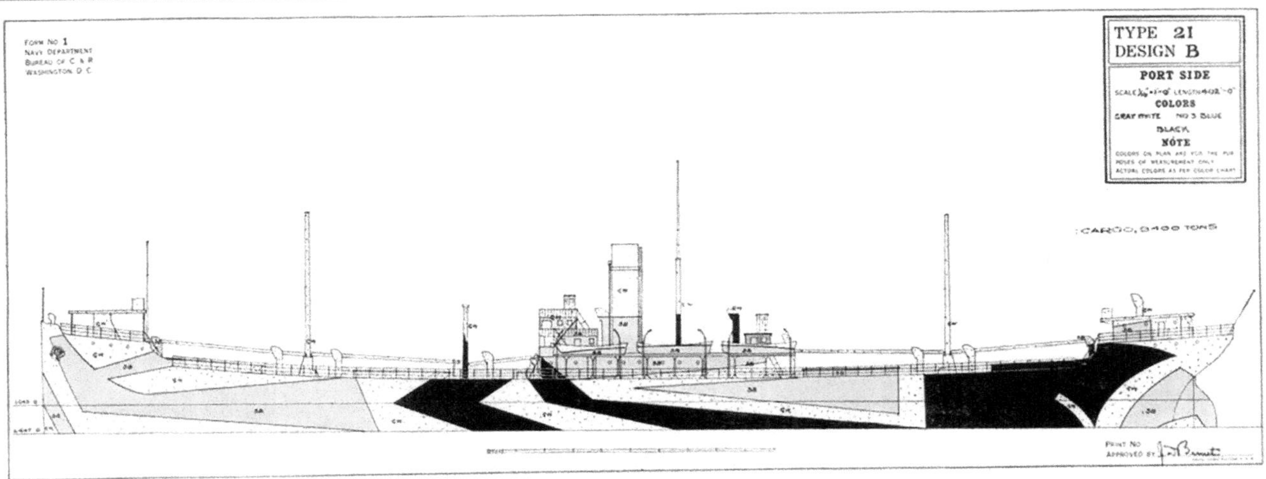

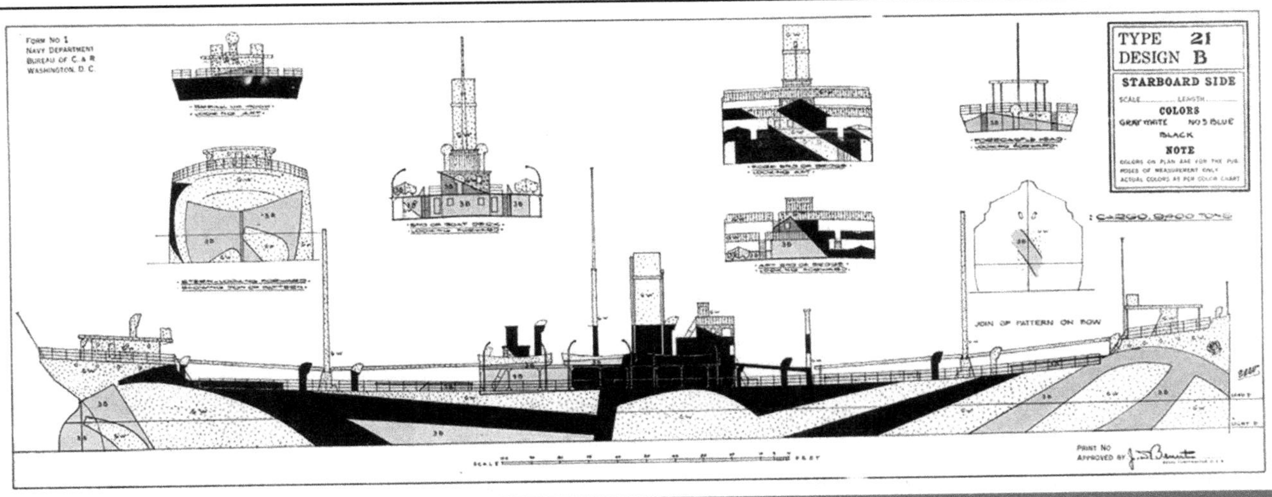

T21 C

Colors used	Ships painted with this pattern
BLACK	ID 3797 OSKAWA
GREY-WHITE	ID 3806 YAMHILL
#3 BLUE	

TYPE 21
DESIGN C
PORT SIDE
SCALE 1/16"=1'0" LENGTH 402'0"
COLORS
BLACK NO. 3 BLUE
GRAY WHITE
NOTE
COLORS ON PLAN ARE FOR THE PURPOSES OF MEASUREMENT ONLY
ACTUAL COLORS AS PER COLOR CHART

TYPE 21
DESIGN C
STARBOARD SIDE
SCALE 1/16"=1'0" LENGTH 402'0"
COLORS
BLACK NO. 3 BLUE
GRAY WHITE
NOTE
COLORS ON PLAN ARE FOR THE PURPOSES OF MEASUREMENT ONLY
ACTUAL COLORS AS PER COLOR CHART

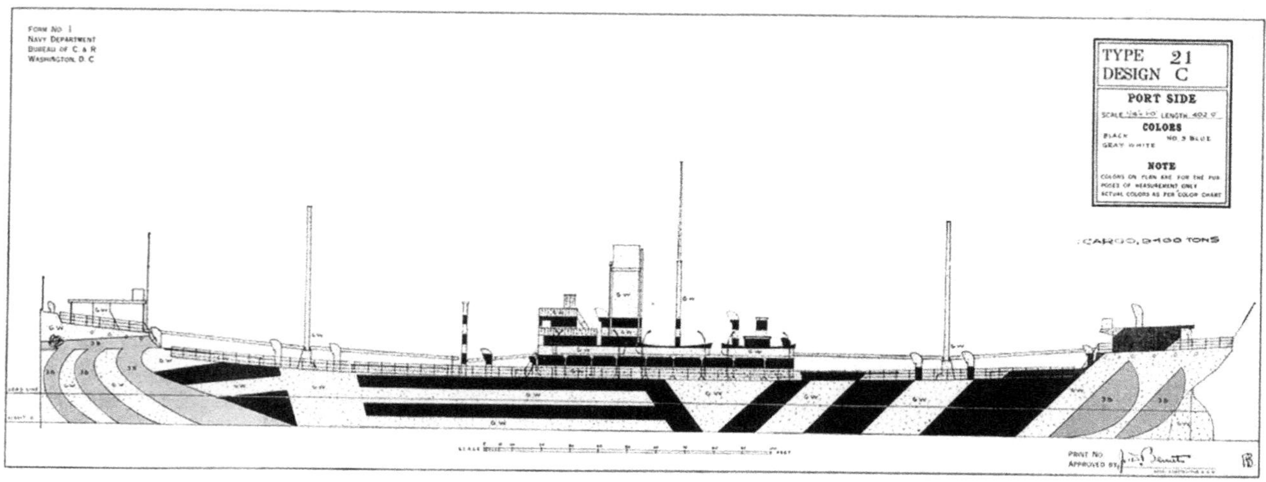

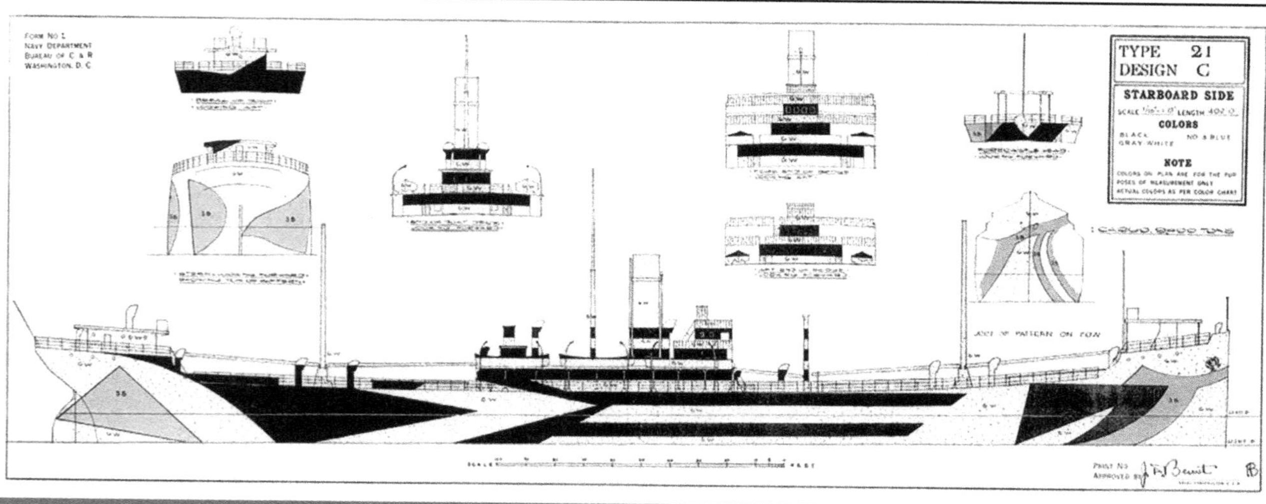

T21 D

Colors used	Ships painted with this pattern
BLACK	ID 3620 CAPE MAY
WHITE	
#3 BLUE	
#1 BLUE	

TYPE 21
DESIGN D
PORT SIDE
SCALE 1/16"-1'-0" LENGTH 402'-0"
COLORS
BLACK
WHITE
NO 1 BLUE
NO 3 BLUE
NOTE
COLORS ON PLAN ARE FOR THE PURPOSES OF MEASUREMENT ONLY
ACTUAL COLORS AS PER COLOR CHART

TYPE 21
DESIGN D
STARBOARD SIDE
SCALE 1/16"-1'-0" LENGTH 402'-0"
COLORS
BLACK
WHITE
NO 1 BLUE
NO 3 BLUE
NOTE
COLORS ON PLAN ARE FOR THE PURPOSES OF MEASUREMENT ONLY
ACTUAL COLORS AS PER COLOR CHART

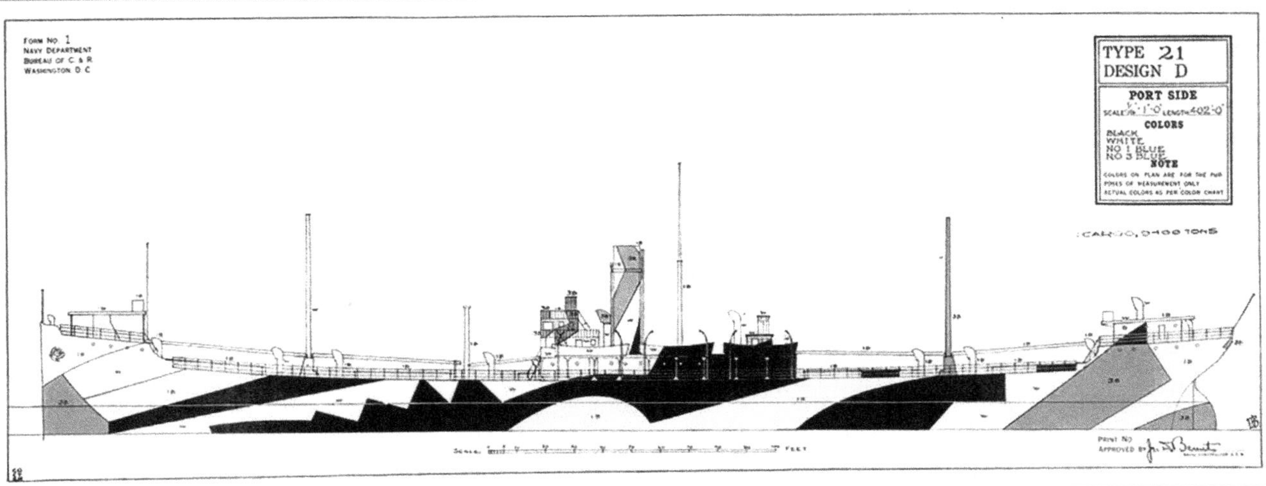

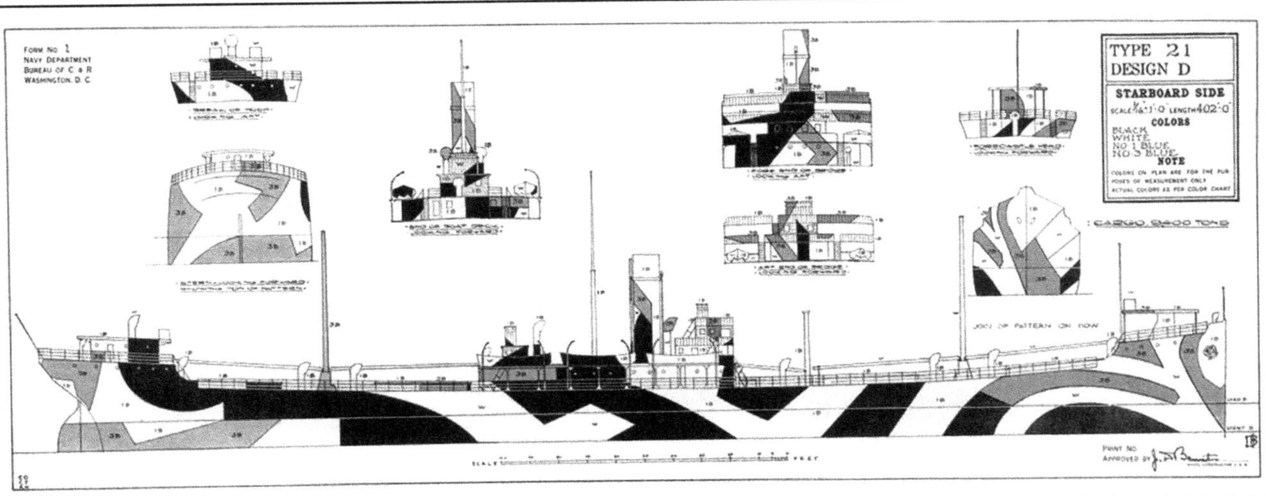

T27 A

Colors used	Ships painted with this pattern
BLACK	
GREY-WHITE	
#3 BLUE	
#1 GREEN	

TYPE 27
DESIGN A
PORT SIDE
SCALE 1/16" = 1'-0" LENGTH 390-0" BP
COLORS
3 BLUE GRAY-WHITE
1 GREEN BLACK
NOTE
COLORS ON PLAN ARE FOR THE PURPOSES OF MEASUREMENT ONLY
ACTUAL COLORS AS PER COLOR CHART

TYPE 27
DESIGN A
STARBOARD SIDE
SCALE 1/16" = 1'-0" LENGTH 390 0" BP
COLORS
3 BLUE GRAY-WHITE
1 GREEN BLACK
NOTE
COLORS ON PLAN ARE FOR THE PURPOSES OF MEASUREMENT ONLY
ACTUAL COLORS AS PER COLOR CHART

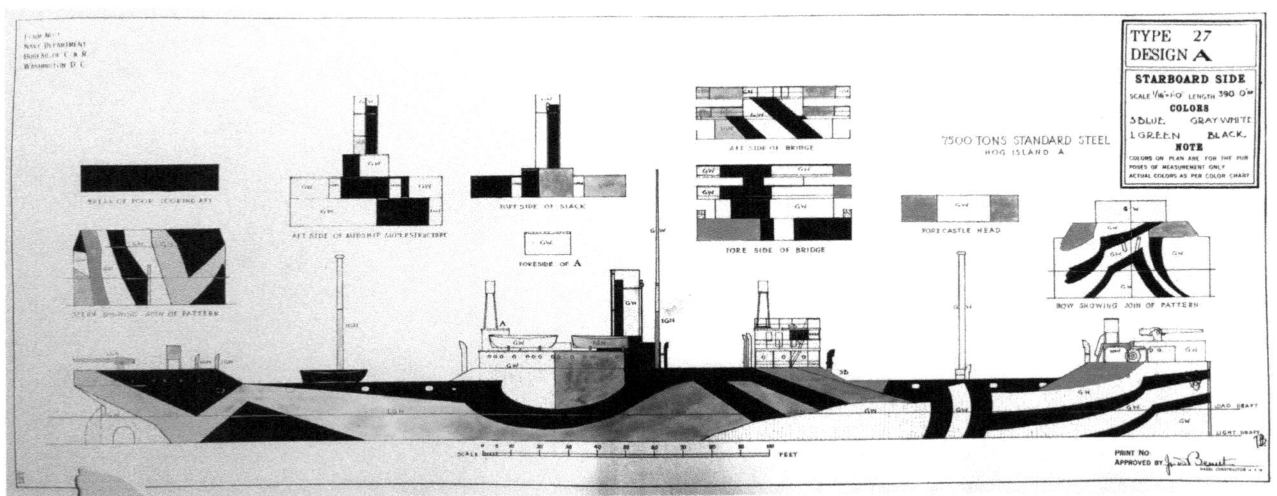

TOCH

Ships painted with this pattern	
DARK GREY	ID 3005 AEOLUS
AERIAL GREY	ID 1408 HURON
PINK	SP 375 COURTNEY`
DARK OLIVE	SP 389 KAJERUNA

NARA RG38

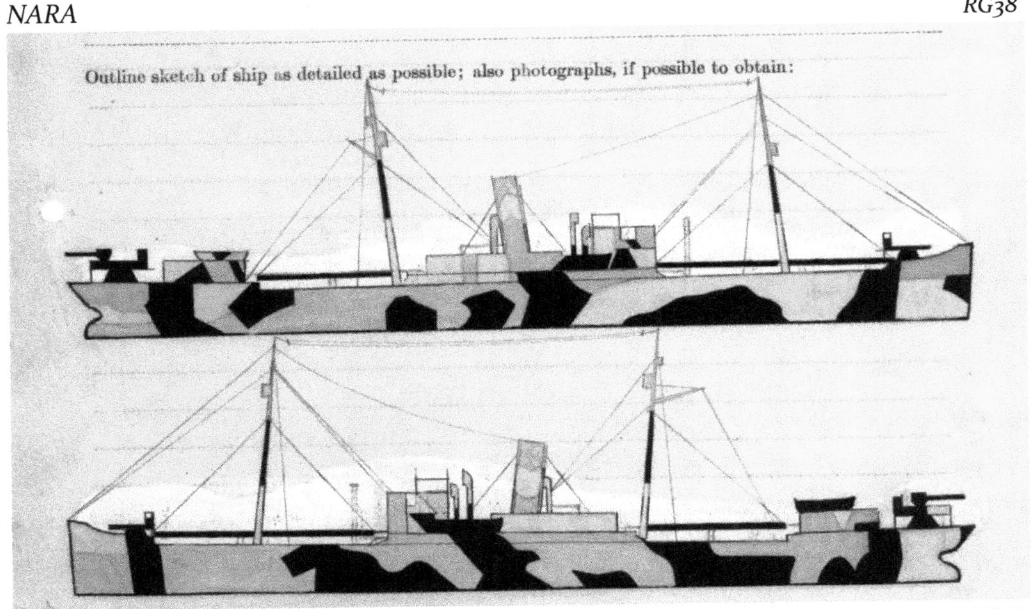

NARA RG38

Bibliography by book

AUTHOR	NAME	PUBLISHER	EDITOR
Patrick Beesley	Room 40	Oxford University Press Oxford 1984	
Roy Behrens	Ship shape	Boblink books, dysart iowa 2012	
Roy Behrens	Camoupedia	Boblink books, dysart iowa 2009	
Leo S. Blodgett	Ship Camouflage	MIT Thesis 1919	
David Bone	Merchantmen Rearmed	Chatto & Windus London 1949	
	Brassey's Naval Annual 1905	J Griffin & Co. Portsmouth 1905	
Jan Breemer	Defeating the U-boat	USNWC press Newport 2010	
CDR Burdick H Brittin and L B Watson	International Law for Seagoing Officers	USNI Annapolis 1956	
RADM W. S. Chalmers	The Life and Letters of David Beatty	Hodder & Stoughton London 1951	
Norman Friedman	British Destroyers from earliest days to the Second World War	USNI Annapolis 2009	
Norman Friedman	Naval Weapons of World War One	Seaforth 2001	
Norman Friedman	U S Destroyers an illustrated design history	USNI Annapolis 1982	
Ian E Gordon	Theories of Visual Perception	John Wiley & sons Chichester UK 1989	
Erich Groener	Die Deutschen Kriegsschiffe	J F Lehmanns verlag Munich 1966	
Guy Hartcup	Camouflage	Scribners NY 1980	
Archibald Hurd	The Merchant Navy	John Murray London 1921	
Edward N. Hurley	The Bridge to France	Lippincott London 1927	
Joseph Husband	On the Coast of France	A. C. McClurg & co Chicago 1919	
L S Howeth CAPT USN	History of Communications-Electronics in the U S Navy	USGPO Washington 1963	
International Committee of the Red Cross,	Protocols additional to the Geneva Conventions of 12 August 1949	Geneva 1970	
Paul Kemp and Michael Wilson	Meditrranean Submarines	Crecy publishing Cheshire UK 1997	
Roger Keyes	The Naval Memoirs 1916-1918	Thornton Butterworth London 1935	

AUTHOR	NAME	PUBLISHER	EDITOR
Erik Larson	Dead Wake	Crown publishers NY 2015	
H. M. Le Fleming	Warships of World War i	Ian allen London	
Arnold Lott	Most Dangerous Sea	USNI Annapolis 1959	
Melvin Maddocks	The Great Liners	Time-Life books Alexandria, VA 1978	
Arthur Marder	From the Dreadnought to Scapa Flow 5 vols.	Seaforth publishing 2013	
Harold Martin and Joseph Baker	Laws of Maritime Warfare	USGPO May 1918	
W H Mitchell and L A Sawyer	British Standard Ships of World War I vol 3	SeaBreezes liverpool 1968	
Naval Advisory Board	Bulletin no 2 - The Enemy Submarine	NY 1918	
Henry Newbolt	Naval Operations	Longmans Green & co London 1931	
ONI publication 42	Antisubmarine Tactics	Washington DC Oct 1918	
Lawrence Perry	Our Navy in the War	Charles Scribner's & sons NY 1918	
Norman Polmar and Edward Whitman	Hunters and Killers	USNI Annapolis 2015	
RDM S S Robinson	History of Naval Tactics	USNI Annapolis 1940	
Stephen Roskill	Churchill and the Admirals	William Morrow & co NY 1978	
Carleton Savage	Policy of the United States Toward Maritime Commerce in War Vol II 1914-18	USGPO 1936	
LLoyd N. Scott	Naval Consulting Board of the United States	GPO Washington 1920	
Paul Silverstone	U S Warships of World War I	Doubleday & co NY 1970	
Colin Simpson	The Lusitania	Ballantine books NY 1972	
Joseph Taussig	The Queenstown patrol 1917	NWC press Newport RI 1996	*William N Still jr*
John Terraine	The U-boat Wars	G. P. Putnam's sons, NY 1989	
Lowell Thomas	Raiders of the deep	Sun Dial Press NY 1940	
David Williams	Liners in Battedress	Conway Maritime London 1989	
David Williams	Naval Camouflage 1914-1945	USNI Annapolis 2001	
	General Instructions for Painting and Cementing Vessels of the U S Navy	GPO Washington 1918	
Jonathan Black	Chapter in Contested Objects: Material Memories of the Great War	Routledge NY 2009	*Nicolas Saunders*
Maurice Prendergrast and R H Gibson	The German Submarine War 1914-18	Penzance 1931	

Bibliography by Magazine

AUTHOR	ARTICLE	MAGAZINE
Robert C Murphy	Marine Camouflage	in Sea Power Jan 1919 p 28-33
Hugh Murphy and Martin Bellamy	The Dazzling Zoologist, John Graham Kerr and the Early Development of Ship Camouflage	in The Northern Mariner/le marin du nord, XIX No. 2, (April 2009), 171-192
Robert F Sumrall	Ship Camouflage deceptive art	in USNIP Jul 1971
Waldemar Kaempffert	Fighting the U-boat with Paint	in Popular Science Monthly Apr 1919 p17-19
Roy R Behrens	The Role of Artists in Ship Camouflage during World War	Leonardo, Vol. 32, No. 1 (1999), pp. 53-59
Everett Warner	Painting Battleships	Illuminating Engineering jul 1919 pp 220-224
Everett Warner	The Science of Marine Camouflage	Illuminating Engineering jul 1919 pp 215-219
Harold Van Buskirk	Camouflage	Illuminating Engineering jul 1919 pp 225-233

Bibliography by Newspaper

PAPER	DATE & PAGES
Baltimore Sun	12 Sep 1915 p4
Boston Evening Globe	7 May 1915 p1
Brattleboro daily defender	16 jul 1918 p6
Bridgeport Times	22 july 1918 p 6
Illinois Republican	8 dec 1917 p
Monroe NC Journal	17 Sep 1918 p 2
New York Times	8 May 1915 p 1
NY Evening World - Daily Magazine	6 Mar 1919 p 1
NY Sun	19 Jan 19 p11
NY Sun	9 Sep 1917 section 5 P3

PAPER	DATE & PAGES
NY Tribune	25 aug 1918 p 6
NY Tribune	27 Aug 1918 p 6
San Antonio Evening News	
Washington evening star	19 nov 1916 p 4
Washington Herald	10 May 1918 p 1
Washington Sunday Star	17 Mar 1918 p 6
Washington Times	19 apr 1919 p 6
Washington Times	7 May 1915 p1
El Paso Herald	13 dec 1918 p 6
Pittsburgh Daily Post	28 jul 1919 p

Index of unknown patterns

ID	NAME	PATTERN
ID 2296	A C BEDFORD	(t)
ID 3321	ACCOMA	?
ID 2185	AMABALA	?
none	ANTILLA	?
ID 4576	APACHE	?
	ASTERIA	
	BAYLEAF	
	BELLAIR	
ID NONE	BLACKFORD	(t)
ID 3526	BLANDON	(t)
ID 3774	BOULTON	(t)
ID 1335	BUENA VENTURA	?
ID 3472	COWETA	(t)
ID 3357	COYOTE	(t)
SP 321	DRUID	IWM MOD 2408
ID 3021	GOLD SHELL	?
ID 2931	GULFLAND	(t)
ID 1609	S V HARKNESS	(t)
ID 1411	HAVERFORD	
	HOLBROOK	IWM ORD 92X
ID 2250	J C DONNELL	(t)
ID 2218	J E O'NEIL	(t)
ID 4535	J W VAN DYKE	(t)
ID 1473	KERMANSHA	?
ID 4268	LAKE CAYUGA	(t)
ID 4427A	LAKE CHARLES	(t)
ID 4406A	LAKE CHELAN	(t)
	LAKE CITY	(t)
ID 4410A	LAKE COMO	(t)
ID 4388	LAKE DUNCAN	(t)
ID 3765D	LAKE ENNIS	(t)
	LAKE FELICITY	(t)
ID 4086A	LAKE GARZA	(t)
ID 4215	LAKE GENEVA	(t)
ID 2278	LAKE GEORGE	(t)
ID 4368	LAKE GREENWOOD	(t)
ID 4054	LAKE HEMLOCK	(t)

ID	NAME	PATTERN
ID 4027	LAKE LOUISE	(t)
ID 2177	LAKE MOHUNK	(t)
ID 4368A	LAKE MONROE	(t)
ID 4333	LAKE NARKA	(t)
ID 4143	LAKE PEARL,	(t)
ID 4345	LAKE PICKAWAY	(t)
ID 3834	LAKEHURST	(t)
	LONE STAR	(t)
USCG	MANNING	?
UK	MATTAWA	
ID 4651	MINNEKHADA	(t)
ID 3358B	MOJAVE	(t)
	PHILADELPHIAN	
ID 3428	POINT ADAMS	(t)
ID 2512	POINT ARENA	(t)
ID 3334	POINT JUDITH	(t)
ID 3494	POINT LOBOS	(t)
ID 2537	POINT LOMA	(t)
ID 3616	QUOQUE	(t)
ID 2740	SANTA CLARA	(t)
ID 1503	SANTA ROSALIA	(t)
D 2450	TRONTOLITE	(t)
ID 3315	WEST COAST	(t)
ID 2775	WEST DURFEE	(t)
ID 3661	WEST ELCASCO	(t)
ID 3718	WEST HUMHAW	(t)
ID 3639	WEST LOQUASSUC	(t)
ID 3254	WEST POINT	(t)
ID 3203	WEST BROOK	(t)
ID 3551	WESTERN BELL	(t)
ID 3272	WESTERN CITY	(t)
ID 3771	WESTERN HOPE	(t)
ID 2889	WESTERN KING	(t)
ID 3741	WESTERN PLAINS	(t)
ID 3728	WESTERN PRIDE	(t)
ID 3527	WESTERN SCOUT	(t)
ID 3550	WESTMEAD	(t)
ID 3675	WESTPOOL	(t)

Index by name

NAME	ID	DESIGN NUMBER
DOCHRA (t)	ID 1758	T4-B
DOLPHIN	PG 24	N86-A
DOWNES	DD 45	N24-ADM2
DRECHTERLAND (t)	ID 2793	T3-G
DYER	DD 84	N12-C
EASTERN CHIEF	ID 3390	T5-C
EASTERNER	ID 3331	T11-D
EASTPORT	ID 3342	T11-E
EDGAR F LUCKENBACH	ID 4587	T5-C
EDITH (t)	ID 3459	T6-B
EDWARD L DOHENEY III	ID 3835	T7-E
EDWARD LUCKENBACH	ID 1662	T5-C
EDWARD PIERCE	ID 4526A	T7-E
EL ALMIRANTE	ID 1341	T4-E
EL CAPITAIN	ID 1407	N55-A
ELINOR (t)	ID 2465	T3-C
ELIZABETH (t)	ID NONE	T3-A
ERICSSON	DD 56	RN
ERNY	ID 1619	T3-B
EVELYN	ID 2228	T6-B
EVERGLADES	ID NONE	T2-I
F J LUCKENBACH	ID 2160	T5-B
FAIRFAX	DD 93	N12-A
FAIRMONT (t)	ID 2429	T3-A
FALMOUTH	ID 3759	T10-H
FANNING	DD 37	N10-ADM
FAVORITE	ID 1385	N34-A
FEDERAL	ID 3657	T4-I
FELIX TAUSSIG	ID 2282	T11-A
FINLAND (t)	ID 4543	N56-A
FINLAND	ID 4543	MACKAY
FIRMORE	ID 3047	T7-B
FLORENCE LUCKENBACH (t)	ID 1606	T5-C
FRANK H BUCK	ID 1613	T7-A
FREDERICK	ACR 8	N73-D
FREDERICK R KELLOG	ID NONE	T7-E
FRESNO	ID 3063	T9-B

NAME	ID	DESIGN NUMBER
FULTON	AS 1	N96-A
GALATEA	SP 714	MACKAY
GEM	SP 41	Exp.
GEORGE W BARNES	ID NONE	T1-A
GEORGE WASHINGTON	ID 3018	N43-A
GLACIER	AF 4	N7-B
GLEN WHITE (t)	ID 2068	T4-B
GOOILAND (t)	ID 2582	T6-G
GORGONTALO (t)	ID 2682	N70-A
GORREDIJK (t)	ID 2482	T9-F
GREAT NORTHERN	ID 4569	N13-A
GREGORY	DD 82	N12-C
GREY FOX	SP 52	MACKAY
GUANTANAMO (t)	ID 1637	T3-B
GULFPORT	ID 2989	T3-A
H B HUBBARD	SP 416	TOCH
H M FLAGLER	ID 4712	T7-B
HANCOCK	AP 3	N59-A
HARISH	ID 3523	T9-K
HARRISBURG	ID 1663	N49-B
HATTERAS (t)	ID 2143	T4-B
HATTIE LUCKENBACH (t)	ID 2486	T3-A
HENDERSON	AP 1	N11-A
HENLEY	DD 39	N10-A
HENLEY	DD 39	RN
HENRY R MALLORY	ID 1280	N61-A
HERBERT L PRATT	ID 2339	T7-B
HICKMAN	ID 3554	T4-J
HISKO	ID 1953	T7-B
HOUSATONIC	ID 1897	N1-D
HOUSTON	ID 4283E	T4-C
HOWICK HALL	ID 1303	T15-A text
HUNTINGTON	ACR 5	N73-ADM
HUNTINGTON	ACR 5	N73-E
HURON	ID 1408	N38-A
HURON	ID 1408	TOCH
IDAHO	ID NONE	T8-A
INDEPENDENCE	ID 3676	T9-P
INDIANA (t)	ID 1787	T4-K text
INDIANAPOLIS	ID 3865	T17-D

NAME	ID	DESIGN NUMBER
LAKE PEPIN (t)	ID 2125	T2-H
LAKE PEWAUKEE	ID 2906	T2-B
LAKE PLACID (t)	ID 1788	T2-E
LAKE PLEASANT	ID 1785A	T2-I
LAKE PORTAGE	ID NONE	T2-B
LAKE SHORE (t)	ID 1792	T2-A
LAKE SIDE (t)	ID 2152	T2-A
LAKE SILVER	ID NONE	T2-G
LAKE SUPERIOR	ID 2995	T2-F text
LAKE TAHOE (t)	ID 2996	T2-C
LAKE VIEW	ID 2186	T2-G
LAKE WASHBURN	ID 4368A	T2-E
LAKE WIMICO	ID 4410G	T2-G
LAKE WINONA	ID 2954	T2-B
LAKE WINOOSKI	ID 4311H	T10-M
LAKE WOOD	ID NONE	T2-C
LAKE WORTH	ID 2997	T2-B
LAKE YAHARA	ID 3974	T2-I
LAKE YEMASSEE	ID 4276D	T8-C
LAKEPORT (t)	ID 2994	T2-D
LAMBERTON	DD 119	N12-J
LANCASTER	ID 2953	T11-A
LARENBURG (t)	ID 2525	T9-B
LAWRENCE	DD 8	N25-A
LEA	DD 118	N12-K
LEBANON	ID 4239G	T12-A
LEERSUM	ID 2683	T11-B text
LENAPE	ID 2700	N57-A
LEVIATHAN	ID 1326	RN
LIBERATOR	ID 3134	T5-B
LIBERTY	ID 3461	T4-G
LITTLE	DD 79	N12-A
LOS ANGELES	ID 1470	T7-A
LOUISVILLE	ID 1644	BRUSH
LOUISVILLE	ID 1644	MACKAY
LOUISVILLE	ID 1644	N50-B
LUCE	DD 99	N12-M
LUCIA (t)	ID 3090	T9-A
LUELLA	ID 2691	T3-B
M J SCANLON	ID 3513	T7-J
MAARTENSDIJK	ID 2497	T6-E

NAME	ID	DESIGN NUMBER
MADAWASKA	ID 3011	N18-A
MAGDALENA (t)	ID 2538	T2-E
MAHAN	DD 102	N12-H
MAJOR WHEELER	ID 3637	T6-J
MALANG	ID 2623	T3-C
MANCHURIA	ID 1633	N44-A
MANTA	ID 2036	T2-D
MARE	ID NONE	T7-C
MARGARET	ID 2510	T3-E
MARIANNA	ID 3944	T3-A
MARIETTA	PG 18	RN
MARSHFIELD	ID 3601	T10-G
MARTHA WASHINGTON	ID 3019	N51-A
MARYANNE	ID 2077	T10-D
MATILDA WEEMS	ID NONE	T3-C
MATSONIA	ID 1589	N15-B
MAUI	ID 1514	N15-B
MAUMEE	AO 2	N42-A
MCDOUGAL	DD 54	RN
MCKEE	DD 87	N12-J
MERCURINE	ID NONE	T3-E
MERCURY	ID 3012	N48-A
MERUAKE	ID NONE	T12-A
MEXICAN	ID 1655	N62-B
MEXICO	ID NONE	T14-A
MIDDLESEX	ID NONE	T7-G
MIJDRECHT (t)	ID 3846	T7-F
MILTON	ID NONE	T10-L
MINEOLA	ID 2142	T9-D
MINNEAPOLIS	C 13	N75-A
MINNEOLA	ID 3142	T9-K
MINNESOTAN (t)	ID 4545	T9-B
MIRACH	ID 2545	T3-G
MIZAR	ID 2549	T10-B
MONGOLIA	ID 1615	N44-A
MONTANA	ACR 13	N73-B
MONTCLAIR	ID 3497	T10-A
MONTICELLO (t)	ID 1307	T4-B
MONTOSO	ID NONE	N49-A
MONTPELIER	ID 1954	T5-A

NAME	ID	DESIGN NUMBER
PROTEUS	AC 9	N39-A
QUINCY	ID 4928	T4-B
QUINNEBAUG	ID 1687	N2-A
QUISTCONCK	ID 3826	T6-G
RADNOR	ID 3023	T5-A
RAINBOW	AS 7	N74-A
RALEIGH	C 8	N80-A
RAPPAHANNOCK	ID 1854	T12-A
RATHBURNE	DD 114	N12-B
RED CLOUD	ID NONE	T10-B
RHODE ISLAND	BB 17	N5-A
RIJNDAM	ID 2505	N53-A
RIJNDIJK (t)	ID 2493	T6-K
RIJSWIJK	ID NONE	T10-C
RINGGOLD	DD 89	N12-I
ROANOKE	ID 1695	N1-C
ROBINSON	DD 88	N12-K
ROCHESTER	ACR 2	N72-A
ROE	DD 24	RN
RONDO	ID 2488	T11-A
ROY H BEATTIE	ID NONE	T10-I
S V HARKNESS	ID NONE	T7-G
SAETIA	ID 2317	T9-B
SAG HARBOR	ID 3352	T10-E
SAGADAHOCK	ID 3311	T9-B
SAINT PAUL (t)	ID 1643	T9-D
SAMARINDA	ID 2511	T9-F
SAN MATEO	ID NONE	T6-E
SANTA BARBARA	ID 4522	T3-D
SANTA LUISA (t)	ID 2873	T14-E
SANTA OLIVIA	ID 3125	T6-D
SANTA PAULA (t)	ID 1580	T9-D
SANTA TECLA	ID 3165	T6-G
SANTA TERESA	ID 3804	T14-E
SANTIAGO (t)	ID 2253	T3-A
SARA THOMPSON	ID 3148	T7-F
SARANAC	ID 1704	N2-B
SASSENHEIM (t)	ID 2454	T2-J
SAVANNAH	ID 3015	N9-A
SC 5	SC 5	MACKAY
SCHLEY	DD 103	N12-E

NAME	ID	DESIGN NUMBER
SEATTLE	ACR 11	N73-F
SERTIA	ID NONE	T9-B
SHAWMUT	ID 1255	N4-A
SHERMAN	ID 3345	T7-A
SHOSHONE	ID 1670	T6-D
SIBONEY	ID 2999	N3-A
SIERRA	ID 1634	N40-B
SILVER SHELL	ID 2270	T1-C
SILVERADO	ID NONE	T8-E
SIOUX	ID NONE	T2-D
SIXAOLA	ID 2777	T14-A
SOCONY	ID 3451	T8-B mod
SOESTDIJK	ID 3413	T9-D
ST LOUIS	C 20	N60-A
ST LOUIS	ID 1644	TOCH
STANDARD ARROW	ID 1532	T7-A
STEPHEN R JONES (T)	ID 4526	T7-E
STERRETT	DD 27	RN
STEVENS	DD 86	N12-B
STURGEON BAY	IX 27	T7-D
SUDBURY (t)	ID 2149	T9-B
SUPPLY	AF	N27-A
SURUGA (t)	ID NONE	BRUSH
SUSQUEHANNA	ID 3016	N54-A
SUWANEE (t)	ID 1320	T4-A
SYLVAN ARROW	ID 2150	T1-A
TALBOT	DD 114	N12-C
TAYLOR	DD 94	N12-A
TENEDORES	ID NONE	N40-A
TERRY	DD 25	RN
TEXAN (t)	ID 1354	T5-B
THUBAN (t)	ID 2893	T4-C
TONOPAH	BM 8	MACKAY
TOPLA (t)	ID 3001	T7-E
TRIPPE	DD 33	RN
TRITON	ID 2467	T2-F text
TROY	ID 1614	MACKAY
VEELHAVEN (t)	ID NONE	T6-D
VEENDIJK	ID 2515	T4-J
VEERHAVEN (t)	ID 2539	T10-D

NAME	ID	DESIGN NUMBER
WINSLOW	DD 53	RN
WINTERSWIJK	ID 2567	T3-D
WISHKAH	ID 3346	T10-A
WOOLSEY	DD 77	N12-K
WYANDOTTE	ID NONE	T3-C
YACONA	SP 617	Exp.
YALE	ID 1672	N36-B

NAME	ID	DESIGN NUMBER
YAMHILL	ID 3806	T21-C
YSELHAVEN	ID NONE	T6-D
ZACA	ID 3792	T21-B
ZEELANDIA	ID 2507	N20-A
ZIRKEL	ID 3407	T21-A
ZUIDERDIJK (t)	ID 2724	T9-G

Index by Pattern

DESIGN NUMBER	NAME	ID
BRUSH	JUPITER	ID 2216
	LOUISVILLE	ID 1644
	SURUGA (t)	ID NONE
	WICO (t)	ID 1278
DD SILHOUETTE	ANTIGONE	ID 3007
	DE KALB	ID 3010
	VON STEUBEN	ID 3017
Exp.	AZTEC	SP 570
	GEM	SP 41
	NARKEETA	YT 3
	YACONA	SP 617
HERZOG	WESTOIL (t)	ID 1621
MACKAY	ANTIGONE	ID 3007
	BUFFALO	AD 8
	CALDWELL	DD 69
	CAROLA IV	SP 812
	CONNER	DD 72
	CORNING (t)	ID NONE
	DE KALB	ID 3010
	FINLAND	ID 4543
	GALATEA	SP 714
	GREY FOX	SP 52
	ISABEL	SP 521
	J L LUCKENBACH	ID 1563
	KROONLAND	ID 1541
	LOUISVILLE	ID 1644
	NEW JERSEY	BB 16
	OLEAN	SP 1630
	PHILADELPHIA	ID 1663
	PLATTSBURG	ID 1645
	POLARINE (t)	ID NONE
	SC 5	SC 5
MACKAY	TONOPAH	BM 8
	TROY	ID 1614
	VENETIA	SP 431
	WINFIELD S CAHILL	SP 493
N1-A	CANANDAIGUA	ID 1694

DESIGN NUMBER	NAME	ID
N1-B	CANONICUS	ID 1686
N1-C	ROANOKE	ID 1695
N1-D	HOUSATONIC	ID 1897
N10-A	HENLEY	DD 39
N10-ADM	FANNING	DD 37
N11-A	HENDERSON	AP 1
N12-A	FAIRFAX	DD 93
	LITTLE	DD 79
	TAYLOR	DD 94
N12-ADM	ALLEN	DD 66
	CALDWELL	DD 69
N12-B	KIMBERLY	DD 80
	RATHBURNE	DD 114
	STEVENS	DD 86
	WARD	DD 139
N12-C	DYER	DD 84
	GREGORY	DD 82
	TALBOT	DD 114
N12-D	DENT	DD 116
	WATERS	DD 115
	WICKES	DD 75
N12-E	SCHLEY	DD 103
N12-F	KILTY	DD 137
N12-H	CHAMPLIN	DD 104
	DELPHY	DD 261
	MAHAN	DD 102
N12-I	PHILIP	DD 76
	RINGGOLD	DD 89
	BELL	DD 95
	ISRAEL	DD 98
	LAMBERTON	DD 119
	MCKEE	DD 87
N12-K	BREESE	DD 122
	COLHOUN	DD 85
	LEA	DD 118
	ROBINSON	DD 88
	WOOLSEY	DD 77

DESIGN NUMBER	NAME	ID
N12-L	MUGFORD	DD 105
N12-M	LUCE	DD 99
N12-N	CRAVEN	DD 70
N13-A	GREAT NORTHERN	ID 4569
N13-B	NORTHERN PACIFIC	ID NONE
N14-A	BLACK HAWK	ID 2140
N15-A	WILHELMINA	ID 2168
N15-B	MATSONIA	ID 1589
	MAUI	ID 1514
N16-B	PRESIDENT GRANT	ID 3014
N17-A	POCAHONTAS	ID 3044
N17-C	POWHATAN	ID 3013
N18-A	MADAWASKA	ID 3011
N19-A	AGAMEMNON	ID 3004
N19-B	MOUNT VERNON	ID 4508
N2-A	QUINNEBAUG	ID 1687
N2-B	SARANAC	ID 1704
N20-A	ZEELANDIA	ID 2507
N21-A	AMERICA	ID 3006
N22-A	PRINCESS MATOIKA	ID 2290
N24-A	PATTERSON	DD 36
N24-ADM2	DOWNES	DD 45
N25-A	LAWRENCE	DD 8
N27-A	SUPPLY	AF
N28-A	NOPATIN	ID 2195
N28-B	NARRAGANSET	ID 2196
N3-A	SIBONEY	ID 2999
N3-B	ORIZABA	ID 1536
N34-A	FAVORITE	ID 1385
N35-A	VON STEUBEN	ID 3017
N36-A	CHARLES	ID 1298
N36-B	YALE	ID 1672
N37-A	AEOLUS	ID 3005
N38-A	HURON	ID 1408
N39-A	PROTEUS	AC 9
N4-A	SHAWMUT	ID 1255
N4-B	AROOSTOOK	ID 1256
N40-A	CALAMARES	ID 3662
	TENEDORES	ID NONE
N40-B	SIERRA	ID 1634
N41-A	ISABELLA	ID NONE

DESIGN NUMBER	NAME	ID
N41-A var	COROZAL	ID NONE
N42-A	CUYAMA	AO 3
	KANAWHA	AO 1
	MAUMEE	AO 2
N43-A	GEORGE WASHINGTON	ID 3018
N44-A	MANCHURIA	ID 1633
	MONGOLIA	ID 1615
N45-A	ANTIGONE	ID 3007
N46-A	ALLIANCA	ID 1636
	ANDALUSIA	ID 2276
N46-A	COLON	ID NONE
	DE KALB	ID 3010
N48-A	MERCURY	ID 3012
N49-A	MONTOSO	ID NONE
N49-B	HARRISBURG	ID 1663
N49-C	PLATTSBURG	ID 1645
N5-A	RHODE ISLAND	BB 17
N50-B	LOUISVILLE	ID 1644
N51-A	MARTHA WASHINGTON	ID 3019
N53-A	CARTER HALL	
N53-A	RIJNDAM	ID 2505
N54-A	SUSQUEHANNA	ID 3016
N55-A	EL CAPITAIN	ID 1407
N55-A var	CELEBES	ID 2680
N56-A	FINLAND (t)	ID 4543
N56-B	KROONLAND	ID 1541
N57-A	LENAPE	ID 2700
N58-A	BAVARIA (t)	ID 2179
N59-A	HANCOCK	AP 3
N6-A	PRAIRIE	AD 5
N6-B	BUFFALO	AD 8
N60-A	ST LOUIS	C 20
N61-A	HENRY R MALLORY	ID 1280
N62-A	DAKOTAN (t)	
	IOWAN	ID 3002
	PENNSYLVANIAN (t)	ID 3511
N62-B	ALASKAN	ID 4542
	MEXICAN	ID 1655
N63-A	CHARLTON HALL (t)	ID 1349
	CRASTER HALL	ID 1486

DESIGN NUMBER	NAME	ID
N64-A	BRIDGE	AF 1
N65-A	CULGOA	AF 3
N66-A	NEPTUNE	AC 8
N66-B	CYCLOPS	AC 4
	JASON (t)	AC 3
	JUPITER (t)	ID 2216
N67-A	BEAVER	ID 2302
N68-A	KONINGEN DER NEDERLANDEN	ID 2708
N69-A	KITTERY	AK 2
N7-B	GLACIER	AF 4
N70-A	GORGONTALO (t)	ID 2682
	VESTAL	AR 4
N72-A	ROCHESTER	ACR 2
N73-A	CHARLOTTE	ACR 12
N73-ADM	HUNTINGTON	ACR 5
N73-B	MONTANA	ACR 13
N73-D	FREDERICK	ACR 8
N73-E	HUNTINGTON	ACR 5
N73-F	SEATTLE	ACR 11
N74-A	RAINBOW	AS 7
N75-A	MINNEAPOLIS	C 13
N76-ADM	BIRMINGHAM	CL 2
N77-A	WILMETTE	IX 49
N8-A	PAUL JONES	DD 10
N8-B	PREBLE	DD 12
N80-A	RALEIGH	C 8
N80-B	CINCINNATI	C 7
N86-A	DOLPHIN	PG 24
N87-A	CITY OF SOUTH HAVEN	ID 2537
N88-A	BLUE RIDGE	ID 2432
N9-A	SAVANNAH	ID 3015
N96-A	FULTON	AS 1
NORFOLK-WATSON	ANNISTON	C 9
	NEBRASKA	BB 14
RN	BALCH	DD 50
	BEALE	DD 40
	BENHAM	DD 49
	CASSIN	DD 43
	CONYNGHAM	DD 58
RN	CUSHING	DD 55
	CYTHERA	SP 575
	DAVIS	DD 65
	DUNCAN	DD 46
	ERICSSON	DD 56
	HENLEY	DD 39
	JARVIS	DD 38
	LEVIATHAN	ID 1326
	MANLEY	DD 74
	MARIETTA	PG 18
	MCDOUGAL	DD 54
	MONAGHAN	DD 32
	NICHOLSON	DD 52
	OBRIEN	DD 51
	PARKER	DD 48
	PATTERSON	DD 36
	PAULDING	DD 22
	PERKINS	DD 26
	PIQUA	SP 139
	PRESTON	DD 23
	ROE	DD 24
	ROWAN	DD 64
	SHAW	DD 68
	STERRETT	DD 27
	TERRY	DD 25
	TRIPPE	DD 33
	WADSWORTH	DD 60
	WAINWRIGHT	DD 62
	WALKE	DD 34
	WARRINGTON	DD 30
	WINSLOW	DD 53
T1-A	AMPETCO	ID 2925
	GEORGE W BARNES	ID NONE
	JOHN M CONNOLLEY	ID 2703
	SYLVAN ARROW	ID 2150
T1-B	ABSECON	ID 3131
	CALALA	ID 3344
T1-C	SILVER SHELL	ID 2270
T1-D	ARDMORE	ID 1543
T10-A	MONTCLAIR	ID 3497
	WESTWARD HO	ID 3098

DESIGN NUMBER	NAME	ID
	WISHKAH	ID 3346
T10-B	LAKE DAMITA	ID NONE
	MIZAR	ID 2549
	RED CLOUD	ID NONE
	WEST EEKONK	ID 3313
T10-C	ALIOTH	ID 2223
	COOS BAY	ID NONE
	LAKE HARRIS	ID 4429A
	LAKE ORMOC	ID NONE
	NAMECKI	ID 3455
	RIJSWIJK	ID NONE
T10-D	LAKE BERDAN	ID 4276C
	MARYANNE	ID 2077
	VEERHAVEN (t)	ID 2539
T10-E	CHIBIABOS	ID 3490
	PASCAGOULA	ID NONE
	SAG HARBOR	ID 3352
T10-F	CATAWBA	ID 3470
	CUMBERLAND	ID 3270
T10-G	ADVANCE	ID NONE
	BANANGO	ID 3810
	BUSHRAM	ID N/A
	MARSHFIELD	ID 3601
	BASSAN	ID 3392
T10-H	AGRIA	ID NONE
	ALABET	ID 3574
	FALMOUTH	ID 3759
T10-H	LAKE DANCEY	ID 4407L
T10-I	CARIBOU	ID 3626
	ROY H BEATTIE	ID NONE
T10-I	BAYOU TECHE	ID 4055
	COLUMBINE	ID 3672
T10-K	LAKE ARLINE (t)	ID 4155
T10-L	ALPACO	ID NONE
	BAXLEY	ID 4449
	BOTSFORD (t)	ID 3546
	MILTON	ID NONE
T10-M	BALINO	ID 3779
	LAKE WINOOSKI	ID 4311H
T11-A	BASCO (t)	ID 1957
	BATH	ID 1997
T11-A	BATJAN (t)	ID NONE
	BUITENZORG (t)	ID 2544
	FELIX TAUSSIG	ID 2282
	LANCASTER	ID 2953
	RONDO	ID 2488
T11-B text	LEERSUM	ID 2683
T11-C	DEFIANCE	ID 3327
T11-D	EASTERNER	ID 3331
T11-E	CHIPPEWA	ID 1419
	EASTPORT	ID 3342
T11-F	CHALLANGER	ID 3630
T12-A	ADONIS	ID 2689
	ANACORTES (t)	ID 4254
	LEBANON	ID 4239G
	MERUAKE	ID NONE
	RAPPAHANNOCK	ID 1854
T12-B	WEST HOSOKIE	ID 3695
T12-C	NEPONSET	ID 3581
T13-A	NORTHERN WIND	ID NONE
T13-B	MONTROLITE	ID 3356
T14-A	KILPATRICK	ID NONE
	KIRKPATRICK	ID NONE
	MEXICO	ID NONE
T14-A	PRINS DER NEDERLANDEN (t)	ID 2752
	SIXAOLA	ID 2777
T14-B	CARILLO (t)	ID 1406
	COMANCHE	ID NONE
T14-E	SANTA LUISA (t)	ID 2873
	SANTA TERESA	ID 3804
T15-A text	HOWICK HALL	ID 1303
T15-D text	CAMDEN (t)	ID 3243
T16-A text	PEQOUT (t)	ID 1400
T17-A text	MOUNT SHASTA	ID 1822
T17-D	INDIANAPOLIS	ID 3865
T17-D	WEST KYSKA	ID 3701
T17-E text	WESTOVER (t)	ID 2867
T2-A	LAKE ARTHUR	ID 2915
	LAKE CHAMPLAIN	ID 1791
	LAKE CLEAR	ID 3597
	LAKE SHORE (t)	ID 1792

DESIGN NUMBER	NAME	ID
	LAKE SIDE (t)	ID 2152
T2-B	BELLA	ID 2211
	LAKE PEWAUKEE	ID 2906
	LAKE PORTAGE	ID NONE
	LAKE WINONA	ID 2954
	LAKE WORTH	ID 2997
T2-C	LAKE MARKHAM	ID 4215C
	LAKE ONTARIO (t)	ID 2992
	LAKE TAHOE (t)	ID 2996
	LAKE WOOD	ID NONE
	NICKERIE	ID NONE
	PLIEADES (t)	ID 1616
	LAKE LARGA	ID 3765A
T2-D	CARIB (t)	ID 1765
	LAKE CAPENS	ID 4358
	LAKE FOREST	ID 2991
T2-D	LAKE HARNEY	ID 4410C
	LAKE LESA	ID 4099
	LAKEPORT (t)	ID 2994
	MANTA	ID 2036
	NACODOCHES	ID NONE
	OZAMA	ID NONE
	SIOUX	ID NONE
T2-E	CHOCTAW (t)	ID 1648
	KIOWA (t)	ID 1942
	KRALINGEN	ID 2521
T2-E	LAKE BENBOW	ID NONE
	LAKE BRIDGE(t)	ID 2990
	LAKE FURNAS	ID NONE
	LAKE HURON (t)	ID 2144
	LAKE PACHUTA	ID 4267
	LAKE PLACID (t)	ID 1788
	LAKE WASHBURN	ID 4368A
	MAGDALENA (t)	ID 2538
	WEST GAMBO	ID 3230
	WESTERN STAR	ID 4210
	WESTFORD (t)	ID 3198
T2-F text	LAKE DARAGA	ID 4428
	LAKE ERIE	ID 2190
	LAKE SUPERIOR	ID 2995
	TRITON	ID 2467

DESIGN NUMBER	NAME	ID
T2-G	ANDRA	ID NONE
	LA FORGE	ID NONE
	LAKE BLEDSOE	ID 4094A
	LAKE BLOOMINGTON	ID NONE
	LAKE BORGNE	ID NONE
	LAKE SILVER	ID NONE
	LAKE VIEW	ID 2186
	LAKE WIMICO	ID 4410G
T2-H	ALVADO	ID 3369
T2-H	BEDMINSTER	ID NONE
	LAKE EKHART	ID 4363Z
	LAKE OSWEYO	ID 4311G
	LAKE PEPIN (t)	ID 2125
	PHECDA	ID 2723
T2-I	BEAUMONT	ID 3097
	EVERGLADES	ID NONE
	LAKE GARDNER	ID 4117
	LAKE PLEASANT	ID 1785A
	LAKE YAHARA	ID 3974
T2-J	ALPAHA	ID 3394
	CRAWL KEYS	ID 3789A
	SASSENHEIM (t)	ID 2454
T2-K	ALANTHUS	ID 3593
	LAKE DYMER	ID 4131
	LAKE GEDNEY (t)	ID 3765C
T2-L text	LAKE ELIKO	ID 4353AA
T2-N text	LAKE ELSINORE	ID 3765B
	LAKE MICHIGAN	ID 2993
T2-Q	ANOKA	ID NONE
T2-S	LAKE AGOMAK	ID NONE
T2-T	LAKE EDON	ID NONE
T2-X	LAKE MATTATO	ID 4276E
T21-A	ZIRKEL	ID 3407
T21-B	ZACA	ID 3792
T21-C	OSKAWA	ID 3797
	YAMHILL	ID 3806
T21-D	CAPE MAY	ID 3620
T3-A	AMERICAN (t)	ID 2292
	ELIZABETH (t)	ID NONE
	FAIRMONT (t)	ID 2429
	GULFPORT	ID 2989

DESIGN NUMBER	NAME	ID
	HATTIE LUCKENBACH (t)	ID 2486
	MARIANNA	ID 3944
	MUNDALE	ID NONE
T3-A	PLUTO (t)	ID 2667
	POSEIDON	ID NONE
	SANTIAGO (t)	ID 2253
	WEST ALSEK	ID 3119
T3-B	CANTON (t)	ID 2508
	ERNY	ID 1619
	GUANTANAMO (t)	ID 1637
	LUELLA	ID 2691
	PANUCO (t)	ID 1533
	PASADENA (t)	ID 2943
	PIMICO	ID NONE
	WACHUSETT (t)	ID 1840
	WATANGA	ID NONE
	WEST COHAS	ID 3253
T3-C	ASTORIA ((t)	ID 2005
	ELINOR (t)	ID 2465
	JOBSHAVEN	ID 2485
	MALANG	ID 2623
	MATILDA WEEMS	ID NONE
	POLAR SEA	ID 3301
	WESTERN OCEAN (t)	ID 3151
	WESTERN QUEEN	ID 2793
	WYANDOTTE	ID NONE
T3-D	ARETHUSA	ID 4688
	NEPTUNUS	ID 2529
	SANTA BARBARA	ID 4522
	WESTERDIJK	ID 2514
	WESTERN WAVE	ID 3154
	WINTERSWIJK	ID 2567
T3-E	MARGARET	ID 2510
	MERCURINE	ID NONE
T3-G	DRECHTERLAND (t)	ID 2793
T3-G	MIRACH	ID 2545
	OZAUKEE	ID 3439
	WALTER D MUNSON	ID 1510
T3-I text	ARAKAN	ID 2224
	BESOEKI	ID 2543
T3-K	AURORA	ID 3325
	CRUSO	ID 3693
T3-R	POLAR LAND	ID 3651
T4-A	ALCOR	ID NONE
	ASCUTNEY	ID NONE
	MUSCATINE (t)	ID 2126
	PLYMOUTH	ID 3308
	SUWANEE (t)	ID 1320
T4-B	ARTEMIS (t)	ID 2197
	CELTIC	AF 2
	DOCHRA (t)	ID 1758
	GLEN WHITE (t)	ID 2068
	HATTERAS (t)	ID 2143
	LAKE LEDAN	ID 3833
	MONTICELLO (t)	ID 1307
	PRINS FREDERICK HENDRICK	ID 2465
	QUINCY	ID 4928
	VITTORIO EMMANUELLE II	ID 3095
T4-C	ALFENOS	ID NONE
	ARUNDO	ID 2674
	BALI (t)	ID 2483
	BELLATRIX (t)	ID 2568
	CAPE ROMAIN	ID 2970
	HOUSTON	ID 4283E
	KERESAN	ID 1806
	LAKE BENTON	ID 4410B
	LAKE CATHERINE	ID 3568
T4-C	THUBAN (t)	ID 2893
T4-D	LAKE JANET	ID 4054A
T4-E	EL ALMIRANTE	ID 1341
	JAN VAN NASSAU (t)	ID 2805
	LAKE BLANCHESTER (t)	ID 3547C
	NORLINA (t)	ID 1597
	WAALHAVEN (t)	ID 2479
T4-F	WEST GOTOMSKA	ID 3322
T4-G	BERWYN	ID 3565
	CLARK	ID NONE
	LIBERTY	ID 3461
T4-H	CANIBAS	ID 3401

DESIGN NUMBER	NAME	ID
	STEPHEN R JONES (T)	ID 4526
	TOPLA (t)	ID 3001
	VULCAN (t)	ID 2756
T7-F	ALLENTOWN	ID 3443
	MIJDRECHT (t)	ID 3846
T7-F	SARA THOMPSON	ID 3148
T7-G	MIDDLESEX	ID NONE
	S V HARKNESS	ID NONE
T7-I	CHESTNUT HILL	ID 2526
	L J DRAKE	ID 3541
T7-J	M J SCANLON	ID 3513
	W D STEED	ID 3449
	WIELDRECHT (t)	ID 2518
T8-A	IDAHO	ID NONE
	WILLIAM ISOM (t)	ID 1555
T8-B mod	SOCONY	ID 3451
T8-C	LAKE YEMASSEE	ID 4276D
	PERFECTION	ID 1551
T8-E	SILVERADO	ID NONE
T8-G	LAKE ONEIDA	ID NONE
T8-I	COSTILLA	ID NONE
T9-A	ACCOMAC	ID 3041
	AUSABLE (t)	ID 1631
	LUCIA (t)	ID 3090
	OAKLAND	ID 2847
	VIRGINIA (t)	ID 2021
	WAKULLA	ID 3147
	WEST BRIDGE	ID 2888
	WEST MOUNT (t)	ID 3202
	WIERINGER (t)	ID 2547
T9-B	ALLOWAY	ID 3138
	BUFORD (t)	ID 3818
	FRESNO	ID 3063
	LARENBURG (t)	ID 2525
	MINNESOTAN (t)	ID 4545
	PETER H CROWELL	ID 2987
	SAETIA	ID 2317
	SAGADAHOCK	ID 3311
	SERTIA	ID NONE
T9-B	SUDBURY (t)	ID 2149

DESIGN NUMBER	NAME	ID
	WEST APAUM	ID 3221
	WINNEBAGO (t)	ID 2353
T9-C	IROQUOIS (t)	ID 4806
	POINT BONITA	ID 3496
	WESTERN SEA	ID 3153
T9-D	ANIWA	ID 3146
	MINEOLA	ID 2142
	OOSTERDIJK (t)	ID 2586
	SAINT PAUL (t)	ID 1643
	SANTA PAULA (t)	ID 1580
	SOESTDIJK	ID 3413
	WASSAIC	ID 3230
	WEST HAVEN	ID 2159
	WEST LIANGA	ID 2758
T9-E	KERESASPA	ID 1484
	WATONWAN	ID 3876
	WESTERN LIGHT (t)	ID 3300
T9-F	ARCADIA	ID 1605
	GORREDIJK (t)	ID 2482
	SAMARINDA	ID 2511
	VOLUNTEER	ID 3242
T9-G	CAPE LOOKOUT (t)	ID 3214
	WEST GALETA	ID 3330
	WEST GALOC	ID 3347
	WEST WIND (t)	ID 3121
	WESTERN MAID (t)	ID 3703
	ZUIDERDIJK (t)	ID 2724
T9-H	WEST ZULA	ID 3501
T9-I	INVINCIBLE	ID 3671
T9-J	AMELAND	ID 2550
	NYANZA	ID 1821
	WEST ZUCKER	ID 3584
T9-K	HARISH	ID 3523
T9-K	ISANTI	ID 3423
	MINNEOLA	ID 3142
	WEST SHORE	ID 3170
	WESTERN COMET	ID 3569
	WESTERN FRONT(t)	ID 1787
T9-L	ARACAJU	Brazil
	VICTORIOUS	ID 3514
T9-O	NAIWA	ID 3512

DESIGN NUMBER	NAME	ID
	NANTAHALA	ID 3519
	NANTASKET	ID 3478
T9-P	INDEPENDENCE	ID 3676
T9-S	WEST MAHOMET	ID 3681
T9-T	WEST MADAKET	ID 3636
T9-U	NEWBURGH	ID 3768
	WEST VIEW	ID NONE
TOCH	AEOLUS	ID 3005
	AMAGANSETT	SP 693

DESIGN NUMBER	NAME	ID
	COLORIA (t)	ID NONE
	COURTNEY`	SP 375
	H B HUBBARD	SP 416
	HURON	ID 1408
	JASON	AC 3
	KAJERUNA	SP 389
	PARTHENIA	SP 671
	ST LOUIS	ID 1644
	WILBERT A EDWARDS	SP 115

CPSIA information can be obtained
at www.ICGtesting.com
Printed in the USA
BVHW020958291020
592123BV00016B/2285

9 789659 274703